Blackstone's

UK & EU Competition Documents

Blackstone's Statutes Series

The number 1 choice for over 20 years

Trusted in over
a million exams

Contents

Preface to the seventh edition

As I indicated in my Preface to the sixth edition, certain EU regulations would be expiring in 2010 that would necessitate a significant review of the material to be included in any new edition. It was also clear that the sixth edition was in danger of exceeding its optimum length. I have therefore trimmed existing material extensively and removed the EU Specialisation, R & D and Technology Block Exemptions. I have also not included the Motor Vehicle Block Exemption despite several requests to do so. Whilst undoubtedly useful to have in a statute collection, this material is not essential for core EU competition modules and will be available in the future on the accompanying website managed by OUP. I have also made the necessary amendments to the key Treaty articles introduced by the Treaty of Lisbon. Readers would be advised to purchase Nigel Foster's *Blackstone's Statutes on EU Treaties & Legislation* for the full scope of the Treaty of Lisbon amendments. New material of particular note includes the new Guidelines on Vertical Restraints and Block Exemption Regulation 330/2010.

I would like to take this opportunity to thank my peers who took the time to complete a comprehensive review of this text by way of a questionnaire compiled by the OUP team. The information received was invaluable in determining what to include and what to omit. Whilst I have not been able to meet each and every request, I am confident that the editorial decisions reflected in this new edition will meet the needs of the vast majority of EU competition modules taught across the UK and indeed beyond.

Feedback is essential to ensure the text continues to meet its objectives and I encourage all comments, constructive or otherwise! As editor, however, I remain responsible for any errors or omissions in the material included.

Kirsty Dougan (née Middleton)
Hong Kong
1 July 2011

New to this edition

The seventh edition of *Blackstone's UK & EU Competition Documents* has been fully revised and updated to include all relevant legislation through to May 2011 including:

- Commission Regulations (EU) No 330/2010 of 20 April 2010 on the application of Article 101(3) of the Treaty on the Functioning of the European Union to categories of vertical agreements and concerted practices
- Guidelines on Vertical Restraints 2010

Part I

UK Statutes

Competition Act 1998

(1998, c. 41)

An Act to make provision about competition and the abuse of a dominant position in the market; to confer powers in relation to investigations conducted in connection with Article 81 or 82 of the Treaty establishing the European Community; to amend the Fair Trading Act 1973 in relation to information which may be required in connection with investigations under that Act; to make provision with respect to the meaning of 'supply of services' in the Fair Trading Act 1973; and for connected purposes.   [9 November 1998]

PART I COMPETITION

Chapter I Agreements

Introduction

1 Enactments replaced

The following shall cease to have effect—

    (a) the Restrictive Practices Court Act 1976 (c. 33),

    (b) the Restrictive Trade Practices Act 1976 (c. 34),

    (c) the Resale Prices Act 1976 (c. 53), and

    (d) the Restrictive Trade Practices Act 1977 (c. 19).

The prohibition

2 Agreements etc. preventing, restricting or distorting competition

(1) Subject to section 3, agreements between undertakings, decisions by associations of undertakings or concerted practices which—

    (a) may affect trade within the United Kingdom, and

    (b) have as their object or effect the prevention, restriction or distortion of competition within the United Kingdom,

are prohibited unless they are exempt in accordance with the provisions of this Part.

(2) Subsection (1) applies, in particular, to agreements, decisions or practices which—

    (a) directly or indirectly fix purchase or selling prices or any other trading conditions;

    (b) limit or control production, markets, technical development or investment;

    (c) share markets or sources of supply;

    (d) apply dissimilar conditions to equivalent transactions with other trading parties, thereby placing them at a competitive disadvantage;

    (e) make the conclusion of contracts subject to acceptance by the other parties of supplementary obligations which, by their nature or according to commercial usage, have no connection with the subject of such contracts.

(3) Subsection (1) applies only if the agreement, decision or practice is, or is intended to be, implemented in the United Kingdom.

(4) Any agreement or decision which is prohibited by subsection (1) is void.

(5) A provision of this Part which is expressed to apply to, or in relation to, an agreement is to be read as applying equally to, or in relation to, a decision by an association of undertakings or a concerted practice (but with any necessary modifications).

(6) Subsection (5) does not apply where the context otherwise requires.

(7) In this section 'the United Kingdom' means, in relation to an agreement which operates or is intended to operate only in a part of the United Kingdom, that part.

(8) The prohibition imposed by subsection (1) is referred to in this Act as 'the Chapter I prohibition'.

Excluded agreements

3 Excluded agreements

(1) The Chapter I prohibition does not apply in any of the cases in which it is excluded by or as a result of—

    (a) Schedule 1 (mergers and concentrations);

    (b) Schedule 2 (competition scrutiny under other enactments); or

    (c) Schedule 3 (planning obligations and other general exclusions).

(2) The Secretary of State may at any time by order amend Schedule 1, with respect to the Chapter I prohibition, by—

(a) providing for one or more additional exclusions; or

(b) amending or removing any provision (whether or not it has been added by an order under this subsection).

(3) The Secretary of State may at any time by order amend Schedule 3, with respect to the Chapter I prohibition, by—

(a) providing for one or more additional exclusions; or

(b) amending or removing any provision—

    (i)   added by an order under this subsection; or

    (ii) included in paragraph 1, 2, 8 or 9 of Schedule 3.

(4) The power under subsection (3) to provide for an additional exclusion may be exercised only if it appears to the Secretary of State that agreements which fall within the additional exclusion—

(a) do not in general have an adverse effect on competition, or

(b) are, in general, best considered under Chapter II or the Enterprise Act 2002.

(5) An order under subsection (2)(a) or (3)(a) may include provision (similar to that made with respect to any other exclusion provided by the relevant Schedule) for the exclusion concerned to cease to apply to a particular agreement.

(6) Schedule 3 also gives the Secretary of State power to exclude agreements from the Chapter I prohibition in certain circumstances.

Exemptions

6   Block exemptions

(1) If agreements which fall within a particular category of agreement are, in the opinion of the OFT, likely to be agreements to which section 9 applies, the OFT may recommend that the Secretary of State make an order specifying that category for the purposes of this section.

(2) The Secretary of State may make an order ('a block exemption order') giving effect to such a recommendation—

(a) in the form in which the recommendation is made; or

(b) subject to such modifications as he considers appropriate.

(3) An agreement which falls within a category specified in a block exemption order is exempt from the Chapter I prohibition.

(4) An exemption under this section is referred to in this Part as a block exemption.

(5) A block exemption order may impose conditions or obligations subject to which a block exemption is to have effect.

(6) A block exemption order may provide—

(a) that breach of a condition imposed by the order has the effect of cancelling the block exemption in respect of an agreement;

(b) that if there is a failure to comply with an obligation imposed by the order, the OFT may, by notice in writing, cancel the block exemption in respect of the agreement;

(c) that if the OFT considers that a particular agreement is not one to which section 9 applies, it may cancel the block exemption in respect of that agreement.

(7) A block exemption order may provide that the order is to cease to have effect at the end of a specified period.

(8) In this section—

'exempt agreement' means an agreement which is exempt from the Chapter I prohibition as a result of section 9; and

'specified' means specified in a block exemption order.

8   Block exemptions: procedure

(1) Before making a recommendation under section 6(1), the OFT must—

(a) publish details of its proposed recommendation in such a way as it thinks most suitable for bringing it to the attention of those likely to be affected; and

(b) consider any representations about it which are made to it.

(2) If the Secretary of State proposes to give effect to such a recommendation subject to modifications, he must inform the OFT of the proposed modifications and take into account any comments made by the OFT.

(3) If, in the opinion of the OFT, it is appropriate to vary or revoke a block exemption order it may make a recommendation to that effect to the Secretary of State.

(4) Subsection (1) also applies to any proposed recommendation under subsection (3).

(5) Before exercising his power to vary or revoke a block exemption order (in a case where there has been no recommendation under subsection (3)), the Secretary of State must—

(a) inform the OFT of the proposed variation or revocation; and

(b) take into account any comments made by the OFT.

(6) A block exemption order may provide for a block exemption to have effect from a date earlier than that on which the order is made.

9 Exempt agreements

(1) An agreement is exempt from the Chapter I prohibition if it—

(a) contributes to—

(i) improving production or distribution, or

(ii) promoting technical or economic progress, while allowing consumers a fair share of the resulting benefit; and

(b) does not—

(i) impose on the undertakings concerned restrictions which are not indispensable to the attainment of those objectives; or

(ii) afford the undertakings concerned the possibility of eliminating competition in respect of a substantial part of the products in question.

(2) In any proceedings in which it is alleged that the Chapter I prohibition is being or has been infringed by an agreement, any undertaking or association of undertakings claiming the benefit of subsection (1) shall bear the burden of proving that the conditions of that subsection are satisfied.

10 Parallel exemptions

(1) An agreement is exempt from the Chapter I prohibition if it is exempt from the Community prohibition—

(a) by virtue of a Regulation,

(b) because it has been given exemption by the Commission, or

(c) because it has been notified to the Commission under the appropriate opposition or objection procedure and—

(i) the time for opposing, or objecting to, the agreement has expired and the Commission has not opposed it; or

(ii) the Commission has opposed, or objected to, the agreement but has withdrawn its opposition or objection.

(2) An agreement is exempt from the Chapter I prohibition if it does not affect trade between Member States but otherwise falls within a category of agreement which is exempt from the Community prohibition by virtue of a Regulation.

(3) An exemption from the Chapter I prohibition under this section is referred to in this Part as a parallel exemption.

(4) A parallel exemption—

(a) takes effect on the date on which the relevant exemption from the Community prohibition takes effect or, in the case of a parallel exemption under subsection (2), would take effect if the agreement in question affected trade between Member States; and

(b) ceases to have effect—

(i) if the relevant exemption from the Community prohibition ceases to have effect; or

(ii) on being cancelled by virtue of subsection (5) or (7).

(5) In such circumstances and manner as may be specified in rules made under section 51, the OFT may—

(a) impose conditions or obligations subject to which a parallel exemption is to have effect;

(b) vary or remove any such condition or obligation;

(c) impose one or more additional conditions or obligations;

(d) cancel the exemption.

(6) In such circumstances as may be specified in rules made under section 51, the date from which cancellation of an exemption is to take effect may be earlier than the date on which notice of cancellation is given.

(7) Breach of a condition imposed by the OFT has the effect of cancelling the exemption.

(8) In exercising its powers under this section, the OFT may require any person who is a party to the agreement in question to give it such information as it may require.

(9) For the purpose of this section references to an agreement being exempt from the Community prohibition are to be read as including references to the prohibition being inapplicable to the agreement by virtue of a Regulation other than the EC Competition Regulation or a decision by the Commission.

(10) In this section— 'the Community prohibition' means the prohibition contained in—

(a) paragraph 1 of Article 85;

(b) any corresponding provision replacing, or otherwise derived from, that provision;

(c) such other Regulation as the Secretary of State may by order specify; and 'Regulation' means a Regulation adopted by the Commission or by the Council.

(11) This section has effect in relation to the prohibition contained in paragraph 1 of Article 53 of the EEA Agreement (and the EFTA Surveillance Authority) as it has effect in relation to the Community prohibition (and the Commission) subject to any modifications which the Secretary of State may by order prescribe.

11   Exemption for certain other agreements

(1) The fact that a ruling may be given by virtue of Article 84 of the Treaty on the question whether or not agreements of a particular kind are prohibited by Article 81(1) does not prevent such agreements from being subject to the Chapter I prohibition.

(2) But the Secretary of State may by regulations make such provision as he considers appropriate for the purpose of granting an exemption from the Chapter I prohibition, in prescribed circumstances, in respect of such agreements.

(3) An exemption from the Chapter I prohibition by virtue of regulations under this section is referred to in this Part as a section 11 exemption.

Notification

12–16   [repealed]

Chapter II Abuse of dominant position

Introduction

17   Enactments replaced

Sections 2 to 10 of the Competition Act 1980 (control of anti-competitive practices) shall cease to have effect.

The prohibition

18   Abuse of dominant position

(1) Subject to section 19, any conduct on the part of one or more undertakings which amounts to the abuse of a dominant position in a market is prohibited if it may affect trade within the United Kingdom.

(2) Conduct may, in particular, constitute such an abuse if it consists in—

(a) directly or indirectly imposing unfair purchase or selling prices or other unfair trading conditions;

(b) limiting production, markets or technical development to the prejudice of consumers;

(c) applying dissimilar conditions to equivalent transactions with other trading parties, thereby placing them at a competitive disadvantage;

(d) making the conclusion of contracts subject to acceptance by the other parties of supplementary obligations which, by their nature or according to commercial usage, have no connection with the subject of the contracts.

(3) In this section—

'dominant position' means a dominant position within the United Kingdom; and

'the United Kingdom' means the United Kingdom or any part of it.

(4) The prohibition imposed by subsection (1) is referred to in this Act as 'the Chapter II prohibition'.

Excluded cases

19 Excluded cases

(1) The Chapter II prohibition does not apply in any of the cases in which it is excluded by or as a result of—

(a) Schedule 1 (mergers and concentrations); or

(b) Schedule 3 (general exclusions).

(2) The Secretary of State may at any time by order amend Schedule 1, with respect to the Chapter II prohibition, by—

(a) providing for one or more additional exclusions; or

(b) amending or removing any provision (whether or not it has been added by an order under this subsection).

(3) The Secretary of State may at any time by order amend paragraph 8 of Schedule 3 with respect to the Chapter II prohibition.

(4) Schedule 3 also gives the Secretary of State power to provide that the Chapter II prohibition is not to apply in certain circumstances.

Notification

20–24 [repealed]

Chapter III Investigation and enforcement

Investigations

25 Power of OFT to investigate

(1) In any of the following cases, the OFT may conduct an investigation.

(2) The first case is where there are reasonable grounds for suspecting that there is an agreement which—

(a) may affect trade within the United Kingdom; and

(b) has as its object or effect the prevention, restriction or distortion of competition within the United Kingdom.

(3) The second case is where there are reasonable grounds for suspecting that there is an agreement which—

(a) may affect trade between Member States; and

(b) has as its object or effect the prevention, restriction or distortion of competition within the Community.

(4) The third case is where there are reasonable grounds for suspecting that the Chapter II prohibition has been infringed.

(5) The fourth case is where there are reasonable grounds for suspecting that the prohibition in Article 82 has been infringed.

(6) The fifth case is where there are reasonable grounds for suspecting that, at some time in the past, there was an agreement which at that time—

(a) may have affected trade within the United Kingdom; and

(b) had as its object or effect the prevention, restriction or distortion of competition within the United Kingdom.

(7) The sixth case is where there are reasonable grounds for suspecting that, at some time in the past, there was an agreement which at that time—

(a) may have affected trade between Member States; and

(b) had as its object or effect the prevention, restriction or distortion of competition within the Community.

(8) Subsection (2) does not permit an investigation to be conducted in relation to an agreement if the OFT—

(a) considers that the agreement is exempt from the Chapter I prohibition as a result of a block exemption or a parallel exemption; and

(b) does not have reasonable grounds for suspecting that the circumstances may be such that it could exercise its power to cancel the exemption.

(9) Subsection (3) does not permit an investigation to be conducted if the OFT—

(a) considers that the agreement is an agreement to which the prohibition in Article 81(1) is inapplicable by virtue of a regulation of the Commission ('the relevant regulation'); and

(b) does not have reasonable grounds for suspecting that the conditions set out in Article 29(2) of the EC Competition Regulation for the withdrawal of the benefit of the relevant regulation may be satisfied in respect of that agreement.

(10) Subsection (6) does not permit an investigation to be conducted in relation to any agreement if the OFT considers that, at the time in question, the agreement was exempt from the Chapter I prohibition as a result of a block exemption or a parallel exemption.

(11) Subsection (7) does not permit an investigation to be conducted in relation to any agreement if the OFT considers that, at the time in question, the agreement was an agreement to which the prohibition in Article 81(1) was inapplicable by virtue of a regulation of the Commission.

(12) It is immaterial for the purposes of subsection (6) or (7) whether the agreement in question remains in existence.

26   Powers when conducting investigations

(1) For the purposes of an investigation, the OFT may require any person to produce to the OFT a specified document, or to provide it with specified information, which it considers relates to any matter relevant to the investigation.

(2) The power conferred by subsection (1) is to be exercised by a notice in writing.

(3) A notice under subsection (2) must indicate—

(a) the subject matter and purpose of the investigation; and

(b) the nature of the offences created by sections 42 to 44.

(4) In subsection (1) 'specified' means—

(a) specified, or described, in the notice; or

(b) falling within a category which is specified, or described, in the notice.

(5) The OFT may also specify in the notice—

(a) the time and place at which any document is to be produced or any information is to be provided;

(b) the manner and form in which it is to be produced or provided.

(6) The power under this section to require a person to produce a document includes power—

(a) if the document is produced—

(i) to take copies of it or extracts from it;

(ii) to require him, or any person who is a present or past officer of his, or is or was at any time employed by him, to provide an explanation of the document;

(b) if the document is not produced, to require him to state, to the best of his knowledge and belief, where it is.

27 Power to enter business premises without a warrant

(1) Any officer of the OFT who is authorised in writing by the OFT to do so ('an investigating officer') may enter any business premises in connection with an investigation.

(2) No investigating officer is to enter any premises in the exercise of his powers under this section unless he has given to the occupier of the premises a written notice which—

    (a) gives at least two working days' notice of the intended entry;

    (b) indicates the subject matter and purpose of the investigation; and

    (c) indicates the nature of the offences created by sections 42 to 44.

(3) Subsection (2) does not apply—

    (a) if the OFT has a reasonable suspicion that the premises are, or have been, occupied by—

        (i) a party to an agreement which it is investigating under section 25; or

        (ii) an undertaking the conduct of which it is investigating under section 25; or

    (b) if the investigating officer has taken all such steps as are reasonably practicable to give notice but has not been able to do so.

(4) In a case falling within subsection (3), the power of entry conferred by subsection (1) is to be exercised by the investigating officer on production of—

    (a) evidence of his authorisation; and

    (b) a document containing the information referred to in subsection (2)(b) and (c).

(5) An investigating officer entering any premises under this section may—

    (a) take with him such equipment as appears to him to be necessary;

    (b) require any person on the premises—

        (i) to produce any document which he considers relates to any matter relevant to the investigation; and

        (ii) if the document is produced, to provide an explanation of it;

    (c) require any person to state, to the best of his knowledge and belief, where any such document is to be found;

    (d) take copies of, or extracts from, any document which is produced;

    (e) require any information which is held in a computer and is accessible from the premises and which the investigating officer considers relates to any matter relevant to the investigation, to be produced in a form—

        (i) in which it can be taken away, and

        (ii) in which it is visible and legible;

    (f) take any steps which appear to be necessary for the purpose of preserving or preventing interference with any document which he considers relates to any matter relevant to the investigation.

(6) In this section 'business premises' means premises (or any part of premises) not used as a dwelling.

28 Power to enter business premises under a warrant

(1) On an application made by the OFT to the court in accordance with rules of court, a judge may issue a warrant if he is satisfied that—

    (a) there are reasonable grounds for suspecting that there are on any business premises documents—

        (i) the production of which has been required under section 26 or 27; and

        (ii) which have not been produced as required;

    (b) there are reasonable grounds for suspecting that—

        (i) there are on any business premises documents which the OFT has power under section 26 to require to be produced; and

        (ii) if the documents were required to be produced, they would not be produced but would be concealed, removed, tampered with or destroyed; or

    (c) an investigating officer has attempted to enter premises in the exercise of his powers under section 27 but has been unable to do so and that there are reasonable grounds for suspecting that there are on the premises documents the production of which could have been required under that section.

(2) A warrant under this section shall authorise a named officer of the OFT, and any other of the OFT's officers whom the OFT has authorised in writing to accompany the named officer—

(a) to enter the premises specified in the warrant, using such force as is reasonably necessary for the purpose;

(b) to search the premises and take copies of, or extracts from, any document appearing to be of a kind in respect of which the application under subsection (1) was granted ('the relevant kind');

(c) to take possession of any documents appearing to be of the relevant kind if—

(i)   such action appears to be necessary for preserving the documents or preventing interference with them; or

(ii)   it is not reasonably practicable to take copies of the documents on the premises;

(d) to take any other steps which appear to be necessary for the purpose mentioned in paragraph (c)(i);

(e) to require any person to provide an explanation of any document appearing to be of the relevant kind or to state, to the best of his knowledge and belief, where it may be found;

(f) to require any information which is held in a computer and is accessible from the premises and which the named officer considers relates to any matter relevant to the investigation, to be produced in a form—

(i)   in which it can be taken away, and

(ii)   in which it is visible and legible.

(3) If, in the case of a warrant under subsection (1)(b), the judge is satisfied that it is reasonable to suspect that there are also on the premises other documents relating to the investigation concerned, the warrant shall also authorise action mentioned in subsection (2) to be taken in relation to any such document.

(3A) A warrant under this section may authorise persons specified in the warrant to accompany the named officer who is executing it.

(4) Any person entering premises by virtue of a warrant under this section may take with him such equipment as appears to him to be necessary.

(5) On leaving any premises which he has entered by virtue of a warrant under this section, the named officer must, if the premises are unoccupied or the occupier is temporarily absent, leave them as effectively secured as he found them.

(6) A warrant under this section continues in force until the end of the period of one month beginning with the day on which it is issued.

(7) Any document of which possession is taken under subsection (2)(c) may be retained for a period of three months.

(8) In this section 'business premises' has the same meaning as in section 27.

28A   Power to enter domestic premises under a warrant

(1) On an application made by the OFT to the court in accordance with rules of court, a judge may issue a warrant if he is satisfied that—

(a) there are reasonable grounds for suspecting that there are on any domestic premises documents—

(i)   the production of which has been required under section 26; and

(ii)   which have not been produced as required; or

(b) there are reasonable grounds for suspecting that—

(i)   there are on any domestic premises documents which the OFT has power under section 26 to require to be produced; and

(ii)   if the documents were required to be produced, they would not be produced but would be concealed, removed, tampered with or destroyed.

(2) A warrant under this section shall authorise a named officer of the OFT, and any other of its officers whom the OFT has authorised in writing to accompany the named officer—

    (a) to enter the premises specified in the warrant, using such force as is reasonably necessary for the purpose;

    (b) to search the premises and take copies of, or extracts from, any document appearing to be of a kind in respect of which the application under subsection (1) was granted ('the relevant kind');

    (c) to take possession of any documents appearing to be of the relevant kind if—

        (i) such action appears to be necessary for preserving the documents or preventing interference with them; or

        (ii) it is not reasonably practicable to take copies of the documents on the premises;

    (d) to take any other steps which appear to be necessary for the purpose mentioned in paragraph (c)(i);

    (e) to require any person to provide an explanation of any document appearing to be of the relevant kind or to state, to the best of his knowledge and belief, where it may be found;

    (f) to require any information which is stored in any electronic form and is accessible from the premises and which the named officer considers relates to any matter relevant to the investigation, to be produced in a form—

        (i) in which it can be taken away, and

        (ii) in which it is visible and legible or from which it can readily be produced in a visible and legible form.

(3) If, in the case of a warrant under subsection (1)(b), the judge is satisfied that it is reasonable to suspect that there are also on the premises other documents relating to the investigation concerned, the warrant shall also authorise action mentioned in subsection (2) to be taken in relation to any such document.

(4) A warrant under this section may authorise persons specified in the warrant to accompany the named officer who is executing it.

(5) Any person entering premises by virtue of a warrant under this section may take with him such equipment as appears to him to be necessary.

(6) On leaving any premises which he has entered by virtue of a warrant under this section, the named officer must, if the premises are unoccupied or the occupier is temporarily absent, leave them as effectively secured as he found them.

(7) A warrant under this section continues in force until the end of the period of one month beginning with the day on which it is issued.

(8) Any document of which possession is taken under subsection (2)(c) maybe retained for a period of three months.

(9) In this section, 'domestic premises' means premises (or any part of premises) that are used as a dwelling and are—

    (a) premises also used in connection with the affairs of an undertaking or association of undertakings; or

    (b) premises where documents relating to the affairs of an undertaking or association of undertakings are kept.

29 Entry of premises under warrant: supplementary

(1) A warrant issued under section 28 or 28A must indicate—

    (a) the subject matter and purpose of the investigation;

    (b) the nature of the offences created by sections 42 to 44.

(2) The powers conferred by section 28 or 28A are to be exercised on production of a warrant issued under that section.

(3) If there is no one at the premises when the named officer proposes to execute such a warrant he must, before executing it—

    (a) take such steps as are reasonable in all the circumstances to inform the occupier of the intended entry; and

    (b) if the occupier is informed, afford him or his legal or other representative a reasonable opportunity to be present when the warrant is executed.

(4) If the named officer is unable to inform the occupier of the intended entry he must, when executing the warrant, leave a copy of it in a prominent place on the premises.

(5) In this section—

'named officer' means the officer named in the warrant; and

'occupier', in relation to any premises, means a person whom the named officer reasonably believes is the occupier of those premises.

30   Privileged communications

(1) A person shall not be required, under any provision of this Part, to produce or disclose a privileged communication.

(2) 'Privileged communication' means a communication—

(a) between a professional legal adviser and his client, or

(b) made in connection with, or in contemplation of, legal proceedings and for the purposes of those proceedings,

which in proceedings in the High Court would be protected from disclosure on grounds of legal professional privilege.

(3) In the application of this section to Scotland—

(a) references to the High Court are to be read as references to the Court of Session; and

(b) the reference to legal professional privilege is to be read as a reference to confidentiality of communications.

30A   Use of statements in prosecution

A statement made by a person in response to a requirement imposed by virtue of any of sections 26 to 28A may not be used in evidence against him on a prosecution for an offence under section 188 of the Enterprise Act 2002 unless, in the proceedings—

(a) in giving evidence, he makes a statement inconsistent with it, and

(b) evidence relating to it is adduced, or a question relating to it is asked, by him or on his behalf.

31   Decisions following an investigation

(1) If as a result of an investigation the OFT proposes to make a decision, the OFT must—

(a) give written notice to the person (or persons) likely to be affected by the proposed decision; and

(b) give that person (or those persons) an opportunity to make representations.

(2) For the purposes of this section and sections 31A and 31B 'decision' means a decision of the OFT—

(a) that the Chapter I prohibition has been infringed;

(b) that the Chapter II prohibition has been infringed;

(c) that the prohibition in Article 81(1) has been infringed; or

(d) that the prohibition in Article 82 has been infringed.

31A   Commitments

(1) Subsection (2) applies in a case where the OFT has begun an investigation under section 25 but has not made a decision (within the meaning given by section 31(2)).

(2) For the purposes of addressing the competition concerns it has identified, the OFT may accept from such person (or persons) concerned as it considers appropriate commitments to take such action (or refrain from taking such action) as it considers appropriate.

(3) At any time when commitments are in force the OFT may accept from the person (or persons) who gave the commitments—

(a) a variation of them if it is satisfied that the commitments as varied will address its current competition concerns;

(b) commitments in substitution for them if it is satisfied that the new commitments will address its current competition concerns.

(4) Commitments under this section—

    (a) shall come into force when accepted; and

    (b) may be released by the OFT where—

        (i)   it is requested to do so by the person (or persons) who gave the commitments; or

        (ii) it has reasonable grounds for believing that the competition concerns referred to in subsection (2) or (3) no longer arise.

(5) The provisions of Schedule 6A to this Act shall have effect with respect to procedural requirements for the acceptance, variation and release of commitments under this section.

31B   Effect of commitments under section 31A

(1) Subsection (2) applies if the OFT has accepted commitments under section 31A (and has not released them).

(2) In such a case, the OFT shall not—

    (a) continue the investigation,

    (b) make a decision (within the meaning of section 31(2)), or

    (c) give a direction under section 35,

in relation to the agreement or conduct which was the subject of the investigation (but this subsection is subject to subsections (3) and (4)).

(3) Nothing in subsection (2) prevents the OFT from taking any action in relation to competition concerns which are not addressed by commitments accepted by it.

(4) Subsection (2) also does not prevent the OFT from continuing the investigation, making a decision, or giving a direction where—

    (a) it has reasonable grounds for believing that there has been a material change of circumstances since the commitments were accepted;

    (b) it has reasonable grounds for suspecting that a person has failed to adhere to one or more of the terms of the commitments; or

    (c) it has reasonable grounds for suspecting that information which led it to accept the commitments was incomplete, false or misleading in a material particular.

(5) If, pursuant to subsection (4), the OFT makes a decision or gives a direction the commitments are to be treated as released from the date of that decision or direction.

31C   Review of commitments

(1) Where the OFT is reviewing or has reviewed the effectiveness of commitments accepted under section 31A it must, if requested to do so by the Secretary of State, prepare a report of its findings.

(2) The OFT must—

    (a) give any report prepared by it under subsection (1) to the Secretary of State; and

    (b) publish the report.

31D   Guidance

(1) The OFT must prepare and publish guidance as to the circumstances in which it may be appropriate to accept commitments under section 31A.

(2) The OFT may at any time alter the guidance.

(3) If the guidance is altered, the OFT must publish it as altered.

(4) No guidance is to be published under this section without the approval of the Secretary of State.

(5) The OFT may, after consulting the Secretary of State, choose how it publishes its guidance.

(6) If the OFT is preparing or altering guidance under this section it must consult such persons as it considers appropriate.

(7) If the proposed guidance or alteration relates to a matter in respect of which a regulator exercises concurrent jurisdiction, those consulted must include that regulator.

(8) When exercising its discretion to accept commitments under section 31A, the OFT must have regard to the guidance for the time being in force under this section.

31E   Enforcement of commitments

(1) If a person from whom the OFT has accepted commitments fails without reasonable excuse to adhere to the commitments (and has not been released from them), the OFT may apply to the court for an order—

    (a) requiring the defaulter to make good his default within a time specified in the order; or

    (b) if the commitments relate to anything to be done in the management or administration of an undertaking, requiring the undertaking or any of its officers to do it.

(2) An order of the court under subsection (1) may provide for all the costs of, or incidental to, the application for the order to be borne by—

    (a) the person in default; or

    (b) any officer of an undertaking who is responsible for the default.

(3) In the application of subsection (2) to Scotland, the reference to 'costs' is to be read as a reference to 'expenses'.

Enforcement

32   Directions in relation to agreements

(1) If the OFT has made a decision that an agreement infringes the Chapter I prohibition or that it infringes the prohibition in Article 81(1), it may give to such person or persons as it considers appropriate such directions as it considers appropriate to bring the infringement to an end.

(3) A direction under this section may, in particular, include provision—

    (a) requiring the parties to the agreement to modify the agreement; or

    (b) requiring them to terminate the agreement.

(4) A direction under this section must be given in writing.

33   Directions in relation to conduct

(1) If the OFT has made a decision that conduct infringes the Chapter II prohibition or that it infringes the prohibition in Article 82, it may give to such person or persons as it considers appropriate such directions as it considers appropriate to bring the infringement to an end.

(3) A direction under this section may, in particular, include provision—

    (a) requiring the person concerned to modify the conduct in question; or

    (b) requiring him to cease that conduct.

(4) A direction under this section must be given in writing.

34   Enforcement of directions

(1) If a person fails, without reasonable excuse, to comply with a direction under section 32 or 33, the OFT may apply to the court for an order—

    (a) requiring the defaulter to make good his default within a time specified in the order; or

    (b) if the direction related to anything to be done in the management or administration of an undertaking, requiring the undertaking or any of its officers to do it.

(2) An order of the court under subsection (1) may provide for all of the costs of, or incidental to, the application for the order to be borne by—

    (a) the person in default; or

    (b) any officer of an undertaking who is responsible for the default.

(3) In the application of subsection (2) to Scotland, the reference to 'costs' is to be read as a reference to 'expenses'.

35   Interim measures

(1) Subject to subsections (8) and (9), this section applies if the OFT has begun an investigation under section 25 and not completed it (but only applies so long as the OFT has power under section 25 to conduct that investigation).

(2) If the OFT considers that it is necessary for it to act under this section as a matter of urgency for the purpose—

    (a) of preventing serious, irreparable damage to a particular person or category of person, or

(b) of protecting the public interest, it may give such directions as it considers appropriate for that purpose.

(3) Before giving a direction under this section, the OFT must—

(a) give written notice to the person (or persons) to whom it proposes to give the direction; and

(b) give that person (or each of them) an opportunity to make representations.

(4) A notice under subsection (3) must indicate the nature of the direction which the OFT is proposing to give and its reasons for wishing to give it.

(5) A direction given under this section may if the circumstances permit be replaced by—

(a) a direction under section 32 or (as appropriate) section 33, or

(b) commitments accepted under section 31A, but, subject to that, has effect while this section applies.

(6) In the cases mentioned in section 25(2), (3), (6) and (7), sections 32(3) and 34 also apply to directions given under this section.

(7) In the cases mentioned in section 25(4) and (5), sections 33(3) and 34 also apply to directions given under this section.

(8) In the case of an investigation conducted by virtue of section 25(2) or (6), this section does not apply if a person has produced evidence to the OFT in connection with the investigation that satisfies it on the balance of probabilities that, in the event of it reaching the basic infringement conclusion, it would also reach the conclusion that the suspected agreement is exempt from the Chapter I prohibition as a result of section 9(1); and in this subsection 'the basic infringement conclusion' is the conclusion that there is an agreement which—

(a) may affect trade within the United Kingdom, and

(b) has as its object or effect the prevention, restriction or distortion of competition within the United Kingdom.

(9) In the case of an investigation conducted by virtue of section 25(3) or (7), this section does not apply if a person has produced evidence to the OFT in connection with the investigation that satisfies it on the balance of probabilities that, in the event of it reaching the basic infringement conclusion, it would also reach the conclusion that the suspected agreement is an agreement to which the prohibition in Article 81(1) is inapplicable because the agreement satisfies the conditions in Article 81(3); and in this subsection 'the basic infringement conclusion' is the conclusion that there is an agreement which—

(a) may affect trade between Member States, and

(b) has as its object or effect the prevention, restriction or distortion of competition within the Community.

36 Penalties

(1) On making a decision that an agreement has infringed the Chapter I prohibition or that it has infringed the prohibition in Article 81(1), the OFT may require an undertaking which is a party to the agreement to pay the OFT a penalty in respect of the infringement.

(2) On making a decision that conduct has infringed the Chapter II prohibition or that it has infringed the prohibition in Article 82, the OFT may require the undertaking concerned to pay the OFT a penalty in respect of the infringement.

(3) The OFT may impose a penalty on an undertaking under subsection (1) or (2) only if the OFT is satisfied that the infringement has been committed intentionally or negligently by the undertaking.

(4) Subsection (1) is subject to section 39 and does not apply in relation to a decision that an agreement has infringed the Chapter I prohibition if the OFT is satisfied that the undertaking acted on the reasonable assumption that that section gave it immunity in respect of the agreement.

(5) Subsection (2) is subject to section 40 and does not apply in relation to a decision that conduct has infringed the Chapter II prohibition if the OFT is satisfied that the undertaking acted on the reasonable assumption that that section gave it immunity in respect of the conduct.

(6) Notice of a penalty under this section must—
    (a) be in writing; and
    (b) specify the date before which the penalty is required to be paid.

(7) The date specified must not be earlier than the end of the period within which an appeal against the notice may be brought under section 46.

(8) No penalty fixed by the OFT under this section may exceed 10% of the turnover of the undertaking (determined in accordance with such provisions as may be specified in an order made by the Secretary of State).

(9) Any sums received by the OFT under this section are to be paid into the Consolidated Fund.

37   Recovery of penalties

(1) If the specified date in a penalty notice has passed and—
    (a) the period during which an appeal against the imposition, or amount, of the penalty may be made has expired without an appeal having been made, or
    (b) such an appeal has been made and determined, the OFT may recover from the undertaking, as a civil debt due to the OFT, any amount payable under the penalty notice which remains outstanding.

(2) In this section—
'penalty notice' means a notice given under section 36; and
'specified date' means the date specified in the penalty notice.

38   The appropriate level of a penalty

(1) The OFT must prepare and publish guidance as to the appropriate amount of any penalty under this Part.

(1A) The guidance must include provision about the circumstances in which, in determining a penalty under this Part, the OFT may take into account effects in another Member State of the agreement or conduct concerned.

(2) The OFT may at any time alter the guidance.

(3) If the guidance is altered, the OFT must publish it as altered.

(4) No guidance is to be published under this section without the approval of the Secretary of State.

(5) The OFT may, after consulting the Secretary of State, choose how it publishes its guidance.

(6) If the OFT is preparing or altering guidance under this section it must consult such persons as it considers appropriate.

(7) If the proposed guidance or alteration relates to a matter in respect of which a regulator exercises concurrent jurisdiction, those consulted must include that regulator.

(8) When setting the amount of a penalty under this Part, the OFT must have regard to the guidance for the time being in force under this section.

(9) If a penalty or a fine has been imposed by the Commission, or by a court or other body in another Member State, in respect of an agreement or conduct, the OFT, an appeal tribunal or the appropriate court must take that penalty or fine into account when setting the amount of a penalty under this Part in relation to that agreement or conduct.

(10) In subsection (9) 'the appropriate court' means—
    (a) in relation to England and Wales, the Court of Appeal;
    (b) in relation to Scotland, the Court of Session;
    (c) in relation to Northern Ireland, the Court of Appeal in Northern Ireland;
    (d) the House of Lords.

39   Limited immunity in relation to the Chapter I prohibition

(1) In this section 'small agreement' means an agreement—
    (a) which falls within a category prescribed for the purposes of this section; but
    (b) is not a price fixing agreement.

(2) The criteria by reference to which a category of agreement is prescribed may, in particular, include—

    (a) the combined turnover of the parties to the agreement (determined in accordance with prescribed provisions);

    (b) the share of the market affected by the agreement (determined in that way).

(3) A party to a small agreement is immune from the effect of section 36(1) so far as that provision relates to decisions about infringement of the Chapter I prohibition; but the OFT may withdraw that immunity under subsection (4).

(4) If the OFT has investigated a small agreement, it may make a decision withdrawing the immunity given by subsection (3) if, as a result of its investigation, it considers that the agreement is likely to infringe the Chapter I prohibition.

(5) The OFT must give each of the parties in respect of which immunity is withdrawn written notice of its decision to withdraw the immunity.

(6) A decision under subsection (4) takes effect on such date ('the withdrawal date') as may be specified in the decision.

(7) The withdrawal date must be a date after the date on which the decision is made.

(8) In determining the withdrawal date, the OFT must have regard to the amount of time which the parties are likely to require in order to secure that there is no further infringement of the Chapter I prohibition with respect to the agreement.

(9) In subsection (1) 'price fixing agreement' means an agreement which has as its object or effect, or one of its objects or effects, restricting the freedom of a party to the agreement to determine the price to be charged (otherwise than as between that party and another party to the agreement) for the product, service or other matter to which the agreement relates.

40   Limited immunity in relation to the Chapter II prohibition

(1) In this section 'conduct of minor significance' means conduct which falls within a category prescribed for the purposes of this section.

(2) The criteria by reference to which a category is prescribed may, in particular, include—

    (a) the turnover of the person whose conduct it is (determined in accordance with prescribed provisions);

    (b) the share of the market affected by the conduct (determined in that way).

(3) A person is immune from the effect of section 36(2), so far as that provision relates to decisions about infringement of the Chapter II prohibition; if his conduct is conduct of minor significance; but the OFT may withdraw that immunity under subsection (4).

(4) If the OFT has investigated conduct of minor significance, it may make a decision withdrawing the immunity given by subsection (3) if, as a result of its investigation, it considers that the conduct is likely to infringe the Chapter II prohibition.

(5) The OFT must give the person, or persons, whose immunity has been withdrawn written notice of its decision to withdraw the immunity.

(6) A decision under subsection (4) takes effect on such date ('the withdrawal date') as may be specified in the decision.

(7) The withdrawal date must be a date after the date on which the decision is made.

(8) In determining the withdrawal date, the OFT must have regard to the amount of time which the person or persons affected are likely to require in order to secure that there is no further infringement of the Chapter II prohibition.

41   [repealed]

Offences

42   Offences

(1) A person is guilty of an offence if he fails to comply with a requirement imposed on him under section 26, 27, 28 or 28A.

(2) If a person is charged with an offence under subsection (1) in respect of a requirement to produce a document, it is a defence for him to prove—

    (a) that the document was not in his possession or under his control; and

    (b) that it was not reasonably practicable for him to comply with the requirement.

(3) If a person is charged with an offence under subsection (1) in respect of a requirement—

    (a) to provide information,

    (b) to provide an explanation of a document, or

    (c) to state where a document is to be found, it is a defence for him to prove that he had a reasonable excuse for failing to comply with the requirement.

(4) Failure to comply with a requirement imposed under section 26 or 27 is not an offence if the person imposing the requirement has failed to act in accordance with that section.

(5) A person is guilty of an offence if he intentionally obstructs an officer acting in the exercise of his powers under section 27.

(6) A person guilty of an offence under subsection (1) or (5) is liable—

    (a) on summary conviction, to a fine not exceeding the statutory maximum;

    (b) on conviction on indictment, to a fine.

(7) A person who intentionally obstructs an officer in the exercise of his powers under a warrant issued under section 28 or 28A is guilty of an offence and liable—

    (a) on summary conviction, to a fine not exceeding the statutory maximum;

    (b) on conviction on indictment, to imprisonment for a term not exceeding two years or to a fine or to both.

43   Destroying or falsifying documents

(1) A person is guilty of an offence if, having been required to produce a document under section 26, 27, 28 or 28A—

    (a) he intentionally or recklessly destroys or otherwise disposes of it, falsifies it or conceals it, or

    (b) he causes or permits its destruction, disposal, falsification or concealment.

(2) A person guilty of an offence under subsection (1) is liable—

    (a) on summary conviction, to a fine not exceeding the statutory maximum;

    (b) on conviction on indictment, to imprisonment for a term not exceeding two years or to a fine or to both.

44   False or misleading information

(1) If information is provided by a person to the OFT in connection with any function of the OFT under this Part, that person is guilty of an offence if—

    (a) the information is false or misleading in a material particular, and

    (b) he knows that it is or is reckless as to whether it is.

(2) A person who—

    (a) provides any information to another person, knowing the information to be false or misleading in a material particular, or

    (b) recklessly provides any information to another person which is false or misleading in a material particular,

knowing that the information is to be used for the purpose of providing information to the OFT in connection with any of its functions under this Part, is guilty of an offence.

(3) A person guilty of an offence under this section is liable—

    (a) on summary conviction, to a fine not exceeding the statutory maximum;

    (b) on conviction on indictment, to imprisonment for a term not exceeding two years or to a fine or to both.

Chapter IV The Competition Commission and appeals

The Commission

45 The Competition Commission

(1) There is to be a body corporate known as the Competition Commission.

(2) The Commission is to have such functions as are conferred on it by or as a result of this Act.

(3) The Monopolies and Mergers Commission is dissolved and its functions are transferred to the Competition Commission.

(4) In any enactment, instrument or other document, any reference to the Monopolies and Mergers Commission which has continuing effect is to be read as a reference to the Competition Commission.

(5) The Secretary of State may by order make such consequential, supplemental and incidental provision as he considers appropriate in connection with—

    (a) the dissolution of the Monopolies and Mergers Commission; and

    (b) the transfer of functions effected by subsection (3).

(6) An order made under subsection (5) may, in particular, include provision—

    (a) for the transfer of property, rights, obligations and liabilities and the continuation of proceedings, investigations and other matters; or

    (b) amending any enactment which makes provision with respect to the Monopolies and Mergers Commission or any of its functions.

(7) Schedules 7 and 7A make further provision about the Competition Commission.

(8) The Secretary of State may by order make such modifications in Part 2 of Schedule 7 and in Schedule 7A (performance of the Competition Commission's general functions) as he considers appropriate for improving the performance by the Competition Commission of its functions.

Appeals

46 Appealable decisions

(1) Any party to an agreement in respect of which the OFT has made a decision may appeal to the Tribunal against, or with respect to, the decision.

(2) Any person in respect of whose conduct the OFT has made a decision may appeal to the Tribunal against, or with respect to, the decision.

(3) In this section 'decision' means a decision of the OFT—

    (a) as to whether the Chapter I prohibition has been infringed,

    (b) as to whether the prohibition in Article 81(1) has been infringed,

    (c) as to whether the Chapter II prohibition has been infringed,

    (d) as to whether the prohibition in Article 82 has been infringed,

    (e) cancelling a block or parallel exemption,

    (f) withdrawing the benefit of a regulation of the Commission pursuant to Article 29(2) of the EC Competition Regulation,

    (g) not releasing commitments pursuant to a request made under section 31A(4)(b)(i),

    (h) releasing commitments under section 31A(4)(b)(ii),

    (i) as to the imposition of any penalty under section 36 or as to the amount of any such penalty,

and includes a direction under section 32, 33 or 35 and such other decisions under this Part as may be prescribed.

(4) Except in the case of an appeal against the imposition, or the amount, of a penalty, the making of an appeal under this section does not suspend the effect of the decision to which the appeal relates.

(5) Part I of Schedule 8 makes further provision about appeals.

47   Third party appeals

(1) A person who does not fall within section 46(1) or (2) may appeal to the Tribunal with respect to—

(a) a decision falling within paragraphs (a) to (f) of section 46(3);

(b) a decision falling within paragraph (g) of section 46(3);

(c) a decision of the OFT to accept or release commitments under section 31A, or to accept a variation of such commitments other than a variation which is not material in any respect;

(d) a decision of the OFT to make directions under section 35;

(e) a decision of the OFT not to make directions under section 35; or

(f) such other decision of the OFT under this Part as may be prescribed.

(2) A person may make an appeal under subsection (1) only if the Tribunal considers that he has a sufficient interest in the decision with respect to which the appeal is made, or that he represents persons who have such an interest.

(3) The making of an appeal under this section does not suspend the effect of the decision to which the appeal relates.

47A   Monetary claims before Tribunal

(1) This section applies to—

(a) any claim for damages, or

(b) any other claim for a sum of money,

which a person who has suffered loss or damage as a result of the infringement of a relevant prohibition may make in civil proceedings brought in any part of the United Kingdom.

(2) In this section 'relevant prohibition' means any of the following—

(a) the Chapter I prohibition;

(b) the Chapter II prohibition;

(c) the prohibition in Article 81(1) of the Treaty;

(d) the prohibition in Article 82 of the Treaty;

(e) the prohibition in Article 65(1) of the Treaty establishing the European Coal and Steel Community;

(f) the prohibition in Article 66(7) of that Treaty.

(3) For the purpose of identifying claims which may be made in civil proceedings, any limitation rules that would apply in such proceedings are to be disregarded.

(4) A claim to which this section applies may (subject to the provisions of this Act and Tribunal rules) be made in proceedings brought before the Tribunal.

(5) But no claim may be made in such proceedings—

(a) until a decision mentioned in subsection (6) has established that the relevant prohibition in question has been infringed; and

(b) otherwise than with the permission of the Tribunal, during any period specified in subsection (7) or (8) which relates to that decision.

(6) The decisions which may be relied on for the purposes of proceedings under this section are—

(a) a decision of the OFT that the Chapter I prohibition or the Chapter II prohibition has been infringed;

(b) a decision of the OFT that the prohibition in Article 81(1) or Article 82 of the Treaty has been infringed;

(c) a decision of the Tribunal (on an appeal from a decision of the OFT) that the Chapter I prohibition, the Chapter II prohibition or the prohibition in Article 81(1) or Article 82 of the Treaty has been infringed;

(d) a decision of the European Commission that the prohibition in Article 81(1) or Article 82 of the Treaty has been infringed; or

(e) a decision of the European Commission that the prohibition in Article 65(1) of the Treaty establishing the European Coal and Steel Community has been infringed, or a finding made by the European Commission under Article 66(7) of that Treaty.

(7) The periods during which proceedings in respect of a claim made in reliance on a decision mentioned in subsection (6)(a), (b) or (c) may not be brought without permission are—

(a) in the case of a decision of the OFT, the period during which an appeal may be made to the Tribunal under section 46 or section 47;

(b) in the case of a decision of the OFT which is the subject of an appeal mentioned in paragraph (a), the period following the decision of the Tribunal on the appeal during which a further appeal may be made under section 49;

(c) in the case of a decision of the Tribunal mentioned in subsection (6)(c), the period during which a further appeal may be made under section 49;

(d) in the case of any decision which is the subject of a further appeal, the period during which an appeal may be made to the House of Lords from a decision on the further appeal; and, where any appeal mentioned in paragraph (a), (b), (c) or (d) is made, the period specified in that paragraph includes the period before the appeal is determined.

(8) The periods during which proceedings in respect of a claim made in reliance on a decision or finding of the European Commission may not be brought without permission are—

(a) the period during which proceedings against the decision or finding may be instituted in the European Court; and

(b) if any such proceedings are instituted, the period before those proceedings are determined.

(9) In determining a claim to which this section applies the Tribunal is bound by any decision mentioned in subsection (6) which establishes that the prohibition in question has been infringed.

(10) The right to make a claim to which this section applies in proceedings before the Tribunal does not affect the right to bring any other proceedings in respect of the claim.

47B Claims brought on behalf of consumers

(1) A specified body may (subject to the provisions of this Act and Tribunal rules) bring proceedings before the Tribunal which comprise consumer claims made or continued on behalf of at least two individuals.

(2) In this section 'consumer claim' means a claim to which section 47A applies which an individual has in respect of an infringement affecting (directly or indirectly) goods or services to which subsection (7) applies.

(3) A consumer claim may be included in proceedings under this section if it is—

(a) a claim made in the proceedings on behalf of the individual concerned by the specified body; or

(b) a claim made by the individual concerned under section 47A which is continued in the proceedings on his behalf by the specified body;

and such a claim may only be made or continued in the proceedings with the consent of the individual concerned.

(4) The consumer claims included in proceedings under this section must all relate to the same infringement.

(5) The provisions of section 47A(5) to (10) apply to a consumer claim included in proceedings under this section as they apply to a claim made in proceedings under that section.

(6) Any damages or other sum (not being costs or expenses) awarded in respect of a consumer claim included in proceedings under this section must be awarded to the individual concerned; but the Tribunal may, with the consent of the specified body and the individual, order that the sum awarded must be paid to the specified body (acting on behalf of the individual).

(7) This subsection applies to goods or services which—

     (a) the individual received, or sought to receive, otherwise than in the course of a business carried on by him (notwithstanding that he received or sought to receive them with a view to carrying on a business); and

     (b) were, or would have been, supplied to the individual (in the case of goods whether by way of sale or otherwise) in the course of a business carried on by the person who supplied or would have supplied them.

  (8) A business includes—

     (a) a professional practice;

     (b) any other undertaking carried on for gain or reward;

     (c) any undertaking in the course of which goods or services are supplied otherwise than free of charge.

  (9) 'Specified' means specified in an order made by the Secretary of State, in accordance with criteria to be published by the Secretary of State for the purposes of this section.

  (10) An application by a body to be specified in an order under this section is to be made in a form approved by the Secretary of State for the purpose.

49   Further appeals

  (1) An appeal lies to the appropriate court—

     (a) from a decision of the Tribunal as to the amount of a penalty under section 36;

     (b) from a decision of the Tribunal as to the award of damages or other sum in respect of a claim made in proceedings under section 47A or included in proceedings under section 47B (other than a decision on costs or expenses) or as to the amount of any such damages of other sum; and

     (c) on a point of law arising from any other decision of the Tribunal on an appeal under section 46 or 47.

  (2) An appeal under this section—

     (a) may be brought by a party to the proceedings before the Tribunal or by a person who has a sufficient interest in the matter; and

     (b) requires the permission of the Tribunal or the appropriate court.

  (3) In this section 'the appropriate court' means the Court of Appeal or, in the case of an appeal from Tribunal proceedings in Scotland, the Court of Session.

Chapter V Miscellaneous

Vertical agreements and land agreements

50   Vertical agreements and land agreements

  (1) The Secretary of State may by order provide for any provision of this Part to apply in relation to—

     (a) vertical agreements, or

     (b) land agreements,

with such modifications as may be prescribed.

  (2) An order may, in particular, provide for exclusions or exemptions, or otherwise provide for prescribed provisions not to apply, in relation to—

     (a) vertical agreements, or land agreements, in general; or

     (b) vertical agreements, or land agreements, of any prescribed description.

  (3) An order may empower the OFT to give directions to the effect that in prescribed circumstances an exclusion, exemption or modification is not to apply (or is to apply in a particular way) in relation to an individual agreement.

  (4) Subsections (2) and (3) are not to be read as limiting the powers conferred by section 71.

  (5) In this section—

'land agreement' and 'vertical agreement' have such meaning as may be prescribed; and

'prescribed' means prescribed by an order.

OFT's rules, guidance and fees

51 Rules

(1) The OFT may make such rules about procedural and other matters in connection with the carrying into effect of the provisions of this Part as it considers appropriate.

(2) Schedule 9 makes further provision about rules made under this section but is not to be taken as restricting the OFT's powers under this section.

(3) If the OFT is preparing rules under this section it must consult such persons as it considers appropriate.

(4) If the proposed rules relate to a matter in respect of which a regulator exercises concurrent jurisdiction, those consulted must include that regulator.

(5) No rule made by the OFT is to come into operation until it has been approved by an order made by the Secretary of State.

(6) The Secretary of State may approve any rule made by the OFT—

(a) in the form in which it is submitted; or

(b) subject to such modifications as he considers appropriate.

(7) If the Secretary of State proposes to approve a rule subject to modifications he must inform the OFT of the proposed modifications and take into account any comments made by the OFT.

(8) Subsections (5) to (7) apply also to any alteration of the rules made by the OFT.

(9) The Secretary of State may, after consulting the OFT, by order vary or revoke any rules made under this section.

(10) If the Secretary of State considers that rules should be made under this section with respect to a particular matter he may direct the OFT to exercise its powers under this section and make rules about that matter.

52 Advice and information

(1) As soon as is reasonably practicable after the passing of this Act, the OFT must prepare and publish general advice and information about—

(a) the application of the Chapter I prohibition and the Chapter II prohibition; and

(b) the enforcement of those prohibitions.

(1A) As soon as is reasonably practicable after 1st May 2004, the OFT must prepare and publish general advice and information about—

(a) the application of the prohibitions in Article 81(1) and Article 82; and

(b) the enforcement by it of those prohibitions.

(2) The OFT may at any time publish revised, or new, advice or information.

(3) Advice and information published under this section must be prepared with a view to—

(a) explaining provisions of this Part to persons who are likely to be affected by them; and

(b) indicating how the OFT expects such provisions to operate.

(4) Advice (or information) published by virtue of subsection (3)(b) may include advice (or information) about the factors which the OFT may take into account in considering whether, and if so how, to exercise a power conferred on it by Chapter I, II or III.

(5) Any advice or information published by the OFT under this section is to be published in such form and in such manner as it considers appropriate.

(6) If the OFT is preparing any advice or information under this section it must consult such persons as it considers appropriate.

(7) If the proposed advice or information relates to a matter in respect of which a regulator exercises concurrent jurisdiction, those consulted must include that regulator.

(8) In preparing any advice or information under this section about a matter in respect of which he may exercise functions under this Part, a regulator must consult—

(a) the OFT;

(b) the other regulators; and

(c) such other persons as he considers appropriate.

53   [repealed]

Regulators

54   Regulators

(1) In this part 'regulator' means—

   (a) the Office of Communications;

   (b) the Gas and Electricity Markets Authority;

   (c) the Director General of Electricity Supply for Northern Ireland;

   (d) the Director General of Water Services;

   (e) the Office of Rail Regulation;

   (f) the Director General of Gas for Northern Ireland; and

   (g) the Civil Aviation Authority.

(2) Parts II and III of Schedule 10 provide for functions of the OFT under this Part to be exercisable concurrently by regulators.

(3) Parts IV and V of Schedule 10 make minor and consequential amendments in connection with the regulators' competition functions.

(4) The Secretary of State may make regulations for the purpose of coordinating the performance of functions under this Part ('Part I functions') which are exercisable concurrently by two or more competent persons as a result of any enactment (including any subordinate legislation) whenever passed or made.

(5) The regulations may, in particular, make provision—

   (a) as to the procedure to be followed by competent persons when determining who is to exercise Part I functions in a particular case;

   (b) as to the steps which must be taken before a competent person exercises, in a particular case, such Part I functions as may be prescribed;

   (c) as to the procedure for determining, in a particular case, questions arising as to which competent person is to exercise Part I functions in respect of the case;

   (d) for Part I functions in a particular case to be exercised jointly—

      (i) by the OFT and one or more regulators, or

      (ii) by two or more regulators,

   and as to the procedure to be followed in such cases;

   (e) as to the circumstances in which the exercise by a competent person of such Part I functions as may be prescribed is to preclude the exercise of such functions by another such person;

   (f) for cases in respect of which Part I functions are being, or have been, exercised by a competent person to be transferred to another such person;

   (g) for the person ('A') exercising Part I functions in a particular case—

      (i) to appoint another competent person ('B') to exercise Part I functions on A's behalf in relation to the case; or

      (ii) to appoint officers of B (with B's consent) to act as officers of A in relation to the case;

   (h) for notification as to who is exercising Part I functions in respect of a particular case.

(6) Provision made by virtue of subsection (5)(c) may provide for questions to be referred to and determined by the Secretary of State or by such other person as may be prescribed.

(7) 'Competent person' means the OFT or any of the regulators.

(8) In this section, 'subordinate legislation' has the same meaning as in section 21(1) of the Interpretation Act 1978 (c 30) and includes an instrument made under—

   (a) an Act of the Scottish Parliament;

   (b) Northern Ireland legislation.

Confidentiality and immunity from defamation

57   Defamation

For the purposes of the law relating to defamation, absolute privilege attaches to any advice, guidance, notice or direction given, or decision made, by the OFT in the exercise of any of its functions under this Part.

Findings of fact by OFT

58   Findings of fact by OFT

(1) Unless the court directs otherwise, an OFT's finding which is relevant to an issue arising in Part I proceedings is binding on the parties if—

  (a) the time for bringing an appeal under section 46 or 47 in respect of the finding has expired and the relevant party has not brought such an appeal under section 46 or 47; or

  (b) the decision of the Tribunal on such an appeal has confirmed the finding.

(2) In this section—

'an OFT's finding' means a finding of fact made by the OFT in the course of 'conducting an investigation';

'Part 1 proceedings' means proceedings brought otherwise than by the OFT—

  (a) in respect of an alleged infringement of the Chapter I prohibition or of the Chapter II prohibition; or

  (b) in respect of an alleged infringement of the prohibitions in Article 81(1) or Article 82;

'relevant party' means—

  (a) in relation to the Chapter I prohibition or the prohibition in Article 81(1) a party to the agreement which is alleged to have infringed the prohibition; and—

  (b) in relation to the Chapter II prohibition or the prohibition in Article 82 the undertaking whose conduct is alleged to have infringed the prohibition.

(3) Rules of court may make provision in respect of assistance to be given by the Director to the court in Part I proceedings.

Findings of infringements

58A   Findings of infringements

(1) This section applies to proceedings before the court in which damages or any other sum of money is claimed in respect of an infringement of—

  (a) the Chapter I prohibition;

  (b) the Chapter II prohibition;

  (c) the prohibition in Article 81(1) of the Treaty;

  (d) the prohibition in Article 82 of the Treaty.

(2) In such proceedings, the court is bound by a decision mentioned in subsection (3) once any period specified in subsection (4) which relates to the decision has elapsed.

(3) The decisions are—

  (a) a decision of the OFT that the Chapter I prohibition or the Chapter II prohibition has been infringed;

  (b) a decision of the OFT that the prohibition in Article 81(1) or Article 82 of the Treaty has been infringed;

  (c) a decision of the Tribunal (or an appeal from a decision of the OFT) that the Chapter I prohibition or the Chapter II prohibition has been infringed, or that the prohibition in Article 81(1) or Article 82 of the Treaty has been infringed.

(4) The periods mentioned in subsection (2) are—

  (a) in the case of a decision of the OFT, the period during which an appeal may be made to the Tribunal under section 46 or 47;

(b) in the case of a decision of the Tribunal mentioned in subsection (3)(c), the period during which a further appeal may be made under section 49;

(c) in the case of any decision which is the subject of a further appeal, the period during which an appeal may be made to the House of Lords from a decision on the further appeal;

and, where any appeal mentioned in paragraph (a), (b) or (c) is made, the period specified in that paragraph includes the period before the appeal is determined.

(2) Section 58A does not apply in relation to decisions made before the commencement of this section.

(3) In section 59(1) of that Act (interpretation), in the definition of 'the court', after '58' there is inserted, '58A'.

Interpretation and governing principles

59   Interpretation of Part I

(1) In this Part—

'agreement' is to be read with section 2(5) and (6);

'Article 81(1)' means Article 81(1) of the Treaty;

'Article 81(3)' means Article 81(3) of the Treaty;

'Article 82' means Article 82 of the Treaty;

'block exemption' has the meaning given in section 6(4);

'block exemption order' has the meaning given in section 6(2);

'the Chapter I prohibition' has the meaning given in section 2(8);

'the Chapter II prohibition' has the meaning given in section 18(4);

'the Commission' (except in relation to the Competition Commission) means the European Commission;

'the Council' means the Council of the European Union;

'the court', except in sections 58, 58A and 60 and the expression 'European Court', means—

(a) in England and Wales, the High Court;

(b) in Scotland, the Court of Session; and

(c) in Northern Ireland, the High Court;

'document' includes information recorded in any form;

'the EEA Agreement' means the Agreement on the European Economic Area signed at Oporto on 2nd May 1992 as it has effect for the time being;

'the European Court' means the Court of Justice of the European Communities and includes the Court of First Instance;

'the EC Competition Regulation' means Council Regulation (EC) No. 1/2003 of 16th December 2002 on the implementation of the rules on competition laid down in Articles 81 and 82 of the Treaty;

'information' includes estimates and forecasts;

'investigating officer' has the meaning given in section 27(1);

'investigation' means an investigation under section 25;

'Minister of the Crown' has the same meaning as in the Ministers of the Crown Act 1975;

'OFCOM' means the Office of Communications;

'officer', in relation to a body corporate, includes a director, manager or secretary and, in relation to a partnership in Scotland, includes a partner;

'the OFT' means the Office of Fair Trading;

'parallel exemption' has the meaning given in section 10(3);

'person', in addition to the meaning given by the Interpretation Act 1978, includes any undertaking;

'premises' includes any land or means of transport;

'prescribed' means prescribed by regulations made by the Secretary of State;

'regulator' has the meaning given by section 54;

'section 11 exemption' has the meaning given in section 11(3);

'the Treaty' means the treaty establishing the European Community;

'the Tribunal' means the Competition Appeal Tribunal; and

'Tribunal Rules' means rules under section 15 of the Enterprise Act 2002.

'working day' means a day which is not—

(a) Saturday,

(b) Sunday,

(c) Christmas Day,

(d) Good Friday, or

(e) a day which is a bank holiday under the Banking and Financial Dealings Act 1971 (c. 80) in any part of the United Kingdom.

(2) The fact that to a limited extent the Chapter I prohibition does not apply to an agreement, because of an exclusion provided by or under this Part or any other enactment, does not require those provisions of the agreement to which the exclusion relates to be disregarded when considering whether the agreement infringes the prohibition for other reasons.

(3) For the purposes of this Part, the power to require information, in relation to information recorded otherwise than in a legible form, includes power to require a copy of it in a legible form.

(4) Any power conferred on the OFT by this Part to require information includes power to require any document which it believes may contain that information.

60   Principles to be applied in determining questions

(1) The purpose of this section is to ensure that so far as is possible (having regard to any relevant differences between the provisions concerned), questions arising under this Part in relation to competition within the United Kingdom are dealt with in a manner which is consistent with the treatment of corresponding questions arising in Community law in relation to competition within the Community.

(2) At any time when the court determines a question arising under this Part, it must act (so far as is compatible with the provisions of this Part and whether or not it would otherwise be required to do so) with a view to securing that there is no inconsistency between—

(a) the principles applied, and decision reached, by the court in determining that question; and—

(b) the principles laid down by the Treaty and the European Court, and any relevant decision of that Court, as applicable at that time in determining any corresponding question arising in Community law.

(3) The court must, in addition, have regard to any relevant decision or statement of the Commission.

(4) Subsections (2) and (3) also apply to—

(a) the OFT; and

(b) any person acting on behalf of the OFT, in connection with any matter arising under this Part.

(5) In subsections (2) and (3), 'court' means any court or tribunal.

(6) In subsections (2)(b) and (3), 'decision' includes a decision as to—

(a) the interpretation of any provision of Community law;

(b) the civil liability of an undertaking for harm caused by its infringement of Community law.

PART II   INSPECTIONS UNDER ARTICLES 20, 21 AND 22(2)

61   Interpretation of Part 2

In this Part—

'Article 20 inspection' means an inspection ordered by a decision of the Commission under Article 20(4) of the EC Competition Regulation which is not an Article 22(2) inspection;

'Article 21 inspection' means an inspection ordered by a decision of the Commission under Article 21 of the EC Competition Regulation;

'Article 22(2) inspection' means an inspection requested by the Commission under Article 22(2) of the EC Competition Regulation;

'books and records' includes books and records stored on any medium;

'the Commission' means the European Commission;

'the EC Competition Regulation' means Council Regulation (EC) No. 1/2003 of 16th December 2002 on the implementation of the rules on competition laid down in Articles 81 and 82 of the Treaty;

'the OFT' means the Office of Fair Trading;

'premises' includes any land or means of transport;

'the Treaty' means the treaty establishing the European Community.

62   Power to enter business premises under a warrant: Article 20 inspections

(1) A judge of the High Court shall issue a warrant if satisfied, on an application made to the High Court in accordance with rules of court by the OFT, that

    (a) the Commission has ordered an Article 20 inspection;

    (b) the Article 20 inspection is being, or is likely to be, obstructed; and

    (c) the measures that would be authorised by the warrant are neither arbitrary nor excessive having regard to the subject matter of the Article 20 inspection.

(2) An Article 20 inspection is being obstructed if—

    (a) a Commission official exercising his power in accordance with Article 20(3) of the EC Competition Regulation has attempted to enter any business premises but has been unable to do so; and

    (b) there are reasonable grounds for suspecting that there are on any business premises books or records which the Commission official has power to examine.

(3) An Article 20 inspection is also being obstructed if there are reasonable grounds for suspecting that there are on any business premises books or records—

    (a) the production of which has been required by a Commission official exercising his power in accordance with Article 20(3) of the EC Competition Regulation; and

    (b) which have not been produced as required.

(4) An Article 20 inspection is likely to be obstructed if—

    (b) there are reasonable grounds for suspecting that there are on any business premises books or records which a Commission official has power to examine; and

    (c) there are also reasonable grounds for suspecting that, if the Commission official attempted to exercise his power to examine any of the books or records, they would not be produced but would be concealed, removed, tampered with or destroyed.

(5) A warrant under this section shall authorise a named officer of the OFT and any other OFT officer, or Commission official, accompanying the named officer—

    (a) to enter any business premises specified in the warrant using such force as is reasonably necessary for the purpose;

    (b) to search for books and records which a Commission official has power to examine, using such force as is reasonably necessary for the purpose;

    (c) to take or obtain copies of or extracts from such books and records;

    (d) to seal the premises, any part of the premises or any books or records which a Commission official has power to seal, for the period and to the extent necessary for the inspection.

(5A) A warrant under this section may authorise persons specified in the warrant to accompany the named officer who is executing it.

(6) Any person entering any premises by virtue of a warrant under this section may take with him such equipment as appears to him to be necessary.

(7) On leaving any premises entered by virtue of the warrant the named officer must, if the premises are unoccupied or the occupier is temporarily absent, leave them as effectively secured as he found them.

(8) A warrant under this section continues in force until the end of the period of one month beginning with the day on which it is issued.

(9) In the application of this section to Scotland, references to the High Court are to be read as references to the Court of Session.

(10) In this section—

'business premises' means any premises of an undertaking or association of undertakings which a Commission official has under Article 20 of the EC Competition Regulation power to enter in the course of the Article 20 inspection;

'Commission official' means any of the persons authorised by the Commission to conduct the Article 20 inspection; and

'OFT officer' means any officer of the OFT whom the OFT has authorised in writing to accompany the named officer.

(11) In subsection (10), the reference in the definition of 'business premises' to Article 20 of the EC Competition Regulation does not include a reference to that Article as applied by Article 21 of that Regulation.

62A Power to enter non-business premises under a warrant: Article 21 inspections

(1) A judge of the High Court shall issue a warrant if satisfied, on an application made to the High Court in accordance with the rules of court by the OFT, that—

(a) the Commission has ordered an Article 21 inspection; and

(b) the measures that would be authorised by the warrant are neither arbitrary nor excessive having regard in particular to the matters mentioned in subsection (2).

(2) Those matters are—

(a) the seriousness of the suspected infringement of Article 81(1) or 82 of the Treaty;

(b) the importance of the evidence sought;

(c) the involvement of the undertaking or association of undertakings concerned; and

(d) whether it is reasonably likely that business books and records relating to the subject matter of the Article 21 inspection are kept on the non-business premises that would be specified in the warrant.

(3) A warrant under this section shall authorise a named officer of the OFT and any other OFT officer, or Commission official, accompanying the named officer to enter any non-business premises specified in the warrant.

(4) A warrant under this section may authorise a named officer of the OFT and any other OFT officer, or Commission official, accompanying the named officer to search for books or records which a Commission official has power to examine.

(5) A warrant under this section may authorise a named officer of the OFT and any other OFT officer, or Commission official, accompanying the named officer to take or obtain copies of books or records of which a Commission official has power to take or obtain copies.

(6) A warrant granted under this section may authorise the use, for either or both of the purposes mentioned in subsections (3) and (4), of such force as is reasonably necessary.

(7) A warrant under this section may authorise persons specified in the warrant to accompany the named officer who is executing it.

(8) Any person entering any premises by virtue of a warrant under this section may take with him such equipment as appears to him to be necessary.

(9) On leaving any premises entered by virtue of a warrant the named officer must, if the premises are unoccupied or the occupier is temporarily absent, leave them as effectively secured as he found them.

(10) A warrant under this section continues in force until the end of the period of one month beginning with the day on which it is issued.

(11) In the application of this section to Scotland, references to the High Court are to be read as references to the Court of Session.

(12) In this section—

'non-business premises' means any premises to which a decision of the Commission ordering the Article 21 inspection relates;

'Commission official' means any of the persons authorised by the Commission to conduct the Article 21 inspection; and

'OFT officer' means any officer of the OFT whom the OFT has authorised in writing to accompany the named officer.

62B   Powers when conducting an Article 22(2) inspection

(1) For the purposes of an Article 22(2) inspection, an authorised officer of the OFT has the powers specified in Article 20(2) of the EC Competition Regulation.

(2) For the purposes of this section and section 63—

'authorised officer of the OFT' means any officer of the OFT to whom an authorisation has been given; and

'authorisation' means an authorisation given in writing by the OFT for the purposes of the Article 22(2) inspection which—

    (i)   identifies the officer;

    (ii) indicates the subject matter and purpose of the inspection; and

    (iii) draws attention to any penalties which a person may incur under the EC Competition Regulation in connection with the inspection.

63   Power to enter business premises under a warrant: Article 22(2) inspections

(1) A judge of the High Court shall issue a warrant if satisfied, on an application made to the High Court in accordance with rules of court by the OFT, that

    (a) the Commission has requested the OFT to conduct an Article 22(2) inspection which the Commission has ordered by a decision under Article 20(4) of the EC Competition Regulation;

    (b) the Article 22(2) inspection is being, or is likely to be, obstructed; and

    (c) the measures that would be authorised by the warrant are neither arbitrary nor excessive having regard to the subject matter of the Article 22(2) inspection.

(2) An Article 22(2) inspection is being obstructed if—

    (a) an authorised officer of the OFT has attempted to enter any business premises but has been unable to do so;

    (b) the officer has produced his authorisation to the undertaking, or association of undertakings, concerned; and

    (c) there are reasonable grounds for suspecting that there are on any business premises books or records which the officer has power to examine.

(3) An Article 22(2) inspection is also being obstructed if—

    (a) there are reasonable grounds for suspecting that there are on any business premises books or records which an authorised officer of the OFT has power to examine;

    (b) the officer has produced his authorisation to the undertaking, or association of undertakings, and has required production of the books or records; and

    (c) the books and records have not been produced as required.

(4) An Article 22(2) inspection is likely to be obstructed if—

    (a) there are reasonable grounds for suspecting that there are on any business premises books or records which an authorised officer of the OFT has power to examine; and

(b) there are also reasonable grounds for suspecting that, if the officer attempted to exercise his power to examine any of the books or records, they would not be produced but would be concealed, removed, tampered with or destroyed.

(5) A warrant under this section shall authorise a named authorised officer of the OFT and any other authorised officer of the OFT, or Commission official, accompanying the named authorised officer—

(a) to enter any business premises specified in the warrant using such force as is reasonably necessary for the purpose;

(b) to search for books and records which an authorised officer of the OFT has power to examine, using such force as is reasonably necessary for the purpose;

(c) to take or obtain copies of or extracts from such books and records; and

(d) to seal the premises, any part of the premises or any books or records which an authorised officer of the OFT has power to seal, for the period and to the extent necessary for the inspection.

(5A) A warrant under this section may authorise persons specified in the warrant to accompany the named authorised officer who is executing it.

(6) Any person entering any premises by virtue of a warrant under this section may take with him such equipment as appears to him to be necessary.

(7) On leaving any premises which he has entered by virtue of the warrant the named authorised officer must, if the premises are unoccupied or the occupier is temporarily absent, leave them as effectively secured as he found them.

(8) A warrant under this section continues in force until the end of the period of one month beginning with the day on which it is issued.

(9) In the application of this section to Scotland, references to the High Court are to be read as references to the Court of Session.

(10) In this section—

'business premises' means any premises of an undertaking or association of undertakings which a Commission official has under Article 20 of the EC Competition Regulation power to enter in the course of the Article 20 inspection;

'Commission official' means any of the persons authorised by the Commission to assist with the Article 22(2) inspection.

64   Entry of premises under sections 62, 62A and 63: supplementary

(1) A warrant issued under section 62 or 63 must indicate—

(a) the subject matter and purpose of the inspection;

(b) the nature of the offence created by section 65.

(2) The powers conferred by section 62 or 63 are to be exercised on production of a warrant issued under that section.

(3) If there is no one at the premises when the named officer proposes to execute such a warrant he must, before executing it—

(a) take such steps as are reasonable in all the circumstances to inform the occupier of the intended entry; and

(b) if the occupier is informed, afford him or his legal or other representative a reasonable opportunity to be present when the warrant is executed.

(4) If the named officer is unable to inform the occupier of the intended entry he must, when executing the warrant, leave a copy of it in a prominent place on the premises.

(5) In this section—

'named officer' means—

(a) for the purposes of a warrant issued under section 62 or 62A, the officer named in the warrant; and

(b) for the purposes of a warrant issued under section 63, the authorised officer named in the warrant.

65   Offences

(1) A person is guilty of an offence if he intentionally obstructs any person in the exercise of his powers under a warrant issued under section 62, 62A or 63.

(2) A person guilty of an offence under subsection (1) is liable—

(a) on summary conviction, to a fine not exceeding the statutory maximum;

(b) on conviction on indictment, to imprisonment for a term not exceeding two years or to a fine or to both.

65A Privileged communications: Article 22(2) inspections

(1) A person shall not be required, by virtue of any provision of section 62B or 63, to produce or disclose a privileged communication.

(2) 'Privileged communication' means a communication—

(a) between a professional legal adviser and his client, or

(b) made in connection with, or in contemplation of, legal proceedings and for the purposes of those proceedings,

which in proceedings in the High Court would be protected from disclosure on grounds of legal professional privilege.

(3) In the application of this section to Scotland—

(a) the reference to the High Court is to be read as a reference to the Court of Session; and

(b) the reference to legal professional privilege is to be read as a reference to confidentiality of communications.

65B Use of statements in prosecution: Article 22(2) inspections

A statement made by a person in response to a requirement imposed by virtue of section 62B or 63 may not be used in evidence against him on a prosecution for an offence under section 188 of the Enterprise Act 2002 unless, in the proceedings—

(a) in giving evidence, he makes a statement inconsistent with it, and

(b) evidence relating to it is adduced, or a question relating to it is asked, by him or on his behalf.

PART 2A ARTICLE 22(1) INVESTIGATIONS

65C   Interpretation of Part 2A

(1) In this Part—

'Article 22(1) investigation' means an investigation conducted by the OFT on behalf and for the account of a competition authority of another Member State pursuant to Article 22(1) of the EC Competition Regulation;

'the Commission' means the European Commission;

'competition authority of another Member State' means a competition authority designated as such under Article 35 of the EC Competition Regulation by a Member State other than the United Kingdom;

'the EC Competition Regulation' means Council Regulation (EC) No. 1/2003 of 16th December 2002 on the implementation of the rules on competition laid down in Articles 81 and 82 of the Treaty; and

'investigating officer' has the meaning given in section 65F(1).

(2) In this Part, the following expressions have the same meanings as in Part 1—

'Article 81(1)';

'Article 82';

'the court';

'document';

'information';

'officer';

(3) If there is no one at the premises when the named officer proposes to execute such a warrant he must, before executing it—

    (a) take such steps as are reasonable in all the circumstances to inform the occupier of the intended entry; and

    (b) if the occupier is informed, afford him or his legal or other representative a reasonable opportunity to be present when the warrant is executed.

(4) If the named officer is unable to inform the occupier of the intended entry he must, when executing the warrant, leave a copy of it in a prominent place on the premises.

(5) In this section—

'named officer' means the officer named in the warrant; and

'occupier', in relation to any premises, means a person whom the named officer reasonably believes is the occupier of those premises.

65J Privileged communications

(1) A person shall not be required, under any provision of this Part, to produce or disclose a privileged communication.

(2) 'Privileged communication' means a communication—

    (a) between a professional legal adviser and his client, or

    (b) made in connection with, or in contemplation of, legal proceedings and for the purposes of those proceedings,

which in proceedings in the High Court would be protected from disclosure on grounds of legal professional privilege.

(3) In the application of this section to Scotland—

    (a) the reference to the High Court is to be read as a reference to the Court of Session; and

    (b) the reference to legal professional privilege is to be read as a reference to confidentiality of communications.

65K Use of statements in prosecution

A statement made by a person in response to a requirement imposed by virtue of any of sections 65E to 65H may not be used in evidence against him on a prosecution for an offence under section 188 of the Enterprise Act 2002 unless, in the proceedings—

    (a) in giving evidence, he makes a statement inconsistent with it, and

    (b) evidence relating to it is adduced, or a question relating to it is asked, by him or on his behalf.

65L Offences

(1) A person is guilty of an offence if he fails to comply with a requirement imposed on him under section 65E, 65F, 65G or 65H.

(2) If a person is charged with an offence under subsection (1) in respect of a requirement to produce a document, it is a defence for him to prove—

    (a) that the document was not in his possession or under his control; and

    (b) that it was not reasonably practicable for him to comply with the requirement.

(3) If a person is charged with an offence under subsection (1) in respect of a requirement—

    (a) to provide information,

    (b) to provide an explanation of a document, or

    (c) to state where a document is to be found,

it is a defence for him to prove that he had a reasonable excuse for failing to comply with the requirement.

(4) Failure to comply with a requirement imposed under section 65E or 65F is not an offence if the person imposing the requirement has failed to act in accordance with that section.

(5) A person is guilty of an offence if he intentionally obstructs an officer acting in the exercise of his powers under section 65F.

(6) A person guilty of an offence under subsection (1) or (5) is liable—

(a) on summary conviction, to a fine not exceeding the statutory maximum;

(b) on conviction on indictment, to a fine.

(7) A person who intentionally obstructs an officer in the exercise of his powers under a warrant issued under section 65G or 65H is guilty of an offence and liable—

(a) on summary conviction, to a fine not exceeding the statutory maximum;

(b) on conviction on indictment, to imprisonment for a term not exceeding two years or to a fine or to both.

65M   Destroying or falsifying documents

(1) A person is guilty of an offence if, having been required to produce a document under section 65E, 65F, 65G or 65H—

(a) he intentionally or recklessly destroys or otherwise disposes of it, falsifies it or conceals it, or

(b) he causes or permits its destruction, disposal, falsification or concealment.

(2) A person guilty of an offence under subsection (1) is liable—

(a) on summary conviction, to a fine not exceeding the statutory maximum;

(b) on conviction on indictment, to imprisonment for a term not exceeding two years or to a fine or to both.

65N   False or misleading information

(1) If information is provided by a person to the OFT in connection with any function of the OFT under this Part, that person is guilty of an offence if—

(a) the information is false or misleading in a material particular; and

(b) he knows that it is or is reckless as to whether it is.

(2) A person who—

(a) provides any information to another person, knowing the information to be false or misleading in a material particular, or

(b) recklessly provides any information to another person which is false or misleading in a material particular,

knowing that the information is to be used for the purpose of providing information to the OFT in connection with any of its functions under this Part, is guilty of an offence.

(3) A person guilty of an offence under this section is liable—

(a) on summary conviction, to a fine not exceeding the statutory maximum;

(b) on conviction on indictment, to imprisonment for a term not exceeding two years or to a fine or to both.

PART IV   SUPPLEMENTAL AND TRANSITIONAL

70   Contracts as to patented products etc.

Sections 44 and 45 of the Patents Act 1977 shall cease to have effect.

71   Regulations, orders and rules

(1) Any power to make regulations or orders which is conferred by this Act is exercisable by statutory instrument.

(2) The power to make rules which is conferred by section 48 is exercisable by statutory instrument.

(3) Any statutory instrument made under this Act may—

(a) contain such incidental, supplemental, consequential and transitional provision as the Secretary of State considers appropriate; and

(b) make different provision for different cases.

(4) No order is to be made under—

(a) section 3,

    (b)   section 19,

    (c)   section 36(8),

    (ca)   section 45(8),

    (d)   section 50, or

    (e)   paragraph 6(3) of Schedule 4,

unless a draft of the order has been laid before Parliament and approved by a resolution of each House.

    (5) Any statutory instrument made under this Act, apart from one made—

    (a) under any of the provisions mentioned in subsection (4), or

    (b) under section 76(3),

shall be subject to annulment by a resolution of either House of Parliament.

72 Offences by bodies corporate etc.

    (1) This section applies to an offence under any of sections 42 to 44, 65 or 65L to 65N.

    (2) If an offence committed by a body corporate is proved—

    (a) to have been committed with the consent or connivance of an officer, or

    (b) to be attributable to any neglect on his part,

the officer as well as the body corporate is guilty of the offence and liable to be proceeded against and punished accordingly.

    (3) In subsection (2) 'officer', in relation to a body corporate, means a director, manager, secretary or other similar officer of the body, or a person purporting to act in any such capacity.

    (4) If the affairs of a body corporate are managed by its members, subsection (2) applies in relation to the acts and defaults of a member in connection with his functions of management as if he were a director of the body corporate.

    (5) If an offence committed by a partnership in Scotland is proved—

    (a) to have been committed with the consent or connivance of a partner, or

    (b) to be attributable to any neglect on his part,

the partner as well as the partnership is guilty of the offence and liable to be proceeded against and punished accordingly.

    (6) In subsection (5) 'partner' includes a person purporting to act as a partner.

73 Crown application

    (1) Any provision made by or under this Act binds the Crown except that—

    (a) the Crown is not criminally liable as a result of any such provision;

    (b) the Crown is not liable for any penalty under any such provision; and

    (c) nothing in this Act affects Her Majesty in her private capacity.

    (2) Subsection (1)(a) does not affect the application of any provision of this Act in relation to persons in the public service of the Crown.

    (3) Subsection (1)(c) is to be interpreted as if section 38(3) of the Crown Proceedings Act 1947 (interpretation of references in that Act to Her Majesty in her private capacity) were contained in this Act.

    (4) If an investigation is conducted under section 25 or 65D in respect of an agreement where none of the parties is the Crown or a person in the public service of the Crown, or in respect of conduct otherwise than by the Crown or such a person—

    (a) the power conferred by section 27 or (as the case may be) section 65F may not be exercised in relation to land which is occupied by a government department, or otherwise for purposes of the Crown, without the written consent of the appropriate person; and

    (b) none of sections 28, 28A, 65G and 65H applies in relation to land so occupied.

    (5) In any case in which consent is required under subsection (4), the person who is the appropriate person in relation to that case is to be determined in accordance with regulations made by the Secretary of State.

    (6) Sections 62, 62A and 63 do not apply in relation to land which is occupied by a government department, or otherwise for purposes of the Crown, unless the matter being investigated is an

agreement to which the Crown or a person in the service of the Crown is a party, or conduct by the Crown or such a person.

(6A) In subsections (4) and (6) 'agreement' includes a suspected agreement and is to be read as applying equally to, or in relation to, a decision by an association of undertakings or a concerted practice; and 'conduct' includes suspected conduct.

(7) [repealed]

(8) If the Secretary of State certifies that it appears to him to be in the interests of national security that the powers of entry—

(a) conferred by section 27 or 65F, or

(b) that may be conferred by a warrant under section 28, 28A, 62, 62A, 63, 65G or 65H;

should not be exercisable in relation to premises held or used by or on behalf of the Crown and which are specified in the certificate, those powers are not exercisable in relation to those premises.

(9) Any amendment, repeal or revocation made by this Act binds the Crown to the extent that the enactment amended, repealed or revoked binds the Crown.

74   Amendments, transitional provisions, savings and repeals

(1) The minor and consequential amendments set out in Schedule 12 are to have effect.

(2) The transitional provisions and savings set out in Schedule 13 are to have effect.

(3) The enactments set out in Schedule 14 are repealed.

75   Consequential and supplementary provision

(1) The Secretary of State may by order make such incidental, consequential, transitional or supplemental provision as he thinks necessary or expedient for the general purposes, or any particular purpose, of this Act or in consequence of any of its provisions or for giving full effect to it.

(2) An order under subsection (1) may, in particular, make provision—

(a) for enabling any person by whom any powers will become exercisable, on a date specified by or under this Act, by virtue of any provision made by or under this Act to take before that date any steps which are necessary as a preliminary to the exercise of those powers;

(b) for making savings, or additional savings, from the effect of any repeal made by or under this Act.

(3) Amendments made under this section shall be in addition, and without prejudice, to those made by or under any other provision of this Act.

(4) No other provision of this Act restricts the powers conferred by this section.

75A   Rules in relation to Part 2 and Part 2A

(1) The OFT may make such rules about procedural and other matters in connection with the carrying into effect of the provisions of Parts 2 and 2A as it considers appropriate.

(2) If the OFT is preparing rules under this section it must consult such persons as it considers appropriate.

(3) No rule made by the OFT is to come into operation until it has been approved by an order made by the Secretary of State.

(4) The Secretary of State may approve any rule made by the OFT—

(a) in the form in which it is submitted; or

(b) subject to such modifications as he considers appropriate.

(5) If the Secretary of State proposes to approve a rule subject to modifications he must inform the OFT of the proposed modifications and take into account any comments made by the OFT.

(6) Subsections (3) to (5) apply also to any alteration of the rules made by the OFT.

(7) The Secretary of State may, after consulting the OFT, by order vary or revoke any rules made under this section.

(8) If the Secretary of State considers that rules should be made under this section with respect to a particular matter he may direct the OFT to exercise its powers under this section and make rules about that matter.

76   Short title, commencement and extent

(1) This Act may be cited as the Competition Act 1998.

(2) Sections 71 and 75 and this section and paragraphs 1 to 7 and 35 of Schedule 13 come into force on the passing of this Act.

(3) The other provisions of this Act come into force on such day as the Secretary of State may by order appoint; and different days may be appointed for different purposes.

(4) This Act extends to Northern Ireland.

SCHEDULES

Sections 3(1)(a) and 19(1)(a)   **SCHEDULE 1**

EXCLUSIONS: MERGERS AND CONCENTRATIONS

PART I   MERGERS

Enterprises ceasing to be distinct: the Chapter I prohibition

1.—(1) To the extent to which an agreement (either on its own or when taken together with another agreement) results, or if carried out would result, in any two enterprises ceasing to be distinct enterprises for the purposes of Part III of the Enterprise Act 2002 ('the 2002 Act'), the Chapter I prohibition does not apply to the agreement.

(2) The exclusion provided by sub-paragraph (1) extends to any provision directly related and necessary to the implementation of the merger provisions.

(3) In sub-paragraph (2) 'merger provisions' means the provisions of the agreement which cause, or if carried out would cause, the agreement to have the result mentioned in sub-paragraph (1).

(4) Section 25 of the 2002 Act applies for the purposes of this paragraph as if—

    (a) in subsection (3) (circumstances in which a person or group of persons may be treated as having control of an enterprise), and

    (b) in subsection (4) (circumstances in which a person or group of persons may be treated as bringing an enterprise under their control),

for 'may' there were substituted 'must'.

Enterprises ceasing to be distinct: the Chapter II prohibition

2.—(1) To the extent to which conduct (either on its own or when taken together with other conduct)—

    (a) results in any two enterprises ceasing to be distinct enterprises for the purposes of Part III of the 2002 Act, or

    (b) is directly related and necessary to the attainment of the result mentioned in paragraph (a),

the Chapter II prohibition does not apply to that conduct.

(2) Section 25 of the 2002 Act applies for the purposes of this paragraph as it applies for the purposes of paragraph 1.

Transfer of a newspaper or of newspaper assets

3. [repealed]

Withdrawal of the paragraph 1 exclusion

4.—(1) The exclusion provided by paragraph 1 does not apply to a particular agreement if the OFT gives a direction under this paragraph to that effect.

(2) If the OFT is considering whether to give a direction under this paragraph, it may by notice in writing require any party to the agreement in question to give the OFT such information in connection with the agreement as it may require.

(3) The OFT may give a direction under this paragraph only as provided in sub-paragraph (4) or (5).

(4) If at the end of such period as may be specified in rules under section 51 a person has failed, without reasonable excuse, to comply with a requirement imposed under sub-paragraph (2), the OFT may give a direction under this paragraph.

(5) The OFT may also give a direction under this paragraph if—

(a) it considers that the agreement will, if not excluded, infringe the Chapter I prohibition; and

(b) the agreement is not a protected agreement.

(6) [repealed]

(7) A direction under this paragraph—

(a) must be in writing;

(b) may be made so as to have effect from a date specified in the direction (which may not be earlier than the date on which it is given).

Protected agreements

5. An agreement is a protected agreement for the purposes of paragraph 4 if—

(a) the OFT or (as the case may be) the Secretary of State has published its or his decision not to make a reference to the Competition Commission under section 21, 32, 44 or 61 of the 2002 Act in connection with the agreement;

(b) the OFT or (as the case may be) the Secretary of State has made a reference to the Competition Commission under section 21, 32, 44 or 61 of the 2002 Act in connection with the agreement and the Commission has found that the agreement has given rise to, or would if carried out give rise to, a relevant merger situation or (as the case may be) a special merger situation;

(c) the agreement does not fall within paragraph (a) or (b) but has given rise to, or would if carried out give rise to, enterprises to which it relates being regarded under section 25 of the 2002 act as ceasing to be distinct enterprises (otherwise than as the result of subsection (3) or (4)(b) of that section);

(d) the OFT has made a reference to the Competition Commission under section 32 of the Water Industry Act 1991 in connection with the agreement and the Commission has found that the agreement has given rise to, or would if carried out give rise to, a merger of any two or more water enterprises; or

(e) the Secretary of State has made a reference to the Competition Commission under Part 3 of the 2002 Act as applied by virtue of paragraph 1 of Schedule 6 to that Act (application of Part 3 to water mergers) in connection with the agreement and the Commission has found that the agreement has given rise to, or would if carried out give rise to, a merger of any two or more water enterprises.

PART II CONCENTRATIONS SUBJECT TO EC CONTROLS

6.—(1) To the extent to which an agreement (either on its own or when taken together with another agreement) gives rise to, or would if carried out give rise to, a concentration, the Chapter I prohibition does not apply to the agreement if the Merger Regulation gives the Commission exclusive jurisdiction in the matter.

(2) To the extent to which conduct (either on its own or when taken together with other conduct) gives rise to, or would if pursued give rise to, a concentration, the Chapter II prohibition does not apply to the conduct if the Merger Regulation gives the Commission exclusive jurisdiction in the matter.

(3) In this paragraph—

'concentration' means a concentration with a Community dimension within the meaning of Articles 1 and 3 of the Merger Regulation; and

'Merger Regulation' means Council Regulation (EEC) No. 4064/89 of 21st December 1989 on the control of concentrations between undertakings as amended by Council Regulation (EC) No. 1310/97 of 30th June 1997.

Sections 3(1)(c) and 19(1)(b) **SCHEDULE 3**

GENERAL EXCLUSIONS

Planning obligations

1.—(1) The Chapter I prohibition does not apply to an agreement—

    (a) to the extent to which it is a planning obligation;

    (b) which is made under section 75 (agreements regulating development or use of land) or 246 (agreements relating to Crown land) of the Town and Country Planning (Scotland) Act 1997; or

    (c) which is made under Article 40 of the Planning (Northern Ireland) Order 1991.

(2) In sub-paragraph (1)(a), 'planning obligation' means—

    (a) a planning obligation for the purposes of section 106 of the Town and Country Planning Act 1990; or

    (b) a planning obligation for the purposes of section 299A of that Act.

Section 21(2) agreements

3. [repealed]

EEA regulated markets

3.—(1) The Chapter I prohibition does not apply to an agreement for the constitution of an EEA regulated market to the extent to which the agreement relates to any of the rules made, or guidance issued, by that market.

(2) The Chapter I prohibition does not apply to a decision made by an EEA regulated market, to the extent to which the decision relates to any of the market's regulating provisions.

(3) The Chapter I prohibition does not apply to—

    (a) any practices of an EEA regulated market; or

    (b) any practices which are trading practices in relation to an EEA regulated market.

(4) The Chapter I prohibition does not apply to an agreement the parties to which are or include—

    (a) an EEA regulated market, or

    (b) a person who is subject to the rules of that market,

to the extent to which the agreement consists of provisions the inclusion of which is required or contemplated by the regulating provisions of that market.

(5) In this paragraph—

'EEA regulated market' is a market which—

    (a) is listed by an EEA State other than the United Kingdom pursuant to Article 47 of Directive 2004/39/EC of the European Parliament and of the Council of 21 April 2004 on markets in financial instruments; and

    (b) operates without any requirement that a person dealing on the market should have a physical presence in the EEA State from which any trading facilities are provided or on any trading floor that the market may have;

'EEA State' means a State which is a contracting party to the EEA Agreement;

'regulating provisions', in relation to an EEA regulated market, means—

    (a) rules made, or guidance issued, by that market,

    (b) practices of that market, or

(c) practices which, in relation to that market, are trading practices;

'trading practices', in relation to an EEA regulated market, means practices of persons who are subject to the rules made by that market, and

(a) which relate to business in respect of which those persons are subject to the rules of that market, and which are required or contemplated by those rules or by guidance issued by that market; or

(b) which are otherwise attributable to the conduct of that market as such.

Services of general economic interest etc.

4. Neither the Chapter I prohibition nor the Chapter II prohibition applies to an undertaking entrusted with the operation of services of general economic interest or having the character of a revenue-producing monopoly in so far as the prohibition would obstruct the performance, in law or in fact, of the particular tasks assigned to that undertaking.

Compliance with legal requirements

5.—(1) The Chapter I prohibition does not apply to an agreement to the extent to which it is made in order to comply with a legal requirement.

(2) The Chapter II prohibition does not apply to conduct to the extent to which it is engaged in an order to comply with a legal requirement.

(3) In this paragraph 'legal requirement' means a requirement

(a) imposed by or under any enactment in force in the United Kingdom;

(b) imposed by or under the Treaty or the EEA Agreement and having legal effect in the United Kingdom without further enactment; or

(c) imposed by or under the law in force in another Member State and having legal effect in the United Kingdom.

Avoidance of conflict with international obligations

6.—(1) If the Secretary of State is satisfied that, in order to avoid a conflict between provisions of this Part and an international obligation of the United Kingdom, it would be appropriate for the Chapter I prohibition not to apply to—

(a) a particular agreement, or

(b) any agreement of a particular description, he may by order exclude the agreement, or agreements of that description, from the Chapter I prohibition.

(2) An order under sub-paragraph (1) may make provision for the exclusion of the agreement or agreements to which the order applies, or of such of them as may be specified, only in specified circumstances.

(3) An order under sub-paragraph (1) may also provide that the Chapter I prohibition is to be deemed never to have applied in relation to the agreement or agreements, or in relation to such of them as may be specified.

(4) If the Secretary of State is satisfied that, in order to avoid a conflict between provisions of this Part and an international obligation of the United Kingdom, it would be appropriate for the Chapter II prohibition not to apply in particular circumstances, he may by order provide for it not to apply in such circumstances as may be specified.

(5) An order under sub-paragraph (4) may provide that the Chapter II prohibition is to be deemed never to have applied in relation to specified conduct.

(6) An international arrangement relating to civil aviation and designated by an order made by the Secretary of State is to be treated as an international obligation for the purposes of this paragraph.

(7) In this paragraph and paragraph 7 'specified' means specified in the order.

Public policy

7.—(1) If the Secretary of State is satisfied that there are exceptional and compelling reasons of public policy why the Chapter I prohibition ought not to apply to—

(a) a particular agreement, or

(b) any agreement of a particular description,

he may by order exclude the agreement, or agreements of that description, from the Chapter I prohibition.

(2) An order under sub-paragraph (1) may make provision for the exclusion of the agreement or agreements to which the order applies, or of such of them as may be specified, only in specified circumstances.

(3) An order under sub-paragraph (1) may also provide that the Chapter I prohibition is to be deemed never to have applied in relation to the agreement or agreements, or in relation to such of them as may be specified.

(4) If the Secretary of State is satisfied that there are exceptional and compelling reasons of public policy why the Chapter II prohibition ought not to apply in particular circumstances, he may by order provide for it not to apply in such circumstances as may be specified.

(5) An order under sub-paragraph (4) may provide that the Chapter II prohibition is to be deemed never to have applied in relation to specified conduct.

Coal and steel

8.—(1) The Chapter I prohibition does not apply to an agreement which relates to a coal or steel product to the extent to which the ECSC Treaty gives the Commission exclusive jurisdiction in the matter.

(2) Sub-paragraph (1) ceases to have effect on the date on which the ECSC Treaty expires ('the expiry date').

(3) The Chapter II prohibition does not apply to conduct which relates to a coal or steel product to the extent to which the ECSC Treaty gives the Commission exclusive jurisdiction in the matter.

(4) Sub-paragraph (3) ceases to have effect on the expiry date.

(5) In this paragraph—

'coal or steel product' means any product of a kind listed in Annex I to the ECSC Treaty; and

'ECSC Treaty' means the Treaty establishing the European Coal and Steel Community.

Agricultural products

9.—(1) The Chapter I prohibition does not apply to an agreement to the extent to which it relates to production of or trade in an agricultural product and—

(a) forms an integral part of a national market organisation;

(b) is necessary for the attainment of the objectives set out in Article 33 of the Treaty; or

(c) is an agreement of farmers or farmers' associations (or associations of such associations) belonging to a single member State which concerns—

(i) the production or sale of agricultural products, or

(ii) the use of joint facilities for the storage, treatment or processing of agricultural products,

and under which there is no obligation to charge identical prices.

(2) If the Commission determines that an agreement does not fulfil the conditions specified by the provision for agricultural products for exclusion from Article 81(1), the exclusion provided by this paragraph ('the agriculture exclusion') is to be treated as ceasing to apply to the agreement on the date of the decision.

(3) The agriculture exclusion does not apply to a particular agreement if the OFT gives a direction under this paragraph to that effect.

(4) If the OFT is considering whether to give a direction under this paragraph, it may by notice in writing require any party to the agreement in question to give the OFT such information in connection with the agreement as it may require.

(5) The OFT may give a direction under this paragraph only as provided in sub-paragraph (6) or (7).

(6) If at the end of such period as may be specified in rules under section 51 a person has failed, without reasonable excuse, to comply with a requirement imposed under sub-paragraph (4), the OFT may give a direction under this paragraph.

(7) The OFT may also give a direction under this paragraph if it considers that an agreement (whether or not it considers that it infringes the Chapter I prohibition) is likely, or is intended, substantially and unjustifiably to prevent, restrict or distort competition in relation to an agricultural product.

(8) A direction under this paragraph—

(a) must be in writing;

(b) may be made so as to have effect from a date specified in the direction (which may not be earlier than the date on which it is given).

(9) In this paragraph—

'agricultural product' means any product of a kind listed in Annex I to the Treaty; and

'provision for agricultural products' means Council Regulation (EEC) No. 26/62 of 4th April 1962 applying certain rules of competition to production of and trade in agricultural products.

SCHEDULE 5

[repealed]

SCHEDULE 6

[repealed]

Section 31A

SCHEDULE 6A

COMMITMENTS

PART 1 PROCEDURAL REQUIREMENTS FOR THE ACCEPTANCE AND VARIATION OF COMMITMENTS

1. Paragraph 2 applies where the OFT proposes to—

(a) accept any commitments under section 31A; or

(b) accept any variation of such commitments other than a variation which is not material in any respect.

2.—(1) Before accepting the commitments or variation, the OFT must—

(a) give notice under this paragraph; and

(b) consider any representations made in accordance with the notice and not withdrawn.

(2) A notice under this paragraph must state—

(a) that the OFT proposes to accept the commitments or variation;

(b) the purpose of the commitments or variation and the way in which the commitments or variation would meet the OFT's competition concerns;

(c) any other facts which the OFT considers are relevant to the acceptance or variation of the commitments; and

(d) the period within which representations may be made in relation to the proposed commitments or variation.

(3) The period stated for the purposes of sub-paragraph (2)(d) must be at least 11 working days starting with the date the notice is given or, if that date is not a working day, with the date of the first working day after that date.

3.—(1) The OFT must not accept the commitments or variation of which notice has been given under paragraph 2(1) with modifications unless it—

(a) gives notice under this paragraph of the proposed modifications; and

(b) considers any representations made in accordance with the notice and not withdrawn.

(2) A notice under this paragraph must state—

(a) the proposed modifications;

(b) the reasons for them; and

(c) the period within which representations may be made in relation to the proposed modifications.

(3) The period stated for the purposes of sub-paragraph (2)(c) must be at least 6 working days starting with the date the notice is given or, if that date is not a working day, with the date of the first working day after that date.

4. If, after giving notice under paragraph 2 or 3 the OFT decides—

(a) not to accept the commitments or variation concerned, and

(b) not to proceed by virtue of paragraph 5 or 6, the OFT must give notice that it has so decided.

5. The requirements of paragraph 3 shall not apply if the OFT—

(a) has already given notice under paragraph 2 but not under paragraph 3; and

(b) considers that the modifications which are now being proposed are not material in any respect.

6. The requirements of paragraph 3 shall not apply if the OFT—

(a) has already given notices under paragraphs 2 and 3; and

(b) considers that the further modifications which are now being proposed are not material in any respect or do not differ in any material respect from the modifications in relation to which notice was last given under paragraph 3.

7. As soon as practicable after accepting commitments or a variation under section 31A the OFT must publish the commitments or the variation in such manner as the OFT considers appropriate.

8. A notice under paragraph 2 or 3 shall be given by—

(a) sending a copy of the notice to such person or persons as the OFT considers appropriate for the purpose of bringing the matter to which it relates to the attention of those likely to be affected by it; or

(b) publishing the notice in such manner as the OFT considers appropriate for the purpose of bringing the matter to which it relates to the attention of those likely to be affected by it.

PART 2 PROCEDURAL REQUIREMENTS FOR THE RELEASE OF COMMITMENTS

10. Paragraph 11 applies where the OFT proposes to release any commitments under section 31A.

11.—(1) Before releasing the commitments, the OFT must—

(a) give notice under this paragraph;

(b) send a copy of the notice to the person (or persons) who gave the commitments; and

(c) consider any representations made in accordance with the notice and not withdrawn.

(2) A notice under this paragraph must state—

(a) the fact that a release is proposed;

(b) the reasons for it; and

(c) the period within which representations may be made in relation to the proposed release.

(3) The period stated for the purposes of sub-paragraph (2) (c) must be at least 11 working days starting with the date the notice is given or, if that date is not a working day, with the date of the first working day after that date.

12. If after giving notice under paragraph 11 the OFT decides not to proceed with the release, it must—

(a) give notice that it has so decided; and

(b) send a copy of the notice to the person (or persons) who gave the commitments.

13. As soon as practicable after releasing the commitments, the OFT must—

(a) publish the release in such manner as it considers appropriate; and

(b) send a copy of the release to the person (or persons) who gave the commitments.

14. A notice under paragraph 11 or 12 shall be given by—

(a) sending a copy of the notice to such other person or persons as the OFT considers appropriate for the purpose of bringing the matter to which it relates to the attention of those likely to be affected by it; or

(b) publishing the notice in such manner as the OFT considers appropriate for the purpose of bringing the matter to which it relates to the attention of those likely to be affected by it.

<table>
<tr><td>Section 45(7)</td><td style="text-align:center">SCHEDULE 7</td></tr>
</table>

THE COMPETITION COMMISSION

PART I GENERAL

Interpretation

1. In this Schedule—

'the 1973 Act' means the Fair Trading Act 1973;

'Chairman' means the chairman of the Commission;

'the Commission' means the Competition Commission;

'Council' has the meaning given in paragraph 5;

'general functions' means any functions of the Commission other than functions—

(b) which are to be discharged by the Council;

'member' means a member of the Commission;

'newspaper merger reference' means a reference under section 45 of the Enterprise Act 2002 which specifies a newspaper public interest consideration (within the meaning of paragraph 20A of Schedule 8 to that Act) or a reference under section 62 of that Act which specifies a consideration specified in section 58(2A) or (2B) of that Act;

'newspaper panel member' means a member of the panel maintained under paragraph 22;

'reporting panel member' means a member appointed under paragraph 2(1)(b);

'secretary' means the secretary of the Commission appointed under paragraph 9; and

'specialist panel member' means a member appointed under any of the provisions mentioned in paragraph 2(1)(d).

Membership of the Commission

2.—(1) The Commission is to consist of—

(b) members appointed by the Secretary of State to form a panel for the purposes of the Commission's general functions;

(c) the members of the panel maintained under paragraph 22;

(d) members appointed by the Secretary of State under or by virtue of—

(i)   section 12(4) or 14(8) of the Water Industry Act 1991;

(ii) section 12(9) of the Electricity Act 1989;

(iii) section 194(1) of the Communications Act 2003;

(iv) Article 15(9) of the Electricity (Northern Ireland) Order 1992.

(1A) A person may not be, at the same time, a member of the Commission and a member of the Tribunal.

(2) A person who is appointed as a member of a kind mentioned in one of paragraphs (aa) to (c) of sub-paragraph (3) may also be appointed as a member of either or both of the other kinds mentioned in those paragraphs.

(3) The kinds of member are—

 (aa) a newspaper panel member;

 (b) a reporting panel member;

 (c) a specialist panel member.

(5) The validity of the Commission's proceedings is not affected by a defect in the appointment of a member.

Chairman and deputy chairmen

3.—(1) The Commission is to have a chairman appointed by the Secretary of State from among the reporting panel members.

(2) The Secretary of State may appoint one or more of the reporting panel members to act as deputy chairman.

(3) The Chairman, and any deputy chairman, may resign that office at any time by notice in writing addressed to the Secretary of State.

(4) If the Chairman (or a deputy chairman) ceases to be a member he also ceases to be Chairman (or a deputy chairman).

(5) If the Chairman is absent or otherwise unable to act, or there is no chairman, any of his functions may be performed—

 (a) if there is one deputy chairman, by him;

 (b) if there is more than one—

  (i) by the deputy chairman designated by the Secretary of State; or

  (ii) if no such designation has been made, by the deputy chairman designated by the deputy chairmen;

 (c) if there is no deputy chairman able to act—

  (i) by the member designated by the Secretary of State; or

  (ii) if no such designation has been made, by the member designated by the Commission.

The Council

5.—(1) The Commission is to have a board to be known as the Competition Commission Council (but referred to in this Schedule as 'the Council').

(2) The Council is to consist of—

 (a) the Chairman and any deputy chairmen of the Commission;

 (bb) the member or members appointed under paragraph 2(1) (e);

 (c) such other members as the Secretary of State may appoint; and

 (d) the secretary.

(3) In exercising its functions under paragraphs 3 and 7 to 12, the Commission is to act through the Council.

(3A) Without prejudice to the question whether any other functions of the Commission are to be so discharged, the functions of the Commission under sections 103, 113, and 166 of the Enterprise Act 2002 (and under section 113 as applied for the purposes of references under Part 4 of that Act by section 171 of that Act) are to be discharged by the Council.

(4) The Council may determine its own procedure including, in particular, its quorum.

(5) The Chairman (and any person acting as Chairman) is to have a casting vote on any question being decided by the Council.

Term of office

6.—(1) Subject to the provisions of this Schedule, each member is to hold and vacate office in accordance with the terms of his appointment.

(2) A person is not to be appointed as a member for more than eight years (but this does not prevent a re-appointment for the purpose only of continuing to act as a member of a group selected under paragraph 15 before the end of his term of office).

(3) Any member may at any time resign by notice in writing addressed to the Secretary of State.

(4) The Secretary of State may remove a member on the ground of incapacity or misbehaviour.

Expenses, remuneration and pensions

7.—(1) The Secretary of State shall pay to the Commission such sums as he considers appropriate to enable it to perform its functions.

(2) The Commission may pay, or make provision for paying, to or in respect of each member such salaries or other remuneration and such pensions, allowances, fees, expenses or gratuities as the Secretary of State may determine.

(3) If a person ceases to be a member otherwise than on the expiry of his term of office and it appears to the Secretary of State that there are special circumstances which make it right for him to receive compensation, the Commission may make a payment to him of such amount as the Secretary of State may determine.

7A. The Commission may publish advice and information in relation to any matter connected with the exercise of its functions.

The Commission's powers

8. Subject to the provisions of this Schedule, the Commission has power to do anything (except borrow money)—

(a) calculated to facilitate the discharge of its functions; or

(b) incidental or conducive to the discharge of its functions.

Staff

9.—(1) The Commission is to have a secretary, appointed by the Secretary of State on such terms and conditions of service as he considers appropriate.

(3) Before appointing a person to be secretary, the Secretary of State must consult the Chairman.

(4) Subject to obtaining the approval of the Secretary of State as to numbers and terms and conditions of service, the Commission may appoint such staff as it thinks appropriate.

Application of seal and proof of instruments

11.—(1) The application of the seal of the Commission must be authenticated by the signature of the secretary or of some other person authorised for the purpose.

(2) Sub-paragraph (1) does not apply in relation to any document which is or is to be signed in accordance with the law of Scotland.

(3) A document purporting to be duly executed under the seal of the Commission—

(a) is to be received in evidence; and

(b) is to be taken to have been so executed unless the contrary is proved.

Accounts

12.—(1) The Commission must—

(a) keep proper accounts and proper records in relation to its accounts;

(b) prepare a statement of accounts in respect of each of its financial years; and

(c) send copies of the statement to the Secretary of State and to the Comptroller and Auditor General before the end of the month of August next following the financial year to which the statement relates.

(2) The statement of accounts must comply with any directions given by the Secretary of State with the approval of the Treasury as to—

(a) the information to be contained in it,

(b) the manner in which the information contained in it is to be presented, or

(c) the methods and principles according to which the statement is to be prepared,

and must contain such additional information as the Secretary of State may with the approval of the Treasury require to be provided for informing Parliament.

(3) The Comptroller and Auditor General must—

(a) examine, certify and report on each statement received by him as a result of this paragraph; and

(b) lay copies of each statement and of his report before each House of Parliament.

(4) In this paragraph 'financial year' means the period beginning with the date on which the Commission is established and ending with March 31st next, and each successive period of twelve months.

Annual reports

12A.—(1) The Commission shall make to the Secretary of State a report for each financial year on its activities during the year.

(2) The annual report must be made before the end of August next following the financial year to which it relates.

(3) The Secretary of State shall lay a copy of the annual report before Parliament and arrange for the report to be published.

Status

13.—(1) The Commission is not to be regarded as the servant or agent of the Crown or as enjoying any status, privilege or immunity of the Crown.

(2) The Commission's property is not to be regarded as property of, or held on behalf of, the Crown.

PART II PERFORMANCE OF THE COMMISSION'S GENERAL FUNCTIONS

Interpretation

14. In this Part of this Schedule 'group' means a group selected under paragraph 15.

Discharge of certain functions by groups

15.—(1) Except where sub-paragraph (7) or (8) gives the Chairman power to act on his own, any general function of the Commission must be performed through a group selected for the purpose by the Chairman.

(2) The group must consist of at least three persons one of whom may be the Chairman.

(3) In selecting the members of the group, the Chairman must comply with any requirement as to its constitution imposed by any enactment applying to specialist panel members.

(4) If the functions to be performed through the group relate to a newspaper merger reference, the group must, subject to sub-paragraph (5), consist of such reporting panel members as the Chairman may select.

(5) The Chairman must select one or more newspaper panel members to be members of the group dealing with functions relating to a newspaper merger reference and, if he selects at least three such members, the group may consist entirely of those members.

(6) Subject to sub-paragraphs (2) to (5), a group must consist of reporting panel members or specialist panel members selected by the Chairman.

(7) While a group is being constituted to perform a particular general function of the Commission, the Chairman may—

(a) take such steps (falling within that general function) as he considers appropriate to facilitate the work of the group when it has been constituted.

(8) The Chairman may exercise the power conferred by section 36(1), 47(1) or 63(1) of the Enterprise Act 2002 while a group is being constituted to perform a relevant general function of the Commission or, when it has been so constituted; before it has held its first meeting.

Chairmen of groups

16. The Chairman must appoint one of the members of a group to act as the chairman of the group.

Replacement of member of group

17.—(1) If, during the proceedings of a group—

    (a) a member of the group ceases to be a member of the Commission,

    (b) the Chairman is satisfied that a member of the group will be unable for a substantial period to perform his duties as a member of the group, or

    (c) it appears to the Chairman that because of a particular interest of a member of the group it is inappropriate for him to remain in the group,

the Chairman may appoint a replacement.

(2) The Chairman may also at any time appoint any reporting panel member to be an additional member of a group.

Attendance of other members

18.—(1) At the invitation of the chairman of a group, any reporting panel member who is not a member of the group may attend meetings or otherwise take part in the proceedings of the group.

(2) But any person attending in response to such an invitation may not—

    (a) vote in any proceedings of the group; or

    (b) have a statement of his dissent from a conclusion of the group included in a report made by them.

(3) Nothing in sub-paragraph (1) is to be taken to prevent a group, or a member of a group, from consulting any member of the Commission with respect to any matter or question with which the group is concerned.

Procedure

19.—(1) Subject to any special or general directions given by the Secretary of State, each group may determine its own procedure.

(2) Each group may, in particular, determine its quorum and determine—

    (a) the extent, if any, to which persons interested or claiming to be interested in the subject-matter of the reference are allowed—

        (i)   to be present or to be heard, either by themselves or by their representatives;

        (ii) to cross-examine witnesses; or

        (iii) otherwise to take part; and

    (b) the extent, if any, to which sittings of the group are to be held in public.

(3) In determining its procedure a group must have regard to any guidance issued by the Chairman.

(4) Before issuing any guidance for the purposes of this paragraph the Chairman must consult the members of the Commission.

(5) This paragraph does not apply to groups for which rules must be made under paragraph 19A.

19A.—(1) The Chairman must make rules of procedure in relation to merger reference groups, market reference groups and special reference groups.

(2) Schedule 7A makes further provision about rules made under this paragraph but is not to be taken as restricting the Chairman's powers under this section.

(3) The Chairman must publish rules made under this paragraph in such manner as he considers appropriate for the purpose of bringing them to the attention of those likely to be affected by them.

(4) The Chairman must consult the members of the Commission and such other persons as he considers appropriate before making rules under this paragraph.

(5) Rules under this paragraph may—

    (a) make different provision for different cases or different purposes;

    (b) be varied or revoked by subsequent rules made under this paragraph.

(6) Subject to rules made under this paragraph, each merger reference group, market reference group and special reference group may determine its own procedure.

(7) In determining how to proceed in accordance with rules made under this paragraph and in determining its procedure under subparagraph (6), a group must have regard to any guidance issued by the Chairman.

(8) Before issuing any guidance for the purposes of this paragraph the Chairman shall consult the members of the Commission and such other persons as he considers appropriate.

(9) In this paragraph and in Schedule 7A—

'market reference group' means any group constituted in connection with a reference under section 126 or 127 of the Enterprise Act 2002 (including that section as it has effect by virtue of another enactment);

'merger reference group' means any group constituted in connection with a reference under section 32 of the Water Industry Act 1991 (c. 56) or section 21, 32, 44 or 61 of the Enterprise Act 2002; and

'special reference group' means any group constituted in connection with a reference or (in the case of the Financial Services and Markets Act 2000 (c. 8)) an investigation under—

(a)   section 11 of the Competition Act 1980 (c. 21);
(c)   section 43 of the Airports Act 1986 (c. 31);
(d)   section 24 or 41E of the Gas Act 1986 (c. 44);
(e)   section 12 or 56C of the Electricity Act 1989 (c. 29);
(g)   section 12 or 14 of the Water Industry Act 1991 (c. 56);
(h)   article 15 of the Electricity (Northern Ireland) Order 1992 (S.I. 1992/231 (N.I.1));
(i)   section 13 of, or Schedule 4A to, the Railways Act 1993 (c. 43);
(j)   article 34 of the Airports (Northern Ireland) Order 1994 (S.I. 1994/426 (N.I.1));
(k)   article 15 of the Gas (Northern Ireland) Order 1996 (S.I. 1996/275 (N.I. 2));
(l)   section 15 of the Postal Services Act 2000 (c. 26);
(m)   section 162 or 306 of the Financial Services and Markets Act 2000 (c. 8);
(n)   section 12 of the Transport Act 2000 (c. 38); or
(o)   section 193 of the Communications Act 2003.

Effect of exercise of functions by group

20.—(1) Subject to sub-paragraphs (2)–(9), anything done by or in relation to a group in, or in connection with, the performance of functions to be performed by the group is to have the same effect as if done by or in relation to the Commission.

(2) For the purposes of Part 3 of the Enterprise Act 2002 (mergers) any decision of a group under section 34(1) or 35(1) of that Act (questions to be decided on non-public interest merger references) that there is an anti-competitive outcome is to be treated as a decision under that section that there is not an anti-competitive outcome if the decision is not that of at least two-thirds of the members of the group.

(3) For the purposes of Part 3 of the Act of 2002, if the decision is not that of at least two-thirds of the members of the group—

(a) any decision of a group under section 47 of that Act (questions to be decided on public interest merger references) that a relevant merger situation has been created is to be treated as a decision under that section that no such situation has been created;

(b) any decision of a group under section 47 of that Act that the creation of a relevant merger situation has resulted, or may be expected to result, in a substantial lessening of competition within any market or markets in the United Kingdom for goods or services is to be treated as a decision under that section that the creation of that situation has not resulted, or may be expected not to result, in such a substantial lessening of competition;

(c) any decision of a group under section 47 of that Act that arrangements are in progress or in contemplation which, if carried into effect, will result in the creation of a relevant merger situation is to be treated as a decision under that section that no such arrangements are in progress or in contemplation; and

(d) any decision of a group under section 47 of that Act that the creation of such a situation as is mentioned in paragraph (c) may be expected to result in a substantial lessening of competition within any market or markets in the United Kingdom for goods or services is to be treated as a decision under that section that the creation of that situation may be expected not to result in such a substantial lessening of competition.

(4) For the purposes of Part 3 of the Act of 2002, if the decision is not that of at least two-thirds of the members of the group—

(a) any decision of a group under section 63 of that Act (questions to be decided on special public interest merger references) that a special merger situation has been created is to be treated as a decision under that section that no such situation has been created; and

(b) any decision of a group under section 63 of that Act that arrangements are in progress or in contemplation which, if carried into effect, will result in the creation of a special merger situation is to be treated as a decision under that section that no such arrangements are in progress or in contemplation.

(5) For the purposes of Part 4 of the Act of 2002 (market investigations), if the decision is not that of at least two-thirds of the members of the group, any decision of a group under section 134 or 141 (questions to be decided on market investigation references) that a feature, or combination of features, of a relevant market prevents, restricts or distorts competition in connection with the supply or acquisition of any goods or services in the United Kingdom or a part of the United Kingdom is to be treated as a decision that the feature or (as the case may be) combination of features does not prevent, restrict or distort such competition.

(6) Accordingly, for the purposes of Part 4 of the Act of 2002, a group is to be treated as having decided under section 134 or 141 that there is no adverse effect on competition if—

(a) one or more than one decision of the group is to be treated as mentioned in sub-paragraph (5); and

(b) there is no other relevant decision of the group.

(7) In sub-paragraph (6) 'relevant decision' means a decision which is not to be treated as mentioned in sub-paragraph (5) and which is that a feature, or combination of features, of a relevant market prevents, restricts or distorts competition in connection with the supply or acquisition of any goods or services in the United Kingdom or a part of the United Kingdom.

(8) Expressions used in sub-paragraphs (2) to (7) shall be construed in accordance with Part 3 or (as the case may be) 4 of the Act of 2002.

(9) Sub-paragraph (1) is also subject to specific provision made by or under other enactments about decisions which are not decisions of at least two-thirds of the members of a group.

Casting votes

21. The chairman of a group is to have a casting vote on any question to be decided by the group.

Newspaper merger references

22. There are to be members of the Commission appointed by the Secretary of State to form a panel of persons available for selection as members of a group constituted in connection with a newspaper merger reference.

SCHEDULE 7A

THE COMPETITION COMMISSION: PROCEDURAL RULES FOR MERGERS AND MARKET REFERENCES ETC.

1. In this Schedule—

'market investigation' means an investigation carried out by a market reference group in connection with a reference under section 126 or 127 of the Enterprise Act 2002 (including that section as it has effect by virtue of another enactment);

'market reference group' has the meaning given by paragraph 19A(9) of Schedule 7 to this Act;

'merger investigation' means an investigation carried out by a merger reference group in connection with a reference under section 21, 32, 44 or 61 of the Act of 2002;

'merger reference group' has the meaning given by paragraph 19A(9) of Schedule 7 to this Act;

'relevant group' means a market reference group, merger reference group or special reference group;

'special investigation' means an investigation carried out by a special reference group—

    (a) in connection with a reference under a provision mentioned in any of paragraphs (a) to (1), (n) and (o) of the definition of 'special reference group' in paragraph 19A(9) of Schedule 7 to this Act; or

    (b) under a provision mentioned in paragraph (m) of that definition; and

'special reference group' has the meaning given by paragraph 19A(9) of Schedule 7 to this Act.

  2. Rules may make provision—

    (a) for particular stages of a merger investigation, a market investigation or a special investigation to be dealt with in accordance with a timetable and for the revision of that timetable;

    (b) as to the documents and information which must be given to a relevant group in connection with a merger investigation, a market investigation or a special investigation;

    (c) as to the documents or information which a relevant group must give to other persons in connection with such an investigation.

  3. Rules made by virtue of paragraph 2(a) and (b) may, in particular, enable or require a relevant group to disregard documents or information given after a particular date.

  4. Rules made by virtue of paragraph 2(c) may, in particular, make provision for the notification or publication of, and for consultation about, provisional findings of a relevant group.

  5. Rules may make provision as to the quorum of relevant groups.

  6. Rules may make provision—

    (a) as to the extent (if any) to which persons interested or claiming to be interested in a matter under consideration which is specified or described in the rules are allowed—

      (i) to be (either by themselves or by their representatives) present before a relevant group or heard by that group;

      (ii) to cross-examine witnesses; or

      (iii) otherwise to take part;

    (b) as to the extent (if any) to which sittings of a relevant group are to be held in public; and

    (c) generally in connection with any matters permitted by rules made under paragraph (a) or (b) (including, in particular, provision for a record of any hearings).

  7. Rules may make provision for—

    (a) the notification or publication of information in relation to merger investigations, market investigations or special investigations;

    (b) consultation about such investigations.

Sections 46(5) and 48(4)
SCHEDULE 8

APPEALS

PART I GENERAL

General procedure

  2.—(1) An appeal to the Tribunal under section 46 or 47 must be made by sending a notice of appeal to it within the specified period.

  (2) The notice of appeal must set out the grounds of appeal in sufficient detail to indicate—

    (a) under which provision of this Act the appeal is brought;

(b) to what extent (if any) the appellant contends that the decision against, or with respect to which, the appeal is brought was based on an error of fact or was wrong in law; and

(c) to what extent (if any) the appellant is appealing against the OFT's exercise of its discretion in making the disputed decision.

(3) The Tribunal may give an appellant leave to amend the grounds of appeal identified in the notice of appeal.

(4) In this paragraph references to the Tribunal are to the Tribunal as constituted (in accordance with section 14 of the Enterprise Act 2002) for the purposes of the proceedings in question.

(5) Nothing in this paragraph restricts the power under section 15 of the Enterprise Act 2002 (tribunal rules) to make provision as to the manner of instituting proceedings before the Tribunal.

Decisions of the Tribunal

3.—(A1) This paragraph applies to any appeal under section 46 or 47 other than—

(a) an appeal under section 46 against, or with respect to, a decision of the kind specified in subsection (3) (g) or (h) of that section, and

(b) an appeal under section 47(1)(b) or (c).

(1) The Tribunal must determine the appeal on the merits by reference to the grounds of appeal set out in the notice of appeal.

(2) The Tribunal may confirm or set aside the decision which is the subject of the appeal, or any part of it, and may—

(a) remit the matter to the OFT,

(b) impose or revoke, or vary the amount of, a penalty,

(d) give such directions, or take such other steps, as the OFT could itself have given or taken, or

(e) make any other decision which the OFT could itself have made.

(3) Any decision of the Tribunal on an appeal has the same effect, and may be enforced in the same manner, as a decision of the OFT.

(4) If the Tribunal confirms the decision which is the subject of the appeal it may nevertheless set aside any finding of fact on which the decision was based.

3A.—(1) This paragraph applies to—

(a) any appeal under section 46 against, or with respect to, a decision of the kind specified in subsection (3) (g) or (h) of that section, and

(b) any appeal under section 47(1)(b) or (c).

(2) The Tribunal must, by reference to the grounds of appeal set out in the notice of appeal, determine the appeal by applying the same principles as would be applied by a court on an application for judicial review.

(3) The Tribunal may—

(a) dismiss the appeal or quash the whole or part of the decision to which it relates; and

(b) where it quashes the whole or part of that decision, remit the matter back to the OFT with a direction to reconsider and make a new decision in accordance with the ruling of the Tribunal.

Section 51(2)   # SCHEDULE 9

OFT'S RULES

General

1. In this Schedule—
'rules' means rules made by the OFT under section 51.

Application

2. [repealed]

Provisional decisions

3. [repealed]

Guidance

4. [repealed]

Decisions

5.—(1) Rules may make provision as to—
- (a) the form and manner in which notice of any decision is to be given;
- (b) the person or persons to whom the notice is to be given;
- (c) the manner in which the OFT is to publish a decision;
- (d) the procedure to be followed if—
    - (i) the OFT takes further action with respect to an agreement after having decided that it does not infringe the Chapter I prohibition;
    - (ii) the OFT takes further action with respect to an agreement after having decided that it does not infringe the prohibition in Article 81(1);
    - (iii) the OFT takes further action with respect to conduct after having decided that it does not infringe the Chapter II prohibition; or
    - (iv) the OFT takes further action with respect to conduct after having decided that it does not infringe the prohibition in Article 82.

(2) In this paragraph 'decision' means a decision of the OFT—
- (a) as to whether or not an agreement has infringed the Chapter I prohibition;
- (b) as to whether or not an agreement has infringed the prohibition in Article 81(1);
- (c) as to whether or not conduct has infringed the Chapter II prohibition; or
- (d) as to whether or not conduct has infringed the prohibition in Article 82.

Individual exemptions

6–7. [repealed]

Block exemptions

8. Rules may make provision as to—
- (a) the procedure to be followed by the OFT if it cancels a block exemption;
- (b) the procedure to be followed by the OFT if it withdraws the benefit of a regulation of the Commission pursuant to Article 29(2) of the EC Competition Regulation.

Parallel exemptions

9. Rules may make provision as to—
- (a) the circumstances in which the OFT may—
    - (i) impose conditions or obligations in relation to a parallel exemption,
    - (ii) vary or remove any such conditions or obligations,
    - (iii) impose additional conditions or obligations, or
    - (iv) cancel the exemption;
- (b) as to the procedure to be followed by the OFT if it is acting under section 10(5);
- (c) the form and manner in which notice of a decision to take any of the steps in sub-paragraph (a) is to be given;
- (d) the circumstances in which an exemption may be cancelled with retrospective effect.

Section 11 exemptions

10. Rules may, with respect to any exemption provided by regulations made under section 11, make provision similar to that made with respect to parallel exemptions by section 10 or by rules under paragraph 9.

Directions withdrawing exclusions

11. Rules may make provision as to the factors which the OFT may take into account when he is determining the date on which a direction given under paragraph 4(1) of Schedule 1 or paragraph 9(3) of Schedule 3 is to have effect.

Disclosure of information

12.—(1) Rules may make provision as to the circumstances in which the OFT is to be required, before disclosing information given to it by a third party in connection with the exercise of any of the OFT's functions under Part I, to give notice, and an opportunity to make representations, to the third party.

(2) In relation to the agreement (or conduct) concerned, 'third party' means a person who is not a party to the agreement (or who has not engaged in the conduct).

Applications under section 47

13. Rules may make provision as to—
    (a) the period within which an application under section 47(1) must be made;
    (b) the procedure to be followed by the OFT in dealing with the application;
    (c) the person or persons to whom notice of the OFT's response to the application is to be given.

Enforcement

14. Rules may make provision as to the procedure to be followed when the OFT takes action under any of sections 32 to 40 with respect to the enforcement of the provisions of this Part.

Enterprise Act 2002

(2002, c. 40)

An Act to establish and provide for the functions of the Office of Fair Trading, the Competition Appeal Tribunal and the Competition Service; to make provision about mergers and market structures and conduct; to amend the constitution and functions of the Competition Commission; to create an offence for those entering into certain anti-competitive agreements; to provide for the disqualification of directors of companies engaging in certain anti-competitive practices; to make other provision about competition law; to amend the law relating to the protection of the collective interests of consumers; to make further provision about the disclosure of information obtained under competition and consumer legislation; to amend the Insolvency Act 1986 and make other provision about insolvency; and for connected purposes

[7 November 2002]

BE IT ENACTED by the Queen's most Excellent Majesty, by and with the advice and consent of the Lords Spiritual and Temporal, and Commons, in this present Parliament assembled, and by the authority of the same, as follows:—

PART I THE OFFICE OF FAIR TRADING

Establishment etc. of Office of Fair Trading

1   The Office of Fair Trading

(1) There shall be a body corporate to be known as the Office of Fair Trading (in this Act referred to as 'the OFT').

(2) The functions of the OFT are carried out on behalf of the Crown.

(3) Schedule 1 (which makes further provision about the OFT) has effect.

(4) In managing its affairs the OFT shall have regard, in addition to any relevant general guidance as to the governance of public bodies, to such generally accepted principles of good corporate governance as it is reasonable to regard as applicable to the OFT.

2   The Director General of Fair Trading

(1) The functions of the Director General of Fair Trading (in this Act referred to as 'the Director'), and his property, rights and liabilities, are transferred to the OFT.

(2) The office of the Director is abolished.

(3) Any enactment, instrument or other document passed or made before the commencement of subsection (1) which refers to the Director shall have effect, so far as necessary for the purposes of or in consequence of anything being transferred, as if any reference to the Director were a reference to the OFT.

3   Annual plan

(1) The OFT shall, before each financial year, publish a document (the 'annual plan') containing a statement of its main objectives and priorities for the year.

(2) The OFT shall for the purposes of public consultation publish a document containing proposals for its annual plan at least two months before publishing the annual plan for any year.

(3) The OFT shall lay before Parliament a copy of each document published under subsection (2) and each annual plan.

4   Annual and other reports

(1) The OFT shall, as soon as practicable after the end of each financial year, make to the Secretary of State a report (the 'annual report') on its activities and performance during that year.

(2) The annual report for each year shall include—

    (a) a general survey of developments in respect of matters relating to the OFT's functions;

    (b) an assessment of the extent to which the OFT's main objectives and priorities for the year (as set out in the annual plan) have been met;

    (c) a summary of the significant decisions, investigations or other activities made or carried out by the OFT during the year;

    (d) a summary of the allocation of the OFT's financial resources to its various activities during the year; and

(e) an assessment of the OFT's performance and practices in relation to its enforcement functions.

(3) The OFT shall lay a copy of each annual report before Parliament and arrange for the report to be published.

(4) The OFT may—

(a) prepare other reports in respect of matters relating to any of its functions; and

(b) arrange for any such report to be published.

General functions of OFT

5   Acquisition of information etc.

(1) The OFT has the function of obtaining, compiling and keeping under review information about matters relating to the carrying out of its functions.

(2) That function is to be carried out with a view to (among other things) ensuring that the OFT has sufficient information to take informed decisions and to carry out its other functions effectively.

(3) In carrying out that function the OFT may carry out, commission or support (financially or otherwise) research.

6   Provision of information etc. to the public

(1) The OFT has the function of—

(a) making the public aware of the ways in which competition may benefit consumers in, and the economy of, the United Kingdom; and

(b) giving information or advice in respect of matters relating to any of its functions to the public.

(2) In carrying out those functions the OFT may—

(a) publish educational materials or carry out other educational activities; or

(b) support (financially or otherwise) the carrying out by others of such activities or the provision by others of information or advice.

7   Provision of information and advice to Ministers etc.

(1) The OFT has the function of—

(a) making proposals, or

(b) giving other information or advice,

on matters relating to any of its functions to any Minister of the Crown or other public authority (including proposals, information or advice as to any aspect of the law or a proposed change in the law).

(2) A Minister of the Crown may request the OFT to make proposals or give other information or advice on any matter relating to any of its functions; and the OFT shall, so far as is reasonably practicable and consistent with its other functions, comply with the request.

8   Promoting good consumer practice

(1) The OFT has the function of promoting good practice in the carrying out of activities which may affect the economic interests of consumers in the United Kingdom.

(2) In carrying out that function the OFT may (without prejudice to the generality of subsection (1)) make arrangements for approving consumer codes and may, in accordance with the arrangements, give its approval to or withdraw its approval from any consumer code.

(3) Any such arrangements must specify the criteria to be applied by the OFT in determining whether to give approval to or withdraw approval from a consumer code.

(4) Any such arrangements may in particular—

(a) specify descriptions of consumer code which may be the subject of an application to the OFT for approval (and any such description may be framed by reference to any feature of a consumer code, including the persons who are, or are to be, subject to the code, the manner in which it is, or is to be, operated and the persons responsible for its operation); and

(b) provide for the use in accordance with the arrangements of an official symbol intended to signify that a consumer code is approved by the OFT.

(5) The OFT shall publish any arrangements under subsection (2) in such manner it considers appropriate.

(6) In this section 'consumer code' means a code of practice or other document (however described) intended, with a view to safeguarding or promoting the interests of consumers, to regulate by any means the conduct of persons engaged in the supply of goods or services to consumers (or the conduct of their employees or representatives).

Miscellaneous

9   Repeal of certain powers of direction

Section 12 of the Fair Trading Act 1973 (in this Act referred to as 'the 1973 Act') and section 13 of the Competition Act 1980 (powers of Secretary of State to give directions) shall cease to have effect.

10   Part II of the 1973 Act

(1) The following provisions of the 1973 Act shall cease to have effect—

    (a) section 3 and Schedule 2 (which establish, and make provision with respect to, the Consumer Protection Advisory Committee);

    (b) sections 13 to 21 (which relate to references made to, and reports of, that Committee); and

    (c) section 22 (power of Secretary of State to make orders in pursuance of a report of that Committee).

11   Super-complaints to OFT

(1) This section applies where a designated consumer body makes a complaint to the OFT that any feature, or combination of features, of a market in the United Kingdom for goods or services is or appears to be significantly harming the interests of consumers.

(2) The OFT must, within 90 days after the day on which it receives the complaint, publish a response stating how it proposes to deal with the complaint, and in particular—

    (a) whether it has decided to take any action, or to take no action, in response to the complaint, and

    (b) if it has decided to take action, what action it proposes to take.

(3) The response must state the OFT's reasons for its proposals.

(4) The Secretary of State may by order amend subsection (2) by substituting any period for the period for the time being specified there.

(5) 'Designated consumer body' means a body designated by the Secretary of State by order.

(6) The Secretary of State—

    (a) may designate a body only if it appears to him to represent the interests of consumers of any description, and

    (b) must publish (and may from time to time vary) other criteria to be applied by him in determining whether to make or revoke a designation.

(7) The OFT—

    (a) must issue guidance as to the presentation by the complainant of a reasoned case for the complaint, and

    (b) may issue such other guidance as appears to it to be appropriate for the purposes of this section.

(8) An order under this section—

    (a) shall be made by statutory instrument, and

    (b) shall be subject to annulment in pursuance of a resolution of either House of Parliament.

(9) In this section—

    (a) references to a feature of a market in the United Kingdom for goods or services have the same meaning as if contained in Part 4, and

    (b) 'consumer' means an individual who is a consumer within the meaning of that Part.

PART II THE COMPETITION APPEAL TRIBUNAL

The Competition Appeal Tribunal

12 The Competition Appeal Tribunal

(1) There shall be a tribunal, to be called the Competition Appeal Tribunal (in this Part referred to as 'the Tribunal').

(2) The Tribunal shall consist of—

(a) a person appointed by the Lord Chancellor to preside over the Tribunal (in this Part referred to as 'the President');

(b) members appointed by the Lord Chancellor to form a panel of chairmen; and

(c) members appointed by the Secretary of State to form a panel of ordinary members.

(3) The Tribunal shall have a Registrar appointed by the Secretary of State.

(4) The expenses of the Tribunal shall be paid by the Competition Service.

(5) Schedule 2 (which makes further provision about the Tribunal) has effect.

13 The Competition Service

(1) There shall be a body corporate called the Competition Service (in this Part referred to as 'the Service').

(2) The purpose of the Service is to fund, and provide support services to, the Competition Appeal Tribunal.

(3) In subsection (2) 'support services' includes the provision of staff, accommodation and equipment and any other services which facilitate the carrying out by the Tribunal of its functions.

(4) The activities of the Service are not carried out on behalf of the Crown (and its property is not to be regarded as held on behalf of the Crown).

(5) The Secretary of State shall pay to the Service such sums as he considers appropriate to enable it to fund the activities of the Tribunal and to carry out its other activities.

(6) Schedule 3 (which makes further provision about the Service) has effect.

14 Constitution of Tribunal for particular proceedings and its decisions

(1) For the purposes of any proceedings before it the Tribunal shall consist of a chairman and two other members.

(2) The chairman must be the President or a member of the panel of chairmen.

(3) The other members may be chosen from either the panel of chairmen or the panel of ordinary members.

(4) If the members of the Tribunal as constituted in accordance with this section are unable to agree on any decision, the decision is to be taken by majority vote.

(5) This section has effect subject to paragraph 17 of Schedule 4 (consequences of a member of the Tribunal being unable to continue after the proceedings have begun to be heard).

(6) Part I of Schedule 4 (which makes further provision about the decisions of the Tribunal and their enforcement) has effect.

15 Tribunal rules

(1) The Secretary of State may, after consulting the President and such other persons as he considers appropriate, make rules (in this Part referred to as 'Tribunal rules') with respect to proceedings before the Tribunal.

(2) Tribunal rules may make provision with respect to matters incidental to or consequential upon appeals provided for by or under any Act to the Court of Appeal or the Court of Session in relation to a decision of the Tribunal.

(3) Tribunal rules may—

(a) specify qualifications for appointment as Registrar;

(b) confer functions on the President or the Registrar in relation to proceedings before the Tribunal; and

(c) contain incidental, supplemental, consequential or transitional provision.

(4) The power to make Tribunal rules is exercisable by statutory instrument subject to annulment in pursuance of a resolution of either House of Parliament.

(5) Part 2 of Schedule 4 (which makes further provision about the rules) has effect, but without prejudice to the generality of subsection (1).

16   Transfers of certain proceedings to and from Tribunal

(1) The Lord Chancellor may by regulations—

    (a) make provision enabling the court—

        (i)   to transfer to the Tribunal for its determination so much of any proceedings before the court as relates to an infringement issue; and

        (ii) to give effect to the determination of that issue by the Tribunal; and

    (b) make such incidental, supplementary, consequential, transitional or saving provision as the Lord Chancellor may consider appropriate.

(2) The power to make regulations under subsection (1) is exercisable by statutory instrument subject to annulment in pursuance of a resolution of either House of Parliament.

(3) Rules of court may prescribe the procedure to be followed in connection with a transfer mentioned in subsection (1).

(4) The court may transfer to the Tribunal, in accordance with rules of court, so much of any proceedings before it as relates to a claim to which section 47A of the 1998 Act applies.

(5) Rules of court may make provision in connection with the transfer from the Tribunal to the High Court or the Court of Session of a claim made in proceedings under section 47A of the 1998 Act.

(6) In this section—

'the court' means—

    (a) the High Court or a county court; or

    (b) the Court of Session or a sheriff court; and

'infringement issue' means any question relating to whether or not an infringement of—

    (a) the Chapter I prohibition or the Chapter II prohibition; or

    (b) Article 81 or 82 of the Treaty, has been or is being committed;

but otherwise any terms used in this section and Part 1 of the 1998 Act have the same meaning as they have in that Part.

Proceedings under Part I of 1998 Act

17   Third party appeals

For section 47 of the 1998 Act (third party appeals) there is substituted—

'47   Third party appeals

(1) A person who does not fall within section 46(1) or (2) may appeal to the Tribunal with respect to a decision falling within paragraphs (a) to (f) of section 46(3) or such other decision of the OFT under this Part as may be prescribed.

(2) A person may make an appeal under subsection (1) only if the Tribunal considers that he has a sufficient interest in the decision with respect to which the appeal is made, or that he represents persons who have such an interest.

(3) The making of an appeal under this section does not suspend the effect of the decision to which the appeal relates.'

18   Damages

After section 47 of the 1998 Act there is inserted—

'47A   Award of damages by the Tribunal

(1) A claim for damages may be made to the Tribunal in respect of an infringement of—

    (a) the Chapter I prohibition;

    (b) the Chapter II prohibition;

(c) the prohibition in Article 81(1) of the Treaty;

(d) the prohibition in Article 82 of the Treaty;

(e) the prohibition in Article 65(1) of the Treaty establishing the European Coal and Steel Community;

(f) the prohibition in Article 66(7) of that Treaty.

(2) Damages may be awarded in respect of an infringement only if—

(a) the OFT has made a decision that the Chapter I prohibition or the Chapter II prohibition has been infringed;

(b) the OFT has made a decision that the prohibition in Article 81(1) or Article 82 of the Treaty has been infringed;

(c) the Tribunal has made a decision that the Chapter I prohibition or the Chapter II prohibition has been infringed, or that the prohibition in Article 81(1) or Article 82 of the Treaty has been infringed;

(d) the European Commission has made a decision that the prohibition in Article 81(1) or Article 82 of the Treaty has been infringed; or

(e) the European Commission has made a decision that the prohibition in Article 65(1) of the Treaty establishing the European Coal and Steel Community has been infringed, or has made a finding under Article 66(7) of that Treaty.

(3) In awarding damages the Tribunal is to apply the same principles as would be applied by a court in awarding damages for a claim in tort or, in Scotland, delict.

(4) Otherwise than with the permission of the Tribunal, where subsection (2) (a), (b) or (c) applies, no claim under this section may be made—

(a) before the end of the period during which an appeal may be made under section 46 or section 47, or under the EC Competition Law (Articles 84 and 85) Enforcement Regulations 2001 (S.I. 2001/2916), with respect to a decision of the OFT;

(b) before the end of the period during which a further appeal may be made under section 49 or under those Regulations with respect to a decision of the Tribunal (whether a decision falling within subsection (2)(c) or a decision on an appeal mentioned in paragraph (a));

(c) before the end of the period during which an appeal may be made to the House of Lords;

and in each case, if any such appeal is made, before the appeal is determined.

(5) Otherwise than with the permission of the Tribunal, where subsection (2)(d) or (e) applies, no claim under this section may be made—

(a) before the end of the period during which proceedings against the decision or finding of the European Commission may be instituted in the European Court;

(b) if any such proceedings are instituted, before those proceedings are determined.

(6) This section does not affect any right a person may have to commence civil proceedings in respect of an infringement mentioned in subsection (1).'

19 Claims on behalf of consumers

After section 47A of the 1998 Act (which is inserted by section 18), there is inserted—

'47B Claims brought on behalf of consumers

(1) A claim may be made under section 47A by a specified body on behalf of two or more individuals who have claims under that section as consumers and in respect of the same infringement.

(2) A claim may be made on behalf of an individual only with his consent.

(3) If two or more individuals have made a claim as consumers under section 47A in respect of the same infringement, a specified body may with the consent of each individual continue the claim on their behalf.

(4) In deciding any claim made or continued under section 47A by virtue of this section, the Tribunal may award damages to an individual on whose behalf a claim is made or continued.

(5) An individual claims as a consumer if the claim is in respect of an infringement affecting (whether directly or indirectly) goods or services to which subsection (6) applies.

(6) This subsection applies to goods or services which—

    (a) the individual received, or sought to receive, otherwise than in the course of a business carried on by him (notwithstanding that he received or sought to receive them with a view to carrying on a business); and

    (b) were, or would have been, supplied to the individual (in the case of goods whether by way of sale or otherwise) in the course of a business carried on by the person who supplied or would have supplied them.

(7) A business includes—

    (a) a professional practice;

    (b) any other undertaking carried on for gain or reward;

    (c) any undertaking in the course of which goods or services are supplied otherwise than free of charge.

(8) 'Specified' means specified in an order made by the Secretary of State, in accordance with criteria to be published by the Secretary of State for the purposes of this section.

(9) An application by a body to be specified in an order under this section is to be made in a form approved by the Secretary of State for the purpose.'

Other amendments of the 1998 Act

20 Findings of infringements

(1) After section 58 of the 1998 Act there is inserted—

'Findings of infringements

58A Findings of infringements

(1) In any proceedings before the court for damages in respect of an infringement of—

    (a) the Chapter I prohibition;

    (b) the Chapter II prohibition;

    (c) the prohibition in Article 81(1) of the Treaty;

    (d) the prohibition in Article 82 of the Treaty;

the court is bound by a decision mentioned in subsection (2) in respect of the infringement.

(2) The decisions are—

    (a) a decision of the OFT that the Chapter I prohibition or the Chapter II prohibition has been infringed;

    (b) a decision of the OFT that the prohibition in Article 81(1) or Article 82 of the Treaty has been infringed;

    (c) a decision of the Tribunal that the Chapter I prohibition or the Chapter II prohibition has been infringed, or that the prohibition in Article 81(1) or Article 82 of the Treaty has been infringed.

(3) Subsection (1) does not have effect in respect of a decision—

    (a) before the end of the period during which an appeal may be made under section 46 or section 47, or under the EC Competition Law (Articles 84 and 85) Enforcement Regulations 2001 (S.I. 2001/2916), with respect to a decision of the OFT;

    (b) before the end of the period during which an appeal may be made under section 49 or under those Regulations with respect to a decision of the Tribunal (whether a decision falling within subsection (2)(c) or a decision on an appeal mentioned in paragraph (a));

    (c) before the end of the period during which an appeal may be made to the House of Lords;

and in each case, if any such appeal is made, before the appeal is determined.'

(2) In section 59(1) of that Act (Interpretation), in the definition of 'the court', after '58' there is inserted ', 58A'.

21 Amendment of 1998 Act relating to the Tribunal

Schedule 5 (which contains amendments of the 1998 Act relating to, and to the proceedings of, the Tribunal) has effect.

PART III MERGERS

Chapter 1 Duty to make references

Duty to make references: completed mergers

22 Duty to make references in relation to completed mergers

    (1) The OFT shall, subject to subsections (2) and (3), make a reference to the Commission if the OFT believes that it is or may be the case that—

        (a) a relevant merger situation has been created; and

        (b) the creation of that situation has resulted, or may be expected to result, in a substantial lessening of competition within any market or markets in the United Kingdom for goods or services.

    (2) The OFT may decide not to make a reference under this section if it believes that—

        (a) the market concerned is not, or the markets concerned are not, of sufficient importance to justify the making of a reference to the Commission; or

        (b) any relevant customer benefits in relation to the creation of the relevant merger situation concerned outweigh the substantial lessening of competition concerned and any adverse effects of the substantial lessening of competition concerned.

    (3) No reference shall be made under this section if—

        (a) the making of the reference is prevented by section 74(1) or 96(3) or paragraph 4 of Schedule 7;

        (b) the OFT is considering whether to accept undertakings under section 73 instead of making such a reference;

        (c) the relevant merger situation concerned is being, or has been, dealt with in connection with a reference made under section 33;

        (d) a notice under section 42(2) is in force in relation to the matter or the matter to which such a notice relates has been finally determined under Chapter 2 otherwise than in circumstances in which a notice is then given to the OFT under section 56(1);

        (e) the matter falls to be dealt with, or has been dealt with, otherwise than under this section by virtue of any provision of Community law (including as a result of a request made by the United Kingdom, whether alone or with others, to the European Commission under article 22(1) of the EC Merger Regulation); or

        (f) subject to subsection (3A), a reasoned submission requesting referral to the European Commission has been submitted to the European Commission under article 4(5) of the EC Merger Regulation.

    (3A) Subsection (3)(f) shall cease to apply if the OFT is informed that a Member State competent to examine the concentration under its national competition law has, within the time permitted by Article 4(5) of the EC Merger Regulation, expressed its disagreement as regards the request to refer the case to the European Commission; and this subsection shall be construed in accordance with that Regulation.

    (4) A reference under this section shall, in particular, specify—

        (a) the enactment under which it is made; and

        (b) the date on which it is made.

    (5) The references in this section to the creation of a relevant merger situation shall be construed in accordance with section 23, the reference in subsection (2) of this section to relevant customer benefits shall be construed in accordance with section 30 and the reference in subsection (3) of this section to a matter to which a notice under section 42(2) relates being finally determined under Chapter 2 shall be construed in accordance with section 42(3) and (4).

    (6) In this Part 'market in the United Kingdom' includes—

        (a) so far as it operates in the United Kingdom or a part of the United Kingdom, any market which operates there and in another country or territory or in a part of another country or territory; and

(b) any market which operates only in a part of the United Kingdom;

and references to a market for goods or services include references to a market for goods and services.

(7) In this Part 'the decision-making authority' means—

(a) in the case of a reference or possible reference under this section or section 33, the OFT or (as the case may be) the Commission; and

(b) in the case of a notice or possible notice under section 42(2) or 59(2) or a reference or possible reference under section 45 or 62, the OFT, the Commission or (as the case may be) the Secretary of State.

23 Relevant merger situations

(1) A relevant merger situation has been created if—

(a) two or more enterprises have ceased to be distinct enterprises at a time or in circumstances falling within section 24; and

(b) the value of the turnover in the United Kingdom of the enterprise being taken over exceeds £70 million.

(2) For the purposes of this Part, a relevant merger situation has also been created if—

(a) two or more enterprises have ceased to be distinct enterprises at a time or in circumstances falling within section 24; and

(b) as a result, one or both of the conditions mentioned in subsections (3) and (4) below prevails or prevails to a greater extent.

(3) The condition mentioned in this subsection is that, in relation to the supply of goods of any description, at least one-quarter of all the goods of that description which are supplied in the United Kingdom, or in a substantial part of the United Kingdom—

(a) are supplied by one and the same person or are supplied to one and the same person; or

(b) are supplied by the persons by whom the enterprises concerned are carried on, or are supplied to those persons.

(4) The condition mentioned in this subsection is that, in relation to the supply of services of any description, the supply of services of that description in the United Kingdom, or in a substantial part of the United Kingdom, is to the extent of at least one-quarter—

(a) supply by one and the same person, or supply for one and the same person; or

(b) supply by the persons by whom the enterprises concerned are carried on, or supply for those persons.

(5) For the purpose of deciding whether the proportion of one-quarter mentioned in subsection (3) or (4) is fulfilled with respect to goods or (as the case may be) services of any description, the decision-making authority shall apply such criterion (whether value, cost, price, quantity, capacity, number of workers employed or some other criterion, of whatever nature), or such combination of criteria, as the decision-making authority considers appropriate.

(6) References in subsections (3) and (4) to the supply of goods or (as the case may be) services shall, in relation to goods or services of any description which are the subject of different forms of supply, be construed in whichever of the following ways the decision-making authority considers appropriate—

(a) as references to any of those forms of supply taken separately;

(b) as references to all those forms of supply taken together; or

(c) as references to any of those forms of supply taken in groups.

(7) For the purposes of subsection (6) the decision-making authority may treat goods or services as being the subject of different forms of supply whenever—

(a) the transactions concerned differ as to their nature, their parties, their terms or their surrounding circumstances; and

(b) the difference is one which, in the opinion of the decision-making authority, ought for the purposes of that subsection to be treated as a material difference.

(8) The criteria for deciding when goods or services can be treated, for the purposes of this section, as goods or services of a separate description shall be such as in any particular case the decision-making authority considers appropriate in the circumstances of that case.

(9) The question whether a relevant merger situation has been created shall be determined as at—

- '(a)   in relation to the giving of a European intervention notice, the time when the notice is given;
- (aa) in relation to the making of a report by the OFT under article 4 of the Enterprise Act 2002 (Protection of Legitimate Interests) Order 2003, the time of the making of the report;
- (ab) in the case of a reference which is treated as having been made under article 5 (2) of the Enterprise Act 2002 (Protection of Legitimate Interests) Order 2003 by virtue of article 7(4) of that Order, such time as the Commission may determine; and';
- (b)   in any other case, immediately before the time when the reference has been, or is to be, made.

24   Time-limits and prior notice

(1) For the purposes of section 23 two or more enterprises have ceased to be distinct enterprises at a time or in circumstances falling within this section if—

- (a) the two or more enterprises ceased to be distinct enterprises before the day on which the reference relating to them is to be made and did so not more than four months before that day; or
- (b) notice of material facts about the arrangements or transactions under or in consequence of which the enterprises have ceased to be distinct enterprises has not been given in accordance with subsection (2).

(2) Notice of material facts is given in accordance with this subsection if—

- (a) it is given to the OFT prior to the entering into of the arrangements or transactions concerned or the facts are made public prior to the entering into of those arrangements or transactions; or
- (b) it is given to the OFT, or the facts are made public, more than four months before the day on which the reference is to be made.

(3) In this section—

'made public' means so publicised as to be generally known or readily ascertainable; and 'notice' includes notice which is not in writing.

25   Extension of time-limits

(1) The OFT and the persons carrying on the enterprises which have or may have ceased to be distinct enterprises may agree to extend by no more than 20 days the four month period mentioned in section 24(1)(a) or (2)(b).

(2) The OFT may by notice to the persons carrying on the enterprises which have or may have ceased to be distinct enterprises extend the four month period mentioned in section 24(1)(a) or (2)(b) if it considers that any of those persons has failed to provide, within the period stated in a notice under section 31 and in the manner authorised or required, information requested of him in that notice.

(3) An extension under subsection (2) shall be for the period beginning with the end of the period within which the information is to be provided and which is stated in the notice under section 31 and ending with—

- (a) the provision of the information to the satisfaction of the OFT; or
- (b) if earlier, the cancellation by the OFT of the extension.

(4) The OFT may by notice to the persons carrying on the enterprises which have or may have ceased to be distinct enterprises extend the four month period mentioned in section 24(1)(a) or (2)(b) if it is seeking undertakings from any of those persons under section 73.

(5) An extension under subsection (4) shall be for the period beginning with the receipt of the notice under that subsection and ending with the earliest of the following events—

- (a) the giving of the undertakings concerned;
- (b) the expiry of the period of 10 days beginning with the first day after the receipt by the OFT of a notice from the person who has been given a notice under subsection (4) and

from whom the undertakings are being sought stating that he does not intend to give the undertakings; or

(c) the cancellation by the OFT of the extension.

(5A) The Secretary of State may by notice to the persons carrying on the enterprises which have or may be ceased to be distinct enterprises extend the four month period mentioned in section 24(1)(a) or (2) (b) if, by virtue of article 5(7) of the Enterprise Act 2002 (Protection of Legitimate Interests) Order 2003 or paragraph 3(5) of Schedule 2 to that Order, he decides to delay a decision as to whether to make a reference under article 5 of that Order.

(5B) An extension under subsection (5A) shall be for the period of the delay.

(6) The OFT may by notice to the persons carrying on the enterprises which have or may have ceased to be distinct enterprises extend the four month period mentioned in section 24(1)(a) or (2)(b) if the European Commission is considering a request made, in relation to the matter concerned, by the United Kingdom (whether alone or with others) under article 22(1) of the EC Merger Regulation or is proceeding with the matter in pursuance of such a request.

(7) An extension under subsection (6) shall be for the period beginning with the receipt of the notice under that subsection and ending with the receipt of a notice under subsection (8).

(8) The OFT shall, in connection with any notice given by it under subsection (6), by notice inform the persons carrying on the enterprises which have or may have ceased to be distinct enterprises of the completion by the European Commission of its consideration of the request of the United Kingdom and of any proceedings undertaken by it in pursuance of that request.

(9) Subject to subsections (10) and (11), where the four month period mentioned in section 24(1)(a) or (2)(b) is extended or further extended by virtue of this section in relation to a particular case, any reference to that period in section 24 or the preceding provisions of this section shall have effect in relation to that case as if it were a reference to a period equivalent to the aggregate of the period being extended and the period of the extension (whether or not those periods overlap in time).

(10) Subsection (11) applies where—

(a) the four month period mentioned in section 24(1)(a) or (2)(b) is further extended;

(b) the further extension and at least one previous extension is made under one or more of subsections (2), (4), (5A) and (6); and

(c) the same days or fractions of days are included in or comprise the further extension and are included in or comprise at least one such previous extension.

(11) In calculating the period of the further extension, any days or fractions of days of the kind mentioned in subsection (10)(c) shall be disregarded.

(12) No more than one extension is possible under subsection (1).

26   Enterprises ceasing to be distinct enterprises

(1) Any two enterprises cease to be distinct enterprises if they are brought under common ownership or common control (whether or not the business to which either of them formerly belonged continues to be carried on under the same or different ownership or control).

(2) Enterprises shall, in particular, be treated as being under common control if they are—

(a) enterprises of interconnected bodies corporate;

(b) enterprises carried on by two or more bodies corporate of which one and the same person or group of persons has control; or

(c) an enterprise carried on by a body corporate and an enterprise carried on by a person or group of persons having control of that body corporate.

(3) A person or group of persons able, directly or indirectly, to control or materially to influence the policy of a body corporate, or the policy of any person in carrying on an enterprise but without having a controlling interest in that body corporate or in that enterprise, may, for the purposes of subsections (1) and (2), be treated as having control of it.

(4) For the purposes of subsection (1), in so far as it relates to bringing two or more enterprises under common control, a person or group of persons may be treated as bringing an enterprise under his or their control if—

(a) being already able to control or materially to influence the policy of the person carrying on the enterprise, that person or group of persons acquires a controlling interest in the enterprise or, in the case of an enterprise carried on by a body corporate, acquires a controlling interest in that body corporate; or

(b) being already able materially to influence the policy of the person carrying on the enterprise, that person or group of persons becomes able to control that policy.

27 Time when enterprises cease to be distinct

(1) Subsection (2) applies in relation to any arrangements or transaction—

(a) not having immediate effect or having immediate effect only in part; but

(b) under or in consequence of which any two enterprises cease to be distinct enterprises.

(2) The time when the parties to any such arrangements or transaction become bound to such extent as will result, on effect being given to their obligations, in the enterprises ceasing to be distinct enterprises shall be taken to be the time at which the two enterprises cease to be distinct enterprises.

(3) In accordance with subsections (1) and (2) (but without prejudice to the generality of those subsections) for the purpose of determining the time at which any two enterprises cease to be distinct enterprises no account shall be taken of any option or other conditional right until the option is exercised or the condition is satisfied.

(4) Subsections (1) to (3) are subject to subsections (5) to (8) and section 28.

(5) The decision-making authority may, for the purposes of a reference, treat successive events to which this subsection applies as having occurred simultaneously on the date on which the latest of the events occurred.

(6) Subsection (5) applies to successive events—

(a) which consist of—

(i) one or more than one event which has occurred within the period of two years before the date of the reference; and

(ii) one or more than one event which will occur;

(b) which are events which have occurred or will occur under or in consequence of the same arrangements or transactions, or successive arrangements or transactions between the same parties or interests; and

(c) by virtue of each of which, under or in consequence of the arrangements or the transaction or transactions concerned, any enterprises cease as between themselves to be distinct enterprises.

(7) The decision-making authority may, for the purposes of subsections (5) and (6), treat such arrangements or transactions as the decision-making authority considers appropriate as arrangements or transactions between the same interests.

(8) In deciding whether it is appropriate to treat arrangements or transactions as arrangements or transactions between the same interests the decision-making authority shall, in particular, have regard to the persons substantially concerned in the arrangements or transactions concerned.

28 Turnover test

(1) For the purposes of section 23 the value of the turnover in the United Kingdom of the enterprise being taken over shall be determined by taking the total value of the turnover in the United Kingdom of the enterprises which cease to be distinct enterprises and deducting—

(a) the turnover in the United Kingdom of any enterprise which continues to be carried on under the same ownership and control; or

(b) if no enterprise continues to be carried on under the same ownership and control, the turnover in the United Kingdom which, of all the turnovers concerned, is the turnover of the highest value.

(2) The turnover in the United Kingdom of an enterprise shall be determined in accordance with such provisions as may be specified in an order made by the Secretary of State.

(3) An order under subsection (2) may, in particular, make provision as to—

    (a) the amounts which are, or which are not, to be treated as comprising an enterprise's turnover;

    (b) the date or dates by reference to which an enterprise's turnover is to be determined;

    (c) the connection with the United Kingdom by virtue of which an enterprise's turnover is turnover in the United Kingdom.

(4) An order under subsection (2) may, in particular, make provision enabling the decision-making authority to determine matters of a description specified in the order (including any of the matters mentioned in paragraphs (a) to (c) of subsection (3)).

(5) The OFT shall—

    (a) keep under review the sum for the time being mentioned in section 22(1)(b); and

    (b) from time to time advise the Secretary of State as to whether the sum is still appropriate.

(6) The Secretary of State may by order amend section 23(1) (b) so as to alter the sum for the time being mentioned there.

29 Obtaining control by stages

'(1) Where an enterprise will be brought under the control of a person or group of persons in the course of two or more transactions (in this section a "series of transactions") to which subsection (2) applies, those transactions may, if the decision-making authority considers it appropriate, be treated for the purposes of a reference as if they will occur simultaneously on the date on which the latest of them will occur.

(2) This subsection applies to—

    (a) any transaction which has occurred or which will occur and which—

        (i) enables that person or group of persons directly or indirectly to control or materially to influence the policy of any person carrying on the enterprise;

        (ii) enables that person or group of persons to do so to a greater degree; or

        (iii) is a step (whether direct or indirect) towards enabling that person or group of persons to do so; and

    (b) any transaction which has occurred or which will occur and by virtue of which that person or group of persons acquires a controlling interest in the enterprise or, where the enterprise is carried on by a body corporate, in that body corporate.

(3) Where a series of transactions includes a transaction falling within subsection (2)(b), any transaction occurring after the occurrence of that transaction is to be disregarded for the purposes of subsection (1).

(4) Where the period within which any relevant transactions have occurred exceeds two years before the date of the reference, the relevant transactions that may be treated as mentioned in subsection (1) are any of those transactions that have occurred within the period of two years.

(4A) In subsection (4) 'relevant transactions' means transactions which have occurred and which are transactions in the series of transactions.'

(5) Sections 25(2) to (4) and 122(1), (2) and (4) to (6) shall apply for the purposes of this section to determine—

    (a) whether an enterprise is brought under the control of a person or group of persons; and

    (b) whether a transaction is one to which subsection (2) applies;

as they apply for the purposes of section 26 to determine whether enterprises are brought under common control.

(6) In determining for the purposes of this section the time at which any transaction occurs, no account shall be taken of any option or other conditional right until the option is exercised or the condition is satisfied.

30 Relevant customer benefits

(1) For the purposes of this Part a benefit is a relevant customer benefit if—

    (a) it is a benefit to relevant customers in the form of—

(i)   lower prices, higher quality or greater choice of goods or services in any market in the United Kingdom (whether or not the market or markets in which the substantial lessening of competition concerned has, or may have, occurred or (as the case may be) may occur); or

(ii) greater innovation in relation to such goods or services; and

(b) the decision-making authority believes—

(i)   in the case of a reference or possible reference under section 22 or 45(2), as mentioned in subsection (2); and

(ii) in the case of a reference or possible reference under section 33 or 45(4), as mentioned in subsection (3).

(2) The belief, in the case of a reference or possible reference under section 22 or section 45(2), is that—

(a) the benefit has accrued as a result of the creation of the relevant merger situation concerned or may be expected to accrue within a reasonable period as a result of the creation of that situation; and

(b) the benefit was, or is, unlikely to accrue without the creation of that situation or a similar lessening of competition.

(3) The belief, in the case of a reference or possible reference under section 33 or 45(4), is that—

(a) the benefit may be expected to accrue within a reasonable period as a result of the creation of the relevant merger situation concerned; and

(b) the benefit is unlikely to accrue without the creation of that situation or a similar lessening of competition.

(4) In subsection (1) 'relevant customers' means—

(a) customers of any person carrying on an enterprise which, in the creation of the relevant merger situation concerned, has ceased to be, or (as the case may be) will cease to be, a distinct enterprise;

(b) customers of such customers; and

(c) any other customers in a chain of customers beginning with the customers mentioned in paragraph (a);

and in this subsection 'customers' includes future customers.

31   Information powers in relation to completed mergers

(1) The OFT may by notice to any of the persons carrying on the enterprises which have or may have ceased to be distinct enterprises request him to provide the OFT with such information as the OFT may require for the purpose of enabling the Secretary of State to decide whether to make a reference under article 5(2) of the Enterprise Act 2002 (Protection of Legitimate Interests) order 2003.

(2) The notice shall state—

(a) the information required;

(b) the period within which the information is to be provided; and

(c) the possible consequences of not providing the information within the stated period and in the authorised or required manner.

32   Supplementary provision for purposes of sections 25 and 31

(1) The Secretary of State may make regulations for the purposes of sections 25 and 31.

(2) The regulations may, in particular—

(a) provide for the manner in which any information requested by the OFT under section 31 is authorised or required to be provided, and the time at which such information is to be treated as provided (including the time at which it is to be treated as provided to the satisfaction of the OFT for the purposes of section 25(3));

(b) provide for the persons carrying on the enterprises which have or may have ceased to be distinct enterprises to be informed, in circumstances in which section 25(3) applies—

> > (i)   of the fact that the OFT is satisfied as to the provision of the information requested by it or (as the case may be) of the OFT's decision to cancel the extension; and
> > (ii) of the time at which the OFT is to be treated as so satisfied or (as the case may be) of the time at which the cancellation is to be treated as having effect;
> (c) provide for the persons carrying on the enterprises which have or may have ceased to be distinct enterprises to be informed, in circumstances in which section 25(5) applies—
> > (i)   of the OFT's decision to cancel the extension; and
> > (ii) of the time at which the cancellation is to be treated as having effect;
> (d) provide for the time at which any notice under section 25(4), (5)(b), (6) or (8) is to be treated as received;
> (e) provide that a person is, or is not, to be treated, in such circumstances as may be specified in the regulations, as acting on behalf of a person carrying on an enterprise which has or may have ceased to be a distinct enterprise.

(3) A notice under section 25(2)—
> (a) shall be given within 5 days of the end of the period within which the information is to be provided and which is stated in the notice under section 31; and
> (b) shall inform the person to whom it is addressed of—
> > (i)   the OFT's opinion as mentioned in section 25(2); and
> > (ii) the OFT's intention to extend the period for considering whether to make a reference.

(4) In determining for the purposes of section 25(1) or (5)(b) or subsection (3)(a) above any period which is expressed in the enactment concerned as a period of days or number of days no account shall be taken of—
> (a) Saturday, Sunday, Good Friday and Christmas Day; and
> (b) any day which is a bank holiday in England and Wales.

Duty to make references: anticipated mergers

33 Duty to make references in relation to anticipated mergers

(1) The OFT shall, subject to subsections (2) and (3), make a reference to the Commission if the OFT believes that it is or may be the case that—
> (a) arrangements are in progress or in contemplation which, if carried into effect, will result in the creation of a relevant merger situation; and
> (b) the creation of that situation may be expected to result in a substantial lessening of competition within any market or markets in the United Kingdom for goods or services.

(2) The OFT may decide not to make a reference under this section if it believes that—
> (a) the market concerned is not, or the markets concerned are not, of sufficient importance to justify the making of a reference to the Commission;
> (b) the arrangements concerned are not sufficiently far advanced, or are not sufficiently likely to proceed, to justify the making of a reference to the Commission; or
> (c) any relevant customer benefits in relation to the creation of the relevant merger situation concerned outweigh the substantial lessening of competition concerned and any adverse effects of the substantial lessening of competition concerned.

(3) No reference shall be made under this section if—
> (a) the making of the reference is prevented by section 74(1) or 96(3) or paragraph 4 of Schedule 7;
> (b) the OFT is considering whether to accept undertakings under section 73 instead of making such a reference;
> (c) the arrangements concerned are being, or have been, dealt with in connection with a reference made under section 22;
> (d) a notice under section 42(2) is in force in relation to the matter or the matter to which such a notice relates has been finally determined under Chapter 2 otherwise than in circumstances in which a notice is then given to the OFT under section 56(1);

(e) the matter falls to be dealt with, or has been dealt with, otherwise than under this section by virtue of any provision of Community law (including as a result of a request made by the United Kingdom, whether alone or with others, to the European Commission under article 22(1) of the EC Merger Regulation); or

(f) subject to subsection (3A), a reasoned submission requesting referral to the European Commission has been submitted to the European Commission under article 4(5) of the EC Merger Regulation.

(3A) Section 33(3)(f) shall cease to apply if the OFT is informed that a Member State competent to examine the concentration under its national competition law has, within the time permitted by Article 4(5) of the EC Merger Regulation, expressed its disagreement as regards the request to refer the case to the European Commission; and this subsection shall be construed in accordance with that Regulation.

(4) A reference under this section shall, in particular, specify—

(a) the enactment under which it is made; and

(b) the date on which it is made.

34 Supplementary provision in relation to anticipated mergers

(1) The Secretary of State may by order make such provision as he considers appropriate about the operation of sections 27 and 29 in relation to—

(a) references under this Part which relate to arrangements which are in progress or in contemplation; or

(b) notices under section 42(2), 59(2) or 67(2) which relate to such arrangements.

(2) An order under subsection (1) may, in particular—

(a) provide for sections 27(5) to (8) and 29 to apply with modifications in relation to such references or notices or in relation to particular descriptions of such references or notices;

(b) enable particular descriptions of events, arrangements or transactions which have already occurred—

(i) to be taken into account for the purposes of deciding whether to make such references or such references of a particular description or whether to give such notices or such notices of a particular description;

(ii) to be dealt with under such references or such references of a particular description or under such notices of a particular description.

Cases referred by European Commission under EC Merger Regulation

34A Duty of OFT where case referred by the European Commission

(1) Subsection (2) applies if the European Commission has by a decision referred the whole or part of a case to the OFT under Article 4(4) or 9 of the EC Merger Regulation, or is deemed to have taken such a decision, unless an intervention notice is in force in relation to that case.

(2) Before the end of the preliminary assessment period, the OFT shall—

(a) decide whether to make a reference to the Commission under section 22 or 33; and

(b) inform the persons carrying on the enterprises concerned by notice of that decision and of the reasons for it.

(3) The OFT may, for the purposes of subsection (2), decide not to make a reference on the basis that it is considering whether to seek or accept undertakings under section 73 instead of making a reference; but a decision taken on that basis does not prevent the OFT from making a reference under section 22 or 33 in the event of no such undertakings being offered or accepted.

(4) In this section—

'the preliminary assessment period' means, subject to subsection (5), the period of 45 working days beginning with the day after the day on which the decision of the European Commission to refer the case is taken (or is deemed to have been taken); and 'working day' means any day which is not—

(a) a Saturday;

(b) a Sunday; or

(c) a day which is a European Commission holiday (as published in the Official Journal of the European Communities before the beginning of the year in which it occurs).

(5) If the OFT has imposed a requirement under section 34B and it considers that the person on whom that requirement was imposed has failed to comply with it, the OFT may, by notice to the persons carrying on the enterprises concerned, extend the preliminary assessment period.

(6) The period of an extension under subsection (5) shall—

(a) begin with the end of the period within which the requirement under section 34B could be complied with; and

(b) end with the earlier of either compliance with the requirement to the satisfaction of the OFT or cancellation by the OFT of the extension.

(7) A notice under subsection (6) shall—

(a) be given within 5 working days of the end of the period mentioned in paragraph (a) of that subsection; and

(b) inform the person to whom it is addressed that the OFT is of the opinion mentioned in subsection (5) and that it intends to extend the preliminary assessment period.

34B   Power to request information in referred cases

(1) In a case mentioned in section 34A(1), the OFT may by notice to any of the persons carrying on the enterprises concerned request him to provide the OFT with such information as the OFT may require for the purpose of making a decision for the purposes of section 34A(2).

(2) The notice shall state—

(a) the information required;

(b) the period within which the information is to be provided;

(c) the manner (if any) in which the information is required to be provided; and

(d) the possible consequences—

(i) of not providing the information within the stated period; and

(ii) if a manner for its provision is stated in the notice, of not providing it in that manner.

Determination of references

35   Questions to be decided in relation to completed mergers

(1) Subject to subsections (6) and (7) and section 127(3), the Commission shall, on a reference under section 22, decide the following questions—

(a) whether a relevant merger situation has been created; and

(b) if so, whether the creation of that situation has resulted, or may be expected to result, in a substantial lessening of competition within any market or markets in the United Kingdom for goods or services.

(2) For the purposes of this Part there is an anti-competitive outcome if—

(a) a relevant merger situation has been created and the creation of that situation has resulted, or may be expected to result, in a substantial lessening of competition within any market or markets in the United Kingdom for goods or services; or

(b) arrangements are in progress or in contemplation which, if carried into effect, will result in the creation of a relevant merger situation and the creation of that situation may be expected to result in a substantial lessening of competition within any market or markets in the United Kingdom for goods or services.

(3) The Commission shall, if it has decided on a reference under section 22 that there is an anti-competitive outcome (within the meaning given by subsection (2)(a)), decide the following additional questions—

(a) whether action should be taken by it under section 41(2) for the purpose of remedying, mitigating or preventing the substantial lessening of competition concerned or any adverse effect which has resulted from, or may be expected to result from, the substantial lessening of competition;

    (b) whether it should recommend the taking of action by others for the purpose of remedy-
        ing, mitigating or preventing the substantial lessening of competition concerned or any
        adverse effect which has resulted from, or may be expected to result from, the substantial
        lessening of competition; and
    (c) in either case, if action should be taken, what action should be taken and what is to be
        remedied, mitigated or prevented.

(4) In deciding the questions mentioned in subsection (3) the Commission shall, in particular, have regard to the need to achieve as comprehensive a solution as is reasonable and practicable to the substantial lessening of competition and any adverse effects resulting from it.

(5) In deciding the questions mentioned in subsection (3) the Commission may, in particular, have regard to the effect of any action on any relevant customer benefits in relation to the creation of the relevant merger situation concerned.

(6) In relation to the question whether a relevant merger situation has been created, a reference under section 22 may be framed so as to require the Commission to exclude from consideration—
    (a) subsection (1) of section 23;
    (b) subsection (2) of that section; or
    (c) cone of those subsections if the Commission finds that the other is satisfied.

(7) In relation to the question whether any such result as is mentioned in section 23(2)(b) has arisen, a reference under section 22 may be framed so as to require the Commission to confine its investigation to the supply of goods or services in a part of the United Kingdom specified in the reference.

36 Questions to be decided in relation to anticipated mergers

(1) Subject to subsections (5) and (6) and section 127(3), the Commission shall, on a reference under section 33, decide the following questions—
    (a) whether arrangements are in progress or in contemplation which, if carried into effect,
        will result in the creation of a relevant merger situation; and
    (b) if so, whether the creation of that situation may be expected to result in a substantial
        lessening of competition within any market or markets in the United Kingdom for goods
        or services.

(2) The Commission shall, if it has decided on a reference under section 33 that there is an anti-competitive outcome (within the meaning given by section 35(2)(b)), decide the following additional questions—
    (a) whether action should be taken by it under section 41(2) for the purpose of remedy-
        ing, mitigating or preventing the substantial lessening of competition concerned or
        any adverse effect which may be expected to result from the substantial lessening of
        competition;
    (b) whether it should recommend the taking of action by others for the purpose of remedying,
        mitigating or preventing the substantial lessening of competition concerned or any adverse
        effect which may be expected to result from the substantial lessening of competition; and
    (c) in either case, if action should be taken, what action should be taken and what is to be
        remedied, mitigated or prevented.

(3) In deciding the questions mentioned in subsection (2) the Commission shall, in particular, have regard to the need to achieve as comprehensive a solution as is reasonable and practicable to the substantial lessening of competition and any adverse effects resulting from it.

(4) In deciding the questions mentioned in subsection (2) the Commission may, in particular, have regard to the effect of any action on any relevant customer benefits in relation to the creation of the relevant merger situation concerned.

(5) In relation to the question whether a relevant merger situation will be created, a reference under section 33 may be framed so as to require the Commission to exclude from consideration—
    (a) subsection (1) of section 23;
    (b) subsection (2) of that section; or
    (c) one of those subsections if the Commission finds that the other is satisfied.

(6) In relation to the question whether any such result as is mentioned in section 23(2)(b) will arise, a reference under section 33 may be framed so as to require the Commission to confine its investigation to the supply of goods or services in a part of the United Kingdom specified in the reference.

37 Cancellation and variation of references under section 22 or 33

(1) The Commission shall cancel a reference under section 33 if it considers that the proposal to make arrangements of the kind mentioned in the reference has been abandoned.

(2) The Commission may, if it considers that doing so is justified by the facts (including events occurring on or after the making of the reference concerned), treat a reference made under section 22 or 33 as if it had been made under section 33 or (as the case may be) 22; and, in such cases, references in this Part to references under those sections shall, so far as may be necessary, be construed accordingly.

(3) Where, by virtue of subsection (2), the Commission treats a reference made under section 22 or 33 as if it had been made under section 33 or (as the case may be) 22, sections 77 to 81 shall, in particular, apply as if the reference had been made under section 33 or (as the case may be) 22 instead of under section 22 or 33.

(4) Subsection (5) applies in relation to any undertaking accepted under section 80, or any order made under section 81, which is in force immediately before the Commission, by virtue of subsection (2), treats a reference made under section 22 or 33 as if it had been made under section 33 or (as the case may be) 22.

(5) The undertaking or order shall, so far as applicable, continue in force as if—

    (a) in the case of an undertaking or order which relates to a reference made under section 22, accepted or made in relation to a reference made under section 33; and

    (b) in the case of an undertaking or order which relates to a reference made under section 33, accepted or made in relation to a reference made under section 22;

and the undertaking or order concerned may be varied, superseded, released or revoked accordingly.

(6) The OFT may at any time vary a reference under section 22 or 33.

(7) The OFT shall consult the Commission before varying any such reference.

(8) Subsection (7) shall not apply if the Commission has requested the variation concerned.

(9) No variation by the OFT under this section shall be capable of altering the period permitted by section 39 within which the report of the Commission under section 38 is to be prepared and published.

38 Investigations and reports on references under section 22 or 33

(1) The Commission shall prepare and publish a report on a reference under section 22 or 33 within the period permitted by section 39.

(2) [repealed]

(3) The Commission shall carry out such investigations as it considers appropriate for the purposes of preparing a report under this section.

(4) The Commission shall, at the same time as a report prepared under this section is published, give it to the OFT.

39 Time-limits for investigations and reports

(1) The Commission shall prepare and publish its report under section 38 within the period of 24 weeks beginning with the date of the reference concerned.

(2) Where article 9(6) of the European Merger Regulations applies in relation to the reference under section 22 or 33, the Commission shall prepare and publish its report under section 38—

    (a) within the period of 24 weeks beginning with the date of the reference; or

    (b) if it is a shorter period, within such period as is necessary to ensure compliance with that article.

(3) The Commission may extend, by no more than 8 weeks, the period within which a report under section 38 is to be prepared and published if it considers that there are special reasons why the report cannot be prepared and published within that period.

(4) The Commission may extend the period within which a report under section 38 is to be prepared and published if it considers that a relevant person has failed (whether with or without a reasonable excuse) to comply with any requirement of a notice under section 109.

(5) In subsection (4) 'relevant person' means—

(a) any person carrying on any of the enterprises concerned;

(b) any person who (whether alone or as a member of a group) owns or has control of any such person; or

(c) any officer, employee or agent of any person mentioned in paragraph (a) or (b).

(6) For the purposes of subsection (5) a person or group of persons able, directly or indirectly, to control or materially to influence the policy of a body of persons corporate or unincorporate, but without having a controlling interest in that body of persons, may be treated as having control of it.

(7) An extension under subsection (3) or (4) shall come into force when published under section 107.

(8) An extension under subsection (4) shall continue in force until—

(a) the person concerned provides the information or documents to the satisfaction of the Commission or (as the case may be) appears as a witness in accordance with the requirements of the Commission; or

(b) the Commission publishes its decision to cancel the extension.

(9) References in this Part to the date of a reference shall be construed as references to the date specified in the reference as the date on which it is made.

(10) This section is subject to section 40.

40   Section 39: supplementary

(1)–(3) [repealed]

(3) A period extended under subsection (3) of section 39 may also be extended under subsection (4) of that section and a period extended under subsection (4) of that section may also be extended under subsection (3) of that section.

(4) No more than one extension is possible under section 39(3).

(5) Where a period within which a report under section 38 is to be prepared and published is extended or further extended under section 39(3) or (4), the period as extended or (as the case may be) further extended shall, subject to subsections (6) and (7), be calculated by taking the period being extended and adding to it the period of the extension (whether or not those periods overlap in time).

(6) Subsection (7) applies where—

(a) the period within which the report under section 38 is to be prepared and published is further extended;

(b) the further extension and at least one previous extension is made under section 39(4); and

(c) the same days or fractions of days are included in or comprise the further extension and are included in or comprise at least one such previous extension.

(7) In calculating the period of the further extension, any days or fractions of days of the kind mentioned in subsection (6)(c) shall be disregarded.

(8) The Secretary of State may by order amend section 39 so as to alter any one or more of the following periods—

(a) the period of 24 weeks mentioned in subsection (1) of that section or any period for the time being mentioned in that subsection in substitution for that period;

(c) the period of 8 weeks mentioned in subsection (3) of that section or any period for the time being mentioned in that subsection in substitution for that period.

(9) No alteration shall be made by virtue of subsection (8) which results in the period for the time being mentioned in subsection (1) of section 39 exceeding 24 weeks or the period for the time being mentioned in subsection (3) of that section exceeding 8 weeks.

(10) An order under subsection (8) shall not affect any period of time within which the Commission is under a duty to prepare and publish its report under section 38 in relation to a reference

under section 22 or 33 if the Commission is already under that duty in relation to that reference when the order is made.

(11) Before making an order under subsection (8) the Secretary of State shall consult the Commission and such other persons as he considers appropriate.

(12) The Secretary of State may make regulations for the purposes of section 39(8).

(13) The regulations may, in particular—

(a) provide for the time at which information or documents are to be treated as provided (including the time at which they are to be treated as provided to the satisfaction of the Commission for the purposes of section 39(8));

(b) provide for the time at which a person is to be treated as appearing as a witness (including the time at which he is to be treated as appearing as a witness in accordance with the requirements of the Commission for the purposes of section 39(8));

(c) provide for the persons carrying on the enterprises which have or may have ceased to be, or may cease to be, distinct enterprises to be informed, in circumstances in which section 39(8) applies, of the fact that—

(i) the Commission is satisfied as to the provision of the information or documents required by it; or

(ii) the person concerned has appeared as a witness in accordance with the requirements of the Commission;

(d) provide for the persons carrying on the enterprises which have or may have ceased to be, or may cease to be, distinct enterprises to be informed, in circumstances in which section 39(8) applies, of the time at which the Commission is to be treated as satisfied as mentioned in paragraph (c)(i) above or the person concerned is to be treated as having appeared as mentioned in paragraph (c)(ii) above.

41   Duty to remedy effects of completed or anticipated mergers

(1) Subsection (2) applies where a report of the Commission has been prepared and published under section 37 within the period permitted by section 38 and contains the decision that there is an anti-competitive outcome.

(2) The Commission shall take such action under section 82 or 84 as it considers to be reasonable and practicable—

(a) to remedy, mitigate or prevent the substantial lessening of competition concerned; and

(b) to remedy, mitigate or prevent any adverse effects which have resulted from, or may be expected to result from, the substantial lessening of competition.

(3) The decision of the Commission under subsection (2) shall be consistent with its decisions as included in its report by virtue of section 35(3) or (as the case may be) 36(2) unless there has been a material changes of circumstances since the preparation of the report or the commission otherwise has a special reason for deciding differently.

(4) In making a decision under subsection (2), the Commission shall, in particular, have regard to the need to achieve as comprehensive a solution as is reasonable and practicable to the substantial lessening of competition and any adverse effects resulting from it. regard to the effect of any action on any relevant customer benefits in relation to the creation of the relevant merger situation concerned.

Chapter 2 Public interest cases

Power to make references

42   Intervention by Secretary of State in certain public interest cases

(1) Subsection (2) applies where—

(a) the Secretary of State has reasonable grounds for suspecting that it is or may be the case that a relevant merger situation has been created or that arrangements are in progress or in contemplation which, if carried into effect, will result in the creation of a relevant merger situation;

(b) no reference under section 22 or 33 has been made in relation to the relevant merger situation concerned;

(c) no decision has been made not to make such a reference (other than a decision made by virtue of subsection (2)(b) of section 33 or a decision to accept undertakings under section 73 instead of making such a reference); and

(d) no reference is prevented from being made under section 22 or 33 by virtue of

(i)   section 22(3) (a) or (e) or (as the case may be) 33(3)(a) or (e); or

(ii)   Community law or anything done under or in accordance with it.

(2) The Secretary of State may give a notice to the OFT (in this Part 'an intervention notice') if he believes that it is or may be the case that one or more than one public interest consideration is relevant to a consideration of the relevant merger situation concerned.

(3) For the purposes of this Part a public interest consideration is a consideration which, at the time of the giving of the intervention notice concerned, is specified in section 58 or is not so specified but, in the opinion of the Secretary of State, ought to be so specified.

(4) No more than one intervention notice shall be given under subsection (2) in relation to the same relevant merger situation.

(5) For the purposes of deciding whether a relevant merger situation has been created or whether arrangements are in progress or in contemplation which, if carried into effect, will result in the creation of a relevant merger situation, sections 23 to 32 (read together with section 34) shall apply for the purposes of this Chapter as they do for the purposes of Chapter 1 but subject to subsection (6).

(6) In their application by virtue of subsection (5) sections 23 to 32 shall have effect as if—

(a) for paragraph (a) of section 23(9) there were substituted—

'(a)   in relation to the giving of an intervention notice, the time when the notice is given;

(aa) in relation to the making of a report by the OFT under section 44, the time of the making of the report;

(ab) in the case of a reference which is treated as having been made under section 45(2) or (3) by virtue of section 49(1), such time as the Commission may determine; and';

(b) the references to the OFT in sections 25(1) to (3), (6) and (8) and 31 included references to the Secretary of State;

(c) the references to the OFT in section 25(4) and (5) were references to the Secretary of State;

(d) the reference in section 25(4) to section 73 were a reference to paragraph 3 of Schedule 7;

(e) after section, 25(5) there were inserted—

'(5A) The Secretary of State may by notice to the persons carrying on the enterprises which have or may have ceased to be distinct enterprises extend the four month period mentioned in section 24(1)(a) or (2)(b) if, by virtue of section 46(5) or paragraph 3(6) of Schedule 7, he decides to delay a decision as to whether to make a reference under section 45.

(5B) An extension under subsection (5A) shall be for the period of the delay.';

(f) in section 25(10)(b) after the word '(4)' there were inserted ', (5A)';

(g) the reference in section 25(12) to one extension were a reference to one extension by the OFT and one extension by the Secretary of State; and

(h) the references to the OFT in section 31(2)(a) to (c) and (3) were construed in accordance with the above modifications;

(i) the existing time-limits in relation to possible references under section 22 or 33 (except for extensions under section 25(4)) remained applicable on and after the giving of an intervention notice as if any extensions were made under section 25 as applied by subsection (5) above but subject to further alteration by the OFT or the Secretary of State under section 25 as so applied;

(j) in subsection (1) of section 31 for the words 'section 22' there were substituted 'section 45(2) or (3)' and, in the application of that subsection to the OFT, for the word 'deciding' there were substituted 'enabling the Secretary of State to decide';

(k) in the case of the giving of intervention notices, the references in sections 23 to 32 to the making of a reference or a reference were, so far as necessary, references to the giving of an intervention notice or an intervention notice; and

(l) the references to the OFT in section 32(2)(a) to (c) and (3) were construed in accordance with the above modifications.

(7) Where the Secretary of State has given an intervention notice mentioning a public interest consideration which, at that time, is not finalised, he shall, as soon as practicable, take such action as is within his power to ensure that it is finalised.

(8) For the purposes of this Part a public interest consideration is finalised if—

    (a) it is specified in section 58 otherwise than by virtue of an order under subsection (3) of that section; or

    (b) it is specified in that section by virtue of an order under subsection (3) of that section and the order providing for it to be so specified has been laid before, and approved by, Parliament in accordance with subsection (7) of section 124 and within the period mentioned in that subsection.

43 Intervention notices under section 42

(1) An intervention notice shall state—

    (a) the relevant merger situation concerned;

    (b) the public interest consideration or considerations which are, or may be, relevant to a consideration of the relevant merger situation concerned; and

    (c) where any public interest consideration concerned is not finalised, the proposed timetable for finalising it.

(2) Where the Secretary of State believes that it is or may be the case that two or more public interest considerations are relevant to a consideration of the relevant merger situation concerned, he may decide not to mention in the intervention notice such of those considerations as he considers appropriate.

(3) An intervention notice shall come into force when it is given and shall cease to be in force when the matter to which it relates is finally determined under this Chapter.

(4) For the purposes of this Part, a matter to which an intervention notice relates is finally determined under this Chapter if—

    (a) the time within which the OFT or (if relevant) OFCOM is to report to the Secretary of State under section 44 or (as the case may be) 44A has expired and no such report has been made;

    (b) the Secretary of State decides to accept an undertaking under paragraph 3 of Schedule 7 instead of making a reference under section 45;

    (c) the Secretary of State otherwise decides not to make a reference under that section;

    (d) the Commission cancels such a reference under section 48(1) or 53(1);

    (e) the time within which the Commission is to prepare a report under section 50 and give it to the Secretary of State has expired and no such report has been prepared and given to the Secretary of State;

    (f) the time within which the Secretary of State is to make and publish a decision under section 54(2) has expired and no such decision has been made and published;

    (g) the Secretary of State decides under section 54(2) to make no finding at all in the matter;

    (h) the Secretary of State otherwise decides under section 54(2) not to make an adverse public interest finding;

    (i) the Secretary of State decides under section 54(2) to make an adverse public interest finding but decides neither to accept an undertaking under paragraph 9 of Schedule 7 nor to make an order under paragraph 11 of that Schedule; or

    (j) the Secretary of State decides under section 54(2) to make an adverse public interest finding and accepts an undertaking under paragraph 9 of Schedule 7 or makes an order under paragraph 11 of that Schedule.

(5) For the purposes of this Part the time when a matter to which an intervention notice relates is finally determined under this Chapter is—

(a) in a case falling within subsection (4)(a), (e) or (f), the expiry of the time concerned;

(b) in a case falling within subsection (4)(b), the acceptance of the undertaking concerned;

(c) in a case falling within subsection (4)(c), (d), (g) or (h), the making of the decision concerned;

(d) in a case falling within subsection (4)(i), the making of the decision neither to accept an undertaking under paragraph 9 of Schedule 7 nor to make an order under paragraph 11 of that Schedule; and

(e) in a case falling within subsection (4)(j), the acceptance of the undertaking concerned or (as the case may be) the making of the order concerned.

(6) In this Part 'OFCOM' means the Office of Communications.

44   Investigation and report by OFT

(1) Subsection (2) applies where the Secretary of State has given an intervention notice in relation to a relevant merger situation.

(2) The OFT shall, within such period as the Secretary of State may require, give a report to the Secretary of State in relation to the case.

(3) The report shall contain—

(a) advice from the OFT on the considerations relevant to the making of a reference under section 22 or 33 which are also relevant to the Secretary of State's decision as to whether to make a reference under section 45; and

(b) a summary of any representations about the case which have been received by the OFT and which relate to any public interest consideration mentioned in the intervention notice concerned (other than a media public interest consideration) and which is or may be relevant to the Secretary of State's decision as to whether to make a reference under section 45.

(4) The report shall, in particular, include decisions as to whether the OFT believes that it is, or may be, the case that—

(a) a relevant merger situation has been created or arrangements are in progress or in contemplation which, if carried into effect, will result in the creation of a relevant merger situation;

(b) the creation of that situation has resulted, or may be expected to result, in a substantial lessening of competition within any market or markets in the United Kingdom for goods or services;

(c) the market or markets concerned would not be of sufficient importance to justify the making of a reference to the Commission under section 22 or 33;

(d) in the case of arrangements which are in progress or in contemplation, the arrangements are not sufficiently far advanced, or not sufficiently likely to proceed, to justify the making of such a reference;

(e) any relevant customer benefits in relation to the creation of the relevant merger situation concerned outweigh the substantial lessening of competition and any adverse effects of the substantial lessening of competition; or

(f) it would be appropriate to deal with the matter (disregarding any public interest considerations mentioned in the intervention notice concerned) by way of undertakings under paragraph 3 of Schedule 7.

(5) If the OFT believes that it is or may be the case that it would be appropriate to deal with the matter (disregarding any public interest considerations mentioned in the intervention notice concerned) by way of undertakings under paragraph 3 of Schedule 7, the report shall contain descriptions of the undertakings which the OFT believes are, or may be, appropriate.

(5A) The report may, in particular, contain a summary of any representations about the case which have been received by the OFT and which relate to any media public interest consideration mentioned in the intervention notice concerned and which is or may be relevant to the Secretary of State's decision as to whether to make a reference under section 45.

(6) The report may, in particular, include advice and recommendations on any public interest consideration mentioned in the intervention notice concerned and which is or may be relevant to the Secretary of State's decision as to whether to make a reference under section 45.

(7) The OFT shall carry out such investigations as it considers appropriate for the purposes of producing a report under this section.

(8) In this Part 'media public interest consideration' means any consideration which, at the time of the giving of the intervention notice concerned—

    (a) is specified in section 58(2A) to (2C); or

    (b) in the opinion of the Secretary of State, is concerned with broadcasting or newspapers and ought to be specified in section 58.

(9) In this Part 'broadcasting' means the provision of services the provision of which—

    (a) is required to be licensed under Part 1 or 3 of the Broadcasting Act 1990 or Part 1 or 2 of the Broadcasting Act 1996; or

    (b) would be required to be so licensed if provided by a person subject to licensing under the Part in question.

(10) In this Part 'newspaper' means a daily, Sunday or local (other than daily or Sunday) newspaper circulating wholly or mainly in the United Kingdom or in a part of the United Kingdom.

(11) The Secretary of State may by order amend subsections (9) and (10).

44A Additional investigation and report by OFCOM: media mergers

(1) Subsection (2) applies where—

    (a) the Secretary of State has given an intervention notice in relation to a relevant merger situation; and

    (b) the intervention notice mentions any media public interest consideration.

(2) OFCOM shall, within such period as the Secretary of State may require, give a report to the Secretary of State on the effect of the consideration or considerations concerned on the case.

(3) The report shall contain—

    (a) advice and recommendations on any media public interest consideration mentioned in the intervention notice concerned and which is or may be relevant to the Secretary of State's decision as to whether to make a reference under section 45; and

    (b) a summary of any representations about the case which have been received by OFCOM and which relate to any such consideration.

(4) OFCOM shall carry out such investigations as they consider appropriate for the purposes of producing a report under this section.

45 Power of Secretary of State to refer matter to Commission

(1) Subsections (2) to (5) apply where the Secretary of State—

    (a) has given an intervention notice in relation to a relevant merger situation; and

    (b) has received a report of the OFT under section 44, and any report of OFCOM which is required by virtue of section 44A, in relation to the matter.

(2) The Secretary of State may make a reference to the Commission if he believes that it is or may be the case that—

    (a) a relevant merger situation has been created;

    (b) the creation of that situation has resulted, or may be expected to result, in a substantial lessening of competition within any market or markets in the United Kingdom for goods or services;

    (c) one or more than one public interest consideration mentioned in the intervention notice is relevant to a consideration of the relevant merger situation concerned; and

    (d) taking account only of the substantial lessening of competition and the relevant public interest consideration or considerations concerned, the creation of that situation operates or may be expected to operate against the public interest.

(3) The Secretary of State may make a reference to the Commission if he believes that it is or may be the case that—

    (a) a relevant merger situation has been created;

    (b) the creation of that situation has not resulted, and may be expected not to result, in a substantial lessening of competition within any market or markets in the United Kingdom for goods or services;

    (c) one or more than one public interest consideration mentioned in the intervention notice is relevant to a consideration of the relevant merger situation concerned; and

    (d) taking account only of the relevant public interest consideration or considerations concerned, the creation of that situation operates or may be expected to operate against the public interest.

  (4) The Secretary of State may make a reference to the Commission if he believes that it is or may be the case that—

    (a) arrangements are in progress or in contemplation which, if carried into effect, will result in the creation of a relevant merger situation;

    (b) the creation of that situation may be expected to result in a substantial lessening of competition within any market or markets in the United Kingdom for goods or services;

    (c) one or more than one public interest consideration mentioned in the intervention notice is relevant to a consideration of the relevant merger situation concerned; and

    (d) taking account only of the substantial lessening of competition and the relevant public interest consideration or considerations concerned, the creation of the relevant merger situation may be expected to operate against the public interest.

  (5) The Secretary of State may make a reference to the Commission if he believes that it is or may be the case that—

    (a) arrangements are in progress or in contemplation which, if carried into effect, will result in the creation of a relevant merger situation;

    (b) the creation of that situation may be expected not to result in a substantial lessening of competition within any market or markets in the United Kingdom for goods or services;

    (c) one or more than one public interest consideration mentioned in the intervention notice is relevant to a consideration of the relevant merger situation concerned; and

    (d) taking account only of the relevant public interest consideration or considerations concerned, the creation of the relevant merger situation may be expected to operate against the public interest.

  (6) For the purposes of this Chapter any anti-competitive outcome shall be treated as being adverse to the public interest unless it is justified by one or more than one public interest consideration which is relevant.

  (7) This section is subject to section 46.

46 References under section 45: supplementary

  (1) No reference shall be made under section 45 if—

    (a) the making of the reference is prevented by section 74(1) or 96(3) or paragraph 4 of Schedule 7;

    (b) the European Commission is considering a request made, in relation to the matter concerned, by the United Kingdom (whether alone or with others) under article 22(1) of the EC Merger Regulation, is proceeding with the matter in pursuance of such a request or has dealt with the matter in pursuance of such a request; or

    (c) subject to subsection (1A), a reasoned submission requesting referral to the European Commission has been submitted to the European Commission under article 4(5) of the EC Merger Regulation.

  (1A) Subsection (1)(c) shall cease to apply if the Secretary of State is informed that a Member State competent to examine the concentration under its national competition law has, within the time permitted by Article 4(5) of the EC Merger Regulation, expressed its disagreement as regards the request to refer the case to the European Commission; and this subsection shall be construed in accordance with that Regulation.

(2) The Secretary of State, in deciding whether to make a reference under section 45, shall accept the decisions of the OFT included in its report by virtue of subsection (4) of section 44 and any descriptions of undertakings as mentioned in subsection (5) of that section.

(3) Where the decision to make a reference under section 45 is made at any time on or after the end of the period of 24 weeks beginning with the giving of the intervention notice concerned, the Secretary of State shall, in deciding whether to make such a reference, disregard any public interest consideration which is mentioned in the intervention notice but which has not been finalised before the end of that period.

(4) Subject to subsection (5), where the decision to make a reference under section 45(2) or (4) is made at any time before the end of the period of 24 weeks beginning with the giving of the intervention notice concerned, the Secretary of State shall, in deciding whether to make such a reference, disregard any public interest consideration which is mentioned in the intervention notice but which has not been finalised if its effect would be to prevent, or to help to prevent, an anticompetitive outcome from being adverse to the public interest.

(5) The Secretary of State may, if he believes that there is a realistic prospect of the public interest consideration mentioned in subsection (4) being finalised within the period of 24 weeks beginning with the giving of the intervention notice concerned, delay deciding whether to make the reference concerned until the public interest consideration is finalised or, if earlier, the period expires.

(6) A reference under section 45 shall, in particular, specify—

    (a) the subsection of that section under which it is made;

    (b) the date on which it is made; and

    (c) the public interest consideration or considerations mentioned in the intervention notice concerned which the Secretary of State is not under a duty to disregard by virtue of subsection (3) above and which he believes are or may be relevant to a consideration of the relevant merger situation concerned.

Cases referred by European Commission under the EC Merger Regulation

46A   Cases referred by the European Commission where intervention notice is in force

(1) Subsection (2) applies if the European Commission has by a decision referred the whole or part of a case to the OFT under Article 4(4) or 9 of the EC Merger Regulation, or is deemed to have taken such a decision, and an intervention notice is in force in relation to that case.

(2) Before the end of the preliminary assessment period, the Secretary of State shall—

    (a) decide whether to make a reference to the Commission under section 45; and

    (b) inform the persons carrying on the enterprises concerned by notice of that decision and of the reasons for it.

(3) The Secretary of State may, for the purposes of subsection (2), decide not to make a reference on the basis that he is considering whether to seek or accept undertakings under paragraph 3 of Schedule 7 instead of making a reference; but a decision taken on that basis does not prevent the Secretary of State from making a reference under section 45 in the event of no such undertakings being offered or accepted.

(4) In this section—

'the preliminary assessment period' means, subject to section 46B, the period of 45 working days beginning with the day after the day on which the decision of the European Commission to refer the case is taken (or is deemed to have been taken); and

'working day' means any day which is not—

    (a) a Saturday;

    (b) a Sunday; or

    (c) a day which is a European Commission holiday (as published in the Official Journal of the European Communities before the beginning of the year in which it occurs).

46B Extension of preliminary assessment period

(1) If the OFT has imposed a requirement under section 46C and it considers that the person on whom that requirement was imposed has failed to comply with it, the OFT may, by notice to the persons carrying on the enterprises concerned, extend the preliminary assessment period.

(2) If the Secretary of State has imposed a requirement under section 46C and he considers that the person on whom that requirement was imposed has failed to comply with it, he may, by notice to the persons carrying on the enterprises concerned, extend the preliminary assessment period.

(3) The period of an extension under this section shall—

  (a) begin with the end of the period within which the requirement under section 46C could be complied with; and

  (b) end with—

    (i) in the case of a notice under subsection (1), the earlier of either compliance with the requirement to the satisfaction of the OFT or cancellation by the OFT of the extension;

    (ii) in the case of a notice under subsection (2), the earlier of either compliance with the requirement to the satisfaction of the Secretary of State or cancellation by him of the extension.

(4) A notice under this section shall—

  (a) be given within 5 working days of the end of the period mentioned in subsection (3)(a); and

  (b) inform the person to whom it is addressed—

    (i) in the case of a notice under subsection (1), that the OFT is of the opinion mentioned in that subsection and that it intends to extend the preliminary assessment period;

    (ii) in the case of a notice under subsection (2), that the Secretary of State is of the opinion mentioned in that subsection and that he intends to extend the preliminary assessment period.

46C Power to request information in referred cases

(1) In a case mentioned in section 46A(1), the OFT may by notice to any of the persons carrying on the enterprises concerned request him to provide the OFT with such information as the OFT may require for the purpose of enabling the Secretary of State to make a decision for the purposes of section 46A(2).

(2) In such a case, the Secretary of State may by notice to any of the persons carrying on the enterprises concerned request him to provide the Secretary of State with such information as he may require for the purpose of enabling him to make a decision for the purposes of section 46A(2).

(3) A notice under subsection (1) or (2) shall state—

  (a) the information required;

  (b) the period within which the information is to be provided; and

  (c) the manner (if any) in which the information is required to be provided; and

  (d) the possible consequences—

    (i) of not providing the information within the stated period; and

    (ii) if a manner for its provision is stated in the notice, of not providing it in that manner.

Reports on references

47 Questions to be decided on references under section 45

(1) The Commission shall, on a reference under section 45(2) or (3), decide whether a relevant merger situation has been created.

(2) If the Commission decides that such a situation has been created, it shall, on a reference under section 45(2), decide the following additional questions—

  (a) whether the creation of that situation has resulted, or may be expected to result, in a substantial lessening of competition within any market or markets in the United Kingdom for goods or services; and

    (b) whether, taking account only of any substantial lessening of competition and the admissible public interest consideration or considerations concerned, the creation of that situation may be expected to operate against the public interest.

(3) If the Commission decides that a relevant merger situation has been created, it shall, on a reference under section 45(3), decide whether, taking account only of the admissible public interest consideration or considerations concerned, the creation of that situation operates or may be expected to operate against the public interest.

(4) The Commission shall, on a reference under section 45(4) or (5), decide whether arrangements are in progress or in contemplation which, if carried into effect, will result in the creation of a relevant merger situation.

(5) If the Commission decides that such arrangements are in progress or in contemplation, it shall, on a reference under section 45(4), decide the following additional questions—

    (a) whether the creation of that situation may be expected to result in a substantial lessening of competition within any market or markets in the United Kingdom for goods or services; and

    (b) whether, taking account only of any substantial lessening of competition and the admissible public interest consideration or considerations concerned, the creation of that situation operates or may expected to operate against the public interest.

(6) If the Commission decides that arrangements are in progress or in contemplation which, if carried into effect, will result in the creation of a relevant merger situation, it shall, on a reference under section 45(5), decide whether, taking account only of the admissible public interest consideration or considerations concerned, the creation of that situation may be expected to operate against the public interest.

(7) The Commission shall, if it has decided on a reference under section 45 that the creation of a relevant merger situation operates or may be expected to operate against the public interest, decide the following additional questions—

    (a) whether action should be taken by the Secretary of State under section 55 for the purpose of remedying, mitigating or preventing any of the effects adverse to the public interest which have resulted from, or may be expected to result from, the creation of the relevant merger situation;

    (b) whether the Commission should recommend the taking of other action by the Secretary of State or action by persons other than itself and the Secretary of State for the purpose of remedying, mitigating or preventing any of the effects adverse to the public interest which have resulted from, or may be expected to result from, the creation of the relevant merger situation; and

    (c) in either case, if action should be taken, what action should be taken and what is to be remedied, mitigated or prevented.

(8) Where the Commission has decided by virtue of subsection (2)(a) or (5)(a) that there is or will be a substantial lessening of competition within any market or markets in the United Kingdom for goods or services, it shall also decide separately the following questions (on the assumption that it is proceeding as mentioned in section 56(6))—

    (a) whether action should be taken by it under section 41 for the purpose of remedying, mitigating or preventing the substantial lessening of competition concerned or any adverse effect which has resulted from, or may be expected to result from, the substantial lessening of competition;

    (b) whether the Commission should recommend the taking of action by other persons for the purpose of remedying, mitigating or preventing the substantial lessening of competition concerned or any adverse effect which has resulted from, or may be expected to result from, the substantial lessening of competition; and

    (c) in either case, if action should be taken, what action should be taken and what is to be remedied, mitigated or prevented.

(9) In deciding the questions mentioned in subsections (7) and (8) the Commission shall, in particular, have regard to the need to achieve as comprehensive a solution as is reasonable and practicable to—

    (a) the adverse effects to the public interest; or

    (b) (as the case may be) the substantial lessening of competition and any adverse effects resulting from it.

    (10) In deciding the questions mentioned in subsections (7) and (8) in a case where it has decided by virtue of subsection (2)(a) or (5)(a) that there is or will be a substantial lessening of competition, the Commission may, in particular, have regard to the effect of any action on any relevant customer benefits in relation to the creation of the relevant merger situation concerned.

    (11) In this section 'admissible public interest consideration' means any public interest consideration which is specified in the reference under section 45 and which the Commission is not under a duty to disregard.

48 Cases where references or certain questions need not be decided

    (1) The Commission shall cancel a reference under section 45(4) or (5) if it considers that the proposal to make arrangements of the kind mentioned in that reference has been abandoned.

    (2) In relation to the question whether a relevant merger situation has been created or the question whether a relevant merger situation will be created, a reference under section 45 may be framed so as to require the Commission to exclude from consideration—

    (a) subsection (1) of section 23;

    (b) subsection (2) of that section; or

    (c) one of those subsections if the Commission finds that the other is satisfied.

    (3) In relation to the question whether any such result as is mentioned in section 23(2)(b) has arisen or the question whether any such result will arise, a reference under section 45 may be framed so as to require the Commission to confine its investigation to the supply of goods or services in a part of the United Kingdom specified in the reference.

49 Variation of references under section 45

    (1) The Commission may, if it considers that doing so is justified by the facts (including events occurring on or after the making of the reference concerned), treat—

    (a) a reference made under subsection (2) or (3) of section 45 as if it had been made under subsection (4) or (as the case may be) (5) of that section; or

    (b) a reference made under subsection (4) or (5) of section 45 as if it had been made under subsection (2) or (as the case may be) (3) of that section;

and, in such cases, references in this Part to references under those enactments shall, so far as may be necessary, be construed accordingly.

    (2) Where, by virtue of subsection (1), the Commission treats a reference made under subsection (2) or (3) of section 45 as if it had been made under subsection (4) or (as the case may be) (5) of that section, paragraphs 1, 2, 7 and 8 of Schedule 7 shall, in particular, apply as if the reference had been made under subsection (4) or (as the case may be) (5) of that section instead of under subsection (2) or (3) of that section.

    (3) Where, by virtue of subsection (1), the Commission treats a reference made under subsection (4) or (5) of section 45 as if it had been made under subsection (2) or (as the case may be) (3) of that section, paragraphs 1, 2, 7 and 8 of Schedule 7 shall, in particular, apply as if the reference had been made under subsection (2) or (as the case may be) (3) of that section instead of under subsection (4) or (5) of that section.

    (4) Subsection (5) applies in relation to any undertaking accepted under paragraph 1 of Schedule 7, or any order made under paragraph 2 of that Schedule, which is in force immediately before the Commission, by virtue of subsection (1), treats a reference as mentioned in subsection (1).

    (5) The undertaking or order shall, so far as applicable, continue in force as if—

    (a) in the case of an undertaking or order which relates to a reference under subsection (2) or (3) of section 45, accepted or made in relation to a reference made under subsection (4) or (as the case may be) (5) of that section; and

    (b) in the case of an undertaking or order which relates to a reference made under subsection (4) or (5) of that section, accepted or made in relation to a reference made under subsection (2) or (as the case may be) (3) of that section;

and the undertaking or order concerned may be varied, superseded, released or revoked accordingly.

(6) The Secretary of State may at any time vary a reference under section 45.

(7) The Secretary of State shall consult the Commission before varying any such reference.

(8) Subsection (7) shall not apply if the Commission has requested the variation concerned.

(9) No variation by the Secretary of State under this section shall be capable of altering the public interest consideration or considerations specified in the reference or the period permitted by section 51 within which the report of the Commission under section 50 is to be prepared and given to the Secretary of State.

50   Investigations and reports on references under section 45

(1) The Commission shall prepare a report on a reference under section 45 and give it to the Secretary of State within the period permitted by section 51.

(2) The report shall, in particular, contain—

    (a) the decisions of the Commission on the questions which it is required to answer by virtue of section 47;

    (b) its reasons for its decisions; and

    (c) such information as the Commission considers appropriate for facilitating a proper understanding of those questions and of its reasons for its decisions.

(2A) Where the report relates to a reference under article 5 which has been made after a report of OFCOM under article 4A, the Commission shall give a copy of its report (whether or not published) to OFCOM.

(3) The Commission shall carry out such investigations as it considers appropriate for the purpose of producing a report under this section.

51   Time-limits for investigations and reports by Commission

(1) The Commission shall prepare its report under section 50 and give it to the Secretary of State under that section within the period of 24 weeks beginning with the date of the reference concerned.

(2) [repealed]

(3) The Commission may extend, by no more than 8 weeks, the period within which a report under section 50 is to be prepared and given to the Secretary of State if it considers that there are special reasons why the report cannot be prepared and given to the Secretary of State within that period.

(4) The Commission may extend the period within which a report under section 50 is to be prepared and given to the Secretary of State if it considers that a relevant person has failed (whether with or without a reasonable excuse) to comply with any requirement of a notice under section 109.

(5) In subsection (4) 'relevant person' means—

    (a) any person carrying on any of the enterprises concerned;

    (b) any person who (whether alone or as a member of a group) owns or has control of any such person; or

    (c) any officer, employee or agent of any person mentioned in paragraph (a) or (b).

(6) For the purposes of subsection (5) a person or group of persons able, directly or indirectly, to control or materially to influence the policy of a body of persons corporate or unincorporate, but without having a controlling interest in that body of persons, may be treated as having control of it.

(7) An extension under subsection (3) or (4) shall come into force when published under section 107.

(8) An extension under subsection (4) shall continue in force until—

    (a) the person concerned provides the information or documents to the satisfaction of the Commission or (as the case may be) appears as a witness in accordance with the requirements of the Commission; or

    (b) the Commission publishes its decision to cancel the extension.

(9) This section is subject to section 52 and 53.

52   Section 51: supplementary

(1)–(2) repealed

(3) A period extended under subsection (3) of section 51 may also be extended under subsection (4) of that section and a period extended under subsection (4) of that section may also be extended under subsection (3) of that section.

(4) No more than one extension is possible under section 51(3).

(5) Where a period within which a report under section 50 is to be prepared and given to the Secretary of State is extended or further extended under section 51(3) or (4), the period as extended or (as the case may be) further extended shall, subject to subsections (6) and (7), be calculated by taking the period being extended and adding to it the period of the extension (whether or not those periods overlap in time).

(6) Subsection (7) applies where—

(a) the period within which the report under section 50 is to be prepared and given to the Secretary of State is further extended;

(b) the further extension and at least one previous extension is made under section 51(4); and

(c) the same days or fractions of days are included in or comprise the further extension and are included in or comprise at least one such previous extension.

(7) In calculating the period of the further extension, any days or fractions of days of the kind mentioned in subsection (6)(c) shall be disregarded.

(8) The Secretary of State may by order amend section 51 so as to alter any one or more of the following periods—

(a) the period of 24 weeks mentioned in subsection (1) of that section or any period for the time being mentioned in that subsection in substitution for that period;

(b) [repealed]

(c) the period of 8 weeks mentioned in subsection (3) of that section or any period for the time being mentioned in that subsection in substitution for that period.

(9) No alteration shall be made by virtue of subsection (8) which results in the period for the time being mentioned in subsection (1) or (2)(a) of section 51 exceeding 24 weeks or the period for the time being mentioned in subsection (3) of that section exceeding 8 weeks.

(10) An order under subsection (8) shall not affect any period of time within which the Commission is under a duty to prepare and give to the Secretary of State its report under section 50 in relation to a reference under section 45 if the Commission is already under that duty in relation to that reference when the order is made.

(11) Before making an order under subsection (8) the Secretary of State shall consult the Commission and such other persons as he considers appropriate.

(12) The Secretary of State may make regulations for the purposes of section 51(8).

(13) The regulations may, in particular—

(a) provide for the time at which information or documents are to be treated as provided (including the time at which they are to be treated as provided to the satisfaction of the Commission for the purposes of section 51(8));

(b) provide for the time at which a person is to be treated as appearing as a witness (including the time at which he is to be treated as appearing as a witness in accordance with the requirements of the Commission for the purposes of section 51(8));

(c) provide for the persons carrying on the enterprises which have or may have ceased to be, or may cease to be, distinct enterprises to be informed, in circumstances in which section 51(8) applies, of the fact that—

(i)   the Commission is satisfied as to the provision of the information or documents required by it; or

(ii) the person concerned has appeared as a witness in accordance with the requirements of the Commission;

(d) provide for the persons carrying on the enterprises which have or may have ceased to be, or may cease to be, distinct enterprises to be informed, in circumstances in which section 51(8) applies, of the time at which the Commission is to be treated as satisfied as mentioned in paragraph (c)(i) above or the person concerned is to be treated as having appeared as mentioned in paragraph (c)(ii) above.

53 Restrictions on action where public interest considerations not finalised

(1) The Commission shall cancel a reference under section 45 if—

(a) the intervention notice concerned mentions a public interest consideration which was not finalised on the giving of that notice or public interest considerations which, at that time, were not finalised;

(b) no other public interest consideration is mentioned in the notice;

(c) at least 24 weeks has elapsed since the giving of the notice; and

(d) the public interest consideration mentioned in the notice has not been finalised within that period of 24 weeks or (as the case may be) none of the public interest considerations mentioned in the notice has been finalised within that period of 24 weeks.

(2) Where a reference to the Commission under section 45 specifies a public interest consideration which has not been finalised before the making of the reference, the Commission shall not give its report to the Secretary of State under section 50 in relation to that reference unless—

(a) the period of 24 weeks beginning with the giving of the intervention notice concerned has expired; or

(b) the public interest consideration concerned has been finalised.

(c) [repealed]

(3) The Commission shall, in reporting on any of the questions mentioned in section 47(2)(b), (3), (5)(b), (6) and (7), disregard any public interest consideration which has not been finalised before the giving of the report.

(4) The Commission shall, in reporting on any of the questions mentioned in section 47(2)(b), (3), (5)(b), (6) and (7), disregard any public interest consideration which was not finalised on the giving of the intervention notice concerned and has not been finalised within the period of 24 weeks beginning with the giving of the notice concerned.

(5) Subsections (1) to (4) are without prejudice to the power of the Commission to carry out investigations in relation to any public interest consideration to which it might be able to have regard in its report.

Decisions of the Secretary of State

54 Decision of Secretary of State in public interest cases

(1) Subsection (2) applies where the Secretary of State has received a report of the Commission under section 50 in relation to a relevant merger situation.

(2) The Secretary of State shall decide whether to make an adverse public interest finding in relation to the relevant merger situation or whether to make no finding at all in the matter.

(3) For the purposes of this Part the Secretary of State makes an adverse public interest finding in relation to a relevant merger situation if, in relation to that situation, he decides—

(a) in connection with a reference to the Commission under subsection (2) of section 45, that it is the case as mentioned in paragraphs (a) to (d) of that subsection or subsection (3) of that section;

(b) in connection with a reference to the Commission under subsection (3) of that section, that it is the case as mentioned in paragraphs (a) to (d) of that subsection;

(c) in connection with a reference to the Commission under subsection (4) of that section, that it is the case as mentioned in paragraphs (a) to (d) of that subsection or subsection (5) of that section; and

(d) in connection with a reference to the Commission under subsection (5) of that section, that it is the case as mentioned in paragraphs (a) to (d) of that subsection.

(4) The Secretary of State may make no finding at all in the matter only if he decides that there is no public interest consideration which is relevant to a consideration of the relevant merger situation concerned.

(5) The Secretary of State shall make and publish his decision under subsection (2) within the period of 30 days beginning with the receipt of the report of the Commission under section 50.

(6) In making a decision under subsections (2) to (4), the Secretary of State shall disregard any public interest consideration not specified in the reference under section 45 and any public interest consideration disregarded by the Commission for the purposes of its report.

(7) In deciding whether to make an adverse public interest finding under subsection (2), the Secretary of State shall accept—

(a) in connection with a reference to the Commission under section 45(2) or (4), the decision of the report of the Commission under section 50 as to whether there is an anti-competitive outcome; and

(b) in connection with a reference to the Commission under section 45(3) or (5)—

(i) the decision of the report of the Commission under section 50 as to whether a relevant merger situation has been created or (as the case may be) arrangements are in progress or in contemplation which, if carried into effect, will result in the creation of a relevant merger situation; and

(ii) the decision of the report of the OFT under section 44 as to the absence of a substantial lessening of competition.

(8) In determining for the purposes of subsection (5) the period of 30 days no account shall be taken of—

(a) Saturday, Sunday, Good Friday and Christmas Day; and

(b) any day which is a bank holiday in England and Wales.

55 Enforcement action by Secretary of State

(1) Subsection (2) applies where the Secretary of State has decided under subsection (2) of section 54 within the period required by subsection (5) of that section to make an adverse public interest finding in relation to a relevant merger situation and has published his decision within the period so required.

(2) The Secretary of State may take such action under paragraph 9 or 11 of Schedule 7 as he considers to be reasonable and practicable to remedy, mitigate or prevent any of the effects adverse to the public interest which have resulted from, or may be expected to result from, the creation of the relevant merger situation concerned.

(3) In making a decision under subsection (2) the Secretary of State shall, in particular, have regard to the report of the Commission under section 50.

(4) In making a decision under subsection (2) in any case of a substantial lessening of competition, the Secretary of State may, in particular, have regard to the effect of any action on any relevant customer benefits in relation to the creation of the relevant merger situation concerned.

Other

56 Competition cases where intervention on public interest grounds ceases

(1) Where the Secretary of State decides not to make a reference under section 45 on the ground that no public interest consideration to which he is able to have regard is relevant to a consideration of the relevant merger situation concerned, he shall by notice require the OFT to deal with the matter otherwise than under this Chapter.

(2) Where a notice is given to the OFT in the circumstances mentioned in subsection (1), the OFT shall decide whether to make a reference under section 22 or 33; and any time-limits in relation to the Secretary of State's decision whether to make a reference under section 45 (including any remaining powers of extension) shall apply in relation to the decision of the OFT whether to make a reference under section 22 or 33.

(3) Where the Commission cancels under section 53(1) a reference under section 44 and the report of the OFT under section 44 contains the decision that it is or may be the case that there is an

anti-competitive outcome in relation to the relevant merger situation concerned, the Commission shall proceed under this Part as if a reference under section 22 or 33 had been made to it by the OFT.

(4) In proceeding by virtue of subsection (3) to prepare and publish a report under section 38, the Commission shall proceed as if—

   (a) the reference under section 22 or 33 had been made at the same time as the reference under section 45;

   (b) the timetable for preparing and giving its report under section 50 (including any remaining powers of extension and as extended by an additional period of 20 days) were the timetable for preparing and publishing its report under section 38; and

   (c) in relation to the question whether a relevant merger situation has been created or the question whether arrangements are in progress or in contemplation which, if carried into effect, will result in the creation of a relevant merger situation, the Commission were confined to the questions on the subject to be investigated by it under section 47.

(5) In determining the period of 20 days mentioned in subsection (4) no account shall be taken of—

   (a) Saturday, Sunday, Good Friday and Christmas Day; and

   (b) any day which is a bank holiday in England and Wales.

(6) Where the Secretary of State decides under section 54(2) to make no finding at all in the matter in connection with a reference under section 45(2) or (4), the Commission shall proceed under this Part as if a reference under section 22 or 33 had been made to it instead of a reference under section 45 and as if its report to the Secretary of State under section 50 had been prepared and published by it under section 38 within the period permitted by section 39.

(7) In relation to proceedings by virtue of subsection (6), the reference in section 41(3) to decisions of the Commission as included in its report by virtue of section 35(3) or 36(2) shall be construed as a reference to decisions which were included in the report of the Commission by virtue of section 47(8).

(8) Where the Commission becomes under a duty to proceed as mentioned in subsection (3) or (6), references in this Part to references under sections 22 and 33 shall, so far as may be necessary, be constituted accordingly; and in particular, sections 77 to 81 shall apply as if a reference has been made to the Commission by the OFT under section 22 or (as the case may be) 33.

57   Duties of OFT and Commission to inform Secretary of State

(1) The OFT shall, in considering whether to make a reference under section 22 or 33, bring to the attention of the Secretary of State any case which it believes raises any consideration specified in section 58 unless it believes that the Secretary of State would consider any such consideration immaterial in the context of the particular case.

(2) The OFT, OFCOM and the Commission shall bring to the attention of the Secretary of State any representations about exercising his powers under section 58(3) which have been made to the OFT, OFCOM or (as the case may be) the Commission.

58   Specified considerations

(1) The interests of national security are specified in this section.

(2) In subsection (1) 'national security' includes public security; and in this subsection 'public security' has the same meaning as in article 21(4) of the EC Merger Regulation.

(2A) The need for—

   (a) accurate presentation of news; and

   (b) free expression of opinion;

in newspapers is specified in this section.

(2B) The need for, to the extent that it is reasonable and practicable, a sufficient plurality of views in newspapers in each market for newspapers in the United Kingdom or a part of the United Kingdom is specified in this section.

(2C) The following are specified in this section—

    (a) the need, in relation to every different audience in the United Kingdom or in a particular area or locality of the United Kingdom, for there to be a sufficient plurality of persons with control of the media enterprises serving that audience;

    (b) the need for the availability throughout the United Kingdom of a wide range of broadcasting which (taken as a whole) is both of high quality and calculated to appeal to a wide variety of tastes and interests; and

    (c) the need for persons carrying on media enterprises, and for those with control of such enterprises, to have a genuine commitment to the attainment in relation to broadcasting of the standards objectives set out in section 319 of the Communications Act 2003.

(3) The Secretary of State may by order modify this section for the purpose of adding to, removing or amending any consideration which is for the time being specified in this section.

(4) An order under this section may, in particular—

    (a) provide for a consideration to be specified in this section for a particular purpose or purposes or for all purposes;

    (b) apply in relation to cases under consideration by the OFT, OFCOM, the Commission or the Secretary of State before the making of the order as well as cases under consideration on or after the making of the order.

(2D) The interest of maintaining the stability of the UK financial system is specified in this section (other than for the purposes of sections 67 and 68 or references made, or deemed to be made, by the European Commission to the OFT under article 4(4) or 9 of the EC Merger Regulation).

58A   Construction of consideration specified in section 58(2C)

(1) For the purposes of section 58 and this section an enterprise is a media enterprise if it consists in or involves broadcasting.

(2) In the case of a merger situation in which at least one of the enterprises ceasing to be distinct consists in or involves broadcasting, the references in section 58(2C)(a) or this section to media enterprises include references to newspaper enterprises.

(3) In this Part 'newspaper enterprise' means an enterprise consisting in or involving the supply of newspapers.

(4) Wherever in a merger situation two media enterprises serving the same audience cease to be distinct, the number of such enterprises serving that audience shall be assumed to be more immediately before they cease to be distinct than it is afterwards.

(5) For the purposes of section 58, where two or more media enterprises—

    (a) would fall to be treated as under common ownership or common control for the purposes of section 26, or

    (b) are otherwise in the same ownership or under the same control,

they shall be treated (subject to subsection (4)) as all under the control of only one person.

(6) A reference in section 58 or this section to an audience shall be construed in relation to a media enterprise in whichever of the following ways the decision-making authority considers appropriate—

    (a) as a reference to any one of the audiences served by that enterprise, taking them separately;

    (b) as a reference to all the audiences served by that enterprise, taking them together;

    (c) as a reference to a number of those audiences taken together in such group as the decision-making authority considers appropriate; or

    (d) as a reference to a part of anything that could be taken to be an audience under any of paragraphs (a) to (c) above.

(7) The criteria for deciding who can be treated for the purposes of this section as comprised in an audience, or as comprised in an audience served by a particular service—

    (a) shall be such as the decision-making authority considers appropriate in the circumstances of the case; and

(b) may allow for persons to be treated as members of an audience if they are only potentially members of it.

(8) In this section 'audience' includes readership.

(9) The power under subsection (3) of section 58 to modify that section includes power to modify this section.

Chapter 3 Other special cases

Special public interest cases

59   Intervention by Secretary of State in special public interest cases

(1) Subsection (2) applies where the Secretary of State has reasonable grounds for suspecting that it is or may be the case that a special merger situation has been created or arrangements are in progress or in contemplation which, if carried into effect, will result in the creation of a special merger situation.

(2) The Secretary of State may give a notice to the OFT (in this Part 'a special intervention notice') if he believes that it is or may be the case that one or more than one consideration specified in section 58 is relevant to a consideration of the special merger situation concerned.

(3) For the purposes of this Part a special merger situation has been created if—

    (a) the condition mentioned in subsection (3A) is satisfied; and

    (b) immediately before the enterprises concerned ceased to be distinct—

        (i)   the conditions mentioned in subsection (3B) were satisfied;

        (ii) the condition mentioned in subsection (3C) was satisfied; or

        (iii) the condition mentioned in subsection (3D) was satisfied.

(3A) The condition mentioned in this subsection is that—

    (a) no relevant merger situation has been created because of section 23(1) (b) and (2)(b); but

    (b) a relevant merger situation would have been created if those enactments were disregarded.

(3B) The conditions mentioned in this subsection are that—

    (a) at least one of the enterprises concerned was carried on in the United Kingdom or by or under the control of a body corporate incorporated in the United Kingdom; and

    (b) a person carrying on one or more of the enterprises concerned was a relevant government contractor.

(3C) The condition mentioned in this subsection is that, in relation to the supply of newspapers of any description, at least one-quarter of all the newspapers of that description which were supplied in the United Kingdom, or in a substantial part of the United Kingdom, were supplied by the person or persons by whom one of the enterprises concerned was carried on.

(3D) The condition mentioned in this subsection is that, in relation to the provision of broadcasting of any description, at least one-quarter of all broadcasting of that description provided in the United Kingdom, or in a substantial part of the United Kingdom, was provided by the person or persons by whom one of the enterprises concerned was carried on.

(5) For the purposes of deciding whether a relevant merger situation has been created or whether arrangements are in progress or in contemplation which, if carried into effect, will result in the creation of a relevant merger situation, sections 23 to 32 (read together with section 34) shall apply for the purposes of this Chapter as they do for the purposes of Chapter 1 but subject to subsection (6).

(6) In their application by virtue of subsection (5) sections 23 to 32 shall have effect as if—

    (a) for paragraph (a) of section 23(9) there were substituted—

        '(a) in relation to the giving of a special intervention notice, the time when the notice is given;

        (aa) in relation to the making of a report by the OFT under section 61, the time of the making of the report;

(ab) in the case of a reference which is treated as having been made under section 62(2) by virtue of section 64(2), such time as the Commission may determine; and';

(c) the references to the OFT in section 24(2)(a) and (b) included references to the Secretary of State;

(d) the references to the OFT in sections 25(1) to (3), (6) and (8) and 31 included references to the Secretary of State;

(e) the references to the OFT in section 25(4) and (5) were references to the Secretary of State;

(f) the reference in section 25(4) to section 73 were a reference to paragraph 3 of Schedule 7;

(g) the reference in section 25(12) to one extension were a reference to one extension by the OFT and one extension by the Secretary of State;

(h) the powers to extend time-limits under section 25 as applied by subsection (5) above, and the power to request information under section 31(1) as so applied, were not exercisable by the OFT or the Secretary of State before the giving of a special intervention notice;

(i) in subsection (1) of section 31 for the words 'section 22' there were substituted 'section 62(2)' and, in the application of that subsection to the OFT, for the word 'deciding' there were substituted 'enabling the Secretary of State to decide';

(j) in the case of the giving of special intervention notices, the references in sections 23 to 32 to the making of a reference or a reference were, so far as necessary, references to the giving of a special intervention notice or a special intervention notice; and

(k) the references to the OFT in section 32(2)(a) to (c) and (3) were construed in accordance with the above modifications.

(6A) The Secretary of State may by order amend the conditions mentioned in subsection (3)(b)(ii) and (iii).

(7) No more than one special intervention notice shall be given under subsection (2) in relation to the same special merger situation.

(8) In this section 'relevant government contractor' means—

(a) a government contractor—

(i) who has been notified by or on behalf of the Secretary of State of information, documents or other articles relating to defence and of a confidential nature which the government contractor or an employee of his may hold or receive in connection with being such a contractor; and

(ii) whose notification has not been revoked by or on behalf of the Secretary of State; or

(b) a former government contractor who was so notified when he was a government contractor and whose notification has not been revoked by or on behalf of the Secretary of State.

(9) In this section—

'defence' has the same meaning as in section 2 of the Official Secrets Act 1989 (c. 6); and

'government contractor' has the same meaning as in the Act of 1989 and includes any subcontractor of a government contractor, any subcontractor of that sub-contractor and any other subcontractor in a chain of sub-contractors which begins with the sub-contractor of the government contractor.

59A Construction of conditions in section 59(3C) and (3D)

(1) For the purpose of deciding whether the proportion of one-quarter mentioned in section 59(3C) or (3D) is fulfilled with respect to—

(a) newspapers of any description, or

(b) broadcasting of any description,

the decision-making authority shall apply such criterion (whether value, cost, price, quantity, capacity, number of workers employed or some other criterion, of whatever nature), or such combination of criteria, as the decision-making authority considers appropriate.

(2) References in section 59(3C) to the supply of newspapers shall, in relation to newspapers of any description which are the subject of different forms of supply, be construed in whichever of the following ways the decision-making authority considers appropriate—

(a) as references to any of those forms of supply taken separately;

(b) as references to all those forms of supply taken together; or

(c) as references to any of those forms of supply taken in groups.

(3) For the purposes of subsection (2) the decision-making authority may treat newspapers as being the subject of different forms of supply whenever—

(a) the transactions concerned differ as to their nature, their parties, their terms or their surrounding circumstances; and

(b) the difference is one which, in the opinion of the decision-making authority, ought for the purposes of that subsection to be treated as a material difference.

(4) References in section 59(3D) to the provision of broadcasting shall, in relation to broadcasting of any description which is the subject of different forms of provision, be construed in whichever of the following ways the decision-making authority considers appropriate—

(a) as references to any of those forms of provision taken separately;

(b) as references to all those forms of provision taken together; or

(c) as references to any of those forms of provision taken in groups.

(5) For the purposes of subsection (4) the decision-making authority may treat broadcasting as being the subject of different forms of provision whenever—

(a) the transactions concerned differ as to their nature, their parties, their terms or their surrounding circumstances; and

(b) the difference is one which, in the opinion of the decision-making authority, ought for the purposes of that subsection to be treated as a material difference.

(6) The criteria for deciding when newspapers or broadcasting can be treated, for the purposes of section 59, as newspapers or broadcasting of a separate description shall be such as in any particular case the decision-making authority considers appropriate in the circumstances of that case.

(7) In section 59 and this section 'provision' and cognate expressions have the same meaning in relation to broadcasting as in Part 3 of the Communications Act 2003; but this subsection is subject to subsections (4) and (5) of this section.

60   Special intervention notices under section 59

(1) A special intervention notice shall state—

(a) the special merger situation concerned; and

(b) the consideration specified in section 60 or considerations so specified which are, or may be, relevant to the special merger situation concerned.

(2) Where the Secretary of State believes that it is or may be the case that two or more considerations specified in section 58 are relevant to a consideration of the special merger situation concerned, he may decide not to mention in the special intervention notice such of those considerations as he considers appropriate.

(3) A special intervention notice shall come into force when it is given and shall cease to be in force when the matter to which it relates is finally determined under this Chapter.

(4) For the purposes of this Part, a matter to which a special intervention notice relates is finally determined under this Chapter if—

(a) the time within which the OFT or (if relevant) OFCOM is to report to the Secretary of State under section 61 or (as the case may be) 61A has expired and no such report has been made;

(b) the Secretary of State decides to accept an undertaking or group of undertakings under paragraph 3 of Schedule 7 instead of making a reference under section 62;

(c) the Secretary of State otherwise decides not to make a reference under that section;

(d) the Commission cancels such a reference under section 64(1);

(e) the time within which the Commission is to prepare a report under section 65 and give it to the Secretary of State has expired and no such report has been prepared and given to the Secretary of State;

(f) the time within which the Secretary of State is to make and publish a decision under section 66(2) has expired and no such decision has been made and published;

(g) the Secretary of State decides under subsection (2) of section 66 otherwise than as mentioned in subsection (5) of that section;

(h) the Secretary of State decides under subsection (2) of section 66 as mentioned in subsection (5) of that section but decides neither to accept an undertaking under paragraph 9 of Schedule 7 nor to make an order under paragraph 11 of that Schedule; or

(i) the Secretary of State decides under subsection (2) of section 66 as mentioned in subsection (5) of that section and accepts an undertaking under paragraph 9 of Schedule 7 or makes an order under paragraph 11 of that Schedule.

(5) For the purposes of this Part the time when a matter to which a special intervention notice relates is finally determined under this Chapter is—

(a) in a case falling within subsection (4)(a), (e) or (f), the expiry of the time concerned;

(b) in a case falling within subsection (4)(b), the acceptance of the undertaking or group of undertakings concerned;

(c) in a case falling within subsection (4)(c), (d) or (g), the making of the decision concerned;

(d) in a case falling within subsection (4)(h), the making of the decision neither to accept an undertaking under paragraph 9 of Schedule 7 nor to make an order under paragraph 11 of that Schedule; and

(e) in a case falling within subsection (4)(i), the acceptance of the undertaking concerned or (as the case may be) the making of the order concerned.

61   Initial investigation and report by OFT

(1) Subsection (2) applies where the Secretary of State has given a special intervention notice in relation to a special merger situation.

(2) The OFT shall, within such period as the Secretary of State may require, give a report to the Secretary of State in relation to the case.

(3) The report shall contain—

(a) advice from the OFT on the considerations relevant to the making of a reference under section 22 or 33 which are also relevant to the Secretary of State's decision as to whether to make a reference under section 62; and

(b) a summary of any representations about the case which have been received by the OFT and which relate to any consideration mentioned in the special intervention notice concerned (other than a consideration which, at the time of the giving of the notice, was specified in section 58(2A) to (2C)) and which is or may be relevant to the Secretary of State's decision as to whether to make a reference under section 62.

(4) The report shall, in particular, include a decision as to whether the OFT believes (disregarding section 59(3B)(b)) that it is, or may be, the case that a special merger situation has been created or (as the case may be) arrangements are in progress or in contemplation which, if carried into effect, will result in the creation of a special merger situation.

(4A) The report may, in particular, contain a summary of any representations about the case which have been received by the OFT and which relate to any consideration which—

(a) is mentioned in the special intervention notice concerned and, at the time of the giving of that notice, was specified in section 58(2A) to (2C); and

(b) is or may be relevant to the Secretary of State's decision as to whether to make a reference under section 62.

(5) The report may, in particular, include advice and recommendations on any consideration mentioned in the special intervention notice concerned and which is or may be relevant to the Secretary of State's decision as to whether to make a reference under section 62.

(6) The OFT shall carry out such investigations as it considers appropriate for the purposes of producing a report under this section.

61A   Additional investigation and report by OFCOM: certain media mergers

(1) Subsection (2) applies where—

    (a) the Secretary of State has given a special intervention notice in relation to a special merger situation; and

    (b) the special intervention notice mentions any consideration which, at the time of the giving of the notice, was specified in section 58(2A) to (2C).

(2) OFCOM shall, within such period as the Secretary of State may require, give a report to the Secretary of State on the effect of the consideration or considerations concerned on the case.

(3) The report shall contain—

    (a) advice and recommendations on any consideration which—

        (i)   is mentioned in the special intervention notice concerned and, at the time of the giving of that notice, was specified in section 58(2A) to (2C); and

        (ii) is or may be relevant to the Secretary of State's decision as to whether to make a reference under section 62; and

    (b) a summary of any representations about the case which have been received by OFCOM and which relate to any such consideration.

(4) OFCOM shall carry out such investigations as they consider appropriate for the purposes of producing a report under this section.

62   Power of Secretary of State to refer the matter

(1) Subsection (2) applies where the Secretary of State—

    (a) has given a special intervention notice in relation to a special merger situation; and

    (b) has received a report of the OFT under section 61, and any report of OFCOM which is required by virtue of section 61A in relation to the matter.

(2) The Secretary of State may make a reference to the Commission if he believes that it is or may be the case that—

    (a) a special merger situation has been created;

    (b) one or more than one consideration mentioned in the special intervention notice is relevant to a consideration of the special merger situation concerned; and

    (c) taking account only of the relevant consideration or considerations concerned, the creation of that situation operates or may be expected to operate against the public interest.

(3) The Secretary of State may make a reference to the Commission if he believes that it is or may be the case that—

    (a) arrangements are in progress or in contemplation which, if carried into effect, will result in the creation of a special merger situation;

    (b) one or more than one consideration mentioned in the special intervention notice is relevant to a consideration of the special merger situation concerned; and

    (c) taking account only of the relevant consideration or considerations concerned, the creation of that situation may be expected to operate against the public interest.

(4) No reference shall be made under this section if the making of the reference is prevented by paragraph 4 of Schedule 7.

(5) The Secretary of State, in deciding whether to make a reference under this section, shall accept the decision of the OFT included in its report under section 61 by virtue of subsection (4) of that section.

(6) A reference under this section shall, in particular, specify—

    (a) the subsection of this section under which it is made;

    (b) the date on which it is made; and

    (c) the consideration or considerations mentioned in the special intervention notice which the Secretary of State believes are, or may be, relevant to a consideration of the special merger situation concerned.

63   Questions to be decided on references under section 62

(1) The Commission shall, on a reference under section 62(2), decide whether a special merger situation has been created.

(2) The Commission shall, on a reference under section 62(3), decide whether arrangements are in progress or in contemplation which, if carried into effect, will result in the creation of a special merger situation.

(3) If the Commission decides that a special merger situation has been created or that arrangements are in progress or in contemplation which, if carried into effect, will result in the creation of a special merger situation, it shall, on a reference under section 62, decide whether, taking account only of the consideration or considerations mentioned in the reference, the creation of that situation operates or may be expected to operate against the public interest.

(4) The Commission shall, if it has decided on a reference under section 62 that the creation of a special merger situation operates or may be expected to operate against the public interest, decide the following additional questions—

> (a) whether action should be taken by the Secretary of State under section 66 for the purpose of remedying, mitigating or preventing any of the effects adverse to the public interest which have resulted from, or may be expected to result from, the creation of the special merger situation concerned;
>
> (b) whether the Commission should recommend the taking of other action by the Secretary of State or action by persons other than itself and the Secretary of State for the purpose of remedying, mitigating or preventing any of the effects adverse to the public interest which have resulted from, or may be expected to result from, the creation of the special merger situation concerned; and
>
> (c) in either case, if action should be taken, what action should be taken and what is to be remedied, mitigated or prevented.

64   Cancellation or variation of references under section 62

(1) The Commission shall cancel a reference under section 62(3) if it considers that the proposal to make arrangements of the kind mentioned in that reference has been abandoned.

(2) The Commission may, if it considers that doing so is justified by the facts (including events occurring on or after the making of the reference concerned), treat a reference made under subsection (2) or (3) of section 62 as if it had been made under subsection (3) or (as the case may be) (2) of that section; and, in such cases, references in this Part to references under those enactments shall, so far as may be necessary, be construed accordingly.

(3) Where, by virtue of subsection (2), the Commission treats a reference made under subsection (2) or (3) of section 62 as if it had been made under subsection (3) or (as the case may be) (2) of that section, paragraphs 1, 2, 7 and 8 of Schedule 7 shall, in particular, apply as if the reference had been made under subsection (3) or (as the case may be) (2) of that section instead of under subsection (2) or (3) of that section.

(4) Subsection (5) applies in relation to any undertaking accepted under paragraph 1 of Schedule 7, or any order made under paragraph 2 of that Schedule, which is in force immediately before the Commission, by virtue of subsection (2), treats a reference made under subsection (2) or (3) of section 62 as if it had been made under subsection (3) or (as the case may be) (2) of that section.

(5) The undertaking or order shall, so far as applicable, continue in force as if—

> (a) in the case of an undertaking or order which relates to a reference under subsection (2) or section 62, accepted or made in relation to a reference made under subsection (3) of that section; and
>
> (b) in the case of an undertaking or order which relates to a reference made under subsection (3) of that section, accepted or made in relation to a reference made under subsection (2) of that section;

and the undertaking or order concerned may be varied, superseded, released or revoked accordingly.

(6) The Secretary of State may at any time vary a reference under section 62.

(7) The Secretary of State shall consult the Commission before varying any such reference.

(8) Subsection (7) shall not apply if the Commission has requested the variation concerned.

(9) No variation by the Secretary of State under this section shall be capable of altering the consideration or considerations specified in the reference or the period permitted by virtue of section 65 within which the report of the Commission under that section is to be prepared and given to the Secretary of State.

65   Investigations and reports on references under section 62

(1) The Commission shall prepare a report on a reference under section 62 and give it to the Secretary of State within the period permitted by virtue of this section.

(2) The report shall, in particular, contain—

    (a) the decisions of the Commission on the questions which it is required to answer by virtue of section 63;

    (b) its reasons for its decisions; and

    (c) such information as the Commission considers appropriate for facilitating a proper understanding of those questions and of its reasons for its decisions.

(2A) Where the report relates to a reference under section 62 which has been made after a report of OFCOM under section 61A, the Commission shall give a copy of its report (whether or not published) to OFCOM.

(3) Sections 51 and 52 (but not section 53) shall apply for the purposes of a report under this section as they apply for the purposes of a report under section 50.

(4) The Commission shall carry out such investigations as it considers appropriate for the purpose of producing a report under this section.

66   Decision and enforcement action by Secretary of State

(1) Subsection (2) applies where the Secretary of State has received a report of the Commission under section 65 in relation to a special merger situation.

(2) The Secretary of State shall, in connection with a reference under section 62(2) or (3), decide the questions which the Commission is required to decide by virtue of section 63(1) to (3).

(3) The Secretary of State shall make and publish his decision under subsection (2) within the period of 30 days beginning with the receipt of the report of the Commission under section 65; and subsection (8) of section 54 shall apply for the purposes of this subsection as it applies for the purposes of subsection (5) of that section.

(4) In making his decisions under subsection (2), the Secretary of State shall accept the decisions of the report of the Commission under section 65 as to whether a special merger situation has been created or whether arrangements are in progress or in contemplation which, if carried into effect, will result in the creation of a special merger situation.

(5) Subsection (6) applies where the Secretary of State has decided under subsection (2) that—

    (a) a special merger situation has been created or arrangements are in progress or in contemplation which, if carried into effect, will result in the creation of a special merger situation;

    (b) at least one consideration which is mentioned in the intervention notice concerned is relevant to a consideration of the special merger situation concerned; and

    (c) taking account only of the relevant consideration or considerations concerned, the creation of that situation operates or may be expected to operate against the public interest;

and has so decided, and published his decision, within the period required by subsection (3).

(6) The Secretary of State may take such action under paragraph 9 or 11 of Schedule 7 as he considers to be reasonable and practicable to remedy, mitigate or prevent any of the effects adverse to the public interest which have resulted from, or may be expected to result from, the creation of the special merger situation concerned.

(7) In making a decision under subsection (6), the Secretary of State shall, in particular, have regard to the report of the Commission under section 65.

European mergers

67 Intervention to protect legitimate interests

(1) Subsection (2) applies where—

  (a) the Secretary of State has reasonable grounds for suspecting that it is or may be the case that—

    (i) a relevant merger situation has been created or that arrangements are in progress or in contemplation which, if carried into effect, will result in the creation of a relevant merger situation; and

    (ii) a concentration with a Community dimension (within the meaning of the EC Merger Regulation), or a part of such a concentration, has thereby arisen or will thereby arise;

  (b) a reference is prevented from being made under section 22 or 33 in relation to the relevant merger situation concerned (whether or not there would otherwise have been a duty to make such a reference) by virtue of Community law or anything done under or in accordance with it; and

  (c) the Secretary of State is considering whether to take appropriate measures to protect legitimate interests as permitted by article 21(4) of the EC Merger Regulation.

(2) The Secretary of State may give a notice to the OFT (in this section 'a European intervention notice') if he believes that it is or may be the case that one or more than one public interest consideration is relevant to a consideration of the relevant merger situation concerned.

(3) A European intervention notice shall state—

  (a) the relevant merger situation concerned;

  (b) the public interest consideration or considerations which are, or may be, relevant to a consideration of the relevant merger situation concerned; and

  (c) where any public interest consideration concerned is not finalised, the proposed timetable for finalising it.

(4) Where the Secretary of State believes that it is or may be the case that two or more public interest considerations are relevant to a consideration of the relevant merger situation concerned, he may decide not to mention in the intervention notice such of those considerations as he considers appropriate.

(5) No more than one European intervention notice shall be given under subsection (2) in relation to the same relevant merger situation.

(6) Where the Secretary of State has given a European intervention notice mentioning a public interest consideration which, at that time, is not finalised, he shall, as soon as practicable, take such action as is within his power to ensure that it is finalised.

(7) For the purposes of deciding whether a relevant merger situation has been created or whether arrangements are in progress or in contemplation which, if carried into effect, will result in the creation of a relevant merger situation, sections 23 to 32 (read together with section 34) shall apply for the purposes of this section as they do for the purposes of Chapter 1 but subject to subsection (8).

(8) In their application by virtue of subsection (7) sections 23 to 32 shall have effect as if—

  (a) references in those sections to the decision-making authority were references to the Secretary of State;

  (b) for paragraphs (a) and (b) of section 23(9) there were substituted ', in relation to the giving of a European intervention notice, the time when the notice is given';

  (c) the references to the OFT in section 24(2)(a) and (b) included references to the Secretary of State;

  (d) section 25, 31 and 32 were omitted; and

  (e) the references in sections 23 to 29 to the making of a reference or a reference were, so far as necessary, references to the giving of a European intervention notice or a European intervention notice.

(9) Section 42(3) shall, in its application to this section and section 68, have effect as if for the words 'intervention notice' there were substituted 'European intervention notice'.

68   Scheme for protecting legitimate interests

(1) The Secretary of State may by order provide for the taking of action, where a European intervention notice has been given, to remedy, mitigate or prevent effects adverse to the public interest which have resulted from, or may be expected to result from, the creation of a European relevant merger situation.

(2) In subsection (1) 'European relevant merger situation' means a relevant merger situation—

    (a) which has been created or will be created if arrangements which are in progress or in contemplation are carried into effect;

    (b) by virtue of which a concentration with a Community dimension (within the meaning of the 'EC Merger Regulation'), or a part of such a concentration, has arisen or will arise; and

    (c) in relation to which a reference was prevented from being made under section 22 or 33 (whether or not there would otherwise have been a duty to make such a reference) by virtue of Community law or anything done under or in accordance with it.

(3) Provision made under subsection (1) shall include provision ensuring that considerations which are not public interest considerations mentioned in the European intervention notice concerned may not be taken into account in determining whether anything operates, or may be expected to operate, against the public interest.

(4) Provision made under subsection (1) shall include provision—

    (a) applying with modifications sections 23 to 32 for the purposes of deciding for the purposes of this section whether a relevant merger situation has been created or whether arrangements are in progress or in contemplation which, if carried into effect, will result in the creation of a relevant merger situation;

    (b) requiring the OFT to make a report to the Secretary of State before a reference is made;

    (c) enabling the Secretary of State to make a reference to the Commission;

    (d) requiring the Commission to investigate and report to the Secretary of State on such a reference;

    (e) enabling the taking of interim and final enforcement action.

(5) An order under this section may include provision (including provision for the creation of offences and penalties, the payment of fees and the delegation of functions) corresponding to any provision made in, or in connection with, this Part in relation to intervention notices or special intervention notices and the cases to which they relate.

(6) In this section 'European intervention notice' has the same meaning as in section 67.

Other

69   [repealed]

Chapter 4 Enforcement

Powers exercisable before references under section 22 or 33

71   Initial undertakings: completed mergers

(1) Subsection (2) applies where the OFT is considering whether to make a reference under section 22.

(2) The OFT may, for the purpose of preventing pre-emptive action, accept from such of the parties concerned as it considers appropriate undertakings to take such action as it considers appropriate.

(3) No undertaking shall be accepted under subsection (2) unless the OFT has reasonable grounds for suspecting that it is or may be the case that a relevant merger situation has been created.

(4) An undertaking under this section—
- (a) shall come into force when accepted;
- (b) may be varied or superseded by another undertaking; and
- (c) may be released by the OFT.

(5) An undertaking which—
- (a) is in force under this section in relation to a possible reference or reference under section 22; and
- (b) has not been adopted under section 80 or paragraph 1 of Schedule 7;

shall cease to be in force if an order under section 72 or 81 comes into force in relation to that reference or an order under paragraph 2 of that Schedule comes into force in relation to the matter.

(6) An undertaking under this section shall, if it has not previously ceased to be in force and if it has not been adopted under section 80 or paragraph 1 of Schedule 7, cease to be in force—
- (a) where the OFT has decided to make the reference concerned under section 22, at the end of the period of 7 days beginning with the making of the reference;
- (b) where the OFT has decided to accept an undertaking under section 73 instead of making that reference, on the acceptance of that undertaking;
- (c) where an intervention notice is in force, at the end of the period of 7 days beginning with the giving of that notice; and
- (d) where the OFT has otherwise decided not to make the reference concerned under section 22, on the making of that decision.

(7) The OFT shall, as soon as reasonably practicable, consider any representations received by it in relation to varying or releasing an undertaking under this section.

(8) In this section and section 72 'pre-emptive action' means action which might prejudice the reference concerned or impede the taking of any action under this Part which may be justified by the Commission's decisions on the reference.

72 Initial enforcement orders: completed mergers

(1) Subsection (2) applies where the OFT is considering whether to make a reference under section 22.

(2) The OFT may by order, for the purpose of preventing pre-emptive action—
- (a) prohibit or restrict the doing of things which the OFT considers would constitute pre-emptive action;
- (b) impose on any person concerned obligations as to the carrying on of any activities or the safeguarding of any assets;
- (c) provide for the carrying on of any activities or the safeguarding of any assets either by the appointment of a person to conduct or supervise the conduct of any activities (on such terms and with such powers as may be specified or described in the order) or in any other manner;
- (d) do anything which may be done by virtue of paragraph 19 of Schedule 8.

(3) No order shall be made under subsection (2) unless the OFT has reasonable grounds for suspecting that it is or may be the case that—
- (a) a relevant merger situation has been created; and
- (b) pre-emptive action is in progress or in contemplation.

(4) An order under this section—
- (a) shall come into force at such time as is determined by or under the order; and
- (b) may be varied or revoked by another order.

(5) An order which—
- (a) is in force under this section in relation to a possible reference or a reference under section 22; and
- (b) has not been adopted under section 81 or paragraph 2 of Schedule 7;

shall cease to be in force if an undertaking under section 71 or 80 comes into force in relation to that reference or an undertaking under paragraph 1 of that Schedule comes into force in relation to the matter.

(6) An order under this section shall, if it has not previously ceased to be in force and if it is not adopted under section 81 or paragraph 2 of Schedule 7, cease to be in force—

    (a) where the OFT has decided to make the reference concerned under section 22, at the end of the period of 7 days beginning with the making of the reference;

    (b) where the OFT has decided to accept an undertaking under section 73 instead of making that reference, on the acceptance of that undertaking;

    (c) where an intervention notice is in force, at the end of the period of 7 days beginning with the giving of that notice; and

    (d) where the OFT has otherwise decided not to make the reference concerned under section 22, on the making of that decision.

(7) The OFT shall, as soon as reasonably practicable, consider any representations received by it in relation to varying or revoking an order under this section.

73   Undertakings in lieu of references under section 22 or 33

(1) Subsection (2) applies if the OFT considers that it is under a duty to make a reference under section 22 or 33 (disregarding the operation of section 22(3)(b) or (as the case may be) 33(3)(b) but taking account of the power of the OFT under section 22(2) or (as the case may be) 33(2) to decide not to make such a reference).

(2) The OFT may, instead of making such a reference and for the purpose of remedying, mitigating or preventing the substantial lessening of competition concerned or any adverse effect which has or may have resulted from it or may be expected to result from it, accept from such of the parties concerned as it considers appropriate undertakings to take such action as it considers appropriate.

(3) In proceeding under subsection (2), the OFT shall, in particular, have regard to the need to achieve as comprehensive a solution as is reasonable and practicable to the substantial lessening of competition and any adverse effects resulting from it.

(4) In proceeding under subsection (2), the OFT may, in particular, have regard to the effect of any action on any relevant customer benefits in relation to the creation of the relevant merger situation concerned.

(5) An undertaking under this section—

    (a) shall come into force when accepted;

    (b) may be varied or superseded by another undertaking; and

    (c) may be released by the OFT.

(6) An undertaking under this section which is in force in relation to a relevant merger situation shall cease to be in force if an order comes into force under section 75 or 76 in relation to that undertaking.

(7) The OFT shall, as soon as reasonably practicable, consider any representations received by it in relation to varying or releasing an undertaking under this section.

74   Effect of undertakings under section 73

(1) The relevant authority shall not make a reference under section 22, 33 or 45 in relation to the creation of a relevant merger situation if—

    (a) the OFT has accepted an undertaking under section 73; and

    (b) the relevant merger situation is the situation by reference to which the undertaking was accepted.

(2) Subsection (1) does not prevent the making of a reference if material facts about relevant arrangements or transactions, or relevant proposed arrangements or transactions, were not notified (whether in writing or otherwise) to the OFT or made public before the undertaking concerned was accepted.

(3) For the purposes of subsection (2) arrangements or transactions, or proposed arrangements or transactions, are relevant if they are the ones in consequence of which the enterprises concerned ceased or may have ceased, or may cease, to be distinct enterprises.

(4) In subsection (2) 'made public' means so publicised as to be generally known or readily ascertainable.

(5) In this section 'relevant authority' means—

    (a) in relation to a possible reference under section 22 or 33, the OFT; and

    (b) in relation to a possible reference under section 45, the Secretary of State.

75 Order-making power where undertakings under section 73 not fulfilled etc.

(1) Subsection (2) applies where the OFT considers that—

    (a) an undertaking accepted by it under section 73 has not been, is not being or will not be fulfilled; or

    (b) in relation to an undertaking accepted by it under that section, information which was false or misleading in a material respect was given to the OFT by the person giving the undertaking before the OFT decided to accept the undertaking.

(2) The OFT may, for any of the purposes mentioned in section 73(2), make an order under this section.

(3) Subsections (3) and (4) of section 73 shall apply for the purposes of subsection (2) above as they apply for the purposes of subsection (2) of that section.

(4) An order under this section may contain—

    (a) anything permitted by Schedule 8; and

    (b) such supplementary, consequential or incidental provision as the OFT considers appropriate.

(5) An order under this section—

    (a) shall come into force at such time as is determined by or under the order;

    (b) may contain provision which is different from the provision contained in the undertaking concerned; and

    (c) may be varied or revoked by another order.

(6) The OFT shall, as soon as reasonably practicable, consider any representations received by it in relation to varying or revoking an order under this section.

76 Supplementary interim order-making power

(1) Subsection (2) applies where—

    (a) the OFT has the power to make an order under section 75 in relation to a particular undertaking and intends to make such an order; or

    (b) the Commission has the power to make an order under section 83 in relation to a particular undertaking and intends to make such an order.

(2) The OFT or (as the case may be) the Commission may, for the purpose of preventing any action which might prejudice the making of that order, make an order under this section.

(3) No order shall be made under subsection (2) unless the OFT or (as the case may be) the Commission has reasonable grounds for suspecting that it is or may be the case that action which might prejudice the making of the order under section 75 or (as the case may be) 83 is in progress or in contemplation.

(4) An order under subsection (2) may—

    (a) prohibit or restrict the doing of things which the OFT or (as the case may be) the Commission considers would prejudice the making of the order under section 75 or (as the case may be) 83;

    (b) impose on any person concerned obligations as to the carrying on of any activities or the safeguarding of any assets;

    (c) provide for the carrying on of any activities or the safeguarding of any assets either by the appointment of a person to conduct or supervise the conduct of any activities (on such terms and with such powers as may be specified or described in the order) or in any other manner;

    (d) do anything which may be done by virtue of paragraph 19 of Schedule 8.

(5) An order under this section—

    (a) shall come into force at such time as is determined by or under the order; and

(b) may be varied or revoked by another order.

(6) An order under this section shall, if it has not previously ceased to be in force, cease to be in force on—

    (a) the coming into force of an order under section 75 or (as the case may be) 83 in relation to the undertaking concerned; or

    (b) the making of the decision not to proceed with such an order.

(7) The OFT or (as the case may be) the Commission shall, as soon as reasonably practicable, consider any representations received by it in relation to varying or revoking an order under this section.

Interim restrictions and powers

77 Restrictions on certain dealings: completed mergers

(1) Subsections (2) and (3) apply where—

    (a) a reference has been made under section 22 but not finally determined; and

    (b) no undertakings under section 71 or 80 are in force in relation to the relevant merger situation concerned and no orders under section 72 or 81 are in force in relation to that situation.

(2) No relevant person shall, without the consent of the Commission—

    (a) complete any outstanding matters in connection with any arrangements which have resulted in the enterprises concerned ceasing to be distinct enterprises;

    (b) make any further arrangements in consequence of that result (other than arrangements which reverse that result); or

    (c) transfer the ownership or control of any enterprises to which the reference relates.

(3) No relevant person shall, without the consent of the Commission, assist in any of the activities mentioned in paragraphs (a) to (c) of subsection (2).

(4) The prohibitions in subsections (2) and (3) do not apply in relation to anything which the person concerned is required to do by virtue of any enactment.

(5) The consent of the Commission under subsection (2) or (3)—

    (a) may be general or special;

    (b) may be revoked by the Commission; and

    (c) shall be published in such manner as the Commission considers appropriate for the purpose of bringing it to the attention of any person entitled to the benefit of it.

(6) Paragraph (c) of subsection (5) shall not apply if the Commission considers that publication is not necessary for the purpose mentioned in that paragraph.

(7) Subsections (2) and (3) shall apply to a person's conduct outside the United Kingdom if (and only if) he is—

    (a) a United Kingdom national;

    (b) a body incorporated under the law of the United Kingdom or of any part of the United Kingdom; or

    (c) a person carrying on business in the United Kingdom.

(8) In this section 'relevant person' means—

    (a) any person who carries on any enterprise to which the reference relates or who has control of any such enterprise;

    (b) any subsidiary of any person falling within paragraph (a); or

    (c) any person associated with any person falling within paragraph (a) or any subsidiary of any person so associated.

78 Restrictions on certain share dealings: anticipated mergers

(1) Subsection (2) applies where—

    (a) a reference has been made under section 33; and

    (b) no undertakings under section 80 are in force in relation to the relevant merger situation concerned and no orders under section 81 are in force in relation to that situation.

(2) No relevant person shall, without the consent of the Commission, directly or indirectly acquire during the relevant period an interest in shares in a company if any enterprise to which the reference relates is carried on by or under the control of that company.

(3) The consent of the Commission under subsection (2)—

    (a) may be general or special;

    (b) may be revoked by the Commission; and

    (c) shall be published in such manner as the Commission considers appropriate for bringing it to the attention of any person entitled to the benefit of it.

(4) Paragraph (c) of subsection (3) shall not apply if the Commission considers that publication is not necessary for the purpose mentioned in that paragraph.

(5) Subsection (2) shall apply to a person's conduct outside the United Kingdom if (and only if) he is—

    (a) a United Kingdom national;

    (b) a body incorporated under the law of the United Kingdom or of any part of the United Kingdom; or

    (c) a person carrying on business in the United Kingdom.

(6) In this section and section 79—

'company' includes any body corporate;

'relevant period' means the period beginning with the making of the reference concerned and ending when the reference is finally determined; 'relevant person' means—

    (a) any person who carries on any enterprise to which the reference relates or who has control of any such enterprise;

    (b) any subsidiary of any person falling within paragraph (a); or

    (c) any person associated with any person falling within paragraph (a) or any subsidiary of any person so associated; and

'share' means share in the capital of a company, and includes stock

79 Sections 77 and 78: further interpretation provisions

(1) For the purposes of this Part a reference under section 22 or 33 is finally determined if—

    (a) the reference is cancelled under section 37(1);

    (b) the time within which the Commission is to prepare and publish a report under section 38 in relation to the reference has expired and no such report has been prepared and published;

    (c) the report of the Commission under section 38 contains the decision that there is not an anti-competitive outcome;

    (d) the report of the Commission under section 38 contains the decision that there is an anti-competitive outcome and the Commission has decided under section 41(2) neither to accept an undertaking under section 82 nor to make an order under section 84; or

    (e) the report of the Commission under section 38 contains the decision that there is an anti-competitive outcome and the Commission has decided under section 41(2) to accept an undertaking under section 82 or to make an order under section 84.

(2) For the purposes of this Part the time when a reference under section 22 or 33 is finally determined is—

    (a) in a case falling within subsection (1)(a), the making of the decision concerned;

    (b) in a case falling within subsection (1)(b), the expiry of the time concerned;

    (c) in a case falling within subsection (1)(c), the publication of the report;

    (d) in a case falling within subsection (1)(d), the making of the decision under section 41(2); and

    (e) in a case falling within subsection (1)(e), the acceptance of the undertaking concerned or (as the case may be) the making of the order concerned.

(3) For the purposes of section 78 and subject to subsection (4) below, the circumstances in which a person acquires an interest in shares include those where—

(a) he enters into a contract to acquire the shares (whether or not for cash);

(b) he is not the registered holder but acquires the right to exercise, or to control the exercise of, any right conferred by the holding of the shares; or

(c) he—

    (i) acquires a right to call for delivery of the shares to himself or to his order or to acquire an interest in the shares; or

    (ii) assumes an obligation to acquire such an interest.

(4) The circumstances in which a person acquires an interest in shares for the purposes of section 78 do not include those where he acquires an interest in pursuance of an obligation assumed before the publication by the OFT of the reference concerned.

(5) The circumstances in which a person acquires a right mentioned in subsection (3)—

(a) include those where he acquires a right, or assumes an obligation, whose exercise or fulfilment would give him that right; but

(b) do not include those where he is appointed as proxy to vote at a specified meeting of a company or of any class of its members or at any adjournment of the meeting or he is appointed by a corporation to act as its representative at any meeting of the company or of any class of its members.

(6) References to rights and obligations in subsections (3) to (5) include conditional rights and conditional obligations.

(7) References in sections 77 and 78 to a person carrying on or having control of any enterprise includes a group of persons carrying on or having control of an enterprise and any member of such a group.

(8) Sections 26(2) to (4) and 127(1), (2) and (4) to (6) shall apply for the purposes of sections 77 and 78 to determine whether any person or group of persons has control of any enterprise and whether persons are associated as they apply for the purposes of section 26 to determine whether enterprises are brought under common control.

(9) Section 736 and 736A of the Companies Act 1985 (c. 6) shall apply for the purposes of sections 77 and 78 to determine whether a company is a subsidiary of an individual or of a group of persons as they apply to determine whether it is a subsidiary of a company; and references to a subsidiary in subsections (8) and (9) of section 736A as so applied shall be construed accordingly.

80   Interim undertakings

(1) Subsections (2) and (3) apply where a reference under section 22 or 33 has been made but is not finally determined.

(2) The Commission may, for the purpose of preventing pre-emptive action, accept from such of the parties concerned as it considers appropriate undertakings to take such action as it considers appropriate.

(3) The Commission may, for the purpose of preventing pre-emptive action, adopt an undertaking accepted by the OFT under section 71 if the undertaking is still in force when the Commission adopts it.

(4) An undertaking adopted under subsection (3)—

(a) shall continue in force, in accordance with its terms, when adopted;

(b) may be varied or superseded by an undertaking under this section; and

(c) may be released by the Commission.

(5) Any other undertaking under this section—

(a) shall come into force when accepted;

(b) may be varied or superseded by another undertaking; and

(c) may be released by the Commission.

(6) References in this Part to undertakings under this section shall, unless the context otherwise requires, include references to undertakings adopted under this section; and references to the acceptance or giving of undertakings under this section shall be construed accordingly.

(7) An undertaking which is in force under this section in relation to a reference under section 22 or 33 shall cease to be in force if an order under section 81 comes into force in relation to that reference.

(8) An undertaking under this section shall, if it has not previously ceased to be in force, cease to be in force when the reference under section 22 or 33 is finally determined.

(9) The Commission shall, as soon as reasonably practicable, consider any representations received by it in relation to varying or releasing an undertaking under this section.

(10) In this section and section 81 'pre-emptive action' means action which might prejudice the reference concerned or impede the taking of any action under this Part which may be justified by the Commission's decisions on the reference.

81 Interim orders

(1) Subsections (2) and (3) apply where a reference has been made under section 22 or 33 but is not finally determined.

(2) The Commission may by order, for the purpose of preventing pre-emptive action—

- (a) prohibit or restrict the doing of things which the Commission considers would constitute pre-emptive action;
- (b) impose on any person concerned obligations as to the carrying on of any activities or the safeguarding of any assets;
- (c) provide for the carrying on of any activities or the safeguarding of any assets either by the appointment of a person to conduct or supervise the conduct of any activities (on such terms and with such powers as may be specified or described in the order) or in any other manner;
- (d) do anything which may be done by virtue of paragraph 19 of Schedule 8.

(3) The Commission may, for the purpose of preventing pre-emptive action, adopt an order made by the OFT under section 72 if the order is still in force when the Commission adopts it.

(4) An order adopted under subsection (3)—

- (a) shall continue in force, in accordance with its terms, when adopted; and
- (b) may be varied or revoked by an order under this section.

(5) Any other order under this section—

- (a) shall come into force at such time as is determined by or under the order; and
- (b) may be varied or revoked by another order.

(6) References in this Part to orders under this section shall, unless the context otherwise requires, include references to orders adopted under this section; and references to the making of orders under this section shall be construed accordingly.

(7) An order which is in force under this section in relation to a reference under section 22 or 33 shall cease to be in force if an undertaking under section 80 comes into force in relation to that reference.

(8) An order under this section shall, if it has not previously ceased to be in force, cease to be in force when the reference under section 22 or 33 is finally determined.

(9) The Commission shall, as soon as reasonably practicable, consider any representations received by it in relation to varying or revoking an order under this section.

Final powers

82 Final undertakings

(1) The Commission may, in accordance with section 41, accept, from such persons as it considers appropriate, undertakings to take action specified or described in the undertakings.

(2) An undertaking under this section—

- (a) shall come into force when accepted;
- (b) may be varied or superseded by another undertaking; and
- (c) may be released by the Commission.

(3) An undertaking which is in force under this section in relation to a reference under section 22 or 33 shall cease to be in force if an order under section 76(1)(b) or 83 comes into force in relation to that reference.

(4) No undertaking shall be accepted under this section in relation to a reference under section 22 or 33 if an order has been made under—

    (a) section 76(1)(b) or 83 in relation to the subject-matter of the undertaking; or

    (b) section 84 in relation to that reference.

(5) The Commission shall, as soon as reasonably practicable, consider any representations received by it in relation to varying or releasing an undertaking under this section.

83   Order-making power where final undertakings not fulfilled

(1) Subsection (2) applies where the Commission considers that—

    (a) an undertaking accepted by it under section 82 has not been, is not being or will not be fulfilled; or

    (b) in relation to an undertaking accepted by it under that section, information which was false or misleading in a material respect was given to the Commission or the OFT by the person giving the undertaking before the Commission decided to accept the undertaking.

(2) The Commission may, for any of the purposes mentioned in section 41(2), make an order under this section.

(3) Subsections (3) to (5) of section 41 shall apply for the purposes of subsection (2) above as they apply for the purposes of subsection (2) of that section.

(4) An order under this section may contain—

    (a) anything permitted by Schedule 8; and

    (b) such supplementary, consequential or incidental provision as the Commission considers appropriate.

(5) An order under this section—

    (a) shall come into force at such time as is determined by or under the order;

    (b) may contain provision which is different from the provision contained in the undertaking concerned; and

    (c) may be varied or revoked by another order.

(6) No order shall be varied or revoked under this section unless the OFT advises that such a variation or revocation is appropriate by reason of a change of circumstances.

84   Final orders

(1) The Commission may, in accordance with section 41, make an order under this section.

(2) An order under this section may contain—

    (a) anything permitted by Schedule 8; and

    (b) such supplementary, consequential or incidental provision as the Commission considers appropriate.

(3) An order under this section—

    (a) shall come into force at such time as is determined by or under the order; and

    (b) may be varied or revoked by another order.

(4) No order shall be varied or revoked under this section unless the OFT advises that such a variation or revocation is appropriate by reason of a change of circumstances.

(5) No order shall be made under this section in relation to a reference under section 22 or 33 if an undertaking has been accepted under section 82 in relation to that reference.

Public interest and special public interest cases

85   Enforcement regime for public interest and special public interest cases

(1) Schedule 7 (which provides for the enforcement regime in public interest and special public interest cases) shall have effect.

(2) The OFT may advise the Secretary of State in relation to the taking by him of enforcement action under Schedule 7.

Undertakings and orders: general provisions

86   Enforcement orders: general provisions

(1) An enforcement order may extend to a person's conduct outside the United Kingdom if (and only if) he is—

(a) a United Kingdom national;

(b) a body incorporated under the law of the United Kingdom or of any part of the United Kingdom; or

(c) a person carrying on business in the United Kingdom.

(2) Nothing in an enforcement order shall have effect so as to—

(a) cancel or modify conditions in licences granted—

(i)   under a patent granted under the Patents Act 1977 (c. 37) or a European patent (UK) (within the meaning of the Act of 1977); or

(ii)   in respect of a design registered under the Registered Designs Act 1949 (c. 88); by the proprietor of the patent or design; or

(b) require an entry to be made in the register of patents or the register of designs to the effect that licences under such a patent or such a design are to be available as of right.

(3) An enforcement order may prohibit the performance of an agreement already in existence when the order is made.

(4) Schedule 8 (which provides for the contents of certain enforcement orders) shall have effect.

(5) Part 1 of Schedule 9 (which enables certain enforcement orders to modify licence conditions etc. in regulated markets) shall have effect.

(6) In this Part 'enforcement order' means an order made under section 72, 75, 76, 81, 83 or 84 or under paragraph 2, 5, 6, 10 or 11 of Schedule 7.

87   Delegated power of directions

(1) An enforcement order may authorise the person making the order to give directions falling within subsection (2) to—

(a) a person specified in the directions; or

(b) the holder for the time being of an office so specified in any body of persons corporate or unincorporate.

(2) Directions fall within this subsection if they are directions—

(a) to take such action as may be specified or described in the directions for the purpose of carrying out, or ensuring compliance with, the enforcement order concerned; or

(b) to do, or refrain from doing, anything so specified or described which the person might be required by that order to do or refrain from doing.

(3) An enforcement order may authorise the person making the order to vary or revoke any directions so given.

(4) The court may by order require any person who has failed to comply with directions given by virtue of this section to comply with them, or otherwise remedy his failure, within such time as may be specified in the order.

(5) Where the directions related to anything done in the management or administration of a body of persons corporate or unincorporate, the court may by order require the body of persons concerned or any officer of it to comply with the directions, or otherwise remedy the failure to comply with them, within such time as may be specified in the order.

(6) An order under subsection (4) or (5) shall be made on the application of the person authorised by virtue of this section to give the directions concerned.

(7) An order under subsection (4) or (5) may provide for all the costs or expenses of, or incidental to, the application for the order to be met by any person in default or by any officers of a body of persons corporate or unincorporate who are responsible for its default.

(8) In this section 'the court' means—

    (a) in relation to England and Wales or Northern Ireland, the High Court; and

    (b) in relation to Scotland, the Court of Session.

88   Contents of certain enforcement orders

(1) This section applies in relation to any order under section 75, 83 or 84 or under paragraph 5, 10 or 11 of Schedule 7.

(2) The order or any explanatory material accompanying the order shall state—

    (a) the actions that the persons or description of persons to whom the order is addressed must do or (as the case may be) refrain from doing;

    (b) the date on which the order comes into force;

    (c) the possible consequences of not complying with the order; and

    (d) the section of this Part under which a review can be sought in relation to the order.

89   Subject-matter of undertakings

(1) The provision which may be contained in an enforcement undertaking is not limited to the provision which is permitted by Schedule 8.

(2) In this Part 'enforcement undertaking' means an undertaking under section 71, 73, 80 or 82 or under paragraph 1, 3 or 9 of Schedule 7.

90   Procedural requirements for certain undertakings and orders

Schedule 10 (which provides for the procedure for accepting certain enforcement undertakings and making certain enforcement orders and for their termination) shall have effect.

91   Register of undertakings and orders

(1) The OFT shall compile and maintain a register for the purposes of this Part.

(2) The register shall be kept in such form as the OFT considers appropriate.

(3) The OFT shall ensure that the following matters are entered in the register—

    (a) the provisions of any enforcement undertaking accepted under this Part;

    (b) the provisions of any enforcement order made under this Part;

    (c) the details of any variation, release or revocation of such an undertaking or order; and

    (d) the details of any consent given by the Commission under section 77(2) or (3) or 78(2) or by the Secretary of State under paragraph 7(2) or (3) or 8(2) of Schedule 7.

(4) The duty in subsection (3) does not extend to anything of which the OFT is unaware.

(5) The Commission and the Secretary of State shall inform the OFT of any matters which are to be included in the register by virtue of subsection (3) and which relate to enforcement undertakings accepted by them, enforcement orders made by them or consents given by them.

(6) The OFT shall ensure that the contents of the register are available to the public—

    (a) during (as a minimum) such hours as may be specified in an order made by the Secretary of State; and

    (b) subject to such reasonable fees (if any) as the OFT may determine.

(7) If requested by any person to do so and subject to such reasonable fees (if any) as the OFT may determine, the OFT shall supply the person concerned with a copy (certified to be true) of the register or of an extract from it.

Enforcement functions of OFT

92   Duty of OFT to monitor undertakings and orders

(1) The OFT shall keep under review—

    (a) the carrying out of any enforcement undertaking or any enforcement order; and

    (b) compliance with the prohibitions in sections 77(2) and (3) and 78(2) and in paragraphs 7(2) and (3) and 8(2) of Schedule 7.

(2) The OFT shall, in particular, from time to time consider—

    (a) whether an enforcement undertaking or enforcement order has been or is being complied with;

(b) whether, by reason of any change of circumstances, an enforcement undertaking is no longer appropriate and—

    (i)   one or more of the parties to it can be released from it; or

    (ii) it needs to be varied or to be superseded by a new enforcement undertaking; and

(c) whether, by reason of any change of circumstances, an enforcement order is no longer appropriate and needs to be varied or revoked.

(3) The OFT shall give the Commission or (as the case may be) the Secretary of State such advice as it considers appropriate in relation to—

(a) any possible variation or release by the Commission or (as the case may be) the Secretary of State of an enforcement undertaking accepted by it or (as the case may be) him;

(b) any possible new enforcement undertaking to be accepted by the Commission or (as the case may be) the Secretary of State so as to supersede another enforcement undertaking given to the Commission or (as the case may be) the Secretary of State;

(c) any possible variation or revocation by the Commission or (as the case may be) the Secretary of State of an enforcement order made by the Commission or (as the case may be) the Secretary of State;

(d) any possible enforcement undertaking to be accepted by the Commission or (as the case may be) the Secretary of State instead of an enforcement order or any possible enforcement order to be made by the Commission or (as the case may be) the Secretary of State instead of an enforcement undertaking;

(e) the enforcement by virtue of section 94(6) to (8) of any enforcement undertaking or enforcement order; or

(f) the enforcement by virtue of section 95(4) and (5) of the prohibitions in sections 77(2) and (3) and 78(2) and in paragraphs 7(2) and (3) and 8(2) of Schedule 7.

(4) The OFT shall take such action as it considers appropriate in relation to—

(a) any possible variation or release by it of an enforcement undertaking accepted by it;

(b) any possible new enforcement undertaking to be accepted by it so as to supersede another enforcement undertaking given to it;

(c) any possible variation or revocation by it of an enforcement order made by it;

(d) any possible enforcement undertaking to be accepted by it instead of an enforcement order or any possible enforcement order to be made by it instead of an enforcement undertaking;

(e) the enforcement by it by virtue of section 94(6) of any enforcement undertaking or enforcement order; or

(f) the enforcement by it by virtue of section 95 (4) and (5) of the prohibitions in sections 77(2) and (3) and 78(2) and in paragraphs 7(2) and (3) and 8(2) of Schedule 7.

(5) The OFT shall keep under review the effectiveness of enforcement undertakings accepted under this Part and enforcement orders made under this Part.

(6) The OFT shall, whenever requested to do so by the Secretary of State and otherwise from time to time, prepare a report of its findings under subsection (5).

(7) The OFT shall—

(a) give any report prepared by it under subsection (6) to the Commission;

(b) give a copy of the report to the Secretary of State; and

(c) publish the report.

93 Further role of OFT in relation to undertakings and orders

(1) Subsections (2) and (3) apply where—

(a) the Commission is considering whether to accept undertakings under section 80 or 82; or

(b) the Secretary of State is considering whether to accept undertakings under paragraph 1, 3 or 9 of Schedule 7.

(2) The Commission or (as the case may be) the Secretary of State (in this section 'the relevant authority') may require the OFT to consult with such persons as the relevant authority considers appropriate with a view to discovering whether they will offer undertakings which the relevant a a view to discovering whether they will offer undertakings which the relevant authority would be prepared to accept under section 80 or 82 or (as the case may be) paragraph 1, 3 or 9 of Schedule 7.

(3) The relevant authority may require the OFT to report to the relevant authority on the outcome of the OFT's consultations within such period as the relevant authority may require.

(4) A report under subsection (3) shall, in particular, contain advice from the OFT as to whether any undertakings offered should be accepted by the relevant authority under section 80 or 82 or (as the case may be) paragraph 1, 3 or 9 of Schedule 7.

(5) The powers conferred on the relevant authority by subsections (1) to (4) are without prejudice to the power of the relevant authority to consult the persons concerned itself.

(6) If asked by the relevant authority for advice in relation to the taking of enforcement action (whether or not by way of undertaking) in a particular case, the OFT shall give such advice as it considers appropriate.

Other

94   Rights to enforce undertakings and orders

(1) This section applies to any enforcement undertaking or enforcement order.

(2) Any person to whom such an undertaking or order relates shall have a duty to comply with it.

(3) The duty shall be owed to any person who may be affected by a contravention of the undertaking or (as the case may be) order.

(4) Any breach of the duty which causes such a person to sustain loss or damage shall be actionable by him.

(5) In any proceedings brought under subsection (4) against a person to whom an enforcement undertaking or an enforcement order relates it shall be a defence for that person to show that he took all reasonable steps and exercised all due diligence to avoid contravening the
undertaking or (as the case may be) order.

(6) Compliance with an enforcement undertaking or an enforcement order shall also be enforceable by civil proceedings brought by the OFT for an injunction or for interdict or for any other appropriate relief or remedy.

(7) Compliance with an undertaking under section 80 or 82, an order made by the Commission under section 76 or an order under section 81, 83 or 84, shall also be enforceable by civil proceedings brought by the Commission for an injunction or for interdict or for any other appropriate relief or remedy.

(8) Compliance with an undertaking under paragraph 1, 3 or 9 of Schedule 7, an order made by the Secretary of State under paragraph 2 of that Schedule or an order under paragraph 5, 6, 10 or 11 of that Schedule, shall also be enforceable by civil proceedings brought by the Secretary of State for an injunction or for interdict or for any other appropriate relief or remedy.

(9) Subsections (6) to (8) shall not prejudice any right that a person may have by virtue of subsection (4) to bring civil proceedings for contravention or apprehended contravention of an enforcement undertaking or an enforcement order.

95   Rights to enforce statutory restrictions

(1) The obligation to comply with section 77(2) or (3) or 78(2) or paragraph 7(2) or (3) or 8(2) of Schedule 7 shall be a duty owed to any person who may be affected by a contravention of the enactment concerned.

(2) Any breach of the duty which causes such a person to sustain loss or damage shall be actionable by him.

(3) In any proceedings brought under subsection (2) against a person who has an obligation to comply with section 77(2) or (3) or 78(2) or paragraph 7(2) or (3) or 8(2) of Schedule 7 it shall be a defence for that person to show that he took all reasonable steps and exercised all due diligence to avoid contravening the enactment concerned.

(4) Compliance with section 77(2) or (3) or 78(2) shall also be enforceable by civil proceedings brought by the OFT or the Commission for an injunction or for interdict or for any other appropriate relief or remedy.

(5) Compliance with paragraph 7(2) or (3) or 8(2) of Schedule 7 shall also be enforceable by civil proceedings brought by the OFT or the Secretary of State for an injunction or for interdict or for any other appropriate relief or remedy.

(6) Subsections (4) and (5) shall not prejudice any right that a person may have by virtue of subsection (2) to bring civil proceedings for contravention or apprehended contravention of section 77(2) or (3) or 78(2) or paragraph 7(2) or (3) or 8(2) of Schedule 7.

Chapter 5 Supplementary

Merger notices

96 Merger notices

(1) A person authorised to do so by regulations under section 101 may give notice to the OFT of proposed arrangements which might result in the creation of a relevant merger situation.

(2) Any such notice (in this Part a 'merger notice')—

(a) shall be in the prescribed form; and

(b) shall state that the existence of the proposal has been made public.

(3) No reference shall be made under section 22, 33 or 45 in relation to—

(a) arrangements of which notice is given under subsection (1) above or arrangements which do not differ from them in any material respect; or

(b) the creation of any relevant merger situation which is, or may be, created in consequence of carrying such arrangements into effect;

if the period for considering the merger notice has expired without a reference being made under that section in relation to those arrangements.

(4) Subsection (3) is subject to section 100.

(5) In this section and section 99(5)(c) and 100(1)(c) 'prescribed' means prescribed by the OFT by notice having effect for the time being and published in the London, Edinburgh and Belfast Gazettes.

(6) In this Part 'notified arrangements' means arrangements of which notice is given under subsection (1) above or arrangements not differing from them in any material respect.

97 Period for considering merger notices

(1) The period for considering a merger notice is, subject as follows, the period of 20 days beginning with the first day after—

(a) the notice has been received by the OFT; and

(b) any fee payable by virtue of section 118 to the OFT in respect of the notice has been paid.

(2) Where no intervention notice is in force in relation to the matter concerned, the OFT may by notice to the person who gave the merger notice extend by a further 10 days the period for considering the merger notice.

(3) Where an intervention notice is in force in relation to the matter concerned and there has been no extension under subsection (2), the OFT may by notice to the person who gave the merger notice extend by a further 20 days the period for considering the merger notice.

(4) Where an intervention notice is in force in relation to the matter concerned and there has been an extension under subsection (2), the OFT may by notice to the person who gave the merger notice extend the period for considering the merger notice by a further number of days which, including any extension already made under subsection (2), does not exceed 20 days.

(5) The OFT may by notice to the person who gave the merger notice extend the period for considering a merger notice if the OFT considers that the person has failed to provide, within the period stated in a notice under section 99(2) and in the authorised or required manner, information requested of him in that notice.

(6) An extension under subsection (5) shall be for the period until the person concerned provides the information to the satisfaction of the OFT or, if earlier, the cancellation by the OFT of the extension.

(7) The OFT may by notice to the person who gave the merger notice extend the period for considering a merger notice if the OFT is seeking undertakings under section 73 or (as the case may be) the Secretary of State is seeking undertakings under paragraph 3 of Schedule 7.

(8) An extension under subsection (7) shall be for the period beginning with the receipt of the notice under that subsection and ending with the earliest of the following events—

> (a) the giving of the undertakings concerned;
> (b) the expiry of the period of 10 days beginning with the first day after the receipt by the OFT of a notice from the person from whom the undertakings are being sought stating that he does not intend to give the undertakings; or
> (c) the cancellation by the OFT of the extension.

(9) The Secretary of State may by notice to the person who gave the merger notice extend the period for considering a merger notice if, by virtue of paragraph 3(6) of Schedule 7, he decides to delay a decision as to whether to make a reference under section 45.

(10) An extension under subsection (9) shall be for the period of the delay.

(11) The OFT may by notice to the person who gave the merger notice extend the period for considering a merger notice if the European Commission is considering a request made, in relation to the matter concerned, by the United Kingdom (whether alone or with others) under article 22(1) of the EC Merger Regulation or is proceeding with the matter in pursuance of such a request.

(12) An extension under subsection (11) shall be for the period beginning with the receipt of the notice under that subsection and ending with the receipt of a notice under subsection (13).

(13) The OFT shall, in connection with any notice given by it under subsection (11), by notice inform the person who gave the merger notice of the completion by the European Commission of its consideration of the request of the United Kingdom and of any proceedings undertaken by it in pursuance of that request.

98   Section 97: supplementary

(1) A notice under section 97(2), (3), (4), (5), (7), (9) or (11) shall be given, before the end of the period for considering the merger notice, to the person who gave the merger notice.

(2) A notice under section 97(5)—

> (a) shall also be given within 5 days of the end of the period within which the information is to be provided and which is stated in the notice under section 99(2); and
> (b) shall also inform the person who gave the merger notice of—
>> (i)   the OFT's opinion as mentioned in section 97(5); and
>> (ii) the OFT's intention to extend the period for considering a merger notice.

(3) In determining for the purposes of section 97(1), (2), (3), (4) or (8)(b) or subsection (2)(a) above any period which is expressed in the enactment concerned as a period of days or number of days no account shall be taken of—

> (a) Saturday, Sunday, Good Friday and Christmas Day; and
> (b) any day which is a bank holiday in England and Wales.

(4) Any reference in this Part (apart from in section 97(1) and section 99(1)) to the period for considering a merger notice shall, if that period is extended by virtue of any one or more of subsections (2), (3), (4) (5), (7), (9) and (11) of section 97 in relation to a particular case, be construed in relation to that case as a reference to that period as so extended; but only one extension is possible under section 97(2), (3) or (4).

(5) Where the period for considering a merger notice is extended or further extended by virtue of section 97, the period as extended or (as the case may be) further extended shall, subject to subsections (6) and (7), be calculated by taking the period being extended and adding to it the period of the extension (whether or not those periods overlap in time).

(6) Subsection (7) applies where—

> (a) the period for considering a merger notice is further extended;

(b) the further extension and at least one previous extension is made under one or more of subsections (5), (7), (9) and (11) of section 97; and

(c) the same days or fractions of days are included in or comprise the further extension and are included in or comprise at least one such previous extension.

(7) In calculating the period of the further extension, any days or fractions of days of the kind mentioned in subsection (6)(c) shall be disregarded.

99　Certain functions of OFT and Secretary of State in relation to merger notices

(1) The OFT shall, so far as practicable and when the period for considering any merger notice begins, take such action as the OFT considers appropriate to bring—

(a) the existence of the proposal;

(b) the fact that the merger notice has been given; and

(c) the date on which the period for considering the notice may expire; to the attention of those whom the OFT considers would be affected if the arrangements were carried into effect.

(2) The OFT may by notice to the person who gave the merger notice request him to provide the OFT with such information as the OFT or (as the case may be) the Secretary of State may require for the purpose of carrying out its or (as the case may be) his functions in relation to the merger notice.

(3) A notice under subsection (2) shall state—

(a) the information required;

(b) the period within which the information is to be provided; and

(c) the possible consequences of not providing the information within the stated period and in the authorised or required manner.

(4) A notice by the OFT under subsection (2) shall be given, before the end of the period for considering the merger notice, to the person who gave the merger notice.

(5) The OFT may, at any time before the end of the period for considering any merger notice, reject the notice if—

(a) the OFT suspects that any information given in respect of the notified arrangements (whether in the merger notice or otherwise) by the person who gave the notice or any connected person is in any material respect false or misleading;

(b) the OFT suspects that it is not proposed to carry the notified arrangements into effect;

(c) any prescribed information is not given in the merger notice or any information requested by notice under subsection (2) is not provided as required; or

(d) the OFT considers that the notified arrangements are, or if carried into effect would result in, a concentration with a Community dimension within the meaning of the EC Merger Regulation.

(6) In this section and section 100 'connected person', in relation to the person who gave a merger notice, means—

(a) any person who, for the purposes of section 127, is associated with him; or

(b) any subsidiary of the person who gave the merger notice or of any person so associated with him.

100　Exceptions to protection given by merger notices

(1) Section 96(3) does not prevent any reference being made to the Commission if—

(a) before the end of the period for considering the merger notice, the OFT rejects the notice under section 99(5);

(b) before the end of that period, any of the enterprises to which the notified arrangements relate cease to be distinct from each other;

(c) any information (whether prescribed information or not) that—

(i) is, or ought to be, known to the person who gave the merger notice or any connected person; and

(ii) is material to the notified arrangements;

is not disclosed to the OFT by such time before the end of that period as may be specified in regulations under section 101;

    (d) at any time after the merger notice is given but before the enterprises to which the notified arrangements relate cease to be distinct from each other, any of those enterprises ceases to be distinct from any enterprise other than an enterprise to which those arrangements relate;

    (e) the six months beginning with the end of the period for considering the merger notice expires without the enterprises to which the notified arrangements relate ceasing to be distinct from each other;

    (f) the merger notice is withdrawn; or

    (g) any information given in respect of the notified arrangements (whether in the merger notice or otherwise) by the person who gave the notice or any connected person is in any material respect false or misleading.

  (2) Subsection (3) applies where—

    (a) two or more transactions which have occurred, or, if any arrangements are carried into effect, will occur, may be treated for the purposes of a reference under section 22, 33 or 45 as having occurred simultaneously on a particular date; and

    (b) section 96(3) does not prevent such a reference in relation to the last of those transactions.

  (3) Section 96(3) does not prevent such a reference in relation to any of those transactions which actually occurred less than six months before—

    (a) that date; or

    (b) the actual occurrence of another of those transactions in relation to which such a reference may be made (whether or not by virtue of this subsection).

  (4) In determining for the purposes of subsections (2) and (3) the time at which any transaction actually occurred, no account shall be taken of any option or other conditional right until the option is exercised or the condition is satisfied.

  (5) In this section references to the enterprises to which the notified arrangements relate are references to those enterprises that would have ceased to be distinct from one another if the arrangements mentioned in the merger notice concerned had been carried into effect at the time when the notice was given.

101   Merger notices: regulations

  (1) The Secretary of State may make regulations for the purposes of sections 96 to 100.

  (2) The regulations may, in particular—

    (a) provide for section 97(1), (2), (3) or (4) or section 100(1)(e) to apply as if any reference to a period of days or months were a reference to a period specified in the regulations for the purposes of the enactment concerned;

    (b) provide for the manner in which any merger notice is authorised or required to be rejected or withdrawn, and the time at which any merger notice is to be treated as received or rejected;

    (c) provide for the time at which any notice under section 97(7), (8)(b), (11) or (13) is to be treated as received;

    (d) provide for the manner in which any information requested by the OFT or any other material information is authorised or required to be provided or disclosed, and the time at which such information is to be treated as provided or disclosed (including the time at which it is to be treated as provided to the satisfaction of the OFT for the purposes of section 97(6));

    (e) provide for the person who gave the merger notice to be informed, in circumstances in which section 97(6) applies—

      (i) of the fact that the OFT is satisfied as to the provision of the information requested by the OFT or (as the case may be) of the OFT's decision to cancel the extension; and

    (ii) of the time at which the OFT is to be treated as so satisfied or (as the case may be) of the time at which the cancellation is to be treated as having effect;

  (f) provide for the person who gave the merger notice to be informed, in circumstances in which section 97(8) applies—

    (i) of any decision by the OFT to cancel the extension; and

    (ii) of the time at which such a cancellation is to be treated as having effect;

  (g) provide for the time at which any fee is to be treated as paid;

  (h) provide that a person is, or is not, to be treated, in such circumstances as may be specified in the regulations, as acting on behalf of a person authorised by regulations under this section to give a merger notice or a person who has given such a notice.

102   Power to modify sections 97 to 101

The Secretary of State may, for the purposes of determining the effect of giving a merger notice and the action which may be or is to be taken by any person in connection with such a notice, by order modify sections 97 to 101.

General duties in relation to references

103   Duty of expedition in relation to references

(1) In deciding whether to make a reference under section 22 or 33 the OFT shall have regard, with a view to the prevention or removal of uncertainty, to the need for making a decision as soon as reasonably practicable.

(2) In deciding whether to make a reference under section 45 or 62 the Secretary of State shall have regard, with a view to the prevention or removal of uncertainty, to the need for making a decision as soon as reasonably practicable.

104   Certain duties of relevant authorities to consult

(1) Subsection (2) applies where the relevant authority is proposing to make a relevant decision in a way which the relevant authority considers is likely to be adverse to the interests of a relevant party.

(2) The relevant authority shall, so far as practicable, consult that party about what is proposed before making that decision.

(3) In consulting the party concerned, the relevant authority shall, so far as practicable, give the reasons of the relevant authority for the proposed decision.

(4) In considering what is practicable for the purposes of this section the relevant authority shall, in particular, have regard to—

  (a) any restrictions imposed by any timetable for making the decision; and

  (b) any need to keep what is proposed, or the reasons for it, confidential.

(5) The duty under this section shall not apply in relation to the making of any decision so far as particular provision is made elsewhere by virtue of this Part for consultation before the making of that decision.

(6) In this section—

'the relevant authority' means the OFT, the Commission or the Secretary of State;

'relevant decision' means—

  (a) in the case of the OFT, any decision by the OFT—

    (i) as to whether to make a reference under section 22 or 33 or accept undertakings under section 73 instead of making such a reference; or

    (ii) to vary under section 37 such a reference;

  (b) in the case of the Commission, any decision on the questions mentioned in section 35(1) or (3), 36(1) or (2), 47 or 63; and

  (c) in the case of the Secretary of State, any decision by the Secretary of State—

    (i) as to whether to make a reference under section 45 or 62; or

    (ii) to vary under section 49 or (as the case may be) 64 such a reference; and 'relevant party' means any person who appears to the relevant authority to control enterprises which are the subject of the reference or possible reference concerned.

104A   Public consultation in relation to media mergers

(1) Subsection (2) applies where the Commission—

    (a) is preparing—

        (i) a report under section 50 on a reference which specifies a media public interest consideration; or

        (ii) a report under section 65 on a reference which specifies a consideration specified in section 58(2A) to (2C); and

    (b) is not under a duty to disregard the consideration concerned.

(2) The Commission shall have regard (among other things) to the need to consult the public so far as they might be affected by the creation of the relevant merger situation or special merger situation concerned and so far as such consultation is practicable.

(3) Any consultation of the kind mentioned in subsection (2) may be undertaken by the Commission by consulting such representative sample of the public or section of the public concerned as the Commission considers appropriate.

Information and publicity requirements

105   General information duties of OFT and Commission

(1) Where the OFT decides to investigate a matter so as to enable it to decide whether to make a reference under section 22 or 33, or so as to make a report under section 44 or 61, it shall, so far as practicable, take such action as it considers appropriate to bring information about the investigation to the attention of those whom it considers might be affected by the creation of the relevant merger situation concerned or (as the case may be) the special merger situation concerned.

(1A) Where OFCOM decide to investigate a matter so as to make a report under section 44A or 61A, they shall, so far as practicable, take such action as they consider appropriate to bring information about the investigation to the attention of those who they consider might be affected by the creation of the relevant merger situation concerned or (as the case may be) the special merger situation concerned.

(2) Subsections 1 and 1A do not apply in relation to arrangements which might result in the creation of a relevant merger situation if a merger notice has been given in relation to those arrangements under section 96.

(3) The OFT shall give the Commission or OFCOM—

    (a) such information in its possession as the Commission or (as the case may be) OFCOM may reasonably require to enable the Commission or (as the case may be) OFCOM to carry out its functions under this Part; and

    (b) any other assistance which the Commission or (as the case may be) OFCOM may reasonably require for the purpose of assisting it in carrying out its functions under this Part and which it is within the power of the OFT to give.

(3A) OFCOM shall give the Commission or the OFT—

    (a) such information in their possession as the Commission or (as the case may be) the OFT may reasonably require to enable the Commission or (as the case may be) the OFT to carry out its functions under this Part; and

    (b) any other assistance which the Commission or (as the case may be) the OFT may reasonably require for the purpose of assisting it in carrying out its functions under this Part and which it is within the power of OFCOM to give.

(4) The OFT shall give the Commission or OFCOM any information in its possession which has not been requested by the Commission or (as the case may be) OFCOM but which, in the opinion of the OFT, would be appropriate to give to the Commission or (as the case may be) OFCOM for the purpose of assisting it in carrying out its functions under this Part.

(4A) OFCOM shall give the Commission or the OFT any information in their possession which has not been requested by the Commission or (as the case may be) the OFT but which, in the opinion of OFCOM, would be appropriate to give to the Commission or (as the case may be) the OFT for the purpose of assisting it in carrying out its functions under this Part.

(5) The OFT, OFCOM and the Commission shall give the Secretary of State—

    (a) such information in their possession as the Secretary of State may by direction reasonably require to enable him to carry out his functions under this Part; and

    (b) any other assistance which the Secretary of State may by direction reasonably require for the purpose of assisting him in carrying out his functions under this Part and which it is within the power of the OFT, OFCOM or (as the case may be) the Commission to give.

(6) The OFT and OFCOM shall give the Secretary of State any information in their possession which has not been requested by the Secretary of State but which, in the opinion of the OFT or (as the case may be) OFCOM, would be appropriate to give to the Secretary of State for the purpose of assisting him in carrying out his functions under this Part.

(7) The Commission shall have regard to any information given to it under subsection (3), and the Secretary of State shall have regard to any information given to him under subsection, (3A), (4) or (4A) (5) or (6).

(7A) OFCOM shall have regard to any information given to them under subsection (3) or (4); and the OFT shall have regard to any information given to it under subsection (3A) or (4A).

(8) Any direction given under subsection (5)—

    (a) shall be in writing; and

    (b) may be varied or revoked by a subsequent direction.

106   Advice and information about references under sections 22 and 33

(1) As soon as reasonably practicable after the passing of this Act, the OFT shall prepare and publish general advice and information about the making of references by it under section 22 or 33.

(2) The OFT may at any time publish revised, or new, advice or information.

(3) As soon as reasonably practicable after the passing of this Act, the Commission shall prepare and publish general advice and information about the consideration by it of references under section 22 or 33 and the way in which relevant customer benefits may affect the taking of enforcement action in relation to such references.

(4) The Commission may at any time publish revised, or new, advice or information.

(5) Advice and information published under this section shall be prepared with a view to—

    (a) explaining relevant provisions of this Part to persons who are likely to be affected by them; and

    (b) indicating how the OFT or (as the case may be) the Commission expects such provisions to operate.

(6) Advice (or information) published by virtue of subsection (1) or (3) may include advice (or information) about the factors which the OFT or (as the case may be) the Commission may take into account in considering whether, and if so how, to exercise a function conferred by this Part.

(7) Any advice or information published by the OFT or the Commission under this section shall be published in such manner as the OFT or (as the case may be) the Commission considers appropriate.

(8) In preparing any advice or information under this section, the OFT shall consult the Commission and such other persons as it considers appropriate.

(9) In preparing any advice or information under this section, the Commission shall consult the OFT and such other persons as it considers appropriate.

106A   Advice and information in relation to media mergers

(1) The Secretary of State may prepare and publish general advice and information about the considerations specified in section 58(2A) to (2C).

(2) The Secretary of State may at any time publish revised, or new, advice or information.

(3) Advice or information published under this section shall be prepared with a view to—

    (a) explaining the considerations specified in section 58(2A) to (2C) to persons who are likely to be affected by them; and

(b) indicating how the Secretary of State expects this Part to operate in relation to such considerations.

(4) Any advice or information published by the Secretary of State under this section shall be published in such manner as the Secretary of State considers appropriate.

(5) In preparing any advice or information under this section, the Secretary of State shall consult the OFT, OFCOM, the Commission and such other persons as he considers appropriate.

106B   General advisory functions of OFCOM

(1) OFCOM may, in connection with any case on which they are required to give a report by virtue of section 44A or 61A, give such advice as they consider appropriate to the Secretary of State in relation to—

(a) any report made in such a case by the Commission under section 50 or 65; and

(b) the taking by the Secretary of State of enforcement action under Schedule 7.

(2) OFCOM may, if requested to do so by the Secretary of State, give such other advice as they consider appropriate to the Secretary of State in connection with any case on which they are required to give a report by virtue of section 44A or 61A.

(3) OFCOM shall publish any advice given by them under this section but advice given by them in relation to a report of the Commission under section 50 or 65 or related enforcement action shall not be published before the report itself is published.

107   Further publicity requirements

(1) The OFT shall publish—

(a) any reference made by it under section 22 or 33 or any decision made by it not to make such a reference;

(b) any variation made by it under section 37 of a reference under section 22 or 33;

(c) such information as it considers appropriate about any decision made by it under section 57(1) to bring a case to the attention of the Secretary of State;

(d) any enforcement undertaking accepted by it under section 71;

(e) any enforcement order made by it under section 72 or 76 or paragraph 2 of Schedule 7;

(f) any variation, release or revocation of such an undertaking or order;

(g) any decision made by it as mentioned in section 76(6)(b); and

(h) any decision made by it to dispense with the requirements of Schedule 10.

(2) The Commission shall publish—

(a) any cancellation by it under section 37(1) of a reference under section 33;

(b) any decision made by it under section 37(2) to treat a reference made under section 22 or 33 as if it had been made under section 32 or (as the case may be) 22;

(c) any extension by it under section 39 of the period within which a report under section 38 is to be prepared and published;

(d) any decision made by it to cancel an extension as mentioned in section 39(8)(b);

(e) any decision made by it under section 41(2) neither to accept an undertaking under section 82 nor to make an order under section 84;

(f) any decision made by it that there has been a material change of circumstances as mentioned in subsection (3) of section 41 or there is another special reason as mentioned in that subsection of that section;

(g) any cancellation by it under section 48(1) or 53(1) of a reference under section 45 or any cancellation by it under section 64(1) of a reference under section 62;

(h) any decision made by it under section 49(1) to treat—

(i) a reference made under subsection (2) or (3) of section 45 as if it had been made under subsection (4) or (as the case may be) (5) of that section; or

(ii) a reference made under subsection (4) or (5) of section 45 as if it had been made under subsection (2) or (as the case may be) (3) of that section;

(i) any extension by it under section 51 of the period within which a report under section 50 is to be prepared and published;

(j) any decision made by it under section 51(8)(b) to cancel such an extension;

(k) any extension by it under section 51 as applied by section 65 (3) of the period within which a report under section 65 is to be prepared and published;

(l) any decision made by it under section 51(8)(b) as applied by section 65(3) to cancel such an extension;

(m) any decision made by it under section 64(2) to treat a reference made under subsection (2) or (3) of section 62 as if it had been made under subsection (3) or (as the case may be) (2) of that section;

(n) any decision made by it as mentioned in section 76(6)(b);

(o) any enforcement order made by it under section 76 or 81;

(p) any enforcement undertaking accepted by it under section 80;

(q) any variation, release or revocation of such an order or undertaking; and

(r) any decision made by it to dispense with the requirements of Schedule 10.

(3) The Secretary of State shall publish—

(a) any intervention notice or special intervention notice given by him;

(b) any report of the OFT under section 44 or 61 which has been received by him;

(ba) any report of OFCOM under section 44A or 61A which has been received by him;

(c) any reference made by him under section 45 or 62 or any decision made by him not to make such a reference;

(d) any variation made by him under section 49 of a reference under section 45 or under section 64 of a reference under section 62;

(e) any report of the Commission under section 50 or 65 which has been received by him;

(f) any decision made by him neither to accept an undertaking under paragraph 9 of Schedule 7 nor to make an order under paragraph 11 of that Schedule;

(g) any notice given by him under section 56(1);

(h) any enforcement undertaking accepted by him under paragraph 1 of Schedule 7;

(i) any variation or release of such an undertaking;

(j) any decision made by him as mentioned in paragraph 6(6)(b) of Schedule 7; and

(k) any decision made by him to dispense with the requirements of Schedule 10.

(4) Where any person is under a duty by virtue of subsection (1), (2) or (3) to publish the result of any action taken by that person or any decision made by that person, the person concerned shall, subject to subsections (5) and (6), also publish that person's reasons for the action concerned or (as the case may be) the decision concerned.

(5) Such reasons need not, if it is not reasonably practicable to do so, be published at the same time as the result of the action concerned or (as the case may be) as the decision concerned.

(6) Subsections (4) and (5) shall not apply in relation to any information published under subsection (1)(c).

(7) The Secretary of State shall publish his reasons for—

(a) any decision made by him under section 54(2) or 66(2); or

(b) any decision to make an order under section 58(3) or vary or revoke such an order.

(8) Such reasons may be published after—

(a) in the case of subsection (7)(a), the publication of the decision concerned; and

(b) in the case of subsection (7)(b), the making of the order or of the variation or revocation; if it is not reasonably practicable to publish them at the same time as the publication of the decision or (as the case may be) the making of the order or variation or revocation.

(9) The Secretary of State shall publish—

(a) the report of the OFT under section 44, and any report of OFCOM under section 61A in relation to a matter no later than publication of his decision as to whether to make a reference under section 45 in relation to that matter; and

(b) the report of the Commission under section 50 in relation to a matter no later than publication of his decision under section 54(2) in relation to that matter.

(10) The Secretary of State shall publish—

    (a) the report of the OFT under section 61, and any report of OFCOM under section 61A in relation to a matter no later than publication of his decision as to whether to make a reference under section 62 in relation to that matter; and

    (b) the report of the Commission under section 65 in relation to a matter no later than publication of his decision under section 66(2) in relation to that matter.

(11) Where the Secretary of State has decided under section 55(2) or 66(6) to accept an undertaking under paragraph 9 of Schedule 7 or to make an order under paragraph 11 of that Schedule, he shall lay details of his decision and his reasons for it, and the Commission's report under section 50 or (as the case may be) 65, before each House of Parliament.

108 Defamation

For the purposes of the law relating to defamation, absolute privilege attaches to any advice, guidance, notice or direction given, or decision or report made, by the OFT, OFCOM, the Commission or the Secretary of State in the exercise of any of their functions under this Part.

Investigation powers

109 Attendance of witnesses and production of documents etc.

(1) The Commission may, for the purpose of any investigation on a reference made to it under this Part, give notice to any person requiring him—

    (a) to attend at a time and place specified in the notice; and

    (b) to give evidence to the Commission or a person nominated by the Commission for the purpose.

(2) The Commission may, for the purpose of any investigation on a reference made to it under this Part, give notice to any person requiring him—

    (a) to produce any documents which—

        (i) are specified or described in the notice, or fall within a category of document which is specified or described in the notice; and

        (ii) are in that person's custody or under his control; and

    (b) to produce them at a time and place so specified and to a person so specified.

(3) The Commission may, for the purpose of any investigation on a reference made to it under this Part, give notice to any person who carries on any business requiring him—

    (a) to supply to the Commission such estimates, forecasts, returns or other information as may be specified or described in the notice; and

    (b) to supply it at a time and place, and in a form and manner, so specified and to a person so specified.

(4) A notice under this section shall include information about the possible consequences of not complying with the notice.

(5) The Commission or any person nominated by it for the purpose may, for the purpose of any investigation on a reference made to it under this Part, take evidence on oath, and for that purpose may administer oaths.

(6) The person to whom any document is produced in accordance with a notice under this section may, for the purpose of any investigation on a reference made to it under this Part, copy the document so produced.

(7) No person shall be required under this section—

    (a) to give any evidence or produce any documents which he could not be compelled to give or produce in civil proceedings before the court; or

    (b) to supply any information which he could not be compelled to supply in evidence in such proceedings.

(8) No person shall be required, in compliance with a notice under this section, to go more than 10 miles from his place of residence unless his necessary travelling expenses are paid or offered to him.

(9) Any reference in this section to the production of a document includes a reference to the production of a legible and intelligible copy of information recorded otherwise than in legible form.

(10) In this section 'the court' means—

    (a) in relation to England and Wales or Northern Ireland, the High Court; and

    (b) in relation to Scotland, the Court of Session.

110 Enforcement of powers under section 109: general

(1) Where the Commission considers that a person has, without reasonable excuse, failed to comply with any requirement of a notice under section 109, it may impose a penalty in accordance with section 111.

(2) The Commission may proceed (whether at the same time or at different times) under subsection (1) and section 39(4) or (as the case may be) 51(4) (including that enactment as applied by section 65(3)) in relation to the same failure.

(3) Where the Commission considers that a person has intentionally obstructed or delayed another person in the exercise of his powers under section 109(6), it may impose a penalty in accordance with section 111.

(4) No penalty shall be imposed by virtue of subsection (1) or (3) if more than 4 weeks have passed since the publication of the report of the Commission on the reference concerned; but this subsection shall not apply in relation to any variation or substitution of the penalty which is permitted by virtue of this Part.

(5) A person, subject to subsection (6), commits an offence if he intentionally alters, suppresses or destroys any document which he has been required to produce by a notice under section 106.

(6) A person does not commit an offence under subsection (5) in relation to any act which constitutes a failure to comply with a notice under section 109 if the Commission has proceeded against that person under subsection (1) above in relation to that failure.

(7) A person who commits an offence under subsection (5) shall be liable—

    (a) on summary conviction, to a fine not exceeding the statutory maximum;

    (b) on conviction on indictment, to imprisonment for a term not exceeding two years or to a fine or to both.

(8) The Commission shall not proceed against a person under subsection (1) in relation to an act which constitutes an offence under subsection (5) if that person has been found guilty of that offence.

(9) In deciding whether and, if so, how to proceed under subsection (1) or (3) or section 39(4) or 51(4) (including that enactment as applied by section 65(3)), the Commission shall have regard to the statement of policy which was most recently published under section 116 at the time when the failure concerned or (as the case may be) the obstruction or delay concerned occurred.

(10) The reference in this section to the production of a document includes a reference to the production of a legible and intelligible copy of information recorded otherwise than in legible form; and the reference to suppressing a document includes a reference to destroying the means of reproducing information recorded otherwise than in legible form.

111 Penalties

(1) A penalty imposed under section 110(1) or (3) shall be of such amount as the Commission considers appropriate.

(2) The amount may, in the case of a penalty imposed under section 110(1), be a fixed amount, an amount calculated by reference to a daily rate or a combination of a fixed amount and an amount calculated by reference to a daily rate.

(3) The amount shall, in the case of a penalty imposed under section 110(3), be a fixed amount.

(4) No penalty imposed under section 110(1) shall—

    (a) in the case of a fixed amount, exceed such amount as the Secretary of State may by order specify;

(b) in the case of an amount calculated by reference to a daily rate, exceed such amount per day as the Secretary of State may so specify; and

(c) in the case of a fixed amount and an amount calculated by reference to a daily rate, exceed such fixed amount and such amount per day as the Secretary of State may so specify.

(5) In imposing a penalty by reference to a daily rate—

(a) no account shall be taken of any days before the service of the notice under section 112 on the person concerned; and

(b) unless the Commission determines an earlier date (whether before or after the penalty is imposed), the amount payable shall cease to accumulate at the beginning of—

(i) the day on which the requirement of the notice concerned under section 109 is satisfied or (as the case may be) the obstruction or delay is removed; or

(ii) if earlier, the day on which the report of the Commission on the reference concerned is published (or, in the case of a report under section 50 or 65, given) or, if no such report is published (or given) within the period permitted for that purpose by this Part, the latest day on which the report may be published (or given) within the permitted period.

(6) No penalty imposed under section 110(3) shall exceed such amount as the Secretary of State may by order specify.

(7) An order under subsection (4) or (6) shall not specify—

(a) in the case of a fixed amount, an amount exceeding £30,000;

(b) in the case of an amount calculated by reference to a daily rate, an amount per day exceeding £15,000; and

(c) in the case of a fixed amount and an amount calculated by reference to a daily rate, a fixed amount exceeding £30,000 and an amount per day exceeding £15,000.

(8) Before making an order under subsection (4) or (6) the Secretary of State shall consult the Commission and such other persons as he considers appropriate.

112   Penalties: main procedural requirements

(1) As soon as practicable after imposing a penalty under section 110(1) or (3), the Commission shall give notice of the penalty.

(2) The notice shall state—

(a) that the Commission has imposed a penalty on the person concerned;

(b) whether the penalty is of a fixed amount, of an amount calculated by reference to a daily rate or of both a fixed amount and an amount calculated by reference to a daily rate;

(c) the amount or amounts concerned and, in the case of an amount calculated by reference to a daily rate, the day on which the amount first starts to accumulate and the day or days on which it might cease to accumulate;

(d) the failure or (as the case may be) the obstruction or delay which the Commission considers gave it the power to impose the penalty;

(e) any other facts which the Commission considers justify the imposition of a penalty and the amount or amounts of the penalty;

(f) the manner in which, and place at which, the penalty is required to be paid to the Commission;

(g) the date or dates, no earlier than the end of the relevant period beginning with the date of service of the notice on the person concerned, by which the penalty or (as the case may be) different portions of it are required to be paid;

(h) that the penalty or (as the case may be) different portions of it may be paid earlier than the date or dates by which it or they are required to be paid; and

(i) that the person concerned has the right to apply under subsection (3) below or to appeal under section 114 and the main details of those rights.

(3) The person against whom the penalty was imposed may, within 14 days of the date of service on him of a notice under subsection (1), apply to the Commission for it to specify a different date or

(as the case may be) different dates by which the penalty or (as the case may be) different portions of it are to be paid.

(4) A notice under this section shall be given by—

(a) serving a copy of the notice on the person on whom the penalty was imposed; and

(b) publishing the notice.

(5) In this section 'relevant period' means the period of 28 days mentioned in subsection (3) of section 114 or, if another period is specified by the Secretary of State under that subsection, that period.

113 Payments and interest by instalments

(1) If the whole or any portion of a penalty is not paid by the date by which it is required to be paid, the unpaid balance from time to time shall carry interest at the rate for the time being specified in section 17 of the Judgments Act 1838 (c. 110).

(2) Where an application has been made under section 112(3), the penalty shall not be required to be paid until the application has been determined, withdrawn or otherwise dealt with.

(3) If a portion of a penalty has not been paid by the date required for it, the Commission may, where it considers it appropriate to do so, require so much of the penalty as has not already been paid (and is capable of being paid immediately) to be paid immediately.

(4) Any sums received by the Commission in or towards the payment of a penalty, or interest on a penalty, shall be paid into the Consolidated Fund.

114 Appeals in relation to penalties

(1) This section applies if a person on whom a penalty is imposed under section 110(1) or (3) is aggrieved by—

(a) the imposition or nature of the penalty;

(b) the amount or amounts of the penalty; or

(c) the date by which the penalty is required to be paid or (as the case may be) the different dates by which portions of the penalty are required to be paid.

(2) The person aggrieved may apply to the Competition Appeal Tribunal.

(3) If a copy of the notice under section 112(1) was served on the person on whom the penalty was imposed, the application to the Competition Appeal Tribunal shall, subject to subsection (4), be made within—

(a) the period of 28 days starting with the day on which the copy was served on the person concerned; or

(b) such other period as the Secretary of State may by order specify.

(4) If the application relates to a decision of the Commission on an application by the person on whom the penalty was imposed under section 112(3), the application to the Competition Appeal Tribunal shall be made within—

(a) the period of 28 days starting with the day on which the person concerned is notified of the decision; or

(b) such other period as the Secretary of State may by order specify.

(5) On an application under this section, the Competition Appeal Tribunal may—

(a) quash the penalty;

(b) substitute a penalty of a different nature or of such lesser amount or amounts as the Competition Appeal Tribunal considers appropriate; or

(c) in a case falling within subsection (1)(c), substitute for the date or dates imposed by the Commission an alternative date or dates;

if it considers it appropriate to do so.

(6) The Competition Appeal Tribunal shall not substitute a penalty of a different nature under subsection (5)(b) unless it considers that the person on whom the penalty is imposed will, or is likely to, pay less under the substituted penalty than he would have paid under the original penalty.

(7) Where an application has been made under this section—

> (a) the penalty shall not be required to be paid until the application has been determined, withdrawn or otherwise dealt with; and
>
> (b) the Commission may agree to reduce the amount or amounts of the penalty in settlement of the application.

(8) Where the Competition Appeal Tribunal substitutes a penalty of a different nature or of a lesser amount or amounts it may require the payment of interest on the substituted penalty at such rate or rates, and from such date or dates, as it considers appropriate.

(9) Where the Competition Appeal Tribunal specifies as a date by which the penalty, or a portion of the penalty, is to be paid a date before the determination of the application under this section it may require the payment of interest on the penalty, or portion, from that date at such rate as it considers appropriate.

(10) An appeal lies to the appropriate court—

> (a) on a point of law arising from a decision of the Tribunal in proceedings under this section; or
>
> (b) from a decision of the Tribunal in such proceedings as to the amount or amounts of a penalty.

(11) An appeal under subsection (10)—

> (a) may be brought by a party to the proceedings before the Tribunal; and
>
> (b) requires the permission of the Tribunal or the appropriate court.

(12) In this section 'the appropriate court' means the Court of Appeal or, in the case of Tribunal proceedings in Scotland, the Court of Session.

115   Recovery of penalties

Where a penalty imposed under section 110(1) or (3), or any portion of such a penalty, has not been paid by the date on which it is required to be paid and—

> (a) no application relating to the penalty has been made under section 114 during the period within which such an application may be made, or
>
> (b) any such application which has been made has been determined, withdrawn or otherwise dealt with, the Commission may recover from the person on whom the penalty was imposed any of the penalty and any interest which has not been paid; and in England and Wales and Northern Ireland such penalty and interest may be recovered as a civil debt due to the Commission.

116   Statement of policy

(1) The Commission shall prepare and publish a statement of policy in relation to the enforcement of notices under section 109.

(2) The statement shall, in particular, include a statement about the considerations relevant to the determination of the nature and amount of any penalty imposed under section 110(1) or (3).

(3) The Commission may revise its statement of policy and, where it does so, it shall publish the revised statement.

(4) The Commission shall consult such persons as it considers appropriate when preparing or revising its statement of policy.

117   False or misleading information

(1) A person commits an offence if—

> (a) he supplies any information to the OFT, OFCOM, the Commission or the Secretary of State in connection with any of their functions under this Part;
>
> (b) the information is false or misleading in a material respect; and
>
> (c) he knows that it is false or misleading in a material respect or is reckless as to whether it is false or misleading in a material respect.

(2) A person commits an offence if he—

> (a) supplies any information to another person which he knows to be false or misleading in a material respect; or

(b) recklessly supplies any information to another person which is false or misleading in a material respect;

knowing that the information is to be used for the purpose of supplying information to the OFT, OFCOM, the Commission or the Secretary of State in connection with any of their functions under this Part.

(3) A person who commits an offence under subsection (1) or (2) shall be liable—

    (a) on summary conviction, to a fine not exceeding the statutory maximum;

    (b) on conviction on indictment, to imprisonment for a term not exceeding two years or to a fine or to both.

Reports

118 Excisions from reports

(1) Subsection (2) applies where the Secretary of State is under a duty to publish—

    (a)   a report of the OFT under section 44 or 61;

    (aa) a report of OFCOM under section 44A or 61A; or

    (b)   a report of the Commission under section 50 or 65.

(2) The Secretary of State may exclude a matter from the report concerned if he considers that publication of the matter would be inappropriate.

(3) In deciding what is inappropriate for the purposes of subsection (2) the Secretary of State shall have regard to the considerations mentioned in section 244.

(4) The body which has prepared the report shall advise the Secretary of State as to the matters (if any) which it considers should be excluded by him under subsection (2).

(5) References in sections 38(4) and 107(11) to the giving or laying of a report of the Commission shall be construed as references to the giving or laying of the report as published.

119 Minority reports of Commission

(1) Subsection (2) applies where, on a reference to the Commission under this Part, a member of a group constituted in connection with the reference in pursuance of paragraph 15 of Schedule 7 to the Competition Act 1998 (c. 41), disagrees with any decisions contained in the report of the Commission under this Part as the decisions of the Commission.

(2) The report shall, if the member so wishes, include a statement of his disagreement and of his reasons for disagreeing.

Further provision about media mergers

119A Other general functions of OFCOM in relation to this Part

(1) OFCOM have the function of obtaining, compiling and keeping under review information about matters relating to the carrying out of their functions under this Part.

(2) That function is to be carried out with a view to (among other things) ensuring that OFCOM have sufficient information to take informed decisions and to carry out their other functions effectively.

(3) In carrying out that function OFCOM may carry out, commission or support (financially or otherwise) research.

(4) Section 3 of the Communications Act 2003 (general duties of OFCOM) shall not apply in relation to functions of OFCOM under this Part.

119B Monitoring role for OFT in relation to media mergers

(1) The OFT has the function of obtaining, compiling and keeping under review information about matters which may be relevant to the Secretary of State in deciding whether to give a special intervention notice mentioning a consideration specified in section 58(2A) to (2C).

(2) That function is to be carried out with a view to (among other things) ensuring that the Secretary of State is aware of cases where, in the opinion of the OFT, he might wish to consider giving such a notice.

(3) That function does not extend to obtaining, compiling or keeping under review information with a view to carrying out a detailed analysis in each case of the operation in relation to that case of the consideration specified in section 58(2A) to (2C).

Other

120 Review of decisions under Part 3

(1) Any person aggrieved by a decision of the OFT, OFCOM, the Secretary of State or the Commission under this Part in connection with a reference or possible reference in relation to a relevant merger situation or a special merger situation may apply to the Competition Appeal Tribunal for a review of that decision.

(2) For this purpose 'decision'—

(a) does not include a decision to impose a penalty under section 110(1) or (3); but

(b) includes a failure to take a decision permitted or required by this Part in connection with a reference or possible reference.

(3) Except in so far as a direction to the contrary is given by the Competition Appeal Tribunal, the effect of the decision is not suspended by reason of the making of the application.

(4) In determining such an application the Competition Appeal Tribunal shall apply the same principles as would be applied by a court on an application for judicial review.

(5) The Competition Appeal Tribunal may—

(a) dismiss the application or quash the whole or part of the decision to which it relates; and

(b) where it quashes the whole or part of that decision, refer the matter back to the original decision maker with a direction to reconsider and make a new decision in accordance with the ruling of the Competition Appeal Tribunal.

(6) An appeal lies on any point of law arising from a decision of the Competition Appeal Tribunal under this section to the appropriate court.

(7) An appeal under subsection (6) requires the permission of the Tribunal or the appropriate court.

(8) In this section—

'the appropriate court' means the Court of Appeal or, in the case of Tribunal proceedings in Scotland, the Court of Session; and

'Tribunal rules' has the meaning given by section 15(1).

121 Fees

(1) The Secretary of State may by order require the payment to him or the OFT of such fees as may be prescribed by the order in connection with the exercise by the Secretary of State, the OFT, OFCOM and the Commission of their functions under or by virtue of this Part and sections 32 to 34 of, and Schedule 4ZA to, the Water Industry Act 1991 (c. 56).

(2) An order under this section may, in particular, provide for fees to be payable—

(a) in respect of a merger notice; or

(b) [repealed]

(c) on the occurrence of any event specified in the order.

(3) The events that may be specified in an order under this section by virtue of subsection (2)(c) include, in particular—

(a) the decision by the OFT in relation to a possible reference under section 22 or 33 that it is or may be the case that a relevant merger situation has been created or (as the case may be) that arrangements are in progress or in contemplation which, if carried into effect, will result in the creation of a relevant merger situation;

(b) the decision by the Secretary of State in relation to a possible reference under section 45 that it is or may be the case that a relevant merger situation has been created or (as the case may be) that arrangements are in progress or in contemplation which, if carried into effect, will result in the creation of a relevant merger situation;

(c) the decision by the Secretary of State in relation to a possible reference under section 62 that—

    (i) it is or may be the case that a special merger situation has been created or (as the case may be) that arrangements are in progress or in contemplation which, if carried into effect, will result in the creation of a special merger situation; and

    (ii) one or more than one consideration mentioned in the intervention notice is relevant to a consideration of the special merger situation concerned; and

(d) the decision by the OFT in relation to a possible reference under section 32 of the Act of 1991 that it is or may be the case that arrangements are in progress which, if carried into effect, will result in a merger of any two or more water enterprises or that such a merger has taken place otherwise than as a result of the carrying into effect of arrangements that have been the subject of a reference by virtue of paragraph (a) of that section.

(4) An order under this section may, in particular, contain provision—

(a) for ascertaining the persons by whom fees are payable;

(b) specifying whether any fee is payable to the Secretary of State or the OFT;

(c) for the amount of any fee to be calculated by reference to matters which may include—

    (i) [repealed]

    (ii) the value of the turnover of the enterprises concerned;

(d) as to the time when any fee is to be paid; and

(e) for the repayment by the Secretary of State or the OFT of the whole or part of any fee in specified circumstances.

(5) For the purposes of subsection (4)(c)(ii) the turnover of an enterprise shall be determined in accordance with such provisions as may be specified in an order under this section.

(6) Provision made by virtue of subsection (5) may, in particular, include provision—

(a) as to the amounts which are, or which are not, to be treated as comprising an enterprise's turnover;

(b) as to the date or dates by reference to which an enterprise's turnover is to be determined;

(c) restricting the turnover to be taken into consideration to turnover which has a connection of a particular description with the United Kingdom.

(7) An order under this section may, in particular, in connection with provisions of the kind mentioned in subsection (5) make provision enabling the Secretary of State or the OFT to determine matters of a description specified in the order (including any of the matters mentioned in paragraphs (a) to (c) of subsection (6)).

(8) In determining the amount of any fees to be prescribed by an order under this section, the Secretary of State may take into account all costs incurred by him and by the OFT in respect of the exercise by him, the OFT, OFCOM and the Commission of their respective functions under or by virtue of this Part and sections 32 to 34 of, and Schedule 4ZA to, the Act of 1991.

(9) Fees paid to the Secretary of State or the OFT under this section shall be paid into the Consolidated Fund.

(10) [repealed]

122 Primacy of Community law

(1) Advice and information published by virtue of section 106(1) or (3) shall include such advice and information about the effect of Community law, and anything done under or in accordance with it, on the provisions of this Part as the OFT or (as the case may be) the Commission considers appropriate.

(2) Advice and information published by the OFT by virtue of section 106(1) shall, in particular, include advice and information about the circumstances in which the duties of the OFT under sections 22 and 33 do not apply as a result of the EC Merger Regulation or anything done under or in accordance with them.

(3) The duty or power to make a reference under section 22 or 45(2) or (3), and the power to give an intervention notice under section 42, shall apply in a case in which the relevant enterprises

ceased to be distinct enterprises at a time or in circumstances not falling within section 24 if the condition mentioned in subsection (4) is satisfied.

(4) The condition mentioned in this subsection is that, because of the EC Merger Regulation or anything done under or in accordance with them, the reference, or (as the case may be) the reference under section 22 to which the intervention notice relates, could not have been made earlier than 4 months before the date on which it is to be made.

(5) Where the duty or power to make a reference under section 22 or 45(2) or (3), or the power to give an intervention notice under section 42, applies as mentioned in subsection (3), references in this Part to the creation of a relevant merger situation shall be construed accordingly.

123   Power to alter share of supply test

(1) The Secretary of State may by order amend or replace the conditions which determine for the purposes of this Part whether a relevant merger situation has been created.

(2) The Secretary of State shall not exercise his power under subsection (1)—

   (a) to amend or replace the conditions mentioned in paragraphs (a) and (b) of subsection (1) of section 23;

   (b) to amend or replace the condition mentioned in paragraph (a) of subsection (2) of that section.

(3) In exercising his power under subsection (1) to amend or replace the condition mentioned in paragraph (b) of subsection (2) of section 23 or any condition which for the time being applies instead of it, the Secretary of State shall, in particular, have regard to the desirability of ensuring that any amended or new condition continues to operate by reference to the degree of commercial strength which results from the enterprises concerned having ceased to be distinct.

(4) Before making an order under this section the Secretary of State shall consult the OFT and the Commission.

(5) An order under this section may provide for the delegation of functions to the decision-making authority.

124   Orders and regulations under Part 3

(1) Any power of the Secretary of State to make an order or regulations under this Part shall be exercisable by statutory instrument.

(2) Any power of the Secretary of State to make an order or regulations under this Part—

   (a) may be exercised so as to make different provision for different cases or different purposes; and

   (b) includes power to make such incidental, supplementary, consequential, transitory, transitional or saving provision as the Secretary of State considers appropriate.

(3) The power of the Secretary of State under section 34, 59(6A) or 123 (including that power as extended by subsection (2) above) may be exercised by modifying any enactment comprised in or made under this Act, or any other enactment.

(4) The power of the Secretary of State under section 40(8), 44(11), 52(8) (including that enactment as applied by section 65(3)), 58(3), 68 or 102 as extended by subsection (2) above may be exercised by modifying any enactment comprised in or made under this Act, or any other enactment.

(5) An order made by the Secretary of State under section 28, (including that enactment as applied by section 42(5), 59(5) and 67(7), 40(8), 52(8) including that enactment as applied by section 65(3), 111(4) or (6), 114(3)(b) or (4)(b) or 121 or Schedule 7 shall be subject to annulment in pursuance of a resolution of either House of Parliament.

(6) No order shall be made by the Secretary of State under section 34, 44(11), 59(6A), 68, 102, 123 or 128(6) unless a draft of it has been laid before, and approved by a resolution of, each House of Parliament.

(7) An order made by the Secretary of State under section 58(3) shall be laid before Parliament after being made and shall cease to have effect unless approved, within the period of 28 days beginning with the day on which it is made, by a resolution of each House of Parliament.

(8) In calculating the period of 28 days mentioned in subsection (7), no account shall be taken of any time during which Parliament is dissolved or prorogued or during which both Houses are adjourned for more than four days.

(9) If an order made by the Secretary of State ceases to have effect by virtue of subsection (7), any modification made by it of an enactment is repealed (and the previous enactment revived) but without prejudice to the validity of anything done in connection with that modification before the order ceased to have effect and without prejudice to the making of a new order.

(10) If, apart from this subsection an order made by the Secretary of State under section 58 (3) would be treated for the purposes of the standing orders of either House of Parliament as a hybrid instrument, it shall proceed in that House as if it were not such an instrument.

125   Offences by bodies corporate

(1) Where an offence under this Part committed by a body corporate is proved to have been committed with the consent or connivance of, or to be attributable to any neglect on the part of—

    (a) a director, manager, secretary or other similar officer of the body corporate, or

    (b) a person purporting to act in such a capacity,

he as well as the body corporate commits the offence and shall be liable to be proceeded against and punished accordingly.

(2) Where the affairs of a body corporate are managed by its members, subsection (1) applies in relation to the acts and defaults of a member in connection with his functions of management as if he were a director of the body corporate.

(3) Where an offence under this Part is committed by a Scottish partnership and is proved to have been committed with the consent or connivance of a partner, or to be attributable to any neglect on the part of a partner, he as well as the partnership commits the offence and shall be liable to be proceeded against and punished accordingly.

(4) In subsection (3) 'partner' includes a person purporting to act as a partner.

126   Service of documents

(1) Any document required or authorised by virtue of this Part to be served on any person may be served—

    (a) by delivering it to him or by leaving it at his proper address or by sending it by post to him at that address;

    (b) if the person is a body corporate other than a limited liability partnership, by serving it in accordance with paragraph (a) on the secretary of the body;

    (c) if the person is a limited liability partnership, by serving it in accordance with paragraph (a) on a member of the partnership; or

    (d) if the person is a partnership, by serving it in accordance with paragraph (a) on a partner or a person having the control or management of the partnership business.

(2) For the purposes of this section and section 7 of the Interpretation Act 1978 (c. 30) (service of documents by post) in its application to this section, the proper address of any person on whom a document is to be served shall be his last known address, except that—

    (a) in the case of service on a body corporate (other than a limited liability partnership) or its secretary, it shall be the address of the registered or principal office of the body;

    (b) in the case of service on a limited liability partnership or a member of the partnership, it shall be the address of the registered or principal office of the partnership;

    (c) in the case of service on a partnership or a partner or a person having the control or management of a partnership business, it shall be the address of the principal office of the partnership.

(3) For the purposes of subsection (2) the principal office of a company constituted under the law of a country or territory outside the United Kingdom or of a partnership carrying on business outside the United Kingdom is its principal office within the United Kingdom.

(4) Subsection (5) applies if a person to be served under this Part with any document by another has specified to that other an address within the United Kingdom other than his proper address (as

determined under subsection (2)) as the one at which he or someone on his behalf will accept documents of the same description as that document.

(5) In relation to that document, that address shall be treated as his proper address for the purposes of this section and section 7 of the Interpretation Act 1978 in its application to this section, instead of that determined under subsection (2).

(6) Any notice in writing or other document required or authorised by virtue of this Part to be served on any person may be served on that person by transmitting the text of the notice or other document to him by means of an electronic communications network or by other means but while in electronic form provided the text is received by that person in legible form and is capable of being used for subsequent reference.

(7) This section does not apply to any document if rules of court make provision about its service.

(8) In this section references to serving include references to similar expressions (such as giving or sending).

127   Associated persons

(1) Associated persons, and any bodies corporate which they or any of them control, shall be treated as one person—

    (a) for the purpose of deciding under section 26 whether any two enterprises have been brought under common ownership or common control;

    (aa) for the purposes of section 58(2C); and

    (b) for the purpose of determining what activities are carried on by way of business by any one person so far as that question arises in connection with paragraph 13(2) of Schedule 8.

(2) Subsection (1) shall not exclude from section 26 any case which would otherwise fall within that section.

(3) A reference under section 22, 33, 45 or 62 (whether or not made by virtue of this section) may be framed so as to exclude from consideration, either altogether or for a specified purpose or to a specified extent, any matter which, apart from this section, would not have been taken into account on that reference.

(4) For the purposes of this section—

    (a) any individual and that individual's spouse or partner and any relative, or spouse or partner of a relative, of that individual or of that individual's spouse or partner;

    (b) any person in his capacity as trustee of a settlement and the settlor or grantor and any person associated with the settlor or grantor;

    (c) persons carrying on business in partnership and the spouse or partner and relatives of any of them; or

    (d) two or more persons acting together to secure or exercise control of a body of persons corporate or unincorporate or to secure control of any enterprise or assets,

shall be regarded as associated with one another.

(5) The reference in subsection (1) to bodies corporate which associated persons control shall be construed in accordance with section 26(3) and (4).

(6) In this section 'relative' means a brother, sister, uncle, aunt, nephew, niece, lineal ancestor or descendant (the stepchild of any person, or anyone adopted by a person, whether legally or otherwise, as his child being regarded as a relative or taken into account to trace a relationship in the same way as that person's child); and references to a spouse or partner shall include a former spouse or partner.

128   Supply of services and market for services etc.

(1) References in this Part to the supply of services shall be construed in accordance with this section; and references in this Part to a market for services and other related expressions shall be construed accordingly.

(2) The supply of services does not include the provision of services under a contract of service or of apprenticeship whether it is express or implied and (if it is express) whether it is oral or in writing.

(3) The supply of services includes—

(a) performing for gain or reward any activity other than the supply of goods;

(b) rendering services to order;

(c) the provision of services by making them available to potential users.

(4) The supply of services includes making arrangements for the use of computer software or for granting access to data stored in any form which is not readily accessible.

(5) The supply of services includes making arrangements by means of a relevant agreement (within the meaning of paragraph 29 of Schedule 2 to the Telecommunications Act 1984 for sharing the use of telecommunications apparatus.

(6) The supply of services includes permitting or making arrangements to permit the use of land in such circumstances as the Secretary of State may by order specify.

129 Other interpretation provisions

(1) In this Part, unless the context otherwise requires—

'action' includes omission; and references to the taking of action include references to refraining from action;

'agreement' means any agreement or arrangement, in whatever way and whatever form it is made, and whether it is, or is intended to be, legally enforceable or not;

'business' includes a professional practice and includes any other undertaking which is carried on for gain or reward or which is an undertaking in the course of which goods or services are supplied otherwise than free of charge;

'change of circumstances' includes any discovery that information has been supplied which is false or misleading in a material respect;

'Community law' means—

(a) all the rights, powers, liabilities, obligations and restrictions from time to time created or arising by or under the Community Treaties; and

(b) all the remedies and procedures from time to time provided for by or under the Community Treaties;

'consumer' means any person who is—

(a) a person to whom goods are or are sought to be supplied (whether by way of sale or otherwise) in the course of a business carried on by the person supplying or seeking to supply them; or

(b) a person for whom services are or are sought to be supplied in the course of a business carried on by the person supplying or seeking to supply them;

and who does not receive or seek to receive the goods or services in the course of a business carried on by him;

'customer' includes a customer who is not a consumer;

'the EC Merger Regulation' means Council Regulation (EC) No 139/2004 of 20th January 2004 on the control of concentrations between undertakings;

'enactment' includes an Act of the Scottish Parliament, Northern Ireland legislation and an enactment comprised in subordinate legislation, and includes an enactment whenever passed or made;

'enterprise' means the activities, or part of the activities, of a business;

'goods' includes buildings and other structures, and also includes ships, aircraft and hovercraft;

'modify' includes amend or repeal;

'notice' means notice in writing;

'price' includes any charge or fee (however described);

'subordinate legislation' has the same meaning as in the Interpretation Act 1978 (c. 30) and also includes an instrument made under an Act of the Scottish Parliament and an instrument made under Northern Ireland legislation;

'subsidiary' has the meaning given by section 736 of the Companies Act 1985 (c. 6);

'supply', in relation to the supply of goods, includes supply by way of sale, lease, hire or hire-purchase, and, in relation to buildings or other structures, includes the construction of them by a person for another person;

'the UK financial system' means the financial system in the United Kingdom and

'United Kingdom national' means an individual who is—

(a) a British citizen, a British overseas territories citizen, a British National (Overseas) or a British Overseas citizen;

(b) a person who under the British Nationality Act 1981 (c. 61) is a British subject; or

(c) a British protected person within the meaning of that Act.

(2) For the purposes of this Part any two bodies corporate are interconnected if—

(a) one of them is a body corporate of which the other is a subsidiary; or

(b) both of them are subsidiaries of one and the same body corporate;

and in this Part 'interconnected bodies corporate' shall be construed accordingly and 'group of interconnected bodies corporate' means a group consisting of two or more bodies corporate all of whom are interconnected with each other.

(3) References in this Part to a person carrying on business include references to a person carrying on business in partnership with one or more other persons.

(4) Any duty to publish which is imposed on a person by this Part shall, unless the context otherwise requires, be construed as a duty on that person to publish in such manner as he considers appropriate for the purpose of bringing the matter concerned to the attention of those likely to be affected by it.

PART IV MARKET INVESTIGATIONS

Chapter 1 Market investigation references

Making of references

131 Power of OFT to make references

(1) The OFT may, subject to subsection (4), make a reference to the Commission if the OFT has reasonable grounds for suspecting that any feature, or combination of features, of a market in the United Kingdom for goods or services prevents, restricts or distorts competition in connection with the supply or acquisition of any goods or services in the United Kingdom or a part of the United Kingdom.

(2) For the purposes of this Part any reference to a feature of a market in the United Kingdom for goods or services shall be construed as a reference to—

(a) the structure of the market concerned or any aspect of that structure;

(b) any conduct (whether or not in the market concerned) of one or more than one person who, in the course of business, supplies or acquires goods or services in the market concerned; or

(c) any conduct relating to the market concerned of customers of any person who, in the course of business, supplies or acquires goods or services.

(3) In subsection (2) 'conduct' includes any failure to act (whether or not intentional) and any other unintentional conduct.

(4) No reference shall be made under this section if—

(a) the making of the reference is prevented by section 156(1); or

(b) a reference has been made under section 132 in relation to the same matter but has not been finally determined.

(5) References in this Part to a market investigation reference being finally determined shall be construed in accordance with section 183(3) to (5).

(6) In this Part—

'market in the United Kingdom' includes—

> (a) so far as it operates in the United Kingdom or a part of the United Kingdom, any market which operates there and in another country or territory or in a part of another country or territory; and
>
> (b) any market which operates only in a part of the United Kingdom;

'market investigation reference' means a reference under this section or section 132;

and references to a market for goods or services include references to a market for goods and services.

132   Ministerial power to make references

(1) Subsection (3) applies where, in relation to any goods or services, the appropriate Minister is not satisfied with a decision of the OFT not to make a reference under section 126.

(2) Subsection (3) also applies where, in relation to any goods or services, the appropriate Minister—

> (a) has brought to the attention of the OFT information which the appropriate Minister considers to be relevant to the question of whether the OFT should make a reference under section 131; but
>
> (b) is not satisfied that the OFT will decide, within such period as the appropriate Minister considers to be reasonable, whether to make such a reference.

(3) The appropriate Minister may, subject to subsection (4), make a reference to the Commission if he has reasonable grounds for suspecting that any feature, or combination of features, of a market in the United Kingdom for goods or services prevents, restricts or distorts competition in connection with the supply or acquisition of any goods or services in the United Kingdom or a part of the United Kingdom.

(4) No reference shall be made under this section if the making of the reference is prevented by section 156(1).

(5) In this Part 'the appropriate Minister' means—

> (a) the Secretary of State; or
>
> (b) the Secretary of State and one or more than one other Minister of the Crown acting jointly.

133   Contents of references

(1) A market investigation reference shall, in particular, specify—

> (a) the enactment under which it is made;
>
> (b) the date on which it is made; and
>
> (c) the description of goods or services to which the feature or combination of features concerned relates.

(2) A market investigation reference may be framed so as to require the Commission to confine its investigation into the effects of features of markets in the United Kingdom for goods or services of a description specified in the reference to the effects of features of such of those markets as exist in connection with—

> (a) a supply, of a description specified in the reference, of the goods or services concerned; or
>
> (b) an acquisition, of a description specified in the reference, of the goods or services concerned.

(3) A description of the kind mentioned in subsection (2)(a) or (b) may, in particular, be by reference to—

> (a) the place where the goods or services are supplied or acquired; or
>
> (b) the persons to whom they are supplied or from whom they are acquired.

Determination of references

134   Questions to be decided on market investigation references

(1) The Commission shall, on a market investigation reference, decide whether any feature, or combination of features, of each relevant market prevents, restricts or distorts competition in

connection with the supply or acquisition of any goods or services in the United Kingdom or a part of the United Kingdom.

(2) For the purposes of this Part, in relation to a market investigation reference, there is an adverse effect on competition if any feature, or combination of features, of a relevant market prevents, restricts or distorts competition in connection with the supply or acquisition of any goods or services in the United Kingdom or a part of the United Kingdom.

(3) In subsections (1) and (2) 'relevant market' means—

    (a) in the case of subsection (2) so far as it applies in connection with a possible reference, a market in the United Kingdom—

        (i)   for goods or services of a description to be specified in the reference; and

        (ii) which would not be excluded from investigation by virtue of section 128(2); and

    (b) in any other case, a market in the United Kingdom—

        (i)   for goods or services of a description specified in the reference concerned; and

        (ii) which is not excluded from investigation by virtue of section 128(2).

(4) The Commission shall, if it has decided on a market investigation reference that there is an adverse effect on competition, decide the following additional questions—

    (a) whether action should be taken by it under section 138 for the purpose of remedying, mitigating or preventing the adverse effect on competition concerned or any detrimental effect on customers so far as it has resulted from, or may be expected to result from, the adverse effect on competition;

    (b) whether it should recommend the taking of action by others for the purpose of remedying, mitigating or preventing the adverse effect on competition concerned or any detrimental effect on customers so far as it has resulted from, or may be expected to result from, the adverse effect on competition; and

    (c) in either case, if action should be taken, what action should be taken and what is to be remedied, mitigated or prevented.

(5) For the purposes of this Part, in relation to a market investigation reference, there is a detrimental effect on customers if there is a detrimental effect on customers or future customers in the form of—

    (a) higher prices, lower quality or less choice of goods or services in any market in the United Kingdom (whether or not the market to which the feature or features concerned relate); or

    (b) less innovation in relation to such goods or services.

(6) In deciding the questions mentioned in subsection (4), the Commission shall, in particular, have regard to the need to achieve as comprehensive a solution as is reasonable and practicable to the adverse effect on competition and any detrimental effects on customers so far as resulting from the adverse effect on competition.

(7) In deciding the questions mentioned in subsection (4), the Commission may, in particular, have regard to the effect of any action on any relevant customer benefits of the feature or features of the market concerned.

(8) For the purposes of this Part a benefit is a relevant customer benefit of a feature or features of a market if—

    (a) it is a benefit to customers in the form of—

        (i)   lower prices, higher quality or greater choice of goods or services in any market in the United Kingdom (whether or not the market to which the feature or features concerned relate); or

        (ii) greater innovation in relation to such goods or services; and

    (b) the Commission, Secretary of State or (as the case may be) the OFT believes that—

        (i)   the benefit has accrued as a result (whether wholly or partly) of the feature or features concerned or may be expected to accrue within a reasonable period as a result (whether wholly or partly) of that feature or those features; and

        (ii) the benefit was, or is, unlikely to accrue without the feature or features concerned.

135   Variation of market investigation references

(1) The OFT or (as the case may be) the appropriate Minister may at any time vary a market investigation reference made by it or (as the case may be) him.

(2) The OFT or (as the case may be) the appropriate Minister shall consult the Commission before varying any such reference.

(3) Subsection (2) shall not apply if the Commission has requested the variation concerned.

(4) No variation under this section shall be capable of altering the period permitted by section 137 within which the report of the Commission under section 136 is to be prepared and published or (as the case may be) the period permitted by section 144 within which the report of the Commission under section 142 is to be prepared and published or given.

136   Investigations and reports on market investigation references

(1) The Commission shall prepare and publish a report on a market investigation reference within the period permitted by section 137.

(2) The report shall, in particular, contain—

    (a) the decisions of the Commission on the questions which it is required to answer by virtue of section 134;

    (b) its reasons for its decisions; and

    (c) such information as the Commission considers appropriate for facilitating a proper understanding of those questions and of its reasons for its decisions.

(3) The Commission shall carry out such investigations as it considers appropriate for the purposes of preparing a report under this section.

(4) The Commission shall, at the same time as a report under this section is published—

    (a) in the case of a reference under section 131, give it to the OFT; and

    (b) in the case of a reference under section 131, give it to the appropriate Minister and give a copy of it to the OFT.

(5) Where a reference has been made by the OFT under section 131 or by the appropriate Minister under section 132 in circumstances in which a reference could have been made by a relevant sectoral regulator under section 131 as it has effect by virtue of a relevant sectoral enactment, the Commission shall, at the same time as the report under this section is published, give a copy of it to the relevant sectoral regulator concerned.

(6) Where a reference has been made by a relevant sectoral regulator under section 131 as it has effect by virtue of a relevant sectoral enactment, the Commission shall, at the same time as the report under this section is published, give a copy of it to the OFT.

(7) In this Part 'relevant sectoral enactment' means—

    (a) [repealed]

    (b) in relation to the Gas and Electricity Markets Authority, section 36A of the Gas Act 1986 (c. 44) or (as the case may be) section 43 of the Electricity Act 1989 (c. 29);

    (c) in relation to the Director General of Water Services, section 31 of the Water Industry Act 1991 (c. 56);

    (d) in relation to the Director General of Electricity Supply for Northern Ireland, article 46 of the Electricity (Northern Ireland) Order 1992 (S.I. 1992/231 (N.I.1));

    (e) in relation to the Rail Regulator, section 67 of the Railways Act 1993 (c. 43);

    (f) in relation to the Director General of Gas for Northern Ireland, article 23 of the Gas (Northern Ireland) Order 1996 (S.I. 1996/275 (N.I. 2));

    (g) in relation to the Civil Aviation Authority, section 86 of the Transport Act 2000 (c. 38);

    (h) in relation to the Office of Communications, sections 370 and 371 of the Communications Act 2003.

(8) In this Part 'relevant sectoral regulator' means the Gas and Electricity Markets Authority, the Director General of Water Services, the Director General of Electricity Supply for Northern Ireland, the Rail Regulator, the Director General of Gas for Northern Ireland, the Civil Aviation Authority or the Office of Communications.

(9) The Secretary of State may by order modify subsection (7) or (8).

137 Time-limits for market investigations and reports

(1) The Commission shall prepare and publish its report under section 136 within the period of two years beginning with the date of the market investigation reference concerned.

(2) Subsection (1) is subject to section 151(3) and (5).

(3) The Secretary of State may by order amend subsection (1) so as to alter the period of two years mentioned in that subsection or any period for the time being mentioned in that subsection in substitution for that period.

(4) No alteration shall be made by virtue of subsection (3) which results in the period for the time being mentioned in subsection (1) exceeding two years.

(5) An order under subsection (3) shall not affect any period of time within which the Commission is under a duty to prepare and publish its report under section 131 in relation to a market investigation reference if the Commission is already under that duty in relation to that reference when the order is made.

(6) Before making an order under subsection (3) the Secretary of State shall consult the Commission and such other persons as he considers appropriate.

(7) References in this Part to the date of a market investigation reference shall be construed as references to the date specified in the reference as the date on which it is made.

138 Duty to remedy adverse effects

(1) Subsection (2) applies where a report of the Commission has been prepared and published under section 136 within the period permitted by section 137 and contains the decision that there is one or more than one adverse effect on competition.

(2) The Commission shall, in relation to each adverse effect on competition, take such action under section 159 or 161 as it considers to be reasonable and practicable—

(a) to remedy, mitigate or prevent the adverse effect on competition concerned; and

(b) to remedy, mitigate or prevent any detrimental effects on customers so far as they have resulted from, or may be expected to result from, the adverse effect on competition.

(3) The decisions of the Commission under subsection (2) shall be consistent with its decisions as included in its report by virtue of section 134(4) unless there has been a material change of circumstances since the preparation of the report or the Commission otherwise has a special reason for deciding differently.

(4) In making a decision under subsection (2), the Commission shall, in particular, have regard to the need to achieve as comprehensive a solution as is reasonable and practicable to the adverse effect on competition concerned and any detrimental effects on customers so far as resulting from the adverse effect on competition.

(5) In making a decision under subsection (2), the Commission may, in particular, have regard to the effect of any action on any relevant customer benefits of the feature or features of the market concerned.

(6) The Commission shall take no action under subsection (2) to remedy, mitigate or prevent any detrimental effect on customers so far as it may be expected to result from the adverse effect on competition concerned if—

(a) no detrimental effect on customers has resulted from the adverse effect on competition; and

(b) the adverse effect on competition is not being remedied, mitigated or prevented.

Chapter II Public interest cases

Intervention notices

139 Public interest intervention by Secretary of State

(1) The Secretary of State may give a notice to the Commission if—

(a) a market investigation reference has been made to the Commission;

(b) no more than four months has passed since the date of the reference;

(c) the reference is not finally determined; and

(d) the Secretary of State believes that it is or may be the case that one or more than one public interest consideration is relevant to the case.

(2) The Secretary of State may give a notice to the OFT if—

(a) the OFT is considering whether to accept if—

  (i) an undertaking under section 154 instead of making a reference under section 131; or

  (ii) an undertaking varying or superseding any such undertaking;

(b) the OFT has published a notice under section 155(1) or (4); and

(c) the Secretary of State believes that it is or may be the case that one or more than one public interest consideration is relevant to the case.

(3) In this Part 'intervention notice' means a notice under subsection (1) or (2).

(4) No more than one intervention notice shall be given under subsection (1) in relation to the same market investigation reference and no more than one intervention notice shall be given under subsection (2) in relation to the same proposed undertaking or in relation to proposed undertakings which do not differ from each other in any material respect.

(5) For the purposes of this Part a public interest consideration is a consideration which, at the time of the giving of the intervention notice concerned, is specified in section 153 or is not so specified but, in the opinion of the Secretary of State, ought to be so specified.

(6) Where the Secretary of State has given an intervention notice mentioning a public interest consideration which, at that time, is not finalised, he shall, as soon as practicable, take such action as is within his power to ensure that it is finalised.

(7) For the purposes of this Part a public interest consideration is finalised if—

(a) it is specified in section 153 otherwise than by virtue of an order under subsection (3) of that section; or

(b) it is specified in that section by virtue of an order under subsection (3) of that section and the order providing for it to be so specified has been laid before, and approved by, Parliament in accordance with subsection (6) of section 181 and within the period mentioned in that subsection.

Intervention notices under section 139(1)

140   Intervention notices under section 139(1)

(1) An intervention notice under section 139(1) shall state—

(a) the market investigation reference concerned;

(b) the date of the market investigation reference concerned;

(c) the public interest consideration or considerations which are, or may be, relevant to the case; and

(d) where any public interest consideration concerned is not finalised, the proposed timetable for finalising it.

(2) Where the Secretary of State believes that it is or may be the case that two or more public interest considerations are relevant to the case, he may decide not to mention in the intervention notice such of those considerations as he considers appropriate.

(3) The Secretary of State may at any time revoke an intervention notice which has been given under section 134(1) and which is in force.

(4) An intervention notice under section 139(1) shall come into force when it is given and shall cease to be in force when the matter to which it relates is finally determined under this Chapter.

(5) For the purposes of subsection (4) a matter to which an intervention notice under section 139(1) relates is finally determined under this Chapter if—

(a) the period permitted by section 144 for the preparation of the report of the Commission under section 142 and for action to be taken in relation to it under section 143 (1) or (3) has expired and no such report has been so prepared or no such action has been taken;

    (b) the Commission decides under section 145(1) to terminate its investigation;

    (c) the report of the Commission has been prepared under section 142 and published under section 143(1) within the period permitted by section 144;

    (d) the Secretary of State fails to make and publish a decision under subsection (2) of section 146 within the period required by subsection (3) of that section;

    (e) the Secretary of State decides under section 146(2) that no eligible public interest consideration is relevant;

    (f) the Secretary of State decides under section 147(2) neither to accept an undertaking under section 159 nor to make an order under section 161;

    (g) the Secretary of State accepts an undertaking under section 159 or makes an order under section 161; or

    (h) the Secretary of State decides to revoke the intervention notice concerned.

(6) For the purposes of subsections (4) and (5) the time when a matter to which an intervention notice under section 139(1) relates is finally determined under this Chapter is—

    (a) in a case falling within subsection (5)(a) or (d), the expiry of the period concerned;

    (b) in a case falling within subsection (5)(b), (e), (f) or (h), the making of the decision concerned;

    (c) in a case falling within subsection (5)(c), the publication of the report concerned; and

    (d) in a case falling within subsection (5)(g), the acceptance of the undertaking concerned or (as the case may be) the making of the order concerned.

141   Questions to be decided by Commission

(1) This section applies where an intervention notice under section 139(1) is in force in relation to a market investigation reference.

(2) The Commission shall decide whether any feature, or combination of features, of each relevant market (within the meaning given by section 134(3)) prevents, restricts or distorts competition in connection with the supply or acquisition of any goods or services in the United Kingdom or a part of the United Kingdom.

(3) The Commission shall, if it has decided that there is an adverse effect on competition, decide the following additional questions—

    (a) whether action should be taken by the Secretary of State under section 147 for the purpose of remedying, mitigating or preventing the adverse effect on competition concerned or any detrimental effect on customers so far as it has resulted from, or may be expected to result from, the adverse effect on competition;

    (b) whether the Commission should recommend the taking of other action by the Secretary of State or action by persons other than itself and the Secretary of State for the purpose of remedying, mitigating or preventing the adverse effect on competition concerned or any detrimental effect on customers so far as it has resulted from, or may be expected to result from, the adverse effect on competition; and

    (c) in either case, if action should be taken, what action should be taken and what is to be remedied, mitigated or prevented.

(4) The Commission shall, if it has decided that there is an adverse effect on competition, also decide separately the following questions (on the assumption that it is proceeding as mentioned in section 148(1))—

    (a) whether action should be taken by it under section 138 for the purpose of remedying, mitigating or preventing the adverse effect on competition concerned or any detrimental effect on customers so far as it has resulted from, or may be expected to result from, the adverse effect on competition;

    (b) whether the Commission should recommend the taking of action by other persons for the purpose of remedying, mitigating or preventing the adverse effect on competition concerned or any detrimental effect on customers so far as it has resulted from, or may be expected to result from, the adverse effect on competition; and

(c) in either case, if action should be taken, what action should be taken and what is to be remedied, mitigated or prevented.

(5) In deciding the questions mentioned in subsections (3) and (4), the Commission shall, in particular, have regard to the need to achieve as comprehensive a solution as is reasonable and practicable to the adverse effect on competition concerned and any detrimental effect on customers so far as resulting from the adverse effect on competition.

(6) In deciding the questions mentioned in subsections (3) and (4), the Commission may, in particular, have regard to the effect of any action on any relevant customer benefits of the feature or features of the market concerned.

142   Investigations and reports by Commission

(1) Where an intervention notice under section 139(1) is in force in relation to a market investigation reference, the Commission shall prepare a report on the reference and take action in relation to it under section 143(1) or (3) within the period permitted by section 144.

(2) The report shall, in particular, contain—
   (a) the decisions of the Commission on the questions which it is required to answer by virtue of section 141;
   (b) its reasons for its decisions; and
   (c) such information as the Commission considers appropriate for facilitating a proper understanding of those questions and of its reasons for its decisions.

(3) The Commission shall carry out such investigations as it considers appropriate for the purposes of preparing a report under this section.

143   Publication etc. of reports of Commission

(1) The Commission shall publish a report under section 142 if it contains—
   (a) the decision of the Commission that there is no adverse effect on competition; or
   (b) the decisions of the Commission that there is one or more than one adverse effect on competition but, on the question mentioned in section 141(4)(a) and in relation to each adverse effect on competition, that no action should be taken by it.

(2) The Commission shall, at the same time as the report is published under subsection (1)—
   (a) in the case of a reference under section 131, give it to the OFT; and
   (b) in the case of a reference under section 132, give it to the appropriate Minister and give a copy of it to the OFT.

(3) Where a report under section 142 contains the decisions of the Commission that there is one or more than one adverse effect on competition and, on the question mentioned in section 141(4)(a) and in relation to at least one such adverse effect, that action should be taken by it, the Commission shall give the report to the Secretary of State.

(4) The Secretary of State shall publish, no later than publication of his decision under section 146(2) in relation to the case, a report of the Commission given to him under subsection (3) and not required to be published by virtue of section 148(2).

(5) The Secretary of State shall, at the same time as a report of the Commission given to him under subsection (3) is published under subsection (4), give a copy of it—
   (a) in the case of a reference under section 131, to the OFT; and
   (b) in the case of a reference under section 132, to any other Minister of the Crown who made the reference and to the OFT.

(6) Where a reference has been made by the OFT under section 131 or by the appropriate Minister under section 132 in circumstances in which a reference could have been made by a relevant sectoral regulator under section 131 as it has effect by virtue of a relevant sectoral enactment, the relevant authority shall, at the same time as the report under section 142 is published under subsection (1) or (4), give a copy of it to the relevant sectoral regulator concerned.

(7) Where a reference has been made by a relevant sectoral regulator under section 131 as it has effect by virtue of a relevant sectoral enactment, the relevant authority shall, at the same time as the report under section 142 is published under subsection (1) or (4), give a copy of it to the OFT.

(8) In subsections (6) and (7) 'the relevant authority' means—

(a) in the case of a report published under subsection (1), the Commission; and

(b) in the case of a report published under subsection (4), the Secretary of State.

144   Time-limits for investigations and reports: Part IV

(1) The Commission shall, within the period of two years beginning with the date of the reference, prepare its report under section 142 and publish it under subsection (1) of section 143 or (as the case may be) give it to the Secretary of State under subsection (3) of that section.

(2) The Secretary of State may by order amend subsection (1) so as to alter the period of two years mentioned in that subsection or any period for the time being mentioned in that subsection in substitution for that period.

(3) No alteration shall be made by virtue of subsection (2) which results in the period for the time being mentioned in subsection (1) exceeding two years.

(4) An order under subsection (2) shall not affect any period of time within which, in relation to a market investigation reference, the Commission is under a duty to prepare its report under section 142 and take action in relation to it under section 143(1) or (3) if the Commission is already under that duty in relation to that reference when the order is made.

(5) Before making an order under subsection (2) the Secretary of State shall consult the Commission and such other persons as he considers appropriate.

145   Restrictions where public interest considerations not finalised: Part IV

(1) The Commission shall terminate its investigation under section 142 if—

(a) the intervention notice concerned mentions a public interest consideration which was not finalised on the giving of that notice or public interest considerations which, at that time, were not finalised;

(b) no other public interest consideration is mentioned in the notice;

(c) at least 24 weeks has elapsed since the giving of the notice; and

(d) the public interest consideration mentioned in the notice has not been finalised within that period of 24 weeks or (as the case may be) none of the public interest considerations mentioned in the notice has been finalised within that period of 24 weeks.

(2) Where the intervention notice concerned mentions a public interest consideration which is not finalised on the giving of the notice, the Commission shall not give its report under section 142 to the Secretary of State in accordance with section 143(3) unless the period of 24 weeks beginning with the giving of the intervention notice concerned has expired or the public interest consideration concerned has been finalised.

(3) The Commission shall, in reporting on any of the questions mentioned in section 141(3), disregard any public interest consideration which has not been finalised before the giving of the report.

(4) The Commission shall, in reporting on any of the questions mentioned in section 141(3), disregard any public interest consideration which was not finalised on the giving of the intervention notice concerned and has not been finalised within the period of 24 weeks beginning with the giving of the notice concerned.

(5) Subsections (1) to (4) are without prejudice to the power of the Commission to carry out investigations in relation to any public interest consideration to which it might be able to have regard in its report.

146   Decision of Secretary of State

(1) Subsection (2) applies where the Secretary of State has received a report of the Commission which—

(a) has been prepared under section 142;

(b) contains the decisions that there is one or more than one adverse effect on competition and, on the question mentioned in section 141(4) (a) and in relation to at least one such adverse effect, that action should be taken by it; and

   (c) has been given to the Secretary of State as required by section 143(3).
   (2) The Secretary of State shall decide whether—
      (a) any eligible public interest consideration is relevant; or
      (b) any eligible public interest considerations are relevant;
to any action which is mentioned in the report by virtue of section 141(4)(a) and (c) and which the Commission should take for the purpose of remedying mitigating or preventing any adverse effect on competition concerned or any detrimental effect on customers so far as it has resulted or may be expected to result from any adverse effect on competition.
   (3) The Secretary of State shall make and publish his decision under subsection (2) within the period of 90 days beginning with the receipt of the report of the Commission under section 142.
   (4) In this section 'eligible public interest consideration' means a public interest consideration which—
      (a) was mentioned in the intervention notice concerned; and
      (b) was not disregarded by the Commission for the purposes of its report under section 142.

147   Remedial action by Secretary of State

   (1) Subsection (2) applies where the Secretary of State has decided under subsection (2) of section 146 within the period required by subsection (3) of that section that an eligible public interest consideration is relevant as mentioned in subsection (2) of that section or eligible public interest considerations are so relevant.
   (2) The Secretary of State may, in relation to any adverse effect on competition identified in the report concerned, take such action under section 159 or 161 as he considers to be—
      (a) reasonable and practicable—
         (i)   to remedy, mitigate or prevent the adverse effect on competition concerned; or
         (ii)   to remedy, mitigate or prevent any detrimental effect on customers so far as it has resulted from, or may be expected to result from the adverse effect on competition; and
      (b) appropriate in the light of the eligible public interest consideration concerned or (as the case may be) the eligible public interest considerations concerned.
   (3) In making a decision under subsection (2), the Secretary of State shall, in particular, have regard to—
      (a) the need to achieve as comprehensive a solution as is reasonable and practicable to the adverse effect on competition concerned and any detrimental effects on customers so far as resulting from the adverse effect on competition; and
      (b) the report of the Commission under section 142.
   (4) In having regard by virtue of subsection (3) to the report of the Commission under section 142, the Secretary of State shall not challenge the decision of the Commission contained in the report that there is one or more than one adverse effect on competition.
   (5) In making a decision under subsection (2), the Secretary of State may, in particular, have regard to the effect of any action on any relevant customer benefits of the feature or features of the market concerned.
   (6) The Secretary of State shall take no action under subsection (2) to remedy, mitigate or prevent any detrimental effect on customers so far as it may be expected to result from the adverse effect on competition concerned if—
      (a) no detrimental effect on customers has resulted from the adverse effect on competition; and
      (b) the adverse effect on competition is not being remedied, mitigated or prevented.
   (7) In this section 'eligible public interest consideration' has the same meaning as in section 146.

148   Reversion of the matter to the Commission

   (1) If—
      (a) the Secretary of State fails to make and publish his decision under subsection (2) of section 146 within the period required by subsection (3) of that section; or

(b) the Secretary of State decides that no eligible public interest consideration is relevant as mentioned in subsection (2) of that section;

the Commission shall proceed under section 138 as if the report had been prepared and published under section 136 within the period permitted by section 137.

(2) The Commission shall publish the report which has been prepared by it under section 142 (if still unpublished) as soon as it becomes able to proceed by virtue of subsection (1).

(3) The Commission shall, at the same time as its report is published under subsection (2), give a copy of it—

(a) in the case of a reference under section 131, to the OFT; and

(b) in the case of a reference under section 132, to any Minister of the Crown who made the reference (other than the Secretary of State) and to the OFT.

(4) Where a reference has been made by the OFT under section 131 or by the appropriate Minister under section 132 in circumstances in which a reference could have been made by a relevant sectoral regulator under section 131 as it has effect by virtue of a relevant sectoral enactment, the Commission shall, at the same time as its report is published under subsection (2), give a copy of it to the relevant sectoral regulator concerned.

(5) Where a reference has been made by a relevant sectoral regulator under section 131 as it has effect by virtue of a relevant sectoral enactment, the Commission shall, at the same time as its report is published under subsection (2), give a copy of it to the OFT.

(6) In relation to proceedings by virtue of subsection (1), the reference in section 138(3) to decisions of the Commission included in its report by virtue of section 134(4) shall be construed as a reference to decisions which were included in the report of the Commission by virtue of section 141(4).

(7) Where the Commission, in proceeding by virtue of subsection (1), intends to proceed in a way which is not consistent with its decisions as included in its report by virtue of section 141(4), it shall not so proceed without the consent of the Secretary of State.

(8) The Secretary of State shall not withhold his consent under subsection (7) unless he believes that the proposed alternative way of proceeding will operate against the public interest.

(9) For the purposes of subsection (8) a proposed alternative way of proceeding will operate against the public interest only if any eligible public interest consideration or considerations outweigh the considerations which have led the Commission to propose proceeding in that way.

(10) In deciding whether to withhold his consent under subsection (7), the Secretary of State shall accept the Commission's view of what, if the only relevant consideration were how to remedy, mitigate or prevent the adverse effect on competition concerned or any detrimental effect on customers so far as resulting from the adverse effect on competition, would be the most appropriate way to proceed.

(11) In this section 'eligible public interest consideration' has the same meaning as in section 146.

Intervention notices under section 139(2)

149   Intervention notices under section 139(2)

(1) An intervention notice under section 139(2) shall state—

(a) the proposed undertaking which may be accepted by the OFT;

(b) the notice under section 155(1) or (4);

(c) the public interest consideration or considerations which are, or may be, relevant to the case; and

(d) where any public interest consideration concerned is not finalised, the proposed timetable for finalising it.

(2) Where the Secretary of State believes that it is or may be the case that two or more public interest considerations are relevant to the case, he may decide not to mention in the intervention notice such of those considerations as he considers appropriate.

(3) The Secretary of State may at any time revoke an intervention notice which has been given under section 139(2) and which is in force.

(4) An intervention notice under section 139(2) shall come into force when it is given and shall cease to be in force on the occurrence of any of the events mentioned in subsection (4).

(5) The events are the—

(a) acceptance by the OFT with the consent of the Secretary of State of an undertaking which is the same as the proposed undertaking mentioned in the intervention notice by virtue of subsection (1)(a) or which does not differ from it in any material respect;

(b) the decision of the OFT to proceed neither with the proposed undertaking mentioned in the intervention notice by virtue of subsection (1)(a) nor a proposed undertaking which does not differ from it in any material respect; or

(c) the decision of the Secretary of State to revoke the intervention notice concerned.

150   Power of veto of Secretary of State

(1) Where an intervention notice under section 139(2) is in force, the OFT shall not, without the consent of the Secretary of State, accept the proposed undertaking concerned or a proposed undertaking which does not differ from it in any material respect.

(2) The Secretary of State shall withhold his consent if he believes that it is or may be the case that the proposed undertaking will, if accepted, operate against the public interest.

(3) For the purposes of subsection (2) a proposed undertaking will, if accepted, operate against the public interest only if any public interest consideration which is mentioned in the intervention notice concerned and has been finalised, or any public interest considerations which are so mentioned and have been finalised, outweigh the considerations which have led the OFT to propose accepting the undertaking.

(4) In making his decision under subsection (2) the Secretary of State shall accept the OFT's view of what undertakings, if the only relevant consideration were how to remedy, mitigate or prevent the adverse effect on competition concerned or any detrimental effect on customers so far as resulting from the adverse effect on competition, would be most appropriate.

(5) Where a public interest consideration which is mentioned in the intervention notice concerned is not finalised on the giving of the notice, the Secretary of State shall not make his decision as to whether to give his consent under this section before—

(a) the end of the period of 24 weeks beginning with the giving of the intervention notice; or

(b) if earlier, the date on which the public interest consideration concerned has been finalised.

(6) Subject to subsections (2) to (5), the Secretary of State shall not withhold his consent under this section.

Other

151   Further interaction of intervention notices with general procedure

(1) Where an intervention notice under section 139(1) comes into force in relation to a market investigation reference, sections 134(1), (4), (6) and (7), 136(1) to (6), 137(1) to (6) and 138 shall cease to apply in relation to that reference.

(2) Where the Secretary of State revokes an intervention notice which has been given under section 139(1), the Commission shall instead proceed under sections 134 and 136 to 138.

(3) Where the Commission is proceeding by virtue of subsection (2), the period within which the Commission shall prepare and publish its report under section 136 shall be extended by an additional period of 20 days.

(4) Where the Commission terminates its investigation under section 145(1), the Commission shall proceed under sections 134 and 136 to 138.

(5) Where the Commission is proceeding by virtue of subsection (4), the period within which the Commission shall prepare and publish its report under section 136 shall be extended by an additional period of 20 days.

(6) In determining the period of 20 days mentioned in subsection (3) or (5) no account shall be taken of—

(a) Saturday, Sunday, Good Friday and Christmas Day; and

(b) any day which is a bank holiday in England and Wales.

152   Certain duties of OFT and Commission

(1) The OFT shall, in considering whether to make a reference under section 131, bring to the attention of the Secretary of State any case which it believes raises any consideration specified in section 153 unless it believes that the Secretary of State would consider any such consideration immaterial in the context of the particular case.

(2) The Commission shall, in investigating any reference made to it under section 131 or 132 within the previous four months, bring to the attention of the Secretary of State any case which it believes raises any consideration specified in section 153 unless it believes that the Secretary of State would consider any such consideration immaterial in the context of the particular case.

(3) The OFT and the Commission shall bring to the attention of the Secretary of State any representations about exercising his power under section 153(3) which have been made to the OFT or (as the case may be) the Commission.

153   Specified considerations: Part IV

(1) The interests of national security are specified in this section.

(2) In subsection (1) 'national security' includes public security; and in this subsection 'public security' has the same meaning as in article 21(4) of Council Regulation (EC) No 139/2004 of 20th January 2004 on the control of concentrations between undertakings.

(3) The Secretary of State may by order modify this section for the purpose of adding to, removing or amending any consideration which is for the time being specified in this section.

(4) An order under this section may apply in relation to cases under consideration by the OFT, by the Secretary of State, by the appropriate Minister (other than the Secretary of State acting alone) or by the Commission before the making of the order as well as cases under consideration on or after the making of the order.

Chapter 3 Enforcement

Undertakings and orders

154   Undertakings in lieu of market investigation references

(1) Subsection (2) applies if the OFT considers that it has the power to make a reference under section 131 and otherwise intends to make such a reference.

(2) The OFT may, instead of making such a reference and for the purpose of remedying, mitigating or preventing—

(a) any adverse effect on competition concerned; or

(b) any detrimental effect on customers so far as it has resulted from, or may be expected to result from, the adverse effect on competition;

accept, from such persons as it considers appropriate, undertakings to take such action as it considers appropriate.

(3) In proceeding under subsection (2), the OFT shall, in particular, have regard to the need to achieve as comprehensive a solution as is reasonable and practicable to the adverse effect on competition concerned and any detrimental effects on customers so far as resulting from the adverse effect on competition.

(4) In proceeding under subsection (2), the OFT may, in particular, have regard to the effect of any action on any relevant customer benefits of the feature or features of the market concerned.

(5) The OFT shall take no action under subsection (2) to remedy, mitigate or prevent any detrimental effect on customers so far as it may be expected to result from the adverse effect on competition concerned if—

(a) no detrimental effect on customers has resulted from the adverse effect on competition; and

(b) the adverse effect on competition is not being remedied, mitigated or prevented.

(6) An undertaking under this section—

    (a) shall come into force when accepted;

    (b) may be varied or superseded by another undertaking; and

    (c) may be released by the OFT.

(7) The OFT shall, as soon as reasonably practicable, consider any representations received by it in relation to varying or releasing an undertaking under this section.

(8) This section is subject to sections 150 and 155.

155 Undertakings in lieu: procedural requirements

(1) Before accepting an undertaking under section 154 (other than an undertaking under that section which varies an undertaking under that section but not in any material respect), the OFT shall—

    (a) publish notice of the proposed undertaking; and

    (b) consider any representations made in accordance with the notice and not withdrawn.

(2) A notice under subsection (1) shall state—

    (a) that the OFT proposes to accept the undertaking;

    (b) the purpose and effect of the undertaking;

    (c) the situation that the undertaking is seeking to deal with;

    (d) any other facts which the OFT considers justify the acceptance of the undertaking;

    (e) a means of gaining access to an accurate version of the proposed undertaking at all reasonable times; and

    (f) the period (not less than 15 days starting with the date of publication of the notice) within which representations may be made in relation to the proposed undertaking.

(3) The matters to be included in a notice under subsection (1) by virtue of subsection (2) shall, in particular, include—

    (a) the terms of the reference under section 131 which the OFT considers that it has power to make and which it otherwise intends to make; and

    (b) the adverse effect on competition, and any detrimental effect on customers so far as resulting from the adverse effect on competition, which the OFT has identified.

(4) The OFT shall not accept the undertaking with modifications unless it—

    (a) publishes notice of the proposed modifications; and

    (b) considers any representations made in accordance with the notice and not withdrawn.

(5) A notice under subsection (4) shall state—

    (a) the proposed modifications;

    (b) the reasons for them; and

    (c) the period (not less than 7 days starting with the date of the publication of the notice under subsection (4)) within which representations may be made in relation to the proposed modifications.

(6) If, after publishing notice under subsection (1) or (4), the OFT decides—

    (a) not to accept the undertaking concerned; and

    (b) not to proceed by virtue of subsection (8) or (9);it shall publish notice of that decision.

(7) As soon as practicable after accepting an undertaking to which this section applies, the OFT shall—

    (a) serve a copy of the undertaking on any person by whom it is given; and

    (b) publish the undertaking.

(8) The requirements of subsection (4) (and those of subsection (1)) shall not apply if the OFT—

    (a) has already published notice under subsection (1) but not subsection (4) in relation to the proposed undertaking; and

    (b) considers that the modifications which are now being proposed are not material in any respect.

(9) The requirements of subsection (4) (and those of subsection (1)) shall not apply if the OFT—

    (a) has already published notice under subsections (1) and (4) in relation to the matter concerned; and

    (b) considers that the further modifications which are now being proposed do not differ in any material respect from the modifications in relation to which notice was last given under subsection (4).

(10) Paragraphs 6 to 8 (but not paragraph 9) of Schedule 10 (procedural requirements before terminating undertakings) shall apply in relation to the proposed release of undertakings under section 154 (other than in connection with accepting an undertaking under that section which varies or supersedes an undertaking under that section) as they apply in relation to the proposed release of undertakings under section 73.

156   Effect of undertakings under section 154

(1) No market investigation reference shall be made by the OFT or the appropriate Minister in relation to any feature, or combination of features, of a market in the United Kingdom for goods or services if—

    (a) the OFT has accepted an undertaking under section 154 within the previous 12 months; and

    (b) the goods or services to which the undertaking relates are of the same description as the goods or services to which the feature, or combination of features, relates.

(2) Subsection (1) does not prevent the making of a market investigation reference if—

    (a) the OFT considers that the undertaking has been breached and has given notice of that fact to the person responsible for giving the undertaking; or

    (b) the person responsible for giving the undertaking supplied, in connection with the matter, information to the OFT which was false or misleading in a material respect.

157   Interim undertakings: Part IV

(1) Subsection (2) applies where—

    (a) a market investigation reference has been made;

    (b) a report has been published under section 136 within the period permitted by section 137 or (as the case may be) a report prepared under section 142 and given to the Secretary of State under section 143(3) within the period permitted by section 144 has been published; and

    (c) the market investigation reference concerned is not finally determined.

(2) The relevant authority may, for the purpose of preventing pre-emptive action, accept, from such persons as the relevant authority considers appropriate, undertakings to take such action as the relevant authority considers appropriate.

(3) An undertaking under this section—

    (a) shall come into force when accepted;

    (b) may be varied or superseded by another undertaking; and

    (c) may be released by the relevant authority.

(4) An undertaking under this section shall, if it has not previously ceased to be in force, cease to be in force when the market investigation reference is finally determined.

(5) The relevant authority shall, as soon as reasonably practicable, consider any representations received by the relevant authority in relation to varying or releasing an undertaking under this section.

(6) In this section and section 158—

'pre-emptive action' means action which might impede the taking of any action under section 138(2) or (as the case may be) 147(2) in relation to the market investigation reference concerned; and

'the relevant authority' means—

    (a) where an intervention notice is in force in relation to the market investigation reference, the Secretary of State;

    (b) in any other case, the Commission.

158 Interim orders: Part IV

(1) Subsection (2) applies where—

    (a) a market investigation reference has been made;

    (b) a report has been published under section 136 within the period permitted by section 137 or (as the case may be) a report prepared under section 142 and given to the Secretary of State under section 143(3) within the period permitted by section 144 has been published; and

    (c) the market investigation reference concerned is not finally determined.

(2) The relevant authority may by order, for the purpose of preventing pre-emptive action—

    (a) prohibit or restrict the doing of things which the relevant authority considers would constitute pre-emptive action;

    (b) impose on any person concerned obligations as to the carrying on of any activities or the safeguarding of any assets;

    (c) provide for the carrying on of any activities or the safeguarding of any assets either by the appointment of a person to conduct or supervise the conduct of any activities (on such terms and with such powers as may be specified or described in the order) or in any other manner;

    (d) do anything which may be done by virtue of paragraph 19 of Schedule 8.

(3) An order under this section—

    (a) shall come into force at such time as is determined by or under the order; and

    (b) may be varied or revoked by another order.

(4) An order under this section shall, if it has not previously ceased to be in force, cease to be in force when the market investigation reference is finally determined.

(5) The relevant authority shall, as soon as reasonably practicable, consider any representations received by the relevant authority in relation to varying or revoking an order under this section.

159 Final undertakings: Part IV

(1) The Commission may, in accordance with section 138, accept, from such persons as it considers appropriate, undertakings to take action specified or described in the undertakings.

(2) The Secretary of State may, in accordance with section 147, accept, from such persons as he considers appropriate, undertakings to take action specified or described in the undertakings.

(3) An undertaking under this section shall come into force when accepted.

(4) An undertaking under subsection (1) or (2) may be varied or superseded by another undertaking under that subsection.

(5) An undertaking under subsection (1) may be released by the Commission and an undertaking under subsection (2) may be released by the Secretary of State.

(6) The Commission or (as the case may be) the Secretary of State shall, as soon as reasonably practicable, consider any representations received by it or (as the case may be) him in relation to varying or releasing an undertaking under this section.

160 Order-making power where final undertakings not fulfilled: Part IV

(1) Subsection (2) applies where the relevant authority considers that—

    (a) an undertaking accepted by the relevant authority under section 159 has not been, is not being or will not be fulfilled; or

    (b) in relation to an undertaking accepted by the relevant authority under that section, information which was false or misleading in a material respect was given to the relevant authority or the OFT by the person giving the undertaking before the relevant authority decided to accept the undertaking.

(2) The relevant authority may, for any of the purposes mentioned in section 138(2) or (as the case may be) 147(2), make an order under this section.

(3) Subsections (3) to (6) of section 138 or (as the case may be) 147 shall apply for the purposes of subsection (2) above as they apply for the purposes of that section.

(4) An order under this section may contain—

    (a) anything permitted by Schedule 8; and

    (b) such supplementary, consequential or incidental provision as the relevant authority considers appropriate.

(5) An order under this section—

    (a) shall come into force at such time as is determined by or under the order;

    (b) may contain provision which is different from the provision contained in the undertaking concerned; and

    (c) may be varied or revoked by another order.

(6) No order shall be varied or revoked under this section unless the OFT advises that such a variation or revocation is appropriate by reason of a change of circumstances.

(7) In this section 'the relevant authority' means—

    (a) in the case of an undertaking accepted under section 159 by the Commission, the Commission; and

    (b) in the case of an undertaking accepted under that section by the Secretary of State, the Secretary of State.

161 Final orders: Part IV

(1) The Commission may, in accordance with section 138, make an order under this section.

(2) The Secretary of State may, in accordance with section 147, make an order under this section.

(3) An order under this section may contain—

    (a) anything permitted by Schedule 8; and

    (b) such supplementary, consequential or incidental provision as the person making it considers appropriate.

(4) An order under this section—

    (a) shall come into force at such time as is determined by or under the order; and

    (b) may be varied or revoked by another order.

(5) No order shall be varied or revoked under this section unless the OFT advises that such a variation or revocation is appropriate by reason of a change of circumstances.

Enforcement functions of OFT

162 Duty of OFT to monitor undertakings and orders: Part IV

(1) The OFT shall keep under review the carrying out of any enforcement undertaking or any enforcement order.

(2) The OFT shall, in particular, from time to time consider—

    (a) whether an enforcement undertaking or enforcement order has been or is being complied with;

    (b) whether, by reason of any change of circumstances, an enforcement undertaking is no longer appropriate and—

        (i) one or more of the parties to it can be released from it; or

        (ii) it needs to be varied or to be superseded by a new enforcement undertaking; and

    (c) whether, by reason of any change of circumstances, an enforcement order is no longer appropriate and needs to be varied or revoked.

(3) The OFT shall give the Commission or (as the case may be) the Secretary of State such advice as it considers appropriate in relation to—

    (a) any possible variation or release by the Commission or (as the case may be) the Secretary of State of an enforcement undertaking accepted by it or (as the case may be) him;

    (b) any possible new enforcement undertaking to be accepted by the Commission or (as the case may be) the Secretary of State so as to supersede another enforcement undertaking given to the Commission or (as the case may be) the Secretary of State;

(c) any possible variation or revocation by the Commission or (as the case may be) the Secretary of State of an enforcement order made by the Commission or (as the case may be) the Secretary of State;

(d) any possible enforcement undertaking to be accepted by the Commission or (as the case may be) the Secretary of State instead of an enforcement order or any possible enforcement order to be made by the Commission or (as the case may be) the Secretary of State instead of an enforcement undertaking; or

(e) the enforcement by virtue of section 167(6) to (8) of any enforcement undertaking or enforcement order.

(4) The OFT shall take such action as it considers appropriate in relation to—

(a) any possible variation or release by it of an undertaking accepted by it under section 154;

(b) any possible new undertaking to be accepted by it under section 154 so as to supersede another undertaking given to it under that section; or

(c) the enforcement by it by virtue of section 167(6) of any enforcement undertaking or enforcement order.

(5) The OFT shall keep under review the effectiveness of enforcement undertakings accepted under this Part and enforcement orders made under this Part.

(6) The OFT shall, whenever requested to do so by the Secretary of State and otherwise from time to time, prepare a report of its findings under subsection (5).

(7) The OFT shall—

(a) give any report prepared by it under subsection (6) to the Commission;

(b) give a copy of the report to the Secretary of State; and

(c) publish the report.

(8) In this Part—

'enforcement order' means an order made under section 158, 160 or 161; and

'enforcement undertaking' means an undertaking accepted under section 154, 157 or 159.

163 Further role of OFT in relation to undertakings and orders: Part IV

(1) Subsections (2) and (3) apply where the Commission or the Secretary of State (in this section 'the relevant authority') is considering whether to accept undertakings under section 157 or 159.

(2) The relevant authority may require the OFT to consult with such persons as the relevant authority considers appropriate with a view to discovering whether they will offer undertakings which the relevant authority would be prepared to accept under section 157 or (as the case may be) 159.

(3) The relevant authority may require the OFT to report to the relevant authority on the outcome of the OFT's consultations within such period as the relevant authority may require.

(4) A report under subsection (3) shall, in particular, contain advice from the OFT as to whether any undertakings offered should be accepted by the relevant authority under section 157 or (as the case may be) 159.

(5) The powers conferred on the relevant authority by subsections (1) to (4) are without prejudice to the power of the relevant authority to consult the persons concerned itself.

(6) If asked by the relevant authority for advice in relation to the taking of enforcement action (whether or not by way of undertakings) in a particular case, the OFT shall give such advice as it considers appropriate.

Supplementary

164 Enforcement undertakings and orders under this Part: general provisions

(1) The provision which may be contained in an enforcement undertaking is not limited to the provision which is permitted by Schedule 8.

(2) The following enactments in Part 3 shall apply in relation to enforcement orders under this Part as they apply in relation to enforcement orders under that Part—

    (a) section 86(1) to (5) (enforcement orders: general provisions); and

    (b) section 87 (power of directions conferred by enforcement order).

(3) An enforcement order under section 160 or 161 or any explanatory material accompanying the order shall state—

    (a) the actions that the persons or description of persons to whom the order is addressed must do or (as the case may be) refrain from doing;

    (b) the date on which the order comes into force;

    (c) the possible consequences of not complying with the order; and

    (d) the section of this Part under which a review can be sought in relation to the order.

165   Procedural requirements for certain undertakings and orders: Part IV

Schedule 10 (procedural requirements for certain undertakings and orders), other than paragraph 9 of that Schedule, shall apply in relation to undertakings under section 159 and orders under section 160 or 161 as it applies in relation to undertakings under section 82 and orders under section 83 or 84.

166   Register of undertakings and orders: Part IV

(1) The OFT shall compile and maintain a register for the purposes of this Part.

(2) The register shall be kept in such form as the OFT considers appropriate.

(3) The OFT shall ensure that the following matters are entered in the register—

    (a) the provisions of any enforcement undertaking accepted by virtue of this Part (whether by the OFT, the Commission, the Secretary of State or a relevant sectoral regulator);

    (b) the provisions of any enforcement order made by virtue of this Part (whether by the Commission, the Secretary of State or a relevant sectoral regulator); and

    (c) the details of any variation, release or revocation of such an undertaking or order.

(4) The duty in subsection (3) does not extend to anything of which the OFT is unaware.

(5) The Commission, the Secretary of State and any relevant sectoral regulator shall inform the OFT of any matters which are to be included in the register by virtue of subsection (3) and which relate to enforcement undertakings accepted by them or enforcement orders made by them.

(6) The OFT shall ensure that the contents of the register are available to the public—

    (a) during (as a minimum) such hours as may be specified in an order made by the Secretary of State; and

    (b) subject to such reasonable fees (if any) as the OFT may determine.

(7) If requested by any person to do so and subject to such reasonable fees (if any) as the OFT may determine, the OFT shall supply the person concerned with a copy (certified to be true) of the register or of an extract from it.

167   Rights to enforce undertakings and orders under this Part

(1) This section applies to any enforcement undertaking or enforcement order.

(2) Any person to whom such an undertaking or order relates shall have a duty to comply with it.

(3) The duty shall be owed to any person who may be affected by a contravention of the undertaking or (as the case may be) order.

(4) Any breach of the duty which causes such a person to sustain loss or damage shall be actionable by him.

(5) In any proceedings brought under subsection (4) against a person to whom an enforcement undertaking or enforcement order relates it shall be a defence for that person to show that he took all reasonable steps and exercised all due diligence to avoid contravening the undertaking or (as the case may be) order.

(6) Compliance with an enforcement undertaking or an enforcement order shall also be enforceable by civil proceedings brought by the OFT for an injunction or for interdict or for any other appropriate relief or remedy.

(7) Compliance with an undertaking accepted under section 157 or 159, or an order under section 158, 160 or 161, shall also be enforceable by civil proceedings brought by the relevant authority for an injunction or for interdict or for any other appropriate relief or remedy.

(8) In subsection (7) 'the relevant authority' means—

    (a) in the case of an undertaking accepted by the Commission or an order made by the Commission, the Commission; and

    (b) in the case of an undertaking accepted by the Secretary of State or an order made by the Secretary of State, the Secretary of State.

(9) Subsections (6) to (8) shall not prejudice any right that a person may have by virtue of subsection (4) to bring civil proceedings for contravention or apprehended contravention of an enforcement undertaking or an enforcement order.

Chapter 4 Supplementary

Regulated markets

168 Regulated markets

(1) Subsection (2) applies where the Commission or the Secretary of State is considering for the purposes of this Part whether relevant action would be reasonable and practicable for the purpose of remedying, mitigating or preventing an adverse effect on competition or any detrimental effect on customers so far as resulting from such an effect.

(2) The Commission or (as the case may be) the Secretary of State shall, in deciding whether such action would be reasonable and practicable, have regard to the relevant statutory functions of the sectoral regulator concerned.

(3) In this section 'relevant action' means—

    (b) modifying conditions in force under Part 4 of the Airports Act 1986 (c. 31) other than any conditions imposed or modified in pursuance of section 40(3) or (4) of that Act;

    (c) modifying the conditions of a licence granted under section 7 or 7A of the Gas Act 1986 (c. 44);

    (d) modifying the conditions of a licence granted under section 6 of the Electricity Act 1989 (c. 29);

    (e) modifying networking arrangements (within the meaning given by section 290 of the Communications Act 2003);

    (f) modifying the conditions of a company's appointment under Chapter 1 of Part 2 of the Water Industry Act 1991 (c. 56);

    (g) modifying the conditions of a licence granted under article 10 of the Electricity (Northern Ireland) Order 1992 (S.I. 1992/231 (N.I. 1));

    (h) modifying the conditions of a licence granted under section 8 of the Railways Act 1993 (c. 43);

    (i) modifying an access agreement (within the meaning given by section 83(1) of the Act of 1993) or a franchise agreement (within the meaning given by section 23(3) of that Act);

    (j) modifying conditions in force under Part 4 of the Airports (Northern Ireland) Order 1994 (S.I. 1994/426 (N.I.1)) other than any conditions imposed or modified in pursuance of article 40(3) or (4) of that Order;

    (k) modifying the conditions of a licence granted under article 8 of the Gas (Northern Ireland) Order 1996 (S.I. 1996/275 (N.I. 2));

    (l) modifying the conditions of a licence granted under section 11 of the Postal Services Act 2000 (c. 26); or

    (m) modifying the conditions of a licence granted under section 5 of the Transport Act 2000 (c. 38).

(4) In this section 'relevant statutory functions' means—

(b) in relation to conditions in force under Part 4 of the Airports Act 1986 other than any conditions imposed or modified in pursuance of section 40(3) or (4) of that Act, the duties of the Civil Aviation Authority under section 39(2) and (3) of that Act;

(c) in relation to any licence granted under section 7 or 7A of the Gas Act 1986, the objectives and duties of the Gas and Electricity Markets Authority under section 4AA and 4AB(2) of that Act;

(d) in relation to any licence granted under section 6 of the Electricity Act 1989 (c. 29), the objectives and duties of the Gas and Electricity Markets Authority under section 3A and 3B(2) of that Act;

(e) in relation to any networking arrangements (within the meaning given by section 290 of the Communications Act 2003), the duty of the Office of Communications under subsection (1) of section 3 of that Act to secure the matters mentioned in subsection (2) (c) of that section;

(f) in relation to a company's appointment under Chapter 1 of Part 2 of the Water Industry Act 1991 (c. 56), the duties of the Director General of Water Services under section 2 of that Act;

(g) in relation to any licence granted under article 10 of the Electricity (Northern Ireland) Order 1992 (S.I. 1992/231 (N.I. 1)), the duty of the Director General of Electricity Supply for Northern Ireland under article 6 of that Order;

(h) in relation to any licence granted under section 8 of the Railways Act 1993 (c. 43) where none of the conditions of the licence relate to consumer protection, the duties of the Rail Regulator under section 4 of that Act;

(i) in relation to any licence granted under section 8 of the Act of 1993 where one or more than one condition of the licence relates to consumer protection, the duties of the Rail Regulator under section 4 of that Act and the duties of the Strategic Rail Authority under section 207 of the Transport Act 2000 (c. 38);

(j) in relation to any access agreement (within the meaning given by section 83(1) of the Act of 1993), the duties of the Rail Regulator under section 4 of the Act of 1993;

(k) in relation to any franchise agreement (within the meaning given by section 23(3) of the Act of 1993), the duties of the Strategic Rail Authority under section 207 of the Act of 2000;

(l) in relation to conditions in force under Part 4 of the Airports (Northern Ireland) Order 1994 (S.I. 1994/426 (N.I.1)) other than any conditions imposed or modified in pursuance of article 40(3) or (4) of that Order, the duties of the Civil Aviation Authority under article 30(2) and (3) of that Order;

(m) in relation to any licence granted under article 8 of the Gas (Northern Ireland) Order 1996 (S.I. 1996/275 (N.I. 2)), the duties of the Director General of Gas for Northern Ireland under article 5 of that Order;

(n) in relation to any licence granted under section 11 of the Postal Services Act 2000 (c. 26), the duties of the Postal Services Commission under section 3 and 5 of that Act; and

(o) in relation to any licence granted under section 5 of the Transport Act 2000, the duties of the Civil Aviation Authority under section 87 of that Act.

(5) In this section 'sectoral regulator' means—

(a) the Civil Aviation Authority;

(b) the Director General of Electricity Supply for Northern Ireland;

(c) the Director General of Gas for Northern Ireland;

(e) the Director General of Water Services;

(f) the Gas and Electricity Markets Authority;

(g) the Office of Communications;

(h) the Postal Services Commission;

(i) the Rail Regulator; or

(j) the Strategic Rail Authority.

(6) Subsection (7) applies where the Commission or the Secretary of State is considering for the purposes of this Part whether modifying the conditions of a licence granted under section 7 or 7A of the Gas Act 1986 (c. 44) would be reasonable and practicable for the purpose of remedying, mitigating or preventing an adverse effect on competition or any detrimental effect on customers so far as resulting from such an effect.

(7) The Commission or (as the case may be) the Secretary of State may, in deciding whether modifying the conditions of such a licence would be reasonable and practicable, have regard to those matters to which the Gas and Electricity Markets Authority may have regard by virtue of section 4AA(4) of the Act of 1986.

(8) The Secretary of State may by order modify subsection (3), (4), (5), (6) or (7).

(9) Part 2 of Schedule 9 (which makes provision for functions under this Part to be exercisable by various sectoral regulators) shall have effect.

Consultation, information and publicity

169   Certain duties of relevant authorities to consult: Part IV

(1) Subsection (2) applies where the relevant authority is proposing to make a relevant decision in a way which the relevant authority considers is likely to have a substantial impact on the interests of any person.

(2) The relevant authority shall, so far as practicable, consult that person about what is proposed before making that decision.

(3) In consulting the person concerned, the relevant authority shall, so far as practicable, give the reasons of the relevant authority for the proposed decision.

(4) In considering what is practicable for the purposes of this section the relevant authority shall, in particular, have regard to—

    (a) any restrictions imposed by any timetable for making the decision; and

    (b) any need to keep what is proposed, or the reasons for it, confidential.

(5) The duty under this section shall not apply in relation to the making of any decision so far as particular provision is made elsewhere by virtue of this Part for consultation before the making of that decision.

(6) In this section—

'the relevant authority' means the OFT, the appropriate Minister or the Commission; and

'relevant decision' means—

    (a) in the case of the OFT, any decision by the OFT—

        (i)   as to whether to make a reference under section 131 or accept undertakings under section 154 instead of making such a reference; or

        (ii) to vary under section 135 such a reference;

    (b) in the case of the appropriate Minister, any decision by the appropriate Minister—

        (i)   as to whether to make a reference under section 132; or

        (ii) to vary under section 135 such a reference; and

    (c) in the case of the Commission, any decision on the questions mentioned in section 134 or 141.

170   General information duties

(1) The OFT shall give the Commission—

    (a) such information in its possession as the Commission may reasonably require to enable the Commission to carry out its functions under this Part; and

    (b) any other assistance which the Commission may reasonably require for the purpose of assisting it in carrying out its functions under this Part and which it is within the power of the OFT to give.

(2) The OFT shall give the Commission any information in its possession which has not been requested by the Commission but which, in the opinion of the OFT, would be appropriate to give to the Commission for the purpose of assisting it in carrying out its functions under this Part.

(3) The OFT and the Commission shall give the Secretary of State or the appropriate Minister so far as he is not the Secretary of State acting alone—

(a) such information in their possession as the Secretary of State or (as the case may be) the appropriate Minister concerned may by direction reasonably require to enable him to carry out his functions under this Part; and

(b) any other assistance which the Secretary of State or (as the case may be) the appropriate Minister concerned may by direction reasonably require for the purpose of assisting him in carrying out his functions under this Part and which it is within the power of the OFT or (as the case may be) the Commission to give.

(4) The OFT shall give the Secretary of State or the appropriate Minister so far as he is not the Secretary of State acting alone any information in its possession which has not been requested by the Secretary of State or (as the case may be) the appropriate Minister concerned but which, in the opinion of the OFT, would be appropriate to give to the Secretary of State or (as the case may be) the appropriate Minister concerned for the purpose of assisting him in carrying out his functions under this Part.

(5) The Commission shall have regard to any information given to it under subsection (1) or (2); and the Secretary of State or (as the case may be) the appropriate Minister concerned shall have regard to any information given to him under subsection (3) or (4).

(6) Any direction given under subsection (3)—

(a) shall be in writing; and

(b) may be varied or revoked by a subsequent direction.

171   Advice and information: Part IV

(1) As soon as reasonably practicable after the passing of this Act, the OFT shall prepare and publish general advice and information about the making of references by it under section 131.

(2) The OFT may at any time publish revised, or new, advice or information.

(3) As soon as reasonably practicable after the passing of this Act, the Commission shall prepare and publish general advice and information about the consideration by it of market investigation references and the way in which relevant customer benefits may affect the taking of enforcement action in relation to such references.

(4) The Commission may at any time publish revised, or new, advice or information.

(5) Advice and information published under this section shall be prepared with a view to—

(a) explaining relevant provisions of this Part to persons who are likely to be affected by them; and

(b) indicating how the OFT or (as the case may be) the Commission expects such provisions to operate.

(6) Advice and information published by virtue of subsection (1) or (3) may include such advice and information about the effect of Community law, and anything done under or in accordance with it, on the provision of this Part as the OFT (as the case may be) or the Commission considers appropriate.

(7) Advice (or information) published by virtue of subsection (1) or (3) may include advice (or information) about the factors which the OFT or (as the case may be) the Commission may take into account in considering whether, and if so how, to exercise a function conferred by this Part.

(8) Any advice or information published by the OFT or the Commission under this section shall be published in such manner as the OFT or (as the case may be) the Commission considers appropriate.

(9) In preparing any advice or information under this section, the OFT shall consult the Commission and such other persons as it considers appropriate.

(10) In preparing any advice or information under this section, the Commission shall consult the OFT and such other persons as it considers appropriate.

(11) In this section 'Community law' means—

(a) all the rights, powers, liabilities, obligations and restrictions from time to time created or arising by or under the Community Treaties; and

(b) all the remedies and procedures from time to time provided for by or under the Community Treaties.

172   Further publicity requirements: Part IV

(1) The OFT shall publish—

  (a) any reference made by it under section 131;

  (b) any variation made by it under section 135 of a reference under section 131;

  (c) any decision of a kind mentioned in section 149(5)(b); and

  (d) such information as it considers appropriate about any decision made by it under section 152(1) to bring a case to the attention of the Secretary of State.

(2) The Commission shall publish—

  (a) any decision made by it under section 138(2) neither to accept an undertaking under section 159 nor to make an order under section 161;

  (b) any decision made by it that there has been a material change of circumstances as mentioned in section 138(3) or there is another special reason as mentioned in that section;

  (c) any termination under section 145(1) of an investigation by it;

  (d) such information as it considers appropriate about any decision made by it under section 152(2) to bring a case to the attention of the Secretary of State;

  (e) any enforcement undertaking accepted by it under section 157;

  (f) any enforcement order made by it under section 158; and

  (g) any variation, release or revocation of such an undertaking or order.

(3) The Secretary of State shall publish—

  (a) any reference made by him under section 132;

  (b) any variation made by him under section 135 of a reference under section 132;

  (c) any intervention notice given by him;

  (d) any decision made by him to revoke such a notice;

  (e) any decision made by him under section 147(2) neither to accept an undertaking under section 159 nor to make an order under section 161;

  (f) any enforcement undertaking accepted by him under section 157;

  (g) any variation or release of such an undertaking; and

  (h) any direction given by him under section 170(3) in connection with the exercise by him of his functions under section 132(3).

(4) The appropriate Minister (other than the Secretary of State acting alone) shall publish—

  (a) any reference made by him under section 132;

  (b) any variation made by him under section 135 of a reference under section 132; and

  (c) any direction given by him under section 170(3) in connection with the exercise by him of his functions under section 132(3).

(5) Where any person is under an obligation by virtue of subsection (1), (2), (3) or (4) to publish the result of any action taken by that person or any decision made by that person, the person concerned shall, subject to subsections (6) and (7), also publish that person's reasons for the action concerned or (as the case may be) as the decision concerned.

(6) Such reasons need not, if it is not reasonably practicable to do so, be published at the same time as the result of the action concerned or (as the case may be) as the decision concerned.

(7) Subsections (5) and (6) shall not apply in relation to any case falling within subsection (1)(d) or (2)(d).

(8) The Secretary of State shall publish his reasons for—

  (a) any decision made by him under section 146(2); or

  (b) any decision to make an order under section 153(3) or vary or revoke such an order.

(9) Such reasons may be published after—

  (a) in the case of subsection (8)(a), the publication of the decision concerned; and

  (b) in the case of subsection (8)(b), the making of the order or of the variation or revocation;

if it is not reasonably practicable to publish them at the same time as the publication of the decision or (as the case may be) the making of the order or variation or revocation.

(10) Where the Secretary of State has decided under section 147(2) to accept an undertaking under section 159 or to make an order under section 161, he shall lay details of his decision and his reasons for it, and the Commission's report under section 142, before each House of Parliament.

173   Defamation: Part IV

For the purposes of the law relating to defamation, absolute privilege attaches to any advice, guidance, notice or direction given, or decision or report made, by the OFT, by the Secretary of State, by the appropriate Minister (other than the Secretary of State acting alone) or by the Commission in the exercise of any of their functions under this Part.

Investigation powers

174   Investigation powers of OFT

(1) The OFT may exercise any of the powers in subsections (3) to (7) for the purpose of assisting it in deciding whether to make a reference under section 131 or to accept undertakings under section 154 instead of making such a reference.

(2) The OFT shall not exercise any of the powers in subsections (3) to (7) for the purpose of assisting it as mentioned in subsection (1) unless it already believes that it has power to make such a reference.

(3) The OFT may give notice to any person requiring him—
  (a) to attend at a time and place specified in the notice; and
  (b) to give evidence to the OFT or a person nominated by the OFT for the purpose.

(4) The OFT may give notice to any person requiring him—
  (a) to produce any documents which—
    (i) are specified or described in the notice, or fall within a category of document which is specified or described in the notice; and
    (ii) are in that person's custody or under his control; and
  (b) to produce them at a time and place so specified and to a person so specified.

(5) The OFT may give notice to any person who carries on any business requiring him—
  (a) to supply to the OFT such estimates, forecasts, returns or other information as may be specified or described in the notice; and
  (b) to supply it at a time and place, and in a form and manner, so specified and to a person so specified.

(6) A notice under this section shall include information about the possible consequences of not complying with the notice.

(7) The person to whom any document is produced in accordance with a notice under this section may, for the purpose mentioned in subsection (1), copy the document so produced.

(8) No person shall be required under this section—
  (a) to give any evidence or produce any documents which he could not be compelled to give or produce in civil proceedings before the court; or
  (b) to supply any information which he could not be compelled to supply in evidence in such proceedings.

(9) No person shall be required, in compliance with a notice under this section, to go more than 10 miles from his place of residence unless his necessary travelling expenses are paid or offered to him.

(10) Any reference in this section to the production of a document includes a reference to the production of a legible and intelligible copy of information recorded otherwise than in legible form.

(11) In this section 'the court' means—
  (a) in relation to England and Wales or Northern Ireland, the High Court; and
  (b) in relation to Scotland, the Court of Session.

175 Enforcement of powers under section 174: offences

(1) A person commits an offence if he, intentionally and without reasonable excuse, fails to comply with any requirement of a notice under section 174.

(2) A person commits an offence if he intentionally and without reasonable excuse alters, suppresses or destroys any document which he has been required to produce by a notice under section 174.

(3) A person who commits an offence under subsection (1) or (2) shall be liable—

(a) on summary conviction, to a fine not exceeding the statutory maximum;

(b) on conviction on indictment, to imprisonment for a term not exceeding two years or to a fine or to both.

(4) A person commits an offence if he intentionally obstructs or delays—

(a) the OFT in the exercise of its powers under section 174; or

(b) any person in the exercise of his powers under subsection (7) of that section.

(5) A person who commits an offence under subsection (4) shall be liable—

(a) on summary conviction, to a fine not exceeding the statutory maximum;

(b) on conviction on indictment, to a fine.

176 Investigation powers of the Commission

(1) The following sections in Part 3 shall apply, with the modifications mentioned in subsection (2) below, for the purposes of references under this Part as they apply for the purposes of references under that Part—

(a) section 109 (attendance of witnesses and production of documents etc.);

(b) section 110 (enforcement of powers under section 106: general);

(c) section 111 (penalties);

(d) section 112 (penalties: main procedural requirements);

(e) section 113 (payments and interest by instalments);

(f) section 114 (appeals in relation to penalties);

(g) section 115 (recovery of penalties); and

(h) section 116 (statement of policy).

(2) Section 110 shall, in its application by virtue of subsection (1) above, have effect as if—

(a) subsection (2) were omitted; and

(b) in subsection (9) the words from 'or section' to 'section 65(3))' were omitted.

(3) Section 111(5)(b)(ii) shall, in its application by virtue of subsection (1) above, have effect as if—

(a) for the words 'section 50 or 65, given' there were substituted 'section 142, published or given under section 143(1) or (3)'; and

(b) for the words '(or given)', in both places where they appear, there were substituted '(or published or given)'.

Reports

177 Excisions from reports: Part IV

(1) Subsection (2) applies where the Secretary of State is under a duty to publish a report of the Commission under section 142.

(2) The Secretary of State may exclude a matter from the report if he considers that publication of the matter would be inappropriate.

(3) In deciding what is inappropriate for the purposes of subsection (2) the Secretary of State shall have regard to the considerations mentioned in section 244.

(4) The Commission shall advise the Secretary of State as to the matters (if any) which it considers should be excluded by him under subsection (2).

(5) References in sections 136(4) to (6), 143(2) and (5) to (7), 148(3) to (5) and 172(10) to the giving or laying of a report of the Commission shall be construed as references to the giving or laying of the report as published.

178 Minority reports of Commission: Part IV

(1) Subsection (2) applies where, on a market investigation reference, a member of a group constituted in connection with the reference in pursuance of paragraph 15 of Schedule 7 to the Competition Act 1998 (c. 41), disagrees with any decisions contained in the report of the Commission under this Part as the decisions of the Commission.

(2) The report shall, if the member so wishes, include a statement of his disagreement and of his reasons for disagreeing.

Other

179 Review of decisions under Part IV

(1) Any person aggrieved by a decision of the OFT, the appropriate Minister, the Secretary of State or the Commission in connection with a reference or possible reference under this Part may apply to the Competition Appeal Tribunal for a review of that decision.

(2) For this purpose 'decision'—
  (a) does not include a decision to impose a penalty under section 110(1) or (3) as applied by section 176; but
  (b) includes a failure to take a decision permitted or required by this Part in connection with a reference or possible reference.

(3) Except in so far as a direction to the contrary is given by the Competition Appeal Tribunal, the effect of the decision is not suspended by reason of the making of the application.

(4) In determining such an application the Competition Appeal Tribunal shall apply the same principles as would be applied by a court on an application for judicial review.

(5) The Competition Appeal Tribunal may—
  (a) dismiss the application or quash the whole or part of the decision to which it relates; and
  (b) where it quashes the whole or part of that decision, refer the matter back to the original decision maker with a direction to reconsider and make a new decision in accordance with the ruling of the Competition Appeal Tribunal.

(6) An appeal lies on any point of law arising from a decision of the Competition Appeal Tribunal under this section to the appropriate court.

(7) An appeal under subsection (6) requires the permission of the Tribunal or the appropriate court.

(8) In this section—
  'the appropriate court' means the Court of Appeal or, in the case of Tribunal proceedings in Scotland, the Court of Session; and
  'Tribunal rules' has the meaning given by section 15(1).

180 Offences

(1) Sections 117 (false or misleading information) and 125 (offences by bodies corporate) shall apply, with the modifications mentioned in subsection (2) below, for the purposes of this Part as they apply for the purposes of Part 3.

(2) Section 117 shall, in its application by virtue of subsection (1) above, have effect as if references to the Secretary of State included references to the appropriate Minister so far as he is not the Secretary of State acting alone and as if the references to OFCOM were omitted.

181 Orders under Part IV

(1) Any power of the Secretary of State to make an order under this Part shall be exercisable by statutory instrument.

(2) Any power of the Secretary of State to make an order under this Part—
  (a) may be exercised so as to make different provision for different cases or different purposes;
  (b) includes power to make such incidental, supplementary, consequential, transitory, transitional or saving provision as the Secretary of State considers appropriate.

(3) The power of the Secretary of State under section 136(9), 137(3), 144(2), 153(3) or 168(8) as extended by subsection (2) above may be exercised by modifying any enactment comprised in or made under this Act, or any other enactment.

(4) An order made by the Secretary of State under section 137(3), 144(2), 158, 160 or 161, or under section 111(4) or (6) or 114(3)(b) or (4)(b) as applied by section 176, shall be subject to annulment in pursuance of a resolution of either House of Parliament.

(5) No order shall be made by the Secretary of State under section 136(9) or 168(8), or section 128(6) as applied by section 183(2), unless a draft of it has been laid before, and approved by a resolution of, each House of Parliament.

(6) An order made by the Secretary of State under section 153(3) shall be laid before Parliament after being made and shall cease to have effect unless approved, within the period of 28 days beginning with the day on which it is made, by a resolution of each House of Parliament.

(7) In calculating the period of 28 days mentioned in subsection (6), no account shall be taken of any time during which Parliament is dissolved or prorogued or during which both Houses are adjourned for more than four days.

(8) If an order made by the Secretary of State ceases to have effect by virtue of subsection (6), any modification made by it of an enactment is repealed but without prejudice to the validity of anything done in connection with that modification before the order ceased to have effect.

(9) If, apart from this subsection, an order made by the Secretary of State under section 153(3) would be treated for the purposes of the standing orders of either House of Parliament as a hybrid instrument, it shall proceed in that House as if it were not such an instrument.

(10) References in this section to an order made under this Part include references to an order made under section 114(4) or (6) or 114(3)(b) or (4)(b) as applied by section 176 and an order made under section 128(6) as applied by section 183(2).

182   Service of documents: Part IV
Section 126 shall apply for the purposes of this Part as it applies for the purposes of Part 3.

183   Interpretation: Part IV
(1) In this Part, unless the context otherwise requires—

'action' includes omission; and references to the taking of action include references to refraining from action;

'business' includes a professional practice and includes any other undertaking which is carried on for gain or reward or which is an undertaking in the course of which goods or services are supplied otherwise than free of charge;

'change of circumstances' includes any discovery that information has been supplied which is false or misleading in a material respect;

'consumer' means any person who is—

    (a) a person to whom goods are or are sought to be supplied (whether by way of sale or otherwise) in the course of a business carried on by the person supplying or seeking to supply them; or

    (b) a person for whom services are or are sought to be supplied in the course of a business carried on by the person supplying or seeking to supply them;

and who does not receive or seek to receive the goods or services in the course of a business carried on by him;

'customer' includes a customer who is not a consumer;

'enactment' includes an Act of the Scottish Parliament, Northern Ireland legislation and an enactment comprised in subordinate legislation, and includes an enactment whenever passed or made;

'goods' includes buildings and other structures, and also includes ships, aircraft and hovercraft;

'Minister of the Crown' means the holder of an office in Her Majesty's Government in the United Kingdom and includes the Treasury;

'modify' includes amend or repeal;

'notice' means notice in writing;

'subordinate legislation' has the same meaning as in the Interpretation Act 1978 (c. 30) and also includes an instrument made under an Act of the Scottish Parliament and an instrument made under Northern Ireland legislation; and

'supply', in relation to the supply of goods, includes supply by way of sale, lease, hire or hire-purchase, and, in relation to buildings or other structures, includes the construction of them by a person for another person.

(2) Sections 127(1)(b) and (4) to (6) and 128 shall apply for the purposes of this Part as they apply for the purposes of Part 3.

(3) For the purposes of this Part a market investigation reference is finally determined if—

    (a) where no intervention notice has been given in relation to it—

        (i) the period permitted by section 137 for preparing and publishing a report under section 136 has expired and no such report has been prepared and published;

        (ii) such a report has been prepared and published within the period permitted by section 137 and contains the decision that there is no adverse effect on competition;

        (iii) the Commission has decided under section 138(2) neither to accept undertakings under section 159 nor to make an order under section 161; or

        (iv) the Commission has accepted an undertaking under section 159 or made an order under section 161;

    (b) where an intervention notice under section 139(1) has been given in relation to it—

        (i) the period permitted by section 144 for the preparation of the report of the Commission under section 142 and for action to be taken in relation to it under section 143(1) or (3) has expired while the intervention notice is still in force and no such report has been so prepared or no such action has been taken;

        (ii) the Commission has terminated under section 145(1) its investigation and the reference is finally determined under paragraph (a) above (disregarding the fact that the notice was given);

        (iii) the report of the Commission has been prepared under section 142 and published under section 143(1) within the period permitted by section 144;

        (iv) the intervention notice was revoked and the reference is finally determined under paragraph (a) above (disregarding the fact that the notice was given);

        (v) the Secretary of State has failed to make and publish a decision under subsection (2) of section 146 within the period permitted by subsection (3) of that section and the reference is finally determined under paragraph (a) above (disregarding the fact that the notice was given);

        (vi) the Secretary of State has decided under section 146(2) that no eligible public interest consideration is relevant and the reference is finally determined under paragraph (a) above (disregarding the fact that the notice was given);

        (vii) the Secretary of State has decided under 146(2) that a public interest consideration is relevant but has decided under section 147(2) neither to accept an undertaking under section 159 nor to make an order under section 161; or

        (viii) the Secretary of State has decided under section 146(2) that a public interest consideration is relevant and has accepted an undertaking under section 159 or made an order under section 161.

(4) For the purposes of this Part the time when a market investigation reference is finally determined is—

    (a) in a case falling within subsection (3)(a)(i) or (b)(i), the expiry of the time concerned;

    (b) in a case falling within subsection (3)(a)(ii) or (b)(iii), the publication of the report;

    (c) in a case falling within subsection (3)(a)(iv) or (b)(viii), the acceptance of the undertaking concerned or (as the case may be) the making of the order concerned; and

    (d) in any other case, the making of the decision or last decision concerned or the taking of the action concerned.

(5) The references in subsection (4) to subsections (3)(a)(i), (ii) and (iv) include those enactments as applied by subsection (3)(b)(ii), (iv), (v) or (vi).

(6) In subsection (4)(c) the reference to the acceptance of the undertaking concerned or the making of the order concerned shall, in a case where the enforcement action concerned involves the acceptance of a group of undertakings, the making of a group of orders or the acceptance and making of a group of undertakings and orders, be treated as a reference to the acceptance or making of the last undertaking or order in the group; but undertakings or orders which vary, supersede or revoke earlier undertakings or orders shall be disregarded for the purposes of subsections (3)(a)(iv) and (b)(viii) and (4)(c).

(7) Any duty to publish which is imposed on a person by this Part shall, unless the context otherwise requires, be construed as a duty on that person to publish in such manner as that person considers appropriate for the purpose of bringing the matter concerned to the attention of those likely to be affected by it.

184 Index of defined expressions: Part IV

In this Part, the expressions listed in the left-hand column have the meaning given by, or are to be interpreted in accordance with, the provisions listed in the right-hand column.

PART V THE COMPETITION COMMISSION

185 The Commission

Schedule 11 (which amends provisions relating to the constitution and powers of the Commission under Schedule 7 to the 1998 Act) has effect.

186 Annual report of Commission

After paragraph 12 of Schedule 7 to the 1998 Act (the Competition Commission) there is inserted—

'Annual reports

12A (1).—The Commission shall make to the Secretary of State a report for each financial year on its activities during the year.

(2) The annual report must be made before the end of August next following the financial year to which it relates.

(3) The Secretary of State shall lay a copy of the annual report before Parliament and arrange for the report to be published.'

187 Commission rules of procedure

(1) In section 45(7) of the 1998 Act (the Competition Commission) for the words 'Schedule 7 makes' there shall be substituted 'Schedules 7 and 7A make'.

(2) In paragraph 19 of Schedule 7 to that Act, after sub-paragraph (4), there shall be inserted—

'(5) This paragraph does not apply to groups for which rules must be made under paragraph 19A.'

(3) After paragraph 19 of that Schedule to that Act there shall be inserted—

'19A.—(1) The Chairman must make rules of procedure in relation to merger reference groups, market reference groups and special reference groups.

(2) Schedule 7A makes further provision about rules made under this paragraph but is not to be taken as restricting the Chairman's powers under this section.

(3) The Chairman must publish rules made under this paragraph in such manner as he considers appropriate for the purpose of bringing them to the attention of those likely to be affected by them.

(4) The Chairman must consult the members of the Commission and such other persons as he considers appropriate before making rules under this paragraph.

(5) Rules under this paragraph may—

(a) make different provision for different cases or different purposes;

(b) be varied or revoked by subsequent rules made under this paragraph.

(6) Subject to rules made under this paragraph, each merger reference group, market reference group and special reference group may determine its own procedure.

(7) In determining how to proceed in accordance with rules made under this paragraph and in determining its procedure under subparagraph (6), a group must have regard to any guidance issued by the Chairman.

(8) Before issuing any guidance for the purposes of this paragraph the Chairman shall consult the members of the Commission and such other persons as he considers appropriate.

(9) In this paragraph and in Schedule 7A—

'market reference group' means any group constituted in connection with a reference under section 126 or 127 of the Enterprise Act 2002 (including that section as it has effect by virtue of another enactment);

'merger reference group' means any group constituted in connection with a reference under section 59 of the Fair Trading Act 1973 (c. 41), section 32 of the Water Industry Act 1991 (c. 56) or section 21, 32, 44 or 61 of the Enterprise Act 2002; and

'special reference group' means any group constituted in connection with a reference or (in the case of the Financial Services and Markets Act 2000 (c. 8)) an investigation under—

(a) section 11 of the Competition Act 1980 (c. 21);

(b) section 13 of the Telecommunications Act 1984 (c. 12);

(c) section 43 of the Airports Act 1986 (c. 31);

(d) section 24 or 41E of the Gas Act 1986 (c. 44);

(e) section 12 or 56C of the Electricity Act 1989 (c. 29);

(f) Schedule 4 to the Broadcasting Act 1990 (c. 42);

(g) section 12 or 14 of the Water Industry Act 1991 (c. 56);

(h) article 15 of the Electricity (Northern Ireland) Order 1992 (S.I. 1992/231 (N.I.1));

(i) section 13 of, or Schedule 4A to, the Railways Act 1993 (c. 43);

(j) article 34 of the Airports (Northern Ireland) Order 1994 (S.I. 1994/426 (N.I. 1));

(k) article 15 of the Gas (Northern Ireland) Order 1996 (S.I. 1996/275 (N.I. 2));

(l) section 15 of the Postal Services Act 2000 (c. 26);

(m) section 162 or 306 of the Financial Services and Markets Act 2000 (c. 8); or

(n) section 12 of the Transport Act 2000 (c. 38).'

(4) After Schedule 7 to that Act there shall be inserted, as Schedule 7A, the Schedule set out in Schedule 12 to this Act.

PART VI CARTEL OFFENCE

Cartel offence

188 Cartel offence

(1) An individual is guilty of an offence if he dishonestly agrees with one or more other persons to make or implement, or to cause to be made or implemented, arrangements of the following kind relating to at least two undertakings (A and B).

(2) The arrangements must be ones which, if operating as the parties to the agreement intend, would—

(a) directly or indirectly fix a price for the supply by A in the United Kingdom (otherwise than to B) of a product or service,

(b) limit or prevent supply by A in the United Kingdom of a product or service,

(c) limit or prevent production by A in the United Kingdom of a product,

(d) divide between A and B the supply in the United Kingdom of a product or service to a customer or customers,

(e) divide between A and B customers for the supply in the United Kingdom of a product or service, or

(f) be bid-rigging arrangements.

(3) Unless subsection (2)(d), (e) or (f) applies, the arrangements must also be ones which, if operating as the parties to the agreement intend, would—

(a) directly or indirectly fix a price for the supply by B in the United Kingdom (otherwise than to A) of a product or service,

(b) limit or prevent supply by B in the United Kingdom of a product or service, or

(c) limit or prevent production by B in the United Kingdom of a product.

(4) In subsections (2)(a) to (d) and (3), references to supply or production are to supply or production in the appropriate circumstances (for which see section 189).

(5) 'Bid-rigging arrangements' are arrangements under which, in response to a request for bids for the supply of a product or service in the United Kingdom, or for the production of a product in the United Kingdom—

(a) A but not B may make a bid, or

(b) A and B may each make a bid but, in one case or both, only a bid arrived at in accordance with the arrangements.

(6) But arrangements are not bid-rigging arrangements if, under them, the person requesting bids would be informed of them at or before the time when a bid is made.

(7) 'Undertaking' has the same meaning as in Part 1 of the 1998 Act.

189   Cartel offence: supplementary

(1) For section 188(2)(a), the appropriate circumstances are that A's supply of the product or service would be at a level in the supply chain at which the product or service would at the same time be supplied by B in the United Kingdom.

(2) For section 188(2)(b), the appropriate circumstances are that A's supply of the product or service would be at a level in the supply chain—

(a) at which the product or service would at the same time be supplied by B in the United Kingdom, or

(b) at which supply by B in the United Kingdom of the product or service would be limited or prevented by the arrangements.

(3) For section 188(2)(c), the appropriate circumstances are that A's production of the product would be at a level in the production chain—

(a) at which the product would at the same time be produced by B in the United Kingdom, or

(b) at which production by B in the United Kingdom of the product would be limited or prevented by the arrangements.

(4) For section 188(2)(d), the appropriate circumstances are that A's supply of the product or service would be at the same level in the supply chain as B's.

(5) For section 188(3)(a), the appropriate circumstances are that B's supply of the product or service would be at a level in the supply chain at which the product or service would at the same time be supplied by A in the United Kingdom.

(6) For section 183(3)(b), the appropriate circumstances are that B's supply of the product or service would be at a level in the supply chain—

(a) at which the product or service would at the same time be supplied by A in the United Kingdom, or

(b) at which supply by A in the United Kingdom of the product or service would be limited or prevented by the arrangements.

(7) For section 188(3)(c), the appropriate circumstances are that B's production of the product would be at a level in the production chain—

(a) at which the product would at the same time be produced by A in the United Kingdom, or

(b) at which production by A in the United Kingdom of the product would be limited or prevented by the arrangements.

190   Cartel offence: penalty and prosecution

(1) A person guilty of an offence under section 188 is liable—

    (a) on conviction on indictment, to imprisonment for a term not exceeding five years or to a fine, or to both;

    (b) on summary conviction, to imprisonment for a term not exceeding six months or to a fine not exceeding the statutory maximum, or to both.

(2) In England and Wales and Northern Ireland, proceedings for an offence under section 188 may be instituted only—

    (a) by the Director of the Serious Fraud Office, or

    (b) by or with the consent of the OFT.

(3) No proceedings may be brought for an offence under section 188 in respect of an agreement outside the United Kingdom, unless it has been implemented in whole or in part in the United Kingdom.

(4) Where, for the purpose of the investigation or prosecution of offences under section 188, the OFT gives a person written notice under this subsection, no proceedings for an offence under section 188 that falls within a description specified in the notice may be brought against that person in England and Wales or Northern Ireland except in circumstances specified in the notice.

191   [repealed]

Criminal investigations by OFT

192   Investigation of offences under section 188

(1) The OFT may conduct an investigation if there are reasonable grounds for suspecting that an offence under section 188 has been committed.

(2) The powers of the OFT under sections 193 and 194 are exercisable, but only for the purposes of an investigation under subsection (1), in any case where it appears to the OFT that there is good reason to exercise them for the purpose of investigating the affairs, or any aspect of the affairs, of any person ('the person under investigation').

193   Powers when conducting an investigation

(1) The OFT may by notice in writing require the person under investigation, or any other person who it has reason to believe has relevant information, to answer questions, or otherwise provide information, with respect to any matter relevant to the investigation at a specified place and either at a specified time or forthwith.

(2) The OFT may by notice in writing require the person under investigation, or any other person, to produce, at a specified place and either at a specified time or forthwith, specified documents, or documents of a specified description, which appear to the OFT to relate to any matter relevant to the investigation.

(3) If any such documents are produced, the OFT may—

    (a) take copies or extracts from them;

    (b) require the person producing them to provide an explanation of any of them.

(4) If any such documents are not produced, the OFT may require the person who was required to produce them to state, to the best of his knowledge and belief, where they are.

(5) A notice under subsection (1) or (2) must indicate—

    (a) the subject matter and purpose of the investigation; and

    (b) the nature of the offences created by section 201.

194   Power to enter premises under a warrant

(1) On an application made by the OFT to the High Court, or, in Scotland, by the procurator fiscal to the sheriff, in accordance with rules of court, a judge or the sheriff may issue a warrant if he is satisfied that there are reasonable grounds for believing—

    (a) that there are on any premises documents which the OFT has power under section 193 to require to be produced for the purposes of an investigation; and

    (b) that—

        (i) a person has failed to comply with a requirement under that section to produce the documents;

        (ii) it is not practicable to serve a notice under that section in relation to them; or

        (iii) the service of such a notice in relation to them might seriously prejudice the investigation.

(2) A warrant under this section shall authorise a named officer of the OFT, and any other officers of the OFT whom the OFT has authorised in writing to accompany the named officer—

    (a) to enter the premises, using such force as is reasonably necessary for the purpose;

    (b) to search the premises and—

        (i) take possession of any documents appearing to be of the relevant kind, or

        (ii) take, in relation to any documents appearing to be of the relevant kind, any other steps which may appear to be necessary for preserving them or preventing interference with them;

    (c) to require any person to provide an explanation of any document appearing to be of the relevant kind or to state, to the best of his knowledge and belief, where it may be found;

    (d) to require any information which is stored in any electronic form and is accessible from the premises and which the named officer considers relates to any matter relevant to the investigation, to be produced in a form—

        (i) in which it can be taken away, and

        (ii) in which it is visible and legible or from which it can readily be produced in a visible and legible form.

(3) Documents are of the relevant kind if they are of a kind in respect of which the application under subsection (1) was granted.

(4) A warrant under this section may authorise persons specified in the warrant to accompany the named officer who is executing it.

(5) In Part 1 of Schedule 1 to the Criminal Justice and Police Act 2001 (c. 16) (powers of seizure to which section 50 of that Act applies), after paragraph 73 there is inserted—

'Enterprise Act 2002

73A. The power of seizure conferred by section 189(2) of the Enterprise Act 2002 (seizure of documents for the purposes of an investigation under section 187(1) of that Act).'

195 Exercise of powers by authorised person

(1) The OFT may authorise any competent person who is not an officer of the OFT to exercise on its behalf all or any of the powers conferred by section 193 or 194.

(2) No such authority may be granted except for the purpose of investigating the affairs, or any aspect of the affairs, of a person specified in the authority.

(3) No person is bound to comply with any requirement imposed by a person exercising powers by virtue of any authority granted under this section unless he has, if required to do so, produced evidence of his authority.

196 Privileged information etc.

(1) A person may not under section 193 or 194 be required to disclose any information or produce any document which he would be entitled to refuse to disclose or produce on grounds of legal professional privilege in proceedings in the High Court, except that a lawyer may be required to provide the name and address of his client.

(2) A person may not under section 193 or 194 be required to disclose any information or produce any document in respect of which he owes an obligation of confidence by virtue of carrying on any banking business unless—

    (a) the person to whom the obligation of confidence is owed consents to the disclosure or production; or

    (b) the OFT has authorised the making of the requirement.

(3) In the application of this section to Scotland, the reference in subsection (1)—

(a) to proceedings in the High Court is to be read as a reference to legal proceedings generally; and

(b) to an entitlement on grounds of legal professional privilege is to be read as a reference to an entitlement by virtue of any rule of law whereby—

(i) communications between a professional legal adviser and his client, or

(ii) communications made in connection with or in contemplation of legal proceedings and for the purposes of those proceedings,

are in such proceedings protected from disclosure on the ground of confidentiality.

197   Restriction on use of statements in court

(1) A statement by a person in response to a requirement imposed by virtue of section 193 or 194 may only be used in evidence against him—

(a) on a prosecution for an offence under section 201(2); or

(b) on a prosecution for some other offence where in giving evidence he makes a statement inconsistent with it.

(2) However, the statement may not be used against that person by virtue of paragraph (b) of subsection (1) unless evidence relating to it is adduced, or a question relating to it is asked, by or on behalf of that person in the proceedings arising out of the prosecution.

198   Use of statements obtained under Competition Act 1998

In the 1998 Act, after section 30 there is inserted—

'30A   Use of statements in prosecution

A statement made by a person in response to a requirement imposed by virtue of any of sections 26 to 28 may not be used in evidence against him on a prosecution for an offence under section 188 of the Enterprise Act 2002 unless, in the proceedings—

(a) in giving evidence, he makes a statement inconsistent with it, and

(b) evidence relating to it is adduced, or a question relating to it is asked, by him or on his behalf.'

199   Surveillance powers

(1) The Regulation of Investigatory Powers Act 2000 (c. 23) is amended as follows.

(2) In section 32 (authorisation of intrusive surveillance)—

(a) after subsection (3) there is inserted—

'(3A) In the case of an authorisation granted by the chairman of the OFT, the authorisation is necessary on grounds falling within subsection (3) only if it is necessary for the purpose of preventing or detecting an offence under section 188 of the Enterprise Act 2002 (cartel offence).';

(b) in subsection (6) after paragraph (m) there is inserted '; and (n) the chairman of the OFT.'

(3) In section 33 (rules for grant of authorisations) after subsection (4) there is inserted— '(4A) The chairman of the OFT shall not grant an authorisation for the carrying out of intrusive surveillance except on an application made by an officer of the OFT.'

(4) In subsection (5)(a) of that section, after 'officer' there is inserted 'or the chairman or an officer of the OFT'.

(5) In section 34 (grant of authorisation in the senior officer's absence)—

(a) in subsection (1)(a), after 'or by' there is inserted 'an officer of the OFT or';

(b) in subsection (2)(a), after 'may be,' there is inserted 'as chairman of the OFT or';

(c) in subsection (4), after paragraph (1) there is inserted—

'(m) a person is entitled to act for the chairman of the OFT if he is an officer of the OFT designated by it for the purposes of this paragraph as a person entitled so to act in an urgent case.'

(6) In section 35 (notification of authorisations for intrusive surveillance)—

(a) in subsections (1) and (10), for 'or customs' there is substituted, 'customs or OFT';

(b) in subsection (10), after paragraph (b) there is inserted— '(ba) the chairman of the OFT; or';

(c) in paragraph (c) of that subsection, at the end there is inserted 'or for a person falling within paragraph (ba).'

(7) In section 36 (approval required for authorisations to take effect)—

(a) in subsection (1), after paragraph (d) there is inserted '; or (e) an officer of the OFT.';

(b) in subsection (6), after paragraph (g) there is inserted '; and

(h) where the authorisation was granted by the chairman of the OFT or a person entitled to act for him by virtue of section 34(4)(m), that chairman.'

(8) In section 37 (quashing of police and customs authorisations etc.) in subsection (1), after paragraph (d) there is inserted '; or(e) an officer of the OFT.'

(9) In section 40 (information to be provided to Surveillance Commissioners) after paragraph (d) there is inserted ', and (e) every officer of the OFT,'.

(10) In section 46 (restrictions on authorisations extending to Scotland), in subsection (3), after paragraph (d) there is inserted— '(da) the OFT;'.

(11) In section 48 (interpretation of Part 2), in subsection (1), after the entry relating to 'directed' and 'intrusive' there is inserted— '"OFT" means the Office of Fair Trading;'.

200   Authorisation of action in respect of property

(1) Part 3 of the Police Act 1997 (c. 50) (authorisation of action in respect of property) is amended as follows.

(2) In section 93 (authorisation to interfere with property etc.)—

(a) in subsection (1B), after 'customs officer' there is inserted 'or an officer of the Office of Fair Trading';

(b) after subsection (2A) there is inserted—

'(2AA) Where the authorising officer is the chairman of the Office of Fair Trading, the only purpose falling within subsection (2) (a) is the purpose of preventing or detecting an offence under section 188 of the Enterprise Act 2002.';

(c) in subsection (3), after paragraph (d) there is inserted ', or

(e) if the authorising officer is within subsection (5) (i), by an officer of the Office of Fair Trading.';

(d) in subsection (5), after paragraph (h) there is inserted '; or

(i) the chairman of the Office of Fair Trading.'

(3) In section 94 (authorisation given in absence of authorising officer) in subsection (2), after paragraph (f) there is inserted—

'(g) where the authorising officer is within paragraph (i) of that subsection, by an officer of the Office of Fair Trading designated by it for the purposes of this section.'

201   Offences

(1) Any person who without reasonable excuse fails to comply with a requirement imposed on him under section 193 or 194 is guilty of an offence and liable on summary conviction to imprisonment for a term not exceeding six months or to a fine not exceeding level 5 on the standard scale or to both.

(2) A person who, in purported compliance with a requirement under section 193 or 194—

(a) makes a statement which he knows to be false or misleading in a material particular; or

(b) recklessly makes a statement which is false or misleading in a material particular, is guilty of an offence.

(3) A person guilty of an offence under subsection (2) is liable—

(a) on conviction on indictment, to imprisonment for a term not exceeding two years or to a fine or to both; and

(b) on summary conviction, to imprisonment for a term not exceeding six months or to a fine not exceeding the statutory maximum, or to both.

(4) Where any person—

(a) knows or suspects that an investigation by the Serious Fraud Office or the OFT into an offence under section 188 is being or is likely to be carried out; and

(b) falsifies, conceals, destroys or otherwise disposes of, or causes or permits the falsification, concealment, destruction or disposal of documents which he knows or suspects are or would be relevant to such an investigation,

he is guilty of an offence unless he proves that he had no intention of concealing the facts disclosed by the documents from the persons carrying out such an investigation.

(5) A person guilty of an offence under subsection (4) is liable—

(a) on conviction on indictment, to imprisonment for a term not exceeding 5 years or to a fine or to both; and

(b) on summary conviction, to imprisonment for a term not exceeding six months or to a fine not exceeding the statutory maximum, or to both.

(6) A person who intentionally obstructs a person in the exercise of his powers under a warrant issued under section 194 is guilty of an offence and liable—

(a) on conviction on indictment, to imprisonment for a term not exceeding 2 years or to a fine or to both; and

(b) on summary conviction, to a fine not exceeding the statutory maximum.

202 Interpretation of sections 192 to 201

In sections 192 to 201—

'documents' includes information recorded in any form and, in relation to information recorded otherwise than in a form in which it is visible and legible, references to its production include references to producing it in a form in which it is visible and legible or from which it can readily be produced in a visible and legible form;

'person under investigation' has the meaning given in section 192(2).

PART VII MISCELLANEOUS COMPETITION PROVISIONS

Powers of entry under 1998 Act

203 Powers of entry

(1) The 1998 Act is amended as follows.

(2) In section 28 (power to enter premises under a warrant), after subsection (3) there is inserted—

'(3A) A warrant under this section may authorise persons specified in the warrant to accompany the named officer who is executing it.'

(3) In section 62 (power to enter premises: Commission investigations), after subsection (5) there is inserted—

'(5A) A warrant under this section may authorise persons specified in the warrant to accompany the named officer who is executing it.'

(4) In section 63 (power to enter premises: Director's special investigations), after subsection (5) there is inserted—

'(5A) A warrant under this section may authorise persons specified in the warrant to accompany the named authorised officer who is executing it.'

Directors disqualification

204 Disqualification

(1) The Company Directors Disqualification Act 1986 (c. 46) is amended as follows.

(2) The following sections are inserted after section 9 (matters for determining unfitness in certain cases)—

'Disqualification for competition infringements

9A Competition disqualification order

(1) The court must make a disqualification order against a person if the following two conditions are satisfied in relation to him.

(2) The first condition is that an undertaking which is a company of which he is a director commits a breach of competition law.

(3) The second condition is that the court considers that his conduct as a director makes him unfit to be concerned in the management of a company.

(4) An undertaking commits a breach of competition law if it engages in conduct which infringes any of the following—

    (a) the Chapter 1 prohibition (within the meaning of the Competition Act 1998) (prohibition on agreements, etc. preventing, restricting or distorting competition);

    (b) the Chapter 2 prohibition (within the meaning of that Act) (prohibition on abuse of a dominant position);

    (c) Article 81 of the Treaty establishing the European Community (prohibition on agreements, etc. preventing, restricting or distorting competition);

    (d) Article 82 of that Treaty (prohibition on abuse of a dominant position).

(5) For the purpose of deciding under subsection (3) whether a person is unfit to be concerned in the management of a company the court—

    (a) must have regard to whether subsection (6) applies to him;

    (b) may have regard to his conduct as a director of a company in connection with any other breach of competition law;

    (c) must not have regard to the matters mentioned in Schedule 1.

(6) This subsection applies to a person if as a director of the company—

    (a) his conduct contributed to the breach of competition law mentioned in subsection (2);

    (b) his conduct did not contribute to the breach but he had reasonable grounds to suspect that the conduct of the undertaking constituted the breach and he took no steps to prevent it;

    (c) he did not know but ought to have known that the conduct of the undertaking constituted the breach.

(7) For the purposes of subsection (6)(a) it is immaterial whether the person knew that the conduct of the undertaking constituted the breach.

(8) For the purposes of subsection (4)(a) or (c) references to the conduct of an undertaking are references to its conduct taken with the conduct of one or more other undertakings.

(9) The maximum period of disqualification under this section is 15 years.

(10) An application under this section for a disqualification order may be made by the OFT or by a specified regulator.

(11) Section 60 of the Competition Act 1998 (c. 41) (consistent treatment of questions arising under United Kingdom and Community law) applies in relation to any question arising by virtue of subsection (4)(a) or (b) above as it applies in relation to any question arising under Part 1 of that Act.

9B   Competition undertakings

(1) This section applies if—

    (a) the OFT or a specified regulator thinks that in relation to any person the conditions mentioned in section 9A(1) are satisfied, and

    (b) the person offers to give the OFT or the specified regulator (as the case may be) a disqualification undertaking.

(2) The OFT or the specified regulator (as the case may be) may accept a disqualification undertaking from the person instead of applying for or proceeding with an application for a disqualification order.

(3) A disqualification undertaking is an undertaking by a person that for the period specified in the undertaking he will not—

    (a) be a director of a company;

    (b) act as receiver of a company's property;

    (c) in any way, whether directly or indirectly, be concerned or take part in the promotion, formation or management of a company;

(d) act as an insolvency practitioner.

(4) But a disqualification undertaking may provide that a prohibition falling within subsection (3)(a) to (c) does not apply if the person obtains the leave of the court.

(5) The maximum period which may be specified in a disqualification undertaking is 15 years.

(6) If a disqualification undertaking is accepted from a person who is already subject to a disqualification undertaking under this Act or to a disqualification order the periods specified in those undertakings or the undertaking and the order (as the case may be) run concurrently.

9C   Competition investigations

(1) If the OFT or a specified regulator has reasonable grounds for suspecting that a breach of competition law has occurred it or he (as the case may be) may carry out an investigation for the purpose of deciding whether to make an application under section 9A for a disqualification order.

(2) For the purposes of such an investigation sections 26 to 30 of the Competition Act 1998 (c. 41) apply to the OFT and the specified regulators as they apply to the OFT for the purposes of an investigation under section 25 of that Act.

(3) Subsection (4) applies if as a result of an investigation under this section the OFT or a specified regulator proposes to apply under section 9A for a disqualification order.

(4) Before making the application the OFT or regulator (as the case may be) must—

    (a) give notice to the person likely to be affected by the application, and

    (b) give that person an opportunity to make representations.

9D   Co-ordination

(1) The Secretary of State may make regulations for the purpose of co-ordinating the performance of functions under sections 9A to 9C (relevant functions) which are exercisable concurrently by two or more persons.

(2) Section 54(5) to (7) of the Competition Act 1998 (c. 41) applies to regulations made under this section as it applies to regulations made under that section and for that purpose in that section—

    (a) references to Part 1 functions must be read as references to relevant functions;

    (b) references to a regulator must be read as references to a specified regulator;

    (c) a competent person also includes any of the specified regulators.

(3) The power to make regulations under this section must be exercised by statutory instrument subject to annulment in pursuance of a resolution of either House of Parliament.

(4) Such a statutory instrument may—

    (a) contain such incidental, supplemental, consequential and transitional provision as the Secretary of State thinks appropriate;

    (b) make different provision for different cases.

9E   Interpretation

(1) This section applies for the purposes of sections 9A to 9D.

(2) Each of the following is a specified regulator for the purposes of a breach of competition law in relation to a matter in respect of which he or it has a function—

    (a) the Director General of Telecommunications;

    (b) the Gas and Electricity Markets Authority;

    (c) the Director General of Water Services;

    (d) the Rail Regulator;

    (e) the Civil Aviation Authority.

(3) The court is the High Court or (in Scotland) the Court of Session.

(4) Conduct includes omission.

(5) Director includes shadow director.'

(3) In section 1(1) (general provision about disqualification orders) for 'section 6' substitute 'sections 6 and 9A'.

(4) In section 8A (variation etc of disqualification undertaking) after subsection (2) there is inserted the following subsection—

'(2A) Subsection (2) does not apply to an application in the case of an undertaking given under section 9B, and in such a case on the hearing of the application whichever of the OFT or a specified regulator (within the meaning of section 9E) accepted the undertaking—

(a) must appear and call the attention of the court to any matters which appear to it or him (as the case may be) to be relevant;

(b) may give evidence or call witnesses.'

(5) In section 8A for subsection (3) there is substituted—

'(3) In this section "the court"—

(a) in the case of an undertaking given under section 9B means the High Court or (in Scotland) the Court of Session;

(b) in any other case has the same meaning as in section 7(2) or 8 (as the case may be).'

(6) In section 16(3) for 'the Secretary of State or the official receiver or the liquidator' substitute 'a person falling within subsection (4)'.

(7) In section 16 after subsection (3) there is inserted the following subsection—

'(4) The following fall within this subsection—

(a) the Secretary of State;

(b) the official receiver;

(c) the OFT;

(d) the liquidator;

(e) a specified regulator (within the meaning of section 9E).'

(8) In section 17 (applications for leave under an order or undertaking) after subsection (3) there is inserted the following subsection—

'(3A) Where a person is subject to a disqualification undertaking accepted at any time under section 9B any application for leave for the purposes of section 9B(4) must be made to the High Court or (in Scotland) the Court of Session.'

(9) In section 17(4) for 'or 1A(1)(a)' substitute '1A(1)(a) or 9B(4)'.

(10) In section 17 after subsection (5) there are inserted the following subsections—

'(6) Subsection (5) does not apply to an application for leave for the purposes of section 1(1) (a) if the application for the disqualification order was made under section 9A.

(7) In such a case and in the case of an application for leave for the purposes of section 9B(4) on the hearing of the application whichever of the OFT or a specified regulator (within the meaning of section 9E) applied for the order or accepted the undertaking (as the case may be)—

(a) must appear and draw the attention of the court to any matters which appear to it or him (as the case may be) to be relevant;

(b) may give evidence or call witnesses.'

(11) In section 18 (register of disqualification orders and undertakings) for subsection (2A) substitute—

'(2A) The Secretary of State must include in the register such particulars as he considers appropriate of—

(a) disqualification undertakings accepted by him under section 7 or 8;

(b) disqualification undertakings accepted by the OFT or a specified regulator under section 9B;

(c) cases in which leave has been granted as mentioned in subsection (1)(d).'

Miscellaneous

205 Super-complaints to regulators other than OFT

(1) The Secretary of State may by order provide that section 11 is to apply to complaints made to a specified regulator in relation to a market of a specified description as it applies to complaints made to the OFT, with such modifications as may be specified.

(2) An order under this section—

(a) shall be made by statutory instrument, and

(b) shall be subject to annulment in pursuance of a resolution of either House of Parliament.

(3) In this section—

'regulator' has the meaning given in section 54(1) of the 1998 Act; and

'specified' means specified in the order.

206   Power to modify Schedule 8

(1) The Secretary of State may by order made by statutory instrument modify Schedule 8.

(2) An order under this section may make—

    (a) different provision for different cases or different purposes;

    (b) such incidental, supplementary, consequential, transitory, transitional or saving provision as the Secretary of State considers appropriate.

(3) An order under this section may, in particular, modify that Schedule in its application by virtue of Part 3 of this Act, in its application by virtue of Part 4 of this Act, in its application by virtue of any other enactment (whether by virtue of Part 4 of this Act as applied by that enactment or otherwise) or in its application by virtue of every enactment that applies it.

(4) An order under this section as extended by subsection (2) may modify any enactment comprised in or made under this Act, or any other enactment.

(5) No order shall be made under this section unless a draft of it has been laid before, and approved by a resolution of, each House of Parliament.

(6) No modification of Schedule 8 in its application by virtue of Part 3 of this Act shall be made by an order under this section if the modification relates to a relevant merger situation or (as the case may be) a special merger situation which has been created before the coming into force of the order.

(7) No modification shall be made by an order under this section of Schedule 8 in its application in relation to references made under section 22, 33, 45 or 62 before the coming into force of the order.

(8) No modification shall be made by an order under this section of Schedule 8 in its application in relation to references made under section 131 or 132 before the coming into force of the order (including references made under section 131 as applied by another enactment).

(9) Before making an order under this section, the Secretary of State shall consult the OFT and the Commission.

(10) Expressions used in this section which are also used in Part 3 of this Act have the same meaning in this section as in that Part.

207   Repeal of Schedule 4 to the 1998 Act

Section 3(1)(d) of and Schedule 4 to the 1998 Act (which provide for the exclusion from the Chapter 1 prohibition in cases involving designated professional rules) shall cease to have effect.

208   Repeal of Part 6 of Fair Trading Act 1973

Sections 78 to 80 of the 1973 Act (references to Commission other than monopoly and merger references) shall cease to have effect.

209   Reform of Community competition law

(1) The Secretary of State may by regulations make such modifications of the 1998 Act as he considers appropriate for the purpose of eliminating or reducing any differences between—

    (a) the domestic provisions of the 1998 Act, and

    (b) European Community competition law,

which result (or would otherwise result) from a relevant Community instrument made after the passing of this Act.

(2) In this section—

'the domestic provisions of the 1998 Act' means the provisions of the 1998 Act so far as they do not implement or give effect to a relevant Community instrument;

'European Community competition law' includes any Act or subordinate legislation so far as it implements or gives effect to a relevant Community instrument;

'relevant Community instrument' means a regulation or directive under Article 83 of the Treaty establishing the European Community.

(3) The Secretary of State may by regulations repeal or otherwise modify any provision of an Act (other than the 1998 Act) which excludes any matter from the Chapter I prohibition or the Chapter II prohibition (within the meaning of Part 1 of the 1998 Act).

(4) The power under subsection (3) may not be exercised—

(a) before the power under subsection (1) has been exercised; or

(b) so as to extend the scope of any exclusion that is not being removed by the regulations.

(5) Regulations under this section may—

(a) confer power to make subordinate legislation;

(b) make such consequential, supplementary, incidental, transitory, transitional or saving provision as the Secretary of State considers appropriate (including provision modifying any Act or subordinate legislation); and

(c) make different provision for different cases or circumstances.

(6) The power to make regulations under this section is exercisable by statutory instrument.

(7) No regulations may be made under this section unless a draft of them has been laid before and approved by a resolution of each House of Parliament.

(8) Paragraph 1(1)(c) of Schedule 2 to the European Communities Act 1972 (c. 68) (restriction on powers to legislate) shall not apply to regulations which implement or give effect to a relevant Community instrument made after the passing of this Act.

PART XI SUPPLEMENTARY

273 Interpretation

In this Act—

'the 1973 Act' means the Fair Trading Act 1973 (c. 41);

'the 1998 Act' means the Competition Act 1998 (c. 41);

'the Commission' means the Competition Commission;

'the Director' means the Director General of Fair Trading; and

'the OFT' means the Office of Fair Trading.

274 Provision of financial assistance for consumer purposes

The Secretary of State may give financial assistance to any person for the purpose of assisting—

(a) activities which the Secretary of State considers are of benefit to consumers; or

(b) the provision of—

(i) advice or information about consumer matters;

(ii) educational materials relating to consumer matters; or

(iii) advice or information to the Secretary of State in connection with the formulation of policy in respect of consumer matters.

275 Financial provision

There shall be paid out of money provided by Parliament—

(a) any expenditure incurred by the OFT, the Secretary of State, any other Minister of the Crown or a government department by virtue of this Act; and

(b) any increase attributable to this Act in the sums payable out of money so provided by virtue of any other Act.

276 Transitional or transitory provision and savings

(1) Schedule 24 (which makes transitional and transitory provisions and savings) has effect.

(2) The Secretary of State may be order made by statutory instrument make such transitional or transitory provisions and savings as he considers appropriate in connection with the coming into force of any provision of this Act.

(3) An order under subsection (2) may modify any Act or subordinate legislation.

(4) Schedule 24 does not restrict the power under subsection (2) to make other transitional or transitory provisions and savings.

277 Power to make consequential amendments etc.

(1) The Secretary of State may by order make such supplementary, incidental or consequential provision as he thinks appropriate—

    (a) for the general purposes, or any particular purpose, of this Act; or

    (b) in consequence of any provision made by or under this Act or for giving full effect to it.

(2) An order under this section may—

    (a) modify any Act or subordinate legislation (including this Act);

    (b) make incidental, supplementary, consequential, transitional, transitory or saving provision.

(3) The power to make an order under this section is exercisable by statutory instrument subject to annulment in pursuance of a resolution of either House of Parliament.

(4) The power conferred by this section is not restricted by any other provision of this Act.

278 Minor and consequential amendments and repeals

(1) Schedule 25 (which contains minor and consequential amendments) has effect.

(2) Schedule 26 (which contains repeals and revocations) has effect.

279 Commencement

The preceding provisions of this Act shall come into force on such day as the Secretary of State may by order made by statutory instrument appoint; and different days may be appointed for different purposes.

280 Extent

(1) Sections 256 to 265, 267, 269 and 272 extend only to England and Wales.

(2) Sections 204, 248 to 255 and 270 extend only to England and Wales and Scotland (but sub-section (3) of section 415A as inserted by section 270 extends only to England and Wales).

(3) Any other modifications by this Act of an enactment have the same extent as the enactment being modified.

(4) Otherwise, this Act extends to England and Wales, Scotland and Northern Ireland.

281 Short title

This Act may be cited as the Enterprise Act 2002.

SCHEDULES

SCHEDULE 1 THE OFFICE OF FAIR TRADING

Membership

(1) The OFT shall consist of a chairman, and no fewer than four other members, appointed by the Secretary of State.

(2) The Secretary of State shall consult the chairman before appointing any other member.

Terms of appointment, remuneration, pensions etc.

2 (1) Subject to this Schedule, the chairman and other members shall hold and vacate office in accordance with the terms of their respective appointments.

(2) The terms of appointment of the chairman and other members shall be determined by the Secretary of State.

3 (1) An appointment of a person to hold office as chairman or other member shall be for a term not exceeding five years.

(2) A person holding office as chairman or other member—

    (a) may resign that office by giving notice in writing to the Secretary of State; and

    (b) may be removed from office by the Secretary of State on the ground of incapacity or misbehaviour.

(3) A previous appointment as chairman or other member does not affect a person's eligibility for appointment to either office.

4 (1) The OFT shall pay to the chairman and other members such remuneration, and such travelling and other allowances, as may be determined by the Secretary of State.

(2) The OFT shall, if required to do so by the Secretary of State—

(a) pay such pension, allowances or gratuities as may be determined by the Secretary of State to or in respect of a person who holds or has held office as chairman or other member; or

(b) make such payments as may be so determined towards provision for the payment of a pension, allowances or gratuities to or in respect of such a person.

(3) If, where any person ceases to hold office as chairman or other member, the Secretary of State determines that there are special circumstances which make it right that he should receive compensation, the OFT shall pay to him such amount by way of compensation as the Secretary of State may determine.

Staff

5 (1) The Secretary of State shall, after consulting the chairman, appoint a person (who may, subject to sub-paragraph (2), also be a member of the OFT) to act as chief executive of the OFT on such terms and conditions as the Secretary of State may think appropriate.

(2) A person appointed as chief executive after the end of the transitional period may not at the same time be chairman.

(3) In sub-paragraph (2) 'the transitional period' means the period of two years beginning with the day on which this paragraph comes into force.

6 The OFT may, with the approval of the Minister for the Civil Service as to numbers and terms and conditions of service, appoint such other staff as it may determine.

Membership of committees or sub-committees of OFT

7 The members of a committee or sub-committee of the OFT may include persons who are not members of the OFT (and a sub-committee may include persons who are not members of the committee which established it).

Proceedings etc.

8 (1) The OFT may regulate its own procedure (including quorum).

(2) The OFT shall consult the Secretary of State before making or revising its procedures for dealing with conflicts of interest.

9 The validity of anything done by the OFT is not affected by a vacancy among its members or by a defect in the appointment of a member.

10 (1) The application of the seal of the OFT shall be authenticated by the signature of—

(a) any member; or

(b) some other person who has been authorised for that purpose by the OFT, whether generally or specially.

(2) Sub-paragraph (1) does not apply in relation to any document which is, or is to be, signed in accordance with the law of Scotland.

11 A document purporting to be duly executed under the seal of the OFT, or signed on its behalf, shall be received in evidence and, unless the contrary is proved, be taken to be so executed or signed.

Performance of functions

12 (1) Anything authorised or required to be done by the OFT (including exercising the power under this paragraph) may be done by—

(a) any member or employee of the OFT who is authorised for that purpose by the OFT, whether generally or specially;

(b) any committee of the OFT which has been so authorised.

(2) Sub-paragraph (1)(b) does not apply to a committee whose members include any person who is not a member or employee of the OFT.

Supplementary powers

13 The OFT has power to do anything which is calculated to facilitate, or is conducive or incidental to, the performance of its functions.

Parliamentary Commissioner Act 1967 (c. 13)

14 In Schedule 2 to the Parliamentary Commissioner Act 1967 (departments and authorities subject to investigation), there is inserted at the appropriate place—
'Office of Fair Trading.'

House of Commons Disqualification Act 1975 (c. 24)

15 In Part 2 of Schedule 1 to the House of Commons Disqualification Act 1975 (bodies of which all members are disqualified), there is inserted at the appropriate place—
'The Office of Fair Trading.'

Northern Ireland Assembly Disqualification Act 1975 (c. 25)

16 In Part 2 of Schedule 1 to the Northern Ireland Assembly Disqualification Act 1975 (bodies of which all members are disqualified), there is inserted at the appropriate place—
'The Office of Fair Trading.'

SCHEDULE 2 THE COMPETITION APPEAL TRIBUNAL

Appointment, etc. of President and chairmen

1 (1) A person is not eligible for appointment as President unless—
    (a) he satisfies the judicial-appointment eligibility condition on a 7-year basis;
    (b) he is an advocate or solicitor in Scotland of at least 7 years' standing; or
    (c) he is a member of the Bar of Northern Ireland or solicitor of the Supreme Court of Northern Ireland of at least 7 years' standing;
and he appears to the Lord Chancellor to have appropriate experience and knowledge of competition law and practice.

(2) A person is not eligible for appointment as a chairman unless—
    (a) he satisfies the judicial-appointment eligibility condition on a 5-year basis;
    (b) he is an advocate or solicitor in Scotland of at least 5 years' standing; or
    (c) he is a member of the Bar of Northern Ireland or solicitor of the Supreme Court of Northern Ireland of at least 5 years' standing;
and he appears to the Lord Chancellor to have appropriate experience and knowledge (either of competition law and practice or any other relevant law and practice).

(3) Before appointing an advocate or solicitor in Scotland under this paragraph, the Lord Chancellor must consult the Lord President of the Court of Session.

(4) In this paragraph 'general qualification' has the same meaning as in section 71 of the Courts and Legal Services Act 1990 (c. 41).

2 (1) The members appointed as President or as chairmen shall hold and vacate office in accordance with their terms of appointment, subject to the following provisions.

(2) A person may not be a chairman for more than 8 years (but this does not prevent a temporary re-appointment for the purpose of continuing to act as a member of the Tribunal as constituted for the purposes of any proceedings instituted before the end of his term of office).

(3) The President and the chairmen may resign their offices by notice in writing to the Lord Chancellor.

(4) The Lord Chancellor may remove a person from office as President or chairman on the ground of incapacity or misbehaviour.

3 If the President is absent or otherwise unable to act the Lord Chancellor may appoint as acting President any person qualified for appointment as a chairman.

Appointment, etc. of ordinary members

4 (1) Ordinary members shall hold and vacate office in accordance with their terms of appointment, subject to the following provisions.

(2) A person may not be an ordinary member for more than 8 years (but this does not prevent a temporary re-appointment for the purpose of continuing to act as a member of the Tribunal as constituted for the purposes of any proceedings instituted before the end of his term of office).

(3) An ordinary member may resign his office by notice in writing to the Secretary of State.

(4) The Secretary of State may remove a person from office as an ordinary member on the ground of incapacity or misbehaviour.

Remuneration etc. for members

5 (1) The Competition Service shall pay to the President, the chairmen and the ordinary members such remuneration (whether by way of salaries or fees), and such allowances, as the Secretary of State may determine.

(2) The Competition Service shall, if required to do so by the Secretary of State—
- (a) pay such pension, allowances or gratuities as may be determined by the Secretary of State to or in respect of a person who holds or has held office as President, a chairman or an ordinary member; or
- (b) make such payments as may be so determined towards provision for the payment of a pension, allowance or gratuities to or in respect of such a person.

Compensation for loss of office

6 If, where any person ceases to hold office as President, a chairman or ordinary member, the Secretary of State determines that there are special circumstances which make it right that he should receive compensation, the Competition Service shall pay to him such amount by way of compensation as the Secretary of State may determine.

Staff, accommodation and property

7 Any staff, office accommodation or equipment required for the Tribunal shall be provided by the Competition Service.

Miscellaneous

8 The President must arrange such training for members of the Tribunal as he considers appropriate.

9 In this Schedule 'chairman' and 'ordinary member' mean respectively a member of the panel of chairmen, or a member of the panel of ordinary members, appointed under section 12.

10 In Part 2 of Schedule 1 to the House of Commons Disqualification Act 1975 (bodies of which all members are disqualified), there is inserted at the appropriate place—

'The Competition Appeal Tribunal.'

11 In Part 2 of Schedule 1 to the Northern Ireland Assembly Disqualification Act 1975 (bodies of which all members are disqualified), there is inserted at the appropriate place—

'The Competition Appeal Tribunal.'

SCHEDULE 3 THE COMPETITION SERVICE

PART I CONSTITUTION ETC.

Membership of the Service

1 (1) The Service shall consist of—
- (a) the President of the Competition Appeal Tribunal;
- (b) the Registrar of the Competition Appeal Tribunal; and
- (c) one or more appointed members.

(2) An appointed member shall be appointed by the Secretary of State after consulting the President.

Chairman of Service

2 (1) Subject to sub-paragraph (2), the members shall choose one of their number to be chairman of the Service.

(2) The Secretary of State shall designate one of the members to be the first chairman of the Service for such period as the Secretary of State may determine.

Appointed members

3 An appointed member shall hold and vacate office in accordance with the terms of his appointment (and is eligible for re-appointment).

Allowances, etc. for members

4 (1) The Service shall pay—
  (a) such travelling and other allowances to its members; and
  (b) such remuneration to any appointed member,
as may be determined by the Secretary of State.

(2) The Service shall, if required to do so by the Secretary of State—
  (a) pay such pension, allowances or gratuities as may be determined by the Secretary of State to or in respect of a person who holds or has held office as an appointed member; or
  (b) make such payments as may be so determined towards provision for the payment of a pension, allowances or gratuities to or in respect of such a person.

5 If, where any person ceases to hold office as an appointed member, the Secretary of State determines that there are special circumstances which make it right that he should receive compensation, the Service shall pay to him such amount by way of compensation as the Secretary of State may determine.

Staff

6 (1) The Service may, with the approval of the Secretary of State as to numbers and terms and conditions of service, appoint such staff as it may determine.

(2) The persons to whom section 1 of the Superannuation Act 1972 (c. 11) (persons to or in respect of whom benefits may be provided by schemes under that section) applies shall include the staff of the Service.

(3) The Service shall pay to the Minister for the Civil Service, at such times as he may direct, such sums as he may determine in respect of any increase attributable to sub-paragraph (2) in the sums payable out of money provided by Parliament under the Superannuation Act 1972.

Procedure

7 (1) The Service may regulate its own procedure (including quorum).

(2) The validity of anything done by the Service is not affected by a vacancy among its members or by a defect in the appointment of a member.

8 (1) The application of the seal of the Service shall be authenticated by the signature of—
  (a) any member; or
  (b) some other person who has been authorised for that purpose by the Service, whether generally or specially.

(2) Sub-paragraph (1) does not apply in relation to any document which is, or is to be, signed in accordance with the law of Scotland.

9 A document purporting to be duly executed under the seal of the Service, or signed on its behalf, shall be received in evidence and, unless the contrary is proved, be taken to be so executed or signed.

The Service's powers

10 The Service has power to do anything which is calculated to facilitate, or is conducive or incidental to, the performance of its functions.

Accounts

11 (1) The Service shall keep proper accounts and proper records in relation to its accounts.

(2) In performing that duty the Service shall, in addition to accounts and records relating to its own activities (including the services provided to the Tribunal), keep separate accounts and separate records in relation to the activities of the Tribunal.

12 (1) The Service shall—

(a) prepare a statement of accounts in respect of each of its financial years; and

(b) prepare a statement of accounts for the Tribunal for each of its financial years.

(2) The Service must send copies of the accounts required by sub-paragraph (1) to the Secretary of State and to the Comptroller and Auditor General before the end of August following the financial year to which they relate.

(3) Those accounts must comply with any directions given by the Secretary of State with the approval of the Treasury as to—

(a) the information to be contained in them;

(b) the manner in which that information is to be presented; and

(c) the methods and principles according to which they are to be prepared.

(4) The Comptroller and Auditor General shall—

(a) examine, certify and report on each statement of accounts received by him; and

(b) lay copies of each statement before Parliament.

(5) In this paragraph 'financial year' means the period of 12 months ending with 31st March.

PART II TRANSFERS OF PROPERTY ETC. BETWEEN THE COMMISSION AND THE SERVICE

13 (1) The Secretary of State may make one or more schemes for the transfer to the Service of defined property, rights and liabilities of the Commission (including rights and liabilities relating to contracts of employment).

(2) A scheme may define the property, rights and liabilities to be transferred by specifying or describing them or by referring to all (or all except anything specified or described) of the property, rights and liabilities comprised in a specified part of the undertaking of the transferor.

(3) The property, rights and liabilities which may be transferred include any that would otherwise be incapable of being transferred or assigned.

(4) A scheme may include supplementary, incidental, transitional and consequential provision.

14 (1) On the day appointed by a scheme under paragraph 13, the property, rights and liabilities which are the subject of the scheme shall, by virtue of this subparagraph, be transferred in accordance with the provisions of the scheme.

(2) If, after that day, the Commission and the Service so agree in writing, the scheme shall for all purposes be deemed to have come into force on that day with such modification as may be agreed.

(3) An agreement under sub-paragraph (2) may, in connection with giving effect to modifications to the scheme, include supplemental, incidental, transitional and consequential provision.

15 The transfer by paragraph 14(1) of the rights and liabilities relating to an individual's contract of employment does not break the continuity of his employment and, accordingly—

(a) he is not to be regarded for the purposes of Part 11 of the Employment Rights Act 1996 as having been dismissed by virtue of the transfer; and

(b) his period of employment with the transferor counts as a period of employment with the transferee for the purposes of that Act.

16 (1) Anything done by or in relation to the transferor for the purposes of or in connection with anything transferred by paragraph 14(1) which is in effect immediately before it is transferred shall be treated as if done by or in relation to the transferee.

(2) There may be continued by or in relation to the transferee anything (including legal proceedings) relating to anything so transferred which is in the process of being done by or in relation to the transferor immediately before it is transferred.

(3) A reference to the transferor in any document relating to anything so transferred shall be taken (so far as necessary for the purposes of or in consequence of the transfer) as a reference to the transferee.

(4) A transfer under paragraph 14(1) does not affect the validity of anything done by or in relation to the transferor before the transfer takes effect.

SCHEDULE 4 TRIBUNAL: PROCEDURE

PART I GENERAL

Decisions of the Tribunal

1 (1) A decision of the Tribunal in any proceedings before it must—
  (a) state the reasons for the decision and whether it was unanimous or taken by a majority;
  (b) be recorded in a document signed and dated by the chairman of the Tribunal dealing with the proceedings.

(2) In preparing that document the Tribunal shall have regard to the need for excluding, so far as practicable—
  (a) information the disclosure of which would in its opinion be contrary to the public interest;
  (b) commercial information the disclosure of which would or might, in its opinion, significantly harm the legitimate business interests of the undertaking to which it relates;
  (c) information relating to the private affairs of an individual the disclosure of which would, or might, in its opinion, significantly harm his interests.

(3) But the Tribunal shall also have regard to the extent to which any disclosure mentioned in sub-paragraph (2) is necessary for the purpose of explaining the reasons for the decision.

(4) The President shall make such arrangements for the publication of the decisions of the Tribunal as he considers appropriate.

Enforcement of decisions in Great Britain

2 If a decision of the Tribunal is registered in England and Wales in accordance with rules of court or any practice direction—
  (a) payment of damages which are awarded by the decision;
  (b) costs awarded by the decision; and
  (c) any direction given as a result of the decision,
may be enforced by the High Court as if the damages or costs were an amount due in pursuance of a judgment or order of the High Court, or as if the direction were an order of the High Court.

3 If a decision of the Tribunal awards damages, costs or expenses, or results in any direction being given, the decision may be recorded for execution in the Books of Council and Session and shall be enforceable accordingly.

4 Subject to rules of court or any practice direction, a decision of the Tribunal may be registered or recorded for execution—
  (a) for the purpose of enforcing a direction given as a result of the decision, by the Registrar of the Tribunal or a person who was a party to the proceedings;
  (b) by a person to whom damages, costs or expenses have been awarded by the decision.

Enforcement of decisions in Northern Ireland

5 (1) A decision of the Tribunal may be enforced in Northern Ireland with the leave of the High Court in Northern Ireland—
  (a) in the case of a direction given as a result of the decision, by the Registrar of the Tribunal or a person who was a party to the proceedings;

(b) by a person to whom damages, costs or expenses have been awarded by the decision.

(2) For the purpose of enforcing in Northern Ireland a decision to award damages, costs or expenses—

    (a) payment may be enforced as if the damages, costs or expenses were an amount due in pursuance of a judgment or order of the High Court in Northern Ireland; and

    (b) a sum equal to the amount of damages or costs shall be deemed to be payable under a money judgment within the meaning of Article 2(2) of the Judgments Enforcement (Northern Ireland) Order 1981 (S.I. 1981/226 (N.I.6)) (and the provisions of that Order apply accordingly).

(3) For the purpose of enforcing in Northern Ireland a direction given as a result of a decision of the Tribunal, the decision may be enforced as if the direction were an order of the High Court in Northern Ireland.

Miscellaneous

6 A decision of the Tribunal in proceedings under section 47B of the 1998 Act which—

    (a) awards damages to an individual in respect of a claim made or continued on his behalf (but is not the subject of an order under section 47B(6)); or

    (b) awards costs or expenses to an individual in respect of proceedings in respect of a claim made under section 47A of that Act prior to its being continued on his behalf in the proceedings under section 47B,

may only be enforced by the individual concerned with the permission of the High Court or Court of Session.

7 An award of costs or expenses against a specified body in proceedings under section 47B of the 1998 Act may not be enforced against any individual on whose behalf a claim was made or continued in those proceedings.

8 In this Part of this Schedule any reference to damages includes a reference to any sum of money (other than costs or expenses) which may be awarded in respect of a claim made under section 47A of the 1998 Act or included in proceedings under section 47B of that Act.

PART II TRIBUNAL RULES

General

9 In this Schedule 'the Tribunal', in relation to any proceedings before it, means the Tribunal as constituted (in accordance with section 14) for the purposes of those proceedings.

10 Tribunal rules may make different provision for different kinds of proceedings.

Institution of proceedings

11 (1) Tribunal rules may make provision as to the period within which and the manner in which proceedings are to be brought.

(2) That provision may, in particular, provide for the form, contents, amendment and acknowledgement of the documents by which proceedings are to be instituted.

12 Tribunal rules may provide for the Tribunal to reject any proceedings (other than a claim for damages under section 47A of the 1998 Act) if it considers that—

    (a) the person instituting them does not have a sufficient interest in the decision with respect to which the proceedings are brought; or

    (b) the document by which he institutes them discloses no valid grounds for bringing them.

13 Tribunal rules may provide for the Tribunal—

    (a) in the case of a claim for damages under section 47A of the 1998 Act, to reject the claim if it considers that there are no reasonable grounds for making it; and

    (b) in the case of a claim made under section 47B of the 1998 Act, to reject the whole claim if it considers that the person making it is not entitled to bring the claim or to reject the claim of any individual on whose behalf that person is claiming if it considers that there are no reasonable grounds for making that claim.

14 Tribunal rules may provide for the Tribunal to reject any proceedings if it is satisfied that the person instituting the proceedings has habitually and persistently and without any reasonable ground—

(a) instituted vexatious proceedings (whether against the same person or against different persons); or

(b) made vexatious applications in any proceedings.

15 Tribunal rules must ensure that no proceedings are rejected without giving the parties the opportunity to be heard.

Pre-hearing reviews and preliminary matters

16 (1) Tribunal rules may make provision for the carrying out by the Tribunal of a preliminary consideration of proceedings (a 'pre-hearing review').

(2) That provision may include—

(a) provision enabling such powers to be exercised on a pre-hearing review as may be specified in the rules;

(b) provision for security and supplemental provision relating to security.

(3) For the purposes of sub-paragraph (2)(b)—

(a) 'provision for security' means provision authorising the Tribunal, in specified circumstances, to order a party to the proceedings, if he wishes to continue to participate in them, to pay a deposit not exceeding such sum as may be specified or calculated in a specified manner; and

(b) 'supplemental provision', in relation to security, means provision as to—

(i)   the manner in which the amount of a deposit is to be determined;

(ii)   the consequences of non-payment of a deposit;

(iii) the circumstances in which the deposit, or any part of it, may be refunded to the person who paid it or paid to another party to the proceedings.

Conduct of the hearing

17 (1) Tribunal rules may make provision—

(a) as to the manner in which proceedings are to be conducted, including provision for any hearing to be held in private if the Tribunal considers it appropriate because it is considering information of a kind mentioned in paragraph 1(2);

(b) as to the persons entitled to appear on behalf of the parties;

(c) for requiring persons to attend to give evidence and produce documents, and for authorising the administration of oaths to witnesses;

(d) as to the evidence which may be required or admitted and the extent to which it should be oral or written;

(e) allowing the Tribunal to fix time limits with respect to any aspect of proceedings and to extend any time limit (before or after its expiry);

(f) enabling the Tribunal, on the application of any party or on its own initiative, to order—

(i)   the disclosure between, or the production by, the parties of documents or classes of documents; or

(ii)   such recovery or inspection of documents as might be ordered by a sheriff;

(g) for the appointment of experts for the purposes of proceedings;

(h) for the award of costs or expenses, including allowances payable to persons in connection with attendance before the Tribunal;

(i) for taxing or otherwise settling any costs or expenses awarded by the Tribunal or for the enforcement of any order awarding costs or expenses.

(2) Rules under sub-paragraph (1)(h) may provide, in relation to a claim made under section 47A of the 1998 Act which is continued on behalf of an individual in proceedings under section 47B

of that Act, for costs or expenses to be awarded to or against that individual in respect of proceedings on that claim which took place before it was included in the proceedings under section 47B of that Act.

(3) Otherwise Tribunal rules may not provide for costs or expenses to be awarded to or against an individual on whose behalf a claim is made or continued in proceedings under section 47B of the 1998 Act.

(4) Tribunal rules may make provision enabling the Tribunal to refer any matter arising in any proceedings (other than proceedings under section 47A or 47B of the 1998 Act) back to the authority that made the decision to which the proceedings relate, if it appears that the matter has not been adequately investigated.

(5) A person who without reasonable excuse fails to comply with—

  (a) any requirement imposed by virtue of sub-paragraph (1)(c); or
  (b) any requirement with respect to the disclosure, production, recovery or inspection of documents which is imposed by virtue of sub-paragraph (1)(f),

is guilty of an offence and liable on summary conviction to a fine not exceeding level 3 on the standard scale.

Quorum

18 (1) Tribunal rules may make provision as to the consequences of a member of the Tribunal being unable to continue after part of any proceedings have been heard.

(2) The rules may allow the Tribunal to consist of the remaining members for the rest of the proceedings.

(3) The rules may enable the President, if it is the chairman of the Tribunal who is unable to continue—

  (a) to appoint either of the remaining members to chair the Tribunal; or
  (b) if that person is not a member of the panel of chairmen, to appoint himself or some other suitably qualified person to attend the proceedings and advise the remaining members on any questions of law arising.

(4) For the purpose of sub-paragraph (1) a person is 'suitably qualified' if he is, or is qualified for appointment as, a member of the panel of chairmen.

Interest

19 (1) Tribunal rules may make provision allowing the Tribunal to order that interest is payable on any damages or other sum awarded by the Tribunal or on any fees ordered to be paid under paragraph 20.

(2) That provision may include provision—

  (a) as to the circumstances in which such an order maybe made;
  (b) as to the manner in which, and the periods in respect of which, interest is to be calculated and paid.

Fees

20 (1) Tribunal rules may provide—

  (a) for fees to be chargeable in respect of specified costs of proceedings; and
  (b) for the amount of such costs to be determined by the Tribunal.

(2) Any sums received in respect of such fees shall be paid into the Consolidated Fund.

Withdrawal of proceedings

21 Tribunal rules may make provision—

  (a) preventing a party who has instituted proceedings from withdrawing them without the permission of the Tribunal or, in specified circumstances, the President or the Registrar;
  (b) for the Tribunal to grant permission to withdraw proceedings on such conditions as it considers appropriate;

(c) enabling the Tribunal to publish any decision which it would have made in any proceedings, had the proceedings not been withdrawn;

(d) as to the effect of withdrawal of proceedings; and

(e) as to the procedure to be followed if parties to proceedings agree to settle.

(2) Tribunal rules may make, in relation to a claim included in proceedings under section 47B of the 1998 Act, any provision which may be made under sub-paragraph (1) in relation to the whole proceedings.

Interim orders

22 (1) Tribunal rules may provide for the Tribunal to make an order, on an interim basis—

(a) suspending the effect of any decision which is the subject matter of proceedings before it;

(b) in the case of an appeal under section 46 or 47 of the 1998 Act, varying the conditions or obligations attached to an exemption;

(c) granting any remedy which the Tribunal would have had power to grant in its final decision.

(2) Tribunal rules may also make provision giving the Tribunal powers similar to those given to the OFT by section 35 of the 1998 Act.

Miscellaneous

23 (1) Tribunal rules may make provision enabling the Tribunal to decide where to sit for the purposes of, or of any part of, any proceedings before it.

(2) Tribunal rules may make provision enabling the Tribunal to decide that any proceedings before it are to be treated, for purposes connected with—

(a) any appeal from a decision of the Tribunal made in those proceedings; and

(b) any other matter connected with those proceedings, as proceedings in England and Wales, Scotland or Northern Ireland (regardless of the decision made for the purposes of sub-paragraph (1)).

(3) For the purposes of sub-paragraph (2), Tribunal rules may provide for each claim for damages made or continued on behalf of an individual in proceedings under section 47B of the 1998 Act to be treated as separate proceedings.

24 Tribunal rules may make provision—

(a) for a person who is not a party to be joined in any proceedings;

(b) for hearing a person who is not a party where, in any proceedings, it is proposed to make an order or give a direction in relation to that person;

(c) for proceedings to be consolidated on such terms as the Tribunal thinks appropriate in such circumstances as may be specified.

25 Tribunal rules may make provision for the Tribunal to transfer a claim for damages (other than a claim made by virtue of section 47B of the 1998 Act) to—

(a) the High Court or a county court in England and Wales or Northern Ireland; or

(b) the Court of Session or a sheriff court in Scotland.

26 Tribunal rules may make provision in connection with the transfer of any proceedings from a court mentioned in paragraph 25 to the Tribunal under section 16.

SCHEDULE 7 ENFORCEMENT REGIME FOR PUBLIC INTEREST AND SPECIAL PUBLIC INTEREST CASES

Pre-emptive undertakings and orders

1 (1) Sub-paragraph (2) applies where an intervention notice or special intervention notice is in force.

(2) The Secretary of State may, for the purpose of preventing pre-emptive action, accept from such of the parties concerned as he considers appropriate undertakings to take such action as he considers appropriate.

(3) Sub-paragraph (4) applies where an intervention notice is in force.

(4) The Secretary of State may, for the purpose of preventing pre-emptive action, adopt an under-taking accepted by the OFT under section 71 if the undertaking is still in force when the Secretary of State adopts it.

(5) An undertaking adopted under sub-paragraph (4)—

    (a) shall continue in force, in accordance with its terms, when adopted;

    (b) may be varied or superseded by an undertaking under this paragraph; and

    (c) may be released by the Secretary of State.

(6) Any other undertaking under this paragraph—

    (a) shall come into force when accepted;

    (b) may be varied or superseded by another undertaking; and

    (c) may be released by the Secretary of State.

(7) References in this Part to undertakings under this paragraph shall, unless the context otherwise requires, include references to undertakings adopted under this paragraph; and references to the acceptance or giving of undertakings under this paragraph shall be construed accordingly.

(8) An undertaking which is in force under this paragraph in relation to a reference or possible reference under section 45 or (as the case may be) 62 shall cease to be in force if an order under paragraph 2 or an undertaking under paragraph 3 comes into force in relation to that reference.

(9) An undertaking under this paragraph shall, if it has not previously ceased to be in force, cease to be in force when the intervention notice concerned or (as the case may be) special intervention notice concerned ceases to be in force.

(10) No undertaking shall be accepted by the Secretary of State under this paragraph before the making of a reference under section 45 or (as the case may be) 62 unless the undertaking relates to a relevant merger situation which has been, or may have been, created or (as the case may be) a special merger situation which has been, or may have been, created.

(11) The Secretary of State shall, as soon as reasonably practicable, consider any representations received by him in relation to varying or releasing an undertaking under this paragraph.

(12) In this paragraph and paragraph 2 'pre-emptive action' means action which might prejudice the reference or possible reference concerned under section 45 or (as the case may be) 62 or impede the taking of any action under this Part which may be justified by the Secretary of State's decisions on the reference.

2 (1) Sub-paragraph (2) applies where an intervention notice or special intervention notice is in force.

(2) The Secretary of State or the OFT may by order, for the purpose of preventing preemptive action—

    (a) prohibit or restrict the doing of things which the Secretary of State or (as the case may be) the OFT considers would constitute pre-emptive action;

    (b) impose on any person concerned obligations as to the carrying on of any activities or the safeguarding of any assets;

    (c) provide for the carrying on of any activities or the safeguarding of any assets either by the appointment of a person to conduct or supervise the conduct of any activities (on such terms and with such powers as may be specified or described in the order) or in any other manner;

    (d) do anything which may be done by virtue of paragraph 19 of Schedule 8.

(3) Sub-paragraph (4) applies where an intervention notice is in force.

(4) The Secretary of State or the OFT may, for the purpose of preventing preemptive action, adopt an order made by the OFT under section 72 if the order is still in force when the Secretary of State or (as the case may be) the OFT adopts it.

(5) An order adopted under sub-paragraph (4)—

    (a) shall continue in force, in accordance with its terms, when adopted; and

    (b) may be varied or revoked by an order under this paragraph.

(6) Any other order under this paragraph—

(a) shall come into force at such time as is determined by or under the order; and

(b) may be varied or revoked by another order.

(7) References in this Part to orders under this paragraph shall, unless the context otherwise requires, include references to orders adopted under this paragraph; and references to the making of orders under this paragraph shall be construed accordingly.

(8) An order which is in force under this paragraph in relation to a reference or possible reference under section 45 or (as the case may be) 62 shall cease to be in force if an undertaking under paragraph 1 or 3 comes into force in relation to that reference.

(9) An order under this paragraph shall, if it has not previously ceased to be in force, cease to be in force when the intervention notice concerned or (as the case may be) special intervention notice concerned ceases to be in force.

(10) No order shall be made by the Secretary of State or the OFT under this paragraph before the making of a reference under section 45 or (as the case may be) 62 unless the order relates to a relevant merger situation which has been, or may have been, created or (as the case may be) a special merger situation which has been, or may have been, created.

(11) The Secretary of State or (as the case may be) the OFT shall, as soon as reasonably practicable, consider any representations received by that person in relation to varying or revoking an order under this paragraph.

Undertakings in lieu of reference under section 45 or 62

3 (1) Sub-paragraph (2) applies if the Secretary of State has power to make a reference to the Commission under section 45 or 61 and otherwise intends to make such a reference.

(2) The Secretary of State may, instead of making such a reference and for the purpose of remedying, mitigating or preventing any of the effects adverse to the public interest which have or may have resulted, or which may be expected to result, from the creation of the relevant merger situation concerned or (as the case may be) the special merger situation concerned, accept from such of the parties concerned as he considers appropriate undertakings to take such action as he considers appropriate.

(3) In proceeding under sub-paragraph (2), the Secretary of State shall, in particular—

(a) accept the decisions of the OFT included in its report under section 44 so far as they relate to the matters mentioned in subsections (4) and (5) of that section; or

(b) (as the case may be) accept the decisions of the OFT included in its report under section 61 so far as they relate to the matters mentioned in subsection (3) (a) and (4) of that section.

(4) In proceeding under sub-paragraph (2) in relation to an anti-competitive outcome, the Secretary of State may, in particular, have regard to the effect of any action on any relevant customer benefits in relation to the creation of the relevant merger situation concerned.

(5) No undertaking shall be accepted by the Secretary of State under this paragraph in connection with a possible reference under section 45 if a public interest consideration mentioned in the intervention notice concerned has not been finalised and the period of 24 weeks beginning with the giving of that notice has not expired.

(6) The Secretary of State may delay making a decision as to whether to accept any such undertaking (and any related decision as to whether to make a reference under section 45) if he considers that there is a realistic prospect of the public interest consideration being finalised within the period of 24 weeks beginning with the giving of the intervention notice concerned.

(7) A delay under sub-paragraph (6) shall not extend beyond—

(a) the time when the public interest consideration is finalised; or

(b) if earlier, the expiry of the period of 24 weeks mentioned in that sub-paragraph.

(8) An undertaking under this paragraph—

(a) shall come into force when accepted;

(b) may be varied or superseded by another undertaking; or

(c) may be released by the Secretary of State.

(9) An undertaking under this paragraph which is in force in relation to a relevant merger situation or (as the case may be) a special merger situation shall cease to be in force if an order comes into force under paragraph 5 or 6 in relation to that undertaking.

(10) The Secretary of State shall, as soon as reasonably practicable, consider any representations received by him in relation to varying or releasing an undertaking under this section.

4 (1) The relevant authority shall not make a reference under section 22, 33 or 45 in relation to the creation of a relevant merger situation or (as the case may be) a reference under section 62 in relation to the creation of a special merger situation if—

    (a) the Secretary of State has accepted an undertaking under paragraph 3; and

    (b) the relevant merger situation or (as the case may be) the special merger situation is the situation by reference to which the undertaking was accepted.

(2) In sub-paragraph (1) 'the relevant authority' means—

    (a) in relation to a possible reference under section 22 or 33, the OFT; and

    (b) in relation to a possible reference under section 45 or 62, the Secretary of State.

(3) Sub-paragraph (1) does not prevent the making of a reference if material facts about relevant arrangements or transactions, or relevant proposed arrangements or transactions, were not notified (whether in writing or otherwise) to the Secretary of State or the OFT or made public before the undertaking concerned was accepted.

(4) For the purposes of sub-paragraph (3) arrangements or transactions, or proposed arrangements or transactions, are relevant if they are the ones in consequence of which the enterprises concerned ceased or may have ceased, or may cease, to be distinct enterprises.

(5) In sub-paragraph (3) 'made public' means so publicised as to be generally known or readily ascertainable.

5 (1) Sub-paragraph (2) applies where the Secretary of State considers that—

    (a) an undertaking accepted by him under paragraph 3 has not been, is not being or will not be fulfilled; or

    (b) in relation to an undertaking accepted by him under that paragraph, information which was false or misleading in a material respect was given to him or the OFT by the person giving the undertaking before he decided to accept the undertaking.

(2) The Secretary of State may, for any of the purposes mentioned in paragraph 3(2), make an order under this paragraph.

(3) Sub-paragraphs (3) and (4) of paragraph 3 shall apply for the purposes of sub-paragraph (2) above as they apply for the purposes of sub-paragraph (2) of that paragraph.

(4) An order under this paragraph may contain—

    (a) anything permitted by Schedule 8; and

    (b) such supplementary, consequential or incidental provision as the Secretary of State considers appropriate.

(5) An order under this paragraph

    (a) shall come into force at such time as is determined by or under the order; and

    (b) may contain provision which is different from the provision contained in the undertaking concerned.

(6) No order shall be varied or revoked under this paragraph unless the OFT advises that such a variation or revocation is appropriate by reason of a change of circumstances.

6 (1) Sub-paragraph (2) applies where—

    (a) the Secretary of State has the power to make an order under paragraph 5 in relation to a particular undertaking and intends to make such an order; or

    (b) the Secretary of State has the power to make an order under paragraph 10 in relation to a particular undertaking and intends to make such an order.

(2) The Secretary of State may, for the purpose of preventing any action which might prejudice the making of that order, make an order under this paragraph.

(3) No order shall be made under sub-paragraph (2) unless the Secretary of State has reasonable grounds for suspecting that it is or may be the case that action which might prejudice the making of the order under paragraph 5 or (as the case may be) 10 is in progress or in contemplation.

(4) An order under sub-paragraph (2) may—

    (a) prohibit or restrict the doing of things which the Secretary of State considers would prejudice the making of the order under paragraph 5 or 10;

    (b) impose on any person concerned obligations as to the carrying on of any activities or the safeguarding of any assets;

    (c) provide for the carrying on of any activities or the safeguarding of any assets either by the appointment of a person to conduct or supervise the conduct of any activities (on such terms and with such powers as may be specified or described in the order) or in any other manner;

    (d) do anything which may be done by virtue of paragraph 19 of Schedule 8.

(5) An order under this paragraph shall come into force at such time as is determined by or under the order.

(6) An order under this paragraph shall, if it has not previously ceased to be in force, cease to be in force on—

    (a) the coming into force of an order under paragraph 5 or (as the case may be) 10 in relation to the undertaking concerned; or

    (b) the making of the decision not to proceed with such an order.

(7) The Secretary of State shall, as soon as reasonably practicable, consider any representations received by him in relation to varying or revoking an order under this paragraph.

Statutory restrictions following reference under section 45 or 62

7 (1) Sub-paragraphs (2) and (3) apply where—

    (a) a reference has been made under section 45(2) or (3) or 62(2) but not finally determined; and

    (b) no undertakings under paragraph 1 are in force in relation to the relevant merger situation concerned or (as the case may be) the special merger situation concerned and no orders under paragraph 2 are in force in relation to that situation.

(2) No relevant person shall, without the consent of the Secretary of State—

    (a) complete any outstanding matters in connection with any arrangements which have resulted in the enterprises concerned ceasing to be distinct enterprises;

    (b) make any further arrangements in consequence of that result (other than arrangements which reverse that result); or

    (c) transfer the ownership or control of any enterprises to which the reference relates.

(3) No relevant person shall, without the consent of the Secretary of State, assist in any of the activities mentioned in paragraphs (a) to (c) of sub-paragraph (2).

(4) The prohibitions in sub-paragraphs (2) and (3) do not apply in relation to anything which the person concerned is required to do by virtue of any enactment.

(5) The consent of the Secretary of State under sub-paragraph (2) or (3)—

    (a) may be general or specific;

    (b) may be revoked by the Secretary of State; and

    (c) shall be published in such manner as the Secretary of State considers appropriate for bringing it to the attention of any person entitled to the benefit of it.

(6) Paragraph (c) of sub-paragraph (5) shall not apply if the Secretary of State considers that publication is not necessary for the purpose mentioned in that paragraph.

(7) Sub-paragraphs (2) and (3) shall apply to a person's conduct outside the United Kingdom if (and only if) he is—

    (a) a United Kingdom national;

    (b) a body incorporated under the law of the United Kingdom or of any part of the United Kingdom; or

(c) a person carrying on business in the United Kingdom.

(8) For the purpose of this paragraph a reference under section 45(2) or (3) is finally determined if—

(a) the time within which the Commission is to prepare a report under section 50 in relation to the reference and give it to the Secretary of State has expired and no such report has been so prepared and given;

(b) the Commission decides to cancel the reference under section 53(1);

(c) the time within which the Secretary of State is to make and publish a decision under section 54(2) has expired and no such decision has been made and published;

(d) the Secretary of State decides under section 54(2) to make no finding at all in the matter;

(e) the Secretary of State otherwise decides under section 54(2) not to make an adverse public interest finding;

(f) the Secretary of State decides under section 54(2) to make an adverse public interest finding but decides neither to accept an undertaking under paragraph 9 of this Schedule nor to make an order under paragraph 11 of this Schedule; or

(g) the Secretary of State decides under section 54(2) to make an adverse public interest finding and accepts an undertaking under paragraph 9 of this Schedule or makes an order under paragraph 11 of this Schedule.

(9) For the purpose of this paragraph a reference under section 62(2) is finally determined if—

(a) the time within which the Commission is to prepare a report under section 65 in relation to the reference and give it to the Secretary of State has expired and no such report has been so prepared and given;

(b) the time within which the Secretary of State is to make and publish a decision under 66(2) has expired and no such decision has been made and published;

(c) the Secretary of State decides under subsection (2) of section 66 otherwise than as mentioned in subsection (5) of that section;

(d) the Secretary of State decides under subsection (2) of section 66 as mentioned in subsection (5) of that section but decides neither to accept an undertaking under paragraph 9 of this Schedule nor to make an order under paragraph 11 of this Schedule; or

(e) the Secretary of State decides under subsection (2) of section 66 as mentioned in subsection (5) of that section and accepts an undertaking under paragraph 9 of this Schedule or makes an order under paragraph 11 of this Schedule.

(10) For the purposes of this paragraph the time when a reference under section 45(2) or (3) or (as the case may be) 62(2) is finally determined is—

(a) in a case falling within sub-paragraph (8)(a) or (c) or (as the case may be) (9)(a) or (b), the expiry of the time concerned;

(b) in a case falling within sub-paragraph (8)(b), (d) or (e) or (as the case may be) (9)(c), the making of the decision concerned;

(c) in a case falling within sub-paragraph (8)(f) or (as the case may be) (9)(d), the making of the decision neither to accept an undertaking under paragraph 9 of this Schedule nor to make an order under paragraph 11 of this Schedule; and

(d) in a case falling within sub-paragraph (8)(g) or (as the case may be) (9)(e), the acceptance of the undertaking concerned or (as the case may be) the making of the order concerned.

(11) In this paragraph 'relevant person' means—

(a) any person who carries on any enterprise to which the reference relates or who has control of any such enterprise;

(b) any subsidiary of any person falling within paragraph (a); or

(c) any person associated with any person falling within paragraph (a) or any subsidiary of any person so associated.

8 (1) Sub-paragraph (2) applies where—

    (a) a reference has been made under section 45(4) or (5) or 62(3); and

    (b) no undertakings under paragraph 1 are in force in relation to the relevant merger situation concerned or (as the case may be) special merger situation concerned and no orders under paragraph 2 are in force in relation to that situation.

(2) No relevant person shall, without the consent of the Secretary of State, directly or indirectly acquire during the relevant period an interest in shares in a company if any enterprise to which the reference relates is carried on by or under the control of that company.

(3) The consent of the Secretary of State under sub-paragraph (2)—

    (a) may be general or specific;

    (b) may be revoked by the Secretary of State; and

    (c) shall be published in such manner as the Secretary of State considers appropriate for bringing it to the attention of any person entitled to the benefit of it.

(4) Paragraph (c) of sub-paragraph (3) shall not apply if the Secretary of State considers that publication is not necessary for the purpose mentioned in that paragraph.

(5) Sub-paragraph (2) shall apply to a person's conduct outside the United Kingdom if (and only if) he is—

    (a) a United Kingdom national;

    (b) a body incorporated under the law of the United Kingdom or of any part of the United Kingdom; or

    (c) a person carrying on business in the United Kingdom.

(6) In this paragraph—

'company' includes any body corporate;

'relevant period' means the period beginning with the publication of the decision of the Secretary of State to make the reference concerned and ending when the reference is finally determined;

'relevant person' means—

    (a) any person who carries on any enterprise to which the reference relates or who has control of any such enterprise;

    (b) any subsidiary of any person falling within paragraph (a); or

    (c) any person associated with any person falling within paragraph (a) or any subsidiary of any person so associated; and

'share' means share in the capital of a company, and includes stock.

(7) For the purposes of the definition of 'relevant period' in sub-paragraph (6), a reference under section 45(4) or (5) is finally determined if—

    (a) the Commission cancels the reference under section 48(1) or 53(1);

    (b) the time within which the Commission is to prepare a report under section 50 in relation to the reference and give it to the Secretary of State has expired and no such report has been so prepared and given;

    (c) the time within which the Secretary of State is to make and publish a decision under section 54(2) has expired and no such decision has been made and published;

    (d) the Secretary of State decides under section 54(2) to make no finding at all in the matter;

    (e) the Secretary of State otherwise decides under section 54(2) not to make an adverse public interest finding;

    (f) the Secretary of State decides under section 54(2) to make an adverse public interest finding but decides neither to accept an undertaking under paragraph 9 of this Schedule nor to make an order under paragraph 11 of this Schedule; or

    (g) the Secretary of State decides under section 54(2) to make an adverse public interest finding and accepts an undertaking under paragraph 9 of this Schedule or makes an order under paragraph 11 of this Schedule.

(8) For the purposes of the definition of 'relevant period' in sub-paragraph (6), a reference under section 62(3) is finally determined if—

(a) the Commission cancels the reference under section 64(1);

(b) the time within which the Commission is to prepare a report under section 65 in relation to the reference and give it to the Secretary of State has expired and no such report has been so prepared and given;

(c) the time within which the Secretary of State is to make and publish a decision under 66(2) has expired and no such decision has been made and published;

(d) the Secretary of State decides under subsection (2) of section 66 otherwise than as mentioned in subsection (5) of that section;

(e) the Secretary of State decides under subsection (2) of section 66 as mentioned in subsection (5) of that section but decides neither to accept an undertaking under paragraph 9 of this Schedule nor to make an order under paragraph 11 of this Schedule; or

(f) the Secretary of State decides under subsection (2) of section 66 as mentioned in subsection (5) of that section and accepts an undertaking under paragraph 9 of this Schedule or makes an order under paragraph 11 of this Schedule.

(9) For the purposes of the definition of 'relevant period' in sub-paragraph (6) above, the time when a reference under section 45(4) or (5) or (as the case may be) 62(3) is finally determined is—

(a) in a case falling within sub-paragraph (7)(a), (d) or (e) or (as the case may be) (8) (a) or (d), the making of the decision concerned;

(b) in a case falling within sub-paragraph (7)(b) or (c) or (as the case maybe) (8)(b) or (c), the expiry of the time concerned;

(c) in a case falling within sub-paragraph (7)(f) or (as the case may be) (8)(e), the making of the decision neither to accept an undertaking under paragraph 9 of this Schedule nor to make an order under paragraph 11 of this Schedule; and

(d) in a case falling within sub-paragraph (7)(g) or (as the case may be) (8)(f), the acceptance of the undertaking concerned or (as the case may be) the making of the order concerned.

(10) Section 79 shall apply for the purposes of paragraph 7 and this paragraph in relation to a reference under section 45 or 62 as it applies for the purposes of sections 77 and 78 in relation to a reference under section 22 or 33.

(11) In its application by virtue of sub-paragraph (10) section 79 shall have effect as if—

(a) subsections (1) and (2) were omitted; and

(b) for the reference in subsection (4) to the OFT there were substituted a reference to the Secretary of State.

Final undertakings and orders

9 (1) The Secretary of State may, in accordance with section 55 or (as the case may be) 66(5) to (7), accept, from such persons as he considers appropriate, undertakings to take action specified or described in the undertakings.

(2) An undertaking under this paragraph—

(a) shall come into force when accepted;

(b) may be varied or superseded by another undertaking; and

(c) may be released by the Secretary of State.

(3) An undertaking which is in force under this paragraph in relation to a reference under section 45 or 62 shall cease to be in force if an order under paragraph 6(1)(b), 10 or 11 comes into force in relation to that reference.

(4) No undertaking shall be accepted under this paragraph in relation to a reference under section 45 or 62 if an order has been made under paragraph 6(1)(b), 10 or 11 in relation to that reference.

(5) The Secretary of State shall, as soon as reasonably practicable, consider any representations received by him in relation to varying or releasing an undertaking under this section.

10 (1) Sub-paragraph (2) applies where the Secretary of State considers that—

(a) an undertaking accepted by him under paragraph 9 has not been, is not being or will not be fulfilled; or

(b) in relation to an undertaking accepted by him under that paragraph, information which was false or misleading in a material respect was given to him or the OFT by the person giving the undertaking before he decided to accept the undertaking.

(2) The Secretary of State may, for any purpose mentioned in section 55(2) or (as the case may be) 66(6), make an order under this paragraph.

(3) Subsections (3) and (4) of section 55 or (as the case may be) subsection (7) of section 66 shall apply for the purposes of sub-paragraph (2) above as they or it applies for the purposes of section 55(2) or (as the case may be) 66(6).

(4) An order under this paragraph may contain—
  (a) anything permitted by Schedule 8; and
  (b) such supplementary, consequential or incidental provision as the Secretary of State considers appropriate.

(5) An order under this paragraph—
  (a) shall come into force at such time as is determined by or under the order; and
  (b) may contain provision which is different from the provision contained in the undertaking concerned.

(6) No order shall be varied or revoked under this paragraph unless the OFT advises that such a variation or revocation is appropriate by reason of a change of circumstances.

11 (1) The Secretary of State may, in accordance with section 55 or (as the case may be) 66(5) to (7), make an order under this paragraph.

(2) An order under this paragraph may contain—
  (a) anything permitted by Schedule 8; and
  (b) such supplementary, consequential or incidental provision as the Secretary of State considers appropriate.

(3) An order under this paragraph shall come into force at such time as is determined by or under the order.

(4) No order shall be made under this paragraph in relation to a reference under section 45 or (as the case may be) 62 if an undertaking has been accepted under paragraph 9 in relation to that reference.

(5) No order shall be varied or revoked under this paragraph unless the OFT advises that such a variation or revocation is appropriate by reason of a change of circumstances.

SCHEDULE 8 PROVISION THAT MAY BE CONTAINED IN CERTAIN ENFORCEMENT ORDERS

Introductory

1 This Schedule applies in relation to such orders, and to such extent, as is provided by this Part and Part 4 and any other enactment; and references in this Schedule to an order shall be construed accordingly.

General restrictions on conduct

2 (1) An order may—
  (a) prohibit the making or performance of an agreement;
  (b) require any party to an agreement to terminate the agreement.

(2) An order made by virtue of sub-paragraph (1) shall not—
  (a) prohibit the making or performance of; or
  (b) require any person to terminate,
an agreement so far as, if made, the agreement would relate, or (as the case may be) so far as the agreement relates, to the terms and conditions of employment of any workers or to the physical conditions in which any workers are required to work.

3 (1) An order may prohibit the withholding from any person of—
    (a) any goods or services;
    (b) any orders for any such goods or services.
(2) References in sub-paragraph (1) to withholding include references to—
    (a) agreeing or threatening to withhold; and
    (b) procuring others to withhold or to agree or threaten to withhold.

4 An order may prohibit requiring as a condition of the supply of goods or services to any person—
    (a) the buying of any goods;
    (b) the making of any payment in respect of services other than the goods or services supplied;
    (c) the doing of any other such matter or the refraining from doing anything mentioned in paragraph (a) or (b) or any other such matter.

5 An order may prohibit—
    (a) discrimination between persons in the prices charged for goods or services;
    (b) anything which the relevant authority considers to be such discrimination;
    (c) procuring others to do anything which is such discrimination or which the relevant authority considers to be such discrimination.

6 An order may prohibit—
    (a) giving, or agreeing to give in other ways, any preference in respect of the supply of goods or services or in respect of the giving of orders for goods or services;
    (b) giving, or agreeing to give in other ways, anything which the relevant authority considers to be a preference in respect of the supply of goods or services or in respect of the giving of orders for goods or services;
    (c) procuring others to do anything mentioned in paragraph (a) or (b).

7 An order may prohibit—
    (a) charging, for goods or services supplied, prices differing from those in any published list or notification;
    (b) doing anything which the relevant authority considers to be charging such prices.

8 (1) An order may regulate the prices to be charged for any goods or services.
(2) No order shall be made by virtue of sub-paragraph (1) unless the relevant report in relation to the matter concerned identifies the prices charged for the goods or services as requiring remedial action.
(3) In this paragraph 'the relevant report' means the report of the Commission which is required by the enactment concerned before an order can be made under this Schedule.

9 An order may prohibit the exercise of any right to vote exercisable by virtue of the holding of any shares, stock or securities.

General obligations to be performed

10 (1) An order may require a person to supply goods or services or to do anything which the relevant authority considers appropriate to facilitate the provision of goods or services.
(2) An order may require a person who is supplying, or is to supply, goods or services to supply such goods or services to a particular standard or in a particular manner or to do anything which the relevant authority considers appropriate to facilitate the provision of such goods or services to that standard or in that manner.

11 An order may require any activities to be carried on separately from any other activities.

Acquisitions and divisions

12 (1) An order may prohibit or restrict—
    (a) the acquisition by any person of the whole or part of the undertaking or assets of another person's business;
    (b) the doing of anything which will or may result in two or more bodies corporate becoming interconnected bodies corporate.

(2) An order may require that if—

    (a) an acquisition of the kind mentioned in sub-paragraph (1)(a) is made; or

    (b) anything is done which results in two or more bodies corporate becoming interconnected bodies corporate;

the persons concerned or any of them shall observe any prohibitions or restrictions imposed by or under the order.

(3) This paragraph shall also apply to any result consisting in two or more enterprises ceasing to be distinct enterprises (other than any result consisting in two or more bodies corporate becoming interconnected bodies corporate).

13 (1) An order may provide for—

    (a) the division of any business (whether by the sale of any part of the undertaking or assets or otherwise);

    (b) the division of any group of interconnected bodies corporate.

(2) For the purposes of sub-paragraph (1)(a) all the activities carried on by way of business by any one person or by any two or more interconnected bodies corporate may be treated as a single business.

(3) An order made by virtue of this paragraph may contain such provision as the relevant authority considers appropriate to effect or take account of the division, including, in particular, provision as to—

    (a) the transfer or creation of property, rights, liabilities or obligations;

    (b) the number of persons to whom the property, rights, liabilities or obligations are to be transferred or in whom they are to be vested;

    (c) the time within which the property, rights, liabilities or obligations are to be transferred or vested;

    (d) the adjustment of contracts (whether by discharge or reduction of any liability or obligation or otherwise);

    (e) the creation, allotment, surrender or cancellation of any shares, stock or securities;

    (f) the formation or winding up of any company or other body of persons corporate or unincorporate;

    (g) the amendment of the memorandum and articles or other instruments regulating any such company or other body of persons;

    (h) the extent to which, and the circumstances in which, provisions of the order affecting a company or other body of persons corporate or unincorporate in its share capital, constitution or other matters may be altered by the company or other body of persons concerned;

    (i) the registration of the order under any enactment by a company or other body of persons corporate or unincorporate which is affected by it as mentioned in paragraph (h);

    (j) the continuation, with any necessary change of parties, of any legal proceedings;

    (k) the approval by the relevant authority or another person of anything required by virtue of the order to be done or of any person to whom anything is to be transferred, or in whom anything is to be vested, by virtue of the order; or

    (l) the appointment of trustees or other persons to do anything on behalf of another person which is required of that person by virtue of the order or to monitor the doing by that person of any such thing.

14 The references in paragraph 13 to the division of a business as mentioned in sub-paragraph (1)(a) of that paragraph shall, in the case of an order under section 75, 83, 84, 160 or 161, or an order under paragraph 5, 10 or 11 of Schedule 7, be construed as including references to the separation, by the sale of any part of any undertaking or assets concerned or other means, of enterprises which are under common control (within the meaning of section 26) otherwise than by reason of their being enterprises of interconnected bodies corporate.

Supply and publication of information

15 (1) An order may require a person supplying goods or services to publish a list of prices or otherwise notify prices.

(2) An order made by virtue of this paragraph may also require or prohibit the publication or other notification of further information.

16 An order may prohibit any person from notifying (whether by publication or otherwise) to persons supplying goods or services prices recommended or suggested as appropriate to be charged by those persons for those goods or services.

17 (1) An order may require a person supplying goods or services to publish—

(a) accounting information in relation to the supply of the goods or services;

(b) information in relation to the quantities of goods or services supplied;

(c) information in relation to the geographical areas in which they are supplied.

(2) In sub-paragraph (1) 'accounting information', in relation to a supply of goods or services, means information as to—

(a) the costs of the supply, including fixed costs and overheads;

(b) the manner in which fixed costs and overheads are calculated and apportioned for accounting purposes of the supplier; and

(c) the income attributable to the supply.

18 An order made by virtue of paragraph 15 or 17 may provide for the manner in which information is to be published or otherwise notified.

19 An order may—

(a) require any person to supply information to the relevant authority;

(b) where the OFT is not the relevant authority, require any person to supply information to the OFT;

(c) provide for the publication, by the person who has received information by virtue of paragraph (a) or (b), of that information.

National security

20 (1) An order may make such provision as the person making the order considers to be appropriate in the interests of national security (within the meaning of section 58(1)).

(2) Such provision may, in particular, include provision requiring a person to do, or not to do, particular things.

Newspaper mergers

20A (1) This paragraph applies in relation to any order—

(a) which is to be made following the giving of—

(i)   an intervention notice which mentions a newspaper public interest consideration;

(ii) an intervention notice which mentions any other media public interest consideration in relation to a relevant merger situation in which one of the enterprises ceasing to be distinct is a newspaper enterprise;

(iii) a special intervention notice which mentions a consideration specified in section 58(2A) or (2B); or

(iv) a special intervention notice which, in relation to a special merger situation in which one of the enterprises ceasing to be distinct is a newspaper enterprise, mentions a consideration specified in section 58(2C); and

(b) to which the consideration concerned is still relevant.

(2) The order may make such provision as the person making the order considers to be appropriate in all circumstances of the case.

(3) Such provision may, in particular, include provision requiring a person to do, or not to do, particular things.

(4) Provision made by virtue of this paragraph may, in particular, include provision—

(a) altering the constitution of a body corporate (whether in connection with the appointment of directors, the establishment of an editorial board or otherwise);

(b) requiring the agreement of the relevant authority or another person before the taking of particular action (including the appointment or dismissal of an editor, journalists or directors or acting as a shadow director);

(c) attaching conditions to the operation of a newspaper;

(d) prohibiting consultation or co-operation between subsidiaries.

(5) In this paragraph 'newspaper public interest consideration' means a media public interest consideration other than one which is such a consideration—

(a) by virtue of section 58(2C); or

(b) by virtue of having been, in the opinion of the Secretary of State, concerned with broadcasting and a consideration that ought to have been specified in section 58.

(6) This paragraph is without prejudice to the operation of the other paragraphs of this Schedule in relation to the order concerned.

Maintaining the stability of the UK financial system

20B.—(1) This paragraph applies for the purposes of a relevant order under paragraph 5, 10 or 11 of Schedule 7 (enforcement orders in cases relating to the stability of the UK financial system) but not for any other purposes of Part 3 or 4 or any other enactment.

(2) The order may make such provision as the person making the order considers to be appropriate in the interest of maintaining the stability of the UK financial system.

(3) Such provision may, in particular, include provision requiring a person to do, or not to do, particular things.

(4) This paragraph is without prejudice to the operation of the other paragraphs of this Schedule in relation to the order.

(5) In this paragraph "relevant order" means an order—

(a) which is to be made following the giving of an intervention notice or special intervention notice which mentions the consideration specified in section 58(2D) (including, in the case of a notice given before the consideration was so specified, an intervention notice which mentions the consideration as a consideration which ought to be specified in section 58); and

(b) to which the consideration is still relevant.

Supplementary

21 (1) An order, as well as making provision in relation to all cases to which it may extend, may make provision in relation to—

(a) those cases subject to specified exceptions; or

(b) any particular case or class of case.

(2) An order may, in relation to the cases in relation to which it applies, make the full provision which may be made by it or any less provision (whether by way of exception or otherwise).

(3) An order may make provision for matters to be determined under the order.

(4) An order may—

(a) make different provision for different cases or classes of case or different purposes;

(b) make such transitional, transitory or saving provision on the person making it considers appropriate.

22 (1) An order which may prohibit the doing of anything (or the refraining from doing anything) may in particular by virtue of paragraph 21(2) prohibit the doing of that thing (or the refraining from doing of it) except to such extent and in such circumstances as may be provided by or under the order.

(2) Any such order may, in particular, prohibit the doing of that thing (or the refraining from doing of it)—

(a) without the agreement of the relevant authority or another person; or

(b) by or in relation to a person who has not been approved by the relevant authority or another person.

Interpretation

23 References in this Schedule to the notification of prices or other information are not limited to the notification in writing of prices or other information.

24 In this Schedule 'the relevant authority' means—

    (a) in the case of an order to be made by the OFT, the OFT;

    (b) in the case of an order to be made by the Commission, the Commission; and

    (c) in the case of an order to be made by the Secretary of State, the Secretary of State.

SCHEDULE 10 PROCEDURAL REQUIREMENTS FOR CERTAIN ENFORCEMENT UNDERTAKINGS AND ORDERS

Requirements for accepting undertakings and making orders

1 Paragraph 2 applies in relation to—

    (a) any undertaking under section 73 or 82 or paragraph 3 or 9 of Schedule 7 (other than an undertaking under the enactment concerned which varies an undertaking under that enactment but not in any material respect); and

    (b) any order under section 75, 83 or 84 or paragraph 5, 10 or 11 of Schedule 7 (other than an order under the enactment concerned which revokes an order under that enactment).

2 (1) Before accepting an undertaking to which this paragraph applies or making an order to which this paragraph applies, the OFT, the Commission or (as the case may be) the Secretary of State (in this Schedule 'the relevant authority') shall—

    (a) give notice of the proposed undertaking or (as the case may be) order; and

    (b) consider any representations made in accordance with the notice and not withdrawn.

(2) A notice under sub-paragraph (1) shall state—

    (a) that the relevant authority proposes to accept the undertaking or (as the case may be) make the order;

    (b) the purpose and effect of the undertaking or. (as the case may be) order;

    (c) the situation that the undertaking or (as the case may be) order is seeking to deal with;

    (d) any other facts which the relevant authority considers justify the acceptance of the under-taking or (as the case may be) the making of the order;

    (e) a means of gaining access to an accurate version of the proposed undertaking or (as the case may be) order at all reasonable times; and

    (f) the period (not less than 15 days starting with the date of publication of the notice in the case of an undertaking and not less than 30 days starting with that date in the case of an order) within which representations may be made in relation to the proposed undertaking or (as the case may be) order.

(3) A notice under sub-paragraph (1) shall be given by—

    (a) in the case of a proposed order, serving on any person identified in the order as a person on whom a copy of the order should be served a copy of the notice and a copy of the proposed order; and

    (b) in every case, publishing the notice.

(4) The relevant authority shall not accept the undertaking with modifications or (as the case may be) make the order with modifications unless the relevant authority—

    (a) gives notice of the proposed modifications; and

    (b) considers any representations made in accordance with the notice and not withdrawn.

(5) A notice under sub-paragraph (4) shall state—

    (a) the proposed modifications;

    (b) the reasons for them; and

(c) the period (not less than 7 days starting with the date of the publication of the notice under sub-paragraph (4)) within which representations may be made in relation to the proposed modifications.

(6) A notice under sub-paragraph (4) shall be given by—

(a) in the case of a proposed order, serving a copy of the notice on any person identified in the order as a person on whom a copy of the order should be served; and

(b) in every case, publishing the notice.

3 (1) If, after giving notice under paragraph 2(1) or (4), the relevant authority decides—

(a) not to accept the undertaking concerned or (as the case may be) make the order concerned; and

(b) not to proceed by virtue of paragraph 5;

the relevant authority shall give notice of that decision.

(2) A notice under sub-paragraph (1) shall be given by—

(a) in the case of a proposed order, serving a copy of the notice on any person identified in the order as a person on whom a copy of the order should be served; and

(b) in every case, publishing the notice.

4 As soon as practicable after accepting an undertaking to which paragraph 2 applies or (as the case may be) making an order to which that paragraph applies, the relevant authority shall (except in the case of an order which is a statutory instrument)—

(a) serve a copy of the undertaking on any person by whom it is given or (as the case may be) serve a copy of the order on any person identified in the order as a person on whom a copy of the order should be served; and

(b) publish the undertaking or (as the case may be) the order.

5 (1) The requirements of paragraph 2(4) (and those of paragraph 2(1)) shall not apply if the relevant authority—

(a) has already given notice under paragraph 2(1) but not paragraph 2(4) in relation to the proposed undertaking or order; and

(b) considers that the modifications which are now being proposed are not material in any respect.

(2) The requirements of paragraph 2(4) (and those of paragraph 2(1)) shall not apply if the relevant authority—

(a) has already given notice under paragraphs 2(1) and (4) in relation to the matter concerned; and

(b) considers that the further modifications which are now being proposed do not differ in any material respect from the modifications in relation to which notice was last given under paragraph 2(4).

Termination of undertakings and orders

6 Paragraph 7 applies where the relevant authority is proposing to—

(a) release any undertaking under section 73 or 82 or paragraph 3 or 9 of Schedule 7 (other than in connection with accepting an undertaking under the enactment concerned which varies or supersedes an undertaking under that enactment); or

(b) revoke any order under section 75, 83 or 84 or paragraph 5, 10 or 11 of Schedule 7 (other than in connection with making an order under the enactment concerned which varies or supersedes an order under that enactment).

7 (1) Before releasing an undertaking to which this paragraph applies or (as the case may be) revoking an order to which this paragraph applies, the relevant authority shall—

(a) give notice of the proposed release or (as the case may be) revocation; and

(b) consider any representations made in accordance with the notice and not withdrawn.

(2) A notice under sub-paragraph (1) shall state—

(a) the fact that a release or (as the case may be) revocation is proposed;

(b) the reasons for it; and

(c) the period (not less than 15 days starting with the date of publication of the notice in the case of an undertaking and not less than 30 days starting with that date in the case of an order) within which representations may be made in relation to the proposed release or (as the case may be) revocation.

(3) If after giving notice under sub-paragraph (1) the relevant authority decides not to proceed with the release or (as the case may be) the revocation, the relevant authority shall give notice of that decision.

(4) A notice under sub-paragraph (1) or (3) shall be given by—

    (a) serving a copy of the notice on the person who gave the undertaking which is being released or (as the case may be) on any person identified in the order being revoked as a person on whom a copy of the order should be served; and

    (b) publishing the notice.

8 As soon as practicable after releasing the undertaking or making the revoking order, the relevant authority shall (except in the case of an order which is a statutory instrument)—

    (a) serve a copy of the release of the undertaking on the person who gave the undertaking or (as the case may be) serve a copy of the revoking order on any person identified in the order being revoked as a person on whom a copy of that order should be served; and

    (b) publish the release or (as the case may be) the revoking order.

Power to dispense with the requirements of the Schedule

9 The relevant authority may dispense with any or all of the requirements of this Schedule if the relevant authority considers that the relevant authority has special reasons for doing so.

Part II

EU Primary Legislation*

Consolidated version of the Treaty on European Union

(Treaty of Rome, 25 March 1957, revised)

Title I Common Provisions

Article 1   (ex Article 1 TEU)

By this Treaty, the HIGH CONTRACTING PARTIES establish among themselves a EUROPEAN UNION, hereinafter called 'the Union' on which the Member States confer competences to attain objectives they have in common.

This Treaty marks a new stage in the process of creating an ever closer union among the peoples of Europe, in which decisions are taken as openly as possible and as closely as possible to the citizen.

The Union shall be founded on the present Treaty and on the Treaty on the Functioning of the European Union (hereinafter referred to as 'the Treaties'). Those two Treaties shall have the same legal value. The Union shall replace and succeed the European Community.

Article 2   (ex Article 2 TEU)

The Union is founded on the values of respect for human dignity, freedom, democracy, equality, the rule of law and respect for human rights, including the rights of persons belonging to minorities. These values are common to the Member States in a society in which pluralism, non-discrimination, tolerance, justice, solidarity and equality between women and men prevail.

Article 3   (ex Article 2 TEU)

1. The Union's aim is to promote peace, its values and the well-being of its peoples.

2. The Union shall offer its citizens an area of freedom, security and justice without internal frontiers, in which the free movement of persons is ensured in conjunction with appropriate measures with respect to external border controls, asylum, immigration and the prevention and combating of crime.

3. The Union shall establish an internal market. It shall work for the sustainable development of Europe based on balanced economic growth and price stability, a highly competitive social market economy, aiming at full employment and social progress, and a high level of protection and improvement of the quality of the environment. It shall promote scientific and technological advance.

It shall combat social exclusion and discrimination, and shall promote social justice and protection, equality between women and men, solidarity between generations and protection of the rights of the child.

It shall promote economic, social and territorial cohesion, and solidarity among Member States.

It shall respect its rich cultural and linguistic diversity, and shall ensure that Europe's cultural heritage is safeguarded and enhanced.

4. The Union shall establish an economic and monetary union whose currency is the euro.

5. In its relations with the wider world, the Union shall uphold and promote its values and interests and contribute to the protection of its citizens. It shall contribute to peace, security, the sustainable development of the Earth, solidarity and mutual respect among peoples, free and fair trade, eradication of poverty and the protection of human rights, in particular the rights of the child, as well as to the strict observance and the development of international law, including respect for the principles of the United Nations Charter.

6. The Union shall pursue its objectives by appropriate means commensurate with the competences which are conferred upon it in the Treaties.

Article 4

1. In accordance with Article 5, competences not conferred upon the Union in the Treaties remain with the Member States.

2. The Union shall respect the equality of Member States before the Treaties as well as their national identities, inherent in their fundamental structures, political and constitutional, inclusive of regional and local self-government. It shall respect their essential State functions, including ensuring the territorial integrity of the State, maintaining law and order and safeguarding national security. In particular, national security remains the sole responsibility of each Member State.

3. Pursuant to the principle of sincere cooperation, the Union and the Member States shall, in full mutual respect, assist each other in carrying out tasks which flow from the Treaties.

The Member States shall take any appropriate measure, general or particular, to ensure fulfilment of the obligations arising out of the Treaties or resulting from the acts of the institutions of the Union.

The Member States shall facilitate the achievement of the Union's tasks and refrain from any measure which could jeopardise the attainment of the Union's objectives.

Article 5   (ex Article 5 TEC)

1. The limits of Union competences are governed by the principle of conferral. The use of Union competences is governed by the principles of subsidiarity and proportionality.

2. Under the principle of conferral, the Union shall act only within the limits of the competences conferred upon it by the Member States in the Treaties to attain the objectives set out therein. Competences not conferred upon the Union in the Treaties remain with the Member States.

3. Under the principle of subsidiarity, in areas which do not fall within its exclusive competence, the Union shall act only if and in so far as the objectives of the proposed action cannot be sufficiently achieved by the Member States, either at central level or at regional and local level, but can rather, by reason of the scale or effects of the proposed action, be better achieved at Union level.

The institutions of the Union shall apply the principle of subsidiarity as laid down in the Protocol on the application of the principles of subsidiarity and proportionality. National Parliaments ensure compliance with the principle of subsidiarity in accordance with the procedure set out in that Protocol.

4. Under the principle of proportionality, the content and form of Union action shall not exceed what is necessary to achieve the objectives of the Treaties.

The institutions of the Union shall apply the principle of proportionality as laid down in the Protocol on the application of the principles of subsidiarity and proportionality.

Title VII Common rules on competition, taxation and approximation of laws

Chapter 1 Rules on competition

Section 1 Rules applying to undertakings

Article 101 (ex Article 81 TEC)

1. The following shall be prohibited as incompatible with the common market: all agreements between undertakings, decisions by associations of undertakings and concerted practices which may affect trade between Member States and which have as their object or effect the prevention, restriction or distortion of competition within the common market, and in particular those which:

    (a) directly or indirectly fix purchase or selling prices or any other trading conditions;

    (b) limit or control production, markets, technical development, or investment;

    (c) share markets or sources of supply;

    (d) apply dissimilar conditions to equivalent transactions with other trading parties, thereby placing them at a competitive disadvantage;

    (e) make the conclusion of contracts subject to acceptance by the other parties of supplementary obligations which, by their nature or according to commercial usage, have no connection with the subject of such contracts.

2. Any agreements or decisions prohibited pursuant to this Article shall be automatically void.

3. The provisions of paragraph 1 may, however, be declared inapplicable in the case

   – any agreement or category of agreements between undertakings;

   – any decision or category of decisions by associations of undertakings;

   – any concerted practice or category of concerted practices,

which contributes to improving the production or distribution of goods or to promoting technical or economic progress, while allowing consumers a fair share of the resulting benefit, and which does not:

    (a) impose on the undertakings concerned restrictions which are not indispensable to the attainment of these objectives;

    (b) afford such undertakings the possibility of eliminating competition in respect of a substantial part of the products in question.

Article 102 (ex Article 82 TEC)

Any abuse by one or more undertakings of a dominant position within the common market or in a substantial part of it shall be prohibited as incompatible with the common market in so far as it may affect trade between Member States.

   Such abuse may, in particular, consist in:

    (a) directly or indirectly imposing unfair purchase or selling prices or other unfair trading conditions;

    (b) limiting production, markets or technical development to the prejudice of consumers;

    (c) applying dissimilar conditions to equivalent transactions with other trading parties, thereby placing them at a competitive disadvantage;

    (d) making the conclusion of contracts subject to acceptance by the other parties of supplementary obligations which, by their nature or according to commercial usage, have no connection with the subject of such contracts.

Article 103 (ex Article 83 TEC)

1. The appropriate regulations or directives to give effect to the principles set out in Articles 81 and 82 shall be laid down by the Council, acting by a qualified majority on a proposal from the Commission and after consulting the European Parliament.

2. The regulations or directives referred to in paragraph 1 shall be designed in particular:

    (a) to ensure compliance with the prohibitions laid down in Article 101(1) and in Article 102 by making provision for fines and periodic penalty payments;

    (b) to lay down detailed rules for the application of Article 81(3), taking into account the need to ensure effective supervision on the one hand, and to simplify administration to the greatest possible extent on the other;

    (c) to define, if need be, in the various branches of the economy, the scope of the provisions of Articles 101 and 102;

    (d) to define the respective functions of the Commission and of the Court of Justice in applying the provisions laid down in this paragraph;

    (e) to determine the relationship between national laws and the provisions contained in this Section or adopted pursuant to this Article.

Article 104 (ex Article 84 TEC)

Until the entry into force of the provisions adopted in pursuance of Article 103, the authorities in Member States shall rule on the admissibility of agreements, decisions and concerted practices and on abuse of a dominant position in the common market in accordance with the law of their country and with the provisions of Article 101, in particular paragraph 3, and of Article 102.

Article 105 (ex Article 85 TEC)

1. Without prejudice to Article 104, the Commission shall ensure the application of the principles laid down in Articles 101 and 102. On application by a Member State or on its own initiative, and in cooperation with the competent authorities in the Member States, who shall give it their assistance, the Commission shall investigate cases of suspected infringement of these principles. If it finds that there has been an infringement, it shall propose appropriate measures to bring it to an end.

2. If the infringement is not brought to an end, the Commission shall record such infringement of the principles in a reasoned decision. The Commission may publish its decision and authorise Member States to take the measures, the conditions and details of which it shall determine, needed to remedy the situation.

3. The Commission may adopt regulations relating to the categories of agreement in respect of which the Council has adopted a regulation or a directive pursuant to Article 103(2)(b).

Article 106 (ex Article 86 TEC)

1. In the case of public undertakings and undertakings to which Member States grant special or exclusive rights, Member States shall neither enact nor maintain in force any measure contrary to the rules contained in the Treaties, in particular to those rules provided for in Article 18 and Articles 101 to 109.

2. Undertakings entrusted with the operation of services of general economic interest or having the character of a revenue producing monopoly shall be subject to the rules contained in this Treaty, in particular to the rules on competition; insofar as the application of such rules does not obstruct the performance, in law or in fact, of the particular tasks assigned to them. The development of trade must not be affected to such an extent as would be contrary to the interests of the Union.

3. The Commission shall ensure the application of the provisions of this Article and shall, where necessary, address appropriate directives or decisions to Member States.

Section 2   Aids granted by States

Article 107 (ex Article 87 TEC)

1. Save as otherwise provided in the Treaties, any aid granted by a Member State or through State resources in any form whatsoever which distorts or threatens to distort competition by favouring certain undertakings or the production of certain goods shall, in so far as it affects trade between Member States, be incompatible with the internal market.

2. The following shall be compatible with the internal market:

    (a) aid having a social character, granted to individual consumers, provided that such aid is granted without discrimination related to the origin of the products concerned;

(b) aid to make good the damage caused by natural disasters or exceptional occurrences;

(c) aid granted to the economy of certain areas of the Federal Republic of Germany affected by the division of Germany, insofar as such aid is required in order to compensate for the economic disadvantages caused by that division. Five years after the entry into force of the Treaty of Lisbon, the Council, acting on a proposal from the Commission, may adopt a decision repealing this point.

3. The following may be considered to be compatible with the internal market:

(a) aid to promote the economic development of areas where the standard of living is abnormally low or where there is serious underemployment, and of the regions referred to in Article 349, in view of their structural, economic and social situation;

(b) aid to promote the execution of an important project of common European interest or to remedy a serious disturbance in the economy of a Member State;

(c) aid to facilitate the development of certain economic activities or of certain economic areas, where such aid does not adversely affect trading conditions to an extent contrary to the common interest;

(d) aid to promote culture and heritage conservation where such aid does not affect trading conditions and competition in the Union to an extent that is contrary to the common interest;

(e) such other categories of aid as may be specified by decision of the Council on a proposal from the Commission.

Article 108 (ex Article 88 TEC)

1. The Commission shall, in cooperation with Member States, keep under constant review all systems of aid existing in those States. It shall propose to the latter any appropriate measures required by the progressive development or by the functioning of the internal market.

2. If, after giving notice to the parties concerned to submit their comments, the Commission finds that aid granted by a State or through State resources is not compatible with the internal market having regard to Article 107, or that such aid is being misused, it shall decide that the State concerned shall abolish or alter such aid within a period of time to be determined by the Commission.

If the State concerned does not comply with this decision within the prescribed time, the Commission or any other interested State may, in derogation from the provisions of Articles 258 and 259, refer the matter to the Court of Justice of the European Union direct.

On application by a Member State, the Council may, acting unanimously, decide that aid which that State is granting or intends to grant shall be considered to be compatible with the internal market, in derogation from the provisions of Article 107 or from the regulations provided for in Article 109, if such a decision is justified by exceptional circumstances. If, as regards the aid in question, the Commission has already initiated the procedure provided for in the first subparagraph of this paragraph, the fact that the State concerned has made its application to the Council shall have the effect of suspending that procedure until the Council has made its attitude known.

If, however, the Council has not made its attitude known within three months of the said application being made, the Commission shall give its decision on the case.

3. The Commission shall be informed, in sufficient time to enable it to submit its comments, of any plans to grant or alter aid. If it considers that any such plan is not compatible with the common market having regard to Article 87, it shall without delay initiate the procedure provided for in paragraph 2. The Member State concerned shall not put its proposed measures into effect until this procedure has resulted in a final decision.

4. The Commission may adopt regulations relating to the categories of State aid that the Council has, pursuant to Article 109, determined may be exempted from the procedure provided for by paragraph 3 of this Article.

Article 109 (ex Article 89 TEC)

The Council, on a proposal from the Commission and after consulting the European Parliament, may make any appropriate regulations for the application of Articles 107 and 108 and may in particular determine the conditions in which Article 108(3) shall apply and the categories of aid exempted from this procedure.

Part III

EU Secondary Legislation[*]

Council Regulation (EC) No 1/2003 of 16 December 2002 on the implementation of the rules on competition laid down in Articles 81 and 82 of the Treaty

(Text with EEA relevance)

THE COUNCIL OF THE EUROPEAN UNION,

Having regard to the Treaty establishing the European Community, and in particular Article 83 thereof,

Having regard to the proposal from the Commission,

Having regard to the opinion of the European Parliament,

Having regard to the opinion of the European Economic and Social Committee,

Whereas:

(1) In order to establish a system which ensures that competition in the common market is not distorted, Articles 81 and 82 of the Treaty must be applied effectively and uniformly in the Community. Council Regulation No 17 of 6 February 1962, First Regulation implementing Articles 81 and 82 of the Treaty, has allowed a Community competition policy to develop that has helped to disseminate a competition culture within the Community. In the light of experience, however, that Regulation should now be replaced by legislation designed to meet the challenges of an integrated market and a future enlargement of the Community.

(2) In particular, there is a need to rethink the arrangements for applying the exception from the prohibition on agreements, which restrict competition, laid down in Article 81(3) of the Treaty. Under Article 83(2)(b) of the Treaty, account must be taken in this regard of the need to ensure effective super-vision, on the one hand, and to simplify administration to the greatest possible extent, on the other.

(3) The centralised scheme set up by Regulation No 17 no longer secures a balance between those two objectives. It hampers application of the Community competition rules by the courts and competition authorities of the Member States, and the system of notification it involves prevents the Commission from concentrating its resources on curbing the most serious infringements. It also imposes considerable costs on undertakings.

(4) The present system should therefore be replaced by a directly applicable exception system in which the competition authorities and courts of the Member States have the power to apply not only Article 81(1) and Article 82 of the Treaty, which have direct applicability by virtue of the case-law of the Court of Justice of the European Communities, but also Article 81(3) of the Treaty.

(5) In order to ensure an effective enforcement of the Community competition rules and at the same time the respect of fundamental rights of defence, this Regulation should regulate the burden of proof under Articles 81 and 82 of the Treaty. It should be for the party or the authority alleging an infringement of Article 81(1) and Article 82 of the Treaty to prove the existence thereof to the required

legal standard. It should be for the undertaking or association of undertakings invoking the benefit of a defence against a finding of an infringement to demonstrate to the required legal standard that the conditions for applying such defence are satisfied. This Regulation affects neither national rules on the standard of proof nor obligations of competition authorities and courts of the Member States to ascertain the relevant facts of a case, provided that such rules and obligations are compatible with general principles of Community law.

(6) In order to ensure that the Community competition rules are applied effectively, the competition authorities of the Member States should be associated more closely with their application. To this end, they should be empowered to apply Community law.

(7) National courts have an essential part to play in applying the Community competition rules. When deciding disputes between private individuals, they protect the subjective rights under Community law, for example, by awarding damages to the victims of infringements. The role of the national courts here complements that of the competition authorities of the Member States. They should therefore be allowed to apply Articles 81 and 82 of the Treaty in full.

(8) In order to ensure the effective enforcement of the Community competition rules and the proper functioning of the cooperation mechanisms contained in this Regulation, it is necessary to oblige the competition authorities and courts of the Member States to also apply Articles 81 and 82 of the Treaty where they apply national competition law to agreements and practices which may affect trade between Member States. In order to create a level playing field for agreements, decisions by associations of undertakings and concerted practices within the internal market, it is also necessary to determine pursuant to Article 83(2)(e) of the Treaty the relationship between national laws and Community competition law. To that effect it is necessary to provide that the application of national competition laws to agreements, decisions or concerted practices within the meaning of Article 81(1) of the Treaty may not lead to the prohibition of such agreements, decisions and concerted practices if they are not also prohibited under Community competition law. The notions of agreements, decisions and concerted practices are autonomous concepts of Community competition law covering the coordination of behaviour of undertakings on the market as interpreted by the Community Courts. Member States should not under this Regulation be precluded from adopting and applying on their territory stricter national competition laws which prohibit or impose sanctions on unilateral conduct engaged in by undertakings. These stricter national laws may include provisions which prohibit or impose sanctions on abusive behaviour toward economically dependent undertakings. Furthermore, this Regulation does not apply to national laws which impose criminal sanctions on natural persons except to the extent that such sanctions are the means whereby competition rules applying to undertakings are enforced.

(9) Articles 81 and 82 of the Treaty have as their objective the protection of competition on the market. This Regulation, which is adopted for the implementation of these Treaty provisions, does not preclude Member States from implementing on their territory national legislation, which protects other legitimate interests provided that such legislation is compatible with general principles and other provisions of Community law. In so far as such national legislation pursues predominantly an objective different from that of protecting competition on the market, the competition authorities and courts of the Member States may apply such legislation on their territory. Accordingly, Member States may under this Regulation implement on their territory national legislation that prohibits or imposes sanctions on acts of unfair trading practice, be they unilateral or contractual. Such legislation pursues a specific objective, irrespective of the actual or presumed effects of such acts on competition on the market. This is particularly the case of legislation which prohibits undertakings from imposing on their trading partners, obtaining or attempting to obtain from them terms and conditions that are unjustified, disproportionate or without consideration.

(10) Regulations such as 19/65/EEC, (EEC) No 2821/71, (EEC) No 3976/87, (EEC) No 1534/91, or (EEC) No 479/92 empower the Commission to apply Article 81(3) of the Treaty by Regulation to certain categories of agreements, decisions by associations of undertakings and concerted practices. In the areas defined by such Regulations, the Commission has adopted and may continue

to adopt so called 'block' exemption Regulations by which it declares Article 81(1) of the Treaty inapplicable to categories of agreements, decisions and concerted practices. Where agreements, decisions and concerted practices to which such Regulations apply nonetheless have effects that are incompatible with Article 81(3) of the Treaty, the Commission and the competition authorities of the Member States should have the power to withdraw in a particular case the benefit of the block exemption Regulation.

(11) For it to ensure that the provisions of the Treaty are applied, the Commission should be able to address decisions to undertakings or associations of undertakings for the purpose of bringing to an end infringements of Articles 81 and 82 of the Treaty. Provided there is a legitimate interest in doing so, the Commission should also be able to adopt decisions which find that an infringement has been committed in the past even if it does not impose a fine. This Regulation should also make explicit provision for the Commission's power to adopt decisions ordering interim measures, which has been acknowledged by the Court of Justice.

(12) This Regulation should make explicit provision for the Commission's power to impose any remedy, whether behavioural or structural, which is necessary to bring the infringement effectively to an end, having regard to the principle of proportionality. Structural remedies should only be imposed either where there is no equally effective behavioural remedy or where any equally effective behavioural remedy would be more burdensome for the undertaking concerned than the structural remedy. Changes to the structure of an undertaking as it existed before the infringement was committed would only be proportionate where there is a substantial risk of a lasting or repeated infringement that derives from the very structure of the undertaking.

(13) Where, in the course of proceedings which might lead to an agreement or practice being prohibited, undertakings offer the Commission commitments such as to meet its concerns, the Commission should be able to adopt decisions which make those commitments binding on the undertakings concerned. Commitment decisions should find that there are no longer grounds for action by the Commission without concluding whether or not there has been or still is an infringement. Commitment decisions are without prejudice to the powers of competition authorities and courts of the Member States to make such a finding and decide upon the case. Commitment decisions are not appropriate in cases where the Commission intends to impose a fine.

(14) In exceptional cases where the public interest of the Community so requires, it may also be expedient for the Commission to adopt a decision of a declaratory nature finding that the prohibition in Article 81 or Article 82 of the Treaty does not apply, with a view to clarifying the law and ensuring its consistent application throughout the Community, in particular with regard to new types of agreements or practices that have not been settled in the existing case-law and administrative practice.

(15) The Commission and the competition authorities of the Member States should form together a network of public authorities applying the Community competition rules in close cooperation. For that purpose it is necessary to set up arrangements for information and consultation. Further modalities for the cooperation within the network will be laid down and revised by the Commission, in close cooperation with the Member States.

(16) Notwithstanding any national provision to the contrary, the exchange of information and the use of such information in evidence should be allowed between the members of the network even where the information is confidential. This information may be used for the application of Articles 81 and 82 of the Treaty as well as for the parallel application of national competition law, provided that the latter application relates to the same case and does not lead to a different outcome. When the information exchanged is used by the receiving authority to impose sanctions on undertakings, there should be no other limit to the use of the information than the obligation to use it for the purpose for which it was collected given the fact that the sanctions imposed on undertakings are of the same type in all systems. The rights of defence enjoyed by undertakings in the various systems can be considered as sufficiently equivalent. However, as regards natural persons, they may be subject to substantially different types of sanctions across the various systems. Where that is the case, it is necessary to ensure that information can only be used if it has been

collected in a way which respects the same level of protection of the rights of defence of natural persons as provided for under the national rules of the receiving authority.

(17) If the competition rules are to be applied consistently and, at the same time, the network is to be managed in the best possible way, it is essential to retain the rule that the competition authorities of the Member States are automatically relieved of their competence if the Commission initiates its own proceedings. Where a competition authority of a Member State is already acting on a case and the Commission intends to initiate proceedings, it should endeavour to do so as soon as possible. Before initiating proceedings, the Commission should consult the national authority concerned.

(18) To ensure that cases are dealt with by the most appropriate authorities within the network, a general provision should be laid down allowing a competition authority to suspend or close a case on the ground that another authority is dealing with it or has already dealt with it, the objective being that each case should be handled by a single authority. This provision should not prevent the Commission from rejecting a complaint for lack of Community interest, as the case-law of the Court of Justice has acknowledged it may do, even if no other competition authority has indicated its intention of dealing with the case.

(19) The Advisory Committee on Restrictive Practices and Dominant Positions set up by Regulation No 17 has functioned in a very satisfactory manner. It will fit well into the new system of decentralised application. It is necessary, therefore, to build upon the rules laid down by Regulation No 17, while improving the effectiveness of the organisational arrangements. To this end, it would be expedient to allow opinions to be delivered by written procedure. The Advisory Committee should also be able to act as a forum for discussing cases that are being handled by the competition authorities of the Member States, so as to help safeguard the consistent application of the Community competition rules.

(20) The Advisory Committee should be composed of representatives of the competition authorities of the Member States. For meetings in which general issues are being discussed, Member States should be able to appoint an additional representative. This is without prejudice to members of the Committee being assisted by other experts from the Member States.

(21) Consistency in the application of the competition rules also requires that arrangements be established for cooperation between the courts of the Member States and the Commission. This is relevant for all courts of the Member States that apply Articles 81 and 82 of the Treaty, whether applying these rules in lawsuits between private parties, acting as public enforcers or as review courts. In particular, national courts should be able to ask the Commission for information or for its opinion on points concerning the application of Community competition law. The Commission and the competition authorities of the Member States should also be able to submit written or oral observations to courts called upon to apply Article 81 or Article 82 of the Treaty. These observations should be submitted within the framework of national procedural rules and practices including those safeguarding the rights of the parties. Steps should therefore be taken to ensure that the Commission and the competition authorities of the Member States are kept sufficiently well informed of proceedings before national courts.

(22) In order to ensure compliance with the principles of legal certainty and the uniform application of the Community competition rules in a system of parallel powers, conflicting decisions must be avoided. It is therefore necessary to clarify, in accordance with the case-law of the Court of Justice, the effects of Commission decisions and proceedings on courts and competition authorities of the Member States. Commitment decisions adopted by the Commission do not affect the power of the courts and the competition authorities of the Member States to apply Articles 81 and 82 of the Treaty.

(23) The Commission should be empowered throughout the Community to require such information to be supplied as is necessary to detect any agreement, decision or concerted practice prohibited by Article 81 of the Treaty or any abuse of a dominant position prohibited by Article 82 of the Treaty. When complying with a decision of the Commission, undertakings cannot be forced to admit that they have committed an infringement, but they are in any event obliged to answer factual questions and to provide documents, even if this information may be used to establish against them or against another undertaking the existence of an infringement.

(24) The Commission should also be empowered to undertake such inspections as are necessary to detect any agreement, decision or concerted practice prohibited by Article 81 of the Treaty or any abuse of a dominant position prohibited by Article 82 of the Treaty. The competition authorities of the Member States should cooperate actively in the exercise of these powers.

(25) The detection of infringements of the competition rules is growing ever more difficult, and, in order to protect competition effectively, the Commission's powers of investigation need to be supplemented. The Commission should in particular be empowered to interview any persons who may be in possession of useful information and to record the statements made. In the course of an inspection, officials authorised by the Commission should be empowered to affix seals for the period of time necessary for the inspection. Seals should normally not be affixed for more than 72 hours. Officials authorised by the Commission should also be empowered to ask for any information relevant to the subject matter and purpose of the inspection.

(26) Experience has shown that there are cases where business records are kept in the homes of directors or other people working for an undertaking. In order to safeguard the effectiveness of inspections, therefore, officials and other persons authorised by the Commission should be empowered to enter any premises where business records may be kept, including private homes. However, the exercise of this latter power should be subject to the authorisation of the judicial authority.

(27) Without prejudice to the case-law of the Court of Justice, it is useful to set out the scope of the control that the national judicial authority may carry out when it authorises, as foreseen by national law including as a precautionary measure, assistance from law enforcement authorities in order to overcome possible opposition on the part of the undertaking or the execution of the decision to carry out inspections in non-business premises. It results from the case-law that the national judicial authority may in particular ask the Commission for further information which it needs to carry out its control and in the absence of which it could refuse the authorisation. The case-law also confirms the competence of the national courts to control the application of national rules governing the implementation of coercive measures.

(28) In order to help the competition authorities of the Member States to apply Articles 81 and 82 of the Treaty effectively, it is expedient to enable them to assist one another by carrying out inspections and other fact-finding measures.

(29) Compliance with Articles 81 and 82 of the Treaty and the fulfilment of the obligations imposed on undertakings and associations of undertakings under this Regulation should be enforceable by means of fines and periodic penalty payments. To that end, appropriate levels of fine should also be laid down for infringements of the procedural rules.

(30) In order to ensure effective recovery of fines imposed on associations of undertakings for infringements that they have committed, it is necessary to lay down the conditions on which the Commission may require payment of the fine from the members of the association where the association is not solvent. In doing so, the Commission should have regard to the relative size of the undertakings belonging to the association and in particular to the situation of small and medium-sized enterprises. Payment of the fine by one or several members of an association is without prejudice to rules of national law that provide for recovery of the amount paid from other members of the association.

(31) The rules on periods of limitation for the imposition of fines and periodic penalty payments were laid down in Council Regulation (EEC) No 2988/74, which also concerns penalties in the field of transport. In a system of parallel powers, the acts, which may interrupt a limitation period, should include procedural steps taken independently by the competition authority of a Member State. To clarify the legal framework, Regulation (EEC) No 2988/74 should therefore be amended to prevent it applying to matters covered by this Regulation, and this Regulation should include provisions on periods of limitation.

(32) The undertakings concerned should be accorded the right to be heard by the Commission, third parties whose interests may be affected by a decision should be given the opportunity of submitting their observations beforehand, and the decisions taken should be widely publicised. While ensuring the rights of defence of the undertakings concerned, in particular, the

right of access to the file, it is essential that business secrets be protected. The confidentiality of information exchanged in the network should likewise be safeguarded.

(33) Since all decisions taken by the Commission under this Regulation are subject to review by the Court of Justice in accordance with the Treaty, the Court of Justice should, in accordance with Article 229 thereof be given unlimited jurisdiction in respect of decisions by which the Commission imposes fines or periodic penalty payments.

(34) The principles laid down in Articles 81 and 82 of the Treaty, as they have been applied by Regulation No 17, have given a central role to the Community bodies. This central role should be retained, whilst associating the Member States more closely with the application of the Community competition rules. In accordance with the principles of subsidiarity and proportionality as set out in Article 5 of the Treaty, this Regulation does not go beyond what is necessary in order to achieve its objective, which is to allow the Community competition rules to be applied effectively.

(35) In order to attain a proper enforcement of Community competition law, Member States should designate and empower authorities to apply Articles 81 and 82 of the Treaty as public enforcers. They should be able to designate administrative as well as judicial authorities to carry out the various functions conferred upon competition authorities in this Regulation. This Regulation recognises the wide variation which exists in the public enforcement systems of Member States. The effects of Article 11(6) of this Regulation should apply to all competition authorities. As an exception to this general rule, where a prosecuting authority brings a case before a separate judicial authority, Article 11 (6) should apply to the prosecuting authority subject to the conditions in Article 35(4) of this Regulation. Where these conditions are not fulfilled, the general rule should apply. In any case, Article 11(6) should not apply to courts insofar as they are acting as review courts.

(36) As the case-law has made it clear that the competition rules apply to transport, that sector should be made subject to the procedural provisions of this Regulation. Council Regulation No 141 of 26 November 1962 exempting transport from the application of Regulation No 17 should therefore be repealed and Regulations (EEC) No 1017/68, (EEC) No 4056/86 and (EEC) No 3975/ 87 should be amended in order to delete the specific procedural provisions they contain.

(37) This Regulation respects the fundamental rights and observes the principles recognised in particular by the Charter of Fundamental Rights of the European Union. Accordingly, this Regulation should be interpreted and applied with respect to those rights and principles.

(38) Legal certainty for undertakings operating under the Community competition rules contributes to the promotion of innovation and investment. Where cases give rise to genuine uncertainty because they present novel or unresolved questions for the application of these rules, individual undertakings may wish to seek informal guidance from the Commission. This Regulation is without prejudice to the ability of the Commission to issue such informal guidance.

HAS ADOPTED THIS REGULATION:

Chapter 1 Principles

Article 1   Application of Articles 81 and 82 of the Treaty

1. Agreements, decisions and concerted practices caught by Article 81(1) of the Treaty which do not satisfy the conditions of Article 81(3) of the Treaty shall be prohibited, no prior decision to that effect being required.

2. Agreements, decisions and concerted practices caught by Article 81(1) of the Treaty which satisfy the conditions of Article 81 (3) of the Treaty shall not be prohibited, no prior decision to that effect being required.

3. The abuse of a dominant position referred to in Article 82 of the Treaty shall be prohibited, no prior decision to that effect being required.

Article 2   Burden of proof

In any national or Community proceedings for the application of Articles 81 and 82 of the Treaty, the burden of proving an infringement of Article 81(1) or of Article 82 of the Treaty shall rest on the party or the authority alleging the infringement. The undertaking or association of undertakings claiming the benefit of Article 81(3) of the Treaty shall bear the burden of proving that the conditions of that paragraph are fulfilled.

Article 3   Relationship between Articles 81 and 82 of the Treaty and national competition laws

1. Where the competition authorities of the Member States or national courts apply national competition law to agreements, decisions by associations of undertakings or concerted practices within the meaning of Article 81(1) of the Treaty which may affect trade between Member States within the meaning of that provision, they shall also apply Article 81 of the Treaty to such agreements, decisions or concerted practices. Where the competition authorities of the Member States or national courts apply national competition law to any abuse prohibited by Article 82 of the Treaty, they shall also apply Article 82 of the Treaty.

2. The application of national competition law may not lead to the prohibition of agreements, decisions by associations of undertakings or concerted practices which may affect trade between Member States but which do not restrict competition within the meaning of Article 81(1) of the Treaty, or which fulfil the conditions of Article 81(3) of the Treaty or which are covered by a Regulation for the application of Article 81(3) of the Treaty. Member States shall not under this Regulation be precluded from adopting and applying on their territory stricter national laws which prohibit or sanction unilateral conduct engaged in by undertakings.

3. Without prejudice to general principles and other provisions of Community law, paragraphs 1 and 2 do not apply when the competition authorities and the courts of the Member States apply national merger control laws nor do they preclude the application of provisions of national law that predominantly pursue an objective different from that pursued by Articles 81 and 82 of the Treaty.

Chapter II Powers

Article 4   Powers of the Commission

For the purpose of applying Articles 81 and 82 of the Treaty, the Commission shall have the powers provided for by this Regulation.

Article 5   Powers of the competition authorities of the Member States

The competition authorities of the Member States shall have the power to apply Articles 81 and 82 of the Treaty in individual cases. For this purpose, acting on their own initiative or on a complaint, they may take the following decisions:
  – requiring that an infringement be brought to an end,
  – ordering interim measures,
  – accepting commitments,
  – imposing fines, periodic penalty payments or any other penalty provided for in their national law.

Where on the basis of the information in their possession the conditions for prohibition are not met they may likewise decide that there are no grounds for action on their part.

Article 6   Powers of the national courts

National courts shall have the power to apply Articles 81 and 82 of the Treaty.

Chapter III Commission decisions

Article 7   Finding and termination of infringement

1. Where the Commission, acting on a complaint or on its own initiative, finds that there is an infringement of Article 81 or of Article 82 of the Treaty, it maybe decision require the undertakings and associations of undertakings concerned to bring such infringement to an end. For this purpose, it may impose on them any behavioural or structural remedies which are proportionate to the

infringement committed and necessary to bring the infringement effectively to an end. Structural remedies can only be imposed either where there is no equally effective behavioural remedy or where any equally effective behavioural remedy would be more burdensome for the undertaking concerned than the structural remedy. If the Commission has a legitimate interest in doing so, it may also find that an infringement has been committed in the past.

2. Those entitled to lodge a complaint for the purposes of paragraph 1 are natural or legal persons who can show a legitimate interest and Member States.

Article 8   Interim measures

1. In cases of urgency due to the risk of serious and irreparable damage to competition, the Commission, acting on its own initiative may by decision, on the basis of a prima facie finding of infringement, order interim measures.

2. A decision under paragraph I shall apply for a specified period of time and may be renewed in so far this is necessary and appropriate.

Article 9   Commitments

1. Where the Commission intends to adopt a decision requiring that an infringement be brought to an end and the undertakings concerned offer commitments to meet the concerns expressed to them by the Commission in its preliminary assessment, the Commission may by decision make those commitments binding on the undertakings. Such a decision may be adopted for a specified period and shall conclude that there are no longer grounds for action by the Commission.

2. The Commission may, upon request or on its own initiative, reopen the proceedings:
- (a) where there has been a material change in any of the facts on which the decision was based;
- (b) where the undertakings concerned act contrary to their commitments; or
- (c) where the decision was based on incomplete, incorrect or misleading information provided by the parties.

Article 10   Finding of inapplicability

Where the Community public interest relating to the application of Articles 81 and 82 of the Treaty so requires, the Commission, acting on its own initiative, may by decision find that Article 81 of the Treaty is not applicable to an agreement, a decision by an association of undertakings or a concerted practice, either because the conditions of Article 81(1) of the Treaty are not fulfilled, or because the conditions of Article 81(3) of the Treaty are satisfied.

The Commission may likewise make such a finding with reference to Article 82 of the Treaty.

Chapter IV   Cooperation

Article 11   Cooperation between the Commission and the competition authorities of the Member States

1. The Commission and the competition authorities of the Member States shall apply the Community competition rules in close cooperation.

2. The Commission shall transmit to the competition authorities of the Member States copies of the most important documents it has collected with a view to applying Articles 7, 8, 9, 10 and Article 29(1). At the request of the competition authority of a Member State, the Commission shall provide it with a copy of other existing documents necessary for the assessment of the case.

3. The competition authorities of the Member States shall, when acting under Article 81 or Article 82 of the Treaty, inform the Commission in writing before or without delay after commencing the first formal investigative measure. This information may also be made available to the competition authorities of the other Member States.

4. No later than 30 days before the adoption of a decision requiring that an infringement be brought to an end, accepting commitments or withdrawing the benefit of a block exemption Regulation, the competition authorities of the Member States shall inform the Commission. To

that effect, they shall provide the Commission with a summary of the case, the envisaged decision or, in the absence thereof, any other document indicating the proposed course of action. This information may also be made available to the competition authorities of the other Member States. At the request of the Commission, the acting competition authority shall make available to the Commission other documents it holds which are necessary for the assessment of the case. The information supplied to the Commission may be made available to the competition authorities of the other Member States. National competition authorities may also exchange between themselves information necessary for the assessment of a case that they are dealing with under Article 81 or Article 82 of the Treaty.

5. The competition authorities of the Member States may consult the Commission on any case involving the application of Community law.

6. The initiation by the Commission of proceedings for the adoption of a decision under Chapter III shall relieve the competition authorities of the Member States of their competence to apply Articles 81 and 82 of the Treaty. If a competition authority of a Member State is already acting on a case, the Commission shall only initiate proceedings after consulting with that national competition authority.

Article 12   Exchange of information

1. For the purpose of applying Articles 81 and 82 of the Treaty the Commission and the competition authorities of the Member States shall have the power to provide one another with and use in evidence any matter of fact or of law, including confidential information.

2. Information exchanged shall only be used in evidence for the purpose of applying Article 81 or Article 82 of the Treaty and in respect of the subject-matter for which it was collected by the transmitting authority. However, where national competition law is applied in the same case and in parallel to Community competition law and does not lead to a different outcome, information exchanged under this Article may also be used for the application of national competition law.

3. Information exchanged pursuant to paragraph 1 can only be used in evidence to impose sanctions on natural persons where:
   - the law of the transmitting authority foresees sanctions of a similar kind in relation to an infringement of Article 81 or Article 82 of the Treaty or, in the absence thereof,
   - the information has been collected in a way which respects the same level of protection of the rights of defence of natural persons as provided for under the national rules of the receiving authority. However, in this case, the information exchanged cannot be used by the receiving authority to impose custodial sanctions.

Article 13   Suspension or termination of proceedings

1. Where competition authorities of two or more Member States have received a complaint or are acting on their own initiative under Article 81 or Article 82 of the Treaty against the same agreement, decision of an association or practice, the fact that one authority is dealing with the case shall be sufficient grounds for the others to suspend the proceedings before them or to reject the complaint. The Commission may likewise reject a complaint on the ground that a competition authority of a Member State is dealing with the case.

2. Where a competition authority of a Member State or the Commission has received a complaint against an agreement, decision of an association or practice which has already been dealt with by another competition authority, it may reject it.

Article 14   Advisory Committee

1. The Commission shall consult an Advisory Committee on Restrictive Practices and Dominant Positions prior to the taking of any decision under Articles 7, 8, 9, 10, 23, Article 24(2) and Article 29(1).

2. For the discussion of individual cases, the Advisory Committee shall be composed of representatives of the competition authorities of the Member States. For meetings in which issues

other than individual cases are being discussed, an additional Member State representative competent in competition matters may be appointed. Representatives may, if unable to attend, be replaced by other representatives.

3. The consultation may take place at a meeting convened and chaired by the Commission, held not earlier than 14 days after dispatch of the notice convening it, together with a summary of the case, an indication of the most important documents and a preliminary draft decision. In respect of decisions pursuant to Article 8, the meeting may be held seven days after the dispatch of the operative part of a draft decision. Where the Commission dispatches a notice convening the meeting which gives a shorter period of notice than those specified above, the meeting may take place on the proposed date in the absence of an objection by any Member State. The Advisory Committee shall deliver a written opinion on the Commission's preliminary draft decision. It may deliver an opinion even if some members are absent and are not represented. At the request of one or several members, the positions stated in the opinion shall be reasoned.

4. Consultation may also take place by written procedure. However, if any Member State so requests, the Commission shall convene a meeting. In case of written procedure, the Commission shall determine a time-limit of not less than 14 days within which the Member States are to put forward their observations for circulation to all other Member States. In case of decisions to be taken pursuant to Article 8, the time-limit of 14 days is replaced by seven days. Where the Commission determines a time-limit for the written procedure which is shorter than those specified above, the proposed time-limit shall be applicable in the absence of an objection by any Member State.

5. The Commission shall take the utmost account of the opinion delivered by the Advisory Committee. It shall inform the Committee of the manner in which its opinion has been taken into account.

6. Where the Advisory Committee delivers a written opinion, this opinion shall be appended to the draft decision. If the Advisory Committee recommends publication of the opinion, the Commission shall carry out such publication taking into account the legitimate interest of undertakings in the protection of their business secrets.

7. At the request of a competition authority of a Member State, the Commission shall include on the agenda of the Advisory Committee cases that are being dealt with by a competition authority of a Member State under Article 81 or Article 82 of the Treaty. The Commission may also do so on its own initiative. In either case, the Commission shall inform the competition authority concerned.

A request may in particular be made by a competition authority of a Member State in respect of a case where the Commission intends to initiate proceedings with the effect of Article 11(6).

The Advisory Committee shall not issue opinions on cases dealt with by competition authorities of the Member States. The Advisory Committee may also discuss general issues of Community competition law.

Article 15 Cooperation with national courts

1. In proceedings for the application of Article 81 or Article 82 of the Treaty, courts of the Member States may ask the Commission to transmit to them information in its possession or its opinion on questions concerning the application of the Community competition rules.

2. Member States shall forward to the Commission a copy of any written judgment of national courts deciding on the application of Article 81 or Article 82 of the Treaty. Such copy shall be forwarded without delay after the full written judgment is notified to the parties.

3. Competition authorities of the Member States, acting on their own initiative, may submit written observations to the national courts of their Member State on issues relating to the application of Article 81 or Article 82 of the Treaty. With the permission of the court in question, they may also submit oral observations to the national courts of their Member State. Where the coherent application of Article 81 or Article 82 of the Treaty so requires, the Commission, acting on its own initiative, may submit written observations to courts of the Member States. With the permission of the court in question, it may also make oral observations.

For the purpose of the preparation of their observations only, the competition authorities of the Member States and the Commission may request the relevant court of the Member State to transmit or ensure the transmission to them of any documents necessary for the assessment of the case.

4. This Article is without prejudice to wider powers to make observations before courts conferred on competition authorities of the Member States under the law of their Member State.

Article 16   Uniform application of Community competition law

1. When national courts rule on agreements, decisions or practices under Article 81 or Article 82 of the Treaty which are already the subject of a Commission decision, they cannot take decisions running counter to the decision adopted by the Commission. They must also avoid giving decisions which would conflict with a decision contemplated by the Commission in proceedings it has initiated. To that effect, the national court may assess whether it is necessary to stay its proceedings. This obligation is without prejudice to the rights and obligations under Article 234 of the Treaty.

2. When competition authorities of the Member States rule on agreements, decisions or practices under Article 81 or Article 82 of the Treaty which are already the subject of a Commission decision, they cannot take decisions which would run counter to the decision adopted by the Commission.

Chapter V   Powers of investigation

Article 17   Investigations into sectors of the economy and into types of agreements

1. Where the trend of trade between Member States, the rigidity of prices or other circumstances suggest that competition may be restricted or distorted within the common market, the Commission may conduct its inquiry into a particular sector of the economy or into a particular type of agreements across various sectors. In the course of that inquiry, the Commission may request the undertakings or associations of undertakings concerned to supply the information necessary for giving effect to Articles 81 and 82 of the Treaty and may carry out any inspections necessary for that purpose.

The Commission may in particular request the undertakings or associations of undertakings concerned to communicate to it all agreements, decisions and concerted practices.

The Commission may publish a report on the results of its inquiry into particular sectors of the economy or particular types of agreement across various sectors and invite comments from interested parties.

2. Articles 14, 18, 19, 20, 22, 23 and 24 shall apply *mutatis mutandis*.

Article 18   Requests for information

1. In order to carry out the duties assigned to it by this Regulation, the Commission may, by simple request or by decision, require undertakings and associations of undertakings to provide all necessary information.

2. When sending a simple request for information to an undertaking or association of undertakings, the Commission shall state the legal basis and the purpose of the request, specify what information is required and fix the time-limit within which the information is to be provided, and the penalties provided for in Article 23 for supplying incorrect or misleading information.

3. Where the Commission requires undertakings and associations of undertakings to supply information by decision, it shall state the legal basis and the purpose of the request, specify what information is required and fix the time-limit within which it is to be provided. It shall also indicate the penalties provided for in Article 23 and indicate or impose the penalties provided for in Article 24. It shall further indicate the right to have the decision reviewed by the Court of Justice.

4. The owners of the undertakings or their representatives and, in the case of legal persons, companies or firms, or associations having no legal personality, the persons authorised to represent them by law or by their constitution shall supply the information requested on behalf of the undertaking or the association of undertakings concerned. Lawyers duly authorised to act

may supply the information on behalf of their clients. The latter shall remain fully responsible if the information supplied is incomplete, incorrect or misleading.

5. The Commission shall without delay forward a copy of the simple request or of the decision to the competition authority of the Member State in whose territory the seat of the undertaking or association of undertaking is situated and the competition authority of the Member State whose territory is affected.

6. At the request of the Commission the governments and competition authorities of the Member States shall provide the Commission with all necessary information to carry out the duties assigned to it by this Regulation.

Article 19   Power to take statements

1. In order to carry out the duties assigned to it by this Regulation, the Commission may interview any natural or legal person who consents to be interviewed for the purpose of collecting information relating to the subject-matter of an investigation.

2. Where an interview pursuant to paragraph 1 is conducted in the premises of an undertaking, the Commission shall inform the competition authority of the Member State in whose territory the interview takes place. If so requested by the competition authority of that Member State, its officials may assist the officials and other accompanying persons authorised by the Commission to conduct the interview.

Article 20   The Commission's powers of inspection

1. In order to carry out the duties assigned to it by this Regulation, the Commission may conduct all necessary inspections of undertakings and associations of undertakings.

2. The officials and other accompanying persons authorised by the Commission to conduct an inspection are empowered:

   (a) to enter any premises, land and means of transport of undertakings and associations of undertakings;
   (b) to examine the books and other records related to the business, irrespective of the medium on which they are stored;
   (c) to take or obtain in any form copies of or extracts from such books or records;
   (d) to seal any business premises and books or records for the period and to the extent necessary for the inspection;
   (e) to ask any representative or member of staff of the undertaking or association of undertakings for explanations on facts or documents relating to the subject-matter and purpose of the inspection and to record the answers.

3. The officials and other accompanying persons authorised by the Commission to conduct an inspection shall exercise their powers upon production of a written authorisation specifying the subject matter and purpose of the inspection and the penalties provided for in Article 23 in case the production of the required books or other records related to the business is incomplete or where the answers to questions asked under paragraph 2 of the present Article are incorrect or misleading. In good time before the inspection, the Commission shall give notice of the inspection to the competition authority of the Member State in whose territory it is to be conducted.

4. Undertakings and associations of undertakings are required to submit to inspections ordered by decision of the Commission. The decision shall specify the subject matter and purpose of the inspection, appoint the date on which it is to begin and indicate the penalties provided for in Articles 23 and 24 and the right to have the decision reviewed by the Court of Justice. The Commission shall take such decisions after consulting the competition authority of the Member State in whose territory the inspection is to be conducted.

5. Officials of as well as those authorised or appointed by the competition authority of the Member State in whose territory the inspection is to be conducted shall, at the request of that authority or of the Commission, actively assist the officials and other accompanying persons authorised by the Commission. To this end, they shall enjoy the powers specified in paragraph 2.

6. Where the officials and other accompanying persons authorised by the Commission find that an undertaking opposes an inspection ordered pursuant to this Article, the Member State concerned shall afford them the necessary assistance, requesting where appropriate the assistance of the police or of an equivalent enforcement authority, so as to enable them to conduct their inspection.

7. If the assistance provided for in paragraph 6 requires authorisation from a judicial authority according to national rules, such authorisation shall be applied for. Such authorisation may also be applied for as a precautionary measure.

8. Where authorisation as referred to in paragraph 7 is applied for, the national judicial authority shall control that the Commission decision is authentic and that the coercive measures envisaged are neither arbitrary nor excessive having regard to the subject matter of the inspection. In its control of the proportionality of the coercive measures, the national judicial authority may ask the Commission, directly or through the Member State competition authority, for detailed explanations in particular on the grounds the Commission has for suspecting infringement of Articles 81 and 82 of the Treaty, as well as on the seriousness of the suspected infringement and on the nature of the involvement of the undertaking concerned. However, the national judicial authority may not call into question the necessity for the inspection nor demand that it be provided with the information in the Commission's file. The lawfulness of the Commission decision shall be subject to review only by the Court of Justice.

Article 21   Inspection of other premises

1. If a reasonable suspicion exists that books or other records related to the business and to the subject-matter of the inspection, which may be relevant to prove a serious violation of Article 81 or Article 82 of the Treaty, are being kept in any other premises, land and means of transport, including the homes of directors, managers and other members of staff of the undertakings and associations of undertakings concerned, the Commission can by decision order an inspection to be conducted in such other premises, land and means of transport.

2. The decision shall specify the subject matter and purpose of the inspection, appoint the date on which it is to begin and indicate the right to have the decision reviewed by the Court of Justice. It shall in particular state the reasons that have led the Commission to conclude that a suspicion in the sense of paragraph 1 exists. The Commission shall take such decisions after consulting the competition authority of the Member State in whose territory the inspection is to be conducted.

3. A decision adopted pursuant to paragraph 1 cannot be executed without prior authorisation from the national judicial authority of the Member State concerned. The national judicial authority shall control that the Commission decision is authentic and that the coercive measures envisaged are neither arbitrary nor excessive having regard in particular to the seriousness of the suspected infringement, to the importance of the evidence sought, to the involvement of the undertaking concerned and to the reasonable likelihood that business books and records relating to the subject matter of the inspection are kept in the premises for which the authorisation is requested. The national judicial authority may ask the Commission, directly or through the Member State competition authority, for detailed explanations on those elements which are necessary to allow its control of the proportionality of the coercive measures envisaged.

However, the national judicial authority may not call into question the necessity for the inspection nor demand that it be provided with information in the Commission's file. The lawfulness of the Commission decision shall be subject to review only by the Court of Justice.

4. The officials and other accompanying persons authorised by the Commission to conduct an inspection ordered in accordance with paragraph 1 of this Article shall have the powers set out in Article 20(2)(a), (b) and (c). Article 20(5) and (6) shall apply *mutatis mutandis*.

Article 22   Investigations by competition authorities of member states

1. The competition authority of a Member State may in its own territory carry out any inspection or other fact-finding measure under its national law on behalf and for the account of the

competition authority of another Member State in order to establish whether there has been an infringement of Article 81 or Article 82 of the Treaty. Any exchange and use of the information collected shall be carried out in accordance with Article 12.

2. At the request of the Commission, the competition authorities of the Member States shall undertake the inspections which the Commission considers to be necessary under Article 20(1) or which it has ordered by decision pursuant to Article 20(4). The officials of the competition authorities of the Member States who are responsible for conducting these inspections as well as those authorised or appointed by them shall exercise their powers in accordance with their national law.

If so requested by the Commission or by the competition authority of the Member State in whose territory the inspection is to be conducted, officials and other accompanying persons authorised by the Commission may assist the officials of the authority concerned.

Chapter VI Penalties

Article 23   Fines

1. The Commission may by decision impose on undertakings and associations of undertakings fines not exceeding 1% of the total turnover in the preceding business year where, intentionally or negligently:

    (a) they supply incorrect or misleading information in response to a request made pursuant to Article 17 or Article 18(2);

    (b) in response to a request made by decision adopted pursuant to Article 17 or Article 18(3), they supply incorrect, incomplete or misleading information or do not supply information within the required time-limit;

    (c) they produce the required books or other records related to the business in incomplete form during inspections under Article 20 or refuse to submit to inspections ordered by a decision adopted pursuant to Article 20(4);

    (d) in response to a question asked in accordance with Article 20(2)(e),

      – they give an incorrect or misleading answer,

      – they fail to rectify within a time-limit set by the Commission an incorrect, incomplete or misleading answer given by a member of staff, or

      – they fail or refuse to provide a complete answer on facts relating to the subject-matter and purpose of an inspection ordered by a decision adopted pursuant to Article 20(4);

    (e) seals affixed in accordance with Article 20(2) (d) by officials or other accompanying persons authorised by the Commission have been broken.

2. The Commission may by decision impose fines on undertakings and associations of undertakings where, either intentionally or negligently:

    (a) they infringe Article 81 or Article 82 of the Treaty; or

    (b) they contravene a decision ordering interim measures under Article 8; or

    (c) they fail to comply with a commitment made binding by a decision pursuant to Article 9.

For each undertaking and association of undertakings participating in the infringement, the fine shall not exceed 10% of its total turnover in the preceding business year.

Where the infringement of an association relates to the activities of its members, the fine shall not exceed 10% of the sum of the total turnover of each member active on the market affected by the infringement of the association.

3. In fixing the amount of the fine, regard shall be had both to the gravity and to the duration of the infringement.

4. When a fine is imposed on an association of undertakings taking account of the turnover of its members and the association is not solvent, the association is obliged to call for contributions from its members to cover the amount of the fine.

Where such contributions have not been made to the association within a time-limit fixed by the Commission, the Commission may require payment of the fine directly by any of the undertakings whose representatives were members of the decision-making bodies concerned of the association.

After the Commission has required payment under the second subparagraph, where necessary to ensure full payment of the fine, the Commission may require payment of the balance by any of the members of the association which were active on the market on which the infringement occurred.

However, the Commission shall not require payment under the second or the third sub-paragraph from undertakings which show that they have not implemented the infringing decision of the association and either were not aware of its existence or have actively distanced themselves from it before the Commission started investigating the case.

The financial liability of each undertaking in respect of the payment of the fine shall not exceed 10% of its total turnover in the preceding business year.

5. Decisions taken pursuant to paragraphs 1 and 2 shall not be of a criminal law nature.

Article 24   Periodic penalty payments

1. The Commission may, by decision, impose on undertakings or associations of undertakings periodic penalty payments not exceeding 5% of the average daily turnover in the preceding business year per day and calculated from the date appointed by the decision, in order to compel them:

(a) to put an end to an infringement of Article 81 or Article 82 of the Treaty, in accordance with a decision taken pursuant to Article 7;

(b) to comply with a decision ordering interim measures taken pursuant to Article 8;

(c) to comply with a commitment made binding by a decision pursuant to Article 9;

(d) to supply complete and correct information which it has requested by decision taken pursuant to Article 17 or Article 18(3);

(e) to submit to an inspection which it has ordered by decision taken pursuant to Article 20(4).

2. Where the undertakings or associations of undertakings have satisfied the obligation which the periodic penalty payment was intended to enforce, the Commission may fix the definitive amount of the periodic penalty payment at a figure lower than that which would arise under the original decision. Article 23(4) shall apply correspondingly.

Chapter VII Limitation periods

Article 25   Limitation periods for the imposition of penalties

1. The powers conferred on the Commission by Articles 23 and 24 shall be subject to the following limitation periods:

(a) three years in the case of infringements of provisions concerning requests for information or the conduct of inspections;

(b) five years in the case of all other infringements.

2. Time shall begin to run on the day on which the infringement is committed. However, in the case of continuing or repeated infringements, time shall begin to run on the day on which the infringement ceases.

3. Any action taken by the Commission or by the competition authority of a Member State for the purpose of the investigation or proceedings in respect of an infringement shall interrupt the limitation period for the imposition of fines or periodic penalty payments. The limitation period shall be interrupted with effect from the date on which the action is notified to at least one undertaking or association of undertakings which has participated in the infringement. Actions which interrupt the running of the period shall include in particular the following:

(a) written requests for information by the Commission or by the competition authority of a Member State;

(b) written authorisations to conduct inspections issued to its officials by the Commission or by the competition authority of a Member State;

(c) the initiation of proceedings by the Commission or by the competition authority of a Member State;

(d) notification of the statement of objections of the Commission or of the competition authority of a Member State.

4. The interruption of the limitation period shall apply for all the undertakings or associations of undertakings which have participated in the infringement.

5. Each interruption shall start time running afresh. However, the limitation period shall expire at the latest on the day on which a period equal to twice the limitation period has elapsed without the Commission having imposed a fine or a periodic penalty payment. That period shall be extended by the time during which limitation is suspended pursuant to paragraph 6.

6. The limitation period for the imposition of fines or periodic penalty payments shall be suspended for as long as the decision of the Commission is the subject of proceedings pending before the Court of Justice.

Article 26   Limitation period for the enforcement of penalties

1. The power of the Commission to enforce decisions taken pursuant to Articles 23 and 24 shall be subject to a limitation period of five years.

2. Time shall begin to run on the day on which the decision becomes final.

3. The limitation period for the enforcement of penalties shall be interrupted:

(a) by notification of a decision varying the original amount of the fine or periodic penalty payment or refusing an application for variation;

(b) by any action of the Commission or of a Member State, acting at the request of the Commission, designed to enforce payment of the fine or periodic penalty payment.

4. Each interruption shall start time running afresh.

5. The limitation period for the enforcement of penalties shall be suspended for so long as:

(a) time to pay is allowed;

(b) enforcement of payment is suspended pursuant to a decision of the Court of Justice.

Chapter VIII   Hearings and professional secrecy

Article 27   Hearing of the parties, complainants and others

1. Before taking decisions as provided for in Articles 7, 8, 23 and Article 24(2), the Commission shall give the undertakings or associations of undertakings which are the subject of the proceedings conducted by the Commission the opportunity of being heard on the matters to which the Commission has taken objection. The Commission shall base its decisions only on objections on which the parties concerned have been able to comment. Complainants shall be associated closely with the proceedings.

2. The rights of defence of the parties concerned shall be fully respected in the proceedings. They shall be entitled to have access to the Commission's file, subject to the legitimate interest of undertakings in the protection of their business secrets. The right of access to the file shall not extend to confidential information and internal documents of the Commission or the competition authorities of the Member States. In particular, the right of access shall not extend to correspondence between the Commission and the competition authorities of the Member States, or between the latter, including documents drawn up pursuant to Articles 11 and 14. Nothing in this paragraph shall prevent the Commission from disclosing and using information necessary to prove an infringement.

3. If the Commission considers it necessary, it may also hear other natural or legal persons. Applications to be heard on the part of such persons shall, where they show a sufficient interest, be granted. The competition authorities of the Member States may also ask the Commission to hear other natural or legal persons.

4. Where the Commission intends to adopt a decision pursuant to Article 9 or Article 10, it shall publish a concise summary of the case and the main content of the commitments or of the

proposed course of action. Interested third parties may submit their observations within a time limit which is fixed by the Commission in its publication and which may not be less than one month. Publication shall have regard to the legitimate interest of undertakings in the protection of their business secrets.

Article 28   Professional secrecy

1. Without prejudice to Articles 12 and 15, information collected pursuant to Articles 17 to 22 shall be used only for the purpose for which it was acquired.

2. Without prejudice to the exchange and to the use of information foreseen in Articles 11, 12, 14, 15 and 27, the Commission and the competition authorities of the Member States, their officials, servants and other persons working under the supervision of these authorities as well as officials and civil servants of other authorities of the Member States shall not disclose information acquired or exchanged by them pursuant to this Regulation and of the kind covered by the obligation of professional secrecy. This obligation also applies to all representatives and experts of Member States attending meetings of the Advisory Committee pursuant to Article 14.

Chapter IX Exemption Regulations

Article 29   Withdrawal in individual cases

1. Where the Commission, empowered by a Council Regulation, such as Regulations 19/65/EEC, (EEC) No 2821/71, (EEC) No 3976/87, (EEC) No 1534/91 or (EEC) No 479/92, to apply Article 81(3) of the Treaty by regulation, has declared Article 81(1) of the Treaty inapplicable to certain categories of agreements, decisions by associations of undertakings or concerted practices, it may, acting on its own initiative or on a complaint, withdraw the benefit of such an exemption Regulation when it finds that in any particular case an agreement, decision or concerted practice to which the exemption Regulation applies has certain effects which are incompatible with Article 81(3) of the Treaty.

2. Where, in any particular case, agreements, decisions by associations of undertakings or concerted practices to which a Commission Regulation referred to in paragraph 1 applies have effects which are incompatible with Article 81(3) of the Treaty in the territory of a Member State, or in a part thereof, which has all the characteristics of a distinct geographic market, the competition authority of that Member State may withdraw the benefit of the Regulation in question in respect of that territory.

Chapter X General provisions

Article 30   Publication of decisions

1. The Commission shall publish the decisions, which it takes pursuant to Articles 7 to 10, 23 and 24.

2. The publication shall state the names of the parties and the main content of the decision, including any penalties imposed. It shall have regard to the legitimate interest of undertakings in the protection of their business secrets.

Article 31   Review by the Court of Justice

The Court of Justice shall have unlimited jurisdiction to review decisions whereby the Commission has fixed a fine or periodic penalty payment. It may cancel, reduce or increase the fine or periodic penalty payment imposed.

Article 32   Exclusions

This Regulation shall not apply to:

    (a) international tramp vessel services as defined in Article 1(3) (a) of Regulation (EEC) No 4056/86;

    (b) a maritime transport service that takes place exclusively between ports in one and the same Member State as foreseen in Article 1(2) of Regulation (EEC) No 4056/86;

Article 33   Implementing provisions

1. The Commission shall be authorised to take such measures as may be appropriate in order to apply this Regulation. The measures may concern, *inter alia:*

    (a) the form, content and other details of complaints lodged pursuant to Article 7 and the procedure for rejecting complaints;

    (b) the practical arrangements for the exchange of information and consultations provided for in Article 11;

    (c) the practical arrangements for the hearings provided for in Article 27.

2. Before the adoption of any measures pursuant to paragraph 1, the Commission shall publish a draft thereof and invite all interested parties to submit their comments within the time-limit it lays down, which may not be less than one month. Before publishing a draft measure and before adopting it, the Commission shall consult the Advisory Committee on Restrictive Practices and Dominant Positions.

Chapter XI   Transitional, amending and final provisions

Article 34   Transitional provisions

1. Applications made to the Commission under Article 2 of Regulation No 17, notifications made under Articles 4 and 5 of that Regulation and the corresponding applications and notifications made under Regulations (EEC) No 1017/68, (EEC) No 4056/86 and (EEC) No 3975/87 shall lapse as from the date of application of this Regulation.

2. Procedural steps taken under Regulation No 17 and Regulations (EEC) No 1017/68, (EEC) No 4056/86 and (EEC) No 3975/87 shall continue to have effect for the purposes of applying this Regulation.

Article 35   Designation of competition authorities of Member States

1. The Member States shall designate the competition authority or authorities responsible for the application of Articles 81 and 82 of the Treaty in such a way that the provisions of this regulation are effectively complied with. The measures necessary to empower those authorities to apply those Articles shall be taken before 1 May 2004. The authorities designated may include courts.

2. When enforcement of Community competition law is entrusted to national administrative and judicial authorities, the Member States may allocate different powers and functions to those different national authorities, whether administrative or judicial.

3. The effects of Article 11(6) apply to the authorities designated by the Member States including courts that exercise functions regarding the preparation and the adoption of the types of decisions foreseen in Article 5. The effects of Article 11(6) do not extend to courts insofar as they act as review courts in respect of the types of decisions foreseen in Article 5.

4. Notwithstanding paragraph 3, in the Member States where, for the adoption of certain types of decisions foreseen in Article 5, an authority brings an action before a judicial authority that is separate and different from the prosecuting authority and provided that the terms of this paragraph are complied with, the effects of Article 11(6) shall be limited to the authority prosecuting the case which shall withdraw its claim before the judicial authority when the Commission opens proceedings and this withdrawal shall bring the national proceedings effectively to an end.

    ...

Article 43   Repeal of Regulations No 17 and No 141

1. Regulation No 17 is repealed with the exception of Article 8(3) which continues to apply to decisions adopted pursuant to Article 81(3) of the Treaty prior to the date of application of this Regulation until the date of expiration of those decisions.

2. Regulation No 141 is repealed.

3. References to the repealed Regulations shall be construed as references to this Regulation.

Article 44   Report on the application of the present Regulation

Five years from the date of application of this Regulation, the Commission shall report to the European Parliament and the Council on the functioning of this Regulation, in particular on the application of Article 11(6) and Article 17.

On the basis of this report, the Commission shall assess whether it is appropriate to propose to the Council a revision of this Regulation.

Article 45   Entry into force

This Regulation shall enter into force on the 20th day following that of its publication in the *Official Journal of the European Communities.*

It shall apply from 1 May 2004.

This Regulation shall be binding in its entirety and directly applicable in all Member States.

Done at Brussels, 16 December 2002.

For the Council
The President
M. FISCHER BOEL

Council Regulation (EC) No 139/2004 of 20 January 2004 on the control of concentrations between undertakings (the EC Merger Regulation)

(Text with EEA relevance)

THE COUNCIL OF THE EUROPEAN UNION,

Having regard to the Treaty establishing the European Community, and in particular Articles 83 and 308 thereof,

Having regard to the proposal from the Commission,

Having regard to the opinion of the European Parliament,

Having regard to the opinion of the European Economic and Social Committee,

Whereas:

(1) Council Regulation (EEC) No 4064/89 of 21 December 1989 on the control of concentrations between undertakings has been substantially amended. Since further amendments are to be made, it should be recast in the interest of clarity.

(2) For the achievement of the aims of the Treaty, Article 3(1)(g) gives the Community the objective of instituting a system ensuring that competition in the internal market is not distorted. Article 4(1) of the Treaty provides that the activities of the Member States and the Community are to be conducted in accordance with the principle of an open market economy with free competition. These principles are essential for the further development of the internal market.

(3) The completion of the internal market and of economic and monetary union, the enlargement of the European Union and the lowering of international barriers to trade and investment will continue to result in major corporate reorganisations, particularly in the form of concentrations.

(4) Such reorganisations are to be welcomed to the extent that they are in line with the requirements of dynamic competition and capable of increasing the competitiveness of European industry, improving the conditions of growth and raising the standard of living in the Community.

(5) However, it should be ensured that the process of reorganisation does not result in lasting damage to competition; Community law must therefore include provisions governing those concentrations which may significantly impede effective competition in the common market or in a substantial part of it.

(6) A specific legal instrument is therefore necessary to permit effective control of all concentrations in terms of their effect on the structure of competition in the Community and to be the only instrument applicable to such concentrations. Regulation (EEC) No 4064/89 has allowed a Community policy to develop in this field. In the light of experience, however, that Regulation should now be recast into legislation designed to meet the challenges of a more integrated market and the future enlargement of the European Union. In accordance with the principles of subsidiarity and of proportionality as set out in Article 5 of the Treaty, this Regulation does not go beyond what is necessary in order to achieve the objective of ensuring that competition in the common market is not distorted, in accordance with the principle of an open market economy with free competition.

(7) Articles 81 and 82, while applicable, according to the case-law of the Court of Justice, to certain concentrations, are not sufficient to control all operations which may prove to be incompatible with the system of undistorted competition envisaged in the Treaty. This Regulation should therefore be based not only on Article 83 but, principally, on Article 308 of the Treaty, under which the Community may give itself the additional powers of action necessary for the attainment of its objectives, and also powers of action with regard to concentrations on the markets for agricultural products listed in Annex I to the Treaty.

(8) The provisions to be adopted in this Regulation should apply to significant structural changes, the impact of which on the market goes beyond the national borders of any one Member State. Such concentrations should, as a general rule, be reviewed exclusively at Community level, in application of a 'one-stop shop' system and in compliance with the principle of subsidiarity. Concentrations not covered by this Regulation come, in principle, within the jurisdiction of the Member States.

(9) The scope of application of this Regulation should be defined according to the geographical area of activity of the undertakings concerned and be limited by quantitative thresholds in order to cover those concentrations which have a Community dimension. The Commission should report to the Council on the implementation of the applicable thresholds and criteria so that the Council, acting in accordance with Article 202 of the Treaty, is in a position to review them regularly, as well as the rules regarding pre-notification referral, in the light of the experience gained; this requires statistical data to be provided by the Member States to the Commission to enable it to prepare such reports and possible proposals for amendments. The Commission's reports and proposals should be based on relevant information regularly provided by the Member States.

(10) A concentration with a Community dimension should be deemed to exist where the aggregate turnover of the undertakings concerned exceeds given thresholds; that is the case irrespective of whether or not the undertakings effecting the concentration have their seat or their principal fields of activity in the Community, provided they have substantial operations there.

(11) The rules governing the referral of concentrations from the Commission to Member States and from Member States to the Commission should operate as an effective corrective mechanism in the light of the principle of subsidiarity; these rules protect the competition interests of the Member States in an adequate manner and take due account of legal certainty and the 'one-stop shop' principle.

(12) Concentrations may qualify for examination under a number of national merger control systems if they fall below the turnover thresholds referred to in this Regulation. Multiple notification of the same transaction increases legal uncertainty, effort and cost for undertakings and may lead to conflicting assessments. The system whereby concentrations may be referred to the Commission by the Member States concerned should therefore be further developed.

(13) The Commission should act in close and constant liaison with the competent authorities of the Member States from which it obtains comments and information.

(14) The Commission and the competent authorities of the Member States should together form a network of public authorities, applying their respective competences in close cooperation, using efficient arrangements for information-sharing and consultation, with a view to ensuring that a case is dealt with by the most appropriate authority, in the light of the principle of subsidiarity

and with a view to ensuring that multiple notifications of a given concentration are avoided to the greatest extent possible. Referrals of concentrations from the Commission to Member States and from Member States to the Commission should be made in an efficient manner avoiding, to the greatest extent possible, situations where a concentration is subject to a referral both before and after its notification.

(15) The Commission should be able to refer to a Member State notified concentrations with a Community dimension which threaten significantly to affect competition in a market within that Member State presenting all the characteristics of a distinct market. Where the concentration affects competition on such a market, which does not constitute a substantial part of the common market, the Commission should be obliged, upon request, to refer the whole or part of the case to the Member State concerned. A Member State should be able to refer to the Commission a concentration which does not have a Community dimension but which affects trade between Member States and threatens to significantly affect competition within its territory. Other Member States which are also competent to review the concentration should be able to join the request. In such a situation, in order to ensure the efficiency and predictability of the system, national time limits should be suspended until a decision has been reached as to the referral of the case. The Commission should have the power to examine and deal with a concentration on behalf of a requesting Member State or requesting Member States.

(16) The undertakings concerned should be granted the possibility of requesting referrals to or from the Commission before a concentration is notified so as to further improve the efficiency of the system for the control of concentrations within the Community. In such situations, the Commission and national competition authorities should decide within short, clearly defined time limits whether a referral to or from the Commission ought to be made, thereby ensuring the efficiency of the system. Upon request by the undertakings concerned, the Commission should be able to refer to a Member State a concentration with a Community dimension which may significantly affect competition in a market within that Member State presenting all the characteristics of a distinct market; the undertakings concerned should not, however, be required to demonstrate that the effects of the concentration would be detrimental to competition. A concentration should not be referred from the Commission to a Member State which has expressed its disagreement to such a referral. Before notification to national authorities, the undertakings concerned should also be able to request that a concentration without a Community dimension which is capable of being reviewed under the national competition laws of at least three Member States be referred to the Commission. Such requests for pre-notification referrals to the Commission would be particularly pertinent in situations where the concentration would affect competition beyond the territory of one Member State. Where a concentration capable of being reviewed under the competition laws of three or more Member States is referred to the Commission prior to any national notification, and no Member State competent to review the case expresses its disagreement, the Commission should acquire exclusive competence to review the concentration and such a concentration should be deemed to have a Community dimension. Such pre-notification referrals from Member States to the Commission should not, however, be made where at least one Member State competent to review the case has expressed its disagreement with such a referral.

(17) The Commission should be given exclusive competence to apply this Regulation, subject to review by the Court of Justice.

(18) The Member States should not be permitted to apply their national legislation on competition to concentrations with a Community dimension, unless this Regulation makes provision therefor. The relevant powers of national authorities should be limited to cases where, failing intervention by the Commission, effective competition is likely to be significantly impeded within the territory of a Member State and where the competition interests of that Member State cannot be sufficiently protected otherwise by this Regulation. The Member States concerned must act promptly in such cases; this Regulation cannot, because of the diversity of national law, fix a single time limit for the adoption of final decisions under national law.

(19) Furthermore, the exclusive application of this Regulation to concentrations with a Community dimension is without prejudice to Article 296 of the Treaty, and does not prevent the

Member States from taking appropriate measures to protect legitimate interests other than those pursued by this Regulation, provided that such measures are compatible with the general principles and other provisions of Community law.

(20) It is expedient to define the concept of concentration in such a manner as to cover operations bringing about a lasting change in the control of the undertakings concerned and therefore in the structure of the market. It is therefore appropriate to include, within the scope of this Regulation, all joint ventures performing on a lasting basis all the functions of an autonomous economic entity. It is moreover appropriate to treat as a single concentration transactions that are closely connected in that they are linked by condition or take the form of a series of transactions in securities taking place within a reasonably short period of time.

(21) This Regulation should also apply where the undertakings concerned accept restrictions directly related to, and necessary for, the implementation of the concentration. Commission decisions declaring concentrations compatible with the common market in application of this Regulation should automatically cover such restrictions, without the Commission having to assess such restrictions in individual cases. At the request of the undertakings concerned, however, the Commission should, in cases presenting novel or unresolved questions giving rise to genuine uncertainty, expressly assess whether or not any restriction is directly related to, and necessary for, the implementation of the concentration. A case presents a novel or unresolved question giving rise to genuine uncertainty if the question is not covered by the relevant Commission notice in force or a published Commission decision.

(22) The arrangements to be introduced for the control of concentrations should, without prejudice to Article 86(2) of the Treaty, respect the principle of non-discrimination between the public and the private sectors. In the public sector, calculation of the turnover of an undertaking concerned in a concentration needs, therefore, to take account of undertakings making up an economic unit with an independent power of decision, irrespective of the way in which their capital is held or of the rules of administrative supervision applicable to them.

(23) It is necessary to establish whether or not concentrations with a Community dimension are compatible with the common market in terms of the need to maintain and develop effective competition in the common market. In so doing, the Commission must place its appraisal within the general framework of the achievement of the fundamental objectives referred to in Article 2 of the Treaty establishing the European Community and Article 2 of the Treaty on European Union.

(24) In order to ensure a system of undistorted competition in the common market, in furtherance of a policy conducted in accordance with the principle of an open market economy with free competition, this Regulation must permit effective control of all concentrations from the point of view of their effect on competition in the Community. Accordingly, Regulation (EEC) No 4064/89 established the principle that a concentration with a Community dimension which creates or strengthens a dominant position as a result of which effective competition in the common market or in a substantial part of it would be significantly impeded should be declared incompatible with the common market.

(25) In view of the consequences that concentrations in oligopolistic market structures may have, it is all the more necessary to maintain effective competition in such markets. Many oligopolistic markets exhibit a healthy degree of competition. However, under certain circumstances, concentrations involving the elimination of important competitive constraints that the merging parties had exerted upon each other, as well as a reduction of competitive pressure on the remaining competitors, may, even in the absence of a likelihood of coordination between the members of the oligopoly, result in a significant impediment to effective competition. The Community courts have, however, not to date expressly interpreted Regulation (EEC) No 4064/89 as requiring concentrations giving rise to such non-coordinated effects to be declared incompatible with the common market. Therefore, in the interests of legal certainty, it should be made clear that this Regulation permits effective control of all such concentrations by providing that any concentration which would significantly impede effective competition, in the common market or in a substantial part of it, should be declared incompatible with the common market. The

notion of 'significant impediment to effective competition' in Article 2(2) and (3) should be interpreted as extending, beyond the concept of dominance, only to the anti-competitive effects of a concentration resulting from the non-coordinated behaviour of undertakings which would not have a dominant position on the market concerned.

(26) A significant impediment to effective competition generally results from the creation or strengthening of a dominant position. With a view to preserving the guidance that may be drawn from past judgments of the European courts and Commission decisions pursuant to Regulation (EEC) No 4064/89, while at the same time maintaining consistency with the standards of competitive harm which have been applied by the Commission and the Community courts regarding the compatibility of a concentration with the common market, this Regulation should accordingly establish the principle that a concentration with a Community dimension which would significantly impede effective competition, in the common market or in a substantial part thereof, in particular as a result of the creation or strengthening of a dominant position, is to be declared incompatible with the common market.

(27) In addition, the criteria of Article 81(1) and (3) of the Treaty should be applied to joint ventures performing, on a lasting basis, all the functions of autonomous economic entities, to the extent that their creation has as its consequence an appreciable restriction of competition between undertakings that remain independent.

(28) In order to clarify and explain the Commission's appraisal of concentrations under this Regulation, it is appropriate for the Commission to publish guidance which should provide a sound economic framework for the assessment of concentrations with a view to determining whether or not they may be declared compatible with the common market.

(29) In order to determine the impact of a concentration on competition in the common market, it is appropriate to take account of any substantiated and likely efficiencies put forward by the undertakings concerned. It is possible that the efficiencies brought about by the concentration counteract the effects on competition, and in particular the potential harm to consumers, that it might otherwise have and that, as a consequence, the concentration would not significantly impede effective competition, in the common market or in a substantial part of it, in particular as a result of the creation or strengthening of a dominant position. The Commission should publish guidance on the conditions under which it may take efficiencies into account in the assessment of a concentration.

(30) Where the undertakings concerned modify a notified concentration, in particular by offering commitments with a view to rendering the concentration compatible with the common market, the Commission should be able to declare the concentration, as modified, compatible with the common market. Such commitments should be proportionate to the competition problem and entirely eliminate it. It is also appropriate to accept commitments before the initiation of proceedings where the competition problem is readily identifiable and can easily be remedied. It should be expressly provided that the Commission may attach to its decision conditions and obligations in order to ensure that the undertakings concerned comply with their commitments in a timely and effective manner so as to render the concentration compatible with the common market. Transparency and effective consultation of Member States as well as of interested third parties should be ensured throughout the procedure.

(31) The Commission should have at its disposal appropriate instruments to ensure the enforcement of commitments and to deal with situations where they are not fulfilled. In cases of failure to fulfil a condition attached to the decision declaring a concentration compatible with the common market, the situation rendering the concentration compatible with the common market does not materialise and the concentration, as implemented, is therefore not authorised by the Commission. As a consequence, if the concentration is implemented, it should be treated in the same way as a non-notified concentration implemented without authorisation. Furthermore, where the Commission has already found that, in the absence of the condition, the concentration would be incompatible with the common market, it should have the power to directly order the dissolution of the concentration, so as to restore the situation prevailing prior to the implementation

of the concentration. Where an obligation attached to a decision declaring the concentration compatible with the common market is not fulfilled, the Commission should be able to revoke its decision. Moreover, the Commission should be able to impose appropriate financial sanctions where conditions or obligations are not fulfilled.

(32) Concentrations which, by reason of the limited market share of the undertakings concerned, are not liable to impede effective competition may be presumed to be compatible with the common market. Without prejudice to Articles 81 and 82 of the Treaty, an indication to this effect exists, in particular, where the market share of the undertakings concerned does not exceed 25 % either in the common market or in a substantial part of it.

(33) The Commission should have the task of taking all the decisions necessary to establish whether or not concentrations with a Community dimension are compatible with the common market, as well as decisions designed to restore the situation prevailing prior to the implementation of a concentration which has been declared incompatible with the common market.

(34) To ensure effective control, undertakings should be obliged to give prior notification of concentrations with a Community dimension following the conclusion of the agreement, the announcement of the public bid or the acquisition of a controlling interest. Notification should also be possible where the undertakings concerned satisfy the Commission of their intention to enter into an agreement for a proposed concentration and demonstrate to the Commission that their plan for that proposed concentration is sufficiently concrete, for example on the basis of an agreement in principle, a memorandum of understanding, or a letter of intent signed by all undertakings concerned, or, in the case of a public bid, where they have publicly announced an intention to make such a bid, provided that the intended agreement or bid would result in a concentration with a Community dimension. The implementation of concentrations should be suspended until a final decision of the Commission has been taken. However, it should be possible to derogate from this suspension at the request of the undertakings concerned, where appropriate. In deciding whether or not to grant a derogation, the Commission should take account of all pertinent factors, such as the nature and gravity of damage to the undertakings concerned or to third parties, and the threat to competition posed by the concentration. In the interest of legal certainty, the validity of transactions must nevertheless be protected as much as necessary.

(35) A period within which the Commission must initiate proceedings in respect of a notified concentration and a period within which it must take a final decision on the compatibility or incompatibility with the common market of that concentration should be laid down. These periods should be extended whenever the undertakings concerned offer commitments with a view to rendering the concentration compatible with the common market, in order to allow for sufficient time for the analysis and market testing of such commitment offers and for the consultation of Member States as well as interested third parties. A limited extension of the period within which the Commission must take a final decision should also be possible in order to allow sufficient time for the investigation of the case and the verification of the facts and arguments submitted to the Commission.

(36) The Community respects the fundamental rights and observes the principles recognised in particular by the Charter of Fundamental Rights of the European Union. Accordingly, this Regulation should be interpreted and applied with respect to those rights and principles.

(37) The undertakings concerned must be afforded the right to be heard by the Commission when proceedings have been initiated; the members of the management and supervisory bodies and the recognised representatives of the employees of the undertakings concerned, and interested third parties, must also be given the opportunity to be heard.

(38) In order properly to appraise concentrations, the Commission should have the right to request all necessary information and to conduct all necessary inspections throughout the Community. To that end, and with a view to protecting competition effectively, the Commission's powers of investigation need to be expanded. The Commission should, in particular, have the right to interview any persons who may be in possession of useful information and to record the statements made.

(39) In the course of an inspection, officials authorised by the Commission should have the right to ask for any information relevant to the subject matter and purpose of the inspection; they should also have the right to affix seals during inspections, particularly in circumstances where there are reasonable grounds to suspect that a concentration has been implemented without being notified; that incorrect, incomplete or misleading information has been supplied to the Commission; or that the undertakings or persons concerned have failed to comply with a condition or obligation imposed by decision of the Commission. In any event, seals should only be used in exceptional circumstances, for the period of time strictly necessary for the inspection, normally not for more than 48 hours.

(40) Without prejudice to the case-law of the Court of Justice, it is also useful to set out the scope of the control that the national judicial authority may exercise when it authorises, as provided by national law and as a precautionary measure, assistance from law enforcement authorities in order to overcome possible opposition on the part of the undertaking against an inspection, including the affixing of seals, ordered by Commission decision. It results from the case-law that the national judicial authority may in particular ask of the Commission further information which it needs to carry out its control and in the absence of which it could refuse the authorisation. The case-law also confirms the competence of the national courts to control the application of national rules governing the implementation of coercive measures. The competent authorities of the Member States should cooperate actively in the exercise of the Commission's investigative powers.

(41) When complying with decisions of the Commission, the undertakings and persons concerned cannot be forced to admit that they have committed infringements, but they are in any event obliged to answer factual questions and to provide documents, even if this information may be used to establish against themselves or against others the existence of such infringements.

(42) For the sake of transparency, all decisions of the Commission which are not of a merely procedural nature should be widely publicised. While ensuring preservation of the rights of defence of the undertakings concerned, in particular the right of access to the file, it is essential that business secrets be protected. The confidentiality of information exchanged in the network and with the competent authorities of third countries should likewise be safeguarded.

(43) Compliance with this Regulation should be enforceable, as appropriate, by means of fines and periodic penalty payments. The Court of Justice should be given unlimited jurisdiction in that regard pursuant to Article 229 of the Treaty.

(44) The conditions in which concentrations, involving undertakings having their seat or their principal fields of activity in the Community, are carried out in third countries should be observed, and provision should be made for the possibility of the Council giving the Commission an appropriate mandate for negotiation with a view to obtaining non-discriminatory treatment for such undertakings.

(45) This Regulation in no way detracts from the collective rights of employees, as recognised in the undertakings concerned, notably with regard to any obligation to inform or consult their recognised representatives under Community and national law.

(46) The Commission should be able to lay down detailed rules concerning the implementation of this Regulation in accordance with the procedures for the exercise of implementing powers conferred on the Commission. For the adoption of such implementing provisions, the Commission should be assisted by an Advisory Committee composed of the representatives of the Member States as specified in Article 23,

HAS ADOPTED THIS REGULATION:

Article 1   Scope

1. Without prejudice to Article 4(5) and Article 22, this Regulation shall apply to all concentrations with a Community dimension as defined in this Article.

2. A concentration has a Community dimension where:

    (a) the combined aggregate worldwide turnover of all the undertakings concerned is more than EUR 5 000 million; and

    (b) the aggregate Community-wide turnover of each of at least two of the undertakings concerned is more than EUR 250 million,

unless each of the undertakings concerned achieves more than two-thirds of its aggregate Community-wide turnover within one and the same Member State.

    3. A concentration that does not meet the thresholds laid down in paragraph 2 has a Community dimension where:

    (a) the combined aggregate worldwide turnover of all the undertakings concerned is more than EUR 2 500 million;

    (b) in each of at least three Member States, the combined aggregate turnover of all the undertakings concerned is more than EUR 100 million;

    (c) in each of at least three Member States included for the purpose of point (b), the aggregate turnover of each of at least two of the undertakings concerned is more than EUR 25 million; and

    (d) the aggregate Community-wide turnover of each of at least two of the undertakings concerned is more than EUR 100 million,

unless each of the undertakings concerned achieves more than two-thirds of its aggregate Community-wide turnover within one and the same Member State.

    4. On the basis of statistical data that may be regularly provided by the Member States, the Commission shall report to the Council on the operation of the thresholds and criteria set out in paragraphs 2 and 3 by 1 July 2009 and may present proposals pursuant to paragraph 5.

    5. Following the report referred to in paragraph 4 and on a proposal from the Commission, the Council, acting by a qualified majority, may revise the thresholds and criteria mentioned in paragraph 3.

Article 2   Appraisal of concentrations

    1. Concentrations within the scope of this Regulation shall be appraised in accordance with the objectives of this Regulation and the following provisions with a view to establishing whether or not they are compatible with the common market.

In making this appraisal, the Commission shall take into account:

    (a) the need to maintain and develop effective competition within the common market in view of, among other things, the structure of all the markets concerned and the actual or potential competition from undertakings located either within or outwith the Community;

    (b) the market position of the undertakings concerned and their economic and financial power, the alternatives available to suppliers and users, their access to supplies or markets, any legal or other barriers to entry, supply and demand trends for the relevant goods and services, the interests of the intermediate and ultimate consumers, and the development of technical and economic progress provided that it is to consumers' advantage and does not form an obstacle to competition.

    2. A concentration which would not significantly impede effective competition in the common market or in a substantial part of it, in particular as a result of the creation or strengthening of a dominant position, shall be declared compatible with the common market.

    3. A concentration which would significantly impede effective competition, in the common market or in a substantial part of it, in particular as a result of the creation or strengthening of a dominant position, shall be declared incompatible with the common market.

    4. To the extent that the creation of a joint venture constituting a concentration pursuant to Article 3 has as its object or effect the coordination of the competitive behaviour of undertakings that remain independent, such coordination shall be appraised in accordance with the criteria of Article 81(1) and (3) of the Treaty, with a view to establishing whether or not the operation is compatible with the common market.

    5. In making this appraisal, the Commission shall take into account in particular:

- whether two or more parent companies retain, to a significant extent, activities in the same market as the joint venture or in a market which is downstream or upstream from that of the joint venture or in a neighbouring market closely related to this market,
- whether the coordination which is the direct consequence of the creation of the joint venture affords the undertakings concerned the possibility of eliminating competition in respect of a substantial part of the products or services in question.

Article 3   Definition of concentration

1. A concentration shall be deemed to arise where a change of control on a lasting basis results from:

(a) the merger of two or more previously independent undertakings or parts of undertakings; or

(b) the acquisition, by one or more persons already controlling at least one undertaking, or by one or more undertakings, whether by purchase of securities or assets, by contract or by any other means, of direct or indirect control of the whole or parts of one or more other undertakings.

2. Control shall be constituted by rights, contracts or any other means which, either separately or in combination and having regard to the considerations of fact or law involved, confer the possibility of exercising decisive influence on an undertaking, in particular by:

(a) ownership or the right to use all or part of the assets of an undertaking;

(b) rights or contracts which confer decisive influence on the composition, voting or decisions of the organs of an undertaking.

3. Control is acquired by persons or undertakings which:

(a) are holders of the rights or entitled to rights under the contracts concerned; or

(b) while not being holders of such rights or entitled to rights under such contracts, have the power to exercise the rights deriving therefrom.

4. The creation of a joint venture performing on a lasting basis all the functions of an autonomous economic entity shall constitute a concentration within the meaning of paragraph 1(b).

5. A concentration shall not be deemed to arise where:

(a) credit institutions or other financial institutions or insurance companies, the normal activities of which include transactions and dealing in securities for their own account or for the account of others, hold on a temporary basis securities which they have acquired in an undertaking with a view to reselling them, provided that they do not exercise voting rights in respect of those securities with a view to determining the competitive behaviour of that undertaking or provided that they exercise such voting rights only with a view to preparing the disposal of all or part of that undertaking or of its assets or the disposal of those securities and that any such disposal takes place within one year of the date of acquisition; that period may be extended by the Commission on request where such institutions or companies can show that the disposal was not reasonably possible within the period set;

(b) control is acquired by an office-holder according to the law of a Member State relating to liquidation, winding up, insolvency, cessation of payments, compositions or analogous proceedings;

(c) the operations referred to in paragraph 1(b) are carried out by the financial holding companies referred to in Article 5(3) of Fourth Council Directive 78/660/EEC of 25 July 1978 based on Article 54(3)(g) of the Treaty on the annual accounts of certain types of companies provided however that the voting rights in respect of the holding are exercised, in particular in relation to the appointment of members of the management and supervisory bodies of the undertakings in which they have holdings, only to maintain the full value of those investments and not to determine directly or indirectly the competitive conduct of those undertakings.

Article 4   Prior notification of concentrations and pre-notification referral at the request of the notifying parties

1. Concentrations with a Community dimension defined in this Regulation shall be notified to the Commission prior to their implementation and following the conclusion of the agreement, the announcement of the public bid, or the acquisition of a controlling interest.

Notification may also be made where the undertakings concerned demonstrate to the Commission a good faith intention to conclude an agreement or, in the case of a public bid, where they have publicly announced an intention to make such a bid, provided that the intended agreement or bid would result in a concentration with a Community dimension.

For the purposes of this Regulation, the term 'notified concentration' shall also cover intended concentrations notified pursuant to the second subparagraph. For the purposes of paragraphs 4 and 5 of this Article, the term 'concentration' includes intended concentrations within the meaning of the second subparagraph.

2. A concentration which consists of a merger within the meaning of Article 3(1)(a) or in the acquisition of joint control within the meaning of Article 3(1)(b) shall be notified jointly by the parties to the merger or by those acquiring joint control as the case may be. In all other cases, the notification shall be effected by the person or undertaking acquiring control of the whole or parts of one or more undertakings.

3. Where the Commission finds that a notified concentration falls within the scope of this Regulation, it shall publish the fact of the notification, at the same time indicating the names of the undertakings concerned, their country of origin, the nature of the concentration and the economic sectors involved. The Commission shall take account of the legitimate interest of undertakings in the protection of their business secrets.

4. Prior to the notification of a concentration within the meaning of paragraph 1, the persons or undertakings referred to in paragraph 2 may inform the Commission, by means of a reasoned submission, that the concentration may significantly affect competition in a market within a Member State which presents all the characteristics of a distinct market and should therefore be examined, in whole or in part, by that Member State.

The Commission shall transmit this submission to all Member States without delay. The Member State referred to in the reasoned submission shall, within 15 working days of receiving the submission, express its agreement or disagreement as regards the request to refer the case. Where that Member State takes no such decision within this period, it shall be deemed to have agreed.

Unless that Member State disagrees, the Commission, where it considers that such a distinct market exists, and that competition in that market may be significantly affected by the concentration, may decide to refer the whole or part of the case to the competent authorities of that Member State with a view to the application of that State's national competition law.

The decision whether or not to refer the case in accordance with the third subparagraph shall be taken within 25 working days starting from the receipt of the reasoned submission by the Commission. The Commission shall inform the other Member States and the persons or undertakings concerned of its decision. If the Commission does not take a decision within this period, it shall be deemed to have adopted a decision to refer the case in accordance with the submission made by the persons or undertakings concerned.

If the Commission decides, or is deemed to have decided, pursuant to the third and fourth subparagraphs, to refer the whole of the case, no notification shall be made pursuant to paragraph 1 and national competition law shall apply. Article 9(6) to (9) shall apply *mutatis mutandis*.

5. With regard to a concentration as defined in Article 3 which does not have a Community dimension within the meaning of Article 1 and which is capable of being reviewed under the national competition laws of at least three Member States, the persons or undertakings referred to in paragraph 2 may, before any notification to the competent authorities, inform the Commission by means of a reasoned submission that the concentration should be examined by the Commission.

The Commission shall transmit this submission to all Member States without delay.

Any Member State competent to examine the concentration under its national competition law may, within 15 working days of receiving the reasoned submission, express its disagreement as regards the request to refer the case.

Where at least one such Member State has expressed its disagreement in accordance with the third subparagraph within the period of 15 working days, the case shall not be referred. The Commission shall, without delay, inform all Member States and the persons or undertakings concerned of any such expression of disagreement.

Where no Member State has expressed its disagreement in accordance with the third subparagraph within the period of 15 working days, the concentration shall be deemed to have a Community dimension and shall be notified to the Commission in accordance with paragraphs 1 and 2. In such situations, no Member State shall apply its national competition law to the concentration.

6. The Commission shall report to the Council on the operation of paragraphs 4 and 5 by 1 July 2009. Following this report and on a proposal from the Commission, the Council, acting by a qualified majority, may revise paragraphs 4 and 5.

Article 5   Calculation of turnover

1. Aggregate turnover within the meaning of this Regulation shall comprise the amounts derived by the undertakings concerned in the preceding financial year from the sale of products and the provision of services falling within the undertakings' ordinary activities after deduction of sales rebates and of value added tax and other taxes directly related to turnover. The aggregate turnover of an undertaking concerned shall not include the sale of products or the provision of services between any of the undertakings referred to in paragraph 4.

Turnover, in the Community or in a Member State, shall comprise products sold and services provided to undertakings or consumers, in the Community or in that Member State as the case may be.

2. By way of derogation from paragraph 1, where the concentration consists of the acquisition of parts, whether or not constituted as legal entities, of one or more undertakings, only the turnover relating to the parts which are the subject of the concentration shall be taken into account with regard to the seller or sellers.

However, two or more transactions within the meaning of the first subparagraph which take place within a two-year period between the same persons or undertakings shall be treated as one and the same concentration arising on the date of the last transaction. 3. In place of turnover the following shall be used:

(a) for credit institutions and other financial institutions, the sum of the following income items as defined in Council Directive 86/635/EEC, after deduction of value added tax and other taxes directly related to those items, where appropriate:
    (i)   interest income and similar income;
    (ii) income from securities:
        – income from shares and other variable yield securities,
        – income from participating interests,
        – income from shares in affiliated undertakings;
    (iii) commissions receivable;
    (iv) net profit on financial operations;
    (v)   other operating income.
    The turnover of a credit or financial institution in the Community or in a Member State shall comprise the income items, as defined above, which are received by the branch or division of that institution established in the Community or in the Member State in question, as the case may be;

(b) for insurance undertakings, the value of gross premiums written which shall comprise all amounts received and receivable in respect of insurance contracts issued by or on behalf of the insurance undertakings, including also outgoing reinsurance premiums, and after deduction of taxes and parafiscal contributions or levies charged by reference to the amounts of individual premiums or the total volume of premiums; as regards Article 1(2)(b) and

(3)(b), (c) and (d) and the final part of Article 1(2) and (3), gross premiums received from Community residents and from residents of one Member State respectively shall be taken into account.

4. Without prejudice to paragraph 2, the aggregate turnover of an undertaking concerned within the meaning of this Regulation shall be calculated by adding together the respective turnovers of the following:

    (a) the undertaking concerned;

    (b) those undertakings in which the undertaking concerned, directly or indirectly:

        (i)   owns more than half the capital or business assets, or

        (ii) has the power to exercise more than half the voting rights, or

        (iii) has the power to appoint more than half the members of the supervisory board, the administrative board or bodies legally representing the undertakings, or

        (iv) has the right to manage the undertakings' affairs;

    (c) those undertakings which have in the undertaking concerned the rights or powers listed in (b);

    (d) those undertakings in which an undertaking as referred to in (c) has the rights or powers listed in (b);

    (e) those undertakings in which two or more undertakings as referred to in (a) to (d) jointly have the rights or powers listed in (b).

5. Where undertakings concerned by the concentration jointly have the rights or powers listed in paragraph 4(b), in calculating the aggregate turnover of the undertakings concerned for the purposes of this Regulation:

    (a) no account shall be taken of the turnover resulting from the sale of products or the provision of services between the joint undertaking and each of the undertakings concerned or any other undertaking connected with any one of them, as set out in paragraph 4(b) to (e);

    (b) account shall be taken of the turnover resulting from the sale of products and the provision of services between the joint undertaking and any third undertakings. This turnover shall be apportioned equally amongst the undertakings concerned.

Article 6   Examination of the notification and initiation of proceedings

1. The Commission shall examine the notification as soon as it is received.

    (a) Where it concludes that the concentration notified does not fall within the scope of this Regulation, it shall record that finding by means of a decision.

    (b) Where it finds that the concentration notified, although falling within the scope of this Regulation, does not raise serious doubts as to its compatibility with the common market, it shall decide not to oppose it and shall declare that it is compatible with the common market.A decision declaring a concentration compatible shall be deemed to cover restrictions directly related and necessary to the implementation of the concentration.

    (c) Without prejudice to paragraph 2, where the Commission finds that the concentration notified falls within the scope of this Regulation and raises serious doubts as to its compatibility with the common market, it shall decide to initiate proceedings. Without prejudice to Article 9, such proceedings shall be closed by means of a decision as provided for in Article 8(1) to (4), unless the undertakings concerned have demonstrated to the satisfaction of the Commission that they have abandoned the concentration.

2. Where the Commission finds that, following modification by the undertakings concerned, a notified concentration no longer raises serious doubts within the meaning of paragraph 1(c), it shall declare the concentration compatible with the common market pursuant to paragraph 1(b).

The Commission may attach to its decision under paragraph 1(b) conditions and obligations intended to ensure that the undertakings concerned comply with the commitments they have entered into vis-à-vis the Commission with a view to rendering the concentration compatible with the common market.

3. The Commission may revoke the decision it took pursuant to paragraph 1(a) or (b) where:

(a) the decision is based on incorrect information for which one of the undertakings is responsible or where it has been obtained by deceit, or

(b) the undertakings concerned commit a breach of an obligation attached to the decision.

4. In the cases referred to in paragraph 3, the Commission may take a decision under paragraph 1, without being bound by the time limits referred to in Article 10(1).

5. The Commission shall notify its decision to the undertakings concerned and the competent authorities of the Member States without delay.

Article 7   Suspension of concentrations

1. A concentration with a Community dimension as defined in Article 1, or which is to be examined by the Commission pursuant to Article 4(5), shall not be implemented either before its notification or until it has been declared compatible with the common market pursuant to a decision under Articles 6(1)(b), 8(1) or 8(2), or on the basis of a presumption according to Article 10(6).

2. Paragraph 1 shall not prevent the implementation of a public bid or of a series of transactions in securities including those convertible into other securities admitted to trading on a market such as a stock exchange, by which control within the meaning of Article 3 is acquired from various sellers, provided that:

(a) the concentration is notified to the Commission pursuant to Article 4 without delay; and

(b) the acquirer does not exercise the voting rights attached to the securities in question or does so only to maintain the full value of its investments based on a derogation granted by the Commission under paragraph 3.

3. The Commission may, on request, grant a derogation from the obligations imposed in paragraphs 1 or 2. The request to grant a derogation must be reasoned. In deciding on the request, the Commission shall take into account *inter alia* the effects of the suspension on one or more undertakings concerned by the concentration or on a third party and the threat to competition posed by the concentration. Such a derogation may be made subject to conditions and obligations in order to ensure conditions of effective competition. A derogation may be applied for and granted at any time, be it before notification or after the transaction.

4. The validity of any transaction carried out in contravention of paragraph 1 shall be dependent on a decision pursuant to Article 6(1)(b) or Article 8(1), (2) or (3) or on a presumption pursuant to Article 10(6).

This Article shall, however, have no effect on the validity of transactions in securities including those convertible into other securities admitted to trading on a market such as a stock exchange, unless the buyer and seller knew or ought to have known that the transaction was carried out in contravention of paragraph 1.

Article 8   Powers of decision of the Commission

1. Where the Commission finds that a notified concentration fulfils the criterion laid down in Article 2(2) and, in the cases referred to in Article 2(4), the criteria laid down in Article 81(3) of the Treaty, it shall issue a decision declaring the concentration compatible with the common market.

A decision declaring a concentration compatible shall be deemed to cover restrictions directly related and necessary to the implementation of the concentration.

2. Where the Commission finds that, following modification by the undertakings concerned, a notified concentration fulfils the criterion laid down in Article 2(2) and, in the cases referred to in Article 2(4), the criteria laid down in Article 81(3) of the Treaty, it shall issue a decision declaring the concentration compatible with the common market.

The Commission may attach to its decision conditions and obligations intended to ensure that the undertakings concerned comply with the commitments they have entered into vis-a-vis the Commission with a view to rendering the concentration compatible with the common market.

A decision declaring a concentration compatible shall be deemed to cover restrictions directly related and necessary to the implementation of the concentration.

3. Where the Commission finds that a concentration fulfils the criterion defined in Article 2 (3) or, in the cases referred to in Article 2(4), does not fulfil the criteria laid down in Article 81(3) of the Treaty, it shall issue a decision declaring that the concentration is incompatible with the common market.

4. Where the Commission finds that a concentration:

(a) has already been implemented and that concentration has been declared incompatible with the common market, or

(b) has been implemented in contravention of a condition attached to a decision taken under paragraph 2, which has found that, in the absence of the condition, the concentration would fulfil the criterion laid down in Article 2(3) or, in the cases referred to in Article 2(4), would not fulfil the criteria laid down in Article 81 (3) of the Treaty, the Commission may:

– require the undertakings concerned to dissolve the concentration, in particular through the dissolution of the merger or the disposal of all the shares or assets acquired, so as to restore the situation prevailing prior to the implementation of the concentration; in circumstances where restoration of the situation prevailing before the implementation of the concentration is not possible through dissolution of the concentration, the Commission may take any other measure appropriate to achieve such restoration as far as possible,

– order any other appropriate measure to ensure that the undertakings concerned dissolve the concentration or take other restorative measures as required in its decision.

In cases falling within point (a) of the first subparagraph, the measures referred to in that subparagraph may be imposed either in a decision pursuant to paragraph 3 or by separate decision.

5. The Commission may take interim measures appropriate to restore or maintain conditions of effective competition where a concentration:

(a) has been implemented in contravention of Article 7, and a decision as to the compatibility of the concentration with the common market has not yet been taken;

(b) has been implemented in contravention of a condition attached to a decision under Article 6(1)(b) or paragraph 2 of this Article;

(c) has already been implemented and is declared incompatible with the common market.

6. The Commission may revoke the decision it has taken pursuant to paragraphs 1 or 2 where:

(a) the declaration of compatibility is based on incorrect information for which one of the undertakings is responsible or where it has been obtained by deceit; or

(b) the undertakings concerned commit a breach of an obligation attached to the decision.

7. The Commission may take a decision pursuant to paragraphs 1 to 3 without being bound by the time limits referred to in Article 10(3), in cases where:

(a) it finds that a concentration has been implemented

(i)   in contravention of a condition attached to a decision under Article 6(1)(b), or

(ii) in contravention of a condition attached to a decision taken under paragraph 2 and in accordance with Article 10(2), which has found that, in the absence of the condition, the concentration would raise serious doubts as to its compatibility with the common market; or

(b) a decision has been revoked pursuant to paragraph 6.

8. The Commission shall notify its decision to the undertakings concerned and the competent authorities of the Member States without delay.

Article 9   Referral to the competent authorities of the Member States

1. The Commission may, by means of a decision notified without delay to the undertakings concerned and the competent authorities of the other Member States, refer a notified concentration to the competent authorities of the Member State concerned in the following circumstances.

2. Within 15 working days of the date of receipt of the copy of the notification, a Member State, on its own initiative or upon the invitation of the Commission, may inform the Commission, which shall inform the undertakings concerned, that:

(a) a concentration threatens to affect significantly competition in a market within that Member State, which presents all the characteristics of a distinct market; or

(b) a concentration affects competition in a market within that Member State, which presents all the characteristics of a distinct market and which does not constitute a substantial part of the common market.

3. If the Commission considers that, having regard to the market for the products or services in question and the geographical reference market within the meaning of paragraph 7, there is such a distinct market and that such a threat exists, either:

(a) it shall itself deal with the case in accordance with this Regulation; or

(b) it shall refer the whole or part of the case to the competent authorities of the Member State concerned with a view to the application of that State's national competition law.

If, however, the Commission considers that such a distinct market or threat does not exist, it shall adopt a decision to that effect which it shall address to the Member State concerned, and shall itself deal with the case in accordance with this Regulation.

In cases where a Member State informs the Commission pursuant to paragraph 2(b) that a concentration affects competition in a distinct market within its territory that does not form a substantial part of the common market, the Commission shall refer the whole or part of the case relating to the distinct market concerned, if it considers that such a distinct market is affected.

4. A decision to refer or not to refer pursuant to paragraph 3 shall be taken:

(a) as a general rule within the period provided for in Article 10(1), second sub-paragraph, where the Commission, pursuant to Article 6(1) (b), has not initiated proceedings; or

(b) within 65 working days at most of the notification of the concentration concerned where the Commission has initiated proceedings under Article 6(1)(c), without taking the preparatory steps in order to adopt the necessary measures under Article 8(2), (3) or (4) to maintain or restore effective competition on the market concerned.

5. If within the 65 working days referred to in paragraph 4(b) the Commission, despite a reminder from the Member State concerned, has not taken a decision on referral in accordance with paragraph 3 nor has taken the preparatory steps referred to in paragraph 4(b), it shall be deemed to have taken a decision to refer the case to the Member State concerned in accordance with paragraph 3(b).

6. The competent authority of the Member State concerned shall decide upon the case without undue delay.

Within 45 working days after the Commission's referral, the competent authority of the Member State concerned shall inform the undertakings concerned of the result of the preliminary competition assessment and what further action, if any, it proposes to take. The Member State concerned may exceptionally suspend this time limit where necessary information has not been provided to it by the undertakings concerned as provided for by its national competition law.

Where a notification is requested under national law, the period of 45 working days shall begin on the working day following that of the receipt of a complete notification by the competent authority of that Member State.

7. The geographical reference market shall consist of the area in which the undertakings concerned are involved in the supply and demand of products or services, in which the conditions of competition are sufficiently homogeneous and which can be distinguished from neighbouring areas because, in particular, conditions of competition are appreciably different in those areas. This assessment should take account in particular of the nature and characteristics of the products or services concerned, of the existence of entry barriers or of consumer preferences, of appreciable differences of the undertakings' market shares between the area concerned and neighbouring areas or of substantial price differences.

8. In applying the provisions of this Article, the Member State concerned may take only the measures strictly necessary to safeguard or restore effective competition on the market concerned.

9. In accordance with the relevant provisions of the Treaty, any Member State may appeal to the Court of Justice, and in particular request the application of Article 243 of the Treaty, for the purpose of applying its national competition law.

Article 10   Time limits for initiating proceedings and for decisions

1. Without prejudice to Article 6(4), the decisions referred to in Article 6(1) shall be taken within 25 working days at most. That period shall begin on the working day following that of the receipt of a notification or, if the information to be supplied with the notification is incomplete, on the working day following that of the receipt of the complete information.

That period shall be increased to 35 working days where the Commission receives a request from a Member State in accordance with Article 9(2) or where, the undertakings concerned offer commitments pursuant to Article 6(2) with a view to rendering the concentration compatible with the common market.

2. Decisions pursuant to Article 8(1) or (2) concerning notified concentrations shall be taken as soon as it appears that the serious doubts referred to in Article 6(1) (c) have been removed, particularly as a result of modifications made by the undertakings concerned, and at the latest by the time limit laid down in paragraph 3.

3. Without prejudice to Article 8(7), decisions pursuant to Article 8(1) to (3) concerning notified concentrations shall be taken within not more than 90 working days of the date on which the proceedings are initiated. That period shall be increased to 105 working days where the undertakings concerned offer commitments pursuant to Article 8(2), second subparagraph, with a view to rendering the concentration compatible with the common market, unless these commitments have been offered less than 55 working days after the initiation of proceedings.

The periods set by the first subparagraph shall likewise be extended if the notifying parties make a request to that effect not later than 15 working days after the initiation of proceedings pursuant to Article 6(1)(c). The notifying parties may make only one such request. Likewise, at any time following the initiation of proceedings, the periods set by the first subparagraph may be extended by the Commission with the agreement of the notifying parties. The total duration of any extension or extensions effected pursuant to this subparagraph shall not exceed 20 working days.

4. The periods set by paragraphs 1 and 3 shall exceptionally be suspended where, owing to circumstances for which one of the undertakings involved in the concentration is responsible, the Commission has had to request information by decision pursuant to Article 11 or to order an inspection by decision pursuant to Article 13.

The first subparagraph shall also apply to the period referred to in Article 9(4)(b).

5. Where the Court of Justice gives a judgment which annuls the whole or part of a Commission decision which is subject to a time limit set by this Article, the concentration shall be reexamined by the Commission with a view to adopting a decision pursuant to Article 6(1).

The concentration shall be re-examined in the light of current market conditions.

The notifying parties shall submit a new notification or supplement the original notification, without delay, where the original notification becomes incomplete by reason of intervening changes in market conditions or in the information provided. Where there are no such changes, the parties shall certify this fact without delay.

The periods laid down in paragraph 1 shall start on the working day following that of the receipt of complete information in a new notification, a supplemented notification, or a certification within the meaning of the third subparagraph.

The second and third subparagraphs shall also apply in the cases referred to in Article 6(4) and Article 8(7).

6. Where the Commission has not taken a decision in accordance with Article 6(1)(b), (c), 8(1), (2) or (3) within the time limits set in paragraphs 1 and 3 respectively, the concentration shall be deemed to have been declared compatible with the common market, without prejudice to Article 9.

Article 11   Requests for information

1. In order to carry out the duties assigned to it by this Regulation, the Commission may, by simple request or by decision, require the persons referred to in Article 3(1)(b), as well as undertakings and associations of undertakings, to provide all necessary information.

2. When sending a simple request for information to a person, an undertaking or an association of undertakings, the Commission shall state the legal basis and the purpose of the request, specify what information is required and fix the time limit within which the information is to be provided, as well as the penalties provided for in Article 14 for supplying incorrect or misleading information.

3. Where the Commission requires a person, an undertaking or an association of undertakings to supply information by decision, it shall state the legal basis and the purpose of the request, specify what information is required and fix the time limit within which it is to be provided. It shall also indicate the penalties provided for in Article 14 and indicate or impose the penalties provided for in Article 15. It shall further indicate the right to have the decision reviewed by the Court of Justice.

4. The owners of the undertakings or their representatives and, in the case of legal persons, companies or firms, or associations having no legal personality, the persons authorised to represent them by law or by their constitution, shall supply the information requested on behalf of the undertaking concerned. Persons duly authorised to act may supply the information on behalf of their clients. The latter shall remain fully responsible if the information supplied is incomplete, incorrect or misleading.

5. The Commission shall without delay forward a copy of any decision taken pursuant to paragraph 3 to the competent authorities of the Member State in whose territory the residence of the person or the seat of the undertaking or association of undertakings is situated, and to the competent authority of the Member State whose territory is affected. At the specific request of the competent authority of a Member State, the Commission shall also forward to that authority copies of simple requests for information relating to a notified concentration.

6. At the request of the Commission, the governments and competent authorities of the Member States shall provide the Commission with all necessary information to carry out the duties assigned to it by this Regulation.

7. In order to carry out the duties assigned to it by this Regulation, the Commission may interview any natural or legal person who consents to be interviewed for the purpose of collecting information relating to the subject matter of an investigation. At the beginning of the interview, which may be conducted by telephone or other electronic means, the Commission shall state the legal basis and the purpose of the interview.

Where an interview is not conducted on the premises of the Commission or by telephone or other electronic means, the Commission shall inform in advance the competent authority of the Member State in whose territory the interview takes place. If the competent authority of that Member State so requests, officials of that authority may assist the officials and other persons authorised by the Commission to conduct the interview.

Article 12   Inspections by the authorities of the Member States

1. At the request of the Commission, the competent authorities of the Member States shall undertake the inspections which the Commission considers to be necessary under Article 13(1), or which it has ordered by decision pursuant to Article 13(4). The officials of the competent authorities of the Member States who are responsible for conducting these inspections as well as those authorised or appointed by them shall exercise their powers in accordance with their national law.

2. If so requested by the Commission or by the competent authority of the Member State within whose territory the inspection is to be conducted, officials and other accompanying persons authorised by the Commission may assist the officials of the authority concerned.

Article 13   The Commission's powers of inspection

1. In order to carry out the duties assigned to it by this Regulation, the Commission may conduct all necessary inspections of undertakings and associations of undertakings.

2. The officials and other accompanying persons authorised by the Commission to conduct an inspection shall have the power:

    (a) to enter any premises, land and means of transport of undertakings and associations of undertakings;

    (b) to examine the books and other records related to the business, irrespective of the medium on which they are stored;

    (c) to take or obtain in any form copies of or extracts from such books or records;

    (d) to seal any business premises and books or records for the period and to the extent necessary for the inspection;

    (e) to ask any representative or member of staff of the undertaking or association of undertakings for explanations on facts or documents relating to the subject matter and purpose of the inspection and to record the answers.

3. Officials and other accompanying persons authorised by the Commission to conduct an inspection shall exercise their powers upon production of a written authorisation specifying the subject matter and purpose of the inspection and the penalties provided for in Article 14, in the production of the required books or other records related to the business which is incomplete or where answers to questions asked under paragraph 2 of this Article are incorrect or misleading. In good time before the inspection, the Commission shall give notice of the inspection to the competent authority of the Member State in whose territory the inspection is to be conducted.

4. Undertakings and associations of undertakings are required to submit to inspections ordered by decision of the Commission. The decision shall specify the subject matter and purpose of the inspection, appoint the date on which it is to begin and indicate the penalties provided for in Articles 14 and 15 and the right to have the decision reviewed by the Court of Justice. The Commission shall take such decisions after consulting the competent authority of the Member State in whose territory the inspection is to be conducted.

5. Officials of, and those authorised or appointed by, the competent authority of the Member State in whose territory the inspection is to be conducted shall, at the request of that authority or of the Commission, actively assist the officials and other accompanying persons authorised by the Commission. To this end, they shall enjoy the powers specified in paragraph 2.

6. Where the officials and other accompanying persons authorised by the Commission find that an undertaking opposes an inspection, including the sealing of business premises, books or records, ordered pursuant to this Article, the Member State concerned shall afford them the necessary assistance, requesting where appropriate the assistance of the police or of an equivalent enforcement authority, so as to enable them to conduct their inspection.

7. If the assistance provided for in paragraph 6 requires authorisation from a judicial authority according to national rules, such authorisation shall be applied for. Such authorisation may also be applied for as a precautionary measure.

8. Where authorisation as referred to in paragraph 7 is applied for, the national judicial authority shall ensure that the Commission decision is authentic and that the coercive measures envisaged are neither arbitrary nor excessive having regard to the subject matter of the inspection. In its control of proportionality of the coercive measures, the national judicial authority may ask the Commission, directly or through the competent authority of that Member State, for detailed explanations relating to the subject matter of the inspection. However, the national judicial authority may not call into question the necessity for the inspection nor demand that it be provided with the information in the Commission's file. The lawfulness of the Commission's decision shall be subject to review only by the Court of Justice.

Article 14   Fines

1. The Commission may by decision impose on the persons referred to in Article 3(1)b, undertakings or associations of undertakings, fines not exceeding 1% of the aggregate turnover of the undertaking or association of undertakings concerned within the meaning of Article 5 where, intentionally or negligently:

  (a) they supply incorrect or misleading information in a submission, certification, notification or supplement thereto, pursuant to Article 4, Article 10(5) or Article 22(3);

  (b) they supply incorrect or misleading information in response to a request made pursuant to Article 11(2);

  (c) in response to a request made by decision adopted pursuant to Article 11(3), they supply incorrect, incomplete or misleading information or do not supply information within the required time limit;

  (d) they produce the required books or other records related to the business in incomplete form during inspections under Article 13, or refuse to submit to an inspection ordered by decision taken pursuant to Article 13(4);

  (e) in response to a question asked in accordance with Article 13(2)(e),
- they give an incorrect or misleading answer,
- they fail to rectify within a time limit set by the Commission an incorrect, incomplete or misleading answer given by a member of staff, or
- they fail or refuse to provide a complete answer on facts relating to the subject matter and purpose of an inspection ordered by a decision adopted pursuant to Article 13(4);

  (f) seals affixed by officials or other accompanying persons authorised by the Commission in accordance with Article 13(2)(d) have been broken.

2. The Commission may by decision impose fines not exceeding 10% of the aggregate turnover of the undertaking concerned within the meaning of Article 5 on the persons referred to in Article 3(1)b or the undertakings concerned where, either intentionally or negligently, they:

  (a) fail to notify a concentration in accordance with Articles 4 or 22(3) prior to its implementation, unless they are expressly authorised to do so by Article 7(2) or by a decision taken pursuant to Article 7(3);

  (b) implement a concentration in breach of Article 7;

  (c) implement a concentration declared incompatible with the common market by decision pursuant to Article 8(3) or do not comply with any measure ordered by decision pursuant to Article 8(4) or (5);

  (d) fail to comply with a condition or an obligation imposed by decision pursuant to Articles 6(1)(b), Article 7(3) or Article 8(2), second subparagraph.

3. In fixing the amount of the fine, regard shall be had to the nature, gravity and duration of the infringement.

4. Decisions taken pursuant to paragraphs 1, 2 and 3 shall not be of a criminal law nature.

Article 15   Periodic penalty payments

1. The Commission may by decision impose on the persons referred to in Article 3(1)b, undertakings or associations of undertakings, periodic penalty payments not exceeding 5% of the average daily aggregate turnover of the undertaking or association of undertakings concerned within the meaning of Article 5 for each working day of delay, calculated from the date set in the decision, in order to compel them:

  (a) to supply complete and correct information which it has requested by decision taken pursuant to Article 11(3);

  (b) to submit to an inspection which it has ordered by decision taken pursuant to Article 13(4);

  (c) to comply with an obligation imposed by decision pursuant to Article 6(1)(b), Article 7(3) or Article 8(2), second subparagraph; or

  (d) to comply with any measures ordered by decision pursuant to Article 8(4) or (5).

2. Where the persons referred to in Article 3(1) (b), undertakings or associations of undertakings have satisfied the obligation which the periodic penalty payment was intended to enforce, the Commission may fix the definitive amount of the periodic penalty payments at a figure lower than that which would arise under the original decision.

Article 16   Review by the Court of Justice

The Court of Justice shall have unlimited jurisdiction within the meaning of Article 229 of the Treaty to review decisions whereby the Commission has fixed a fine or periodic penalty payments; it may cancel, reduce or increase the fine or periodic penalty payment imposed.

Article 17   Professional secrecy

1. Information acquired as a result of the application of this Regulation shall be used only for the purposes of the relevant request, investigation or hearing.

2. Without prejudice to Article 4(3), Articles 18 and 20, the Commission and the competent authorities of the Member States, their officials and other servants and other persons working under the supervision of these authorities as well as officials and civil servants of other authorities of the Member States shall not disclose information they have acquired through the application of this Regulation of the kind covered by the obligation of professional secrecy.

3. Paragraphs 1 and 2 shall not prevent publication of general information or of surveys which do not contain information relating to particular undertakings or associations of undertakings.

Article 18   Hearing of the parties and of third persons

1. Before taking any decision provided for in Article 6(3), Article 7(3), Article 8(2) to (6), and Articles 14 and 15, the Commission shall give the persons, undertakings and associations of undertakings concerned the opportunity, at every stage of the procedure up to the consultation of the Advisory Committee, of making known their views on the objections against them.

2. By way of derogation from paragraph 1, a decision pursuant to Articles 7(3) and 8(5) may be taken provisionally, without the persons, undertakings or associations of undertakings concerned being given the opportunity to make known their views beforehand, provided that the Commission gives them that opportunity as soon as possible after having taken its decision.

3. The Commission shall base its decision only on objections on which the parties have been able to submit their observations. The rights of the defence shall be fully respected in the proceedings. Access to the file shall be open at least to the parties directly involved, subject to the legitimate interest of undertakings in the protection of their business secrets.

4. In so far as the Commission or the competent authorities of the Member States deem it necessary, they may also hear other natural or legal persons. Natural or legal persons showing a sufficient interest and especially members of the administrative or management bodies of the undertakings concerned or the recognised representatives of their employees shall be entitled, upon application, to be heard.

Article 19   Liaison with the authorities of the Member States

1. The Commission shall transmit to the competent authorities of the Member States copies of notifications within three working days and, as soon as possible, copies of the most important documents lodged with or issued by the Commission pursuant to this Regulation. Such documents shall include commitments offered by the undertakings concerned vis-à-vis the Commission with a view to rendering the concentration compatible with the common market pursuant to Article 6(2) or Article 8(2), second subparagraph.

2. The Commission shall carry out the procedures set out in this Regulation in close and constant liaison with the competent authorities of the Member States, which may express their views upon those procedures. For the purposes of Article 9 it shall obtain information from the competent authority of the Member State as referred to in paragraph 2 of that Article and give it the opportunity to make known its views at every stage of the procedure up to the adoption of a decision pursuant to paragraph 3 of that Article; to that end it shall give it access to the file.

3. An Advisory Committee on concentrations shall be consulted before any decision is taken pursuant to Article 8(1) to (6), Articles 14 or 15 with the exception of provisional decisions taken in accordance with Article 18(2).

4. The Advisory Committee shall consist of representatives of the competent authorities of the Member States. Each Member State shall appoint one or two representatives; if unable to attend, they

may be replaced by other representatives. At least one of the representatives of a Member State shall be competent in matters of restrictive practices and dominant positions.

5. Consultation shall take place at a joint meeting convened at the invitation of and chaired by the Commission. A summary of the case, together with an indication of the most important documents and a preliminary draft of the decision to be taken for each case considered, shall be sent with the invitation. The meeting shall take place not less than 10 working days after the invitation has been sent. The Commission may in exceptional cases shorten that period as appropriate in order to avoid serious harm to one or more of the undertakings concerned by a concentration.

6. The Advisory Committee shall deliver an opinion on the Commission's draft decision, if necessary by taking a vote. The Advisory Committee may deliver an opinion even if some members are absent and unrepresented. The opinion shall be delivered in writing and appended to the draft decision. The Commission shall take the utmost account of the opinion delivered by the Committee. It shall inform the Committee of the manner in which its opinion has been taken into account.

7. The Commission shall communicate the opinion of the Advisory Committee, together with the decision, to the addressees of the decision. It shall make the opinion public together with the decision, having regard to the legitimate interest of undertakings in the protection of their business secrets.

Article 20   Publication of decisions

1. The Commission shall publish the decisions which it takes pursuant to Article 8(1) to (6), Articles 14 and 15 with the exception of provisional decisions taken in accordance with Article 18 (2) together with the opinion of the Advisory Committee in the *Official Journal of the European Union*.

2. The publication shall state the names of the parties and the main content of the decision; it shall have regard to the legitimate interest of undertakings in the protection of their business secrets.

Article 21   Application of the Regulation and jurisdiction

1. This Regulation alone shall apply to concentrations as defined in Article 3, and Council Regulations (EC) No 1/2003, (EEC) No 1017/68, (EEC) No 4056/86 and (EEC) No 3975/87 shall not apply, except in relation to joint ventures that do not have a Community dimension and which have as their object or effect the coordination of the competitive behaviour of undertakings that remain independent.

2. Subject to review by the Court of Justice, the Commission shall have sole jurisdiction to take the decisions provided for in this Regulation.

3. No Member State shall apply its national legislation on competition to any concentration that has a Community dimension.

The first subparagraph shall be without prejudice to any Member State's power to carry out any enquiries necessary for the application of Articles 4(4), 9(2) or after referral, pursuant to Article 9 (3), first subparagraph, indent (b), or Article 9(5), to take the measures strictly necessary for the application of Article 9(8).

4. Notwithstanding paragraphs 2 and 3, Member States may take appropriate measures to protect legitimate interests other than those taken into consideration by this Regulation and compatible with the general principles and other provisions of Community law.

Public security, plurality of the media and prudential rules shall be regarded as legitimate interests within the meaning of the first subparagraph.

Any other public interest must be communicated to the Commission by the Member State concerned and shall be recognised by the Commission after an assessment of its compatibility with the general principles and other provisions of Community law before the measures referred to above may be taken. The Commission shall inform the Member State concerned of its decision within 25 working days of that communication.

Article 22   Referral to the Commission

1. One or more Member States may request the Commission to examine any concentration as defined in Article 3 that does not have a Community dimension within the meaning of Article 1 but affects trade between Member States and threatens to significantly affect competition within the territory of the Member State or States making the request.

Such a request shall be made at most within 15 working days of the date on which the concentration was notified, or if no notification is required, otherwise made known to the Member State concerned.

2. The Commission shall inform the competent authorities of the Member States and the undertakings concerned of any request received pursuant to paragraph 1 without delay.

Any other Member State shall have the right to join the initial request within a period of 15 working days of being informed by the Commission of the initial request.

All national time limits relating to the concentration shall be suspended until, in accordance with the procedure set out in this Article, it has been decided where the concentration shall be examined. As soon as a Member State has informed the Commission and the undertakings concerned that it does not wish to join the request, the suspension of its national time limits shall end.

3. The Commission may, at the latest 10 working days after the expiry of the period set in paragraph 2, decide to examine, the concentration where it considers that it affects trade between Member States and threatens to significantly affect competition within the territory of the Member State or States making the request. If the Commission does not take a decision within this period, it shall be deemed to have adopted a decision to examine the concentration in accordance with the request.

The Commission shall inform all Member States and the undertakings concerned of its decision. It may request the submission of a notification pursuant to Article 4.

The Member State or States having made the request shall no longer apply their national legislation on competition to the concentration.

4. Article 2, Article 4(2) to (3), Articles 5, 6, and 8 to 21 shall apply where the Commission examines a concentration pursuant to paragraph 3. Article 7 shall apply to the extent that the concentration has not been implemented on the date on which the Commission informs the undertakings concerned that a request has been made.

Where a notification pursuant to Article 4 is not required, the period set in Article 10(1) within which proceedings may be initiated shall begin on the working day following that on which the Commission informs the undertakings concerned that it has decided to examine the concentration pursuant to paragraph 3.

5. The Commission may inform one or several Member States that it considers a concentration fulfils the criteria in paragraph 1. In such cases, the Commission may invite that Member State or those Member States to make a request pursuant to paragraph 1.

Article 23   Implementing provisions

1. The Commission shall have the power to lay down in accordance with the procedure referred to in paragraph 2:

    (a) implementing provisions concerning the form, content and other details of notifications and submissions pursuant to Article 4;

    (b) implementing provisions concerning time limits pursuant to Article 4(4), (5) Articles 7, 9, 10 and 22;

    (c) the procedure and time limits for the submission and implementation of commitments pursuant to Article 6(2) and Article 8(2);

    (d) implementing provisions concerning hearings pursuant to Article 18.

2. The Commission shall be assisted by an Advisory Committee, composed of representatives of the Member States.

    (a) Before publishing draft implementing provisions and before adopting such provisions, the Commission shall consult the Advisory Committee.

(b) Consultation shall take place at a meeting convened at the invitation of and chaired by the Commission. A draft of the implementing provisions to be taken shall be sent with the invitation. The meeting shall take place not less than 10 working days after the invitation has been sent.

(c) The Advisory Committee shall deliver an opinion on the draft implementing provisions, if necessary by taking a vote. The Commission shall take the utmost account of the opinion delivered by the Committee.

Article 24   Relations with third countries

1. The Member States shall inform the Commission of any general difficulties encountered by their undertakings with concentrations as defined in Article 3 in a third country.

2. Initially not more than one year after the entry into force of this Regulation and, thereafter periodically, the Commission shall draw up a report examining the treatment accorded to undertakings having their seat or their principal fields of activity in the Community, in the terms referred to in paragraphs 3 and 4, as regards concentrations in third countries. The Commission shall submit those reports to the Council, together with any recommendations.

3. Whenever it appears to the Commission, either on the basis of the reports referred to in paragraph 2 or on the basis of other information, that a third country does not grant undertakings having their seat or their principal fields of activity in the Community, treatment comparable to that granted by the Community to undertakings from that country, the Commission may submit proposals to the Council for an appropriate mandate for negotiation with a view to obtaining comparable treatment for undertakings having their seat or their principal fields of activity in the Community.

4. Measures taken under this Article shall comply with the obligations of the Community or of the Member States, without prejudice to Article 307 of the Treaty, under international agreements, whether bilateral or multilateral.

Article 25   Repeal

1. Without prejudice to Article 26(2), Regulations (EEC) No 4064/89 and (EC) No 1310/97 shall be repealed with effect from 1 May 2004.

2. References to the repealed Regulations shall be construed as references to this Regulation and shall be read in accordance with the correlation table in the Annex.

Article 26   Entry into force and transitional provisions

1. This Regulation shall enter into force on the 20th day following that of its publication in the *Official Journal of the European Union.*

It shall apply from 1 May 2004.

2. Regulation (EEC) No 4064/89 shall continue to apply to any concentration which was the subject of an agreement or announcement or where control was acquired within the meaning of Article 4(1) of that Regulation before the date of application of this Regulation, subject, in particular, to the provisions governing applicability set out in Article 25(2) and (3) of Regulation (EEC) No 4064/89 and Article 2 of Regulation (EEC) No 1310/97.

3. As regards concentrations to which this Regulation applies by virtue of accession, the date of accession shall be substituted for the date of application of this Regulation.

This Regulation shall be binding in its entirety and directly applicable in all Member States. Done at Brussels, 20 January 2004.

For the Council
The President
C McCREEVY

Commission Regulation (EU) No 330/2010 of 20 April 2010 on the application of Article 101(3) of the Treaty on the Functioning of the European Union to categories of vertical agreements and concerted practices

(Text with EEA relevance)

THE EUROPEAN COMMISSION,

Having regard to the Treaty on the Functioning of the European Union,

Having regard to Regulation No 19/65/EEC of the Council of 2 March 1965 on the application of Article 85(3) of the Treaty to certain categories of agreements and concerted practices, and in particular Article 1 thereof,

Having published a draft of this Regulation,

After consulting the Advisory Committee on Restrictive Practices and Dominant Positions,

Whereas:

(1) Regulation No 19/65/EEC empowers the Commission to apply Article 101(3) of the Treaty on the Functioning of the European Union (*) by regulation to certain categories of vertical agreements and corresponding concerted practices falling within Article 10 of the Treaty.

(2) Commission Regulation (EC) No 2790/1999 of 22 December 1999 on the application of Article 81(3) of the Treaty to categories of vertical agreements and concerted practices defines a category of vertical agreements which the Commission regarded as normally satisfying the conditions laid down in Article 101(3) of the Treaty. In view of the overall positive experience with the application of that Regulation, which expires on 31 May 2010, and taking into account further experience acquired since its adoption, it is appropriate to adopt a new block exemption regulation.

(3) The category of agreements which can be regarded as normally satisfying the conditions laid down in Article 101(3) of the Treaty includes vertical agreements for the purchase or sale of goods or services where those agreements are concluded between non-competing undertakings, between certain competitors or by certain associations of retailers of goods. It also includes vertical agreements containing ancillary provisions on the assignment or use of intellectual property rights. The term 'vertical agreements' should include the corresponding concerted practices.

(4) For the application of Article 101(3) of the Treaty by regulation, it is not necessary to define those vertical agreements which are capable of falling within Article 101(1) of the Treaty. In the individual assessment of agreements under Article 101(1) of the Treaty, account has to be taken of several factors, and in particular the market structure on the supply and purchase side.

(5) The benefit of the block exemption established by this Regulation should be limited to vertical agreements for which it can be assumed with sufficient certainty that they satisfy the conditions of Article 101(3) of the Treaty.

(6) Certain types of vertical agreements can improve economic efficiency within a chain of production or distribution by facilitating better coordination between the participating undertakings. In particular, they can lead to a reduction in the transaction and distribution costs of the parties and to an optimisation of their sales and investment levels.

(7) The likelihood that such efficiency-enhancing effects will outweigh any anti-competitive effects due to restrictions contained in vertical agreements depends on the degree of market power of the parties to the agreement and, therefore, on the extent to which those undertakings face competition from other suppliers of goods or services regarded by their customers as interchangeable or substitutable for one another, by reason of the products' characteristics, their prices and their intended use.

(8) It can be presumed that, where the market share held by each of the undertakings party to the agreement on the relevant market does not exceed 30 %, vertical agreements which do not contain certain types of severe restrictions of competition generally lead to an improvement in production or distribution and allow consumers a fair share of the resulting benefits.

(9) Above the market share threshold of 30 %, there can be no presumption that vertical agreements falling within the scope of Article 101(1) of the Treaty will usually give rise to objective advantages of such a character and size as to compensate for the disadvantages which they create for competition. At the same time, there is no presumption that those vertical agreements are either caught by Article 101(1) of the Treaty or that they fail to satisfy the conditions of Article 101(3) of the Treaty.

(10) This Regulation should not exempt vertical agreements containing restrictions which are likely to restrict competition and harm consumers or which are not indispensable to the attainment of the efficiency-enhancing effects. In particular, vertical agreements containing certain types of severe restrictions of competition such as minimum and fixed resale-prices, as well as certain types of territorial protection, should be excluded from the benefit of the block exemption established by this Regulation irrespective of the market share of the undertakings concerned.

(11) In order to ensure access to or to prevent collusion on the relevant market, certain conditions should be attached to the block exemption. To this end, the exemption of non-compete obligations should be limited to obligations which do not exceed a defined duration. For the same reasons, any direct or indirect obligation causing the members of a selective distribution system not to sell the brands of particular competing suppliers should be excluded from the benefit of this Regulation.

(12) The market-share limitation, the non-exemption of certain vertical agreements and the conditions provided for in this Regulation normally ensure that the agreements to which the block exemption applies do not enable the participating undertakings to eliminate competition in respect of a substantial part of the products in question.

(13) The Commission may withdraw the benefit of this Regulation, pursuant to Article 29(1) of Council Regulation (EC) No 1/2003 of 16 December 2002 on the implementation of the rules on competition laid down in Articles 81 and 82 of the Treaty, where it finds in a particular case that an agreement to which the exemption provided for in this Regulation applies nevertheless has effects which are incompatible with Article 101(3) of the Treaty.

(14) The competition authority of a Member State may withdraw the benefit of this Regulation pursuant to Article 29(2) of Regulation (EC) No 1/2003 in respect of the territory of that Member State, or a part thereof where, in a particular case, an agreement to which the exemption provided for in this Regulation applies nevertheless has effects which are incompatible with Article 101(3) of the Treaty in the territory of that Member State, or in a part thereof, and where such territory has all the characteristics of a distinct geographic market.

(15) In determining whether the benefit of this Regulation should be withdrawn pursuant to Article 29 of Regulation (EC) No 1/2003, the anti-competitive effects that may derive from the existence of parallel networks of vertical agreements that have similar effects which significantly restrict access to a relevant market or competition therein are of particular importance. Such cumulative effects may for example arise in the case of selective distribution or non compete obligations.

(16) In order to strengthen supervision of parallel networks of vertical agreements which have similar anti-competitive effects and which cover more than 50 % of a given market, the Commission may by regulation declare this Regulation inapplicable to vertical agreements containing specific restraints relating to the market concerned, thereby restoring the full application of Article 101 of the Treaty to such agreements,

HAS ADOPTED THIS REGULATION:

Article 1   Definitions

1. For the purposes of this Regulation, the following definitions shall apply:
    (a) 'vertical agreement' means an agreement or concerted practice entered into between two or more undertakings each of which operates, for the purposes of the agreement or the concerted practice, at a different level of the production or distribution chain, and relating to the conditions under which the parties may purchase, sell or resell certain goods or services;
    (b) 'vertical restraint' means a restriction of competition in a vertical agreement falling within the scope of Article 101(1) of the Treaty;

   (c) 'competing undertaking' means an actual or potential competitor; 'actual competitor' means an undertaking that is active on the same relevant market; 'potential competitor' means an undertaking that, in the absence of the vertical agreement, would, on realistic grounds and not just as a mere theoretical possibility, in case of a small but permanent increase in relative prices be likely to undertake, within a short period of time, the necessary additional investments or other necessary switching costs to enter the relevant market;

   (d) 'non-compete obligation' means any direct or indirect obligation causing the buyer not to manufacture, purchase, sell or resell goods or services which compete with the contract goods or services, or any direct or indirect obligation on the buyer to purchase from the supplier or from another undertaking designated by the supplier more than 80 % of the buyer's total purchases of the contract goods or services and their substitutes on the relevant market, calculated on the basis of the value or, where such is standard industry practice, the volume of its purchases in the preceding calendar year;

   (e) 'selective distribution system' means a distribution system where the supplier undertakes to sell the contract goods or services, either directly or indirectly, only to distributors selected on the basis of specified criteria and where these distributors undertake not to sell such goods or services to unauthorised distributors within the territory reserved by the supplier to operate that system;

   (f) 'intellectual property rights' includes industrial property rights, know how, copyright and neighbouring rights;

   (g) 'know-how' means a package of non-patented practical information, resulting from experience and testing by the supplier, which is secret, substantial and identified: in this context, 'secret' means that the know-how is not generally known or easily accessible; 'substantial' means that the know-how is significant and useful to the buyer for the use, sale or resale of the contract goods or services; 'identified' means that the know-how is described in a sufficiently comprehensive manner so as to make it possible to verify that it fulfils the criteria of secrecy and substantiality;

   (h) 'buyer' includes an undertaking which, under an agreement falling within Article 101(1) of the Treaty, sells goods or services on behalf of another undertaking;

   (i) 'customer of the buyer' means an undertaking not party to the agreement which purchases the contract goods or services from a buyer which is party to the agreement.

   2. For the purposes of this Regulation, the terms 'undertaking', 'supplier' and 'buyer' shall include their respective connected undertakings.

   'Connected undertakings' means:

   (a) undertakings in which a party to the agreement, directly or indirectly:

      (i) has the power to exercise more than half the voting rights, or

      (ii) has the power to appoint more than half the members of the supervisory board, board of management or bodies legally representing the undertaking, or

      (iii) has the right to manage the undertaking's affairs;

   (b) undertakings which directly or indirectly have, over a party to the agreement, the rights or powers listed in point (a);

   (c) undertakings in which an undertaking referred to in point (b) has, directly or indirectly, the rights or powers listed in point (a);

   (d) undertakings in which a party to the agreement together with one or more of the undertakings referred to in points (a), (b) or (c), or in which two or more of the latter undertakings, jointly have the rights or powers listed in point (a);

   (e) undertakings in which the rights or the powers listed in point (a) are jointly held by:

      (i) parties to the agreement or their respective connected undertakings referred to in points (a) to (d), or

      (ii) one or more of the parties to the agreement or one or more of their connected undertakings referred to in points (a) to (d) and one or more third parties.

Article   Exemption

1. Pursuant to Article 101(3) of the Treaty and subject to the provisions of this Regulation, it is hereby declared that Article 101(1) of the Treaty shall not apply to vertical agreements.

This exemption shall apply to the extent that such agreements contain vertical restraints.

2. The exemption provided for in paragraph 1 shall apply to vertical agreements entered into between an association of undertakings and its members, or between such an association and its suppliers, only if all its members are retailers of goods and if no individual member of the association, together with its connected undertakings, has a total annual turnover exceeding EUR 50 million. Vertical agreements entered into by such associations shall be covered by this Regulation without prejudice to the application of Article 101 of the Treaty to horizontal agreements concluded between the members of the association or decisions adopted by the association.

3. The exemption provided for in paragraph 1 shall apply to vertical agreements containing provisions which relate to the assignment to the buyer or use by the buyer of intellectual property rights, provided that those provisions do not constitute the primary object of such agreements and are directly related to the use, sale or resale of goods or services by the buyer or its customers. The exemption applies on condition that, in relation to the contract goods or services, those provisions do not contain restrictions of competition having the same object as vertical restraints which are not exempted under this Regulation.

4. The exemption provided for in paragraph 1 shall not apply to vertical agreements entered into between competing undertakings. However, it shall apply where competing undertakings enter into a non-reciprocal vertical agreement and:

    (a) the supplier is a manufacturer and a distributor of goods, while the buyer is a distributor and not a competing undertaking at the manufacturing level; or

    (b) the supplier is a provider of services at several levels of trade, while the buyer provides its goods or services at the retail level and is not a competing undertaking at the level of trade where it purchases the contract services.

5. This Regulation shall not apply to vertical agreements the subject matter of which falls within the scope of any other block exemption regulation, unless otherwise provided for in such a regulation.

Article 3   Market share threshold

1. The exemption provided for in Article 2 shall apply on condition that the market share held by the supplier does not exceed 30 % of the relevant market on which it sells the contract goods or services and the market share held by the buyer does not exceed 30 % of the relevant market on which it purchases the contract goods or services.

2. For the purposes of paragraph 1, where in a multi party agreement an undertaking buys the contract goods or services from one undertaking party to the agreement and sells the contract goods or services to another undertaking party to the agreement, the market share of the first undertaking must respect the market share threshold provided for in that paragraph both as a buyer and a supplier in order for the exemption provided for in Article 2 to apply.

Article 4   Restrictions that remove the benefit of the block exemption—
hardcore restrictions

The exemption provided for in Article 2 shall not apply to vertical agreements which, directly or indirectly, in isolation or in combination with other factors under the control of the parties, have as their object:

    (a) the restriction of the buyer's ability to determine its sale price, without prejudice to the possibility of the supplier to impose a maximum sale price or recommend a sale price, provided that they do not amount to a fixed or minimum sale price as a result of pressure from, or incentives offered by, any of the parties;

    (b) the restriction of the territory into which, or of the customers to whom, a buyer party to the agreement, without prejudice to a restriction on its place of establishment, may sell the contract goods or services, except:

        (i) the restriction of active sales into the exclusive territory or to an exclusive customer group reserved to the supplier or allocated by the supplier to another buyer, where such a restriction does not limit sales by the customers of the buyer,

    (ii) the restriction of sales to end users by a buyer operating at the wholesale level of trade,

    (iii) the restriction of sales by the members of a selective distribution system to unauthorised distributors within the territory reserved by the supplier to operate that system, and

    (iv) the restriction of the buyer's ability to sell components, supplied for the purposes of incorporation, to customers who would use them to manufacture the same type of goods as those produced by the supplier;

  (c) the restriction of active or passive sales to end users by members of a selective distribution system operating at the retail level of trade, without prejudice to the possibility of prohibiting a member of the system from operating out of an unauthorised place of establishment;

  (d) the restriction of cross-supplies between distributors within a selective distribution system, including between distributors operating at different level of trade;

  (e) the restriction, agreed between a supplier of components and a buyer who incorporates those components, of the supplier's ability to sell the components as spare parts to end-users or to repairers or other service providers not entrusted by the buyer with the repair or servicing of its goods.

Article 5   Excluded restrictions

1. The exemption provided for in Article 2 shall not apply to the following obligations contained in vertical agreements:

  (a) any direct or indirect non-compete obligation, the duration of which is indefinite or exceeds five years;

  (b) any direct or indirect obligation causing the buyer, after termination of the agreement, not to manufacture, purchase, sell or resell goods or services;

  (c) any direct or indirect obligation causing the members of a selective distribution system not to sell the brands of particular competing suppliers.

For the purposes of point (a) of the first subparagraph, a non- compete obligation which is tacitly renewable beyond a period of five years shall be deemed to have been concluded for an indefinite duration.

2. By way of derogation from paragraph 1(a), the time limitation of five years shall not apply where the contract goods or services are sold by the buyer from premises and land owned by the supplier or leased by the supplier from third parties not connected with the buyer, provided that the duration of the non-compete obligation does not exceed the period of occupancy of the premises and land by the buyer.

3. By way of derogation from paragraph 1(b), the exemption provided for in Article 2 shall apply to any direct or indirect obligation causing the buyer, after termination of the agreement, not to manufacture, purchase, sell or resell goods or services where the following conditions are fulfilled:

  (a) the obligation relates to goods or services which compete with the contract goods or services;

  (b) the obligation is limited to the premises and land from which the buyer has operated during the contract period;

  (c) the obligation is indispensable to protect know-how transferred by the supplier to the buyer;

  (d) the duration of the obligation is limited to a period of one year after termination of the agreement.

Paragraph 1(b) is without prejudice to the possibility of imposing a restriction which is unlimited in time on the use and disclosure of know-how which has not entered the public domain.

Article 6   Non-application of this Regulation

Pursuant to Article 1a of Regulation No 19/65/EEC, the Commission may by regulation declare that, where parallel networks of similar vertical restraints cover more than 50 % of a relevant market, this Regulation shall not apply to vertical agreements containing specific restraints relating to that market.

Article 7 Application of the market share threshold

For the purposes of applying the market share thresholds provided for in Article 3 the following rules shall apply:

(a) the market share of the supplier shall be calculated on the basis of market sales value data and the market share of the buyer shall be calculated on the basis of market purchase value data. If market sales value or market purchase value data are not available, estimates based on other reliable market information, including market sales and purchase volumes, may be used to establish the market share of the undertaking concerned;

(b) the market shares shall be calculated on the basis of data relating to the preceding calendar year;

(c) the market share of the supplier shall include any goods or services supplied to vertically integrated distributors for the purposes of sale;

(d) if a market share is initially not more than 30 % but subsequently rises above that level without exceeding 35 %, the exemption provided for in Article 2 shall continue to apply for a period of two consecutive calendar years following the year in which the 30 % market share threshold was first exceeded;

(e) if a market share is initially not more than 30 % but subsequently rises above 35 %, the exemption provided for in Article 2 shall continue to apply for one calendar year following the year in which the level of 35 % was first exceeded;

(f) the benefit of points (d) and (e) may not be combined so as to exceed a period of two calendar years;

(g) the market share held by the undertakings referred to in point (e) of the second subparagraph of Article 1(2) shall be apportioned equally to each undertaking having the rights or the powers listed in point (a) of the second subparagraph of Article 1(2).

Article 8 Application of the turnover threshold

1. For the purpose of calculating total annual turnover within the meaning of Article 2(2), the turnover achieved during the previous financial year by the relevant party to the vertical agreement and the turnover achieved by its connected undertakings in respect of all goods and services, excluding all taxes and other duties, shall be added together. For this purpose, no account shall be taken of dealings between the party to the vertical agreement and its connected undertakings or between its connected undertakings.

2. The exemption provided for in Article 2 shall remain applicable where, for any period of two consecutive financial years, the total annual turnover threshold is exceeded by no more than 10 %.EN L 102/6 Official Journal of the European Union 23.4.2

Article 9 Transitional period

The prohibition laid down in Article 101(1) of the Treaty shall not apply during the period from 1 June 2010 to 31 May 2011 in respect of agreements already in force on 31 May 2010 which do not satisfy the conditions for exemption provided for in this Regulation but which, on 31 May 2010, satisfied the conditions for exemption provided for in Regulation (EC) No 2790/1999.

Article 10 Period of validity

This Regulation shall enter into force on 1 June 2010.

It shall expire on 31 May 2022.

This Regulation shall be binding in its entirety and directly applicable in all Member States.

Done at Brussels, 20 April 2010.

For the Commission
The President
José Manuel BARROSO

Commission Regulation (EC) No 802/2004 of 7 April 2004 implementing Council Regulation (EC) No 139/2004 on the control of concentrations between undertakings

(Text with EEA relevance)

THE COMMISSION OF THE EUROPEAN COMMUNITIES,

Having regard to the Treaty establishing the European Community,

Having regard to the Agreement on the European Economic Area,

Having regard to Council Regulation (EC) No 139/2004 of 20 January 2004 on the control of concentrations between undertakings (EC Merger Regulation), and in particular Article 23(1) thereof,

Having regard to Council Regulation (EEC) No 4064/89 of 21 December 1989 on the control of concentrations between undertakings, as last amended by Regulation (EC) No 1310/97, and in particular Article 23 thereof,

Having consulted the Advisory Committee,

Whereas:

(1) Council Regulation (EEC) No 4064/89 of 21 December 1989 on the control of concentrations between undertakings has been recast, with substantial amendments to various provisions of that Regulation.

(2) Commission Regulation (EC) No 447/98 of 1 March 1998 on the notifications, time-limits and hearings provided for in Council Regulation (EEC) No 4064/89 must be modified in order to take account of those amendments. For the sake of clarity it should therefore be repealed and replaced by a new regulation.

(3) The Commission has adopted measures concerning the terms of reference of hearing officers in certain competition proceedings.

(4) Regulation (EC) No 139/2004 is based on the principle of compulsory notification of concentrations before they are put into effect. On the one hand, a notification has important legal consequences which are favourable to the parties to the proposed concentration, while, on the other hand, failure to comply with the obligation to notify renders the parties liable to fines and may also entail civil law disadvantages for them. It is therefore necessary in the interests of legal certainty to define precisely the subject matter and content of the information to be provided in the notification.

(5) It is for the notifying parties to make a full and honest disclosure to the Commission of the facts and circumstances which are relevant for taking a decision on the notified concentration.

(6) Regulation (EC) No 139/2004 also allows the undertakings concerned to request, in a reasoned submission, prior to notification, that a concentration fulfilling the requirements of that Regulation be referred to the Commission by one or more Member States, or referred by the Commission to one or more Member States, as the case may be. It is important to provide the Commission and the competent authorities of the Member States concerned with sufficient information, in order to enable them to assess, within a short period of time, whether or not a referral ought to be made. To that end, the reasoned submission requesting the referral should contain certain specific information.

(7) In order to simplify and expedite examination of notifications and of reasoned submissions, it is desirable to prescribe that forms be used.

(8) Since notification sets in motion legal time-limits pursuant to Regulation (EC) No 139/2004, the conditions governing such time-limits and the time when they become effective should also be determined.

(9) Rules must be laid down in the interests of legal certainty for calculating the time-limits provided for in Regulation (EC) No 139/2004. In particular, the beginning and end of time periods and the circumstances suspending the running of such periods must be determined, with due

regard to the requirements resulting from the exceptionally tight legal timeframe available for the proceedings.

(10) The provisions relating to the Commission's procedure must be framed in such a way as to safeguard fully the right to be heard and the rights of defence. For these purposes, the Commission should distinguish between the parties who notify the concentration, other parties involved in the proposed concentration, third parties and parties regarding whom the Commission intends to take a decision imposing a fine or periodic penalty payments.

(11) The Commission should give the notifying parties and other parties involved in the proposed concentration, if they so request, an opportunity before notification to discuss the intended concentration informally and in strict confidence. In addition, the Commission should, after notification, maintain close contact with those parties, to the extent necessary to discuss with them any practical or legal problems which it discovers on a first examination of the case, with a view, if possible, to resolving such problems by mutual agreement.

(12) In accordance with the principle of respect for the rights of defence, the notifying parties must be given the opportunity to submit their comments on all the objections which the Commission proposes to take into account in its decisions. The other parties involved in the proposed concentration should also be informed of the Commission's objections and should be granted the opportunity to express their views.

(13) Third parties demonstrating a sufficient interest must also be given the opportunity of expressing their views, if they make a written application to that effect.

(14) The various persons entitled to submit comments should do so in writing, both in their own interests and in the interests of sound administration, without prejudice to their right to request a formal oral hearing, where appropriate, to supplement the written procedure. In urgent cases, however, the Commission must be enabled to proceed immediately to formal oral hearings of the notifying parties, of other parties involved or of third parties.

(15) It is necessary to define the rights of persons who are to be heard, to what extent they should be granted access to the Commission's file and on what conditions they may be represented or assisted.

(16) When granting access to the file, the Commission should ensure the protection of business secrets and other confidential information. The Commission should be able to ask undertakings that have submitted documents or statements to identify confidential information.

(17) In order to enable the Commission to carry out a proper assessment of commitments offered by the notifying parties with a view to rendering the concentration compatible with the common market, and to ensure due consultation with other parties involved, with third parties and with the authorities of the Member States as provided for in Regulation (EC) No 139/2004, in particular Article 18(1), 18(4), Article 19(1), 19(2), 19(3) and 19(5) thereof, the procedure and time-limits for submitting the commitments referred to in Article 6(2) and Article 8(2) of that Regulation should be laid down.

(18) It is also necessary to define the rules applicable to certain time limits set by the Commission.

(19) The Advisory Committee on Concentrations must deliver its opinion on the basis of a preliminary draft decision. It must therefore be consulted on a case after the inquiry in to that case has been completed. Such consultation does not, however, prevent the Commission from reopening an inquiry if need be.

HAS ADOPTED THIS REGULATION:

Chapter I Scope

Article 1   Scope
This Regulation shall apply to the control of concentrations conducted pursuant to Regulation (EC) No 139/2004.

Chapter II Notifications and other submissions

Article 2   Persons entitled to submit notifications

1. Notifications shall be submitted by the persons or undertakings referred to in Article 4(2) of Regulation (EC) No 139/2004.

2. Where notifications are signed by representatives of persons or of undertakings, such representatives shall produce written proof that they are authorised to act.

3. Joint notifications shall be submitted by a joint representative who is authorised to transmit and to receive documents on behalf of all notifying parties.

Article 3   Submission of notifications

1. Notifications shall be submitted in the manner prescribed by Form CO as set out in Annex I. Under the conditions set out in Annex II, notifications may be submitted in Short Form as defined therein. Joint notifications shall be submitted on a single form.

2. One original and 35 copies of the Form CO and the supporting documents shall be submitted to the Commission. The notification shall be delivered to the address referred to in Article 23 (1) and in the format specified by the Commission.

3. The supporting documents shall be either originals or copies of the originals; in the latter case the notifying parties shall confirm that they are true and complete.

4. Notifications shall be in one of the official languages of the Community. For the notifying parties, this language shall also be the language of the proceeding, as well as that of any subsequent proceedings relating to the same concentration. Supporting documents shall be submitted in their original language. Where the original language is not one of the official languages of the Community, a translation into the language of the proceeding shall be attached.

5. Where notifications are made pursuant to Article 57 of the Agreement on the European Economic Area, they may also be submitted in one of the official languages of the EFTA States or the working language of the EFTA Surveillance Authority. If the language chosen for the notifications is not an official language of the Community, the notifying parties shall simultaneously supplement all documentation with a translation into an official language of the Community. The language which is chosen for the translation shall determine the language used by the Commission as the language of the proceeding for the notifying parties.

Article 4   Information and documents to be provided

1. Notifications shall contain the information, including documents, requested in the applicable forms set out in the Annexes. The information shall be correct and complete.

2. The Commission may dispense with the obligation to provide any particular information in the notification, including documents, or with any other requirement specified in Annexes I and II where the Commission considers that compliance with those obligations or requirements is not necessary for the examination of the case.

3. The Commission shall without delay acknowledge in writing to the notifying parties or their representatives receipt of the notification and of any reply to a letter sent by the Commission pursuant to Article 5(2) and 5(3).

Article 5   Effective date of notification

1. Subject to paragraphs 2, 3 and 4, notifications shall become effective on the date on which they are received by the Commission.

2. Where the information, including documents, contained in the notification is incomplete in any material respect, the Commission shall inform the notifying parties or their representatives in writing without delay. In such cases, the notification shall become effective on the date on which the complete information is received by the Commission.

3. Material changes in the facts contained in the notification coming to light subsequent to the notification which the notifying parties know or ought to know, or any new information coming to light subsequent to the notification which the parties know or ought to know and which would

have had to be notified if known at the time of notification, shall be communicated to the Commission without delay. In such cases, when these material changes or new information could have a significant effect on the appraisal of the concentration, the notification may be considered by the Commission as becoming effective on the date on which the relevant information is received by the Commission; the Commission shall inform the notifying parties or their representatives of this in writing and without delay.

4. Incorrect or misleading information shall be considered to be incomplete information.

5. When the Commission publishes the fact of the notification pursuant to Article 4(3) of Regulation (EC) No 139/2004, it shall specify the date upon which the notification has been received. Where, further to the application of paragraphs 2, 3 and 4 of this Article, the effective date of notification is later than the date specified in that publication, the Commission shall issue a further publication in which it shall state the later date.

Article 6   Specific provisions relating to reasoned submissions, supplements and certifications

1. Reasoned submissions within the meaning of Article 4(4) and 4(5) of Regulation (EC) No 139/2004 shall contain the information, including documents, requested in accordance with Annex III to this Regulation.

2. Article 2, Article 3(1), third sentence, 3(2) to (5), Article 4, Article 5(1), 5(2) first sentence, 5(3), 5(4), Article 21 and Article 23 of this Regulation shall apply *mutatis mutandis* to reasoned submissions within the meaning of Article 4(4) and 4(5) of Regulation (EC) No 139/2004.

Article 2, Article 3(1), third sentence, 3(2) to (5), Article 4, Article 5(1) to (4), Article 21 and Article 23 of this Regulation shall apply *mutatis mutandis* to supplements to notifications and certifications within the meaning of Article 10(5) of Regulation (EC) No 139/2004.

Chapter III Time-limits

Article 7   Beginning of time periods

Time periods shall begin on the working day, as defined in Article 24 of this Regulation, following the event to which the relevant provision of Regulation (EC) No 139/2004 refers.

Article 8   Expiry of time periods

A time period calculated in working days shall expire at the end of its last working day. A time period set by the Commission in terms of a calendar date shall expire at the end of that day.

Article 9   Suspension of time limit

1. The time limits referred to in Articles 9(4), Article 10(1) and 10(3) of Regulation (EC) No 139/2004 shall be suspended where the Commission has to take a decision pursuant to Article 11 (3) or Article 13(4) of that Regulation, on any of the following grounds:

(a) information which the Commission has requested pursuant to Article 11(2) of Regulation (EC) No 139/2004 from one of the notifying parties or another involved party, as defined in Article 11 of this Regulation, is not provided or not provided in full within the time limit fixed by the Commission;

(b) information which the Commission has requested pursuant to Article 11(2) of Regulation (EC) No 139/2004 from a third party, as defined in Article 11 of this Regulation, is not provided or not provided in full within the time limit fixed by the Commission owing to circumstances for which one of the notifying parties or another involved party, as defined in Article 11 of this Regulation, is responsible;

(c) one of the notifying parties or another involved party, as defined in Article 11 of this Regulation, has refused to submit to an inspection deemed necessary by the Commission on the basis of Article 13(1) of Regulation (EC) No 139/2004 or to cooperate in the carrying out of such an inspection in accordance with Article 13(2) of that Regulation;

(d) the notifying parties have failed to inform the Commission of material changes in the facts contained in the notification, or of any new information of the kind referred to in Article 5(3) of this Regulation.

2. The time limits referred to in Articles 9(4), Article 10(1) and 10(3) of Regulation (EC) No 139/2004 shall be suspended where the Commission has to take a decision pursuant to Article 11 (3) of that Regulation, without proceeding first by way of simple request for information, owing to circumstances for which one of the undertakings involved in the concentration is responsible.

3. The time limits referred to in Articles 9(4), Article 10(1) and (3) of Regulation (EC) No 139/2004 shall be suspended:

(a) in the cases referred to in points (a) and (b) of paragraph 1, for the period between the expiry of the time limit set in the simple request for information, and the receipt of the complete and correct information required by decision;

(b) in the cases referred to in point (c) of paragraph 1, for the period between the unsuccessful attempt to carry out the inspection and the completion of the inspection ordered by decision;

(c) in the cases referred to in point (d) of paragraph 1, for the period between the occurrence of the change in the facts referred to therein and the receipt of the complete and correct information;

(d) in the cases referred to in paragraph 2 for the period between the expiry of the time limit set in the decision and the receipt of the complete and correct information required by decision.

4. The suspension of the time limit shall begin on the working day following the date on which the event causing the suspension occurred. It shall expire with the end of the day on which the reason for suspension is removed. Where such a day is not a working day, the suspension of the time-limit shall expire with the end of the following working day.

Article 10   Compliance with the time-limits

1. The time limits referred to in Article 4(4), fourth subparagraph, Article 9(4), Article 10(1) and (3), and Article 22(3) of Regulation (EC) No 139/2004 shall be met where the Commission has taken the relevant decision before the end of the period.

2. The time limits referred to in Article 4(4), second subparagraph, Article 4(5), third subparagraph, Article 9(2), Article 22(1), second subparagraph, and 22(2), second subparagraph, of Regulation (EC) No 139/2004 shall be met by a Member State concerned where that Member State, before the end of the period, informs the Commission in writing or makes or joins the request in writing, as the case may be.

3. The time limit referred to in Article 9(6) of Regulation (EC) No 139/2004 shall be met where the competent authority of a Member State concerned informs the undertakings concerned in the manner set out in that provision before the end of the period.

Chapter IV Exercise of the right to be heard; hearings

Article 11   Parties to be heard

For the purposes of the rights to be heard pursuant to Article 18 of Regulation (EC) No 139/ 2004, the following parties are distinguished:

(a) notifying parties, that is, persons or undertakings submitting a notification pursuant to Article 4(2) of Regulation (EC) No 139/2004;

(b) other involved parties, that is, parties to the proposed concentration other than the notifying parties, such as the seller and the undertaking which is the target of the concentration;

(c) third persons, that is natural or legal persons, including customers, suppliers and competitors, provided they demonstrate a sufficient interest within the meaning of

Article 18(4), second sentence, of Regulation (EC) No 139/2004, which is the case in particular

- for members of the administrative or management bodies of the undertakings concerned or the recognised representatives of their employees;
- for consumer associations, where the proposed concentration concerns products or services used by final consumers;

(d) parties regarding whom the Commission intends to take a decision pursuant to Article 14 or Article 15 of Regulation (EC) No 139/2004.

Article 12   Decisions on the suspension of concentrations

1. Where the Commission intends to take a decision pursuant to Article 7(3) of Regulation (EC) No 139/2004 which adversely affects one or more of the parties, it shall, pursuant to Article 18 (1) of that Regulation, inform the notifying parties and other involved parties in writing of its objections and shall set a time limit within which they may make known their views in writing.

2. Where the Commission, pursuant to Article 18(2) of Regulation (EC) No 139/2004, has taken a decision referred to in paragraph 1 of this Article provisionally without having given the notifying parties and other involved parties the opportunity to make known their views, it shall without delay send them the text of the provisional decision and shall set a time limit within which they may make known their views in writing.

Once the notifying parties and other involved parties have made known their views, the Commission shall take a final decision annulling, amending or confirming the provisional decision. Where they have not made known their views in writing within the time limit set, the Commission's provisional decision shall become final with the expiry of that period.

Article 13   Decisions on the substance of the case

1. Where the Commission intends to take a decision pursuant to Article 6(3) or Article 8(2) to (6) of Regulation (EC) No 139/2004, it shall, before consulting the Advisory Committee on Concentrations, hear the parties pursuant to Article 18(1) and (3) of that Regulation.

Article 12(2) of this Regulation shall apply *mutatis mutandis* where, in application of Article 18(2) of Regulation (EC) No 139/2004, the Commission has taken a decision pursuant to Article 8(5) of that Regulation provisionally.

2. The Commission shall address its objections in writing to the notifying parties.

The Commission shall, when giving notice of objections, set a time limit within which the notifying parties may inform the Commission of their comments in writing.

The Commission shall inform other involved parties in writing of these objections.

The Commission shall also set a time limit within which those other involved parties may inform the Commission of their comments in writing.

The Commission shall not be obliged to take into account comments received after the expiry of a time limit which it has set.

3. The parties to whom the Commission's objections have been addressed or who have been informed of those objections shall, within the time limit set, submit in writing their comments on the objections. In their written comments, they may set out all facts and matters known to them which are relevant to their defence, and shall attach any relevant documents as proof of the facts set out. They may also propose that the Commission hear persons who may corroborate those facts. They shall submit one original and 10 copies of their comments to the Commission to the address of the Commission's Directorate General for Competition. An electronic copy shall also be submitted at the same address and in the format specified by the Commission. The Commission shall forward copies of such written comments without delay to the competent authorities of the Member States.

4. Where the Commission intends to take a decision pursuant to Article 14 or Article 15 of Regulation (EC) No 139/2004, it shall, before consulting the Advisory Committee on Concentrations,

hear pursuant to Article 18(1) and (3) of that Regulation the parties regarding whom the Commission intends to take such a decision.

The procedure provided for in paragraph 2, first and second subparagraphs, and paragraph 3 shall apply, *mutatis mutandis.*

Article 14   Oral hearings

1. Where the Commission intends to take a decision pursuant to Article 6(3) or Article 8(2) to (6) of Regulation (EC) No 139/2004, it shall afford the notifying parties who have so requested in their written comments the opportunity to develop their arguments in a formal oral hearing. It may also, at other stages in the proceedings, afford the notifying parties the opportunity of expressing their views orally.

2. Where the Commission intends to take a decision pursuant to Article 6(3) or Article 8(2) to (6) of Regulation (EC) No 139/2004, it shall also afford other involved parties who have so requested in their written comments the opportunity to develop their arguments in a formal oral hearing. It may also, at other stages in the proceedings, afford other involved parties the opportunity of expressing their views orally.

3. Where the Commission intends to take a decision pursuant to Article 14 or Article 15 of Regulation (EC) No 139/2004, it shall afford parties on whom it proposes to impose a fine or periodic penalty payment the opportunity to develop their arguments in a formal oral hearing, if so requested in their written comments. It may also, at other stages in the proceedings, afford such parties the opportunity of expressing their views orally.

Article 15   Conduct of formal oral hearings

1. Formal oral hearings shall be conducted by the Hearing Officer in full independence.

2. The Commission shall invite the persons to be heard to attend the formal oral hearing on such date as it shall determine.

3. The Commission shall invite the competent authorities of the Member States to take part in any formal oral hearing.

4. Persons invited to attend shall either appear in person or be represented by legal representatives or by representatives authorised by their constitution as appropriate. Undertakings and associations of undertakings may also be represented by a duly authorised agent appointed from among their permanent staff.

5. Persons heard by the Commission may be assisted by their lawyers or other qualified and duly authorised persons admitted by the Hearing Officer.

6. Formal oral hearings shall not be public. Each person may be heard separately or in the presence of other persons invited to attend, having regard to the legitimate interest of the undertakings in the protection of their business secrets and other confidential information.

7. The Hearing Officer may allow all parties within the meaning of Article 11, the Commission services and the competent authorities of the Member States to ask questions during the formal oral hearing.

The Hearing Officer may hold a preparatory meeting with the parties and the Commission services, so as to facilitate the efficient organisation of the formal oral hearing.

8. The statements made by each person heard shall be recorded. Upon request, the recording of the formal oral hearing shall be made available to the persons who attended that hearing. Regard shall be had to the legitimate interest of the undertakings in the protection of their business secrets and other confidential information.

Article 16   Hearing of third persons

1. If third persons apply in writing to be heard pursuant to Article 18(4), second sentence, of Regulation (EC) No 139/2004, the Commission shall inform them in writing of the nature and subject matter of the procedure and shall set a time limit within which they may make known their views.

2. The third persons referred to in paragraph 1 shall make known their views in writing within the time limit set. The Commission may, where appropriate, afford such third parties who have so requested in their written comments the opportunity to participate in a formal hearing. It may also in other cases afford such third parties the opportunity of expressing their views orally.

3. The Commission may likewise invite any other natural or legal person to express its views, in writing as well as orally, including at a formal oral hearing.

Chapter V Access to the file and treatment of confidential information

Article 17   Access to the file and use of documents

1. If so requested, the Commission shall grant access to the file to the parties to whom it has addressed a statement of objections, for the purpose of enabling them to exercise their rights of defence. Access shall be granted after the notification of the statement of objections.

2. The Commission shall, upon request, also give the other involved parties who have been informed of the objections access to the file in so far as this is necessary for the purposes of preparing their comments.

3. The right of access to the file shall not extend to confidential information, or to internal documents of the Commission or of the competent authorities of the Member States. The right of access to the file shall equally not extend to correspondence between the Commission and the competent authorities of the Member States or between the latter.

4. Documents obtained through access to the file pursuant to this Article may only be used for the purposes of the relevant proceeding pursuant to Regulation (EC) No 139/2004.

Article 18 Confidential information

1. Information, including documents, shall not be communicated or made accessible by the Commission in so far as it contains business secrets or other confidential information the disclosure of which is not considered necessary by the Commission for the purpose of the procedure.

2. Any person which makes known its views or comments pursuant to Articles 12, Article 13 and Article 16 of this Regulation, or supplies information pursuant to Article 11 of Regulation (EC) No 139/2004, or subsequently submits further information to the Commission in the course of the same procedure, shall clearly identify any material which it considers to be confidential, giving reasons, and provide a separate nonconfidential version by the date set by the Commission.

3. Without prejudice to paragraph 2, the Commission may require persons referred to in Article 3 of Regulation (EC) No 139/2004, undertakings and associations of undertakings in all cases where they produce or have produced documents or statements pursuant to Regulation (EC) No 139/2004 to identify the documents or parts of documents which they consider to contain business secrets or other confidential information belonging to them and to identify the undertakings with regard to which such documents are to be considered confidential.

The Commission may also require persons referred to in Article 3 of Regulation (EC) No 139/2004, undertakings or associations of undertakings to identify any part of a statement of objections, case summary or a decision adopted by the Commission which in their view contains business secrets.

Where business secrets or other confidential information are identified, the persons, undertakings and associations of undertakings shall give reasons and provide a separate non-confidential version by the date set by the Commission.

4. If persons, undertakings or associations of undertakings fail to comply with paragraphs 2 or 3, the Commission may assume that the documents or statements concerned do not contain confidential information.

Chapter VI Commitments offered by the undertakings concerned

Article 19   Time limits for submission of commitments

1. Commitments offered by the undertakings concerned pursuant to Article 6(2) of Regulation (EC) No 139/2004 shall be submitted to the Commission within not more than 20 working days from the date of receipt of the notification.

2. Commitments offered by the undertakings concerned pursuant to Article 8(2) of Regulation (EC) No 139/2004 shall be submitted to the Commission within not more than 65 working days from the date on which proceedings were initiated.

Where pursuant to Article 10(3), second subparagraph, of Regulation (EC) No 139/2004 the period for the adoption of a decision pursuant to Article 8(1), (2) and (3) is extended, the period of 65 working days for the submission of commitments shall automatically be extended by the same number of working days.

In exceptional circumstances, the Commission may accept commitments offered after the expiry of the time limit for their submission within the meaning of this paragraph provided that the procedure provided for in Article 19(5) of Regulation (EC) No 139/2004 is complied with.

3. Articles 7, 8 and 9 shall apply *mutatis mutandis*.

Article 20   Procedure for the submission of commitments

1. One original and 10 copies of commitments offered by the undertakings concerned pursuant to Article 6(2) or Article 8(2) of Regulation (EC) No 139/2004 shall be submitted to the Commission at the address of the Commission's Directorate General for Competition. An electronic copy shall also be submitted at the same address and in the format specified by the Commission. The Commission shall forward copies of such commitments without delay to the competent authorities of the Member States.

1a. In addition to the requirements set out in paragraph 1, the undertakings concerned shall, at the same time as offering commitments pursuant to Article 6(2) or Article 8(2) of Regulation (EC) No 139/2004, submit one original and 10 copies of the information and documents prescribed by the Form RM relating to remedies (Form RM) as set out in Annex IV to this Regulation. The information submitted shall be correct and complete.

2. When offering commitments pursuant to Articles 6(2) or Article 8(2) of Regulation (EC) No 139/2004, the undertakings concerned shall at the same time clearly identify any information which they consider to be confidential, giving reasons, and shall provide a separate non-confidential version.

Article 20a Trustees

1. The commitments offered by the undertakings concerned pursuant to Article 6(2) or Article 8(2) of Regulation (EC) No 139/2004 may include, at the own expense of the undertakings concerned, the appointment of an independent trustee (or trustees) assisting the Commission in overseeing the parties' compliance with the commitments or having a mandate to implement the commitments. The trustee may be appointed by the parties, after the Commission has approved its identity, or by the Commission. The trustee shall carry out its tasks under the supervision of the Commission.

2. The Commission may attach such trustee-related provisions of the commitments as conditions and obligations pursuant to Article 6(2) or Article 8(2) of Regulation (EC) No 139/2004.

Chapter VII Miscellaneous provisions

Article 21   Transmission of documents

1. Transmission of documents and invitations from the Commission to the addressees maybe effected in any of the following ways:

(a) delivery by hand against receipt;

(b) registered letter with acknowledgement of receipt;

(c) fax with a request for acknowledgement of receipt;

(d) telex;

(e) electronic mail with a request for acknowledgement of receipt.

2. Unless otherwise provided in this Regulation, paragraph 1 also applies to the transmission of documents from the notifying parties, from other involved parties or from third parties to the Commission.

3. Where a document is sent by telex, by fax or by electronic mail, it shall be presumed that it has been received by the addressee on the day on which it was sent.

Article 22   Setting of time limits

In setting the time limits provided for pursuant to Article 12(1) and (2), Article 13(2) and Article 16(1), the Commission shall have regard to the time required for the preparation of statements and to the urgency of the case. It shall also take account of working days as well as public holidays in the country of receipt of the Commission's communication.

Time limits shall be set in terms of a precise calendar date.

Article 23   Receipt of documents by the Commission

1. In accordance with the provisions of Article 5(1) of this Regulation, notifications shall be delivered to the Commission at the address of the Commission's Directorate General for Competition as published by the Commission in the *Official Journal of the European Union*.

2. Additional information requested to complete notifications must reach the Commission at the address referred to in paragraph 1.

3. Written comments on Commission communications pursuant to Article 12(1) and (2), Article 13(2) and Article 16(1) of this Regulation must have reached the Commission at the address referred to in paragraph 1 before the expiry of the time limit set in each case.

Article 24   Definition of working days

The expression working days in Regulation (EC) No 139/2004 and in this Regulation means all days other than Saturdays, Sundays, and Commission holidays as published in the *Official Journal of the European Union* before the beginning of each year.

Article 25   Repeal and transitional provision

1. Without prejudice to paragraphs 2 and 3, Regulation (EC) No 447/98 is repealed with effect from 1 May 2004.

References to the repealed Regulation shall be construed as references to this Regulation.

2. Regulation (EC) No 447/98 shall continue to apply to any concentration falling within the scope of Regulation (EEC) No 4064/89.

3. For the purposes of paragraph 2, Sections 1 to 12 of the Annex to Regulation (EC) No 447/98 shall be replaced by Sections 1 to 11 of Annex I to this Regulation. In such cases references in those sections to the 'EC Merger Regulation' and to the 'Implementing Regulation' shall be read as referring to the corresponding provisions of Regulation (EEC) No 4064/89 and Regulation (EC) No 447/98, respectively.

Article 26   Entry into force

This Regulation shall enter into force on 1 May 2004.

This Regulation shall be binding in its entirety and directly applicable in all Member States.

Done at Brussels, 7 April 2004.

For the Commission
Franz FISCHLER
Member of the Commission

Annex I Form Co-relating to the notification of a concentration pursuant to Regulation (EC) No 139/2004

1 Introduction

1.1 The purpose of this Form

This Form specifies the information that must be provided by notifying parties when submitting a notification to the European Commission of a proposed merger, acquisition or other concentration. The merger control system of the European Union is laid down in Council Regulation (EC) No 139/2004 (hereinafter referred to as "the EC Merger Regulation"), and in Commission Regulation (EC) No 802/2004 (hereinafter referred to as "the Implementing Regulation"), to which this Form CO is annexed. The text of these regulations, as well as other relevant documents, can be found on the Competition page of the Commission's Europa web site. Your attention is drawn to the corresponding provisions of the Agreement on the European Economic Area (hereinafter referred to as "the EEA Agreement").

In order to limit the time and expense involved in complying with various merger control procedures in several individual countries, the European Union has put in place a system of merger control by which concentrations having a Community dimension (normally, where the parties to the concentration fulfil certain turnover thresholds) are assessed by the European Commission in a single procedure (the 'one stop shop' principle). Mergers which do not meet the turnover thresholds may fall within the competence of the Member States' and/or the EFTA States' authorities in charge of merger control.

The EC Merger Regulation requires the Commission to reach a decision within a legal deadline. In an initial phase the Commission normally has 25 working days to decide whether to clear the concentration or to 'initiate proceedings', i.e., to undertake an in-depth investigation. If the Commission decides to initiate proceedings, it normally has to take a final decision on the operation within no more than 90 working days of the date when proceedings are initiated.

In view of these deadlines, and for the 'one stop shop' principle to work, it is essential that the Commission is provided, in a timely fashion, with the information required to carry out the necessary investigation and to assess the impact of the concentration on the markets concerned. This requires that a certain amount of information be provided at the time of notification. It is recognised that the information requested in this Form is substantial. However, experience has shown that, depending on the specific characteristics of the case, not all information is always necessary for an adequate examination of the proposed concentration. Accordingly, if you consider that any particular information requested by this Form may not be necessary for the Commission's examination of the case, you are encouraged to ask the Commission to dispense with the obligation to provide certain information ('waiver'). See Section 1.3 (g) for more details.

Pre-notification contacts are extremely valuable to both the notifying parties and the Commission in determining the precise amount of information required in a notification and, in the majority of cases, will result in a significant reduction of the information required. Notifying parties may refer to the Commission's Best Practices on the Conduct of EC Merger Control Proceedings, which provides guidance on pre-notification contacts and the preparation of notifications.

In addition, it should be noted that certain concentrations, which are unlikely to pose any competition concerns, can be notified using a Short Form, which is attached to the Implementing Regulation, as Annex II.

1.2 Who must notify

In the case of a merger within the meaning of Article 3(1)(a) of the EC Merger Regulation or the acquisition of joint control of an undertaking within the meaning of Article 3(1)(b) of the EC Merger

Regulation, the notification shall be completed jointly by the parties to the merger or by those acquiring joint control, as the case may be.

In case of the acquisition of a controlling interest in one undertaking by another, the acquirer must complete the notification.

In the case of a public bid to acquire an undertaking, the bidder must complete the notification.

Each party completing the notification is responsible for the accuracy of the information which it provides.

1.3 The requirement for a correct and complete notification

All information required by this Form must be correct and complete. The information required must be supplied in the appropriate Section of this Form.

In particular you should note that:

(a) In accordance with Article 10(1) of the EC Merger Regulation and Article 5(2) and (4) of the Implementing Regulation, the time-limits of the EC Merger Regulation linked to the notification will not begin to run until all the information that has to be supplied with the notification has been received by the Commission. This requirement is to ensure that the Commission is able to assess the notified concentration within the strict time-limits provided by the EC Merger Regulation.

(b) The notifying parties should verify, in the course of preparing their notification, that contact names and numbers, and in particular fax numbers and e-mail addresses, provided to the Commission are accurate, relevant and up-to-date.

(c) Incorrect or misleading information in the notification will be considered to be incomplete information (Article 5(4) of the Implementing Regulation).

(d) If a notification is incomplete, the Commission will inform the notifying parties or their representatives in writing and without delay. The notification will only become effective on the date on which the complete and accurate information is received by the Commission (Article 10(1) of the EC Merger Regulation, Articles 5(2) and (4) of the Implementing Regulation).

(e) Under Article 14(1)(a) of the EC Merger Regulation, notifying parties who, either intentionally or negligently, supply incorrect or misleading information, may be liable to fines of up to 1 % of the aggregate turnover of the undertaking concerned. In addition, pursuant to Article 6(3)(a) and Article 8(6)(a) of the EC Merger Regulation the Commission may revoke its decision on the compatibility of a notified concentration where it is based on incorrect information for which one of the undertakings is responsible.

(f) You may request in writing that the Commission accept that the notification is complete notwithstanding the failure to provide information required by this Form, if such information is not reasonably available to you in part or in whole (for example, because of the unavailability of information on a target company during a contested bid). The Commission will consider such a request, provided that you give reasons for the unavailability of that information, and provide your best estimates for missing data together with the sources for the estimates. Where possible, indications as to where any of the requested information that is unavailable to you could be obtained by the Commission should also be provided.

(g) You may request in writing that the Commission accept that the notification is complete notwithstanding the failure to provide information required by this Form, if you consider that any particular information required, in the full or short form version, may not be necessary for the Commission's examination of the case. The Commission will consider such a request, provided that you give adequate reasons why that information is not relevant and necessary to its inquiry into the notified operation. You should explain this during your pre-notification contacts with the Commission and, submit a written request for a waiver, asking the Commission to dispense with the obligation to provide that information, pursuant to Article 4(2) of the Implementing Regulation.

1.4 How to notify

The notification must be completed in one of the official languages of the European Community. This language will thereafter be the language of the proceedings for all notifying parties. Where notifications are made in accordance with Article 12 of Protocol 24 to the EEA Agreement in an official language of an EFTA State which is not an official language of the Community, the notification must simultaneously be supplemented with a translation into an official language of the Community.

The information requested by this Form is to be set out using the sections and paragraph numbers of the Form, signing a declaration as provided in Section 11, and annexing supporting documentation. In completing Sections 7 to 9 of this Form, the notifying parties are invited to consider whether, for purposes of clarity, these sections are best presented in numerical order, or whether they can be grouped together for each individual affected market (or group of affected markets).

For the sake of clarity, certain information may be put in annexes. However, it is essential that all key substantive pieces of information, and in particular market share information for the parties and their largest competitors, are presented in the body of Form CO. Annexes to this Form shall only be used to supplement the information supplied in the Form itself.

Contact details must be provided in a format provided by the Commission's Directorate-General for Competition (DG Competition). For a proper investigatory process, it is essential that the contact details are accurate. Multiple instances of incorrect contact details may be a ground for declaring a notification incomplete.

Supporting documents are to be submitted in their original language; where this is not an official language of the Community, they must be translated into the language of the proceeding (Article 3(4) of the Implementing Regulation).

Supporting documents may be originals or copies of the originals. In the latter case, the notifying party must confirm that they are true and complete.

One original and 35 copies of the Form CO and the supporting documents shall be submitted to the Commission's Directorate-General for Competition.

The notification shall be delivered to the address referred to in Article 23 (1) of the Implementing Regulation and in the format specified by the Commission from time to time. This address is published in the *Official Journal of the European Union*. The notification must be delivered to the Commission on working days as defined by Article 24 of the Implementing Regulation. In order to enable it to be registered on the same day, it must be delivered before 17.00 hrs on Mondays to Thursdays and before 16.00 hrs on Fridays and workdays preceding public holidays and other holidays as determined by the Commission and published in the *Official Journal of the European Union*. The security instructions given on DG Competition's website must be adhered to.

1.5 Confidentiality

Article 287 of the Treaty and Article 17(2) of the EC Merger Regulation as well as the corresponding provisions of the EEA Agreement require the Commission, the Member States, the EFTA Surveillance Authority and the EFTA States, their officials and other servants not to disclose information they have acquired through the application of the Regulation of the kind covered by the obligation of professional secrecy. The same principle must also apply to protect confidentiality between notifying parties.

If you believe that your interests would be harmed if any of the information you are asked to supply were to be published or otherwise divulged to other parties, submit this information separately with each page clearly marked 'Business Secrets'. You should also give reasons why this information should not be divulged or published.

In the case of mergers or joint acquisitions, or in other cases where the notification is completed by more than one of the parties, business secrets may be submitted under separate cover, and referred to in the notification as an annex. All such annexes must be included in the submission in order for a notification to be considered complete.

1.6   Definitions and instructions for purposes of this Form

Notifying party or parties: in cases where a notification is submitted by only one of the undertakings who is a party to an operation, 'notifying parties' is used to refer only to the undertaking actually submitting the notification.

Party(ies) to the concentration or parties: these terms relate to both the acquiring and acquired parties, or to the merging parties, including all undertakings in which a controlling interest is being acquired or which is the subject of a public bid.

Except where otherwise specified, the terms notifying party(ies) and party(ies) to the concentration include all the undertakings which belong to the same groups as those parties.

Affected markets: Section 6 of this Form requires the notifying parties to define the relevant product markets, and further to identify which of those relevant markets are likely to be affected by the notified operation. This definition of affected market is used as the basis for requiring information for a number of other questions contained in this Form. The definitions thus submitted by the notifying parties are referred to in this Form as the affected market (s). This term can refer to a relevant market made up either of products or of services.

Year: all references to the word year in this Form should be read as meaning calendar year, unless otherwise stated. All information requested in this Form must, unless otherwise specified, relate to the year preceding that of the notification.

The financial data requested in Sections 3.3 to 3.5 must be provided in euros at the average exchange rates prevailing for the years or other periods in question.

All references contained in this Form are to the relevant articles and paragraphs of the EC Merger Regulation, unless otherwise stated.

1.7   Provision of information to Employees and their representatives

The Commission would like to draw attention to the obligations to which the parties to a concentration may be subject under Community and/or national rules on information and consultation regarding transactions of a concentrative nature vis-à-vis employees and/or their representatives.

Section 1 Description of the concentration

1.1. Provide an executive summary of the concentration, specifying the parties to the concentration, the nature of the concentration (for example, merger, acquisition, or joint venture), the areas of activity of the notifying parties, the markets on which the concentration will have an impact (including the main affected markets), and the strategic and economic rationale for the concentration.

1.2. Provide a summary (up to 500 words) of the information provided under Section 1.1. It is intended that this summary will be published on the Commission's website at the date of notification. The summary must be drafted so that it contains no confidential information or business secrets.

Section 2 Information about the parties

2.1. Information on notifying party (or parties)

Give details of:

2.1.1. name and address of undertaking;

2.1.2. nature of the undertaking's business;

2.1.3. name, address, telephone number, fax number and e-mail address of, and position held by, the appropriate contact person; and

2.1.4. an address for service of the notifying party (or each of the notifying parties) to which documents and, in particular, Commission decisions may be delivered. The name, telephone number and e-mail address of a person at this address who is authorised to accept service must be provided.

2.2. Information on other parties to the concentration

For each party to the concentration (except the notifying party or parties) give details of:

2.2.1. name and address of undertaking;

2.2.2. nature of undertaking's business;

2.2.3. name, address, telephone number, fax number and e-mail address of, and position held by, the appropriate contact person; and

2.2.4. an address for service of the party (or each of the parties) to which documents and, in particular, Commission Decisions may be delivered. The name, e-mail address and telephone number of a person at this address who is authorised to accept service must be provided.

2.3. Appointment of representatives

Where notifications are signed by representatives of undertakings, such representatives must produce written proof that they are authorised to act. The written proof must contain the name and position of the persons granting such authority.

Provide the following contact details of any representatives who have been authorised to act for any of the parties to the concentration, indicating whom they represent:

2.3.1. name of representative;

2.3.2. address of representative;

2.3.3. name, address, telephone number, fax number and e-mail address of person to be contacted; and

2.3.4. an address of the representative (in Brussels if available) to which correspondence may be sent and documents delivered.

Section 3 Details of the concentration

3.1. Describe the nature of the concentration being notified. In doing so, state:

(a) whether the proposed concentration is a full legal merger, an acquisition of sole or joint control, a full-function joint venture within the meaning of Article 3(4) of the EC Merger Regulation or a contract or other means of conferring direct or indirect control within the meaning of Article 3(2) of the EC Merger Regulation;

(b) whether the whole or parts of parties are subject to the concentration;

(c) a brief explanation of the economic and financial structure of the concentration;

(d) whether any public offer for the securities of one party by another party has the support of the former's supervisory boards of management or other bodies legally representing that party;

(e) the proposed or expected date of any major events designed to bring about the completion of the concentration;

(f) the proposed structure of ownership and control after the completion of the concentration;

(g) any financial or other support received from whatever source (including public authorities) by any of the parties and the nature and amount of this support; and

(h) the economic sectors involved in the concentration.

3.2. State the value of the transaction (the purchase price or the value of all the assets involved, as the case may be).

3.3. For each of the undertakings concerned by the concentration provide the following data for the last financial year:

3.3.1. world-wide turnover;

3.3.2. Community-wide turnover;

3.3.3. EFTA-wide turnover;

3.3.4. turnover in each Member State;

3.3.5. turnover in each EFTA State;

3.3.6. the Member State, if any, in which more than two-thirds of Community-wide turnover is achieved; and

3.3.7. the EFTA State, if any, in which more than two-thirds of EFTA-wide turnover is achieved.

3.4. For the purposes of Article 1(3) of the EC Merger Regulation, if the operation does not meet the thresholds set out in Article 1(2), provide the following data for the last financial year:

3.4.1. the Member States, if any, in which the combined aggregate turnover of all the undertakings concerned is more than EUR 100 million; and

3.4.2. the Member States, if any, in which the aggregate turnover of each of at least two of the undertakings concerned is more than EUR 25 million.

3.5. For the purposes of determining whether the concentration qualifies as an EFTA cooperation case, provide the following information with respect to the last financial year:

3.5.1. does the combined turnover of the undertakings concerned in the territory of the EFTA States equal 25% or more of their total turnover in the EEA territory?

3.5.2. does each of at least two undertakings concerned have a turnover exceeding EUR 250 million in the territory of the EFTA States?

3.6. Describe the economic rationale of the concentration.

Section 4 Ownership and control

4.1. For each of the parties to the concentration provide a list of all undertakings belonging to the same group.

This list must include:

4.1.1. all undertakings or persons controlling these parties, directly or indirectly;

4.1.2. all undertakings active on any affected market that are controlled, directly or indirectly:

(a) by these parties;

(b) by any other undertaking identified in 4.1.1.

For each entry listed above, the nature and means of control should be specified.

The information sought in this section may be illustrated by the use of organization charts or diagrams to show the structure of ownership and control of the undertakings.

4.2. With respect to the parties to the concentration and each undertaking or person identified in response to Section 4.1, provide:

4.2.1. a list of all other undertakings which are active in affected markets (affected markets are defined in Section 6) in which the undertakings, or persons, of the group hold individually or collectively 10% or more of the voting rights, issued share capital or other securities;   in each case, identify the holder and state the percentage held;

4.2.2. a list for each undertaking of the members of their boards of management who are also members of the boards of management or of the supervisory boards of any other undertaking which is active in affected markets; and (where applicable) for each undertaking a list of the members of their supervisory boards who are also members of the boards of management of any other undertaking which is active in affected markets;   in each case, identify the name of the other undertaking and the positions held;

4.2.3. details of acquisitions made during the last three years by the groups identified above (Section 4.1) of undertakings active in affected markets as defined in Section 6.   Information provided here may be illustrated by the use of organization charts or diagrams to give a better understanding.

Section 5 Supporting documentation

Notifying parties must provide the following:

5.1. copies of the final or most recent versions of all documents bringing about the concentration, whether by agreement between the parties to the concentration, acquisition of a controlling interest or a public bid;

5.2. in a public bid, a copy of the offer document; if it is unavailable at the time of notification, it should be submitted as soon as possible and not later than when it is posted to shareholders;

5.3. copies of the most recent annual reports and accounts of all the parties to the concentration; and

5.4. copies of all analyses, reports, studies, surveys, and any comparable documents prepared by or for any member(s) of the board of directors, or the supervisory board, or the other person(s)

exercising similar functions (or to whom such functions have been delegated or entrusted), or the shareholders' meeting, for the purpose of assessing or analysing the concentration with respect to market shares, competitive conditions, competitors (actual and potential), the rationale of the concentration, potential for sales growth or expansion into other product or geographic markets, and/or general market conditions.

For each of these documents, indicate (if not contained in the document itself) the date of preparation, the name and title of each individual who prepared each such document.

Section 6 Market definitions

The relevant product and geographic markets determine the scope within which the market power of the new entity resulting from the concentration must be assessed.

The notifying party or parties must provide the data requested having regard to the following definitions:

I   Relevant product markets:

A relevant product market comprises all those products and/or services which are regarded as interchangeable or substitutable by the consumer, by reason of the products' characteristics, their prices and their intended use. A relevant product market may in some cases be composed of a number of individual products and/or services which present largely identical physical or technical characteristics and are interchangeable.

Factors relevant to the assessment of the relevant product market include the analysis of why the products or services in these markets are included and why others are excluded by using the above definition, and having regard to, for example, substitutability, conditions of competition, prices, cross-price elasticity of demand or other factors relevant for the definition of the product markets (for example, supply-side substitutability in appropriate cases).

II   Relevant geographic markets:

The relevant geographic market comprises the area in which the undertakings concerned are involved in the supply and demand of relevant products or services, in which the conditions of competition are sufficiently homogeneous and which can be distinguished from neighbouring geographic areas because, in particular, conditions of competition are appreciably different in those areas.

Factors relevant to the assessment of the relevant geographic market include inter alia the nature and characteristics of the products or services concerned, the existence of entry barriers, consumer preferences, appreciable differences in the undertakings' market shares between neighbouring geographic areas or substantial price differences.

III   Affected markets:

For purposes of information required in this Form, affected markets consist of relevant product markets where, in the EEA territory, in the Community, in the territory of the EFTA States, in any Member State or in any EFTA State:

(a) two or more of the parties to the concentration are engaged in business activities in the same product market and where the concentration will lead to a combined market share of 15% or more. These are horizontal relationships;

(b) one or more of the parties to the concentration are engaged in business activities in a product market, which is upstream or downstream of a product market in which any other party to the concentration is engaged, and any of their individual or combined market shares at either level is 25% or more, regardless of whether there is or is not any existing supplier/customer relationship between the parties to the concentration. These are vertical relationships.

On the basis of the above definitions and market share thresholds, provide the following information:

– Identify each affected market within the meaning of Section III, at:
– the EEA, Community or EFTA level;
– the individual Member States or EFTA States level.6.2.

In addition, state and explain the parties' view regarding the scope of the relevant geographic market within the meaning of Section II that applies in relation to each affected market identified above.

IV Other markets in which the notified operation may have a significant impact

6.3. On the basis of the above definitions, describe the product and geographic scope of markets other than affected markets identified in Section 6.1 in which the notified operation may have a significant impact, for example, where:

    (a) any of the parties to the concentration has a market share larger than 25% and any other party to the concentration is a potential competitor into that market. A party may be considered a potential competitor, in particular, where it has plans to enter a market, or has developed or pursued such plans in the past two years;

    (b) any of the parties to the concentration has a market share larger than 25% and any other party to the concentration holds important intellectual property rights for that market;

    (c) any of the parties to the concentration is present in a product market, which is a neighbouring market closely related to a product market in which any other party to the concentration is engaged, and the individual or combined market shares of the parties in any one of these markets is 25% or more. Product markets are closely related neighbouring markets when the products are complementary to each other or when they belong to a range of products that is generally purchased by the same set of customers for the same end use;

where such markets include the whole or a part of the EEA.

In order to enable the Commission to consider, from the outset, the competitive impact of the proposed concentration in the markets identified under this Section 6.3, notifying partiesare invited to submit the information under Sections 7 and 8 of this Form in relation to those markets.

Section 7 Information on affected markets

For each affected relevant product market, for each of the last three financial years:

    (a) for the EEA territory;

    (b) for the Community as a whole;

    (c) for the territory of the EFTA States as a whole;

    (d) individually for each Member State and EFTA State where the parties to the concentration do business; and

    (e) where in the opinion of the notifying parties, the relevant geographic market is different; provide the following:

7.1. an estimate of the total size of the market in terms of sales value (in euros) and volume (units). Indicate the basis and sources for the calculations and provide documents where available to confirm these calculations;

7.2. the sales in value and volume, as well as an estimate of the market shares, of each of the parties to the concentration;

7.3. an estimate of the market share in value (and where appropriate, volume) of all competitors (including importers) having at least 5% of the geographic market under consideration. On this basis, provide an estimate of the HHI index pre- and post-merger, and the difference between the two (the delta). Indicate the proportion of market shares used as a basis to calculate the HHI. Identify the sources used to calculate these market shares and provide documents where available to confirm the calculation;

7.4. the name, address, telephone number, fax number and e-mail address of the head of the legal department (or other person exercising similar functions; and in cases where there is no such person, then the chief executive) for the competitors identified under 7.3;

7.5. an estimate of the total value and volume and source of imports from outside the EEA territory and identify:

(a) the proportion of such imports that are derived from the groups to which the parties to the concentration belong;

(b) an estimate of the extent to which any quotas, tariffs or non-tariff barriers to trade, affect these imports; and

(c) an estimate of the extent to which transportation and other costs affect these imports;

7.6. the extent to which trade among States within the EEA territory is affected by:

(a) transportation and other costs; and

(b) other non-tariff barriers to trade;

7.7. the manner in which the parties to the concentration produce, price and sell the products and/or services; for example, whether they manufacture and price locally, or sell through local distribution facilities;

7.8. a comparison of price levels in each Member State and EFTA State by each party to the concentration and a similar comparison of price levels between the Community, the EFTA States and other areas where these products are produced (e.g. Russia, the United States of America, Japan, China, or other relevant areas); and

7.9. the nature and extent of vertical integration of each of the parties to the concentration compared with their largest competitors.

Section 8 General conditions in affected markets

8.1. Identify the five largest independent suppliers to the parties to the concentration and their individual shares of purchases from each of these suppliers (of raw materials or goods used for purposes of producing the relevant products). Provide the name, address, telephone number, fax number and e-mail address of the head of the legal department (or other person exercising similar functions; and in cases where there is no such person, then the chief executive) for each of these suppliers.

Structure of supply in affected markets

8.2. Explain the distribution channels and service networks that exist in the affected markets. In so doing, take account of the following where appropriate:

(a) the distribution systems prevailing in the market and their importance. To what extent is distribution performed by third parties and/or undertakings belonging to the same group as the parties identified in Section 4?

(b) the service networks (for example, maintenance and repair) prevailing and their importance in these markets. To what extent are such services performed by third parties and/or undertakings belonging to the same group as the parties identified in Section 4?

8.3. Provide an estimate of the total Community-wide and EFTA-wide capacity for the last three years. Over this period what proportion of this capacity is accounted for by each of the parties to the concentration, and what have been their respective rates of capacity utilization. If applicable, identify the location and capacity of the manufacturing facilities of each of the parties to the concentration in affected markets.

8.4. Specify whether any of the parties to the concentration, or any of the competitors, have 'pipeline products', products likely to be brought to market in the near term, or plans to expand (or contract) production or sales capacity. If so, provide an estimate of the projected sales and market shares of the parties to the concentration over the next three to five years.

8.5. If you consider any other supply-side considerations to be relevant, they should be specified.

Structure of demand in affected markets

8.6. Identify the five largest independent customers of the parties in each affected market and their individual share of total sales for such products accounted for by each of those customers. Provide the name, address, telephone number, fax number and e-mail address of the head of the legal department (or other person exercising similar functions; and in cases where there is no such person, then the chief executive) for each of these customers.

8.7. Explain the structure of demand in terms of:
  (a) the phases of the markets in terms of, for example, take-off, expansion, maturity and de-
      cline, and a forecast of the growth rate of demand;
  (b) the importance of customer preferences, for example in terms of brand loyalty, the provi-
      sion of pre- and after-sales services, the provision of a full range of products, or network
      effects;
  (c) the role of product differentiation in terms of attributes or quality, and the extent to which
      the products of the parties to the concentration are close substitutes;
  (d) the role of switching costs (in terms of time and expense) for customers when changing
      from one supplier to another;
  (e) the degree of concentration or dispersion of customers;
  (f) segmentation of customers into different groups with a description of the 'typical cus-
      tomer' of each group;
  (g) the importance of exclusive distribution contracts and other types of long-term contracts;
      and
  (h) the extent to which public authorities, government agencies, State enterprises or similar
      bodies are important participants as a source of demand.

Market entry

8.8. Over the last five years, has there been any significant entry into any affected markets?
If so, identify such entrants and provide the name, address, telephone number, fax number and
e-mail address of the head of the legal department (or other person exercising similar functions; and in cases where there is no such person, then the chief executive) and an estimate
of the current market share of each such entrant. If any of the parties to the concentration
entered an affected market in the past five years, provide an analysis of the barriers to entry
encountered.

8.9. In the opinion of the notifying parties, are there undertakings (including those at present operating only outside the Community or the EEA) that are likely to enter the market? If so, identify such
entrants and provide the name, address, telephone number, fax number and e-mail address of the
head of the legal department (or other person exercising similar functions; and in cases where there
is no such person, then the chief executive). Explain why such entry is likely and provide an estimate
of the time within which such entry is likely to occur.

8.10 Describe the various factors influencing entry into affected markets, examining entry
from both a geographical and product viewpoint. In so doing, take account of the following where
appropriate:
  (a) the total costs of entry (R&D, production, establishing distribution systems, promotion,
      advertising, servicing, and so forth) on a scale equivalent to a significant viable com-
      petitor, indicating the market share of such a competitor;
  (b) any legal or regulatory barriers to entry, such as government authorization or standard
      setting in any form, as well as barriers resulting from product certification procedures, or
      the need to have a proven track record;
  (c) any restrictions created by the existence of patents, know-how and other intellectual
      property rights in these markets and any restrictions created by licensing such rights;
  (d) the extent to which each of the parties to the concentration are holders, licensees or licen-
      sors of patents, know-how and other rights in the relevant markets;
  (e) the importance of economies of scale for the production or distribution of products in the
      affected markets; and
  (f) access to sources of supply, such as availability of raw materials and necessary
      infrastructure.

Research and development

8.11. Give an account of the importance of research and development in the ability of a firm operating the relevant market(s) to compete in the long term. Explain the nature of the research and

development in affected markets carried out by the parties to the concentration. In so doing, take account of the following, where appropriate:

    (a) trends and intensities of research and development in these markets and for the parties to the concentration;

    (b) the course of technological development for these markets over an appropriate time period (including developments in products and/or services, production processes, distribution systems, and so on);

    (c) the major innovations that have been made in these markets and the undertakings responsible for these innovations; and

    (d) the cycle of innovation in these markets and where the parties are in this cycle of innovation.

Cooperative agreements

8.12. To what extent do cooperative agreements (horizontal, vertical, or other) exist in the affected markets?

8.13. Give details of the most important cooperative agreements engaged in by the parties to the concentration in the affected markets, such as research and development, licensing, joint production, specialization, distribution, long term supply and exchange of information agreements and, where deemed useful, provide a copy of these agreements.

Trade associations

8.14. With respect to the trade associations in the affected markets:

    (a) identify those of which the parties to the concentration are members; and

    (b) identify the most important trade associations to which the customers and suppliers of the parties to the concentration belong.

Provide the name, address, telephone number, fax number and e-mail address of the appropriate contact person for all trade associations listed above.

Section 9 Overall market context and efficiencies

9.1. Describe the world wide context of the proposed concentration, indicating the position of each of the parties to the concentration outside of the EEA territory in terms of size and competitive strength.

9.2. Describe how the proposed concentration is likely to affect the interests of intermediate and ultimate consumers and the development of technical and economic progress.

9.3. Should you wish the Commission specifically to consider from the outset whether efficiency gains generated by the concentration are likely to enhance the ability and incentive of the new entity to act pro-competitively for the benefit of consumers, please provide a description of, and supporting documents relating to, each efficiency (including cost savings, new product introductions, and service or product improvements) that the parties anticipate will result from the proposed concentration relating to any relevant product.

For each claimed efficiency, provide:

    (i)   a detailed explanation of how the proposed concentration would allow the new entity to achieve the efficiency. Specify the steps that the parties anticipate taking to achieve the efficiency, the risks involved in achieving the efficiency, and the time and costs required to achieve it;

    (ii) where reasonably possible, a quantification of the efficiency and a detailed explanation of how the quantification was calculated. Where relevant, also provide an estimate of the significance of efficiencies related to new product introductions or quality improvements. For efficiencies that involve cost savings, state separately the one-time fixed cost savings, recurring fixed cost savings, and variable cost savings (in euros per unit and euros per year);

    (iii) the extent to which customers are likely to benefit from the efficiency and a detailed explanation of how this conclusion is arrived at; and

    (iv) the reason why the party or parties could not achieve the efficiency to a similar extent by means other than through the concentration proposed, and in a manner that is not likely to raise competition concerns.

Section 10 Cooperative effects of a joint venture

10. For the purpose of Article 2(4) of the EC Merger Regulation, answer the following questions:

    (a) Do two or more parents retain to a significant extent activities in the same market as the joint venture or in a market which is upstream or downstream from that of the joint venture or in a neighbouring market closely related to this market? If the answer is affirmative, please indicate for each of the markets referred to here:

        – the turnover of each parent company in the preceding financial year;

        – the economic significance of the activities of the joint venture in relation to this turnover;

        – the market share of each parent.

    (b) If the answer to (a) is affirmative and in your view the creation of the joint venture does not lead to coordination between independent undertakings that restricts competition within the meaning of Article 81(1) of the EC Treaty, and, where applicable, the corresponding provisions of the EEA Agreement, give your reasons.

    (c) Without prejudice to the answers to (a) and (b) and in order to ensure that a complete assessment of the case can be made by the Commission, please explain how the criteria of Article 81(3) of the EC Treaty and, where applicable, the corresponding provisions of the EEA Agreement apply. Under Article 81(3), the provisions of Article 81(1) may be declared inapplicable if the operation:

      (i)   contributes to improving the production or distribution of goods, or to promoting technical or economic progress;

      (ii)   allows consumers a fair share of the resulting benefit;

      (iii) does not impose on the undertakings concerned restrictions which are not indispensable to the attainment of these objectives; and

      (iv) does not afford such undertakings the possibility of eliminating competition in respect of a substantial part of the products in question.

Section 11 Declaration

Article 2(2) of the Implementing Regulation states that where notifications are signed by representatives of undertakings, such representatives must produce written proof that they are authorized to act. Such written authorization must accompany the notification.

The notification must conclude with the following declaration which is to be signed by or on behalf of all the notifying parties:

The notifying party or parties declare that, to the best of their knowledge and belief, the information given in this notification is true, correct, and complete, that true and complete copies of documents required by Form CO have been supplied, that all estimates are identified as such and are their best estimates of the underlying facts, and that all the opinions expressed are sincere.

They are aware of the provisions of Article 14(1)(a) of the EC Merger Regulation.

Place and date:

Signatures:

Name/s and positions:

On behalf of:

Annex II Short form for the notification of a concentration pursuant to Regulation (EC) No 139/2004

1. Introduction

1.1   The purpose of the Short Form

The Short Form specifies the information that must be provided by the notifying parties when submitting a notification to the European Commission of certain proposed mergers, acquisitions or other concentrations that are unlikely to raise competition concerns.

In completing this Form, your attention is drawn to Council Regulation (EC) No 139/2004 (hereinafter referred to as "the EC Merger Regulation"), and Commission Regulation (EC) No 802/2004 (hereinafter referred to as "the Implementing Regulation"), to which this Form is annexed. The text of these regulations, as well as other relevant documents, can be found on the Competition page of the Commission's Europa web site. Your attention is also drawn to the corresponding provisions of the Agreement on the European Economic Area (hereinafter referred to as "the EEA Agreement").

As a general rule, the Short Form may be used for the purpose of notifying concentrations, where one of the following conditions is met:

1. in the case of a joint venture, the joint venture has no, or negligible, actual or foreseen activities within the territory of the European Economic Area (EEA). Such cases occur where:
   (a) the turnover of the joint venture and/or the turnover of the contributed activities is less than EUR 100 million in the EEA territory; and
   (b) the total value of the assets transferred to the joint venture is less than EUR 100 million in the EEA territory;

2. none of the parties to the concentration are engaged in business activities in the same relevant product and geographic market (no horizontal overlap), or in a market which is upstream or downstream of a market in which another party to the concentration is engaged (no vertical relationship);

3. two or more of the parties to the concentration are engaged in business activities in the same relevant product and geographic market (horizontal relationships), provided that their combined market share is less than 15%; and/or one or more of the parties to the concentration are engaged in business activities in a product market which is upstream or downstream of a product market in which any other party to the concentration is engaged (vertical relationships), and provided that none of their individual or combined market shares at either level is 25% or more; or

4. a party is to acquire sole control of an undertaking over which it already has joint control. The Commission may require a full form notification where it appears either that the conditions for using the Short Form are not met, or, exceptionally, where they are met, the Commission determines, nonetheless, that a notification under Form CO is necessary for an adequate investigation of possible competition concerns.

Examples of cases where a notification under Form CO may be necessary are concentrations where it is difficult to define the relevant markets (for example, in emerging markets or where there is no established case practice); where a party is a new or potential entrant, or an important patent holder; where it is not possible to adequately determine the parties' market shares; in markets with high entry barriers, with a high degree of concentration or known competition problems; where at least two parties to the concentration are present in closely related neighbouring markets; and in concentrations where an issue of coordination arises, as referred to in Article 2(4) of the EC Merger Regulation. Similarly, a Form CO notification may be required in the case of a party acquiring sole control of a joint venture in which it currently holds joint control, where the acquiring party and the joint venture, together, have a strong market position, or the joint venture and the acquiring party have strong positions in vertically related markets.

1.2   Reversion to the full Form CO notification

In assessing whether a concentration may be notified under the Short Form, the Commission will ensure that all relevant circumstances are established with sufficient clarity. In this respect, the responsibility to provide correct and complete information rests with the notifying parties.

If, after the concentration has been notified, the Commission considers that the case is not appropriate for notification under the Short Form, the Commission may require full, or where appropriate partial, notification under Form CO. This may be the case where:

- it appears that the conditions for using the Short Form are not met;
- although the conditions for using the Short Form are met, a full or partial notification under Form CO appears to be necessary for an adequate investigation of possible competition concerns or to establish that the transaction is a concentration within the meaning of Article 3 of the EC Merger Regulation;
- the Short Form contains incorrect or misleading information;
- a Member State or an EFTA State expresses substantiated competition concerns about the notified concentration within 15 working days of receipt of the copy of the notification; or
- a third party expresses substantiated competition concerns within the time-limit laid down by the Commission for such comments.

In such cases, the notification may be treated as being incomplete in a material respect pursuant to Article 5(2) of the Implementing Regulation. The Commission will inform the notifying parties or their representatives of this in writing and without delay. The notification will only become effective on the date on which all information required is received.

1.3   mportance of pre-notification contacts

Experience has shown that pre-notification contacts are extremely valuable to both the notifying parties and the Commission in determining the precise amount of information required in a notification. Also, in cases where the parties wish to submit a Short Form notification, they are advised to engage in pre-notification contacts with the Commission in order to discuss whether the case is one for which it is appropriate to use a Short Form. Notifying parties may refer to the Commission's Best Practices on the Conduct of EC Merger Control Proceedings, which provides guidance on pre-notification contacts and the preparation of notifications.

1.4   Who must notify

In the case of a merger within the meaning of Article 3(1)(a) of the EC Merger Regulation or the acquisition of joint control of an undertaking within the meaning of Article 3(1)(b) of the EC Merger Regulation, the notification shall be completed jointly by the parties to the merger or by those acquiring joint control, as the case may be.

In the case of the acquisition of a controlling interest in one undertaking by another, the acquirer must complete the notification.

In the case of a public bid to acquire an undertaking, the bidder must complete the notification.

Each party completing the notification is responsible for the accuracy of the information which it provides.

1.5   The requirement for a correct and complete notification

All information required by this Form must be correct and complete. The information required must be supplied in the appropriate Section of this Form.

In particular you should note that:

(a) In accordance with Article 10(1) of the EC Merger Regulation and Article 5(2) and (4) of the Implementing Regulation, the time-limits of the EC Merger Regulation linked to the notification will not begin to run until all the information that must be supplied with the notification has been received by the Commission. This requirement is to ensure that the Commission is able to assess the notified concentration within the strict time-limits provided by the EC Merger Regulation.

(b) The notifying parties should verify, in the course of preparing their notification, that contact names and numbers, and in particular fax numbers and e-mail addresses, provided to the Commission are accurate, relevant and up-to-date.

(c) Incorrect or misleading information in the notification will be considered to be incomplete information (Article 5(4) of the Implementing Regulation).

(d) If a notification is incomplete, the Commission will inform the notifying parties or their representatives in writing and without delay. The notification will only become effective on the date on which the complete and accurate information is received by the Commission (Article 10(1) of the EC Merger Regulation, Article 5(2) and (4) of the Implementing Regulation).

(e) Under Article 14(1)(a) of the EC Merger Regulation, notifying parties who, either intentionally or negligently, supply incorrect or misleading information, may be liable to fines of up to 1 % of the aggregate turnover of the undertaking concerned. In addition, pursuant to Article 6(3)(a) and Article 8(6)(a) of the EC Merger Regulation the Commission may revoke its decision on the compatibility of a notified concentration where it is based on incorrect information for which one of the undertakings is responsible.

(f) You may request in writing that the Commission accept that the notification is complete notwithstanding the failure to provide information required by this Form, if such information is not reasonably available to you in part or in whole (for example, because of the unavailability of information on a target company during a contested bid). The Commission will consider such a request, provided that you give reasons for the unavailability of that information, and provide your best estimates for missing data together with the sources for the estimates. Where possible, indications as to where any of the requested information that is unavailable to you could be obtained by the Commission should also be provided.

(g) You may request in writing that the Commission accept that the notification is complete notwithstanding the failure to provide information required by this Form, if you consider that any particular information required may not be necessary for the Commission's examination of the case. The Commission will consider such a request, provided that you give adequate reasons why that information is not relevant and necessary to its inquiry into the notified operation. You should explain this during your prenotification contacts with the Commission and submit a written request for a waiver, asking the Commission to dispense with the obligation to provide that information, pursuant to Article 4(2) of the Implementing Regulation.

1.6   How to notify

The notification must be completed in one of the official languages of the European Community. This language will thereafter be the language of the proceedings for all notifying parties. Where notifications are made in accordance with Article 12 of Protocol 24 to the EEA Agreement in an official language of an EFTA State which is not an official language of the Community, the notification must simultaneously be supplemented with a translation into an official language of the Community.

The information requested by this Form is to be set out using the sections and paragraph numbers of the Form, signing a declaration as provided in Section 9, and annexing supporting documentation. In completing Section 7 of this Form, the notifying parties are invited to consider whether, for purposes of clarity, this section is best presented in numerical order, or whether information can be grouped together for each individual reportable market (or group of reportable markets).

For the sake of clarity, certain information may be put in annexes. However, it is essential that all key substantive pieces of information, in particular, market share information for the parties and their largest competitors, are presented in the body of this Form. Annexes to this Form shall only be used to supplement the information supplied in the Form itself.

Contact details must be provided in a format provided by the Commission's Directorate-General for Competition (DG Competition). For a proper investigatory process, it is essential that the contact details are accurate. Multiple instances of incorrect contact details may be a ground for declaring a notification incomplete.

Supporting documents are to be submitted in their original language; where this is not an official language of the Community, they must be translated into the language of the proceeding (Article 3(4) of the Implementing Regulation).

Supporting documents may be originals or copies of the originals. In the latter case, the notifying party must confirm that they are true and complete.

One original and 35 copies of the Short Form and the supporting documents shall be submitted to the Commission's Directorate-General for Competition.

The notification shall be delivered to the address referred to in Article 23(1) of the Implementing Regulation and in the format specified by the Commission from time to time. This address is published in the *Official Journal of the European Union*. The notification must be delivered to the Commission on working days as defined by Article 24 of the Implementing Regulation. In order to enable it to be registered on the same day, it must be delivered before 17.00 hrs on Mondays to Thursdays and before 16.00 hrs on Fridays and workdays preceding public holidays and other holidays as determined by the Commission and published in the *Official Journal of the European Union*. The security instructions given on DG Competition's website must be adhered to.

1.7 Confidentiality

Article 287 of the Treaty and Article 17(2) of the EC Merger Regulation as well as the corresponding provisions of the EEA Agreement require the Commission, the Member States, the EFTA Surveillance Authority and the EFTA States, their officials and other servants not to disclose information they have acquired through the application of the Regulation of the kind covered by the obligation of professional secrecy. The same principle must also apply to protect confidentiality between notifying parties.

If you believe that your interests would be harmed if any of the information you are asked to supply were to be published or otherwise divulged to other parties, submit this information separately with each page clearly marked 'Business Secrets'. You should also give reasons why this information should not be divulged or published.

In the case of mergers or joint acquisitions, or in other cases where the notification is completed by more than one of the parties, business secrets may be submitted under separate cover, and referred to in the notification as an annex. All such annexes must be included in the submission in order for a notification to be considered complete.

1.8 Definitions and instructions for purposes of this Form

Notifying party or parties: in cases where a notification is submitted by only one of the undertakings who is a party to an operation, 'notifying parties' is used to refer only to the undertaking actually submitting the notification.

Party(ies) to the concentration or parties: these terms relate to both the acquiring and acquired parties, or to the merging parties, including all undertakings in which a controlling interest is being acquired or which is the subject of a public bid.

Except where otherwise specified, the terms notifying party(ies) and party(ies) to the concentration include all the undertakings which belong to the same groups as those parties.

Year: all references to the word year in this Form should be read as meaning calendar year, unless otherwise stated. All information requested in this Form must, unless otherwise specified, relate to the year preceding that of the notification.

The financial data requested in Sections 3.3 to 3.5 must be provided in euros at the average exchange rates prevailing for the years or other periods in question.

All references contained in this Form are to the relevant articles and paragraphs of the EC Merger Regulation, unless otherwise stated.

1.9 Provision of information to employees and their representatives

The Commission would like to draw attention to the obligations to which the parties to a concentration may be subject under Community and/or national rules on information and consultation regarding transactions of a concentrative nature vis-a-vis employees and/or their representatives.

Section 1 Description of the concentration

1.1. Provide an executive summary of the concentration, specifying the parties to the concentration, the nature of the concentration (for example, merger, acquisition, joint venture), the areas of activity of the notifying parties, the markets on which the concentration will have an impact (including the main reportable markets), and the strategic and economic rationale for the concentration.

1.2. Provide a summary (up to 500 words) of the information provided under Section 1.1. It is intended that this summary will be published on the Commission's website at the date of notification. The summary must be drafted so that it contains no confidential information or business secrets.

Section 2 Information about the parties

2.1. Information on notifying party (or parties)

Give details of:

2.1.1. name and address of undertaking;

2.1.2. nature of the undertaking's business;

2.1.3. name, address, telephone number, fax number and e-mail address of, and position held by, the appropriate contact person; and

2.1.4. an address for service of the notifying party (or each of the notifying parties) to which documents and, in particular, Commission Decisions may be delivered. The name, e-mail address and telephone number of a person at this address who is authorised to accept service must be provided.

2.2. Information on other parties to the concentration

For each party to the concentration (except the notifying party or parties) give details of:

2.2.1. name and address of undertaking;

2.2.2. nature of undertaking's business;

2.2.3. name, address, telephone number, fax number and e-mail address of, and position held by, the appropriate contact person; and

2.2.4. an address for service of the party (or each of the parties) to which documents and, in particular, Commission Decisions may be delivered. The name, e-mail address and telephone number of a person at this address who is authorised to accept service must be provided.

2.3. Appointment of representatives

Where notifications are signed by representatives of undertakings, such representatives must produce written proof that they are authorised to act. The written proof must contain the name and position of the persons granting such authority.

Provide the following contact details of information of any representatives who have been authorised to act for any of the parties to the concentration, indicating whom they represent:

2.3.1. name of representative;

2.3.2. address of representative;

2.3.3. name, address, telephone number, fax number and e-mail address of person to be contacted; and

2.3.4. an address of the representative for service (in Brussels if available) to which correspondence may be sent and documents delivered.

Section 3 Details of the concentration

3.1. Describe the nature of the concentration being notified. In doing so state:

   (a) whether the proposed concentration is a full legal merger, an acquisition of sole or joint control, a full-function joint venture within the meaning of Article 3(4) of the EC Merger Regulation or a contract or other means of conferring direct or indirect control within the meaning of Article 3(2) of the EC Merger Regulation;

   (b) whether the whole or parts of parties are subject to the concentration;

   (c) a brief explanation of the economic and financial structure of the concentration;

   (d) whether any public offer for the securities of one party by another party has the support of the former's supervisory boards of management or other bodies legally representing that party;

   (e) the proposed or expected date of any major events designed to bring about the completion of the concentration;

(f) the proposed structure of ownership and control after the completion of the concentration;

(g) any financial or other support received from whatever source (including public authorities) by any of the parties and the nature and amount of this support; and

(h) the economic sectors involved in the concentration.

3.2. State the value of the transaction (the purchase price or the value of all the assets involved, as the case may be);

3.3. For each of the undertakings concerned by the concentration provide the following data for the last financial year:

3.3.1. world-wide turnover;

3.3.2. Community-wide turnover;

3.3.3. EFTA-wide turnover;

3.3.4. turnover in each Member State;

3.3.5. turnover in each EFTA State;

3.3.6. the Member State, if any, in which more than two-thirds of Community-wide turnover is achieved; and

3.3.7. the EFTA State, if any, in which more than two-thirds of EFTA-wide turnover is achieved.

3.4. For the purposes of Article 1(3) of the EC Merger Regulation, if the operation does not meet the thresholds set out in Article 1(2), provide the following data for the last financial year:

3.4.1. the Member States, if any, in which the combined aggregate turnover of all the undertakings concerned is more than EUR 100 million; and

3.4.2. the Member States, if any, in which the aggregate turnover of each of at least two of the undertakings concerned is more than EUR 25 million.

3.5. For the purposes of determining whether the concentration qualifies as an EFTA cooperation case, provide the following information with respect to the last financial year:

3.5.1. does the combined turnover of the undertakings concerned in the territory of the EFTA States equal 25% or more of their total turnover in the EEA territory?

3.5.2. does each of at least two undertakings concerned have a turnover exceeding EUR 250 million in the territory of the EFTA States?

3.6. In case the transaction concerns the acquisition of joint control of a joint venture, provide the following information:

3.6.1. the turnover of the joint venture and/or the turnover of the contributed activities to the joint venture; and/or

3.6.2. the total value of assets transferred to the joint venture.

3.7. Describe the economic rationale of the concentration.

Section 4 Ownership and control

For each of the parties to the concentration provide a list of all undertakings belonging to the same group. This list must include:

4.1. all undertakings or persons controlling these parties, directly or indirectly;

4.2. all undertakings active in any reportable market that are controlled, directly or indirectly:

(a) by these parties;

(b) by any other undertaking identified in 4.1.

For each entry listed above, the nature and means of control should be specified.

The information sought in this section may be illustrated by the use of organisation charts or diagrams to show the structure of ownership and control of the undertakings.

Section 5 Supporting documentation

Notifying parties must provide the following:

5.1. copies of the final or most recent versions of all documents bringing about the concentration, whether by agreement between the parties to the concentration, acquisition of a controlling interest or a public bid; and

5.2. copies of the most recent annual reports and accounts of all the parties to the concentration.

Section 6 Market definitions

The relevant product and geographic markets determine the scope within which the market power of the new entity resulting from the concentration must be assessed. (^{2})

The notifying party or parties must provide the data requested having regard to the following definitions:

I Relevant product markets:

A relevant product market comprises all those products and/or services which are regarded as inter-changeable or substitutable by the consumer, by reason of the products' characteristics, their prices and their intended use. A relevant product market may in some cases be composed of a number of individual products and/or services which present largely identical physical or technical characteristics and are interchangeable.

Factors relevant to the assessment of the relevant product market include the analysis of why the products or services in these markets are included and why others are excluded by using the above definition, and having regard to, for example, substitutability, conditions of competition, prices, cross-price elasticity of demand or other factors relevant for the definition of the product markets (for example, supply-side substitutability in appropriate cases).

II Relevant geographic markets:

The relevant geographic market comprises the area in which the undertakings concerned are involved in the supply and demand of relevant products or services, in which the conditions of competition are sufficiently homogeneous and which can be distinguished from neighbouring geographic areas because, in particular, conditions of competition are appreciably different in those areas.

Factors relevant to the assessment of the relevant geographic market include *inter alia* the nature and characteristics of the products or services concerned, the existence of entry barriers, consumer preferences, appreciable differences in the undertakings' market shares between neighbouring geographic areas or substantial price differences.

III Reportable markets

For purposes of information required in this Form, reportable markets consist of all relevant product and geographic markets, as well as plausible alternative relevant product and geographic market definitions, on the basis of which:

(a) two or more of the parties to the concentration are engaged in business activities in the same relevant market (horizontal relationships);

(b) one or more of the parties to the concentration are engaged in business activities in a product market, which is upstream or downstream of a market in which any other party to the concentration is engaged, regardless of whether there is or is not any existing supplier/customer relationship between the parties to the concentration (vertical relationships).

6.1. On the basis of the above market definitions, identify all reportable markets.

Section 7 Information on markets

For each reportable market described in Section 6, for the year preceding the operation, provide the following:

7.1. an estimate of the total size of the market in terms of sales value (in euros) and volume (units). Indicate the basis and sources for the calculations and provide documents where available to confirm these calculations;

7.2. the sales in value and volume, as well as an estimate of the market shares, of each of the parties to the concentration. Indicate if there have been significant changes to the sales and market shares for the last three financial years; and

7.3. for horizontal and vertical relationships, an estimate of the market share in value (and where appropriate, volume) of the three largest competitors (indicating the basis for the estimates). Provide the name, address, telephone number, fax number and e-mail address of the head of the legal department (or other person exercising similar functions; and in cases where there is no such person, then the chief executive) for these competitors.

Section 8 Cooperative effects of a joint venture

8. For the purpose of Article 2(4) of the EC Merger Regulation, please answer the following questions:

    (a) Do two or more parents retain to a significant extent activities in the same market as the joint venture or in a market which is upstream or downstream from that of the joint venture or in a neighbouring market closely related to this market? If the answer is affirmative, please indicate for each of the markets referred to here:
- the turnover of each parent company in the preceding financial year;
- the economic significance of the activities of the joint venture in relation to this turnover;
- the market share of each parent.

If the answer is negative, please justify your answer.

    (b) If the answer to (a) is affirmative and in your view the creation of the joint venture does not lead to coordination between independent undertakings that restricts competition within the meaning of Article 81(1) of the EC Treaty, and, where applicable, the corresponding provisions of the EEA Agreement, give your reasons.

    (c) Without prejudice to the answers to (a) and (b) and in order to ensure that a complete assessment of the case can be made by the Commission, please explain how the criteria of Article 81(3) of the EC Treaty and, where applicable, the corresponding provisions of the EEA Agreement apply. Under Article 81(3), the provisions of Article 81(1) may be declared inapplicable if the operation:
      (i) contributes to improving the production or distribution of goods, or to promoting technical or economic progress;
      (ii) allows consumers a fair share of the resulting benefit;
      (iii) does not impose on the undertakings concerned restrictions which are not indispensable to the attainment of these objectives; and
      (iv) does not afford such undertakings the possibility of eliminating competition in respect of a substantial part of the products in question.

Section 9 Declaration

Article 2(2) of the Implementing Regulation states that where notifications are signed by representatives of undertakings, such representatives must produce written proof that they are authorized to act. Such written authorization must accompany the notification.

The notification must conclude with the following declaration which is to be signed by or onbehalf of all the notifying parties:

The notifying party or parties declare that, to the best of their knowledge and belief, the information given in this notification is true, correct, and complete, that true and complete copies of documents required by Form CO have been supplied, that all estimates are identified as such and are their best estimates of the underlying facts, and that all the opinions expressed are sincere.

They are aware of the provisions of Article 14(1) (a) of the EC Merger Regulation.

Place and date:

Signatures:

Name/s and positions:

On behalf of:

Annex III Form RS

(RS = reasoned submission pursuant to Article 4(4) and (5) of Council Regulation (EC) No 139/2004)

Form RS Relating to reasoned submissions pursuant to Articles 4(4) and 4(5) of Regulation (EC) No 139/2004

Introduction

A The purpose of this Form

This Form specifies the information that requesting parties should provide when making a reasoned submission for a pre-notification referral under Article 4(4) or (5) of Council Regulation (EC) No 139/2004 (hereinafter referred to as "the EC Merger Regulation"). Your attention is drawn to the EC Merger Regulation and to Commission Regulation (EC) No 802/2004 (hereinafter referred to as "the EC Merger Implementing Regulation"), to which this Form RS is annexed. The text of these regulations, as well as other relevant documents, can be found on the Competition page of the Commission's Europa web site. Your attention is also drawn to the corresponding provisions of the Agreement on the European Economic Area (hereinafter referred to as "the EEA Agreement"). Experience has shown that prior contacts are extremely valuable to both the parties and the relevant authorities in determining the precise amount and type of information required. Accordingly, parties are encouraged to consult the Commission and the relevant Member State/s or EFTA State/s regarding the adequacy of the scope and type of information on which they intend to base their reasoned submission.

B The requirement for a reasoned submission to be correct and complete

All information required by this Form must be correct and complete. The information required must be supplied in the appropriate section of this Form.

Incorrect or misleading information in the reasoned submission will be considered to be incomplete information (Article 5(4) of the EC Merger Implementing Regulation).

If parties submit incorrect information, the Commission will have the power to revoke any Article 6 or 8 decision it adopts following an Article 4(5) referral, pursuant to Article 6(3)(a) or 8(6) (a) of the EC Merger Regulation. Following revocation, national competition laws would once again be applicable to the transaction. In the case of referrals under Article 4(4) made on the basis of incorrect information, the Commission may require a notification pursuant to Article 4(1). In addition, the Commission will have the power to impose fines for submission of incorrect or misleading information pursuant to Article 14(1) (a) of the EC Merger Regulation. (See point d below). Finally, parties should also be aware that, if a referral is made on the basis of incorrect, misleading or incomplete information included in Form RS, the Commission and/or the Member States and the EFTA States may consider making a post-notification referral rectifying any referral made at pre-notification.

In particular you should note that:

(a) In accordance with Articles 4(4) and (5) of the EC Merger Regulation, the Commission is obliged to transmit reasoned submissions to the Member States and the EFTA States without delay. The time limits for considering a reasoned submission will begin upon receipt of the submission by the relevant Member State/s or EFTA State/s.

(b) The submitting parties should therefore verify, in the course of preparing their reasoned submission, that all information and arguments relied upon are sufficiently supported by independent sources.

(c) Under Article 14(1)(a) of the EC Merger Regulation, parties making a reasoned submission who, either intentionally or negligently, provide incorrect or misleading information, may be liable to fines of up to 1 % of the aggregate turnover of the undertaking concerned.

(d) You may request in writing that the Commission accept that the reasoned submission is complete notwithstanding the failure to provide information required by this Form, if such information is not reasonably available to you in part or in whole (for example, because of the unavailability of information on a target company during a contested bid). The Commission will consider such a request, provided that you give reasons for the non-availability of that information, and provide your best estimates for missing data together with the sources for the estimates. Where possible, indications as to where any of the requested information that is unavailable to you could be obtained by the Commission or the relevant Member State/s and EFTA State/s should also be provided.

(e) You may request that the Commission accept that the reasoned submission is complete notwithstanding the failure to provide information required by this Form, if you consider that any particular information requested by this Form may not be necessary for the Commission's or the relevant Member State/s' or EFTA State/s' examination of the case. The Commission will consider such a request, provided that you give adequate reasons why that information is not relevant and necessary to dealing with your request for a pre-notification referral. You should explain this during your prior contacts with the Commission and with the relevant Member State/s and EFTA State/s, and submit a written request for a waiver asking the Commission to dispense with the obligation to provide that information, pursuant to Article 4(2) of the EC Merger Implementing Regulation. The Commission may consult with the relevant Member State or EFTA State authority or authorities before deciding whether to accede to such a request.

C   Persons entitled to submit a reasoned submission

In the case of a merger within the meaning of Article 3(1)(a) of the EC Merger Regulation or the acquisition of joint control of an undertaking within the meaning of Article 3(1)(b) of the Merger Regulation, the reasoned submission must be completed jointly by the parties to the merger or by those acquiring joint control as the case may be.

In case of the acquisition of a controlling interest in one undertaking by another, the acquirer must complete the reasoned submission.

In the case of a public bid to acquire an undertaking, the bidder must complete the reasoned submission.

Each party completing a reasoned submission is responsible for the accuracy of the information which it provides.

D   How to make a reasoned submission

The reasoned submission must be completed in one of the official languages of the European Union. This language will thereafter be the language of the proceedings for all submitting parties.

In order to facilitate treatment of Form RS by Member State and EFTA State authorities, parties are strongly encouraged to provide the Commission with a translation of their reasoned submission in a language or languages which will be understood by all addressees of the information. As regards requests for referral to (a) Member State/s or (an) EFTA State/s, the requesting parties are strongly encouraged to include a copy of the request in the language/s of the Member State/s and EFTA State/s to which referral is being requested.

The information requested by this Form is to be set out using the sections and paragraph numbers of the Form, signing the declaration at the end, and annexing supporting documentation. For the sake of clarity, certain information may be put in annexes. However, it is essential that all key substantive pieces of information are presented in the body of Form RS. Annexes to this Form shall only be used to supplement the information supplied in the Form itself.

Supporting documents are to be submitted in their original language; where this is not an official language of the Community, they must be translated into the language of the proceeding.

Supporting documents may be originals or copies of the originals. In the latter case, the submitting party must confirm that they are true and complete.

One original and 35 copies of the Form RS and of the supporting documents must be submitted to the Commission. The reasoned submission shall be delivered to the address referred to in Article 23 (1) of the EC Merger Implementing Regulation and in the format specified by the Commission services.

The submission must be delivered to the address of the Commission's Directorate-General for Competition (DG Competition). This address is published in the *Official Journal of the European Union.* The submission must be delivered to the Commission on working days as defined by Article 24 of the EC Merger Implementing Regulation. In order to enable it to be registered on the same day, it must be delivered before 17.00 hrs on Mondays to Thursdays and before 16.00 hrs on Fridays and workdays preceding public holidays and other holidays as determined by the Commission and published in the *Official Journal of the European Union.* The security instructions given on DG Competition's website must be adhered to.

E Confidentiality

Article 287 of the Treaty and Article 17(2) of the EC Merger Regulation, as well as the corresponding provisions of the EEA Agreement require the Commission, the Member States, the EFTA Surveillance Authority and the EFTA States, their officials and other servants not to disclose information they have acquired through the application of the Regulation of the kind covered by the obligation of professional secrecy. The same principle must also apply to protect confidentiality between notifying parties.

If you believe that your interests would be harmed if any of the information supplied were to be published or otherwise divulged to other parties, submit this information separately with each page clearly marked 'Business Secrets'. You should also give reasons why this information should not be divulged or published.

In the case of mergers or joint acquisitions, or in other cases where the reasoned submission is completed by more than one of the parties, business secrets may be submitted in separate annexes, and referred to in the submission as an annex. All such annexes must be included in the reasoned submission.

F Definitions and instructions for the purposes of this Form

Submitting party or parties: in cases where a reasoned submission is made by only one of the undertakings who is a party to an operation, 'submitting parties' is used to refer only to the undertaking actually making the submission.

Party(ies) to the concentration or parties: these terms relate to both the acquiring and acquired parties, or to the merging parties, including all undertakings in which a controlling interest is being acquired or which is the subject of a public bid.

Except where otherwise specified, the terms 'submitting party(ies)' and 'party(ies) to the concentration' include all the undertakings which belong to the same groups as those 'parties'.

Affected markets: Section 4 of this Form requires the submitting parties to define the relevant product markets, and further to identify which of those relevant markets are likely to be affected by the operation. This definition of affected market is used as the basis for requiring information for a number of other questions contained in this Form. The definitions thus submitted by the submitting parties are referred to in this Form as the affected market (s). This term can refer to a relevant market made up either of products or of services.

Year: all references to the word 'year' in this Form should be read as meaning calendar year, unless otherwise stated. All information requested in this Form relates, unless otherwise specified, to the year preceding that of the reasoned submission.

The financial data requested in this Form must be provided in Euros at the average exchange rates prevailing for the years or other periods in question.

All references contained in this Form are to the relevant Articles and paragraphs of the EC Merger Regulation, unless otherwise stated.

Section 1 Background information

1.0. Indicate whether the reasoned submission is made under Article 4(4) or (5).
- Article 4(4) referral
- Article 4(5) referral

1.1. Information on the submitting party (or parties)

Give details of:

1.1.1. the name and address of undertaking;

1.1.2. the nature of the undertaking's business;

1.1.3. the name, address, telephone number, fax number and electronic address of, and position held by, the appropriate contact person; and

1.1.4. an address for service of the submitting party (or each of the submitting parties) to which documents and, in particular, Commission decisions may be delivered. The name, telephone number and e-mail address of a person at this address who is authorised to accept service must be provided.

1.2. Information on the other parties to the concentration

For each party to the concentration (except the submitting party or parties) give details of:

1.2.1. the name and address of undertaking;

1.2.2. the nature of undertaking's business;

1.2.3. the name, address, telephone number, fax number and electronic address of, and position held by the appropriate contact person;

1.2.4. an address for service of the party (or each of the parties) to which documents and, in particular, Commission Decisions may be delivered. The name, e-mail address and telephone number of a person at this address who is authorised to accept service must be provided.

1.3. Appointment of representatives

Where reasoned submissions are signed by representatives of undertakings, such representatives must produce written proof that they are authorized to act. The written proof must contain the name and position of the persons granting such authority.

Provide the following contact details of any representatives who have been authorized to act for any of the parties to the concentration, indicating whom they represent:

1.3.1. the name of the representative;

1.3.2. the address of the representative;

1.3.3. the name, address, telephone number, fax number and e-mail address of the person to be contacted; and

1.3.4. an address of the representative (in Brussels if available) to which correspondence may be sent and documents delivered.

Section 2 General background and details of the concentration

2.1. Describe the general background to the concentration. In particular, give an overview of the main reasons for the transaction, including its economic and strategic rationale.

Provide an executive summary of the concentration, specifying the parties to the concentration, the nature of the concentration (for example, merger, acquisition, or joint venture.), the areas of activity of the submitting parties, the markets on which the concentration will have an impact (including the main affected markets), and the strategic and economic rationale for the concentration.

2.2. Describe the legal nature of the transaction which is the subject of the reasoned submission. In doing so, indicate:

(a) whether the whole or parts of the parties are subject to the concentration;

(b) the proposed or expected date of any major events designed to bring about the completion of the concentration;

(c) the proposed structure of ownership and control after the completion of the concentration; and

(d) whether the proposed transaction is a concentration within the meaning of Article 3 of the EC Merger Regulation.

2.3. List the economic sectors involved in the concentration.

2.3.1. State the value of the transaction (the purchase price or the value of all the assets involved, as the case may be).

2.4. Provide sufficient financial or other data to show that the concentration meets OR does not meet the jurisdictional thresholds under Article 1 of the EC Merger Regulation.

2.4.1. Provide a breakdown of the Community-wide turnover achieved by the undertakings concerned, indicating, where applicable, the Member State, if any, in which more than two-thirds of this turnover is achieved.

2.4.2. Provide a breakdown of the EFTA-wide turnover achieved by the undertakings concerned, indicating, where applicable, the EFTA State, if any, in which more than two-thirds of this turnover is achieved.

Section 3 Ownership and control

For each of the parties to the concentration provide a list of all undertakings belonging to the same group.

This list must include:

3.1. all undertakings or persons controlling these parties, directly or indirectly;

3.2. all undertakings active on any affected market that are controlled, directly or indirectly:

(a) by these parties;

(b) by any other undertaking identified in 3.1.

For each entry listed above, the nature and means of control should be specified.

The information sought in this section may be illustrated by the use of organization charts or diagrams to show the structure of ownership and control of the undertakings.

Section 4 Market definitions

The relevant product and geographic markets determine the scope within which the market power of the new entity resulting from the concentration must be assessed.

The submitting party or parties must provide the data requested having regard to the following definitions:

I   Relevant product markets

A relevant product market comprises all those products and/or services which are regarded as interchangeable or substitutable by the consumer, by reason of the products' characteristics, their prices and their intended use. A relevant product market may in some cases be composed of a number of individual products and/or services which present largely identical physical or technical characteristics and are interchangeable.

Factors relevant to the assessment of the relevant product market include the analysis of why the products or services in these markets are included and why others are excluded by using the above definition, and having regard to, for example, substitutability, conditions of competition, prices, cross-price elasticity of demand or other factors relevant for the definition of the product markets (for example, supply-side substitutability in appropriate cases).

II   Relevant geographic markets

The relevant geographic market comprises the area in which the undertakings concerned are involved in the supply and demand of relevant products or services, in which the conditions of competition are sufficiently homogeneous and which can be distinguished from neighbouring geographic areas because, in particular, conditions of competition are appreciably different in those areas.

Factors relevant to the assessment of the relevant geographic market include *inter alia* the nature and characteristics of the products or services concerned, the existence of entry barriers, consumer preferences, appreciable differences in the undertakings' market shares between neighbouring geographic areas, or substantial price differences.

III   Affected markets

For the purposes of the information required in this Form, affected markets consist of relevant product markets where, in the EEA territory, in the Community, in the territory of the EFTA States, in any Member State or in any EFTA State:

> (a) two or more of the parties to the concentration are engaged in business activities in the same product market and where the concentration will lead to a combined market share of 15% or more. These are horizontal relationships;
>
> (b) one or more of the parties to the concentration are engaged in business activities in a product market, which is upstream or downstream of a product market in which any other party to the concentration is engaged, and any of their individual or combined market shares at either level is 25% or more, regardless of whether there is or is not any existing supplier/customer relationship between the parties to the concentration. These are vertical relationships.

On the basis of the above definitions and market share thresholds, provide the following information:

> 4.1.   Identify each affected market within the meaning of Section III:
>
> > (a) at the EEA, Community or EFTA level;
> >
> > (b) in the case of a request for referral pursuant to Article 4(4) of the EC Merger Regulation, at the level of each individual Member State or EFTA State;
> >
> > (c) in the case of a request for referral pursuant to Article 4(5) of the EC Merger Regulation, at the level of each Member State or EFTA State identified at Section 6.3.1 of this Form as capable of reviewing the concentration.
>
> 4.2.   In addition, explain the submitting parties' view as to the scope of the relevant geographic market within the meaning of Section II in relation to each affected market identified at 4.1 above.

Section 5   Information on affected markets

For each affected relevant product market, for the last financial year,

> (a) for the EEA territory, for the Community as a whole and for the EFTA States as a whole;
>
> (b) in the case of a request for referral pursuant to Article 4(4) of the EC Merger Regulation, individually for each Member State/EFTA State where the parties to the concentration do business;
>
> (c) in the case of a request for referral pursuant to Article 4(5) of the EC Merger Regulation, individually for each Member State/EFTA State identified at Section 6.3.1 of this Form as capable of reviewing the concentration where the parties to the concentration do business; and
>
> (d) where in the opinion of the submitting parties, the relevant geographic market is different;

provide the following information:

> 5.1.   an estimate of the total size of the market in terms of sales value (in Euros) and volume (units). Indicate the basis and sources for the calculations and provide documents where available to confirm these calculations;
>
> 5.2.   the sales in value and volume, as well as an estimate of the market shares, of each of the parties to the concentration;
>
> 5.3. an estimate of the market share in value (and where appropriate volume) of all competitors (including importers) having at least 5% of the geographic market under consideration;
>
> On this basis, provide an estimate of the HHI index pre- and post-merger, and the difference between the two (the delta). Indicate the proportion of market shares used as a basis to calculate the HHI; Identify the sources used to calculate these market shares and provide documents where available to confirm the calculation;
>
> 5.4.   the five largest independent customers of the parties in each affected market and their individual share of total sales for such products accounted for by each of those customers;
>
> 5.5.   the nature and extent of vertical integration of each of the parties to the concentration compared with their largest competitors;
>
> 5.6.   identify the five largest independent suppliers to the parties;

5.7. Over the last five years, has there been any significant entry into any affected markets? In the opinion of the submitting parties are there undertakings (including those at present operating only in extra-Community markets) that are likely to enter the market? Please specify.

5.8. To what extent do cooperative agreements (horizontal or vertical) exist in the affected markets?

5.9. If the concentration is a joint venture, do two or more parents retain to a significant extent activities in the same market as the joint venture or in a market which is downstream or upstream from that of the joint venture or in a neighbouring market closely related to this market?

5.10. Describe the likely impact of the proposed concentration on competition in the affected markets and how the proposed concentration is likely to affect the interests of intermediate and ultimate consumers and the development of technical and economic progress.

Section 6 Details of the referral request and reasons why the case should be referred

6.1. Indicate whether the reasoned submission is made pursuant to Article 4(4) or 4(5) of the EC Merger Regulation, and fill in only the relevant sub-section:
  – Article 4.4. referral
  – Article 4.5 referral

Sub-section 6.2

Article 4(4) Referral

6.2.1. Identify the Member State/s and EFTA State/s which, pursuant to Article 4(4) of the EC Merger Regulation, you submit should examine the concentration, indicating whether or not you have made informal contact with this Member State/s and/or EFTA State/s.

6.2.2. Specify whether you are requesting referral of the whole or part of the case.

If you are requesting referral of part of the case, specify clearly the part or parts of the case for which you request the referral.

If you are requesting referral of the whole of the case, you must confirm that there are no affected markets outside the territory of the Member State/s and EFTA State/s to which you request the referral to be made.

6.2.3. Explain in what way each of the affected markets in the Member State/s and EFTA State/s to which referral is requested presents all the characteristics of a distinct market within the meaning of Article 4(4) of the EC Merger Regulation.

6.2.4. Explain in what way competition may be significantly affected in each of the above-mentioned distinct markets within the meaning of Article 4(4).

6.2.5. In the event of a Member State/s and/or EFTA State/s becoming competent to review the whole or part of the case following a referral pursuant to Article 4(4) of the EC Merger Regulation, do you consent to the information contained in this Form being relied upon by the Member State/s and/ or EFTA State/s in question for the purpose of its/their national proceedings relating to that case or part thereof? YES or NO.

Sub-section 6.3

Article 4(5) Referral

6.3.1. For each Member State and/or EFTA State, specify whether the concentration is or is not capable of being reviewed under its national competition law. You must tick one box for each and every Member State and/or EFTA State.

Is the concentration capable of being reviewed under the national competition law of each of the following Member States and/or EFTA States? You must reply for each Member State and/or EFTA State. Only indicate YES or NO for each Member State and/or EFTA State. Failure to indicate YES or NO for any Member State and/or EFTA State shall be deemed to constitute an indication of YES for that Member State and/or EFTA State.

Belgium:	YES	NO
Bulgaria:	YES	NO
Czech Republic:	YES	NO
Denmark:	YES	NO
Germany:	YES	NO
Estonia:	YES	NO
Ireland:	YES	NO
Greece:	YES	NO
Spain:	YES	NO
France:	YES	NO
Italy:	YES	NO
Cyprus:	YES	NO
Latvia:	YES	NO
Lithuania:	YES	NO
Luxembourg:	YES	NO
Hungary:	YES	NO
Malta:	YES	NO
Netherlands:	YES	NO
Austria:	YES	NO
Poland:	YES	NO
Portugal:	YES	NO
Romania:	YES	NO
Slovenia:	YES	NO
Slovakia:	YES	NO
Finland:	YES	NO
Sweden:	YES	NO
United Kingdom:	YES	NO
Iceland:	YES	NO
Norway:	YES	NO
Liechtenstein:	YES	NO

6.3.2. For each Member State and/or EFTA State, provide sufficient financial or other data to show that the concentration meets or does not meet the relevant jurisdictional criteria under the applicable national law.

6.3.3. Explain why the case should be examined by the Commission. Explain in particular whether the concentration might affect competition beyond the territory of one Member State and/or EFTA State.

Section 7 Declaration

It follows from Articles 2(2) and 6(2) of the EC Merger Implementing Regulation that where reasoned submissions are signed by representatives of undertakings, such representatives must produce written proof that they are authorized to act. Such written authorization must accompany the submission.

The reasoned submission must conclude with the following declaration which is to be signed by or on behalf of all the submitting parties:

The submitting party or parties declare that, following careful verification, the information given in this reasoned submission is to the best of their knowledge and belief true, correct, and complete, that true and complete copies of documents required by Form RS, have been supplied, and that all estimates are identified as such and are their best estimates of the underlying facts and that all the opinions expressed are sincere.

They are aware of the provisions of Article 14(1)(a) of the EC Merger Regulation.

Place and date:

Signatures:

Name/s and positions:

On behalf of:

Annex IV

Form RM relating to the information concerning commitments submitted pursuant to Article 6(2) and Article 8(2) of Regulation (EC) No 139/2004

Form RM relating to remedies

Introduction

This form specifies the information and documents to be submitted by the undertakings concerned at the same time as offering commitments pursuant to Article 6(2) or Article 8(2) of Regulation (EC) No 139/2004. The information requested is necessary to allow the Commission to examine whether the commitments are capable of rendering the concentration compatible with the common market in that they will prevent a significant impediment to effective competition. The Commission may dispense with the obligation to provide any particular information in respect of the commitments offered, including documents, or with any other requirement laid down in this form where it considers that compliance with those obligations or requirements is not necessary for the examination of the commitments offered. The level of information required will vary according to the type and structure of the remedy proposed. For example, carve-out remedies will typically require more detailed information than divestitures of stand-alone businesses. The Commission is available to discuss the scope of the information required with the parties upfront. If you consider that any particular information requested by this Form may not be necessary for the Commission's assessment, you may approach the Commission asking to dispense with certain requirements, giving adequate reasons why that information is not relevant.

Section 1

Description of the commitment

1.1. Provide detailed information on
   (i)   the object of the commitments offered, and
   (ii) the conditions for their implementation.

1.2.   Where the commitments offered consist in the divestiture of a business, Section 5 provides for the specific information required.

Section 2

Suitability to remove competition concerns

2. Provide information showing the suitability of the commitments offered to remove the significant impediment of effective competition identified by the Commission.

Section 3

Deviation from Model Texts

3. Identify any deviations of the commitments offered from the pertinent Model Commitments texts published by the Commission's services, as revised from time-to-time, and explain the reasons for the deviations.

Section 4

Summary of the commitments

4. Provide a non-confidential summary of the nature and scope of the commitments offered and why, in your view, they are suitable to remove any significant impediment to effective competition. The Commission may use this summary for the market test of the commitments offered with third parties.

Section 5

Information on a business to be divested

5. Where the commitments offered consist in the divestiture of a business, provide the following information and documents.

General information on the business to be divested

The following information should be provided as to the current operation of the business to be divested and changes already planned for the future:

5.1. Describe the business to be divested generally, including the entities belonging to it, their registered place of business and place of management, other locations for production or provisions of services, the general organisational structure and any other relevant information relating to the administrative structure of the business to be divested.

5.2. State whether there are and describe any legal obstacles for the transfer of the business to be divested or the assets, including third party rights and administrative approvals required.

5.3. List and describe the products manufactured or services provided, in particular their technical and other characteristics, the brands involved, the turnover generated with each of these products or services, and any innovations or new products or services planned.

5.4. Describe the level on which the essential functions of the business to be divested are operated if they are not operated on the level of the business to be divested itself, including such functions as research and development, production, marketing and sales, logistics, relations with customers, relations with suppliers, IT systems, etc. The description should contain the role performed by those other levels, the relations with the business to be divested and the resources (personnel, assets, financial resources, etc.) involved in the function.

5.5. Describe in detail the links between the business to be divested and other undertakings controlled by the notifying parties (irrespective of the direction of the link), such as:

— supply, production, distribution, service or other contracts,
— shared tangible or intangible assets,
— shared or seconded personnel,
— shared IT systems or other systems, and
— shared customers.

5.6. Describe in general terms all relevant tangible and intangible assets used and/or owned by the business to be divested, including, in any case, IP rights and brands.

5.7. Submit an organisational chart identifying the number of personnel currently working in each of the functions of the business to be divested and a list of those employees who are indispensable for the operation of the business to be divested, describing their functions.

5.8. Describe the customers of the business to be divested, including a list of customers, a description of the corresponding records available, and provide the total turnover generated by the business to be divested with each of these customers (in EUR and as percentage of the total turnover of business to be divested).

5.9. Provide financial data for the business to be divested, including the turnover and the EBITDA achieved in the last two years, and the forecast for the next two years.

5.10. Identify and describe any changes that have occurred in the last two years, in the organisation of the business to be divested or in the links with other undertakings controlled by the notifying parties.

5.11. Identify and describe any changes, planned for the next two years, in the organisation of the business to be divested or in the links with other undertakings controlled by the notifying parties.

General information on the business to be divested as described in the commitments

5.12. Describe any areas where the business to be divested as set out in the commitments offered differs from the nature and scope of the business as currently operated.

Acquisition by a suitable purchaser

5.13. Explain the reasons why, in your view, the business will be acquired by a suitable purchaser in the time-frame proposed in the commitments offered.

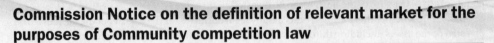

Part IV

EU Commission Notices[*]

Commission Notice on the definition of relevant market for the purposes of Community competition law

(OJ 1997, No. C372/5)

(text with EEA relevance)

I INTRODUCTION

1. The purpose of this notice is to provide guidance as to how the Commission applies the concept of relevant product and geographic market in its ongoing enforcement of Community competition law, in particular the application of Council Regulation No 17 and (EEC) No 4064/89, their equivalents in other sectoral applications such as transport, coal and steel, and agriculture, and the relevant provisions of the EEA Agreement. Throughout this notice, references to Articles 85 and 86 of the Treaty and to merger control are to be understood as referring to the equivalent provisions in the EEA Agreement and the ECSC Treaty.

2. Market definition is a tool to identify and define the boundaries of competition between firms. It serves to establish the framework within which competition policy is applied by the Commission. The main purpose of market definition is to identify in a systematic way the competitive constraints that the undertakings involved face. The objective of defining a market in both its product and geographic dimension is to identify those actual competitors of the undertakings involved that are capable of constraining those undertakings' behaviour and of preventing them from behaving independently of effective competitive pressure. It is from this perspective that the market definition makes it possible *inter alia* to calculate market shares that would convey meaningful information regarding market power for the purposes of assessing dominance or for the purposes of applying Article 85.

3. It follows from point 2 that the concept of 'relevant market' is different from other definitions of market often used in other contexts. For instance, companies often use the term 'market' to refer to the area where it sells its products or to refer broadly to the industry or sector where it belongs.

4. The definition of the relevant market in both its product and its geographic dimensions often has a decisive influence on the assessment of a competition case. By rendering public the procedures which the Commission follows when considering market definition and by indicating the criteria and evidence on which it relies to reach a decision, the Commission expects to increase the transparency of its policy and decision-making in the area of competition policy.

5. Increased transparency will also result in companies and their advisers being able to better anticipate the possibility that the Commission may raise competition concerns in an individual case. Companies could, therefore, take such a possibility into account in their own internal decision-making when contemplating, for instance, acquisitions, the creation of joint ventures, or the establishment of certain agreements. It is also intended that companies should be in a better position to understand what sort of information the Commission considers relevant for the purposes of market definition.

6. The Commission's interpretation of 'relevant market' is without prejudice to the interpretation which may be given by the Court of Justice or the Court of First Instance of the European Communities.

II DEFINITION OF RELEVANT MARKET

Definition of relevant product market and relevant geographic market

7. The Regulations based on Article 85 and 86 of the Treaty, in particular in section 6 of Form A/B with respect to Regulation No 17, as well as in section 6 of Form CO with respect to Regulation (EEC) No 4064/89 on the control of concentrations having a Community dimension have laid down the following definitions, 'Relevant product markets' are defined as follows:

'A relevant product market comprises all those products and/or services which are regarded as interchangeable or substitutable by the consumer, by reason of the products' characteristics, their prices and their intended use'.

8. 'Relevant geographic markets' are defined as follows:
'The relevant geographic market comprises the area in which the undertakings concerned are involved in the supply and demand of products or services, in which the conditions of competition are sufficiently homogeneous and which can be distinguished from neighbouring areas because the conditions of competition are appreciably different in those areas'.

9. The relevant market within which to assess a given competition issue is therefore established by the combination of the product and geographic markets. The Commission interprets the definitions in paragraphs 7 and 8 (which reflect the case-law of the Court of Justice and the Court of First Instance as well as its own decision-making practice) according to the orientations defined in this notice.

Concept of relevant market and objectives of Community competition policy

10. The concept of relevant market is closely related to the objectives pursued under Community competition policy. For example, under the Community's merger control, the objective in controlling structural changes in the supply of a product/service is to prevent the creation or reinforcement of a dominant position as a result of which effective competition would be significantly impeded in a substantial part of the common market. Under the Community's competition rules, a dominant position is such that a firm or group of firms would be in a position to behave to an appreciable extent independently of its competitors, customers and ultimately of its consumers. Such a position would usually arise when a firm or group of firms accounted for a large share of the supply in any given market, provided that other factors analysed in the assessment (such as entry barriers, customers' capacity to react, etc.) point in the same direction.

11. The same approach is followed by the Commission in its application of Article 86 of the Treaty to firms that enjoy a single or collective dominant position. Within the meaning of Regulation No 17, the Commission has the power to investigate and bring to an end abuses of such a dominant position, which must also be defined by reference to the relevant market. Markets may also need to be defined in the application of Article 85 of the Treaty in particular, in determining whether an appreciable restriction of competition exists or in establishing if the condition pursuant to Article 85(3)(b) for an exemption from the application of Article 85(1) is met.

12. The criteria for defining the relevant market are applied generally for the analysis of certain types of behaviour in the market and for the analysis of structural changes in the supply of products. This methodology, though, might lead to different results depending on the nature of the competition

issue being examined. For instance, the scope of the geographic market might be different when analysing a concentration, where the analysis is essentially prospective, from an analysis of past behaviour. The different time horizon considered in each case might lead to the result that different geographic markets are defined for the same products depending on whether the Commission is examining a change in the structure of supply, such as a concentration or a cooperative joint venture, or examining issues relating to certain past behaviour.

Basic principles for market definition

Competitive constraints

13. Firms are subject to three main sources or competitive constraints: demand substitutability, supply substitutability and potential competition. From an economic point of view, for the definition of the relevant market, demand substitution constitutes the most immediate and effective disciplinary force on the suppliers of a given product, in particular in relation to their pricing decisions. A firm or a group of firms cannot have a significant impact on the prevailing conditions of sale, such as prices, if its customers are in a position to switch easily to available substitute products or to suppliers located elsewhere. Basically, the exercise of market definition consists in identifying the effective alternative sources of supply for the customers of the undertakings involved, in terms both of products/services and of geographic location of suppliers.

14. The competitive constraints arising from supply side substitutability other then those described in paragraphs 20 to 23 and from potential competition are in general less immediate and in any case require an analysis of additional factors. As a result such constraints are taken into account at the assessment stage of competition analysis.

Demand substitution

15. The assessment of demand substitution entails a determination of the range of products which are viewed as substitutes by the consumer. One way of making this determination can be viewed as a speculative experiment, postulating a hypothetical small, lasting change in relative prices and evaluating the likely reactions of customers to that increase. The exercise of market definition focuses on prices for operational and practical purposes, and more precisely on demand substitution arising from small, permanent changes in relative prices. This concept can provide clear indications as to the evidence that is relevant in defining markets.

16. Conceptually, this approach means that, starting from the type of products that the undertakings involved sell and the area in which they sell them, additional products and areas will be included in, or excluded from, the market definition depending on whether competition from these other products and areas affect or restrain sufficiently the pricing of the parties' products in the short term.

17. The question to be answered is whether the parties' customers would switch to readily available substitutes or to suppliers located elsewhere in response to a hypothetical small (in the range 5% to 10%) but permanent relative price increase in the products and areas being considered. If substitution were enough to make the price increase unprofitable because of the resulting loss of sales, additional substitutes and areas are included in the relevant market. This would be done until the set of products and geographical areas is such that small, permanent increases in relative prices would be profitable. The equivalent analysis is applicable in cases concerning the concentration of buying power, where the starting point would then be the supplier and the price test serves to identify the alternative distribution channels or outlets for the supplier's products. In the application of these principles, careful account should be taken of certain particular situations as described within paragraphs 56 and 58.

18. A practical example of this test can be provided by its application to a merger of, for instance, soft-drink bottlers. An issue to examine in such a case would be to decide whether different flavours of soft drinks belong to the same market. In practice, the question to address would be whether consumers of flavour A would switch to other flavours when confronted with a permanent price increase of 5% to 10% for flavour A. If a sufficient number of consumers would switch to, say, flavour B, to such an extent that the price increase for flavour A would not be profitable

owing to the resulting loss of sales, then the market would comprise at least flavours A and B. The process would have to be extended in addition to other available flavours until a set of products is identified for which a price rise would not induce a sufficient substitution in demand.

19. Generally, and in particular for the analysis of merger cases, the price to take into account will be the prevailing market price. This may not be the case where the prevailing price has been determined in the absence of sufficient competition. In particular for the investigation of abuses of dominant positions, the fact that the prevailing price might already have been substantially increased will be taken into account.

Supply substitution

20. Supply-side substitutability may also be taken into account when defining markets in those situations in which its effects are equivalent to those of demand substitution in terms of effectiveness and immediacy. This means that suppliers are able to switch production to the relevant products and market them in the short termwithout incurring significant additional costs or risks in response to small and permanent changes in relative prices. When these conditions are met, the additional production that is put on the market will have a disciplinary effect on the competitive behaviour of the companies involved. Such an impact in terms of effectiveness and immediacy is equivalent to the demand substitution effect.

21. These situations typically arise when companies market a wide range of qualities or grades of one product; even if, for a given final customer or group of consumers, the different qualities are not substitutable, the different qualities will be grouped into one product market, provided that most of the suppliers are able to offer and sell the various qualities immediately and without the signifi-cant increases in costs described above. In such cases, the relevant product market will encompass all products that are substitutable in demand and supply, and the current sales of those products will be aggregated so as to give the total value or volume of the market. The same reasoning may lead to group different geographic areas.

22. A practical example of the approach to supply-side substitutability when defining product markets is to be found in the case of paper. Paper is usually supplied in a range of different qualities, from standard writing paper to high quality papers to be used, for instance, to publish art books. From a demand point of view, different qualities of paper cannot be used for any given use, i.e. an art book or a high quality publication cannot be based on lower quality papers. However, paper plants are prepared to manufacture the different qualities, and production can be adjusted with negligible costs and in a short time-frame. In the absence of particular difficulties in distribution, paper manufacturers are able there-fore, to compete for orders of the various qualities, in particular if orders are placed with sufficient lead time to allow for modification of production plans. Under such circumstances, the Commission would not define a separate market for each quality of paper and its respective use. The various qualities of paper are included in the relevant market, and their sales added up to estimate total market value and volume.

23. When supply-side substitutability would entail the need to adjust significantly exist-ing tangible and intangible assets, additional investments, strategic decisions or time delays, it will not be considered at the stage of market definition. Examples where supply-side substitution did not induce the Commission to enlarge the market are offered in the area of consumer prod-ucts, in particular for branded beverages. Although bottling plants may in principle bottle different beverages, there are costs and lead times involved (in terms of advertising, product testing and dis-tribution) before the products can actually be sold. In these cases, the effects of supply-side substitut-ability and other forms of potential competition would then be examined at a later stage.

Potential competition

24. The third source of competitive constraint, potential competition, is not taken into account when defining markets, since the conditions under which potential competition will actually represent an effective competitive constraint depend on the analysis of specific factors and circumstances related to the conditions of entry. If required, this analysis is only carried out at a subsequent stage, in general once the position of the companies involved in the relevant market has already been ascertained, and when such position gives rise to concerns from a competition point of view.

III EVIDENCE RELIED ON TO DEFINE RELEVANT MARKETS

The process of defining the relevant market in practice

Product dimension

25. There is a range of evidence permitting an assessment of the extent to which substitution would take place. In individual cases, certain types of evidence will be determinant, depending very much on the characteristics and specificity of the industry and products or services that are being examined. The same type of evidence may be of no importance in other cases. In most cases, a decision will have to be based on the consideration of a number of criteria and different items of evidence. The Commission follows an open approach to empirical evidence, aimed at making an effective use of all available information which may be relevant in individual cases. The Commission does not follow a rigid hierarchy of different sources of information or types of evidence.

26. The process of defining relevant markets may be summarized as follows: on the basis of the preliminary information available or information submitted by the undertakings involved, the Commission will usually be in a position to broadly establish the possible relevant markets within which, for instance, a concentration or a restriction of competition has to be assessed. In general, and for all practical purposes when handling individual cases, the question will usually be to decide on a few alternative possible relevant markets. For instance, with respect to the product market, the issue will often be to establish whether product A and product B belong or do not belong to the same product market. It is often the case that the inclusion of product B would be enough to remove any competition concerns.

27. In such situations it is not necessary to consider whether the market includes additional products, or to reach a definitive conclusion on the precise product market. If under the conceivable alternative market definitions the operation in question does not raise competition concerns, the question of market definition will be left open, reducing thereby the burden on companies to supply information.

Geographic dimension

28. The Commission's approach to geographic market definition might be summarized as follows: it will take a preliminary view of the scope of the geographic market on the basis of broad indications as to the distribution of market shares between the parties and their competitors, as well as a preliminary analysis of pricing and price differences at national and Community or EEA level. This initial view is used basically as a working hypothesis to focus the Commission's enquiries for the purposes of arriving at a precise geographic market definition.

29. The reasons behind any particular configuration of prices and market shares need to be explored. Companies might enjoy high market shares in their domestic markets just because of the weight of the past, and conversely, a homogeneous presence of companies throughout the EEA might be consistent with national or regional geographic markets. The initial working hypothesis will therefore be checked against an analysis of demand characteristics (importance of national or local preferences, current patterns of purchases of customers, product differentiation/brands, other) in order to establish whether companies in different areas do indeed constitute a real alternative source of supply for consumers. The theoretical experiment is again based on substitution arising from changes in relative prices, and the question to answer is again whether the customers of the parties would switch their orders to companies located elsewhere in the short term and at a negligible cost.

30. If necessary, a further check on supply factors will be carried out to ensure that those companies located in differing areas do not face impediments in developing their sales on competitive terms throughout the whole geographic market. This analysis will include an examination of requirements for a local presence in order to sell in that area the conditions of access to distribution channels, costs associated with setting up a distribution network, and the presence or absence of regulatory

barriers arising from public procurement, price regulations, quotas and tariffs limiting trade or production, technical standards, monopolies, freedom of establishment, requirements for administrative
authorizations, packaging regulations, etc. In short, the Commission will identify possible obstacles
and barriers isolating companies located in a given area from the competitive pressure of companies
located outside that area, so as to determine the precise degree of market interpenetration at national,
European or global level.

31. The actual pattern and evolution of trade flows offers useful supplementary indications as to
the economic importance of each demand or supply factor mentioned above, and the extent to which
they may or may not constitute actual barriers creating different geographic markets. The analysis of
trade flows will generally address the question of transport costs and the extent to which these may
hinder trade between different areas, having regard to plant location, costs of production and relative
price levels.

Market integration in the Community

32. Finally, the Commission also takes into account the continuing process of market integration, in particular in the Community, when defining geographic markets, especially in the area of
concentrations and structural joint ventures. The measures adopted and implemented in the internal
market programme to remove barriers to trade and further integrate the Community markets cannot
be ignored when assessing the effects on competition of a concentration or a structural joint venture. A situation where national markets have been artificially isolated from each other because of
the existence of legislative barriers that have now been removed will generally lead to a cautious
assessment of past evidence regarding prices, market shares or trade patterns. A process of market
integration that would, in the short term, lead to wider geographic markets may therefore be taken
into consideration when defining the geographic market for the purposes of assessing concentrations
and joint ventures.

The process of gathering evidence

33. When a precise market definition is deemed necessary; the Commission will often contact
the main customers and the main companies in the industry to enquire into their views about the
boundaries of product and geographic markets and to obtain the necessary factual evidence to reach
a conclusion. The Commission might also contact the relevant professional associations, and companies active in upstream markets, so as to be able to define, in so far as necessary, separate product
and geographic markets, for different levels of production or distribution of the products/ services in
question. It might also request additional information to the undertakings involved.

34. Where appropriate, the Commission will address written requests for information to the
market players mentioned above. These requests will usually include questions relating to the
perceptions of companies about reactions to hypothetical price increases and their views of
the boundaries of the relevant market. They will also ask for provision of the factual information
the Commission deems necessary to reach a conclusion on the extent of the relevant market. The
Commission might also discuss with marketing directors or other officers of those companies to
gain a better understanding on how negotiations between suppliers and customers take place and
better understand issues relating to the definition of the relevant market. Where appropriate, they
might also carry out visits or inspections to the premises of the parties, their customers and/or their
competitors, in order to better understand how products are manufactured and sold.

35. The type of evidence relevant to reach a conclusion as to the product market can be categorized as follows:

Evidence to define markets—product dimension

36. An analysis of the product characteristics and its intended use allows the Commission, as a
first step, to limit the field of investigation of possible substitutes. However, product characteristics
and intended use are insufficient to show whether two products are demand substitutes. Functional
interchangeability or similarity in characteristics may not, in themselves, provide sufficient criteria,
because the responsiveness of customers to relative price changes may be determined by other
considerations as well. For example, there may be different competitive constraints in the original

equipment market for car components and in spare parts, thereby leading to a separate delineation of two relevant markets. Conversely, differences in product characteristics are not in themselves sufficient to exclude demand substitutability, since this will depend to a large extent on how customers value different characteristics.

37. The type of evidence the Commission considers relevant to assess whether two products are demand substitutes can be categorized as follows:

38. *Evidence of substitution in the recent past.* In certain cases, it is possible to analyse evidence relating to recent past events or shocks in the market that offer actual examples of substitution between two products. When available, this sort of information will normally be fundamental for market definition. If there have been changes in relative prices in the past (all else being equal), the reactions in terms of quantities demanded will be determinant in establishing substitutability. Launches of new products in the past can also offer useful information, when it is possible to precisely analyse which products have lost sales to the new product.

39. There are a number of *quantitative tests* that have specifically been designed for the purpose of delineating markets. These tests consist of various econometric and statistical approaches estimates of elasticities and cross-price elasticities for the demand of a product, tests based on similarity of price movements over time, the analysis of causality between price series and similarity of price levels and/or their convergence. The Commission takes into account the available quantitative evidence capable of withstanding rigorous scrutiny for the purposes of establishing patterns of substitution in the past.

40. *Views of customers and competitors.* The Commission often contacts the main customers and competitors of the companies involved in its enquiries, to gather their views on the boundaries of the product market as well as most of the factual information it requires to reach a conclusion on the scope of the market. Reasoned answers of customers and competitors as to what would happen if relative prices for the candidate products were to increase in the candidate geographic area by a small amount (for instance of 5% to 10%) are taken into account when they are sufficiently backed by factual evidence.

41. *Consumer preferences.* In the case of consumer goods, it may be difficult for the Commission to gather the direct views of end consumers about substitute products. *Marketing studies* that companies have commissioned in the past and that are used by companies in their own decision-making as to pricing of their products and/or marketing actions may provide useful information for the Commission's delineation of the relevant market. Consumer surveys on usage patterns and attitudes, data from consumer's purchasing patterns, the views expressed by retailers and more generally, market research studies submitted by the parties and their competitors are taken into account to establish whether an economically significant proportion of consumers consider two products as substitutable, also taking into account the importance of brands for the products in question. The methodology followed in consumer surveys carried out *ad hoc* by the undertakings involved or their competitors for the purposes of a merger procedure or a procedure pursuant to Regulation No 17 will usually be scrutinized with utmost care. Unlike pre-existing studies, they have not been prepared in the normal course of business for the adoption of business decisions.

42. *Barriers and costs associated with switching demand to potential substitutes.* There are a number of barriers and costs that might prevent the Commission from considering two *prima facie* demand substitutes as belonging to one single product market. It is not possible to provide an exhaustive list of all the possible barriers to substitution and of switching costs. These barriers or obstacles might have a wide range of origins, and in its decisions, the Commission has been confronted with regulatory barriers or other forms of State intervention, constraints arising in downstream markets, need to incur specific capital investment or loss in current output in order to switch to alternative inputs, the location of customers, specific investment in production process, learning and human capital investment, retooling costs or other investments, uncertainty about quality and reputation of unknown suppliers, and others.

43. *Different categories of customers and price discrimination.* The extent of the product market might be narrowed in the presence of distinct groups of customers. A distinct group of customers

for the relevant product may constitute a narrower, distinct market when such a group could be subject to price discrimination. This will usually be the case when two conditions are met: (a) it is possible to identify clearly which group an individual customer belongs to at the moment of selling the relevant products to him, and (b) trade among customers or arbitrage by third parties should not be feasible.

Evidence for defining markets—geographic dimension

44. The type of evidence the Commission considers relevant to reach a conclusion as to the geographic market can be categorized as follows:

45. *Past evidence of diversion of orders to other areas.* In certain cases, evidence on changes in prices between different areas and consequent reactions by customers might be available. Generally, the same quantitative tests used for product market definition might as well be used in geographic market definition, bearing in mind that international comparisons of prices might be more complex due to a number of factors such as exchange rate movements, taxation and product differentiation.

46. Basic *demand characteristics.* The nature of demand for the relevant product may in itself determine the scope of the geographical market. Factors such as national preferences or preferences for national brands, language, culture and life style, and the need for a local presence have a strong potential to limit the geographic scope of competition.

47. *Views of customers and competitors.* Where appropriate, the Commission will contact the main customers and competitors of the parties in its enquiries, to gather their views on the boundaries of the geographic market as well as most of the factual information it requires to reach a conclusion on the scope of the market when they are sufficiently backed by factual evidence.

48. *Current geographic pattern of purchases.* An examination of the customers' current geographic pattern of purchases provides useful evidence as to the possible scope of the geographic market. When customers purchase from companies located anywhere in the Community or the EEA on similar terms, or they procure their supplies through effective tendering procedures in which companies from anywhere in the Community or the EEA submit bids, usually the geographic market will be considered to be Community-wide.

49. *Trade flows/pattern of shipments.* When the number of customers is so large that it is not possible to obtain through them a clear picture of geographic purchasing patterns, information on trade flows might be used alternatively, provided that the trade statistics are available with a sufficient degree of detail for the relevant products. Trade flows, and above all, the rationale behind trade flows provide useful insights and information for the purpose of establishing the scope of the geographic market but are not in themselves conclusive.

50. *Barriers and switching costs associated to divert orders to companies located in other areas.* The absence of trans-border purchases or trade flows, for instance, does not necessarily mean that the market is at most national in scope. Still, barriers isolating the national market have to identified before it is concluded that the relevant geographic market in such a case is national. Perhaps the clearest obstacle for a customer to divert its orders to other areas is the impact of transport costs and transport restrictions arising from legislation or from the nature of the relevant products. The impact of transport costs will usually limit the scope of the geographic market for bulky, low-value products, bearing in mind that a transport disadvantage might also be compensated by a comparative advantage in other costs (labour costs or raw materials). Access to distribution in a given area, regulatory barriers still existing in certain sectors, quotas and custom tariffs might also constitute barriers isolating a geographic area from the competitive pressure of companies located outside that area. Significant switching costs in procuring supplies from companies located in other countries constitute additional sources of such barriers.

51. On the basis of the evidence gathered, the Commission will then define a geographic market that could range from a local dimension to a global one, and there are examples of both local and global markets in past decisions of the Commission.

52. The paragraphs above describe the different factors which might be relevant to define markets. This does not imply that in each individual case it will be necessary to obtain evidence and assess each of these factors. Often in practice the evidence provided by a subset of these factors will be sufficient to reach a conclusion, as shown in the past decisional practice of the Commission.

IV CALCULATION OF MARKET SHARE

53. The definition of the relevant market in both its product and geographic dimensions allows the identification of the suppliers and the customers/consumers active on that market. On that basis, a total market size and market shares for each supplier can be calculated on the basis of their sales of the relevant products in the relevant area. In practice, the total market size and market shares are often available from market sources, i.e. companies' estimates, studies commissioned from industry consultants and/or trade associations. When this is not the case, or when available estimates are not reliable, the Commission will usually ask each supplier in the relevant market to provide its own sales in order to calculate total market size and market shares.

54. If sales are usually the reference to calculate market shares, there are nevertheless other indications that, depending on the specific products or industry in question, can offer useful information such as, in particular, capacity, the number of players in bidding markets, units of fleet as in aerospace, or the reserves held in the case of sectors such as mining.

55. As a rule of thumb, both volume sales and value sales provide useful information. In cases of differentiated products, sales in value and their associated market share will usually be considered to better reflect the relative position and strength of each supplier.

V ADDITIONAL CONSIDERATIONS

56. There are certain areas where the application of the principles above has to be undertaken with care. This is the case when considering primary and secondary markets, in particular, when the behaviour of undertakings at a point in time has to be analysed pursuant to Article 86. The method of defining markets in these cases is the same, i.e. assessing the responses of customers based on their purchasing decisions to relative price changes, but taking into account as well, constraints on substitution imposed by conditions in the connected markets. A narrow definition of market for secondary products, for instance, spare parts, may result when compatibility with the primary product is important. Problems of finding compatible secondary products together with the existence of high prices and a long lifetime of the primary products may render relative price increases of secondary products profitable. A different market definition may result if significant substitution between secondary products is possible or if the characteristics of the primary products make quick and direct consumer responses to relative price increases of the secondary products feasible.

57. In certain cases, the existence of chains of substitution might lead to the definition of a relevant market where products or areas at the extreme of the market are not directly substitutable. An example might be provided by the geographic dimension of a product with significant transport costs. In such cases, deliveries from a given plant are limited to a certain area around each plant by the impact of transport costs. In principle, such an area could constitute the relevant geographic market. However, if the distribution of plants is such that there are considerable overlaps between the areas around different plants, it is possible that the pricing of those products will be constrained by a chain substitution effect, and lead to the definition of a broader geographic market. The same reasoning may apply if product B is a demand substitute for products A and C. Even if products A and C are not direct demand substitutes, they might be found to be in the same relevant product market since their respective pricing might be constrained by substitution to B.

58. From a practical perspective, the concept of chains of substitution has to be corroborated by actual evidence, for instance related to price interdependence at the extremes of the chains of substitution, in order to lead to an extension of the relevant market in an individual case. Price levels at the extremes of the chains would have to be of the same magnitude as well.

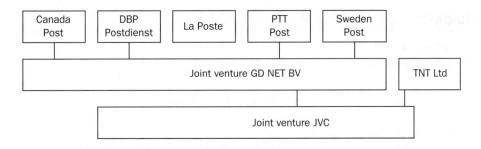

Merger scenario

Before merger

| Company A | | Company B |

After merger

| Merged company |
| Combined assets |

After Breaking up the merger

Company A:	Company B:
Divided assets of merged company	Divided assets of merged company
—some (initial) assets of A	—some (initial) assets of A
—some (initial) assets of B	—some (initial) assets of B
—some (subsequent) assets of the	—some (subsequent) assets of the
merged company	merged company

Joint venture scenario (JV)

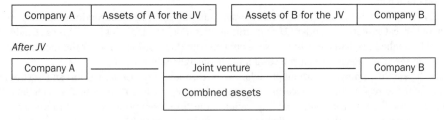

Before JV

| Company A | Assets of A for the JV | | Assets of B for the JV | Company B |

After JV

| Company A | — | Joint venture | — | Company B |
| | | Combined assets | | |

After breaking up the JV

Company A	Divided assets of joint	Divided assets of joint	Company B
	venture:	venture:	
	—some (initial) assets	—some (initial) assets	
	of A	of A	
	—some (initial) assets	—some (initial) assets	
	of B	of B	
	—some (subsequent)	—some (subsequent)	
	assets of the JV	assets of the JV	

Guidelines on Vertical Restraints 2010

(OJ 2010, No. C130/01)

(Text with EEA relevant)

I. INTRODUCTION

1   Purpose of the Guidelines

(1) These Guidelines set out the principles for the assessment of vertical agreements under Article 101 of the Treaty on the Functioning of the European Union (hereinafter 'Article 101'). Article 1(1)(a) of Commission Regulation (EU) No 330/2010 of 20 April 2010 on the application of Article 101(3) of the Treaty on the Functioning of the European Union to categories of vertical agreements and concerted practices (hereinafter referred to as the 'Block Exemption Regulation') (see paragraphs (24) to (46)) defines the term 'vertical agreement'. These Guidelines are without prejudice to the possible parallel application of Article 102 of the Treaty on the Functioning of the European Union (hereinafter 'Article 102') to vertical agreements. These Guidelines are structured in the following way:

- Section II (paragraphs (8) to (22)) describes vertical agreements which generally fall outside Article 101(1);
- Section III (paragraphs (23) to (73)) clarifies the conditions for the application of the Block Exemption Regulation;
- Section IV (paragraphs (74) to (85)) describes the principles concerning the withdrawal of the block exemption and the disapplication of the Block Exemption Regulation;
- Section V (paragraphs (86) to (95)) provides guidance on how to define the relevant market and calculate market shares;
- Section VI (paragraphs (96) to (229)) describes the general framework of analysis and the enforcement policy of the Commission in individual cases concerning vertical agreements.

(2) Throughout these Guidelines, the analysis applies to both goods and services, although certain vertical restraints are mainly used in the distribution of goods. Similarly, vertical agreements can be concluded for intermediate and final goods and services. Unless otherwise stated, the analysis and arguments in these Guidelines apply to all types of goods and services and to all levels of trade. Thus, the term 'products' includes both goods and services. The terms 'supplier' and 'buyer' are used for all levels of trade. The Block Exemption Regulation and these Guidelines do not apply to agreements with final consumers where the latter are not undertakings, since Article 101 only applies to agreements between undertakings.

(3) By issuing these Guidelines, the Commission aims to help companies conduct their own assessment of vertical agreements under EU competition rules. The standards set forth in these Guidelines cannot be applied mechanically, but must be applied with due consideration for the specific circumstances of each case. Each case must be evaluated in the light of its own facts.

(4) These Guidelines are without prejudice to the case-law of the General Court and the Court of Justice of the European Union concerning the application of Article 101 to vertical agreements. The Commission will continue to monitor the operation of the Block Exemption Regulation and Guidelines based on market information from stakeholders and national competition authorities and may revise this notice in the light of future developments and of evolving insight.

2   Applicability of Article 101 to vertical agreements

(5) Article 101 applies to vertical agreements that may affect trade between Member States and that prevent, restrict or distort competition ('vertical restraints'). Article 101 provides a legal framework for the assessment of vertical restraints, which takes into consideration the distinction between anti-competitive and pro-competitive effects. Article 101(1) prohibits those agreements which appreciably restrict or distort competition, while Article 101(3) exempts those agreements which confer sufficient benefits to outweigh the anti-competitive effects.

(6) For most vertical restraints, competition concerns can only arise if there is insufficient competition at one or more levels of trade, that is, if there is some degree of market power at the level of the supplier or the buyer or at both levels. Vertical restraints are generally less harmful than horizontal restraints and may provide substantial scope for efficiencies.

(7) The objective of Article 101 is to ensure that undertakings do not use agreements – in this context, vertical agreements – to restrict competition on the market to the detriment of consumers. Assessing vertical restraints is also important in the context of the wider objective of achieving an integrated internal market. Market integration enhances competition in the European Union. Companies should not be allowed to re-establish private barriers between Member States where State barriers have been successfully abolished.

II. VERTICAL AGREEMENTS WHICH GENERALLY FALL OUTSIDE THE SCOPE OF ARTICLE 101(1)

1   Agreements of minor importance and SMEs

(8) Agreements that are not capable of appreciably affecting trade between Member States or of appreciably restricting competition by object or effect do not fall within the scope of Article 101(1). The Block Exemption Regulation applies only to agreements falling within the scope of application of Article 101(1). These Guidelines are without prejudice to the application of Commission Notice on agreements of minor importance which do not appreciably restrict competition under Article 81(1) of the Treaty establishing the European Community (de minimis) or any future de minimis notice.

(9) Subject to the conditions set out in the de minimis notice concerning hardcore restrictions and cumulative effect issues, vertical agreements entered into by non-competing undertakings whose individual market share on the relevant market does not exceed 15 % are generally considered to fall outside the scope of Article 101(1). There is no presumption that vertical agreements concluded by undertakings having more than 15 % market share automatically infringe Article 101(1). Agreements between undertakings whose market share exceeds the 15 % threshold may still not have an appreciable effect on trade between Member States or may not constitute an appreciable restriction of competition. Such agreements need to be assessed in their legal and economic context. The criteria for the assessment of individual agreements are set out in paragraphs (96) to (229).

(10) As regards hardcore restrictions referred to in the de minimis notice, Article 101(1) may apply below the 15 % threshold, provided that there is an appreciable effect on trade between Member States and on competition. The applicable case-law of the Court of Justice and the General Court is relevant in this respect. Reference is also made to the possible need to assess positive and negative effects of hardcore restrictions as described in particular in paragraph (47) of these Guidelines.

(11) In addition, the Commission considers that, subject to cumulative effect and hardcore restrictions, vertical agreements between small and medium-sized undertakings as defined in the Annex to Commission Recommendation of 6 May 2003 concerning the definition of micro, small and medium-sized enterprises are rarely capable of appreciably affecting trade between Member States or of appreciably restricting competition within the meaning of Article 101(1), and therefore generally fall outside the scope of Article 101(1). In cases where such agreements nonetheless meet the conditions for the application of Article 101(1), the Commission will normally refrain from opening proceedings for lack of sufficient interest for the European Union unless those undertakings collectively or individually hold a dominant position in a substantial part of the internal market.

2   Agency agreements

2.1   *Definition of agency agreements*

(12) An agent is a legal or physical person vested with the power to negotiate and/or conclude contracts on behalf of another person (the principal), either in the agent's own name or in the name of the principal, for the:

- purchase of goods or services by the principal, or
- sale of goods or services supplied by the principal.

(13) The determining factor in defining an agency agreement for the application of Article 101(1) is the financial or commercial risk borne by the agent in relation to the activities for which it has been appointed as an agent by the principal. In this respect it is not material for the assessment whether the agent acts for one or several principals. Neither is material for this assessment the qualification given to their agreement by the parties or national legislation.

(14) There are three types of financial or commercial risk that are material to the definition of an agency agreement for the application of Article 101(1). First, there are the contract-specific risks which are directly related to the contracts concluded and/or negotiated by the agent on behalf of the principal, such as financing of stocks. Secondly, there are the risks related to market-specific investments. These are investments specifically required for the type of activity for which the agent has been appointed by the principal, that is, which are required to enable the agent to conclude and/or negotiate this type of contract. Such investments are usually sunk, which means that upon leaving that particular field of activity the investment cannot be used for other activities or sold other than at a significant loss. Thirdly, there are the risks related to other activities undertaken on the same product market, to the extent that the principal requires the agent to undertake such activities, but not as an agent on behalf of the principal but for its own risk.

(15) For the purposes of applying Article 101(1), the agreement will be qualified as an agency agreement if the agent does not bear any, or bears only insignificant, risks in relation to the contracts concluded and/or negotiated on behalf of the principal, in relation to market-specific investments for that field of activity, and in relation to other activities required by the principal to be undertaken on the same product market. However, risks that are related to the activity of providing agency services in general, such as the risk of the agent's income being dependent upon its success as an agent or general investments in for instance premises or personnel, are not material to this assessment.

(16) For the purpose of applying Article 101(1), an agreement will thus generally be considered an agency agreement where property in the contract goods bought or sold does not vest in the agent, or the agent does not himself supply the contract services and where the agent:

(a) does not contribute to the costs relating to the supply/purchase of the contract goods or services, including the costs of transporting the goods. This does not preclude the agent from carrying out the transport service, provided that the costs are covered by the principal;

(b) does not maintain at its own cost or risk stocks of the contract goods, including the costs of financing the stocks and the costs of loss of stocks and can return unsold goods to the principal without charge, unless the agent is liable for fault (for example, by failing to comply with reasonable security measures to avoid loss of stocks);

(c) does not undertake responsibility towards third parties for damage caused by the product sold (product liability), unless, as agent, it is liable for fault in this respect;

(d) does not take responsibility for customers' non-performance of the contract, with the exception of the loss of the agent's commission, unless the agent is liable for fault (for example, by failing to comply with reasonable security or anti-theft measures or failing to comply with reasonable measures to report theft to the principal or police or to communicate to the principal all necessary information available to him on the customer's financial reliability);

(e) is not, directly or indirectly, obliged to invest in sales promotion, such as contributions to the advertising budgets of the principal;

(f) does not make market-specific investments in equipment, premises or training of personnel, such as for example the petrol storage tank in the case of petrol retailing or specific software to sell insurance policies in case of insurance agents, unless these costs are fully reimbursed by the principal;

(g) does not undertake other activities within the same product market required by the principal, unless these activities are fully reimbursed by the principal.

(17) This list is not exhaustive. However, where the agent incurs one or more of the risks or costs mentioned in paragraphs (14), (15) and (16), the agreement between agent and principal will not be

qualified as an agency agreement. The question of risk must be assessed on a case-by-case basis, and with regard to the economic reality of the situation rather than the legal form. For practical reasons, the risk analysis may start with the assessment of the contract-specific risks. If contract-specific risks are incurred by the agent, it will be enough to conclude that the agent is an independent distributor. On the contrary, if the agent does not incur contract-specific risks, then it will be necessary to continue further the analysis by assessing the risks related to market-specific investments. Finally, if the agent does not incur any contract-specific risks and risks related to market-specific investments, the risks related to other required activities within the same product market may have to be considered.

2.2 The application of Article 101(1) to agency agreements

(18) In the case of agency agreements as defined in section 2.1, the selling or purchasing function of the agent forms part of the principal's activities. Since the principal bears the commercial and financial risks related to the selling and purchasing of the contract goods and services all obligations imposed on the agent in relation to the contracts concluded and/or negotiated on behalf of the principal fall outside Article 101(1). The following obligations on the agent's part will be considered to form an inherent part of an agency agreement, as each of them relates to the ability of the principal to fix the scope of activity of the agent in relation to the contract goods or services, which is essential if the principal is to take the risks and therefore to be in a position to determine the commercial strategy:

> (h) (a) limitations on the territory in which the agent may sell these goods or services;
> (i) (b) limitations on the customers to whom the agent may sell these goods or services;
> (j) (c) the prices and conditions at which the agent must sell or purchase these goods or services.

(19) In addition to governing the conditions of sale or purchase of the contract goods or services by the agent on behalf of the principal, agency agreements often contain provisions which concern the relationship between the agent and the principal. In particular, they may contain a provision preventing the principal from appointing other agents in respect of a given type of transaction, customer or territory (exclusive agency provisions) and/or a provision preventing the agent from acting as an agent or distributor of undertakings which compete with the principal (single branding provisions). Since the agent is a separate undertaking from the principal, the provisions which concern the relationship between the agent and the principal may infringe Article 101(1). Exclusive agency provisions will in general not lead to anti-competitive effects. However, single branding provisions and post-term non-compete provisions, which concern inter-brand competition, may infringe Article 101(1) if they lead to or contribute to a (cumulative) foreclosure effect on the relevant market where the contract goods or services are sold or purchased (see in particular Section VI.2.1). Such provisions may benefit from the Block Exemption Regulation, in particular when the conditions provided in Article 5 of that Regulation are fulfilled. They can also be individually justified by efficiencies under Article 101(3) as for instance described in paragraphs (144) to (148).

(20) An agency agreement may also fall within the scope of Article 101(1), even if the principal bears all the relevant financial and commercial risks, where it facilitates collusion. That could, for instance, be the case when a number of principals use the same agents while collectively excluding others from using these agents, or when they use the agents to collude on marketing strategy or to exchange sensitive market information between the principals.

(21) Where the agent bears one or more of the relevant risks as described in paragraph (16), the agreement between agent and principal does not constitute an agency agreement for the purpose of applying Article 101(1). In that situation, the agent will be treated as an independent undertaking and the agreement between agent and principal will be subject to Article 101(1) as any other vertical agreement.

3 Subcontracting agreements

(22) Subcontracting concerns a contractor providing technology or equipment to a subcontractor that undertakes to produce certain products on the basis thereof (exclusively) for the contractor. Subcontracting is covered by Commission notice of 18 December 1978 concerning the assessment

of certain subcontracting agreements in relation to Article 85(1) of the EEC Treaty (hereinafter 'subcontracting notice'). According to that notice, which remains applicable, subcontracting agreements whereby the subcontractor undertakes to produce certain products exclusively for the contractor generally fall outside the scope of Article 101(1) provided that the technology or equipment is necessary to enable the subcontractor to produce the products. However, other restrictions imposed on the subcontractor such as the obligation not to conduct or exploit its own research and development or not to produce for third parties in general may fall within the scope of Article 101.

III. APPLICATION OF THE BLOCK EXEMPTION REGULATION

1　Safe harbour created by the Block Exemption Regulation

(23) For most vertical restraints, competition concerns can only arise if there is insufficient competition at one or more levels of trade, that is, if there is some degree of market power at the level of the supplier or the buyer or at both levels. Provided that they do not contain hardcore restrictions of competition, which are restrictions of competition by object, the Block Exemption Regulation creates a presumption of legality for vertical agreements depending on the market share of the supplier and the buyer. Pursuant to Article 3 of the Block Exemption Regulation, it is the supplier's market share on the market where it sells the contract goods or services and the buyer's market share on the market where it purchases the contract goods or services which determine the applicability of the block exemption. In order for the block exemption to apply, the supplier's and the buyer's market share must each be 30 % or less. Section V of these Guidelines provides guidance on how to define the relevant market and calculate the market shares. Above the market share threshold of 30 %, there is no presumption that vertical agreements fall within the scope of Article 101(1) or fail to satisfy the conditions of Article 101(3) but there is also no presumption that vertical agreements falling within the scope of Article 101(1) will usually satisfy the conditions of Article 101(3).

2　Scope of the Block Exemption Regulation

2.1　Definition of vertical agreements

(24) Article 1(1)(a) of the Block Exemption Regulation defines a 'vertical agreement' as 'an agreement or concerted practice entered into between two or more undertakings each of which operates, for the purposes of the agreement or the concerted practice, at a different level of the production or distribution chain, and relating to the conditions under which the parties may purchase, sell or resell certain goods or services'.

(25) The definition of 'vertical agreement' referred to in paragraph (24) has four main elements:

    (a) The Block Exemption Regulation applies to agreements and concerted practices. The Block Exemption Regulation does not apply to unilateral conduct of the undertakings concerned. Such unilateral conduct can fall within the scope of Article 102 which prohibits abuses of a dominant position. For there to be an agreement within the meaning of Article 101 it is sufficient that the parties have expressed their joint intention to conduct themselves on the market in a specific way. The form in which that intention is expressed is irrelevant as long as it constitutes a faithful expression of the parties' intention. In case there is no explicit agreement expressing the concurrence of wills, the Commission will have to prove that the unilateral policy of one party receives the acquiescence of the other party. For vertical agreements, there are two ways in which acquiescence with a particular unilateral policy can be established. First, the acquiescence can be deduced from the powers conferred upon the parties in a general agreement drawn up in advance. If the clauses of the agreement drawn up in advance provide for or authorise a party to adopt subsequently a specific unilateral policy which will be binding on the other party, the acquiescence of that policy by the other party can be established on the basis thereof. Secondly, in the absence of such an explicit acquiescence, the Commission can show the existence of tacit acquiescence. For that it is necessary to show first that one party requires explicitly or implicitly the cooperation of the other party for the implementation of its unilateral policy and second that the other party complied with that requirement by implementing that unilateral policy in practice. For instance, if after a supplier's announcement of a unilateral reduction of supplies in order to prevent parallel trade, distributors reduce immediately their orders and stop engaging in parallel trade, then those distributors tacitly acquiesce to the supplier's unilateral policy. This can however not be concluded if the distributors continue to engage in parallel trade or entry to find new ways to engage in parallel trade. Similarly, for vertical agreements, tacit acquiescence may be deduced from the level of coercion exerted by a party to impose its unilateral policy on the other party or parties to the agreement in combination with the number of distributors that are actually implementing in practice the unilateral policy of the supplier. For instance, a system of monitoring and penalties, set up by a supplier to penalise those distributors that do not comply with its unilateral policy, points to tacit acquiescence with the supplier's unilateral policy if this system allows the supplier to implement in practice its policy. The two ways of establishing acquiescence described in this paragraph can be used jointly;

(b) The agreement or concerted practice is between two or more undertakings. Vertical agreements with final consumers not operating as an undertaking are not covered by the Block Exemption Regulation. More generally, agreements with final consumers do not fall under Article 101(1), as that article applies only to agreements between undertakings, decisions by associations of undertakings and concerted practices of undertakings. This is without prejudice to the possible application of Article 102;

(c) The agreement or concerted practice is between undertakings each operating, for the purposes of the agreement, at a different level of the production or distribution chain. This means for instance that one undertaking produces a raw material which the other undertaking uses as an input, or that the first is a manufacturer, the second a wholesaler and the third a retailer. This does not preclude an undertaking from being active at more than one level of the production or distribution chain;

(d) The agreements or concerted practices relate to the conditions under which the parties to the agreement, the supplier and the buyer, 'may purchase, sell or resell certain goods or services'. This reflects the purpose of the Block Exemption Regulation to cover purchase and distribution agreements. These are agreements which concern the conditions for the purchase, sale or resale of the goods or services supplied by the supplier and/or which concern the conditions for the sale by the buyer of the goods or services which incorporate these goods or services. Both the goods or services supplied by the supplier and the resulting goods or services are considered to be contract goods or services under the Block Exemption Regulation. Vertical agreements relating to all final and intermediate goods and services are covered. The only exception is the automobile sector, as long as this sector remains covered by a specific block exemption such as that granted by Commission Regulation (EC) No 1400/2002 of 31 July 2002 on the application of Article 81(3) of the Treaty to categories of vertical agreements and concerted practices in the motor vehicle sector or its successor. The goods or services provided by the supplier may be resold by the buyer or may be used as an input by the buyer to produce its own goods or services.

(26) The Block Exemption Regulation also applies to goods sold and purchased for renting to third parties. However, rent and lease agreements as such are not covered, as no good or service is sold by the supplier to the buyer. More generally, the Block Exemption Regulation does not cover restrictions or obligations that do not relate to the conditions of purchase, sale and resale, such as an obligation preventing parties from carrying out independent research and development which the parties may have included in an otherwise vertical agreement. In addition, Article 2(2) to (5) of the Block Exemption Regulation directly or indirectly excludes certain vertical agreements from the application of that Regulation.

2.2   *Vertical agreements between competitors*

(27) Article 2(4) of the Block Exemption Regulation explicitly excludes 'vertical agreements entered into between competing undertakings' from its application. Vertical agreements between competitors are dealt with, as regards possible collusion effects, in the Commission Guidelines on the applicability of Article 81 of the EC Treaty to horizontal cooperation agreements. However, the vertical aspects of such agreements need to be assessed under these Guidelines. Article 1(1)(c) of the Block Exemption Regulation defines a competing undertaking as 'an actual or potential competitor'. Two companies are treated as actual competitors if they are active on the same relevant market. A company is treated as a potential competitor of another company if, absent the agreement, in case of a small but permanent increase in relative prices it is likely that this first company, within a short period of time normally not longer than one year, would undertake the necessary additional investments or other necessary switching costs to enter the relevant market on which the other company is active. That assessment must be based on realistic grounds; the mere theoretical possibility of entering a market is not sufficient. A distributor that provides specifications to a manufacturer to produce particular goods under the distributor's brand name is not to be considered a manufacturer of such own-brand goods.

(28) Article 2(4) of the Block Exemption Regulation contains two exceptions to the general exclusion of vertical agreements between competitors. These exceptions concern non-reciprocal agreements. Non-reciprocal agreements between competitors are covered by the Block Exemption Regulation where (a) the supplier is a manufacturer and distributor of goods, while the buyer is only a distributor and not also a competing undertaking at the manufacturing level, or (b) the supplier is a provider of services operating at several levels of trade, while the buyer operates at the retail level and is not a competing undertaking at the level of trade where it purchases the contract services. The first exception covers situations of dual distribution, that is, the manufacturer of particular goods also acts as a distributor of the goods in competition with independent distributors of its goods. In case of dual distribution it is considered that in general any potential impact on the competitive relationship between the manufacturer and retailer at the retail level is of lesser importance than the potential impact of the vertical supply agreement on competition in general at the manufacturing or retail level. The second exception covers similar situations of dual distribution, but in this case for services, when the supplier is also a provider of products at the retail level where the buyer operates.

2.3   *Associations of retailers*

(29) Article 2(2) of the Block Exemption Regulation includes in its application vertical agreements entered into by an association of undertakings which fulfils certain conditions and thereby excludes from the Block Exemption Regulation vertical agreements entered into by all other associations. Vertical agreements entered into between an association and its members, or between an association and its suppliers, are covered by the Block Exemption Regulation only if all the members are retailers of goods (not services) and if each individual member of the association has a turnover not exceeding EUR 50 million. Retailers are distributors reselling goods to final consumers. Where only a limited number of the members of the association have a turnover exceeding the EUR 50 million threshold and where these members together represent less than 15 % of the collective turnover of all the members combined, the assessment under Article 101 will normally not be affected.

(30) An association of undertakings may involve both horizontal and vertical agreements. The horizontal agreements must be assessed according to the principles set out in the Guidelines on the applicability of Article 81 of the EC Treaty to horizontal cooperation agreements. If that assessment leads to the conclusion that a cooperation between undertakings in the area of purchasing or selling is acceptable, a further assessment will be necessary to examine the vertical agreements concluded by the association with its suppliers or its individual members. The latter assessment will follow the rules of the Block Exemption Regulation and these Guidelines. For instance, horizontal agreements concluded between the members of the association or decisions adopted by the association, such as the decision to require the members to purchase from the association or the decision to allocate exclusive territories to the members must first be assessed as a horizontal agreement. Once that assessment

leads to the conclusion that the horizontal agreement is not anticompetitive, an assessment of the vertical agreements between the association and individual members or between the association and suppliers is necessary.

2.4 *Vertical agreements containing provisions on intellectual property rights (IPRs)*

(31) Article 2(3) of the Block Exemption Regulation includes vertical agreements containing certain provisions relating to the assignment of IPRs to or use of IPRs by the buyer in its application and thereby excludes all other vertical agreements containing IPR provisions from the Block Exemption Regulation. The Block Exemption Regulation applies to vertical agreements containing IPR provisions where five conditions are fulfilled:

(a) The IPR provisions must be part of a vertical agreement, that is, an agreement with conditions under which the parties may purchase, sell or resell certain goods or services;

(b) The IPRs must be assigned to, or licensed for use by, the buyer;

(c) The IPR provisions must not constitute the primary object of the agreement;

(d) The IPR provisions must be directly related to the use, sale or resale of goods or services by the buyer or its customers. In the case of franchising where marketing forms the object of the exploitation of the IPRs, the goods or services are distributed by the master franchisee or the franchisees;

(e) The IPR provisions, in relation to the contract goods or services, must not contain restrictions of competition having the same object as vertical restraints which are not exempted under the Block Exemption Regulation.

(32) Such conditions ensure that the Block Exemption Regulation applies to vertical agreements where the use, sale or resale of goods or services can be performed more effectively because IPRs are assigned to or licensed for use by the buyer. In other words, restrictions concerning the assignment or use of IPRs can be covered when the main object of the agreement is the purchase or distribution of goods or services.

(33) The first condition makes clear that the context in which the IPRs are provided is an agreement to purchase or distribute goods or an agreement to purchase or provide services and not an agreement concerning the assignment or licensing of IPRs for the manufacture of goods, nor a pure licensing agreement. The Block Exemption Regulation does not cover for instance:

(a) agreements where a party provides another party with a recipe and licenses the other party to produce a drink with this recipe;

(b) agreements under which one party provides another party with a mould or master copy and licenses the other party to produce and distribute copies;

(c) the pure licence of a trade mark or sign for the purposes of merchandising;

(d) sponsorship contracts concerning the right to advertise oneself as being an official sponsor of an event;

(e) copyright licensing such as broadcasting contracts concerning the right to record and/or broadcast an event.

(34) The second condition makes clear that the Block Exemption Regulation does not apply when the IPRs are provided by the buyer to the supplier, no matter whether the IPRs concern the manner of manufacture or of distribution. An agreement relating to the transfer of IPRs to the supplier and containing possible restrictions on the sales made by the supplier is not covered by the Block Exemption Regulation. That means, in particular, that subcontracting involving the transfer of know-how to a subcontractor does not fall within the scope of application of the Block Exemption Regulation (see also paragraph (22)). However, vertical agreements under which the buyer provides only specifications to the supplier which describe the goods or services to be supplied fall within the scope of application of the Block Exemption Regulation.

(35) The third condition makes clear that in order to be covered by the Block Exemption Regulation, the primary object of the agreement must not be the assignment or licensing of IPRs. The primary object must be the purchase, sale or resale of goods or services and the IPR provisions must serve the implementation of the vertical agreement.

(36) The fourth condition requires that the IPR provisions facilitate the use, sale or resale of goods or services by the buyer or its customers. The goods or services for use or resale are usually supplied by the licensor but may also be purchased by the licensee from a third supplier. The IPR provisions will normally concern the marketing of goods or services. An example would be a franchise agreement where the franchisor sells goods for resale to the franchisee and licenses the franchisee to use its trade mark and know-how to market the goods or where the supplier of a concentrated extract licenses the buyer to dilute and bottle the extract before selling it as a drink.

(37) The fifth condition highlights the fact that the IPR provisions should not have the same object as any of the hardcore restrictions listed in Article 4 of the Block Exemption Regulation or any of the restrictions excluded from the coverage of the Block Exemption Regulation by Article 5 of that Regulation (see paragraphs (47) to (69) of these Guidelines).

(38) Intellectual property rights relevant to the implementation of vertical agreements within the meaning of Article 2(3) of the Block Exemption Regulation generally concern three main areas: trade marks, copyright and know-how.

Trade mark

(39) A trade mark licence to a distributor may be related to the distribution of the licensor's products in a particular territory. If it is an exclusive licence, the agreement amounts to exclusive distribution.

Copyright

(40) Resellers of goods covered by copyright (books, software, etc.) may be obliged by the copyright holder only to resell under the condition that the buyer, whether another reseller or the end user, shall not infringe the copyright. Such obligations on the reseller, to the extent that they fall under Article 101(1) at all, are covered by the Block Exemption Regulation.

(41) Agreements, under which hard copies of software are supplied for resale and where the reseller does not acquire a licence to any rights over the software but only has the right to resell the hard copies, are to be regarded as agreements for the supply of goods for resale for the purpose of the Block Exemption Regulation. Under that form of distribution, licensing the software only occurs between the copyright owner and the user of the software. It may take the form of a 'shrink wrap' licence, that is, a set of conditions included in the package of the hard copy which the end user is deemed to accept by opening the package.

(42) Buyers of hardware incorporating software protected by copyright may be obliged by the copyright holder not to infringe the copyright, and must therefore not make copies and resell the software or make copies and use the software in combination with other hardware. Such use-restrictions, to the extent that they fall within Article 101(1) at all, are covered by the Block Exemption Regulation.

Know-how

(43) Franchise agreements, with the exception of industrial franchise agreements, are the most obvious example of where know-how for marketing purposes is communicated to the buyer. Franchise agreements contain licences of intellectual property rights relating to trade marks or signs and know-how for the use and distribution of goods or the provision of services. In addition to the licence of IPR, the franchisor usually provides the franchisee during the life of the agreement with commercial or technical assistance, such as procurement services, training, advice on real estate, financial planning etc. The licence and the assistance are integral components of the business method being franchised.

(44) Licensing contained in franchise agreements is covered by the Block Exemption Regulation where all five conditions listed in paragraph (31) are fulfilled. Those conditions are usually fulfilled as under most franchise agreements, including master franchise agreements, the franchisor provides goods and/or services, in particular commercial or technical assistance services, to the franchisee. The IPRs help the franchisee to resell the products supplied by the franchisor or by a supplier designated by the franchisor or to use those products and sell the resulting goods or services. Where the franchise agreement only or primarily concerns licensing of IPRs, it is not covered by the Block

Exemption Regulation, but the Commission will, as a general rule, apply the principles set out in the Block Exemption Regulation and these Guidelines to such an agreement.

(45) The following IPR-related obligations are generally considered necessary to protect the franchisor's intellectual property rights and are, where these obligations fall under Article 101(1), also covered by the Block Exemption Regulation:

(a) an obligation on the franchisee not to engage, directly or indirectly, in any similar business;

(b) an obligation on the franchisee not to acquire financial interests in the capital of a competing undertaking such as would give the franchisee the power to influence the economic conduct of such undertaking;

(c) an obligation on the franchisee not to disclose to third parties the know-how provided by the franchisor as long as this know-how is not in the public domain;

(d) an obligation on the franchisee to communicate to the franchisor any experience gained in exploiting the franchise and to grant the franchisor, and other franchisees, a non-exclusive licence for the know-how resulting from that experience;

(e) an obligation on the franchisee to inform the franchisor of infringements of licensed intellectual property rights, to take legal action against infringers or to assist the franchisor in any legal actions against infringers;

(f) an obligation on the franchisee not to use know-how licensed by the franchisor for purposes other than the exploitation of the franchise;

(g) an obligation on the franchisee not to assign the rights and obligations under the franchise agreement without the franchisor's consent.

2.5 Relationship to other block exemption regulations

(46) Article 2(5) states that the Block Exemption Regulation does 'not apply to vertical agreements the subject matter of which falls within the scope of any other block exemption regulation, unless otherwise provided for in such a regulation'. The Block Exemption Regulation does not therefore apply to vertical agreements covered by Commission Regulation (EC) No 772/2004 of 27 April 2004 on the application of Article 81(3) of the Treaty to categories of technology transfer agreements, Regulation 1400/2002 on the application of Article 81(3) of the Treaty to categories of vertical agreements and concerted practices in the motor vehicle sector or Commission Regulation (EC) No 2658/2000 of 29 November 2000 on the application of Article 81(3) of the Treaty to categories of specialisation agreements and Commission Regulation (EC) No 2659/2000 of 29 November 2000 on the application of Article 81(3) of the Treaty to categories of research and development agreements exempting vertical agreements concluded in connection with horizontal agreements, or any future regulations of that kind, unless otherwise provided for in such a regulation.

3 Hardcore restrictions under the Block Exemption Regulation

(47) Article 4 of the Block Exemption Regulation contains a list of hardcore restrictions which lead to the exclusion of the whole vertical agreement from the scope of application of the Block Exemption Regulation. Where such a hardcore restriction is included in an agreement, that agreement is presumed to fall within Article 101(1). It is also presumed that the agreement is unlikely to fulfil the conditions of Article 101(3), for which reason the block exemption does not apply. However, undertakings may demonstrate pro-competitive effects under Article 101(3) in an individual case. Where the undertakings substantiate that likely efficiencies result from including the hardcore restriction in the agreement and demonstrate that in general all the conditions of Article 101(3) are fulfilled, the Commission will be required to effectively assess the likely negative impact on competition before making an ultimate assessment of whether the conditions of Article 101(3) are fulfilled.

(48) The hardcore restriction set out in Article 4(a) of the Block Exemption Regulation concerns resale price maintenance (RPM), that is, agreements or concerted practices having as their direct or indirect object the establishment of a fixed or minimum resale price or a fixed or minimum price level to be observed by the buyer. In the case of contractual provisions or concerted practices that directly establish the resale price, the restriction is clear cut. However, RPM can also be achieved through

indirect means. Examples of the latter are an agreement fixing the distribution margin, fixing the maximum level of discount the distributor can grant from a prescribed price level, making the grant of rebates or reimbursement of promotional costs by the supplier subject to the observance of a given price level, linking the prescribed resale price to the resale prices of competitors, threats, intimidation, warnings, penalties, delay or suspension of deliveries or contract terminations in relation to observance of a given price level. Direct or indirect means of achieving price fixing can be made more effective when combined with measures to identify price-cutting distributors, such as the implementation of a price monitoring system, or the obligation on retailers to report other members of the distribution network that deviate from the standard price level. Similarly, direct or indirect price fixing can be made more effective when combined with measures which may reduce the buyer's incentive to lower the resale price, such as the supplier printing a recommended resale price on the product or the supplier obliging the buyer to apply a most-favoured-customer clause. The same indirect means and the same 'supportive' measures can be used to make maximum or recommended prices work as RPM. However, the use of a particular supportive measure or the provision of a list of recommended prices or maximum prices by the supplier to the buyer is not considered in itself as leading to RPM.

(49) In the case of agency agreements, the principal normally establishes the sales price, as the agent does not become the owner of the goods. However, where such an agreement cannot be qualified as an agency agreement for the purposes of applying Article 101(1) (see paragraphs (12) to (21)) an obligation preventing or restricting the agent from sharing its commission, fixed or variable, with the customer would be a hardcore restriction under Article 4(a) of the Block Exemption Regulation. In order to avoid including such a hardcore restriction in the agreement, the agent should thus be left free to lower the effective price paid by the customer without reducing the income for the principal.

(50) The hardcore restriction set out in Article 4(b) of the Block Exemption Regulation concerns agreements or concerted practices that have as their direct or indirect object the restriction of sales by a buyer party to the agreement or its customers, in as far as those restrictions relate to the territory into which or the customers to whom the buyer or its customers may sell the contract goods or services. This hardcore restriction relates to market partitioning by territory or by customer group. That may be the result of direct obligations, such as the obligation not to sell to certain customers or to customers in certain territories or the obligation to refer orders from these customers to other distributors. It may also result from indirect measures aimed at inducing the distributor not to sell to such customers, such as refusal or reduction of bonuses or discounts, termination of supply, reduction of supplied volumes or limitation of supplied volumes to the demand within the allocated territory or customer group, threat of contract termination, requiring a higher price for products to be exported, limiting the proportion of sales that can be exported or profit pass-over obligations. It may further result from the supplier not providing a Union-wide guarantee service under which normally all distributors are obliged to provide the guarantee service and are reimbursed for this service by the supplier, even in relation to products sold by other distributors into their territory. Such practices are even more likely to be viewed as a restriction of the buyer's sales when used in conjunction with the implementation by the supplier of a monitoring system aimed at verifying the effective destination of the supplied goods, such as the use of differentiated labels or serial numbers. However, obligations on the reseller relating to the display of the supplier's brand name are not classified as hardcore. As Article 4(b) only concerns restrictions of sales by the buyer or its customers, this implies that restrictions of the supplier's sales are also not a hardcore restriction, subject to what is stated in paragraph (59) regarding sales of spare parts in the context of Article 4(e) of the Block Exemption Regulation. Article 4(b) applies without prejudice to a restriction on the buyer's place of establishment. Thus, the benefit of the Block Exemption Regulation is not lost if it is agreed that the buyer will restrict its distribution outlet(s) and warehouse(s) to a particular address, place or territory.

(51) There are four exceptions to the hardcore restriction in Article 4(b) of the Block Exemption Regulation. The first exception in Article 4(b)(i) allows a supplier to restrict active sales by a buyer party to the agreement to a territory or a customer group which has been allocated exclusively to another buyer or which the supplier has reserved to itself. A territory or customer group is exclusively allocated when the supplier agrees to sell its product only to one distributor for distribution in a

particular territory or to a particular customer group and the exclusive distributor is protected against active selling into its territory or to its customer group by all the other buyers of the supplier within the Union, irrespective of sales by the supplier. The supplier is allowed to combine the allocation of an exclusive territory and an exclusive customer group by for instance appointing an exclusive distributor for a particular customer group in a certain territory. Such protection of exclusively allocated territories or customer groups must, however, permit passive sales to such territories or customer groups. For the application of Article 4(b) of the Block Exemption Regulation, the Commission interprets 'active' and 'passive' sales as follows:

- 'Active' sales mean actively approaching individual customers by for instance direct mail, including the sending of unsolicited e-mails, or visits; or actively approaching a specific customer group or customers in a specific territory through advertisement in media, on the internet or other promotions specifically targeted at that customer group or targeted at customers in that territory. Advertisement or promotion that is only attractive for the buyer if it (also) reaches a specific group of customers or customers in a specific territory, is considered active selling to that customer group or customers in that territory.

- 'Passive' sales mean responding to unsolicited requests from individual customers including delivery of goods or services to such customers. General advertising or promotion that reaches customers in other distributors' (exclusive) territories or customer groups but which is a reasonable way to reach customers outside those territories or customer groups, for instance to reach customers in one's own territory, are considered passive selling. General advertising or promotion is considered a reasonable way to reach such customers if it would be attractive for the buyer to undertake these investments also if they would not reach customers in other distributors' (exclusive) territories or customer groups.

(52) The internet is a powerful tool to reach a greater number and variety of customers than by more traditional sales methods, which explains why certain restrictions on the use of the internet are dealt with as (re)sales restrictions. In principle, every distributor must be allowed to use the internet to sell products. In general, where a distributor uses a website to sell products that is considered a form of passive selling, since it is a reasonable way to allow customers to reach the distributor. The use of a website may have effects that extend beyond the distributor's own territory and customer group; however, such effects result from the technology allowing easy access from everywhere. If a customer visits the web site of a distributor and contacts the distributor and if such contact leads to a sale, including delivery, then that is considered passive selling. The same is true if a customer opts to be kept (automatically) informed by the distributor and it leads to a sale. Offering different language options on the website does not, of itself, change the passive character of such selling. The Commission thus regards the following as examples of hardcore restrictions of passive selling given the capability of these restrictions to limit the distributor's access to a greater number and variety of customers:

(a) an agreement that the (exclusive) distributor shall prevent customers located in another (exclusive) territory from viewing its website or shall automatically reroute its customers to the manufacturer's or other (exclusive) distributors' websites. This does not exclude an agreement that the distributor's website shall also offer a number of links to websites of other distributors and/or the supplier;

(b) an agreement that the (exclusive) distributor shall terminate consumers' transactions over the internet once their credit card data reveal an address that is not within the distributor's (exclusive) territory;

(c) an agreement that the distributor shall limit its proportion of overall sales made over the internet. This does not exclude the supplier requiring, without limiting the online sales of the distributor, that the buyer sells at least a certain absolute amount (in value or volume) of the products offline to ensure an efficient operation of its brick and mortar shop (physical point of sales), nor does it preclude the supplier from making sure that the online activity of the distributor remains consistent with the supplier's distribution model (see paragraphs (54) and (56)). This absolute amount of required offline sales can be the same for all buyers, or determined individually for each buyer on the basis of objective criteria, such as the buyer's size in the network or its geographic location;

(d) an agreement that the distributor shall pay a higher price for products intended to be re-sold by the distributor online than for products intended to be resold offline. This does not exclude the supplier agreeing with the buyer a fixed fee (that is, not a variable fee where the sum increases with the realised offline turnover as this would amount indirectly to dual pricing) to support the latter's offline or online sales efforts.

(53) A restriction on the use of the internet by distributors that are party to the agreement is compatible with the Block Exemption Regulation to the extent that promotion on the internet or use of the internet would lead to active selling into, for instance, other distributors' exclusive territories or customer groups. The Commission considers online advertisement specifically addressed to certain customers as a form of active selling to those customers. For instance, territory-based banners on third party websites are a form of active sales into the territory where these banners are shown. In general, efforts to be found specifically in a certain territory or by a certain customer group is active selling into that territory or to that customer group. For instance, paying a search engine or online advertisement provider to have advertisements displayed specifically to users in a particular territory is active selling into that territory.

(54) However, under the Block Exemption the supplier may require quality standards for the use of the internet site to resell its goods, just as the supplier may require quality standards for a shop or for selling by catalogue or for advertising and promotion in general. This may be relevant in particular for selective distribution. Under the Block Exemption, the supplier may, for example, require that its distributors have one or more brick and mortar shops or showrooms as a condition for becoming a member of its distribution system. Subsequent changes to such a condition are also possible under the Block Exemption, except where those changes have as their object to directly or indirectly limit the online sales by the distributors. Similarly, a supplier may require that its distributors use third party platforms to distribute the contract products only in accordance with the standards and conditions agreed between the supplier and its distributors for the distributors' use of the internet. For instance, where the distributor's website is hosted by a third party platform, the supplier may require that customers do not visit the distributor's website through a site carrying the name or logo of the third party platform.

(55) There are three further exceptions to the hardcore restriction set out in Article 4(b) of the Block Exemption Regulation. All three exceptions allow for the restriction of both active and passive sales. Under the first exception, it is permissible to restrict a wholesaler from selling to end users, which allows a supplier to keep the wholesale and retail level of trade separate. However, that exception does not exclude the possibility that the wholesaler can sell to certain end users, such as bigger end users, while not allowing sales to (all) other end users. The second exception allows a supplier to restrict an appointed distributor in a selective distribution system from selling, at any level of trade, to unauthorised distributors located in any territory where the system is currently operated or where the supplier does not yet sell the contract products (referred to as 'the territory reserved by the supplier to operate that system' in Article 4(b)(iii)). The third exception allows a supplier to restrict a buyer of components, to whom the components are supplied for incorporation, from reselling them to competitors of the supplier. The term 'component' includes any intermediate goods and the term 'incorporation' refers to the use of any input to produce goods.

(56) The hardcore restriction set out in Article 4(c) of the Block Exemption Regulation excludes the restriction of active or passive sales to end users, whether professional users or final consumers, by members of a selective distribution network, without prejudice to the possibility of prohibiting a member of the network from operating out of an unauthorised place of establishment. Accordingly, dealers in a selective distribution system, as defined in Article 1(1)(e) of the Block Exemption Regulation, cannot be restricted in the choice of users to whom they may sell, or purchasing agents acting on behalf of those users except to protect an exclusive distribution system operated elsewhere (see paragraph (51)). Within a selective distribution system the dealers should be free to sell, both actively and passively, to all end users, also with the help of the internet. Therefore, the Commission considers any obligations which dissuade appointed dealers from using the internet to reach a greater

number and variety of customers by imposing criteria for online sales which are not overall equivalent to the criteria imposed for the sales from the brick and mortar shop as a hardcore restriction. This does not mean that the criteria imposed for online sales must be identical to those imposed for offline sales , but rather that they should pursue the same objectives and achieve comparable results and that the difference between the criteria must be justified by the different nature of these two distribution modes. For example, in order to prevent sales to unauthorised dealers, a supplier can restrict its selected dealers from selling more than a given quantity of contract products to an individual end user. Such a requirement may have to be stricter for online sales if it is easier for an unauthorised dealer to obtain those products by using the internet. Similarly, it may have to be stricter for offline sales if it is easier to obtain them from a brick and mortar shop. In order to ensure timely delivery of contract products, a supplier may impose that the products be delivered instantly in the case of offline sales. Whereas an identical requirement cannot be imposed for online sales, the supplier may specify certain practicable delivery times for such sales. Specific requirements may have to be formulated for an online aftersales help desk, so as to cover the costs of customers returning the product and for applying secure payment systems.

(57) Within the territory where the supplier operates selective distribution, this system may not be combined with exclusive distribution as that would lead to a hardcore restriction of active or passive selling by the dealers under Article 4(c) of the Block Exemption Regulation, with the exception that restrictions can be imposed on the dealer's ability to determine the location of its business premises. Selected dealers may be prevented from operating their business from different premises or from opening a new outlet in a different location. In that context, the use by a distributor of its own website cannot be considered to be the same thing as the opening of a new outlet in a different location. If the dealer's outlet is mobile, an area may be defined outside which the mobile outlet cannot be operated. In addition, the supplier may commit itself to supplying only one dealer or a limited number of dealers in a particular part of the territory where the selective distribution system is applied.

(58) The hardcore restriction set out in Article 4(d) of the Block Exemption Regulation concerns the restriction of cross-supplies between appointed distributors within a selective distribution system. Accordingly, an agreement or concerted practice may not have as its direct or indirect object to prevent or restrict the active or passive selling of the contract products between the selected distributors. Selected distributors must remain free to purchase the contract products from other appointed distributors within the network, operating either at the same or at a different level of trade. Consequently, selective distribution cannot be combined with vertical restraints aimed at forcing distributors to purchase the contract products exclusively from a given source. It also means that within a selective distribution network, no restrictions can be imposed on appointed wholesalers as regards their sales of the product to appointed retailers.

(59) The hardcore restriction set out in Article 4(e) of the Block Exemption Regulation concerns agreements that prevent or restrict end-users, independent repairers and service providers from obtaining spare parts directly from the manufacturer of those spare parts. An agreement between a manufacturer of spare parts and a buyer that incorporates those parts into its own products (original equipment manufacturer (OEM)), may not, either directly or indirectly, prevent or restrict sales by the manufacturer of those spare parts to end users, independent repairers or service providers. Indirect restrictions may arise particularly when the supplier of the spare parts is restricted in supplying technical information and special equipment which are necessary for the use of spare parts by users, independent repairers or service providers. However, the agreement may place restrictions on the supply of the spare parts to the repairers or service providers entrusted by the original equipment manufacturer with the repair or servicing of its own goods. In other words, the original equipment manufacturer may require its own repair and service network to buy spare parts from it.

4   Individual cases of hardcore sales restrictions that may fall outside the scope of Article 101(1) or may fulfil the conditions of Article 101(3)

(60) Hardcore restrictions may be objectively necessary in exceptional cases for an agreement of a particular type or nature and therefore fall outside Article 101(1). For example, a hardcore restriction

may be objectively necessary to ensure that a public ban on selling dangerous substances to certain customers for reasons of safety or health is respected. In addition, undertakings may plead an efficiency defence under Article 101(3) in an individual case. This section provides some examples for (re)sales restrictions, whereas for RPM this is dealt with in section VI.2.10.

(61) A distributor which will be the first to sell a new brand or the first to sell an existing brand on a new market, thereby ensuring a genuine entry on the relevant market, may have to commit substantial investments where there was previously no demand for that type of product in general or for that type of product from that producer. Such expenses may often be sunk and in such circumstances the distributor may not enter into the distribution agreement without protection for a certain period of time against (active and) passive sales into its territory or to its customer group by other distributors. For example such a situation may occur where a manufacturer established in a particular national market enters another national market and introduces its products with the help of an exclusive distributor and where this distributor needs to invest in launching and establishing the brand on this new market. Where substantial investments by the distributor to start up and/or develop the new market are necessary, restrictions of passive sales by other distributors into such a territory or to such a customer group which are necessary for the distributor to recoup those investments generally fall outside the scope of Article 101(1) during the first two years that the distributor is selling the contract goods or services in that territory or to that customer group, even though such hardcore restrictions are in general presumed to fall within the scope of Article 101(1).

(62) In the case of genuine testing of a new product in a limited territory or with a limited customer group and in the case of a staggered introduction of a new product, the distributors appointed to sell the new product on the test market or to participate in the first round(s) of the staggered introduction may be restricted in their active selling outside the test market or the market(s) where the product is first introduced without falling within the scope of Article 101(1) for the period necessary for the testing or introduction of the product.

(63) In the case of a selective distribution system, cross supplies between appointed distributors must normally remain free (see paragraph (58)). However, if appointed wholesalers located in different territories are obliged to invest in promotional activities in 'their' territories to support the sales by appointed retailers and it is not practical to specify in a contract the required promotional activities, restrictions on active sales by the wholesalers to appointed retailers in other wholesalers' territories to overcome possible free riding may, in an individual case, fulfil the conditions of Article 101(3).

(64) In general, an agreement that a distributor shall pay a higher price for products intended to be resold by the distributor online than for products intended to be resold offline ('dual pricing') is a hardcore restriction (see paragraph (52)). However, in some specific circumstances, such an agreement may fulfil the conditions of Article 101(3). Such circumstances may be present where a manufacturer agrees such dual pricing with its distributors, because selling online leads to substantially higher costs for the manufacturer than offline sales. For example, where offline sales include home installation by the distributor but online sales do not, the latter may lead to more customer complaints and warranty claims for the manufacturer. In that context, the Commission will also consider to what extent the restriction is likely to limit internet sales and hinder the distributor to reach more and different customers.

5   Excluded restrictions under the Block Exemption Regulation

(65) Article 5 of the Block Exemption Regulation excludes certain obligations from the coverage of the Block Exemption Regulation even though the market share threshold is not exceeded. However, the Block Exemption Regulation continues to apply to the remaining part of the vertical agreement if that part is severable from the non-exempted obligations.

(66) The first exclusion is provided for in Article 5(1)(a) of the Block Exemption Regulation and concerns non-compete obligations. Non-compete obligations are arrangements that result in the buyer purchasing from the supplier or from another undertaking designated by the supplier more than 80 % of the buyer's total purchases of the contract goods and services and their substitutes during the preceding calendar year (as defined by Article 1(1)(d) of the Block Exemption Regulation),

thereby preventing the buyer from purchasing competing goods or services or limiting such purchases to less than 20 % of total purchases. Where, in the first year after entering in the agreement, for the year preceding the conclusion of the contract no relevant purchasing data for the buyer are available, the buyer's best estimate of its annual total requirements may be used. Such non-compete obligations are not covered by the Block Exemption Regulation where the duration is indefinite or exceeds five years. Non-compete obligations that are tacitly renewable beyond a period of five years are also not covered by the Block Exemption Regulation (see the second subparagraph of Article 5(1)). In general, non-compete obligations are exempted under that Regulation where their duration is limited to five years or less and no obstacles exist that hinder the buyer from effectively terminating the non-compete obligation at the end of the five year period. If, for instance, the agreement provides for a five-year non-compete obligation and the supplier provides a loan to the buyer, the repayment of that loan should not hinder the buyer from effectively terminating the non-compete obligation at the end of the five-year period. Similarly, when the supplier provides the buyer with equipment which is not relationship-specific, the buyer should have the possibility to take over the equipment at its market asset value once the non-compete obligation expires.

(67) The five-year duration limit does not apply when the goods or services are resold by the buyer 'from premises and land owned by the supplier or leased by the supplier from third parties not connected with the buyer'. In such cases the non-compete obligation may be of the same duration as the period of occupancy of the point of sale by the buyer (Article 5(2) of the Block Exemption Regulation). The reason for this exception is that it is normally unreasonable to expect a supplier to allow competing products to be sold from premises and land owned by the supplier without its permission. By analogy, the same principles apply where the buyer operates from a mobile outlet owned by the supplier or leased by the supplier from third parties not connected with the buyer. Artificial ownership constructions, such as a transfer by the distributor of its proprietary rights over the land and premises to the supplier for only a limited period, intended to avoid the five-year limit cannot benefit from this exception.

(68) The second exclusion from the block exemption is provided for in Article 5(1)(b) of the Block Exemption Regulation and concerns post term non-compete obligations on the buyer. Such obligations are normally not covered by the Block Exemption Regulation, unless the obligation is indispensable to protect know-how transferred by the supplier to the buyer, is limited to the point of sale from which the buyer has operated during the contract period, and is limited to a maximum period of one year (see Article 5(3) of the Block Exemption Regulation). According to the definition in Article 1(1)(g) of the Block Exemption Regulation the know-how needs to be 'substantial', meaning that the know-how includes information which is significant and useful to the buyer for the use, sale or resale of the contract goods or services.

(69) The third exclusion from the block exemption is provided for in Article 5(1)(c) of the Block Exemption Regulation and concerns the sale of competing goods in a selective distribution system. The Block Exemption Regulation covers the combination of selective distribution with a non-compete obligation, obliging the dealers not to resell competing brands in general. However, if the supplier prevents its appointed dealers, either directly or indirectly, from buying products for resale from specific competing suppliers, such an obligation cannot enjoy the benefit of the Block Exemption Regulation. The objective of the exclusion of such an obligation is to avoid a situation whereby a number of suppliers using the same selective distribution outlets prevent one specific competitor or certain specific competitors from using these outlets to distribute their products (foreclosure of a competing supplier which would be a form of collective boycott).

6   Severability

(70) The Block Exemption Regulation exempts vertical agreements on condition that no hardcore restriction, as set out in Article 4 of that Regulation, is contained in or practised with the vertical agreement. If there are one or more hardcore restrictions, the benefit of the Block Exemption Regulation is lost for the entire vertical agreement. There is no severability for hardcore restrictions.

(71) The rule of severability does apply, however, to the excluded restrictions set out in Article 5 of the Block Exemption Regulation. Therefore, the benefit of the block exemption is only lost in relation to that part of the vertical agreement which does not comply with the conditions set out in Article 5.

7   Portfolio of products distributed through the same distribution system

(72) Where a supplier uses the same distribution agreement to distribute several goods/services some of these may, in view of the market share threshold, be covered by the Block Exemption Regulation while others may not. In that case, the Block Exemption Regulation applies to those goods and services for which the conditions of application are fulfilled.

(73) In respect of the goods or services which are not covered by the Block Exemption Regulation, the ordinary rules of competition apply, which means:

(a) there is no block exemption but also no presumption of illegality;

(b) if there is an infringement of Article 101(1) which is not exemptible, consideration may be given to whether there are appropriate remedies to solve the competition problem within the existing distribution system;

(c) if there are no such appropriate remedies, the supplier concerned will have to make other distribution arrangements.

Such a situation can also arise where Article 102 applies in respect of some products but not in respect of others.

IV. WITHDRAWAL OF THE BLOCK EXEMPTION AND DISAPPLICATION OF THE BLOCK EXEMPTION REGULATION

1   Withdrawal procedure

(74) The presumption of legality conferred by the Block Exemption Regulation may be withdrawn where a vertical agreement, considered either in isolation or in conjunction with similar agreements enforced by competing suppliers or buyers, comes within the scope of Article 101(1) and does not fulfil all the conditions of Article 101(3).

(75) The conditions of Article 101(3) may in particular not be fulfilled when access to the relevant market or competition therein is significantly restricted by the cumulative effect of parallel networks of similar vertical agreements practised by competing suppliers or buyers. Parallel networks of vertical agreements are to be regarded as similar if they contain restraints producing similar effects on the market. Such a situation may arise for example when, on a given market, certain suppliers practise purely qualitative selective distribution while other suppliers practise quantitative selective distribution. Such a situation may also arise when, on a given market, the cumulative use of qualitative criteria forecloses more efficient distributors. In such circumstances, the assessment must take account of the anti-competitive effects attributable to each individual network of agreements. Where appropriate, withdrawal may concern only a particular qualitative criterion or only the quantitative limitations imposed on the number of authorised distributors.

(76) Responsibility for an anti-competitive cumulative effect can only be attributed to those undertakings which make an appreciable contribution to it. Agreements entered into by undertakings whose contribution to the cumulative effect is insignificant do not fall under the prohibition provided for in Article 101(1) and are therefore not subject to the withdrawal mechanism. The assessment of such a contribution will be made in accordance with the criteria set out in paragraphs (128) to (229).

(77) Where the withdrawal procedure is applied, the Commission bears the burden of proof that the agreement falls within the scope of Article 101(1) and that the agreement does not fulfil one or several of the conditions of Article 101(3). A withdrawal decision can only have ex nunc effect, which means that the exempted status of the agreements concerned will not be affected until the date at which the withdrawal becomes effective.

(78) As referred to in recital 14 of the Block Exemption Regulation, the competition authority of a Member State may withdraw the benefit of the Block Exemption Regulation in respect of vertical agreements whose anti-competitive effects are felt in the territory of the Member State concerned or a part thereof, which has all the characteristics of a distinct geographic market. The Commission has the exclusive power to withdraw the benefit of the Block Exemption Regulation in respect of vertical agreements restricting competition on a relevant geographic market which is wider than the territory of a single Member State. When the territory of a single Member State, or a part thereof, constitutes the relevant geographic market, the Commission and the Member State concerned have concurrent competence for withdrawal.

2   Disapplication of the Block Exemption Regulation

(79) Article 6 of the Block Exemption Regulation enables the Commission to exclude from the scope of the Block Exemption Regulation, by means of regulation, parallel networks of similar vertical restraints where these cover more than 50 % of a relevant market. Such a measure is not addressed to individual undertakings but concerns all undertakings whose agreements are defined in the regulation disapplying the Block Exemption Regulation.

(80) Whereas the withdrawal of the benefit of the Block Exemption Regulation implies the adoption of a decision establishing an infringement of Article 101 by an individual company, the effect of a regulation under Article 6 is merely to remove, in respect of the restraints and the markets concerned, the benefit of the application of the Block Exemption Regulation and to restore the full application of Article 101(1) and (3). Following the adoption of a regulation declaring the Block Exemption Regulation inapplicable in respect of certain vertical restraints on a particular market, the criteria developed by the relevant case-law of the Court of Justice and the General Court and by notices and previous decisions adopted by the Commission will guide the application of Article 101 to individual agreements. Where appropriate, the Commission will take a decision in an individual case, which can provide guidance to all the undertakings operating on the market concerned.

(81) For the purpose of calculating the 50 % market coverage ratio, account must be taken of each individual network of vertical agreements containing restraints, or combinations of restraints, producing similar effects on the market. Article 6 of the Block Exemption Regulation does not entail an obligation on the part of the Commission to act where the 50 % market-coverage ratio is exceeded. In general, disapplication is appropriate when it is likely that access to the relevant market or competition therein is appreciably restricted. This may occur in particular when parallel networks of selective distribution covering more than 50 % of a market are liable to foreclose the market by using selection criteria which are not required by the nature of the relevant goods or which discriminate against certain forms of distribution capable of selling such goods.

(82) In assessing the need to apply Article 6 of the Block Exemption Regulation, the Commission will consider whether individual withdrawal would be a more appropriate remedy. This may depend, in particular, on the number of competing undertakings contributing to a cumulative effect on a market or the number of affected geographic markets within the Union.

(83) Any regulation referred to in Article 6 of the Block Exemption Regulation must clearly set out its scope. Therefore, the Commission must first define the relevant product and geographic market(s) and, secondly, must identify the type of vertical restraint in respect of which the Block Exemption Regulation will no longer apply. As regards the latter aspect, the Commission may modulate the scope of its regulation according to the competition concern which it intends to address. For instance, while all parallel networks of single-branding type arrangements shall be taken into account in view of establishing the 50 % market coverage ratio, the Commission may nevertheless restrict the scope of the disapplication regulation only to non-compete obligations exceeding a certain duration. Thus, agreements of a shorter duration or of a less restrictive nature might be left unaffected, in consideration of the lesser degree of foreclosure attributable to such restraints. Similarly, when on a particular market selective distribution is practised in combination with additional restraints such as non-compete or quantity-forcing on the buyer, the disapplication regulation may concern only such additional restraints. Where appropriate, the Commission may also provide guidance by specifying

the market share level which, in the specific market context, may be regarded as insufficient to bring about a significant contribution by an individual undertaking to the cumulative effect.

(84) Pursuant to Regulation No 19/65/EEC of 2 March 1965 of the Council on the application of Article 85(3) of the Treaty to certain categories of agreements and concerted practices, the Commission will have to set a transitional period of not less than six months before a regulation disapplying the Block Exemption Regulation becomes applicable. This should allow the undertakings concerned to adapt their agreements to take account of the regulation disapplying the Block Exemption Regulation.

(85) A regulation disapplying the Block Exemption Regulation will not affect the exempted status of the agreements concerned for the period preceding its date of application.

V. MARKET DEFINITION AND MARKET SHARE CALCULATION

1   Commission Notice on definition of the relevant market

(86) The Commission Notice on definition of the relevant market for the purposes of Community competition law provides guidance on the rules, criteria and evidence which the Commission uses when considering market definition issues. That Notice will not be further explained in these Guidelines and should serve as the basis for market definition issues. These Guidelines will only deal with specific issues that arise in the context of vertical restraints and that are not dealt with in that notice.

2   The relevant market for calculating the 30 % market share threshold under the Block Exemption Regulation

(87) Under Article 3 of the Block Exemption Regulation, the market share of both the supplier and the buyer are decisive to determine if the block exemption applies. In order for the block exemption to apply, the market share of the supplier on the market where it sells the contract products to the buyer, and the market share of the buyer on the market where it purchases the contract products, must each be 30 % or less. For agreements between small and medium-sized undertakings it is in general not necessary to calculate market shares (see paragraph (11)).

(88) In order to calculate an undertaking's market share, it is necessary to determine the relevant market where that undertaking sells and purchases, respectively, the contract products. Accordingly, the relevant product market and the relevant geographic market must be defined. The relevant product market comprises any goods or services which are regarded by the buyers as interchangeable, by reason of their characteristics, prices and intended use. The relevant geographic market comprises the area in which the undertakings concerned are involved in the supply and demand of relevant goods or services, in which the conditions of competition are sufficiently homogenous, and which can be distinguished from neighbouring geographic areas because, in particular, conditions of competition are appreciably different in those areas.

(89) The product market definition primarily depends on substitutability from the buyers' perspective. When the supplied product is used as an input to produce other products and is generally not recognisable in the final product, the product market is normally defined by the direct buyers' preferences. The customers of the buyers will normally not have a strong preference concerning the inputs used by the buyers. Usually, the vertical restraints agreed between the supplier and buyer of the input only relate to the sale and purchase of the intermediate product and not to the sale of the resulting product. In the case of distribution of final goods, substitutes for the direct buyers will normally be influenced or determined by the preferences of the final consumers. A distributor, as reseller, cannot ignore the preferences of final consumers when it purchases final goods. In addition, at the distribution level the vertical restraints usually concern not only the sale of products between supplier and buyer, but also their resale. As different distribution formats usually compete, markets are in general not defined by the form of distribution that is applied. Where suppliers generally sell a portfolio of

products, the entire portfolio may determine the product market when the portfolios and not the individual products are regarded as substitutes by the buyers. As distributors are professional buyers, the geographic wholesale market is usually wider than the retail market, where the product is resold to final consumers. Often, this will lead to the definition of national or wider wholesale markets. But retail markets may also be wider than the final consumers' search area where homogenous market conditions and overlapping local or regional catchment areas exist.

(90) Where a vertical agreement involves three parties, each operating at a different level of trade, each party's market share must be 30 % or less in order for the block exemption to apply. As specified in Article 3(2) of the Block Exemption Regulation, where in a multi party agreement an undertaking buys the contract goods or services from one undertaking party to the agreement and sells the contract goods or services to another undertaking party to the agreement, the block exemption applies only if its market share does not exceed the 30 % threshold both as a buyer and a supplier. If, for instance, in an agreement between a manufacturer, a wholesaler (or association of retailers) and a retailer, a non-compete obligation is agreed, then the market shares of the manufacturer and the wholesaler (or association of retailers) on their respective downstream markets must not exceed 30 % and the market share of the wholesaler (or association of retailers) and the retailer must not exceed 30 % on their respective purchase markets in order to benefit from the block exemption.

(91) Where a supplier produces both original equipment and the repair or replacement parts for that equipment, the supplier will often be the only or the major supplier on the after-market for the repair and replacement parts. This may also arise where the supplier (OEM supplier) subcontracts the manufacturing of the repair or replacement parts. The relevant market for application of the Block Exemption Regulation may be the original equipment market including the spare parts or a separate original equipment market and after-market depending on the circumstances of the case, such as the effects of the restrictions involved, the lifetime of the equipment and importance of the repair or replacement costs. In practice, the issue is whether a significant proportion of buyers make their choice taking into account the lifetime costs of the product. If so, it indicates there is one market for the original equipment and spare parts combined.

(92) Where the vertical agreement, in addition to the supply of the contract goods, also contains IPR provisions – such as a provision concerning the use of the supplier's trademark – which help the buyer to market the contract goods, the supplier's market share on the market where it sells the contract goods is relevant for the application of the Block Exemption Regulation. Where a franchisor does not supply goods to be resold but provides a bundle of services and goods combined with IPR provisions which together form the business method being franchised, the franchisor needs to take account of its market share as a provider of a business method. For that purpose, the franchisor needs to calculate its market share on the market where the business method is exploited, which is the market where the franchisees exploit the business method to provide goods or services to end users. The franchisor must base its market share on the value of the goods or services supplied by its franchisees on this market. On such a market, the competitors may be providers of other franchised business methods but also suppliers of substitutable goods or services not applying franchising. For instance, without prejudice to the definition of such market, if there was a market for fast-food services, a franchisor operating on such a market would need to calculate its market share on the basis of the relevant sales figures of its franchisees on this market.

3 Calculation of market shares under the Block Exemption Regulation

(93) The calculation of market shares needs to be based in principle on value figures. Where value figures are not available substantiated estimates can be made. Such estimates may be based on other reliable market information such as volume figures (see Article 7(a) of the Block Exemption Regulation).

(94) In-house production, that is, production of an intermediate product for own use, may be very important in a competition analysis as one of the competitive constraints or to accentuate the market position of a company. However, for the purpose of market definition and the calculation of market share for intermediate goods and services, in-house production will not be taken into account.

(95) However, in the case of dual distribution of final goods, that is, where a producer of final goods also acts as a distributor on the market, the market definition and market share calculation need to include sales of their own goods made by the producers through their vertically integrated distributors and agents (see Article 7(c) of the Block Exemption Regulation). 'Integrated distributors' are connected undertakings within the meaning of Article 1(2) of the Block Exemption Regulation.

VI. ENFORCEMENT POLICY IN INDIVIDUAL CASES

1   The framework of analysis

(96) Outside the scope of the block exemption, it is relevant to examine whether in the individual case the agreement falls within the scope of Article 101(1) and if so whether the conditions of Article 101(3) are satisfied. Provided that they do not contain restrictions of competition by object and in particular hardcore restrictions of competition, there is no presumption that vertical agreements falling outside the block exemption because the market share threshold is exceeded fall within the scope of Article 101(1) or fail to satisfy the conditions of Article 101(3). Individual assessment of the likely effects of the agreement is required. Companies are encouraged to do their own assessment. Agreements that either do not restrict competition within the meaning of Article 101(1) or which fulfil the conditions of Article 101(3) are valid and enforceable. Pursuant to Article 1(2) of Council Regulation (EC) No 1/2003 of 16 December 2002 on the implementation of the rules on competition laid down in Articles 81 and 82 of the Treaty no notification needs to be made to benefit from an individual exemption under Article 101(3). In the case of an individual examination by the Commission, the latter will bear the burden of proof that the agreement in question infringes Article 101(1). The undertakings claiming the benefit of Article 101(3) bear the burden of proving that the conditions of that paragraph are fulfilled. When likely anti-competitive effects are demonstrated, undertakings may substantiate efficiency claims and explain why a certain distribution system is indispensable to bring likely benefits to consumers without eliminating competition, before the Commission decides whether the agreement satisfies the conditions of Article 101(3).

(97) The assessment of whether a vertical agreement has the effect of restricting competition will be made by comparing the actual or likely future situation on the relevant market with the vertical restraints in place with the situation that would prevail in the absence of the vertical restraints in the agreement. In the assessment of individual cases, the Commission will take, as appropriate, both actual and likely effects into account. For vertical agreements to be restrictive of competition by effect they must affect actual or potential competition to such an extent that on the relevant market negative effects on prices, output, innovation, or the variety or quality of goods and services can be expected with a reasonable degree of probability. The likely negative effects on competition must be appreciable. Appreciable anticompetitive effects are likely to occur when at least one of the parties has or obtains some degree of market power and the agreement contributes to the creation, maintenance or strengthening of that market power or allows the parties to exploit such market power. Market power is the ability to maintain prices above competitive levels or to maintain output in terms of product quantities, product quality and variety or innovation below competitive levels for a not insignificant period of time. The degree of market power normally required for a finding of an infringement under Article 101(1) is less than the degree of market power required for a finding of dominance under Article 102.

(98) Vertical restraints are generally less harmful than horizontal restraints. The main reason for the greater focus on horizontal restraints is that such restraints may concern an agreement between competitors producing identical or substitutable goods or services. In such horizontal relationships, the exercise of market power by one company (higher price of its product) may benefit its competitors. This may provide an incentive to competitors to induce each other to behave anti-competitively. In vertical relationships, the product of the one is the input for the other-, in other words, the activities of the parties to the agreement are complementary to each other. The exercise of market power by either the upstream or downstream company would therefore normally hurt the demand for the

product of the other. The companies involved in the agreement therefore usually have an incentive to prevent the exercise of market power by the other.

(99) Such self-restraining character should not, however, be over-estimated. When a company has no market power, it can only try to increase its profits by optimising its manufacturing and distribution processes, with or without the help of vertical restraints. More generally, because of the complementary role of the parties to a vertical agreement in getting a product on the market, vertical restraints may provide substantial scope for efficiencies. However, when an undertaking does have market power it can also try to increase its profits at the expense of its direct competitors by raising their costs and at the expense of its buyers and ultimately consumers by trying to appropriate some of their surplus. This can happen when the upstream and downstream company share the extra profits or when one of the two uses vertical restraints to appropriate all the extra profits.

Negative effects of vertical restraints

(100) The negative effects on the market that may result from vertical restraints which EU competition law aims at preventing are the following:

(a) anticompetitive foreclosure of other suppliers or other buyers by raising barriers to entry or expansion;

(b) softening of competition between the supplier and its competitors and/or facilitation of collusion amongst these suppliers, often referred to as reduction of inter-brand competition;

(c) softening of competition between the buyer and its competitors and/or facilitation of collusion amongst these competitors, often referred to as reduction of intra-brand competition if it concerns distributors' competition on the basis of the brand or product of the same supplier;

(d) the creation of obstacles to market integration, including, above all, limitations on the possibilities for consumers to purchase goods or services in any Member State they may choose.

(101) Foreclosure, softening of competition and collusion at the manufacturers' level may harm consumers in particular by increasing the wholesale prices of the products, limiting the choice of products, lowering their quality or reducing the level of product innovation. Foreclosure, softening of competition and collusion at the distributors' level may harm consumers in particular by increasing the retail prices of the products, limiting the choice of price-service combinations and distribution formats, lowering the availability and quality of retail services and reducing the level of innovation of distribution.

(102) On a market where individual distributors distribute the brand(s) of only one supplier, a reduction of competition between the distributors of the same brand will lead to a reduction of intra-brand competition between these distributors, but may not have a negative effect on competition between distributors in general. In such a case, if inter-brand competition is fierce, it is unlikely that a reduction of intra-brand competition will have negative effects for consumers.

(103) Exclusive arrangements are generally more anti-competitive than non-exclusive arrangements. Exclusive arrangements, whether by means of express contractual language or their practical effects, result in one party sourcing all or practically all of its demand from another party. For instance, under a non-compete obligation the buyer purchases only one brand. Quantity forcing, on the other hand, leaves the buyer some scope to purchase competing goods. The degree of foreclosure may therefore be less with quantity forcing.

(104) Vertical restraints agreed for non-branded goods and services are in general less harmful than restraints affecting the distribution of branded goods and services. Branding tends to increase product differentiation and reduce substitutability of the product, leading to a reduced elasticity of demand and an increased possibility to raise price. The distinction between branded and non-branded goods or services will often coincide with the distinction between intermediate goods and services and final goods and services.

(105) In general, a combination of vertical restraints aggravates their individual negative effects. However, certain combinations of vertical restraints are less anti-competitive than their use in isolation. For instance, in an exclusive distribution system, the distributor may be tempted to increase the price of the products as intra-brand competition has been reduced. The use of quantity forcing or the setting of a maximum resale price may limit such price increases. Possible negative effects of vertical restraints are reinforced when several suppliers and their buyers organize their trade in a similar way, leading to so-called cumulative effects.

1.2. *Positive effects of vertical restraints*

(106) It is important to recognise that vertical restraints may have positive effects by, in particular, promoting non-price competition and improved quality of services. When a company has no market power, it can only try to increase its profits by optimizing its manufacturing or distribution processes. In a number of situations vertical restraints may be helpful in this respect since the usual arm's length dealings between supplier and buyer, determining only price and quantity of a certain transaction, can lead to a sub-optimal level of investments and sales.

(107) While trying to give a fair overview of the various justifications for vertical restraints, these Guidelines do not claim to be complete or exhaustive. The following reasons may justify the application of certain vertical restraints:

(a) To solve a 'free-rider' problem. One distributor may free-ride on the promotion efforts of another distributor. That type of problem is most common at the wholesale and retail level. Exclusive distribution or similar restrictions may be helpful in avoiding such free-riding. Free-riding can also occur between suppliers, for instance where one invests in promotion at the buyer's premises, in general at the retail level, that may also attract customers for its competitors. Non-compete type restraints can help to overcome free-riding.

For there to be a problem, there needs to be a real free-rider issue. Free-riding between buyers can only occur on pre-sales services and other promotional activities, but not on after-sales services for which the distributor can charge its customers individually. The product will usually need to be relatively new or technically complex or the reputation of the product must be a major determinant of its demand, as the customer may otherwise very well know what it wants, based on past purchases. And the product must be of a reasonably high value as it is otherwise not attractive for a customer to go to one shop for information and to another to buy. Lastly, it must not be practical for the supplier to impose on all buyers, by contract, effective promotion or service requirements.

Free-riding between suppliers is also restricted to specific situations, namely to cases where the promotion takes place at the buyer's premises and is generic, not brand specific.

(b) To 'open up or enter new markets'. Where a manufacturer wants to enter a new geographic market, for instance by exporting to another country for the first time, this may involve special 'first time investments' by the distributor to establish the brand on the market. In order to persuade a local distributor to make these investments, it may be necessary to provide territorial protection to the distributor so that it can recoup these investments by temporarily charging a higher price. Distributors based in other markets should then be restrained for a limited period from selling on the new market (see also paragraph (61) in Section III.4). This is a special case of the free-rider problem described under point (a).

(c) The 'certification free-rider issue'. In some sectors, certain retailers have a reputation for stocking only 'quality' products. In such a case, selling through those retailers may be vital for the introduction of a new product. If the manufacturer cannot initially limit its sales to the premium stores, it runs the risk of being de-listed and the product introduction may fail. There may, therefore, be a reason for allowing for a limited duration a restriction such as exclusive distribution or selective distribution. It must be enough to guarantee introduction of the new product but not so long as to hinder large-scale dissemination.

Such benefits are more likely with 'experience' goods or complex goods that represent a relatively large purchase for the final consumer.

(d) The so-called 'hold-up problem'. Sometimes there are client-specific investments to be made by either the supplier or the buyer, such as in special equipment or training. For instance, a component manufacturer that has to build new machines and tools in order to satisfy a particular requirement of one of its customers. The investor may not commit the necessary investments before particular supply arrangements are fixed.

However, as in the other free-riding examples, there are a number of conditions that have to be met before the risk of under-investment is real or significant. Firstly, the investment must be relationship-specific. An investment made by the supplier is considered to be relationship-specific when, after termination of the contract, it cannot be used by the supplier to supply other customers and can only be sold at a significant loss. An investment made by the buyer is considered to be relationship-specific when, after termination of the contract, it cannot be used by the buyer to purchase and/or use products supplied by other suppliers and can only be sold at a significant loss. An investment is thus relationship-specific because it can only, for instance, be used to produce a brand-specific component or to store a particular brand and thus cannot be used profitably to produce or resell alternatives. Secondly, it must be a long-term investment that is not recouped in the short run. And thirdly, the investment must be asymmetric, that is, one party to the contract invests more than the other party. Where these conditions are met, there is usually a good reason to have a vertical restraint for the duration it takes to depreciate the investment. The appropriate vertical restraint will be of the non-compete type or quantity forcing type when the investment is made by the supplier and of the exclusive distribution, exclusive customer allocation or exclusive supply type when the investment is made by the buyer.

(e) The 'specific hold-up problem that may arise in the case of transfer of substantial know-how'. The know-how, once provided, cannot be taken back and the provider of the know-how may not want it to be used for or by its competitors. In as far as the know-how was not readily available to the buyer, is substantial and indispensable for the operation of the agreement, such a transfer may justify a non-compete type of restriction, which would normally fall outside Article 101(1).

(f) The 'vertical externality issue'. A retailer may not gain all the benefits of its action taken to improve sales; some may go to the manufacturer. For every extra unit a retailer sells by lowering its resale price or by increasing its sales effort, the manufacturer benefits if its wholesale price exceeds its marginal production costs. Thus, there may be a positive externality bestowed on the manufacturer by such retailer's actions and from the manufacturer's perspective the retailer may be pricing too high and/or making too little sales efforts. The negative externality of too high pricing by the retailer is sometimes called the 'double marginalisation problem' and it can be avoided by imposing a maximum resale price on the retailer. To increase the retailer's sales efforts selective distribution, exclusive distribution or similar restrictions may be helpful.

(g) 'Economies of scale in distribution'. In order to have scale economies exploited and thereby see a lower retail price for its product, the manufacturer may want to concentrate the resale of its products on a limited number of distributors. To do so, it could use exclusive distribution, quantity forcing in the form of a minimum purchasing requirement, selective distribution containing such a requirement or exclusive sourcing.

(h) 'Capital market imperfections'. The usual providers of capital (banks, equity markets) may provide capital sub-optimally when they have imperfect information on the quality of the borrower or there is an inadequate basis to secure the loan. The buyer or supplier may have better information and be able, through an exclusive relationship, to obtain extra security for its investment. Where the supplier provides the loan to the buyer, this may lead to non-compete or quantity forcing on the buyer. Where the buyer provides the loan to the supplier, this may be the reason for having exclusive supply or quantity forcing on the supplier.

(i) 'Uniformity and quality standardisation'. A vertical restraint may help to create a brand image by imposing a certain measure of uniformity and quality standardization on the distributors, thereby increasing the attractiveness of the product to the final consumer and increasing its sales. This can for instance be found in selective distribution and franchising.

(108) The nine situations listed in paragraph (107) make clear that under certain conditions, vertical agreements are likely to help realise efficiencies and the development of new markets and that this may offset possible negative effects. The case is in general strongest for vertical restraints of a limited duration which help the introduction of new complex products or protect relationship-specific investments. A vertical restraint is sometimes necessary for as long as the supplier sells its product to the buyer (see in particular the situations described in paragraph (107)(a), (e), (f), (g) and (i)).

(109) A large measure of substitutability exists between the different vertical restraints. As a result, the same inefficiency problem can be solved by different vertical restraints. For instance, economies of scale in distribution may possibly be achieved by using exclusive distribution, selective distribution, quantity forcing or exclusive sourcing. However, the negative effects on competition may differ between the various vertical restraints, which plays a role when indispensability is discussed under Article 101(3).

1.3. *Methodology of analysis*

(110) The assessment of a vertical restraint generally involves the following four steps:

(a) First, the undertakings involved need to establish the market shares of the supplier and the buyer on the market where they respectively sell and purchase the contract products.

(b) If the relevant market share of the supplier and the buyer each do not exceed the 30 % threshold, the vertical agreement is covered by the Block Exemption Regulation, subject to the hardcore restrictions and excluded restrictions set out in that Regulation.

(c) If the relevant market share is above the 30 % threshold for supplier and/or buyer, it is necessary to assess whether the vertical agreement falls within Article 101(1).

(d) If the vertical agreement falls within Article 101(1), it is necessary to examine whether it fulfils the conditions for exemption under Article 101(3).

1.3.1. *Relevant factors for the assessment under Article 101(1)*

(111) In assessing cases above the market share threshold of 30 %, the Commission will undertake a full competition analysis. The following factors are particularly relevant to establish whether a vertical agreement brings about an appreciable restriction of competition under Article 101(1):

(a) nature of the agreement;
(b) market position of the parties;
(c) market position of competitors;
(d) market position of buyers of the contract products;
(e) entry barriers;
(f) maturity of the market;
(g) level of trade;
(h) nature of the product;
(i) other factors.

(112) The importance of individual factors may vary from case to case and depends on all other factors. For instance, a high market share of the parties is usually a good indicator of market power, but in the case of low entry barriers it may not be indicative of market power. It is therefore not possible to provide firm rules on the importance of the individual factors.

(113) Vertical agreements can take many shapes and forms. It is therefore important to analyse the nature of the agreement in terms of the restraints that it contains, the duration of those restraints and the percentage of total sales on the market affected by those restraints. It may be necessary to go beyond the express terms of the agreement. The existence of implicit restraints may be derived from the way in which the agreement is implemented by the parties and the incentives that they face.

(114) The market position of the parties provides an indication of the degree of market power, if any, possessed by the supplier, the buyer or both. The higher their market share, the greater their market power is likely to be. This is particularly so where the market share reflects cost advantages or other competitive advantages vis à-vis competitors. Such competitive advantages may, for instance, result from being a first mover on the market (having the best site, etc.), from holding essential patents or having superior technology, from being the brand leader or having a superior portfolio.

(115) Such indicators, namely market share and possible competitive advantages, are used to assess the market position of competitors. The stronger the competitors are and the greater their number, the less risk there is that the parties will be able to individually exercise market power and foreclose the market or soft competition. It is also relevant to consider whether there are effective and timely counterstrategies that competitors would be likely to deploy. However, if the number of competitors becomes rather small and their market position (size, costs, R&D potential, etc.) is rather similar, such a market structure may increase the risk of collusion. Fluctuating or rapidly changing market shares are in general an indication of intense competition.

(116) The market position of the parties' customers provides an indication of whether or not one or more of those customers possess buyer power. The first indicator of buyer power is the market share of the customer on the purchase market. That share reflects the importance of its demand for possible suppliers. Other indicators focus on the position of the customer on its resale market, including characteristics such as a wide geographic spread of its outlets, own brands including private labels and its brand image amongst final consumers. In some circumstances, buyer power may prevent the parties from exercising market power and thereby solve a competition problem that would otherwise have existed. This is particularly so when strong customers have the capacity and incentive to bring new sources of supply on to the market in the case of a small but permanent increase in relative prices. Where strong customers merely extract favourable terms for themselves or simply pass on any price increase to their customers, their position does not prevent the parties from exercising market power.

(117) Entry barriers are measured by the extent to which incumbent companies can increase their price above the competitive level without attracting new entry. In the absence of entry barriers, easy and quick entry would render price increases unprofitable. When effective entry, preventing or eroding the exercise of market power, is likely to occur within one or two years, entry barriers can, as a general rule, be said to be low. Entry barriers may result from a wide variety of factors such as economies of scale and scope, government regulations, especially where they establish exclusive rights, state aid, import tariffs, intellectual property rights, ownership of resources where the supply is limited due to for instance natural limitations, essential facilities, a first mover advantage and brand loyalty of consumers created by strong advertising over a period of time. Vertical restraints and vertical integration may also work as an entry barrier by making access more difficult and foreclosing (potential) competitors. Entry barriers may be present at only the supplier or buyer level or at both levels. The question whether certain of those factors should be described as entry barriers depends particularly on whether they entail sunk costs. Sunk costs are those costs that have to be incurred to enter or be active on a market but that are lost when the market is exited. Advertising costs to build consumer loyalty are normally sunk costs, unless an exiting firm could either sell its brand name or use it somewhere else without a loss. The more costs are sunk, the more potential entrants have to weigh the risks of entering the market and the more credibly incumbents can threat that they will match new competition, as sunk costs make it costly for incumbents to leave the market. If, for instance, distributors are tied to a manufacturer via a non-compete obligation, the foreclosing effect will be more significant if setting up its own distributors will impose sunk costs on the potential entrant. In general, entry requires sunk costs, sometimes minor and sometimes major. Therefore, actual competition is in general more effective and will weigh more heavily in the assessment of a case than potential competition.

(118) A mature market is a market that has existed for some time, where the technology used is well known and widespread and not changing very much, where there are no major brand innovations and in which demand is relatively stable or declining. In such a market, negative effects are more likely than in more dynamic markets.

(119) The level of trade is linked to the distinction between intermediate and final goods and services. Intermediate goods and services are sold to undertakings for use as an input to produce other goods or services and are generally not recognisable in the final goods or services. The buyers of intermediate products are usually well-informed customers, able to assess quality and therefore less reliant on brand and image. Final goods are, directly or indirectly, sold to final consumers that often rely more on brand and image. As distributors have to respond to the demand of final consumers, competition may suffer more when distributors are foreclosed from selling one or a number of brands than when buyers of intermediate products are prevented from buying competing products from certain sources of supply.

(120) The nature of the product plays a role in particular for final products in assessing both the likely negative and the likely positive effects. When assessing the likely negative effects, it is important whether the products on the market are more homogeneous or heterogeneous, whether the product is expensive, taking up a large part of the consumer's budget, or is inexpensive and whether the product is a one-off purchase or repeatedly purchased. In general, when the product is more heterogeneous, less expensive and resembles more a one-off purchase, vertical restraints are more likely to have negative effects.

(121) In the assessment of particular restraints other factors may have to be taken into account. Among these factors can be the cumulative effect, that is, the coverage of the market by similar agreements of others, whether the agreement is 'imposed' (mainly one party is subject to the restrictions or obligations) or 'agreed' (both parties accept restrictions or obligations), the regulatory environment and behaviour that may indicate or facilitate collusion like price leadership, pre-announced price changes and discussions on the 'right' price, price rigidity in response to excess capacity, price discrimination and past collusive behaviour.

1.3.2.   *Relevant factors for the assessment under Article 101(3)*

(122) Restrictive vertical agreements may also produce pro-competitive effects in the form of efficiencies, which may outweigh their anti-competitive effects. Such an assessment takes place within the framework of Article 101(3), which contains an exception from the prohibition rule of Article 101(1). For that exception to be applicable, the vertical agreement must produce objective economic benefits, the restrictions on competition must be indispensable to attain the efficiencies, consumers must receive a fair share of the efficiency gains, and the agreement must not afford the parties the possibility of eliminating competition in respect of a substantial part of the products concerned.

(123) The assessment of restrictive agreements under Article 101(3) is made within the actual context in which they occur and on the basis of the facts existing at any given point in time. The assessment is sensitive to material changes in the facts. The exception rule of Article 101(3) applies as long as the four conditions are fulfilled and ceases to apply when that is no longer the case. When applying Article 101(3) in accordance with these principles it is necessary to take into account the investments made by any of the parties and the time needed and the restraints required to commit and recoup an efficiency enhancing investment.

(124) The first condition of Article 101(3) requires an assessment of what are the objective benefits in terms of efficiencies produced by the agreement. In this respect, vertical agreements often have the potential to help realise efficiencies, as explained in section 1.2, by improving the way in which the parties conduct their complementary activities.

(125) In the application of the indispensability test contained in Article 101(3), the Commission will in particular examine whether individual restrictions make it possible to perform the production, purchase and/or (re)sale of the contract products more efficiently than would have been the case in the absence of the restriction concerned. In making such an assessment, the market conditions and the realities facing the parties must be taken into account. Undertakings invoking the benefit of Article 101(3) are not required to consider hypothetical and theoretical alternatives. They must, however, explain and demonstrate why seemingly realistic and significantly less restrictive alternatives would be significantly less efficient. If the application of what appears to be a commercially realistic

and less restrictive alternative would lead to a significant loss of efficacies, the restriction in question is treated as indispensable.

(126) The condition that consumers must receive a fair share of the benefits implies that consumers of the products purchased and/or (re)sold under the vertical agreement must at least be compensated for the negative effects of the agreement. In other words, the efficiency gains must fully off-set the likely negative impact on prices, output and other relevant factors caused by the agreement.

(127) The last condition of Article 101(3), according to which the agreement must not afford the parties the possibility of eliminating competition in respect of a substantial part of the products concerned, presupposes an analysis of remaining competitive pressures on the market and the impact of the agreement on such sources of competition. In the application of the last condition of Article 101(3), the relationship between Article 101(3) and Article 102 must be taken into account. According to settled case law, the application of Article 101(3) cannot prevent the application of Article 102. Moreover, since Articles 101 and 102 both pursue the aim of maintaining effective competition on the market, consistency requires that Article 101(3) be interpreted as precluding any application of the exception rule to restrictive agreements that constitute an abuse of a dominant position. The vertical agreement may not eliminate effective competition, by removing all or most existing sources of actual or potential competition. Rivalry between undertakings is an essential driver of economic efficiency, including dynamic efficacies in the form of innovation. In its absence, the dominant undertaking will lack adequate incentives to continue to create and pass on efficiency gains. Where there is no residual competition and no foreseeable threat of entry, the protection of rivalry and the competitive process outweighs possible efficacy gains. A restrictive agreement which maintains, creates or strengthens a market position approaching that of a monopoly can normally not be justified on the grounds that it also creates efficacy gains.

2   Analysis of specific vertical restraints

(128) The most common vertical restraints and combinations of vertical restraints are analysed in the remainder of these Guidelines following the framework of analysis developed in paragraphs (96) to (127). Other restraints and combinations exist for which no direct guidance is provided in these Guidelines. They will, however, be treated according to the same principles and with the same emphasis on the effect on the market.

2.1.   *Single branding*

(129) Under the heading of 'single branding' fall those agreements which have as their main element the fact that the buyer is obliged or induced to concentrate its orders for a particular type of product with one supplier. That component can be found amongst others in non-compete and quantity-forcing on the buyer. A non-compete arrangement is based on an obligation or incentive scheme which makes the buyer purchase more than 80% of its requirements on a particular market from only one supplier. It does not mean that the buyer can only buy directly from the supplier, but that the buyer will not buy and resell or incorporate competing goods or services. Quantity-forcing on the buyer is a weaker form of non-compete, where incentives or obligations agreed between the supplier and the buyer make the latter concentrate its purchases to a large extent with one supplier. Quantity-forcing may for example take the form of minimum purchase requirements, stocking requirements or non-linear pricing, such as conditional rebate schemes or a two-part tariff (fixed fee plus a price per unit). A so-called 'English clause', requiring the buyer to report any better offer and allowing him only to accept such an offer when the supplier does not match it, can be expected to have the same effect as a single branding obligation, especially when the buyer has to reveal who makes the better offer.

(130) The possible competition risks of single branding are foreclosure of the market to competing suppliers and potential suppliers, softening of competition and facilitation of collusion between suppliers in case of cumulative use and, where the buyer is a retailer selling to final consumers, a loss of in-store inter-brand competition. Such restrictive effects have a direct impact on inter-brand competition.

(131) Single branding is exempted by the Block Exemption Regulation where the supplier's and buyer's market share each do not exceed 30 % and are subject to a limitation in time of five years for

the non-compete obligation. The remainder of this section provides guidance for the assessment of individual cases above the market share threshold or beyond the time limit of five years.

(132) The capacity for single branding obligations of one specific supplier to result in anticompetitive foreclosure arises in particular where, without the obligations, an important competitive constraint is exercised by competitors that either are not yet present on the market at the time the obligations are concluded, or that are not in a position to compete for the full supply of the customers. Competitors may not be able to compete for an individual customer's entire demand because the supplier in question is an unavoidable trading partner at least for part of the demand on the market, for instance because its brand is a 'must stock item' preferred by many final consumers or because the capacity constraints on the other suppliers are such that a part of demand can only be provided for by the supplier in question. The market position of the supplier is thus of main importance to assess possible anti-competitive effects of single branding obligations.

(133) If competitors can compete on equal terms for each individual customer's entire demand, single branding obligations of one specific supplier are generally unlikely to hamper effective competition unless the switching of supplier by customers is rendered difficult due to the duration and market coverage of the single branding obligations. The higher its tied market share, that is, the part of its market share sold under a single branding obligation, the more significant foreclosure is likely to be. Similarly, the longer the duration of the single branding obligations, the more significant foreclosure is likely to be. Single branding obligations shorter than one year entered into by non-dominant companies are generally not considered to give rise to appreciable anti-competitive effects or net negative effects. Single branding obligations between one and five years entered into by non-dominant companies usually require a proper balancing of pro- and anti-competitive effects, while single branding obligations exceeding five years are for most types of investments not considered necessary to achieve the claimed efficacies or the efficacies are not sufficient to outweigh their foreclosure effect. Single branding obligations are more likely to result in anti-competitive foreclosure when entered into by dominant companies.

(134) When assessing the supplier's market power, the market position of its competitors is important. As long as the competitors are sufficiently numerous and strong, no appreciable anti-competitive effects can be expected. Foreclosure of competitors is not very likely where they have similar market positions and can offer similarly attractive products. In such a case, foreclosure may, however, occur for potential entrants when a number of major suppliers enter into single branding contracts with a significant number of buyers on the relevant market (cumulative effect situation). This is also a situation where single branding agreements may facilitate collusion between competing suppliers. If, individually, those suppliers are covered by the Block Exemption Regulation, a withdrawal of the block exemption may be necessary to deal with such a negative cumulative effect. A tied market share of less than 5 % is not considered in general to contribute significantly to a cumulative foreclosure effect.

(135) In cases where the market share of the largest supplier is below 30 % and the market share of the five largest suppliers is below 50 %, there is unlikely to be a single or a cumulative anti-competitive effect situation. Where a potential entrant cannot penetrate the market profitably, it is likely to be due to factors other than single branding obligations, such as consumer preferences.

(136) Entry barriers are important to establish whether there is anticompetitive foreclosure. Wherever it is relatively easy for competing suppliers to create new buyers or find alternative buyers for their product, foreclosure is unlikely to be a real problem. However, there are often entry barriers, both at the manufacturing and at the distribution level.

(137) Countervailing power is relevant, as powerful buyers will not easily allow themselves to be cut off from the supply of competing goods or services. More generally, in order to convince customers to accept single branding, the supplier may have to compensate them, in whole or in part, for the loss in competition resulting from the exclusivity. Where such compensation is given, it may be in the individual interest of a customer to enter into a single branding obligation with the supplier. But it would be wrong to conclude automatically from this that all single branding obligations, taken together, are overall beneficial for customers on that market and for the final consumers. It is in particular unlikely that consumers as a whole will benefit if there are many customers and the single

branding obligations, taken together, have the effect of preventing the entry or expansion of competing undertakings.

(138) Lastly, 'the level of trade' is relevant. Anticompetitive foreclosure is less likely in case of an intermediate product. When the supplier of an intermediate product is not dominant, the competing suppliers still have a substantial part of demand that is free. Below the level of dominance an anticompetitive foreclosure effect may however arise in a cumulative effect situation. A cumulative anticompetitive effect is unlikely to arise as long as less than 50 % of the market is tied.

(139) Where the agreement concerns the supply of a final product at the wholesale level, the question whether a competition problem is likely to arise depends in large part on the type of wholesaling and the entry barriers at the wholesale level. There is no real risk of anticompetitive foreclosure if competing manufacturers can easily establish their own wholesaling operation. Whether entry barriers are low depends in part on the type of wholesaling, that is, whether or not wholesalers can operate efficiently with only the product concerned by the agreement (for example ice cream) or whether it is more efficient to trade in a whole range of products (for example frozen foodstuffs). In the latter case, it is not efficient for a manufacturer selling only one product to set up its own wholesaling operation. In that case, anti-competitive effects may arise. In addition, cumulative effect problems may arise if several suppliers tie most of the available wholesalers.

(140) For final products, foreclosure is in general more likely to occur at the retail level, given the significant entry barriers for most manufacturers to start retail outlets just for their own products. In addition, it is at the retail level that single branding agreements may lead to reduced in-store inter-brand competition. It is for these reasons that for final products at the retail level, significant anti-competitive effects may start to arise, taking into account all other relevant factors, if a non-dominant supplier ties 30 % or more of the relevant market. For a dominant company, even a modest tied market share may already lead to significant anti-competitive effects.

(141) At the retail level, a cumulative foreclosure effect may also arise. Where all suppliers have market shares below 30 %, a cumulative anticompetitive foreclosure effect is unlikely if the total tied market share is less than 40 % and withdrawal of the block exemption is therefore unlikely. That figure may be higher when other factors like the number of competitors, entry barriers etc. are taken into account. Where not all companies have market shares below the threshold of the Block Exemption Regulation but none is dominant, a cumulative anticompetitive foreclosure effect is unlikely if the total tied market share is below 30 %.

(142) Where the buyer operates from premises and land owned by the supplier or leased by the supplier from a third party not connected with the buyer, the possibility of imposing effective remedies for a possible foreclosure effect will be limited. In that case, intervention by the Commission below the level of dominance is unlikely.

(143) In certain sectors, the selling of more than one brand from a single site may be difficult, in which case a foreclosure problem can better be remedied by limiting the effective duration of contracts.

(144) Where appreciable anti-competitive effects are established, the question of a possible exemption under Article 101(3) arises. For non-compete obligations, the efficacies described in points (a) (free riding between suppliers), (d), (e) (hold-up problems) and (h) (capital market imperfections) of paragraph (107), may be particularly relevant.

(145) In the case of an efficacy as described in paragraph (107)(a), (107)(d) and (107)(h), quantity forcing on the buyer could possibly be a less restrictive alternative. A non-compete obligation may be the only viable way to achieve an efficacy as described in paragraph (107)(e), (hold-up problem related to the transfer of know how).

(146) In the case of a relationship-specific investment made by the supplier (see paragraph (107)(d)), a non-compete or quantity forcing agreement for the period of depreciation of the investment will in general fulfil the conditions of Article 101(3). In the case of high relationship-specific investments, a non-compete obligation exceeding five years may be justified. A relationship-specific investment could, for instance, be the installation or adaptation of equipment by the supplier when this equipment can be used afterwards only to produce components for a particular buyer. General

or market-specific investments in (extra) capacity are normally not relationship-specific investments. However, where a supplier creates new capacity specifically linked to the operations of a particular buyer, for instance a company producing metal cans which creates new capacity to produce cans on the premises of or next to the canning facility of a food producer, this new capacity may only be economically viable when producing for this particular customer, in which case the investment would be considered to be relationship-specific.

(147) Where the supplier provides the buyer with a loan or provides the buyer with equipment which is not relationship-specific, this in itself is normally not sufficient to justify the exemption of an anticompetitive foreclosure effect on the market. In case of capital market imperfection, it may be more efficient for the supplier of a product than for a bank to provide a loan (see paragraph (107)(h)). However, in such a case the loan should be provided in the least restrictive way and the buyer should thus in general not be prevented from terminating the obligation and repaying the outstanding part of the loan at any point in time and without payment of any penalty.

(148) The transfer of substantial know-how (paragraph (107)(e)) usually justifies a non-compete obligation for the whole duration of the supply agreement, as for example in the context of franchising.

(149) Example of non-compete obligation

The market leader in a national market for an impulse consumer product, with a market share of 40 %, sells most of its products (90 %) through tied retailers (tied market share 36 %). The agreements oblige the retailers to purchase only from the market leader for at least four years. The market leader is especially strongly represented in the more densely populated areas like the capital. Its competitors, 10 in number, of which some are only locally available, all have much smaller market shares, the biggest having 12 %. Those 10 competitors together supply another 10 % of the market via tied outlets. There is strong brand and product differentiation in the market. The market leader has the strongest brands. It is the only one with regular national advertising campaigns. It provides its tied retailers with special stocking cabinets for its product.

The result on the market is that in total 46 % (36 % + 10 %) of the market is foreclosed to potential entrants and to incumbents not having tied outlets. Potential entrants find entry even more difficult in the densely populated areas where foreclosure is even higher, although it is there that they would prefer to enter the market. In addition, owing to the strong brand and product differentiation and the high search costs relative to the price of the product, the absence of in-store inter-brand competition leads to an extra welfare loss for consumers. The possible efficacies of the outlet exclusivity, which the market leader claims result from reduced transport costs and a possible hold-up problem concerning the stocking cabinets, are limited and do not outweigh the negative effects on competition. The efficacies are limited, as the transport costs are linked to quantity and not exclusivity and the stocking cabinets do not contain special know-how and are not brand specific. Accordingly, it is unlikely that the conditions of Article 101(3) are fulfilled.

(150) Example of quantity forcing

A producer X with a 40 % market share sells 80 % of its products through contracts which specify that the reseller is required to purchase at least 75 % of its requirements for that type of product from X. In return X is offering financing and equipment at favourable rates. The contracts have a duration of five years in which repayment of the loan is foreseen in equal instalments. However, after the first two years buyers have the possibility to terminate the contract with a six-month notice period if they repay the outstanding loan and take over the equipment at its market asset value. At the end of the five-year period the equipment becomes the property of the buyer. Most of the competing producers are small, twelve in total with the biggest having a market share of 20 %, and engage in similar contracts with different durations. The producers with market shares below 10 % often have contracts with longer durations and with less generous termination clauses. The contracts of producer X leave 25 % of requirements free to be supplied by competitors. In the last three years, two new producers have entered the market and gained a combined market share of around 8 %, partly by taking over the loans of a number of resellers in return for contracts with these resellers.

Producer X's tied market share is 24 % (0,75 × 0,80 × 40 %). The other producers' tied market share is around 25 %. Therefore, in total around 49 % of the market is foreclosed to potential entrants and to incumbents not having tied outlets for at least the first two years of the supply contracts. The market shows that the resellers often have difficulty in obtaining loans from banks and are too small in general to obtain capital through other means like the issuing of shares. In addition, producer X is able to demonstrate that concentrating its sales on a limited number of resellers allows him to plan its sales better and to save transport costs. In the light of the efficacies on the one hand and the 25 % non-tied part in the contracts of producer X, the real possibility for early termination of the contract, the recent entry of new producers and the fact that around half the resellers are not tied on the other hand, the quantity forcing of 75 % applied by producer X is likely to fulfil the conditions of Article 101(3).

2.2 Exclusive distribution

(151) In an exclusive distribution agreement, the supplier agrees to sell its products to only one distributor for resale in a particular territory. At the same time, the distributor is usually limited in its active selling into other (exclusively allocated) territories. The possible competition risks are mainly reduced intra-brand competition and market partitioning, which may facilitate price discrimination in particular. When most or all of the suppliers apply exclusive distribution, it may soften competition and facilitate collusion, both at the suppliers' and distributors' level. Lastly, exclusive distribution may lead to foreclosure of other distributors and therewith reduce competition at that level.

(152) Exclusive distribution is exempted by the Block Exemption Regulation where both the supplier's and buyer's market share each do not exceed 30 %, even if combined with other non-hardcore vertical restraints, such as a non-compete obligation limited to five years, quantity forcing or exclusive purchasing. A combination of exclusive distribution and selective distribution is only exempted by the Block Exemption Regulation if active selling in other territories is not restricted. The remainder of this section provides guidance for the assessment of exclusive distribution in individual cases above the 30 % market share threshold.

(153) The market position of the supplier and its competitors is of major importance, as the loss of intra-brand competition can only be problematic if inter-brand competition is limited. The stronger the position of the supplier, the more serious is the loss of intra-brand competition. Above the 30 % market share threshold, there may be a risk of a significant reduction of intra-brand competition. In order to fulfil the conditions of Article 101(3), the loss of intra-brand competition may need to be balanced with real efficacies.

(154) The position of the competitors can have a dual significance. Strong competitors will generally mean that the reduction in intra-brand competition is outweighed by sufficient inter-brand competition. However, if the number of competitors becomes rather small and their market position is rather similar in terms of market share, capacity and distribution network, there is a risk of collusion and/or softening of competition. The loss of intra-brand competition can increase that risk, especially when several suppliers operate similar distribution systems. Multiple exclusive dealerships, that is, when different suppliers appoint the same exclusive distributor in a given territory, may further increase the risk of collusion and/or softening of competition. If a dealer is granted the exclusive right to distribute two or more important competing products in the same territory, inter-brand competition may be substantially restricted for those brands. The higher the cumulative market share of the brands distributed by the exclusive multiple brand dealers, the higher the risk of collusion and/or softening of competition and the more inter-brand competition will be reduced. If a retailer is the exclusive distributor for a number of brands this may have as result that if one producer cuts the wholesale price for its brand, the exclusive retailer will not be eager to transmit this price cut to the final consumer as it would reduce its sales and profits made with the other brands. Hence, compared to the situation without multiple exclusive dealerships, producers have a reduced interest in entering into price competition with one another. Such cumulative effect situations may be a reason to withdraw the benefit of the Block Exemption Regulation where the market shares of the suppliers and buyers are below the threshold of the Block Exemption Regulation.

(155) Entry barriers that may hinder suppliers from creating new distributors or finding alternative distributors are less important in assessing the possible anti-competitive effects of exclusive distribution. Foreclosure of other suppliers does not arise as long as exclusive distribution is not combined with single branding.

(156) Foreclosure of other distributors is not an issue where the supplier which operates the exclusive distribution system appoints a high number of exclusive distributors on the same market and those exclusive distributors are not restricted in selling to other non-appointed distributors. Foreclosure of other distributors may however become an issue where there is buying power and market power downstream, in particular in the case of very large territories where the exclusive distributor becomes the exclusive buyer for a whole market. An example would be a supermarket chain which becomes the only distributor of a leading brand on a national food retail market. The foreclosure of other distributors may be aggravated in the case of multiple exclusive dealership.

(157) Buying power may also increase the risk of collusion on the buyers' side when the exclusive distribution arrangements are imposed by important buyers, possibly located in different territories, on one or several suppliers.

(158) Maturity of the market is important, as loss of intra-brand competition and price discrimination may be a serious problem in a mature market but may be less relevant on a market with growing demand, changing technologies and changing market positions.

(159) The level of trade is important as the possible negative effects may differ between the wholesale and retail level. Exclusive distribution is mainly applied in the distribution of final goods and services. A loss of intra-brand competition is especially likely at the retail level if coupled with large territories, since final consumers may be confronted with little possibility of choosing between a high price/high service and a low price/low service distributor for an important brand.

(160) A manufacturer that chooses a wholesaler to be its exclusive distributor will normally do so for a larger territory, such as a whole Member State. As long as the wholesaler can sell the products without limitation to downstream retailers there are not likely to be appreciable anti-competitive effects. A possible loss of intra-brand competition at the wholesale level may be easily outweighed by efficacies obtained in logistics, promotion etc., especially when the manufacturer is based in a different country. The possible risks for inter-brand competition of multiple exclusive dealerships are however higher at the wholesale than at the retail level. Where one wholesaler becomes the exclusive distributor for a significant number of suppliers, not only is there a risk that competition between these brands is reduced, but also that there is foreclosure at the wholesale level of trade.

(161) As stated in paragraph (155), foreclosure of other suppliers does not arise as long as exclusive distribution is not combined with single branding. But even when exclusive distribution is combined with single branding anticompetitive foreclosure of other suppliers is unlikely, except possibly when the single branding is applied to a dense network of exclusive distributors with small territories or in case of a cumulative effect. In such a case it may be necessary to apply the principles on single branding set out in section 2.1. However, when the combination does not lead to significant foreclosure, the combination of exclusive distribution and single branding may be pro-competitive by increasing the incentive for the exclusive distributor to focus its efforts on the particular brand. Therefore, in the absence of such a foreclosure effect, the combination of exclusive distribution with non-compete may very well fulfil the conditions of Article 101(3) for the whole duration of the agreement, particularly at the wholesale level.

(162) The combination of exclusive distribution with exclusive sourcing increases the possible competition risks of reduced intra-brand competition and market partitioning which may facilitate price discrimination in particular. Exclusive distribution already limits arbitrage by customers, as it limits the number of distributors and usually also restricts the distributors in their freedom of active selling. Exclusive sourcing, requiring the exclusive distributors to buy their supplies for the particular brand directly from the manufacturer, eliminates in addition possible arbitrage by the exclusive distributors, which are prevented from buying from other distributors in the system. As a result, the supplier's possibilities to limit intra-brand competition by applying dissimilar conditions of sale to the

detriment of consumers are enhanced, unless the combination allows the creation of efficacies leading to lower prices to all final consumers.

(163) The nature of the product is not particularly relevant to the assessment of possible anticompetitive effects of exclusive distribution. It is, however, relevant to an assessment of possible efficacies, that is, after an appreciable anti-competitive effect is established.

(164) Exclusive distribution may lead to efficacies, especially where investments by the distributors are required to protect or build up the brand image. In general, the case for efficacies is strongest for new products, complex products, and products whose qualities are difficult to judge before consumption (so-called experience products) or whose qualities are difficult to judge even after consumption (so-called experience products). In addition, exclusive distribution may lead to savings in logistic costs due to economies of scale in transport and distribution.

(165) Example of exclusive distribution at the wholesale level

On the market for a consumer durable, A is the market leader. A sells its product through exclusive wholesalers. Territories for the wholesalers correspond to the entire Member State for small Member States, and to a region for larger Member States. Those exclusive distributors deal with sales to all the retailers in their territories. They do not sell to final consumers. The wholesalers are in charge of promotion in their markets, including sponsoring of local events, but also explaining and promoting the new products to the retailers in their territories. Technology and product innovation are evolving fairly quickly on this market, and pre-sale service to retailers and to final consumers plays an important role. The wholesalers are not required to purchase all their requirements of the brand of supplier A from the producer himself, and arbitrage by wholesalers or retailers is practicable because the transport costs are relatively low compared to the value of the product. The wholesalers are not under a non-compete obligation. Retailers also sell a number of brands of competing suppliers, and there are no exclusive or selective distribution agreements at the retail level. On the EU market of sales to wholesalers A has around 50 % market share. Its market share on the various national retail markets varies between 40 % and 60 %. A has between 6 and 10 competitors on every national market. B, C and D are its biggest competitors and are also present on each national market, with market shares varying between 20 % and 5 %. The remaining producers are national producers, with smaller market shares. B, C and D have similar distribution networks, whereas the local producers tend to sell their products directly to retailers.

On the wholesale market described in this example, the risk of reduced intra-brand competition and price discrimination is low. Arbitrage is not hindered, and the absence of intra-brand competition is not very relevant at the wholesale level. At the retail level, neither intra- nor inter-brand competition are hindered. Moreover, inter-brand competition is largely unaffected by the exclusive arrangements at the wholesale level. Therefore it is likely, even if anti-competitive effects exist, that also the conditions of Article 101(3) are fulfilled.

(166) Example of multiple exclusive dealerships in an oligopolistic market

On a national market for a final product, there are four market leaders, which each have a market share of around 20 %. Those four market leaders sell their product through exclusive distributors at the retail level. Retailers are given an exclusive territory which corresponds to the town in which they are located or a district of the town for large towns. In most territories, the four market leaders happen to appoint the same exclusive retailer ('multiple dealership'), often centrally located and rather specialised in the product. The remaining 20 % of the national market is composed of small local producers, the largest of these producers having a market share of 5 % on the national market. Those local producers sell their products in general through other retailers, in particular because the exclusive distributors of the four largest suppliers show in general little interest in selling less well-known and cheaper brands. There is strong brand and product differentiation on the market. The four market leaders have large national advertising campaigns and strong brand images, whereas the fringe producers do not advertise their products at the national level. The market is rather mature, with stable demand and no major product and technological innovation. The product is relatively simple.

In such an oligopolistic market, there is a risk of collusion between the four market leaders. That risk is increased through multiple dealerships. Intra-brand competition is limited by the territorial exclusivity. Competition between the four leading brands is reduced at the retail level, since one retailer fixes the price of all four brands in each territory. The multiple dealership implies that, if one producer cuts the price for its brand, the retailer will not be eager to transmit this price cut to the final consumer as it would reduce its sales and profits made with the other brands. Hence, producers have a reduced interest in entering into price competition with one another. Inter-brand price competition exists mainly with the low brand image goods of the fringe producers. The possible efficacy arguments for (joint) exclusive distributors are limited, as the product is relatively simple, the resale does not require any specific investments or training and advertising is mainly carried out at the level of the producers. Even though each of the market leaders has a market share below the threshold, the conditions of Article 101(3) may not be fulfilled and withdrawal of the block exemption may be necessary for the agreements concluded with distributors whose market share is below 30 % of the procurement market.

(167) Example of exclusive distribution combined with exclusive sourcing

Manufacturer A is the European market leader for a bulky consumer durable, with a market share of between 40 % and 60 % in most national retail markets. In Member States where it has a high market share, it has less competitors with much smaller market shares. The competitors are present on only one or two national markets. A's long time policy is to sell its product through its national subsidiaries to exclusive distributors at the retail level, which are not allowed to sell actively into each other's territories. Those distributors are thereby incentivised to promote the product and provide pre-sales services. Recently the retailers are in addition obliged to purchase manufacturer A's products exclusively from the national subsidiary of manufacturer A in their own country. The retailers selling the brand of manufacturer A are the main resellers of that type of product in their territory. They handle competing brands, but with varying degrees of success and enthusiasm. Since the introduction of exclusive sourcing, A applies price differences of 10 % to 15 % between markets with higher prices in the markets where it has less competition. The markets are relatively stable on the demand and the supply side, and there are no significant technological changes.

In the high price markets, the loss of intra-brand competition results not only from the territorial exclusivity at the retail level but is aggravated by the exclusive sourcing obligation imposed on the retailers. The exclusive sourcing obligation helps to keep markets and territories separate by making arbitrage between the exclusive retailers, the main resellers of that type of product, impossible. The exclusive retailers also cannot sell actively into each other's territory and in practice tend to avoid delivering outside their own territory. As a result, price discrimination is possible, without it leading to a significant increase in total sales. Arbitrage by consumers or independent traders is limited due to the bulkiness of the product.

While the possible efficacy arguments for appointing exclusive distributors may be convincing, in particular because of the incentivising of retailers, the possible efficacy arguments for the combination of exclusive distribution and exclusive sourcing, and in particular the possible efficiency arguments for exclusive sourcing, linked mainly to economies of scale in transport, are unlikely to outweigh the negative effect of price discrimination and reduced intra-brand competition. Consequently, it is unlikely that the conditions of Article 101(3) are fulfilled.

2.3. *Exclusive customer allocation*

(168) In an exclusive customer allocation agreement, the supplier agrees to sell its products to only one distributor for resale to a particular group of customers. At the same time, the distributor is usually limited in its active selling to other (exclusively allocated) groups of customers. The Block Exemption Regulation does not limit the way an exclusive customer group can be defined; it could for instance be a particular type of customers defined by their occupation but also a list of specific customers selected on the basis of one or more objective criteria. The possible competition risks are mainly reduced intra-brand competition and market partitioning, which may in particular facilitate price discrimination. Where most or all of the suppliers apply exclusive customer allocation, competition

may be softened and collusion, both at the suppliers' and the distributors' level, may be facilitated. Lastly, exclusive customer allocation may lead to foreclosure of other distributors and therewith reduce competition at that level.

(169) Exclusive customer allocation is exempted by the Block Exemption Regulation when both the supplier's and buyer's market share does not exceed the 30 % market share threshold, even if combined with other non-hardcore vertical restraints such as non-compete, quantity-forcing or exclusive sourcing. A combination of exclusive customer allocation and selective distribution is normally a hardcore restriction, as active selling to end-users by the appointed distributors is usually not left free. Above the 30 % market share threshold, the guidance provided in paragraphs (151) to (167) applies also to the assessment of exclusive customer allocation, subject to the specific remarks in the remainder of this section.

(170) The allocation of customers normally makes arbitrage by the customers more difficult. In addition, as each appointed distributor has its own class of customers, non-appointed distributors not falling within such a class may find it difficult to obtain the product. Consequently, possible arbitrage by non-appointed distributors will be reduced.

(171) Exclusive customer allocation is mainly applied to intermediate products and at the wholesale level when it concerns final products, where customer groups with different specific requirements concerning the product can be distinguished.

(172) Exclusive customer allocation may lead to efficacies, especially when the distributors are required to make investments in for instance specific equipment, skills or know-how to adapt to the requirements of their group of customers. The depreciation period of these investments indicates the justified duration of an exclusive customer allocation system. In general the case is strongest for new or complex products and for products requiring adaptation to the needs of the individual customer. Identifiable differentiated needs are more likely for intermediate products, that is, products sold to different types of professional buyers. Allocation of final consumers is unlikely to lead to efficacies.

(173) Example of exclusive customer allocation

A company has developed a sophisticated sprinkler installation. The company has currently a market share of 40 % on the market for sprinkler installations. When it started selling the sophisticated sprinkler it had a market share of 20 % with an older product. The installation of the new type of sprinkler depends on the type of building that it is installed in and on the use of the building (office, chemical plant, hospital etc.). The company has appointed a number of distributors to sell and install the sprinkler installation. Each distributor needed to train its employees for the general and specific requirements of installing the sprinkler installation for a particular class of customers. To sure that distributors would specialise, the company assigned to each distributor an exclusive class of customers and prohibited active sales to each others' exclusive customer classes. After five years, all the exclusive distributors will be allowed to sell actively to all classes of customers, thereby ending the system of exclusive customer allocation. The supplier may then also start selling to new distributors. The market is quite dynamic, with two recent entries and a number of technological developments. Competitors, with market shares between 25 % and 5 %, are also upgrading their products.

As the exclusivity is of limited duration and helps to ensure that the distributors may recoup their investments and concentrate their sales efforts first on a certain class of customers in order to learn the trade, and as the possible anti-competitive effects seem limited in a dynamic market, the conditions of Article 101(3) are likely to be fulfilled.

2.4.   Selective distribution

(174) Selective distribution agreements, like exclusive distribution agreements, restrict the number of authorised distributors on the one hand and the possibilities of resale on the other. The difference with exclusive distribution is that the restriction of the number of dealers does not depend on the number of territories but on selection criteria linked in the first place to the nature of the product. Another difference with exclusive distribution is that the restriction on resale is not a restriction on active selling to a territory but a restriction on any sales to non-authorised distributors, leaving only

appointed dealers and final customers as possible buyers. Selective distribution is almost always used to distribute branded final products.

(175) The possible competition risks are a reduction in intra-brand competition and, especially in case of cumulative effect, foreclosure of certain type(s) of distributors and softening of competition and facilitation of collusion between suppliers or buyers. To assess the possible anti-competitive effects of selective distribution under Article 101(1), a distinction needs to be made between purely qualitative selective distribution and quantitative selective distribution. Purely qualitative selective distribution selects dealers only on the basis of objective criteria required by the nature of the product such as training of sales personnel, the service provided at the point of sale, a certain range of the products being sold etc. The application of such criteria does not put a direct limit on the number of dealers. Purely qualitative selective distribution is in general considered to fall outside Article 101(1) for lack of anti-competitive effects, provided that three conditions are satisfied. First, the nature of the product in question must necessitate a selective distribution system, in the sense that such a system must constitute a legitimate requirement, having regard to the nature of the product concerned, to preserve its quality and ensure its proper use. Secondly, resellers must be chosen on the basis of objective criteria of a qualitative nature which are laid down uniformly for all and made available to all potential resellers and are not applied in a discriminatory manner. Thirdly, the criteria laid down must not go beyond what is necessary. Quantitative selective distribution adds further criteria for selection that more directly limit the potential number of dealers by, for instance, requiring minimum or maximum sales, by fixing the number of dealers, etc.

(176) Qualitative and quantitative selective distribution is exempted by the Block Exemption Regulation as long as the market share of both supplier and buyer each do not exceed 30 %, even if combined with other non-hardcore vertical restraints, such as non-compete or exclusive distribution, provided active selling by the authorised distributors to each other and to end users is not restricted. The Block Exemption Regulation exempts selective distribution regardless of the nature of the product concerned and regardless of the nature of the selection criteria. However, where the characteristics of the product do not require selective distribution or do not require the applied criteria, such as for instance the requirement for distributors to have one or more brick and mortar shops or to provide specific services, such a distribution system does not generally bring about sufficient efficiency enhancing effects to counterbalance a significant reduction in intra-brand competition. Where appreciable anti-competitive effects occur, the benefit of the Block Exemption Regulation is likely to be withdrawn. In addition, the remainder of this section provides guidance for the assessment of selective distribution in individual cases which are not covered by the Block Exemption Regulation or in the case of cumulative effects resulting from parallel networks of selective distribution.

(177) The market position of the supplier and its competitors is of central importance in assessing possible anti-competitive effects, as the loss of intra-brand competition can only be problematic if inter-brand competition is limited. The stronger the position of the supplier, the more problematic is the loss of intra-brand competition. Another important factor is the number of selective distribution networks present in the same market. Where selective distribution is applied by only one supplier on the market, quantitative selective distribution does not normally create net negative effects provided that the contract goods, having regard to their nature, require the use of a selective distribution system and on condition that the selection criteria applied are necessary to ensure efficient distribution of the goods in question. The reality, however, seems to be that selective distribution is often applied by a number of the suppliers on a given market.

(178) The position of competitors can have a dual significance and plays in particular a role in case of a cumulative effect. Strong competitors will mean in general that the reduction in intra-brand competition is easily outweighed by sufficient inter-brand competition. However, when a majority of the main suppliers apply selective distribution, there will be a significant loss of intra-brand competition and possible foreclosure of certain types of distributors as well as an increased risk of collusion between those major suppliers. The risk of foreclosure of more efficient distributors has always been greater with selective distribution than with exclusive distribution, given the restriction on sales to non-authorised dealers in selective distribution. That restriction is designed

to give selective distribution systems a closed character, making it impossible for non-authorised dealers to obtain supplies. Accordingly, selective distribution is particularly well suited to avoid pressure by price discounters (whether offline or online-only distributors) on the margins of the manufacturer, as well as on the margins of the authorised dealers. Foreclosure of such distribution formats, whether resulting from the cumulative application of selective distribution or from the application by a single supplier with a market share exceeding 30 %, reduces the possibilities for consumers to take advantage of the specific benefits offered by these formats such as lower prices, more transparency and wider access.

(179) Where the Block Exemption Regulation applies to individual networks of selective distribution, withdrawal of the block exemption or disapplication of the Block Exemption Regulation may be considered in case of cumulative effects. However, a cumulative effect problem is unlikely to arise when the share of the market covered by selective distribution is below 50 %. Also, no problem is likely to arise where the market coverage ratio exceeds 50 %, but the aggregate market share of the five largest suppliers (CR5) is below 50 %. Where both the CR5 and the share of the market covered by selective distribution exceed 50 %, the assessment may vary depending on whether or not all five largest suppliers apply selective distribution. The stronger the position of the competitors which do not apply selective distribution, the less likely other distributors will be foreclosed. If all five largest suppliers apply selective distribution, competition concerns may arise with respect to those agreements in particular that apply quantitative selection criteria by directly limiting the number of authorised dealers or that apply qualitative criteria, such as a requirement to have one or more brick and mortar shops or to provide specific services, which forecloses certain distribution formats. The conditions of Article 101(3) are in general unlikely to be fulfilled if the selective distribution systems at issue prevent access to the market by new distributors capable of adequately selling the products in question, especially price discounters or online-only distributors offering lower prices to consumers, thereby limiting distribution to the advantage of certain existing channels and to the detriment of final consumers. More indirect forms of quantitative selective distribution, resulting for instance from the combination of purely qualitative selection criteria with the requirement imposed on the dealers to achieve a minimum amount of annual purchases, are less likely to produce net negative effects, if such an amount does not represent a significant proportion of the dealer's total turnover achieved with the type of products in question and it does not go beyond what is necessary for the supplier to recoup its relationship-specific investment and/or realise economies of scale in distribution. As regards individual contributions, a supplier with a market share of less than 5 % is in general not considered to contribute significantly to a cumulative effect.

(180) Entry barriers are mainly of interest in the case of foreclosure of the market to non-authorised dealers. In general, entry barriers will be considerable as selective distribution is usually applied by manufacturers of branded products. It will in general take time and considerable investment for excluded retailers to launch their own brands or obtain competitive supplies elsewhere.

(181) Buying power may increase the risk of collusion between dealers and thus appreciably change the analysis of possible anti-competitive effects of selective distribution. Foreclosure of the market to more efficient retailers may especially result where a strong dealer organisation imposes selection criteria on the supplier aimed at limiting distribution to the advantage of its members.

(182) Article 5(1)(c) of the Block Exemption Regulation provides that the supplier may not impose an obligation causing the authorised dealers, either directly or indirectly, not to sell the brands of particular competing suppliers. Such a condition aims specifically at avoiding horizontal collusion to exclude particular brands through the creation of a selective club of brands by the leading suppliers. That kind of obligation is unlikely to be exemptible when the CR5 is equal to or above 50 %, unless none of the suppliers imposing such an obligation belongs to the five largest suppliers on the market.

(184) Maturity of the market is important, as loss of intra-brand competition and possible foreclosure of suppliers or dealers may be a serious problem on a mature market but is less relevant on a market with growing demand, changing technologies and changing market positions.

(185) Selective distribution may be efficient when it leads to savings in logistical costs due to economies of scale in transport and that may occur irrespective of the nature of the product (paragraph

(107)(g)). However, such an efficiency is usually only marginal in selective distribution systems. To help solve a free-rider problem between the distributors (paragraph (107)(a)) or to help create a brand image (paragraph (107)(i)), the nature of the product is very relevant. In general, the case is strongest for new products, complex products, products whose qualities are difficult to judge before consumption (so-called experience products) or whose qualities are difficult to judge even after consumption (so-called experience products). The combination of selective distribution with a location clause, protecting an appointed dealer against other appointed dealers opening up a shop in its vicinity, may in particular fulfil the conditions of Article 101(3) if the combination is indispensable to protect substantial and relationship-specific investments made by the authorised dealer (paragraph (107)(d)).

(186) To ensure that the least anti-competitive restraint is chosen, it is relevant to see whether the same efficacies can be obtained at a comparable cost by for instance service requirements alone.

(187) Example of quantitative selective distribution

On a market for consumer durables, the market leader (brand A) with a market share of 35 %, sells its product to final consumers through a selective distribution network. There are several criteria for admission to the network: the shop must employ trained staff and provide pre-sales services, there must be a specialised area in the shop devoted to the sales of the product and similar hi-tech products, and the shop is required to sell a wide range of models of the supplier and to display them in an attractive manner. Moreover, the number of admissible retailers in the network is directly limited through the establishment of a maximum number of retailers per number of inhabitants in each province or urban area. Manufacturer A has 6 competitors in that market. Its largest competitors, B, C and D, have market shares of respectively 25, 15 and 10 %, whilst the other producers have smaller market shares. A is the only manufacturer to use selective distribution. The selective distributors of brand A always handle a few competing brands. However, competing brands are also widely sold in shops which are not member of A's selective distribution network. Channels of distribution are various: for instance, brands B and C are sold in most of A's selected shops, but also in other shops providing a high quality service and in hypermarkets. Brand D is mainly sold in high service shops. Technology is evolving quite rapidly in this market, and the main suppliers maintain a strong quality image for their products through advertising.

On that market, the coverage ratio of selective distribution is 35 %. Inter-brand competition is not directly affected by the selective distribution system of A. Intrabrand competition for brand A may be reduced, but consumers have access to low service/low price retailers for brands B and C, which have a comparable quality image to brand A. Moreover, access to high service retailers for other brands is not foreclosed, since there is no limitation on the capacity of selected distributors to sell competing brands, and the quantitative limitation on the number of retailers for brand A leaves other high service retailers free to distribute competing brands. In this case, in view of the service requirements and the efficacies these are likely to provide and the limited effect on intra-brand competition the conditions of Article 101(3) are likely to be fulfilled.

(188) Example of selective distribution with cumulative effects

On a market for a particular sports article, there are seven manufacturers, whose respective market shares are: 25 %, 20 %, 15 %, 15 %, 10 %, 8 % and 7 %. The five largest manufacturers distribute their products through quantitative selective distribution, whilst the two smallest use different types of distribution systems, which results in a coverage ratio of selective distribution of 85 %. The criteria for access to the selective distribution networks are remarkably uniform amongst manufacturers: the distributors are required to have one or more brick and mortar shops, those shops are required to have trained personnel and to provide pre-sale services, there must be a specialised area in the shop devoted to the sales of the article and a minimum size for this area is specified. The shop is required to sell a wide range of the brand in question and to display the article in an attractive manner, the shop must be located in a commercial street, and that type of article must represent at least 30 % of the total turnover of the shop. In general, the same dealer is appointed selective distributor for all five brands. The two brands which do not use selective distribution usually sell through less specialised retailers with lower service levels. The market is stable, both on the supply and on the demand side, and there is strong brand image and product differentiation. The five market leaders have strong brand images, acquired through advertising and sponsoring, whereas the two smaller manufacturers have a strategy of cheaper products, with no strong brand image.

On that market, access by general price discounters and online-only distributors to the five leading brands is denied. Indeed, the requirement that this type of article represents at least 30 % of the activity of the dealers and the criteria on presentation and pre-sales services rule out most price discounters from the network of authorised dealers. The requirement to have one or more brick and mortar shops excludes online-only distributors from the network. As a consequence, consumers have no choice but to buy the five leading brands in high service/high price shops. This leads to reduced inter-brand competition between the five leading brands. The fact that the two smallest brands can be bought in low service/low price shops does not compensate for this, because the brand image of the five market leaders is much better. Inter-brand competition is also limited through multiple dealership. Even though there exists some degree of intra-brand competition and the number of retailers is not directly limited, the criteria for admission are strict enough to lead to a small number of retailers for the five leading brands in each territory.

The efficacies associated with these quantitative selective distribution systems are low: the product is not very complex and does not justify a particularly high service. Unless the manufacturers can prove that there are clear efficacies linked to their network of selective distribution, it is probable that the block exemption will have to be withdrawn because of its cumulative effects resulting in less choice and higher prices for consumers.

2.5. *Franchising*

(189) Franchise agreements contain licences of intellectual property rights relating in particular to trade marks or signs and know-how for the use and distribution of goods or services. In addition to the licence of IPRs, the franchisor usually provides the franchisee during the life of the agreement with commercial or technical assistance. The licence and the assistance are integral components of the business method being franchised. The franchisor is in general paid a franchise fee by the franchisee for the use of the particular business method. Franchising may enable the franchisor to establish, with limited investments, a uniform network for the distribution of its products. In addition to the provision of the business method, franchise agreements usually contain a combination of different vertical restraints concerning the products being distributed, in particular selective distribution and/or non-compete and/or exclusive distribution or weaker forms thereof.

(190) The coverage by the Block Exemption Regulation of the licensing of IPRs contained in franchise agreements is dealt with in paragraphs (24) to (46). As for the vertical restraints on the purchase, sale and resale of goods and services within a franchising arrangement, such as selective distribution, non-compete obligations or exclusive distribution, the Block Exemption Regulation applies up to the 30 % market share threshold. The guidance provided in respect of those types of restraints applies also to franchising, subject to the following two specific remarks:

(a) The more important the transfer of know-how, the more likely it is that the restraints create efficacies and/or are indispensable to protect the know-how and that the vertical restraints fulfil the conditions of Article 101(3);

(b) A non-compete obligation on the goods or services purchased by the franchisee falls outside the scope of Article 101(1) where the obligation is necessary to maintain the common identity and reputation of the franchised network. In such cases, the duration of the non-compete obligation is also irrelevant under Article 101(1), as long as it does not exceed the duration of the franchise agreement itself.

(191) Example of franchising

A manufacturer has developed a new format for selling sweets in so-called fun shops where the sweets can be coloured specially on demand from the consumer. The manufacturer of the sweets has also developed the machines to colour the sweets. The manufacturer also produces the colouring liquids. The quality and freshness of the liquid is of vital importance to producing good sweets. The manufacturer made a success of its sweets through a number of own retail outlets all operating under the same trade name and with the uniform fun image (style of lay-out of the shops, common advertising etc.). In order to expand sales the manufacturer started a franchising system. The franchisees are obliged to buy the sweets, liquid and colouring machine from the manufacturer, to have the same image and operate under the trade name, pay a franchise fee, contribute to common advertising and ensure the confidentiality of the operating manual prepared by the franchisor. In addition, the franchisees are only allowed to sell from the agreed premises, to sell to end users or other franchisees and are not allowed to sell other sweets. The franchisor is obliged not to appoint another franchisee nor operate a retail outlet himself in a given contract territory. The franchisor is also under the obligation to update and further develop its products, the business outlook and the operating manual and make these improvements available to all retail franchisees. The franchise agreements are concluded for a duration of 10 years.

Sweet retailers buy their sweets on a national market from either national producers that cater for national tastes or from wholesalers which import sweets from foreign producers in addition to selling products from national producers. On that market the franchisor's products compete with other brands of sweets. The franchisor has a market share of 30 % on the market for sweets sold to retailers. Competition comes from a number of national and international brands, sometimes produced by large diversified food companies. There are many potential points of sale of sweets in the form of tobacconists, general food retailers, cafeterias and specialised sweet shops. The franchisor's market share of the market for machines for colouring food is below 10 %.

Most of the obligations contained in the franchise agreements can be deemed necessary to protect the intellectual property rights or maintain the common identity and reputation of the franchised network and fall outside Article 101(1). The restrictions on selling (contract territory and selective distribution) provide an incentive to the franchisees to invest in the colouring machine and the franchise concept and, if not necessary to, at least help maintain the common identity, thereby offsetting the loss of intra-brand competition. The non-compete clause excluding other brands of sweets from the shops for the full duration of the agreements does allow the franchisor to keep the outlets uniform and prevent competitors from benefiting from its trade name. It does not lead to any serious foreclosure in view of the great number of potential outlets available to other sweet producers. The franchise agreements of this franchisor are likely to fulfil the conditions for exemption under Article 101(3) in as far as the obligations contained therein fall under Article 101(1).

2.6 *Exclusive supply*

(192) Under the heading of exclusive supply fall those restrictions that have as their main element that the supplier is obliged or induced to sell the contract products only or mainly to one buyer, in general or for a particular use. Such restrictions may take the form of an exclusive supply obligation, restricting the supplier to sell to only one buyer for the purposes of resale or a particular use, but may for instance also take the form of quantity forcing on the supplier, where incentives are agreed between the supplier and buyer which make the former concentrate its sales mainly with one buyer. For intermediate goods or services, exclusive supply is often referred to as industrial supply.

(193) Exclusive supply is exempted by the Block Exemption Regulation where both the supplier's and buyer's market share does not exceed 30 %, even if combined with other non-hardcore vertical restraints such as non-compete. The remainder of this section provides guidance for the assessment of exclusive supply in individual cases above the market share threshold.

(194) The main competition risk of exclusive supply is anti-competitive foreclosure of other buyers. There is a similarity with the possible effects of exclusive distribution, in particular when the exclusive distributor becomes the exclusive buyer for a whole market (see section 2.2, in particular paragraph (156)). The market share of the buyer on the upstream purchase market is obviously important for assessing the ability of the buyer to impose exclusive supply which forecloses other buyers from access to supplies. The importance of the buyer on the downstream market is however the factor which determines whether a competition problem may arise. If the buyer has no market power downstream, then no appreciable negative effects for consumers can be expected. Negative effects may

arise when the market share of the buyer on the downstream supply market as well as the upstream purchase market exceeds 30 %. Where the market share of the buyer on the upstream market does not exceed 30 %, significant foreclosure effects may still result, especially when the market share of the buyer on its downstream market exceeds 30 % and the exclusive supply relates to a particular use of the contract products. Where a company is dominant on the downstream market, any obligation to supply the products only or mainly to the dominant buyer may easily have significant anti-competitive effects.

(195) It is not only the market position of the buyer on the upstream and downstream market that is important but also the extent to and the duration for which it applies an exclusive supply obligation. The higher the tied supply share, and the longer the duration of the exclusive supply, the more significant the foreclosure is likely to be. Exclusive supply agreements shorter than five years entered into by non-dominant companies usually require a balancing of pro- and anti-competitive effects, while agreements lasting longer than five years are for most types of investments not considered necessary to achieve the claimed efficiencies or the efficacies are not sufficient to outweigh the foreclosure effect of such long-term exclusive supply agreements.

(196) The market position of the competing buyers on the upstream market is important as it is likely that competing buyers will be foreclosed for anti-competitive reasons, that is, to increase their costs, if they are significantly smaller than the foreclosing buyer. Foreclosure of competing buyers is not very likely where those competitors have similar buying power and can offer the suppliers similar sales possibilities. In such a case, foreclosure could only occur for potential entrants, which may not be able to secure supplies when a number of major buyers all enter into exclusive supply contracts with the majority of suppliers on the market. Such a cumulative effect may lead to withdrawal of the benefit of the Block Exemption Regulation.

(197) Entry barriers at the supplier level are relevant to establishing whether there is real foreclosure. In as far as it is efficient for competing buyers to provide the goods or services themselves via upstream vertical integration, foreclosure is unlikely to be a real problem. However, there are often significant entry barriers.

(198) Countervailing power of suppliers is relevant, as important suppliers will not easily allow themselves to be cut off from alternative buyers. Foreclosure is therefore mainly a risk in the case of weak suppliers and strong buyers. In the case of strong suppliers, the exclusive supply may be found in combination with non-compete obligations. The combination with non-compete obligations brings in the rules developed for single branding. Where there are relationship-specific investments involved on both sides (hold-up problem) the combination of exclusive supply and non-compete obligations that is, reciprocal exclusivity in industrial supply agreements may often be justified, in particular below the level of dominance.

(199) Lastly, the level of trade and the nature of the product are relevant for foreclosure. Anticompetitive foreclosure is less likely in the case of an intermediate product or where the product is homogeneous. Firstly, a foreclosed manufacturer that uses a certain input usually has more flexibility to respond to the demand of its customers than the wholesaler or retailer has in responding to the demand of the final consumer for whom brands may play an important role. Secondly, the loss of a possible source of supply matters less for the foreclosed buyers in the case of homogeneous products than in the case of a heterogeneous product with different grades and qualities. For final branded products or differentiated intermediate products where there are entry barriers, exclusive supply may have appreciable anti-competitive effects where the competing buyers are relatively small compared to the foreclosing buyer, even if the latter is not dominant on the downstream market.

(200) Efficacies can be expected in the case of a hold-up problem (paragraph (107)(d) and (107)(e)), and such efficacies are more likely for intermediate products than for final products. Other efficacies are less likely. Possible economies of scale in distribution (paragraph (107)(g)) do not seem likely to justify exclusive supply.

(201) In the case of a hold-up problem and even more so in the case of economies of scale in distribution, quantity forcing on the supplier, such as minimum supply requirements, could well be a less restrictive alternative.

(202) Example of exclusive supply

On a market for a certain type of components (intermediate product market) supplier A agrees with buyer B to develop, with its own know-how and considerable investment in new machines and with the help of specifications supplied by buyer B, a different version of the component. B will have to make considerable investments to incorporate the new component. It is agreed that A will supply the new product only to buyer B for a period of five years from the date of first entry on the market. B is obliged to buy the new product only from A for the same period of five years. Both A and B can continue to sell and buy respectively other versions of the component elsewhere. The market share of buyer B on the upstream component market and on the downstream final goods market is 40 %. The market share of the component supplier is 35 %. There are two other component suppliers with around 20-25 % market share and a number of small suppliers.

Given the considerable investments, the agreement is likely to fulfil the conditions of Article 101(3) in view of the efficiencies and the limited foreclosure effect. Other buyers are foreclosed from a particular version of a product of a supplier with 35 % market share and there are other component suppliers that could develop similar new products. The foreclosure of part of buyer B's demand to other suppliers is limited to maximum 40 % of the market.

2.7. *Upfront access payments*

(203) Upfront access payments are fixed fees that suppliers pay to distributors in the framework of a vertical relationship at the beginning of a relevant period, in order to get access to their distribution network and remunerate services provided to the suppliers by the retailers. This category includes various practices such as slotting allowances, the so called pay-to-stay fees, payments to have access to a distributor's promotion campaigns etc. Upfront access payments are exempted under the Block Exemption Regulation when both the supplier's and buyer's market share does not exceed 30 %. The remainder of this section provides guidance for the assessment of upfront access payments in individual cases above the market share threshold.

(204) Upfront access payments may sometimes result in anti-competitive foreclosure of other distributors if such payments induce the supplier to channel its products through only one or a limited number of distributors. A high fee may make that a supplier wants to channel a substantial volume of its sales through this distributor in order to cover the costs of the fee. In such a case, upfront access payments may have the same downstream foreclosure effect as an exclusive supply type of obligation. The assessment of that negative effect is made by analogy to the assessment of exclusive supply obligations (in particular paragraphs (194) to (199)).

(205) Exceptionally, upfront access payments may also result in anticompetitive foreclosure of other suppliers, where the widespread use of upfront access payments increases barriers to entry for small entrants. The assessment of that possible negative effect is made by analogy to the assessment of single branding obligations (in particular paragraphs (132) to (141)).

(206) In addition to possible foreclosure effects, upfront access payments may soften competition and facilitate collusion between distributors. Upfront access payments are likely to increase the price charged by the supplier for the contract products since the supplier must cover the expense of those payments. Higher supply prices may reduce the incentive of the retailers to compete on price on the downstream market, while the profits of distributors are increased as a result of the access payments. Such reduction of competition between distributors through the cumulative use of upfront access payments normally requires the distribution market to be highly concentrated.

(207) However, the use of upfront access payments may in many cases contribute to an efficient allocation of shelf space for new products. Distributors often have less information than suppliers on the potential for success of new products to be introduced on the market and, as a result, the amount of products to be stocked may be sub-optimal. Upfront access payments may be used to reduce this asymmetry in information between suppliers and distributors by explicitly allowing suppliers to compete for shelf space. The distributor may thus receive a signal of which products are most likely to be successful since a supplier would normally agree to pay an upfront access fee if it estimates a low probability of failure of the product introduction.

(208) Furthermore, due to the asymmetry in information mentioned in paragraph (207), suppliers may have incentives to free-ride on distributors' promotional efforts in order to introduce suboptimal products. If a product is not successful, the distributors will pay part of the costs of the product failure. The use of upfront access fees may prevent such free riding by shifting the risk of product failure back to the suppliers, thereby contributing to an optimal rate of product introductions.

2.8. *Category Management Agreements*

(209) Category management agreements are agreements by which, within a distribution agreement, the distributor trusts the supplier (the 'category captain') with the marketing of a category of products including in general not only the supplier's products, but also the products of its competitors. The category captain may thus have an influence on for instance the product placement and product promotion in the shop and product selection for the shop. Category management agreements are exempted under the Block Exemption Regulation when both the supplier's and buyer's market share does not exceed 30 %. The remainder of this section provides guidance for the assessment of category management agreements in individual cases above the market share threshold.

(210) While in most cases category management agreements will not be problematic, they may sometimes distort competition between suppliers, and finally result in anticompetitive foreclosure of other suppliers, where the category captain is able, due to its influence over the marketing decisions of the distributor, to limit or disadvantage the distribution of products of competing suppliers. While in most cases the distributor may not have an interest in limiting its choice of products, when the distributor also sells competing products under its own brand (private labels), the distributor may also have incentives to exclude certain suppliers, in particular intermediate range products. The assessment of such upstream foreclosure effect is made by analogy to the assessment of single branding obligations (in particular paragraphs (132) to (141)) by addressing issues like the market coverage of these agreements, the market position of competing suppliers and the possible cumulative use of such agreements.

(211) In addition, category management agreements may facilitate collusion between distributors when the same supplier serves as a category captain for all or most of the competing distributors on a market and provides these distributors with a common point of reference for their marketing decisions.

(212) Category management may also facilitate collusion between suppliers through increased opportunities to exchange via retailers sensitive market information, such as for instance information related to future pricing, promotional plans or advertising campaigns.

(213) However, the use of category management agreements may also lead to efficiencies. Category management agreements may allow distributors to have access to the supplier's marketing expertise for a certain group of products and to achieve economies of scale as they ensure that the optimal quantity of products is presented timely and directly on the shelves. As category management is based on customers' habits, category management agreements may lead to higher customer satisfaction as they help to better meet demand expectations. In general, the higher the inter-brand competition and the lower consumers' switching costs, the greater the economic benefits achieved through category management.

2.9 *Tying*

(214) Tying refers to situations where customers that purchase one product (the tying product) are required also to purchase another distinct product (the tied product) from the same supplier or someone designated by the latter. Tying may constitute an abuse within the meaning of Article 102. Tying may also constitute a vertical restraint falling under Article 101 where it results in a single branding type of obligation (see paragraphs (129) to (150)) for the tied product. Only the latter situation is dealt with in these Guidelines.

(215) Whether products will be considered as distinct depends on customer demand. Two products are distinct where, in the absence of the tying, a substantial number of customers would purchase or would have purchased the tying product without also buying the tied product from the

same supplier, thereby allowing stand-alone production for both the tying and the tied product. Evidence that two products are distinct could include direct evidence that, when given a choice, customers purchase the tying and the tied products separately from different sources of supply, or indirect evidence, such as the presence on the market of undertakings specialised in the manufacture or sale of the tied product without the tying product, or evidence indicating that undertakings with little market power, particularly on competitive markets, tend not to tie or not to bundle such products. For instance, since customers want to buy shoes with laces and it is not practicable for distributors to lace new shoes with the laces of their choice, it has become commercial usage for shoe manufacturers to supply shoes with laces. Therefore, the sale of shoes with laces is not a tying practice.

(216) Tying may lead to anticompetitive foreclosure effects on the tied market, the tying market, or both at the same time. The foreclosure effect depends on the tied percentage of total sales on the market of the tied product. On the question of what can be considered appreciable foreclosure under Article 101(1), the analysis for single branding can be applied. Tying means that there is at least a form of quantity-forcing on the buyer in respect of the tied product. Where in addition a non-compete obligation is agreed in respect of the tied product, this increases the possible foreclosure effect on the market of the tied product. The tying may lead to less competition for customers interested in buying the tied product, but not the tying product. If there is not a sufficient number of customers that will buy the tied product alone to sustain competitors of the supplier on the tied market, the tying can lead to those customers facing higher prices. If the tied product is an important complementary product for customers of the tying product, a reduction of alternative suppliers of the tied product and hence a reduced availability of that product can make entry onto the tying market alone more difficult.

(217) Tying may also directly lead to prices that are above the competitive level, especially in three situations. Firstly, if the tying and the tied product can be used in variable proportions as inputs to a production process, customers may react to an increase in price for the tying product by increasing their demand for the tied product while decreasing their demand for the tying product. By tying the two products the supplier may seek to avoid this substitution and as a result be able to raise its prices. Secondly, when the tying allows price discrimination according to the use the customer makes of the tying product, for example the tying of ink cartridges to the sale of photocopying machines (metering). Thirdly, when in the case of long-term contracts or in the case of after-markets with original equipment with a long replacement time, it becomes difficult for the customers to calculate the consequences of the tying.

(218) Tying is exempted under the Block Exemption Regulation when the market share of the supplier, on both the market of the tied product and the market of the tying product, and the market share of the buyer, on the relevant upstream markets, do not exceed 30 %. It may be combined with other vertical restraints, which are not hardcore restrictions under that Regulation, such as non-compete obligations or quantity forcing in respect of the tying product, or exclusive sourcing. The remainder of this section provides guidance for the assessment of tying in individual cases above the market share threshold.

(219) The market position of the supplier on the market of the tying product is obviously of central importance to assess possible anti-competitive effects. In general, this type of agreement is imposed by the supplier. The importance of the supplier on the market of the tying product is the main reason why a buyer may find it difficult to refuse a tying obligation.

(220) The market position of the supplier's competitors on the market of the tying product is important in assessing the supplier's market power. As long as its competitors are sufficiently numerous and strong, no anti-competitive effects can be expected, as buyers have sufficient alternatives to purchase the tying product without the tied product, unless other suppliers are applying similar tying. In addition, entry barriers on the market of the tying product are relevant to establish the market position of the supplier. When tying is combined with a non-compete obligation in respect of the tying product, this considerably strengthens the position of the supplier.

(221) Buying power is relevant, as important buyers will not easily be forced to accept tying without obtaining at least part of the possible efficiencies. Tying not based on efficacy is therefore mainly a risk where buyers do not have significant buying power.

(222) Where appreciable anti-competitive effects are established, the question whether the conditions of Article 101(3) are fulfilled arises. Tying obligations may help to produce efficacies arising from joint production or joint distribution. Where the tied product is not produced by the supplier, an efficacy may also arise from the supplier buying large quantities of the tied product. For tying to fulfil the conditions of Article 101(3), it must, however, be shown that at least part of these cost reductions are passed on to the consumer, which is normally not the case when the retailer is able to obtain, on a regular basis, supplies of the same or equivalent products on the same or better conditions than those offered by the supplier which applies the tying practice. Another efficacy may exist where tying helps to ensure a certain uniformity and quality standardisation (see paragraph (107)(i)). However, it needs to be demonstrated that the positive effects cannot be realised equally efficiently by requiring the buyer to use or resell products satisfying minimum quality standards, without requiring the buyer to purchase these from the supplier or someone designated by the latter. The requirements concerning minimum quality standards would not normally fall within the scope of Article 101(1). Where the supplier of the tying product imposes on the buyer the suppliers from which the buyer must purchase the tied product, for instance because the formulation of minimum quality standards is not possible, this may also fall outside the scope of Article 101(1), especially where the supplier of the tying product does not derive a direct (financial) benefit from designating the suppliers of the tied product.

2.10   Resale price restrictions

(223) As explained in section III.3, resale price maintenance (RPM), that is, agreements or concerted practices having as their direct or indirect object the establishment of a fixed or minimum resale price or a fixed or minimum price level to be observed by the buyer, are treated as a hardcore restriction. Where an agreement includes RPM, that agreement is presumed to restrict competition and thus to fall within Article 101(1). It also gives rise to the presumption that the agreement is unlikely to fulfil the conditions of Article 101(3), for which reason the block exemption does not apply. However, undertakings have the possibility to plead an efficiency defence under Article 101(3) in an individual case. It is incumbent on the parties to substantiate that likely efficiencies result from including RPM in their agreement and demonstrate that all the conditions of Article 101(3) are fulfilled. It then falls to the Commission to effectively assess the likely negative effects on competition and consumers before deciding whether the conditions of Article 101(3) are fulfilled.

(224) RPM may restrict competition in a number of ways. Firstly, RPM may facilitate collusion between suppliers by enhancing price transparency on the market, thereby making it easier to detect whether a supplier deviates from the collusive equilibrium by cutting its price. RPM also undermines the incentive for the supplier to cut its price to its distributors, as the fixed resale price will prevent it from benefiting from expanded sales. Such a negative effect is particularly plausible where the market is prone to collusive outcomes, for instance if the manufacturers form a tight oligopoly, and a significant part of the market is covered by RPM agreements. Second, by eliminating intra-brand price competition, RPM may also facilitate collusion between the buyers, that is, at the distribution level. Strong or well organised distributors may be able to force or convince one or more suppliers to fix their resale price above the competitive level and thereby help them to reach or stabilise a collusive equilibrium. The resulting loss of price competition seems especially problematic when the RPM is inspired by the buyers, whose collective horizontal interests can be expected to work out negatively for consumers. Third, RPM may more generally soften competition between manufacturers and/or between retailers, in particular when manufacturers use the same distributors to distribute their products and RPM is applied by all or many of them. Fourth, the immediate effect of RPM will be that all or certain distributors are prevented from lowering their sales price for that particular brand. In other words, the direct effect of RPM is a price increase. Fifth, RPM may lower the pressure on the margin of the manufacturer, in particular where the manufacturer has a commitment problem, that is, where it has

an interest in lowering the price charged to subsequent distributors. In such a situation, the manufacturer may prefer to agree to RPM, so as to help it to commit not to lower the price for subsequent distributors and to reduce the pressure on its own margin. Sixth, RPM may be implemented by a manufacturer with market power to foreclose smaller rivals. The increased margin that RPM may offer distributors, may entice the latter to favour the particular brand over rival brands when advising customers, even where such advice is not in the interest of these customers, or not to sell these rival brands at all. Lastly, RPM may reduce dynamism and innovation at the distribution level. By preventing price competition between different distributors, RPM may prevent more efficient retailers from entering the market or acquiring sufficient scale with low prices. It also may prevent or hinder the entry and expansion of distribution formats based on low prices, such as price discounters.

(225) However, RPM may not only restrict competition but may also, in particular where it is supplier driven, lead to efficacies, which will be assessed under Article 101(3). Most notably, where a manufacturer introduces a new product, RPM may be helpful during the introductory period of expanding demand to induce distributors to better take into account the manufacturer's interest to promote the product. RPM may provide the distributors with the means to increase sales efforts and if the distributors on this market are under competitive pressure this may induce them to expand overall demand for the product and make the launch of the product a success, also for the benefit of consumers. Similarly, fixed resale prices, and not just maximum resale prices, may be necessary to organise in a franchise system or similar distribution system applying a uniform distribution format a coordinated short term low price campaign (2 to 6 weeks in most cases) which will also benefit the consumers. In some situations, the extra margin provided by RPM may allow retailers to provide (additional) pre-sales services, in particular in case of experience or complex products. If enough customers take advantage from such services to make their choice but then purchase at a lower price with retailers that do not provide such services (and hence do not incur these costs), high-service retailers may reduce or eliminate these services that enhance the demand for the supplier's product. RPM may help to prevent such free riding at the distribution level. The parties will have to convincingly demonstrate that the RPM agreement can be expected to not only provide the means but also the inactive to overcome possible free riding between retailers on these services and that the pre-sales services overall benefit consumers as part of the demonstration that all the conditions of Article 101(3) are fulfilled.

(226) The practice of recommending a resale price to a reseller or requiring the reseller to respect a maximum resale price is covered by the Block Exemption Regulation when the market share of each of the parties to the agreement does not exceed the 30 % threshold, provided it does not amount to a minimum or fixed sale price as a result of pressure from, or incentives offered by, any of the parties. The remainder of this section provides guidance for the assessment of maximum or recommended prices above the market share threshold and for cases of withdrawal of the block exemption.

(227) The possible competition risk of maximum and recommended prices is that they will work as a focal point for the resellers and might be followed by most or all of them and/or that maximum or recommended prices may soften competition or facilitate collusion between suppliers.

(228) An important factor for assessing possible anti-competitive effects of maximum or recommended resale prices is the market position of the supplier. The stronger the market position of the supplier, the higher the risk that a maximum resale price or a recommended resale price leads to a more or less uniform application of that price level by the resellers, because they may use it as a focal point. They may find it difficult to deviate from what they perceive to be the preferred resale price proposed by such an important supplier on the market.

(229) Where appreciable anti-competitive effects are established for maximum or recommended resale prices, the question of a possible exemption under Article 101(3) arises. For maximum resale prices, the efficiency described in paragraph (107)(f) (avoiding double marginalisation), may be particularly relevant. A maximum resale price may also help to ensure that the brand in question competes more forcefully with other brands, including own label products, distributed by the same distributor.

Guidelines on the applicability of Article 81 of the EC Treaty to horizontal cooperation agreements

(OJ 2001, No. C3/02)

(Text with EEA relevance)

1. INTRODUCTION

1.1 Purpose

1. These guidelines set out the principles for the assessment of horizontal cooperation agreements under Article 81 of the Treaty. A cooperation is of a 'horizontal nature' if an agreement or concerted practice is entered into between companies operating at the same level(s) in the market. In most instances, horizontal cooperation amounts to cooperation between competitors. It covers, for example, areas such as research and development (R & D), production, purchasing or commercialisation.

2. Horizontal cooperation may lead to competition problems. This is, for example, the case if the parties to a cooperation agree to fix prices or output, to share markets, or if the cooperation enables the parties to maintain, gain or increase market power and thereby causes negative market effects with respect to prices, output, innovation or the variety and quality of products.

3. On the other hand, horizontal cooperation can lead to substantial economic benefits. Companies need to respond to increasing competitive pressure and a changing market place driven by globalisation, the speed of technological progress and the generally more dynamic nature of markets. Cooperation can be a means to share risk, save costs, pool know-how and launch innovation faster. In particular for small and medium-sized enterprises cooperation is an important means to adapt to the changing market place.

4. The Commission, while recognising the economic benefits that can be generated by cooperation, has to ensure that effective competition is maintained. Article 81 provides the legal framework for a balanced assessment taking into account both anti-competitive effects as well as economic benefits.

5. In the past, two Commission notices and two block exemption regulations provided guidance for the assessment of horizontal cooperation under Article 81. Commission Regulation (EEC) No 417/85, as last amended by Regulation (EC) No 223 6/9 7 and Commission Regulation (EEC) No 418/85, as last amended by Regulation (EC) No 2236/97, provided for the exemption of certain forms of specialisation agreement and research and development agreement (R & D) respectively. Those two Regulations have now been replaced by Commission Regulation (EC) No 2658/2000 of 29 November 2000 on the application of Article 81(3) of the Treaty to categories of specialisation agreements ('the Specialisation block exemption Regulation') and Commission Regulation (EC) No 2659/2000 of29 November 2000 on the application of Article 81(3) of the Treaty to categories of research and development agreements ('the R & D block exemption Regulation'). The two notices provided guidance in respect of certain types of cooperation agreement falling outside Article 81 and the assessment of cooperative joint ventures.

6. Changing markets have generated an increasing variety and use of horizontal cooperation. More complete and updated guidance is needed to improve clarity and transparency regarding the applicability of Article 81 in this area. Within the assessment greater emphasis has to be put on economic criteria to better reflect recent developments in enforcement practice and the case law of the Court of Justice and Court of First Instance of the European Communities.

7. The purpose of these guidelines is to provide an analytical framework for the most common types of horizontal cooperation. This framework is primarily based on criteria that help to analyse the economic context of a cooperation agreement. Economic criteria such as the market power of

the parties and other factors relating to the market structure, form a key element of the assessment of the market impact likely to be caused by a cooperation and therefore for the assessment under Article 81. Given the enormous variety in types and combinations of horizontal cooperation and market circumstances in which they operate, it is impossible to provide specific answers for every possible scenario. The present analytical framework based on economic criteria will nevertheless assist businesses in assessing the compatibility of an individual cooperation agreement with Article 81.

8. The guidelines not only replace the Notices referred to in paragraph 5, but also cover a wider range of the most common types of horizontal agreements. They complement the R & D block exemption Regulation and the Specialisation block exemption Regulation.

1.2   Scope of the guidelines

9. These guidelines cover agreements or concerted practices (hereinafter referred to as 'agreements') entered into between two or more companies operating at the same level (s) in the market, e.g. at the same level of production or distribution. Within this context the focus is an cooperation between competitors. The term 'competitors' as used in these guidelines includes both actual and potential.

10. The present guidelines do not, however, address all possible horizontal agreements. They are only concerned with those types of cooperation which potentially generate efficiency gains, namely agreements on R & D, production, purchasing, commercialisation, standardisation, and environmental agreements. Other types of horizontal agreements between competitors, for example on the exchange of information or on minority shareholdings, are to be addressed separately.

11. Agreements that are entered into between companies operating at a different level of the production or distribution chain, that is to say vertical agreements, are in principle excluded from these guidelines and dealt with in Commission Regulation (EC) No 2790/1999 (the 'Block Exemption Regulation on Vertical Restraints') and the Guidelines on vertical restraints. However, to the extent that vertical agreements, e.g. distribution agreements, are concluded between competitors, the effects of the agreement on the market and the possible competition problems can be similar to horizontal agreements. Therefore, these agreements have to be assessed according to the principles described in the present guidelines. This does not exclude the additional application of the Guidelines on Vertical Restraints to these agreements to assess the vertical restraints included in such agreements.

12. Agreements may combine different stages of cooperation, for example, R & D and the production of its results. Unless they fall under Council Regulation (EEC) No 4064/89 of 21 December 1989 on the control of concentrations between undertakings, as last amended by Regulation (EC) No 1310/97 ('the Merger Regulation'), these agreements are covered by the guidelines. The centre of gravity of the cooperation determines which section of the present guidelines applies to the agreement in question. In the determination of the centre of gravity, account is taken in particular of two factors: firstly, the starting point of the cooperation, and, secondly, the degree of integration of the different functions which are being combined. A cooperation involving both joint R & D and joint production of the results would thus normally be covered in the section on 'Agreements on Research and Development', as the joint production will only take place if the joint R & D is successful. This implies that the results of the joint R & D are decisive for production. The R & D agreement can thus be regarded as the starting point of the cooperation. This assessment would change if the agreement foresaw a full integration in the area of production and only a partial integration of some R & D activities. In this case, the possible anticompetitive effects and economic benefits of the cooperation would largely relate to the joint production, and the agreement would therefore be examined according to the principles set out in the section on 'Production Agreements'. More complex arrangements such as strategic alliances that combine a number of different areas and instruments of cooperation in varying ways are not covered by the guidelines. The assessment of each individual area of cooperation within an alliance may be carried out with the help of the corresponding chapter in the guidelines. However, complex arrangements must also be analysed in their totality. Due to the variety of areas an alliance may combine, it is impossible to give general guidance for such an overall

assessment. Alliances or other forms of cooperation that primarily declare intentions are impossible to assess under the competition rules as long as they lack a precise scope.

13. The criteria set out in these guidelines apply to cooperation concerning both goods and services, collectively referred to as 'products'. However, the guidelines do not apply to the extent that sector-specific rules apply, as is the case for agriculture, transport or insurance. Operations that come under the Merger Regulation are also not the subject of the present guidelines.

14. Article 81 only applies to those horizontal cooperation agreements which may affect trade between Member States. These guidelines are not concerned with the analysis of the capability of a given agreement to affect trade. The following principles on the applicability of Article 81 are therefore based on the assumption that trade between Member States is affected. In practice, however, this issue needs to be examined on a case-by-case basis.

15. Article 81 does not apply to agreements which are of minor importance because they are not capable of appreciably restricting competition by object or effect. These guidelines are without prejudice to the application of the present or any future 'de minimis' notice.

16. The assessment under Article 81 as described in these guidelines is without prejudice to the possible parallel application of Article 82 of the Treaty to horizontal cooperation agreements. Furthermore, these guidelines are without prejudice to the interpretation that may be given by the Court of First Instance and the Court of Justice of the European Communities in relation to the application of Article 81 to horizontal cooperation agreements.

1.3 Basic principles for the assessment under Article 81

1.3.1. *Article 81(1)*

17. Article 81(1) applies to horizontal cooperation agreements which have as their object or effect the prevention, restriction or distortion of competition (hereinafter referred to as 'restrictions of competition').

18. In some cases the nature of a cooperation indicates from the outset the applicability of Article 81(1). This is the case for agreements that have as their object a restriction of competition by means of price fixing, output limitation or sharing of markets or customers. These agreements are presumed to have negative market effects. It is therefore not necessary to examine their actual effects on competition and the market in order to establish that they fall within Article 81(1).

19. Many horizontal cooperation agreements, however, do not have as their object a restriction of competition. Therefore, an analysis of the effects of the agreement is necessary. For this analysis it is not sufficient that the agreement limits competition between the parties. It must also be likely to affect competition in the market to such an extent that negative market effects as to prices, output, innovation or the variety or quality of goods and services can be expected.

20. Whether the agreement is able to cause such negative market effects depends on the economic context taking into account both the nature of the agreement and the parties' combined market power which determines—together with other structural factors—the capability of the cooperation to affect overall competition to such a significant extent.

Nature of the agreement

21. The nature of an agreement relates to factors such as the area and objective of the cooperation, the competitive relationship between the parties and the extent to which they combine their activities. These factors indicate the likelihood of the parties coordinating their behaviour in the market.

22. Certain types of agreement, for instance most R & D agreements or cooperation to set standards or improve environmental conditions, are less likely to include restrictions with respect to prices and output. If these types of agreements have negative effects at all these are likely to be on innovation or the variety of products. They may also give rise to foreclosure problems.

23. Other types of cooperation such as agreements on production or purchasing typically cause a certain degree of commonality in (total) costs. If this degree is significant, the parties may more easily coordinate market prices and output. A significant degree of commonality in costs

can only be achieved under certain conditions: First, the area of cooperation, e.g. production and purchasing, has to account for a high proportion of the total costs in a given market. Secondly, the parties need to combine their activities in the area of cooperation to a significant extent. This is, for instance, the case, where they jointly manufacture or purchase an important intermediate product or a high proportion of their total output of a final product.

Agreements that do not fall under Article 81(1)

24. Some categories of agreements do not fall under Article 81(1) because of their very nature. This is normally true for cooperation that does not imply a coordination of the parties' competitive behaviour in the market such as

- cooperation between non-competitors,
- cooperation between competing companies that cannot independently carry out the project or activity covered by the cooperation,
- cooperation concerning an activity which does not influence the relevant parameters of competition.

These categories of cooperation could only come under Article 81(1) if they involve firms with significant market powerand are likely to cause foreclosure problems vis-a-vis third parties.

Agreements that almost always fall under Article 81(1)

25. Another category of agreements can be assessed from the outset as normally falling under Article 81(1). This concerns cooperation agreements that have the object to restrict competition by means of price fixing, output limitation or sharing of markets or customers. These restrictions are considered to be the most harmful, because they directly interfere with the outcome of the competitive process. Price fixing and output limitation directly lead to customers paying higher prices or not receiving the desired quantities. The sharing of markets or customers reduces the choice available to customers and therefore also leads to higher prices or reduced output. It can therefore be presumed that these restrictions have negative market effects. They are therefore almost always prohibited.

Agreements that may fall under Article 81(1)

26. Agreements that do not belong to the above-mentioned categories need further analysis in order to decide whether they fall under Article 81(1). The analysis has to include market-related criteria such as the market position of the parties and other structural factors.

Market power and market structure

27. The starting point for the analysis is the position of the parties in the markets affected by the cooperation. This determines whether or not they are likely to maintain, gain or increase market power through the cooperation, i.e. have the ability to cause negative market effects as to prices, output, innovation or the variety or quality of goods and services. To carry out this analysis the relevant market(s) have to be defined by using the methodology of the Commission's market definition notice. Where specific types of markets are concerned such as purchasing or technology markets, these guidelines will provide additional guidance.

28. If the parties together have a low combined market share, a restrictive effect of the cooperation is unlikely and no further analysis normally is required. If one of just two parties has only an insignificant market share and if it does not possess important resources, even a high combined market share normally cannot be seen as indicating a restrictive effect on competition in the market. Given the variety of cooperation types and the different effects they may cause in different market situations, it is impossible to give a general market share threshold above which sufficient market power for causing restrictive effects can be assumed.

29. In addition to the market position of the parties and the addition of market shares, the market concentration, i.e. the position and number of competitors, may have to be taken into account as an additional factor to assess the impact of the cooperation on market competition. As an indicator the Herfindahl-Hirshman Index ('HHI'), which sums up the squares of the individual market shares of all competitors, can be used: With an HHI below 1 000 the market concentration can be characterised as low, between 1 000 and 1 800 as moderate and above 1 800 as high. Another possible indicator would be the leading firm concentration ratio, which sums up the individual market shares of the leading competitors.

30. Depending on the market position of the parties and the concentration in the market, other factors such as the stability of market shares over time, entry barriers and the likelihood of market entry, the countervailing power of buyers/suppliers or the nature of the products (e.g. homogeneity, maturity) have to be considered as well. Where an impact on competition in innovation is likely and can not be assessed adequately on the basis of existing markets, specific factors to analyse these impacts may have to be taken into account (see Chapter 2, R & D agreements).

1.3.2. *Article 81(3)*

31. Agreements that come under Article 81(1) may be exempted provided the conditions of Article 81(3) are fulfilled. This is the case if the agreement

  – contributes to improving the production or distribution of products or to promoting technical or economic progress
  – allows consumers a fair share of the resulting benefit and does not
  – impose restrictions which are not indispensable to the attainment of the above listed objectives
  – afford the possibility of eliminating competition in respect of a substantial part of the products in question.

Economic benefits

32. The first condition requires that the agreement contributes to improving the production or distribution of products or to promoting technical or economic progress. As these benefits relate to static or dynamic efficiencies, they can be referred to as 'economic benefits'. Economic benefits may outweigh restrictive effects on: competition. For instance, a cooperation may enable firms to offer goods or services at lower prices, better quality or to launch innovation more quickly. Most efficiencies stem from the combination and integration of different skills or resources. The parties must demonstrate that the efficiencies are likely to be caused by the cooperation and cannot be achieved by less restrictive means (see also below). Efficiency claims must be substantiated. Speculations or general statements on cost savings are not sufficient.

33. The Commission does not take into account cost savings that arise from output reduction, market sharing, or from the mere exercise of market power.

Fair share for the consumers

34. Economic benefits have to favour not only the parties to the agreement, but also the consumers. Generally, the transmission of the benefits to the consumers will depend on the intensity of competition within the relevant market. Competitive pressures will normally ensure that cost-savings are passed on by way of lower prices or that companies have an incentive to bring new products to the market as quickly as possible. Therefore, if sufficient competition which effectively constrains the parties to the agreement is maintained on the market, the competitive process will normally ensure that the consumers receive a fair share of the economic benefits.

Indispensability

35. The restriction of competition must be necessary to achieve the economic benefits. If there are less restrictive means to achieve similar benefits, the claimed efficiencies cannot be used to justify the restrictions of competition. Whether or not individual restrictions are necessary depends on market circumstances and on the duration of the agreement. For instance, exclusivity agreements may prevent a participating party from free riding and may therefore be acceptable. Under certain circumstances they may, however, not be necessary and worsen a restrictive effect.

No elimination of competition

36. The last criterion of elimination of competition for a substantial part of the products in question is related to the question of dominance. Where an undertaking is dominant or becoming dominant as a consequence of a horizontal agreement, an agreement which produces anti-competitive effects in the meaning of Article 81 can in principle not be exempted.

Block Exemption Regulations for R & D and Specialisation

37. Under certain conditions the criteria of Article 81(3) can be assumed to be fulfilled for specified categories of agreements. This is in particular the case for R & D and production agreements where the combination of complementary skills or assets can be the source of substantial efficiencies. These guidelines should be seen as a complement to the R & D and Specialisation block exemption Regulations. Those block exemption Regulations exempt most common forms of agreements in the fields of production/specialisation up to a market share threshold of 20% and in the field of R & D up to a market share threshold of 25% provided that the agreements fulfil the conditions for application of the block exemption and do not contain 'hard core' restrictions ('black clauses') that render the block exemption inapplicable. The block exemption Regulations do not provide severability for hardcore restrictions. If there are one or more hardcore restrictions, the benefit of the block exemption Regulation is lost for the entire agreement.

1.4   Structure of the following chapters on types of cooperation

38. The guidelines are divided into chapters relating to certain types of agreements. Each chapter is structured according to the analytical framework described above under point 1.3. Where necessary, specific guidance on the definition of relevant markets is given (e.g. in the field of R & D or with respect to purchasing markets).

2.   AGREEMENTS ON RESEARCH AND DEVELOPMENT

2.1   Definition

39. R & D agreements may vary in form and scope. They range from outsourcing certain R & D activities to the joint improvement of existing technologies or to a cooperation concerning the research, development and marketing of completely new products. They may take the form of a cooperation agreement or of a jointly controlled company. This chapter applies to all forms of R & D agreements including related agreements concerning the production or commercialisation of the R & D results provided that the cooperation's centre of gravity lies in R & D, with the exception of mergers and joint ventures falling under the Merger Regulation.

40. Cooperation in R & D may reduce duplicative, unnecessary costs, lead to significant cross fertilisation of ideas and experience and thus result in products and technologies being developed more rapidly than would otherwise be the case. As a general rule, R & D cooperation tends to increase overall R & D activities.

41. Small and medium-sized enterprises (SMEs) form a dynamic and heterogeneous community which is confronted by many challenges, including the growing demands of larger companies for which they often work as sub-contractors. In R & D intensive sectors, fast growing SMEs, more often called 'start-up companies', also aim at becoming a leader in fast-developing market segments. To meet those challenges and to remain competitive, SMEs need constantly to innovate. Through R & D cooperation there is a likelihood that overall R & D by SMEs will increase and that they will be able to compete more vigorously with stronger market players.

42. Under certain circumstances, however, R & D agreements may cause competition problems such as restrictive effects on prices, output, innovation, or variety or quality of products.

2.2   Relevant markets

43. The key to defining the relevant market when assessing the effects of an R & D agreement is to identify those products, technologies or R & D efforts, that will act as a competitive constraint on the parties. At one end of the spectrum of possible situations, the innovation may result in a product (or technology) which competes in an existing product (or technology) market. This is the case with R & D directed towards slight improvements or variations, such as new models of certain products. Here, possible effects concern the market for existing products. At the other end, innovation may result in an entirely new product which creates its own new market (e.g. of the spectrum of a new vaccine for a previously incurable disease). In such a case, existing markets are only relevant if they are somehow related to the innovation in question. Consequently, and if possible,

the effects of the cooperation on innovation have to be assessed. However, most of the cases probably concern situations in between these two extremes, i.e. situations in which innovation efforts may create products (or technology) which, over time, replace existing ones (e.g. CDs which have replaced records). A careful analysis of those situations may have to cover both existing markets and the impact of the agreement on innovation.

Existing markets
(a) Product markets

44. When the cooperation concerns R & D for the improvement of existing products, these existing products including its close substitutes form the relevant market concerned by the cooperation.

45. If the R & D efforts aim at a significant change of an existing product or even at a new product replacing existing ones, substitution with the existing products may be imperfect or long-term. Consequently, the old and the potentially emerging new products are not likely to belong to the same relevant market. The market for existing products may nevertheless be concerned, if the pooling of R & D efforts is likely to result in the coordination of the parties' behaviour as suppliers of existing products. An exploitation of power in the existing market, however, is only possible if the parties together have a strong position with respect to both the existing product market and R & D efforts.

46. If the R & D concerns an important component of a final product, not only the market for this component may be relevant for the assessment, but the existing market for the final product as well. For instance, if car manufacturers cooperate in R & D related to a new type of engine, the car market may be affected by this R & D cooperation. The market for final products, however, is only relevant for the assessment, if the component at which the R & D is aimed, is technically or economically a key element of these final products and if the parties to the R & D agreement are important competitors with respect to the final products.

(b) Technology markets

47. R & D cooperation may not only concern products but also technology. When rights to intellectual property are marketed separately from the products concerned to which they relate, the relevant technology market has to be defined as well. Technology markets consist of the intellectual property that is licensed and its close substitutes, i.e. other technologies which customers could use as a substitute.

48. The methodology for defining technology markets follows the same principles as product market definition. Starting from the technology which is marketed by the parties, one needs to identify those other technologies to which customers could switch in response to a small but permanent increase in relative prices. Once these technologies are identified, one can calculate market shares by dividing the licensing income generated by the parties with the total licensing income of all sellers of substitutable technologies.

49. The parties' position in the market for existing technology is a relevant assessment criterion where the R & D cooperation concerns the significant improvement of existing technology or a new technology that is likely to replace the existing technology. The parties' market share can however only be taken as a starting point for this analysis. In technology markets, particular emphasis must be put on potential competition. If companies, who do not currently license their technology, are potential entrants on the technology market they could constrain the ability of the parties to raise the price for their technology (see Example 3 below).

Competition in innovation (R & D efforts)

50. R & D cooperation may not—or not only—affect competition in existing markets, but competition in innovation. This is the case where cooperation concerns the development of new products/technology which either may—if emerging—one day replace existing ones or which are being developed for a new intended use and will therefore not replace existing products but create a completely new demand. The effects on competition in innovation are important in these situations, but can in some cases not be sufficiently assessed by analysing actual or potential competition in existing

product/technology markets. In this respect, two scenarios can be distinguished, depending on the nature of the innovative process in a given industry.

51. In the first scenario, which is for instance present in the pharmaceutical industry, the process of innovation is structured in such a way that it is possible at an early stage to identify R & D poles. R & D poles are R & D efforts directed towards a certain new product or technology, and the substitutes for that R & D, i.e. R & D aimed at developing substitutable products or technology for those developed by the cooperation and having comparable access to resources as well as a similar timing. In this case, it can be analysed if after the agreement there will be a sufficient number of R & D poles left. The starting point of the analysis is the R & D of the parties. Then credible competing R & D poles have to be identified. In order to assess the credibility of competing poles, the following aspects have to be taken into account: the nature, scope and size of possible other R & D efforts, their access to financial and human resources, know-how/patents, or other specialised assets as well as their timing and their capability to exploit possible results. An R & D pole is not a credible competitor if it can not be regarded as a close substitute for the parties' R & D effort from the viewpoint of, for instance, access to resources or timing.

52. In the second scenario, the innovative efforts in an industry are not clearly structured so as to allow the identification of R & D poles. In this situation, the Commission would, absent exceptional circumstances, not try to assess the impact of a given R & D cooperation on innovation, but would limit its assessment to product and/or technology markets which are related to the R & D cooperation in question.

Calculation of market shares

53. The calculation of market shares, both for the purposes of the R & D block exemption Regulation and of these guidelines, has to reflect the distinction between existing markets and competition in innovation. At the beginning of a cooperation the reference point is the market for products capable of being improved or replaced by the products under development. If the R & D agreement only aims at improving or refining existing products, this market includes the products directly concerned by the R & D. Market shares can thus be calculated on the basis of the sales value of the existing products. If the R & D aims at replacing an existing product, the new product will, if successful, become a substitute to the existing products. To assess the competitive position of the parties, it is again possible to calculate market shares on the basis of the sales value of the existing products. Consequently, the R & D block exemption Regulation bases its exemption of these situations on the market share in 'the relevant market for the products capable of being improved or replaced by the contract products'. For an automatic exemption, this market share may not exceed 25%.

54. If the R & D aims at developing a product which will create a complete new demand, market shares based on sales cannot be calculated. Only an analysis of the effects of the agreement on competition in innovation is possible. Consequently, the R & D block exemption Regulation exempts these agreements irrespective of market share for a period of seven years after the product is first put on the market. However, the benefit of the block exemption may be withdrawn if the agreement would eliminate effective competition in innovation. After the seven year period, market shares based on sales value can be calculated, and the market share threshold of 25% applies.

2.3 Assessment under Article 81(1)

2.3.1. *Nature of the agreement*

2.3.1.1. *Agreements that do not fall under Article 81(1)*

55. Most R & D agreements do not fall under Article 81(1). First, this can be said for agreements relating to cooperation in R & D at a rather theoretical stage, far removed from the exploitation of possible results.

56. Moreover, R & D cooperation between non-competitors does generally not restrict competition. The competitive relationship between the parties has to be analysed in the context of affected existing markets and/or innovation. If the parties are not able to carry out the necessary R & D independently,

there is no competition to be restricted. This can apply, for example, to firms bringing together complementary skills, technologies and other resources. The issue of potential competition has to be assessed on a realistic basis. For instance, parties cannot be defined as potential competitors simply because the cooperation enables them to carry out the R & D activities. The decisive question is whether each party independently has the necessary means as to assets, know-how and other resources.

57. R & D cooperation by means of outsourcing of previously captive R & D is often carried out by specialised companies, research institutes or academic bodies which are not active in the exploitation of the results. Typically such agreements are combined with a transfer of know-how and/or an exclusive supply clause concerning possible results. Due to the complementary nature of the cooperating parties in these scenarios, Article 81(1) does not apply.

58. R & D cooperation which does not include the joint exploitation of possible results by means of licensing, production and/or marketing rarely falls under Article 81(1). Those 'pure' R & D agreements can only cause a competition problem, if effective competition with respect to innovation is significantly reduced.

2.3.1.2. *Agreements that almost always fall under Article 81(1)*

59. If the true object of an agreement is not R & D but the creation of a disguised cartel, i.e. otherwise prohibited price fixing, output limitation or market allocation, it falls under Article 81(1). However, an R & D agreement which includes the joint exploitation of possible future results is not necessarily restrictive of competition.

2.3.1.3. *Agreements that may fall under Article 81(1)*

60. R & D agreements that cannot be assessed from the outset as clearly non-restrictive may fall under Article 81(1) and have to be analysed in their economic context. This applies to R & D cooperation which is set up at a stage rather close to the market launch and which is agreed between companies that are competitors on either existing product/technology markets or on innovation markets.

2.3.2. *Market power and market structures*

61. R & D cooperation can cause negative market effects in three respects: First, it may restrict innovation, secondly it may cause the coordination of the parties' behaviour in existing markets and thirdly, foreclosure problems may occur at the level of the exploitation of possible results. These types of negative market effects, however, are only likely to emerge when the parties to the cooperation have significant power on the existing markets and/or competition with respect to innovation is significantly reduced. Without market power there is no incentive to coordinate behaviour on existing markets or to reduce or slow down innovation. A foreclosure problem may only arise in the context of cooperation involving at least one player with significant market power for a key technology and the exclusive exploitation of results.

62. There is no absolute market share threshold which indicates that an R & D agreement creates some degree of market power and thus falls under Article 81(1). However, R & D agreements are exempted provided that they are concluded between parties with a combined market share not exceeding 25% and that the other conditions for the application of the R & D Block Exemption Regulation are fulfilled. Therefore, for most R & D agreements, restrictive effects only have to be analysed if the parties' combined market share exceeds 25%.

63. Agreements falling outside the R & D Block Exemption Regulation due to a stronger market position of the parties do not necessarily restrict competition. However, the stronger the combined position of the parties on existing markets and/or the more competition in innovation is restricted, the more likely is the application of Article 81(1) and the assessment requires a more detailed analysis.

64. If the R & D is directed at the improvement or refinement of existing products/technology possible effects concern the relevant market (s) for these existing products/technology. Effects on prices, output and/or innovation in existing markets are, however, only likely if the parties together have a strong position, entry is difficult and few other innovation activities are identifiable. Furthermore, if the R & D only concerns a relatively minor input of a final product, effects as to competition in these final products are, if invariably, very limited. In general, a distinction has to be made between pure R

& D agreements and more comprehensive cooperation involving different stages of the exploitation of results (i.e. licensing, production, marketing). As said above, pure R & D agreements rarely come under Article 81(1). This is in particular true for R & D directed towards a limited improvement of existing products/technology. If, in such a scenario, the R & D cooperation includes joint exploitation only by means of licensing, restrictive effects such as foreclosure problems are unlikely. If, however, joint production and/or marketing of the slightly improved products/technology are included, the cooperation has to be examined more closely. First, negative effects as to prices and output in existing markets are more likely if strong competitors are involved in such a situation. Secondly, the cooperation may come closer to a production agreement because the R & D activities may de facto not form the centre of gravity of such a collaboration.

65. If the R & D is directed at an entirely new product (or technology) which creates its own new market, price and output effects on existing markets are rather unlikely. The analysis has to focus on possible restrictions of innovation concerning, for instance, the quality and variety of possible future products/technology or the speed of innovation. Those restrictive effects can arise where two or more of the few firms engaged in the development of such a new product, start to cooperate at a stage where they are each independently rather near to the launch of the product. In such a case, innovation maybe restricted even by a pure R & D agreement. In general, however, R & D cooperation concerning entirely new products is pro-competitive. This principle does not change significantly if the joint exploitation of the results, even joint marketing, is involved. Indeed, the issue of joint exploitation in these situations is only relevant where foreclosure from key technologies plays a role. Those problems would, however, not arise where the parties grant licences to third parties.

66. Most R & D agreements will lie somewhere in between the two situations described above. They may therefore have effects on innovation as well as repercussions on existing markets. Consequently, both the existing market and the effect on innovation may be of relevance for the assessment with respect to the parties' combined positions, concentration ratios, number of players/ innovators and entry conditions. In some cases there can be restrictive price/output effects on existing markets and a negative impact on innovation by means of slowing down the speed of development. For instance, if significant competitors on an existing technology market cooperate to develop a new technology which may one day replace existing products, this cooperation is likely to have restrictive effects if the parties have significant market power on the existing market (which would give an incentive to exploit it), and if they also have a strong position with respect to R & D. A similar effect can occur, if the major player in an existing market cooperates with a much smaller or even potential competitor who is just about to emerge with a new product/technology which may endanger the incumbent's position.

67. Agreements may also fall outside the block exemption irrespective of the market power of the parties. This applies for instance to agreements which restrict access of a party to the results of the work because they do not, as a general rule, promote technical and economic progress by increasing the dissemination of technical knowledge between the parties. The Block exemption provides for a specific exception to this general rule in the case of academic bodies, research Regulation institutes or specialised companies which provide R & D as a service and which are not active in the industrial exploitation of the results of research and development. Nevertheless, it should be noted that agreements containing exclusive access rights may, where they fall under Article 81(1), meet the criteria for exemption under Article 81(3), particularly where exclusive access rights are economically indispensable in view of the market, risks and scale of the investment required to exploit the results of the research and development.

2.4   Assessment under Article 81(3)

2.4.1. *Economic benefits*

68. Most R & D agreements—with or without joint exploitation of possible results—bring about economic benefits by means of cost savings and cross fertilisation of ideas and experience, thus resulting in improved or new products and technologies being developed more rapidly than would otherwise be the case. Under these conditions it appears reasonable to provide for the exemption of such

agreements which result in a restriction of competition up to a market share threshold below which it can, for the application of Article 81(3), in general, be presumed that the positive effects of research and development agreements will outweigh any negative effects on competition. Therefore, the R & D Block Exemption Regulation exempts those R & D agreements which fulfill certain conditions (see Article 3) and which do not include hard core restrictions (see Article 5), provided that the combined market share of the parties in the affected existing market(s) does not exceed 25%.

69. If considerable market power is created or increased by the cooperation, the parties have to demonstrate significant benefits in carrying out R & D, a quicker launch of new products/ technology or other efficiencies.

2.4.2. *Indispensability*

70. An R & D agreement can not be exempted if it imposes restrictions that are not indispensable to the attainment of the above-mentioned benefits. The individual clauses listed in Article 5 of the R & D block exemption Regulation will in most cases render an exemption impossible following an individual assessment too, and can therefore be regarded as a good indication of restrictions that are not indispensable to the cooperation.

2.4.3. *No elimination of competition*

71. No exemption will be possible, if the parties are afforded the possibility of eliminating competition in respect of a substantial part of the products (or technologies) in question. Where as a consequence of a R & D agreement an undertaking is dominant or becoming dominant either on an existing markets or with respect to innovation, such an agreement which produces anti-competitive effects in the meaning of Article 81 can in principle not be exempted. For innovation this is the case, for example, if the agreement combines the only two existing poles of research.

Time of the assessment and duration of the exemption

72. R & D agreements extending to the joint production and marketing of new products/technology require particular attention as to the time of the assessment.

73. At the beginning of an R & D cooperation, its success and factors such as the parties' future market position as well as the development of future product or technology markets are often not known. Consequently, the assessment at the point in time when the cooperation is formed is limited to the (then) existing product or technology markets and/or innovation markets as described in this chapter. If, on the basis of this analysis, competition is not likely to be eliminated, the R & D agreement can benefit from an exemption. This will normally cover the duration of the R & D phase plus, in as far as the joint production and marketing of the possible results is concerned, an additional phase for a possible launch and market introduction. The reason for this additional exemption phase is that the first companies to reach the market with a new product/technology will often enjoy very high initial market shares and successful R & D is also often rewarded by intellectual property protection. A strong market position due to this 'first mover advantage' cannot normally be interpreted as elimination of competition. Therefore, the block exemption covers R & D agreements for an additional period of seven years (i.e. beyond the R & D phase) irrespective of whether or not the parties obtain with their new products/technology a high share within this period. This also applies to the individual assessment of cases falling outside the block exemption provided that the criteria of Article 81(3) as to the other aspects of the agreement are fulfilled. This does not exclude the possibility that a period of more than 7 years also meets the criteria of Article 81(3) if it can be shown to be the minimum period of time necessary to guarantee an adequate return on the investment involved.

74. If a new assessment of an R & D cooperation is made after that period—for instance, following a complaint—the analysis has to be based on the (then) existing market situation. The block exemption still continues to apply if the parties' share on the (then) relevant market does not exceed 25%. Similarly, Article 81(3) continues to apply to R & D agreements falling outside the block exemption provided that the criteria for an exemption are fulfilled.

2.5 Examples

75. Example 1

Situation: There are two major companies on the European market for the manufacture of existing electronic components: A (30%) and B (30%). They have each made significant investment in the R & D necessary to develop miniaturised electronic components and have developed early prototypes. They now agree to pool these R & D efforts by setting up a JV to complete the R&D and produce the components, which will be sold back to the parents, who will commercialise them separately. The remainder of the market consists of small firms without sufficient resources to undertake the necessary investments.

Analysis: Miniaturised electronic components, while likely to compete with the existing components in some areas, are essentially a new technology and an analysis must be made of the poles of research destined towards this future market. If the JV goes ahead then only one route to the necessary manufacturing technology will exist, whereas it would appear likely that A and B could reach the market individually with separate products. While the agreement could have advantages in bringing a new technology forward quicker, it also reduces variety and creates a commonality of costs between the parties. Furthermore, the possibility for the parties to exploit their strong position on the existing market must be taken into account. Since they would face no competition at the R & D level, their incentives to pursue the new technology at a high pace could be severely reduced. Although some of these concerns could be remedied by requiring the parties to license key know-how for manufacturing miniature components to third parties on reasonable terms, it may not be possible to remedy all concerns and fulfil the conditions for an exemption.

76. Example 2

Situation: A small research company A which does not have its own marketing organisation has discovered and patented a pharmaceutical substance based on new technology that will revolutionise the treatment of a certain disease. Company A enters into an R & D agreement with a large pharmaceutical producer B of products that have so far been used for treating the disease. Company B lacks any similar R & D programme. For the existing products company B has a market share of around 75% in all Member States, but patents are expiring over the next five-year period. There exist two other poles of research at approximately the same stage of development using the same basic new technology. Company B will provide considerable funding and know-how for product development, as well as future access to the market. Company B is granted a license for the exclusive production and distribution of the resulting product for the duration of the patent. It is expected that the parties could jointly bring the product to market in five to seven years.

Analysis: The product is likely to belong to a new relevant market. The parties bring complementary resources and skills to the cooperation, and the probability of the product coming to market increases substantially. Although Company B is likely to have considerable market power on the existing market, this power will be decreasing shortly and the existence of other poles of research are likely to eliminate any incentive to reduce R & D efforts. The exploitation rights during the remaining patent period are likely to be necessary for Company B to make the considerable investments needed and Company A has no own marketing resources. The agreement is therefore unlikely to restrict competition.

77. Example 3

Situation: Two engineering companies that produce vehicle components, agree to set up a JV to combine their R&D efforts to improve the production and performance of an existing component. They also pool their existing technology licensing businesses in this area, but will continue to manufacture separately. The two companies have market shares in Europe of 15% and 20% on the OEM product market. There are two other major competitors together with several in-house research programmes by large vehicle manufacturers. On the world-wide market for the licensing of technology for these products they have shares of 20% and 25%, measured in terms of revenue generated, and there are two other major technologies. The product life cycle for the component is typically two to three years. In each of the last five years one of the major firms has introduced a new version or upgrade.

Analysis: Since neither company's R & D effort is aimed at a completely new product, the markets to consider are for the existing components and for the licensing of relevant technology. Although their existing R&D programmes broadly overlap, the reduced duplication through the cooperation could allow them to spend more on R & D than individually. Several other technologies exist and the parties' combined *market share on the OEM market does not bring them into a dominant position. Although their market share on the technology market, at 45%, is very high, there are competing technologies. In addition, the vehicle manufacturers, who do not currently licence their technology, are also potential entrants on this market thus constraining the ability of the parties to raise price. As described, the JV is likely to benefit from an exemption.*

3. PRODUCTION AGREEMENTS (INCLUDING SPECIALISATION AGREEMENTS)

3.1. Definition

78. Production agreements may vary in form and scope. They may take the form of joint production through a joint venture, i.e. a jointly controlled company that runs one or several production facilities, or can be carried out by means of specialisation or subcontracting agreements whereby one party agrees to carry out the production of a certain product.

79. Generally, one can distinguish three categories of production agreements: Joint production agreements, whereby the parties agree to produce certain products jointly, (unilateral or reciprocal) specialisation agreements, whereby the parties agree unilaterally or reciprocally to cease production of a product and to purchase it from the other party, and subcontracting agreements whereby one party (the 'contractor') entrusts to another party (the 'subcontractor') the production of a product.

80. Subcontracting agreements are vertical agreements. They are therefore, to the extent that they contain restrictions of competition, covered by the Block Exemption Regulation and the Guidelines on Vertical Restraints. There are however two exceptions to this rule: Subcontracting agreements between competitors, and subcontracting agreements between non-competitors involving the transfer of know-how to the subcontractor.

81. Subcontracting agreements between competitors are covered by these guidelines. Guidance for the assessment of subcontracting agreements between non-competitors involving the transfer of know-how to the subcontractor is given in a separate Notice.

3.2. Relevant markets

82. In order to assess the competitive relationship between the cooperating parties, the relevant product and geographic market(s) directly concerned by the cooperation (i.e. the market (s) to which products subject to the agreement belong) must first be defined. Secondly, a production agreement in one market may also affect the competitive behaviour of the parties in a market which is downstream or upstream or a neighbouring market closely related to the market directly concerned by the cooperation (so-called 'spill-over markets'). However, spill-over effects only occur if the cooperation in one market necessarily results in the coordination of competitive behaviour in another market, i.e. if the markets are linked by interdependencies, and if the parties are in a strong position on the spill-over market.

3.3 Assessment under Article 81(1)

3.3.1. *Nature of the agreement*

83. The main source of competition problems that may arise from production agreements is the coordination of the parties' competitive behaviour as suppliers. This type of competition problem arises where the cooperating parties are actual or potential competitors on at least one of these relevant market(s), i.e. on the markets directly concerned by the cooperation and/or on possible spill-over markets.

84. The fact that the parties are competitors does not automatically cause the coordination of their behaviour. In addition, the parties normally need to cooperate with regard to a significant part of their activities in order to achieve a substantial degree of commonality of costs. The higher the degree of commonality of costs, the greater the potential for a limitation of price competition, especially in the case of homogeneous products.

85. In addition to coordination concerns, production agreements may also create foreclosure problems and other negative effects towards third parties. They are not caused by a competitive relationship between the parties, but by a strong market position of at least one of the parties (e.g. on an upstream market for a key component, which enables the parties to raise the costs of their rivals in a downstream market) in the context of a more vertical or complementary relationship between the cooperating parties. Therefore, the possibility of foreclosure mainly needs to be examined in the case of joint production of an important component and of subcontracting agreements (see below).

3.3.1.1. *Agreements that do not fall under Article 81(1)*

86. Unless foreclosure problems arise, production agreements between non-competitors are not normally caught by Article 81(1). This is also true for agreements whereby inputs or components which have so far been manufactured for own consumption (captive production) are purchased from a third party by way of subcontracting or unilateral specialisation, unless there are indications that the company which so far has only produced for own consumption could have entered the merchant market for sales to third parties without incurring significant additional costs or risks in response to small, permanent changes in relative market prices.

87. Even production agreements between competitors do not necessarily come under Article 81(1). First, cooperation between firms which compete on markets closely related to the market directly concerned by the cooperation, cannot be defined as restricting competition, if the cooperation is the only commercially justifiable possible way to enter a new market, to launch a new product or service or to carry out a specific project.

88. Secondly, an effect on the parties' competitive behaviour as market suppliers is highly unlikely if the parties have a small proportion of their total costs in common. For instance, a low degree of commonality in total costs can be assumed where two or more companies agree on specialisation/ joint production of an intermediate product which only accounts for a small proportion of the production costs of the final product and, consequently, the total costs. The same applies to a subcontracting agreement between competitors where the input which one competitor purchases from another only accounts for a small proportion of the production costs of the final product. A low degree of commonality of total costs can also be assumed where the parties jointly manufacture a final product, but only a small proportion as compared to their total output of the final product. Even if a significant proportion is jointly manufactured, the degree of commonality of total costs may nevertheless be low or moderate, if the cooperation concerns heterogeneous products which require costly marketing.

89. Thirdly, subcontracting agreements between competitors do not fall under Article 81(1) if they are limited to individual sales and purchases on the merchant market without any further obligations and without forming part of a wider commercial relationship between the parties.

3.3.1.2. *Agreements that almost always fall under Article 81(1)*

90. Agreements which fix the prices for market supplies of the parties, limit output or share markets or customer groups have the object of restricting competition and almost always fall under Article 81(1). This does, however, not apply to cases

- where the parties agree on the output directly concerned by the production agreement (e.g. the capacity and production volume of a joint venture or the agreed amount of outsourced products), or
- where a production joint venture that also carries out the distribution of the manufactured products sets the sales prices for these products, provided that the price fixing by the joint venture is the effect of integrating the various functions.

In both scenarios the agreement on output or prices will not be assessed separately, but in light of the overall effects of the joint venture on the market in order to determine the applicability of Article 81(1).

3.3.1.3. *Agreements that may fall under Article 81(1)*

91. Production agreements that cannot be characterised as clearly restrictive or non-restrictive on the basis of the above factors may fall under Article 81(1)and have to be analysed in their economic context. This applies to cooperation agreements between competitors which create a significant degree of commonality of costs, but do not involve hard core restrictions as described above.

3.3.2. *Market power and market structures*

92. The starting point for the analysis is the position of the parties in the market(s) concerned. This is due to the fact that without market power the parties to a production agreement do not have an incentive to coordinate their competitive behaviour as suppliers. Secondly, there is no effect on competition in the market without market power of the parties, even if the parties would coordinate their behaviour.

93. There is no absolute market share threshold which indicates that a production agreement creates some degree of market power and thus falls under Article 81(1). However, agreements concerning unilateral or reciprocal specialisation as well as joint production are block exempted provided that they are concluded between parties with a combined market share not exceeding 20% in the relevant market (s) and that the other conditions for the application of the Specialisation block exemption Regulation are fulfilled. Therefore, for agreements covered by the block exemption, restrictive effects only have to be analysed if the parties combined market share exceeds 20%.

94. Agreements which are not covered by the block exemption Regulation require a more detailed analysis. The starting point is the market position of the parties. This will normally be followed by the concentration ratio and the number of players as well as by other factors as described in Chapter 1.

95. Usually the analysis will only involve the relevant market(s) with which the cooperation is directly concerned. Under certain circumstances, e.g. if the parties have a very strong combined position on up- or downstream markets or on markets otherwise closely related to the markets with which the cooperation is directly concerned, these spill-over markets may however have to be analysed as well. This applies in particular to cooperation in upstream markets by firms which also enjoy a strong combined market position further downstream. Similarly, problems of foreclosure may need to be examined if the parties individually have a strong position as either suppliers or buyers of an input.

Market position of the parties, concentration ratio, number of players and other structural factors

96. If the parties' combined market share is larger than 20%, the likely impact of the production agreement on the market must be assessed. In this respect market concentration as well as market shares will be a significant factor. The higher the combined market share of the parties, the higher the concentration in the market concerned. However, a moderately higher market share than allowed for in the block exemption does not necessarily imply a high concentration ratio. Far instance, a combined market share of the parties of slightly more than 20% may occur in a market with a moderate concentration (HHI below 1800). In such a scenario a restrictive effect is unlikely. In a more concentrated market, however, a market share of more than 20% may, alongside other elements, lead to a restriction of competition (see also example 1 below). The picture may nevertheless change, if the market is very dynamic with new participants entering the market and market positions changing frequently.

97. For joint production, network effects, i.e. links between a significant number of competitors, can also play an important role. In a concentrated market the creation of an additional link may tip the balance and make collusion in this market likely, even if the parties have a significant, but still moderate, combined market share (see example 2 below).

98. Under specific circumstances a cooperation between potential competitors may also raise competition concerns. This is, however, limited to cases where a strong player in one market cooperates with a realistic potential entrant, for instance, with a strong supplier of the same product or service in a neighbouring geographic market. The reduction of potential competition creates particular problems if actual competition is already weak and threat of entry is a major source of competition.

Cooperation in upstream markets

99. Joint production of an important component or other input to the parties' final product can cause negative market effects under certain circumstances:
- Foreclosure problems (see example 3 below) provided that the parties have a strong position on the relevant input market (non-captive use) and that switching between captive and non-captive use would not occur in the presence of a small but permanent relative price increase for the product in question.
- Spill-over effects (see example 4 below) provided that the input is an important component of costs and that the parties have a strong position in the downstream market for the final product.

Subcontracting agreements between competitors

100. Similar problems can arise if a competitor subcontracts an important component or other input to its final product from a competitor. This can also lead to:
- Foreclosure problems provided that the parties have a strong position as either suppliers or buyers on the relevant input market (non-captive use). Subcontracting could then either lead to other competitors not being able to obtain this input at a competitive price or to other suppliers not being able to supply the input competitively if they will be losing a large part of their demand.
- Spill-over effects provided that the input is an important component of costs and that the parties have a strong position in the downstream market for the final product.

Specialisation agreements

101. Reciprocal specialisation agreements with market shares beyond the threshold of the block exemption will almost always fall under Article 81(1) and have to be examined carefully because of the risk of market partitioning (see example 5 below).

3.4 Assessment under Article 81(3)

3.4.1. *Economic benefits*

102. Most common types of production agreements can be assumed to cause some economic benefits in the form of economies of scale or scope or better production technologies unless they are an instrument for price fixing, output restriction or market and customer allocation. Under these conditions it appears reasonable to provide for the exemption of such agreements which result in a restriction of competition up to a market share threshold below which it can, for the application of Article 81(3), in general, be presumed that the positive effects of production agreements will outweigh any negative effects on competition. Therefore, agreements concerning unilateral or reciprocal specialisation as well as joint production are block exempted (Specialisation block exemption Regulation) provided that they do not contain hard core restrictions (see Article 5) and that they are concluded between parties with a combined market share not exceeding 20% in the relevant market(s).

103. For those agreements not covered by the block exemption the parties have to demonstrate improvements of production or other efficiencies. Efficiencies that only benefit the parties or cost savings that are caused by output reduction or market allocation cannot be taken into account.

3.4.2. *Indispensability*

104. Restrictions that go beyond what is necessary to achieve the economic benefits described above will not be accepted. For instance, parties should not be restricted in their competitive behaviour on output outside the cooperation.

3.4.3. *No elimination of competition*

105. No exemption will be possible, if the parties are afforded the possibility of eliminating competition in respect of a substantial part of the products in question. Where as a consequence of a production agreement an undertaking is dominant or becoming dominant, such an agreement which produces anti-competitive effects in the meaning of Article 81 can in principle not be exempted. This has to be analysed on the relevant market to which the products subject to the cooperation belong and on possible spill-over markets.

3.5 Examples

Joint production

106. The following two examples concern hypothetical cases causing competition problems on the relevant market to which the jointly manufactured products belong.

107. Example 1

Situation: *Two suppliers, A and B, of the basic chemical product X decide to build a new production plant controlled by a joint venture. This plant will produce roughly 50% of their total output. X is a homogeneous product and is not substitutable with other products, i.e. forms a relevant market on its own. The market is rather stagnant. The parties will not significantly increase total output, but close down two old factories and shift capacity to the new plant. A and B each have a market share of 20%. There are three other significant suppliers each with 10–15% market share and several smaller players.*

Analysis: *It is likely that this joint venture would have an effect on the competitive behaviour of the parties because coordination would give them considerable market power, if not even a dominant position. Severe restrictive effects in the market are probable. High efficiency gains which may outweigh these effects are unlikely in such a scenario where a significant increase in output cannot be expected.*

108. Example 2

Situation: *Two suppliers, A and B, form a production joint venture on the same relevant market as in example 1. The joint venture also produces 50% of the parties' total output. A and B have 15% market share. There are 3 other players: C with a market share of 30%, D with 25% and E with 15%. B already has a joint production plant with E.*

Analysis: *Here the market is characterised by very few players and rather symmetric structures. The joint venture creates an additional link between the players. Coordination between A and B would de facto further increase concentration and also link E to A and B. This cooperation is likely to cause a severe restrictive effect, and—as in example 1—high efficiency gains cannot be expected.*

109. Example 3 also concerns the relevant market to which the jointly manufactured products belong, but demonstrates the importance of criteria other than market share (here: switching between captive and non-captive production).

110. Example 3

Situation: *A and B set up a production joint venture for an intermediate product X through restructuring current plants. The joint venture sells X exclusively to A and B. It produces 40% of A's total output of X and 50% of B's total output. A and B are captive users of X and are also suppliers of the non-captive market. A's share of total industry output of X is 10%, B's share amounts to 20% and the share of the joint venture to 14%. On the non-captive market, however, A and B have respectively 25% and 35% market share.*

Analysis: *Despite the parties' strong position on the non-captive market the cooperation may not eliminate effective competition in the market for X, if switching costs between captive and non-captive use are small. However, only very rapid switching would counteract the high market share of 60%. Otherwise this production venture raises serious competition concerns which cannot be outweighed even by significant economic benefits.*

111. Example 4 concerns cooperation regarding an important intermediate product with *spill-over effects on a downstream market.*

112. Example 4

Situation: *A and B set up a production joint venture for an intermediate product X. They will close their own factories, which have been manufacturing X, and will cover their needs of X exclusively from the joint venture. The intermediate product accounts for 50% of the total costs of the final product Y. A and B each have a share of 20% in the market for Y. There are two other significant suppliers of Y each with 15% market share and several smaller competitors.*

Analysis: *Here the commonality of costs is high; furthermore, the parties would gain market power through coordination of their behaviour on the market Y. The case raises competition problems and the assessment is almost identical to example 1 although here the cooperation is taking place in an up-stream market.*

Reciprocal specialisation

113. Example 5

Situation: *A and B each manufacture and supply the homogeneous products X and Y, which belong to different markets. A's market share of X is 28% and of Y it is 10%. B's share of X is 10% and of Y it is 30%. Because of scale economies they conclude a reciprocal specialisation agreement according to which A will in future only produce X and B will produce only Y. Both agree on cross-supplies so that they will both remain in the markets as suppliers. Due to the homogeneous nature of the products, distribution costs are minor. There are two other manufacturing suppliers of X and Y with market shares of roughly 15% each, the remaining suppliers have 5–10% shares.*

Analysis: *The degree of commonality of costs is extremely high, only the relatively minor distribution costs remain separate. Consequently, there is very little room for competition left. The parties would gain market power through coordination of their behaviour on the markets for X and Y. Furthermore, it is likely that the market supplies of Y from A and X from B will diminish over time. The case raises competition problems which the economies of scale are unlikely to outweigh.*

The scenario may change if X and Y were heterogeneous products with a very high proportion of marketing and distribution costs (e.g. 65–70% of total costs). Furthermore, if the offer of a complete range of the differentiated products was a condition for competing successfully, the withdrawal of one or more parties as suppliers of X and/or Y would be unlikely. In such a scenario the criteria for exemption may be fulfilled (provided that the economies are significant), despite the high market shares.

Subcontracting between competitors

114. Example 6

Situation: *A and B are competitors in the market for the final product X. A has a market share of 15%, B of 20%. Both also produce the intermediate product Y, which is an input into the production of X, but is also used to produce other products. It accounts for 10% of the cost of X. A only products Y for internal consumption, while B is also selling Y to thirdparty customers. Its market share for Y is 10%. A and B agree on a subcontracting agreement, whereby A will purchase 60% of its requirements of Y from B. It will continue to produce 40% of its requirements internally to not lose the know-how related to the production of Y.*

Analysis: *As A has only produced Y for internal consumption, it first needs to be analysed if A is a realistic potential entrant into the merchant market for sales of Y to third parties. If this is not the case, then the agreement does not restrict competition with respect to Y. Spill-over effects into the market for X are also unlikely in view of the low degree of commonality of costs created by the agreement.*

If A were to be regarded a realistic potential entrant into the merchant market for sales of Y to third parties, the market position of B in the market for Y would need to be taken into account. As B's market share is rather low, the result of the analysis would not change.

4. PURCHASING AGREEMENTS

4.1 Definition

115. This chapter focuses on agreements concerning the joint buying of products. Joint buying can be carried out by a jointly controlled company, by a company in which many firms hold a small stake, by a contractual arrangement or even looser form of cooperation.

116. Purchasing agreements are often concluded by small and medium-sized enterprises to achieve volumes and discounts similar to their bigger competitors. These agreements between small and medium-sized enterprises are therefore normally pro-competitive. Even if a moderate degree of market power is created, this may be outweighed by economies of scale provided the parties actually bundle volume.

117. Joint purchasing may involve both horizontal and vertical agreements. In these cases a two-step analysis is necessary. First, the horizontal agreements have to be assessed according to the principles described in the present guidelines. If this assessment leads to the conclusion that a cooperation between competitors in the area of purchasing is acceptable, a further assessment will be necessary to examine the vertical agreements concluded with suppliers or individual sellers. The latter assessment will follow the rules of the Block Exemption Regulation and the Guidelines on Vertical Restraints.

118. An example would be an association formed by a group of retailers for the joint purchasing of products. Horizontal agreements concluded between the members of the association or decisions adopted by the association have to be assessed first as a horizontal agreement according to the present guidelines. Only if this assessment is positive does it become relevant to assess the resulting vertical agreements between the association and an individual members or between the association and suppliers. These agreements are covered—up to a certain limit—by the block exemption for vertical restraints. Those agreements falling outside the vertical block exemption will not be presumed to be illegal but may need individual examination.

4.2 Relevant markets

119. There are two markets which may be affected by joint buying: First, the market(s) with which the cooperation is directly concerned, i.e. the relevant purchasing market(s). Secondly, the selling market(s), i.e. the market(s) downstream where the participants of the joint purchasing arrangement are active as sellers.

120. The definition of relevant purchasing markets follows the principles described in the Commission Notice on the definition of the relevant market and is based on the concept of substitutability to identify competitive constraints. The only difference to the definition of 'selling markets' is that substitutability has to be defined from the viewpoint of supply and not from the viewpoint of demand. In other words: the suppliers' alternatives are decisive in identifying the competitive constraints on purchasers. These could be analysed for instance by examining the suppliers' reaction to a small but lasting price *decrease*. If the market is defined, the market share can be calculated as the percentage for which the purchases by the parties concerned account out of the total sales of the purchased product or service in the relevant market.

121. Example 1

A group of car manufacturers agree to buy product X jointly. Their combined purchases of X account for 15 units. All the sales of X to car manufacturers account for 50 units. However, X is also sold to manufacturers of products other than cars. All sales of X account for 100 units. Thus, the (purchasing) market share of the group is 15%.

122. If the parties are in addition competitors on one or more selling markets, these markets are also relevant for the assessment. Restrictions of competition on these markets are more likely if the parties will achieve market power by coordinating their behaviour and if the parties have a significant proportion of their total costs in common. This is, for instance, the case if retailers which are active in the same relevant retail market(s) jointly purchase a significant amount of the products they offer for resale. It may also be the case if competing manufacturers and sellers of a final product jointly

purchase a high proportion of their input together. The selling markets have to be defined by applying the methodology described in the Commission Notice on the definition of the relevant market.

4.3 Assessment under article 81(1)

4.3.1. *Nature of the agreement*

4.3.1.1. *Agreements that do not fall under article 81(1)*

123. By their very nature joint buying agreements will be concluded between companies that are at least competitors on the purchasing markets. If, however, competing purchasers cooperate who are not active on the same relevant market further downstream (e.g. retailers which are active in different geographic markets and cannot be regarded as realistic potential competitors), Article 81(1) will rarely apply unless the parties have a very strong position in the buying markets, which could be used to harm the competitive position of other players in their respective selling markets.

4.3.1.2. *Agreements that almost always fall under article 81(1)*

124. Purchasing agreements only come under Article 81(1) by their nature if the cooperation does not truly concern joint buying, but serves as a tool to engage in a disguised cartel, i.e. otherwise prohibited price fixing, output limitation or market allocation.

4.3.1.3. *Agreements that may fall under article 81(1)*

125. Most purchasing agreements have to be analysed in their legal and economic context. The analysis has to cover both the purchasing and the selling markets.

4.3.2. *Market power and market structures*

126. The starting point for the analysis is the examination of the parties' buying power. Buying power can be assumed if a purchasing agreement accounts for a sufficiently large proportion of the total volume of a purchasing market so that prices can be driven down below the competitive level or access to the market can be foreclosed to competing buyers. A high degree of buying power over the suppliers of a market may bring about inefficiencies such as quality reductions, lessening of innovation efforts, or ultimately sub-optimal supply. However, the primary concerns in the context of buying power are that lower prices may not be passed on to customers further downstream and that it may cause cost increases for the purchasers' competitors on the selling markets because either suppliers will try to recover price reductions for one group of customers by increasing prices for other customers or competitors have less access to efficient suppliers. Consequently, purchasing markets and selling markets are characterised by interdependencies as set out below.

Interdependencies between purchasing and selling market(s)

127. The cooperation of competing purchasers can appreciably restrict competition by means of creating buying power. Whilst the creation of buying power can lead to lower prices for consumers, buying power is not always pro-competitive and may even, under certain circumstances, cause severe negative effects on competition.

128. First, lower purchasing costs resulting from the exercise of buying power cannot be seen as pro-competitive, if the purchasers together have power on the selling markets. In this case, the cost savings are probably not passed on to consumers. The more combined power the parties have on their selling markets, the higher is the incentive for the parties to coordinate their behaviour as sellers. This may be facilitated if the parties achieve a high degree of commonality of costs through joint purchasing. For instance, if a group of large retailers buys a high proportion of their products together, they will have a high proportion of their total cost in common. The negative effects of joint buying can therefore be rather similar to joint production.

129. Secondly, power on the selling markets may be created or increased through buying power which is used to foreclose competitors or to raise rivals' costs. Significant buying power by one group of customers may lead to foreclosure of competing buyers by limiting their access to efficient suppliers. It can also cause cost increases for its competitors because supplies will try to recover price reductions for one group of customers by increasing prices for other customers (e.g. rebate discrimination

by suppliers of retailers). This is only possible if the suppliers of the purchasing markets also have a certain degree of market power. In both cases, competition in the selling markets can be further restricted by buying power.

130. There is no absolute threshold which indicates that a buying cooperation creates some degree of market power and thus falls under Article 81(1). However, in most cases, it is unlikely that market power exists if the parties to the agreement have a combined market share of below 15% on the purchasing market(s) as well as a combined market share of below 15% on the selling market(s). In any event, at that level of market share it is likely that the conditions of Article 81(3) explained below are fulfilled by the agreement in question.

131. A market share above this threshold does not automatically indicate that a negative market effect is caused by the cooperation but requires a more detailed assessment of the impact of a joint buying agreement on the market, involving factors such as the market concentration and possible countervailing power of strong suppliers. Joint buying that involves parties with a combined market share significantly above 15% in a concentrated market is likely to come under Article 81(1), and efficiencies that may outweigh the restrictive effect have to be shown by the parties.

4.4 Assessment under article 81(3)

4.4.1. *Economic benefits*

132. Purchasing agreements can bring about economic benefits such as economies of scale in ordering or transportation which may outweigh restrictive effects. If the parties together have significant buying or selling power, the issue of efficiencies has to be examined carefully. Cost savings that are caused by the mere exercise of power and which do not benefit consumers cannot be taken into account.

4.4.2. *Indispensability*

133. Purchasing agreements cannot be exempted if they impose restrictions that are not indispensable to the attainment of the above mentioned benefits. An obligation to buy exclusively through the cooperation can in certain cases be indispensable to achieve the necessary volume for the realisation of economies of scale. However, such an obligation has to be assessed in the context of the individual case.

4.4.3. *No elimination of competition*

134. No exemption will be possible, if the parties are afforded the possibility of eliminating competition in respect of a substantial part of the products in question. This assessment has to cover buying and selling markets. The combined market shares of the parties can be regarded as a starting point. It then needs to be evaluated whether these market shares are indicative of a dominant position, and whether there are any mitigating factors, such as countervailing power of suppliers on the purchasing markets or potential for market entry in the selling markets. Where as a consequence of a purchasing agreement an undertaking is dominant or becoming dominant on either the buying or selling market, such an agreement which produces anti-competitive effects in the meaning of Article 81 can in principle not be exempted.

4.5 Examples

135. Example 2

Situation: Two manufacturers, A and B, decide to jointly buy component X. They are competitors on their selling market. Together their purchases represent 35% of the total sales of X in the EEA, which is assumed to be the relevant geographic market. There are 6 other manufacturers (competitors of A and B on their selling market) accounting for the remaining 65% of the purchasing market; one having 25%, the others accounting for significantly less. The supply side is rather concentrated with 6 suppliers of component X, two with 30% market share each, and the rest with between 10 and 15% (HHI of 2300–2500). On their selling market, A and B achieve a combined market share of 35%.

Analysis: Due to the parties' market power in their selling market, the benefits of possible cost savings may not be passed on to final consumers. Furthermore, the joint buying is likely to increase the costs of the parties' smaller competitors because the two powerful suppliers probably recover price reductions for the group by increasing smaller customers' prices. Increasing concentration in the downstream market may be the result. In addition, the cooperation may lead to further concentration among suppliers because smaller ones, which may already work near or below minimum optimal scale, may be driven out of business if they cannot reduce prices further. Such a case probably causes a significant restriction of competition which may not be outweighed by possible efficiency gains from bundling volume.

136. Example 3

Situation: 150 small retailers conclude an agreement to form a joint buying organisation. They are obliged to buy a minimum volume through the organisation which accounts for roughly 50% of each retailer's total costs. The retailers can buy more than the minimum volume through the organisation, and they may also buy outside the cooperation. They have a combined market share of 20% on each of the purchasing and the selling market(s). A and B are their two large competitors, A has a 25% share on each of the markets concerned, B 35%. The remaining smaller competitors have also formed a buying group. The 150 retailers achieve economies by combining a significant amount of volume and buying tasks.

Analysis: The retailers may achieve a high degree of commonality of costs if they ultimately buy more than the agreed minimum volume together. However, together they only have a moderate market position on the buying and the selling market. Furthermore, the cooperation brings about some economies of scale. This cooperation is likely to be exempted.

137. Example 4

Situation: Two supermarket chains conclude an agreement to jointly buy products which account for roughly 50% of their total costs. On the relevant buying markets for the different categories of products the parties have shares between 25% and 40%, on the relevant selling market (assuming there is only one geographic market concerned) they achieve 40%. There are five other significant retailers each with 10–15% market share. Market entry is not likely.

Analysis: It is likely that this joint buying arrangement would have an effect on the competitive behaviour of the parties because coordination would give them significant market power. This is particularly the case if entry is weak. The incentive to coordinate behaviour is higher if the costs are similar. Similar margins of the parties would add an incentive to have the same prices. Even if efficiencies are caused by the cooperation, it is not likely to be exempted due to the high degree of market power.

138. Example 5

Situation: small cooperatives conclude an agreement to form a joint buying organisation. They are obliged to buy a minimum volume through the organisation. The parties can buy more than the minimum volume through the organisation, but they may also buy outside the cooperation. Each of the parties has a total market share of 5% on each of the purchasing and selling markets, giving a combined market share of 25%. There are two other significant retailers each with 20–25% market share and a number of smaller retailers with market shares below 5%.

Analysis: The setting up of the joint buying organisation is likely to give the parties a market position on both the purchasing and selling markets of a degree which enables them to compete with the two largest retailers. Moreover, the presence of these two other players with similar levels of market position is likely to result in the efficiencies of the agreement being passed on to consumers. In such a scenario the agreement is likely to be exempted.

5. COMMERCIALISATION AGREEMENTS

5.1 Definition

139. The agreements covered in this section involve cooperation between competitors in the selling, distribution or promotion of their products. These agreements can have a widely varying scope, depending on the marketing functions which are being covered by the cooperation. At one end of the spectrum, there is joint selling that leads to a joint determination of all commercial aspects related to the sale of the product including price. At the other end, there are more limited agreements that only address one specific marketing function, such as distribution, service, or advertising.

140. The most important of these more limited agreements would seem to be distribution agreements. These agreements are generally covered by the Block Exemption Regulation and Guidelines on Vertical Restraints unless the parties are actual or potential competitors. In this case, the Block Exemption Regulation only covers non-reciprocal vertical agreements between competitors, if (a) the buyer, together with its connected undertakings, has an annual turnover not exceeding EUR 100 million, or (b) the supplier is a manufacturer and a distributor of products and the buyer is a distributor who is not also a manufacturer of products competing with the contract products, or (c) the supplier is a provider of services at several levels of trade, while the buyer does not provide competing services at the level of trade where it purchases the contract services. If competitors agree to distribute their products on a reciprocal basis there is a possibility in certain cases that the agreements have as their object or effect the partitioning of markets between the parties or that they lead to collusion. The same is true for non-reciprocal agreements between competitors exceeding a certain size. These agreements have thus first to be assessed according to the principles set out below. If this assessment leads to the conclusion that a cooperation between competitors in the area of distribution would in principle be acceptable, a further assessment will be necessary to examine the vertical restraints included in such agreements. This assessment should be based on the principles set out in the Guidelines on Vertical Restraints.

141. A further distinction should be drawn between agreements where the parties agree only on joint commercialisation and agreements where the commercialisation is related to another cooperation. This can be for instance the case as regards joint production or joint purchasing. These agreements will be dealt with as in the assessment of those types of cooperation.

5.2 Relevant markets

142. To assess the competitive relationship between the cooperating parties, first the relevant product and geographic market(s) directly concerned by the cooperation (i.e. the market(s) to which products subject to the agreement belong) have to be defined. Secondly, a commercialisation agreement in one market may also affect the competitive behaviour of the parties in a neighbouring market closely related to the market directly concerned by the cooperation.

5.3 Assessment under Article 81(1)

5.3.1. *Nature of the agreement*

5.3.1.1. *Agreements that do not fall under Article 81(1)*

143. The commercialisation agreements covered by this section only fall under the competition rules if the parties to the agreements are competitors. If the parties clearly do not compete with regard to the products or services covered by the agreement, the agreement cannot create competition problems of a horizontal nature. However, the agreement can fall under Article 81(1) if it contains vertical restraints, such as restrictions on passive sales, resale price maintenance, etc. This also applies if a cooperation in commercialisation is objectively necessary to allow one party to enter a market it could not have entered individually, for example, because of the costs involved. A specific application of this principle would be consortia arrangements that allow the companies involved to mount a credible tender for projects that they would not be able to fulfil, or would not have bid for, individually. As they are therefore not potential competitors for the tender, there is no restriction of competition.

5.3.1.2. *Agreements that almost always fall under Article 81(1)*

144. The principal competition concern about a commercialisation agreement between competitors is price fixing. Agreements limited to joint selling have as a rule the object and effect of coordinating the pricing policy of competing manufacturers. In this case they not only eliminate price competition between the parties but also restrict the volume of products to be delivered by the participants within the framework of the system for allocating orders. They therefore restrict competition between the parties on the supply side and limit the choice of purchasers and fall under Article 81(1).

145. This appreciation does not change if the agreement is non-exclusive. Article 81(1) continues to apply even where the parties are free to sell outside the agreement, as long as it can be presumed that the agreement will lead to an overall coordination of the prices charged by the parties.

5.3.1.3. *Agreements that may fall under Article 81(1)*

146. For commercialisation arrangements that fall short of joint selling there will be two major concerns. The first is that the joint commercialisation provides a clear opportunity for exchanges of sensitive commercial information particularly on marketing strategy and pricing. The second is that, depending on the cost structure of the commercialisation, a significant input to the parties' final costs may be common. As a result the actual scope for price competition at the final sales level may be limited. Joint commercialisation agreements therefore can fall under Article 81(1) if they either allow the exchange of sensitive commercial information, or if they influence a significant part of the parties' final cost.

147. A specific concern related to distribution arrangements between competitors which are active in different geographic markets is that they can lead to or be an instrument of market partitioning. In the case of reciprocal agreements to distribute each other's products, the parties to the agreement allocate markets or customers and eliminate competition between themselves. The key question in assessing an agreement of this type is if the agreement in question is objectively necessary for the parties to enter each other's market. If it is, the agreement does not create competition problems of a horizontal nature. However, the distribution agreement can fall under Article 81(1) if it contains vertical restraints, such as restrictions on passive sales, resale price maintenance, etc. If the agreement is not objectively necessary for the parties to enter each other's market, it falls under 81(1). If the agreement is not reciprocal, the risk of market partitioning is less pronounced. It needs however to be assessed if the non-reciprocal agreement constitutes the basis for a mutual understanding to not enter each other's market or is a means to control access to or competition on the 'importing' market.

5.3.2. *Market power and market structure*

148. As indicated above, agreements that involve price fixing will always fall under Article 81(1) irrespective of the market power of the parties. They may, however, be exemptable under Article 81(3) under the conditions described below.

149. Commercialisation agreements between competitors which do not involve price fixing are only subject to Article 81(1) if the parties to the agreement have some degree of market power. In most cases, it is unlikely that market power exists if the parties to the agreement have a combined market share of below 15%. In any event, at that level of market share it is likely that the conditions of Article 81(3) explained below are fulfilled by the agreement in question.

150. If the parties' combined market share is greater than 15%, the likely impact of the joint commercialisation agreement on the market must be assessed. In this respect market concentration, as well as market shares will be a significant factor. The more concentrated the market the more useful information about prices or marketing strategy to reduce uncertainty and the greater the incentive for the parties to exchange such information.

5.4   Assessment under Article 81(3)

5.4.1. *Economic benefits*

151. The efficiencies to be taken into account when assessing whether a joint commercialisation agreement can be exempted will depend upon the nature of the activity. Price fixing can generally not be justified, unless it is indispensable for the integration of other marketing functions, and this integration will generate substantial efficiencies. The size of the efficiencies generated depends *inter alia* on the importance of the joint marketing activities for the overall cost structure of the product in question. Joint distribution is thus more likely to generate significant efficiencies for producers of widely distributed consumer products than for producers of industrial products which are only bought by a limited number of users.

152. In addition, the claimed efficiencies should not be savings which result only from the elimination of costs that are inherently part of competition, but must result from the integration of economic activities. A reduction of transport cost which is only a result of customer allocation without any integration of the logistical system can therefore not be regarded as an efficiency that would make an agreement exemptable.

153. Claimed efficiency benefits must be demonstrated. An important element in this respect would be the contribution by both parties of significant capital, technology, or other assets. Cost savings through reduced duplication of resources and facilities can also be accepted. If, on the other hand, the joint commercialisation represents no more than a sales agency with no investment, it is likely to be a disguised cartel and as such cannot fulfil the conditions of Article 81(3).

5.4.2. *Indispensability*

154. A commercialisation agreement cannot be exempted if it imposes restrictions that are not indispensable to the attainment of the abovementioned benefits. As discussed above, the question of indispensability is especially important for those agreements involving price fixing or the allocation of markets.

5.4.3. *No elimination of competition*

155. No exemption will be possible, if the parties are afforded the possibility of eliminating competition in respect of a substantial part of the products in question. In making this assessment, the combined market shares of the parties can be regarded as a starting point. One then needs to evaluate whether these market shares are indicative of a dominant position, and whether there are any mitigating factors, such as the potential for market entry. Where as a consequence of a commercialisation agreement an undertaking is dominant or becoming dominant, such an agreement which produces anti-competitive effects in the meaning of Article 81 can in principle not be exempted.

5.5   Examples

156. Example 1

Situation: 5 small food producers, each with 2% market share of the overall food market, agree to: combine their distribution facilities; market under a common brand name; and sell their products at a common price. This involves significant investment in warehousing, transport, advertising, marketing and a sales force. It significantly reduces their cost base, representing typically 50% of the price at which they sell, and allows them to offer a quicker, more efficient distribution system. The customers of the food producers are large retail chains.

Three large multinational food groups dominate the market, each with 20% market share. The rest of the market is made up of small independent producers. The product ranges of the parties to this agreement overlap in some significant areas, but in no product market does their combined market share exceed 15%.

Analysis: The agreement involves price fixing and thus falls under Article 81(1), even though the parties to the agreement cannot be considered as having market power. However, the integration of the marketing and distribution appears to provide significant efficiencies which are of benefit to customers both in terms of improved service, and lower costs. The question is therefore whether the agreement is exemptable under Article 81(3). To answer this question it must be established whether the price fixing is indispensable for the integration of the other marketing functions and the attainment of the economic benefits. In this case, the price fixing can be regarded as indispensable, as the clients—large retail chains—do not want to deal with a multitude of prices. It is also indispensable, as the aim—a common brand—can only be credibly achieved if all aspects of marketing, including price, are standardised. As the parties do not have market power and the agreement creates significant efficiencies it is compatible with Article 81.

157. Example 2

Situation: 2 producers of ball bearings, each having a market share of 5%, create a sales joint venture which will market the products, determine the prices and allocate orders to the parent companies. They retain the right to sell outside this structure. Deliveries to customers continue to be made directly from the parents' factories. They claim that this will create efficiencies as the joint sales force can demonstrate the parties' products at the same time to the same client thus eliminating a wasteful duplication of sales efforts. In addition, the joint venture would, wherever possible, allocate orders to the closest factory possible, thus reducing transport costs.

Analysis: The agreement involves price fixing and thus falls under Article 81(1), even though the parties to the agreement cannot be considered as having market power. It is not exemptable under Article 81(3), as the claimed efficiencies are only cost reductions derived from the elimination of competition between the parties.

158. Example 3

Situation: 2 producers of soft drinks are active in 2 different, neighbouring Member States. Both have a market share of 20% in their home market. They agree to reciprocally distribute each other's product in their respective geographic market.

Both markets are dominated by a large multinational soft drink producer, having a market share of 50% in each market.

Analysis: The agreement falls under Article 81(1) if the parties can be presumed to be potential competitors. Answering this question would thus require an analysis of the barriers to entry into the respective geographic markets. If the parties could have entered each other's market independently, then their agreement eliminates competition between them. However, even though the market shares of the parties indicate that they could have some market power, an analysis of the market structure indicates that this is not the case. In addition, the reciprocal distribution agreement benefits customers as it increases the available choice in each geographic market. The agreement would thus be exemptable even if it were considered to be restrictive of competition.

6. AGREEMENT ON STANDARDS

6.1 Definition

159. Standardisation agreements have as their primary objective the definition of technical or quality requirements with which current or future products, production processes or methods may comply. Standardisation agreements can cover various issues, such as standardisation of different grades or sizes of a particular product or technical specifications in markets where compatibility and interoperability with other products or systems is essential. The terms of access to a particular quality mark or for approval by a regulatory body can also be regarded as a standard.

160. Standards related to the provision of professional services, such as rules of admission to a liberal profession, are not covered by these guidelines.

6.2 Relevant markets

161. Standardisation agreements produce their effects on three possible markets, which will be defined according to the Commission notice on market definition. First, the product market(s) to which the standard(s) relates. Standards on entirely new products may raise issues similar to those raised for R & D agreements, as far as market definition is concerned (see Point 2.2). Second, the service market for standard setting, if different standard setting bodies or agreements exist. Third, where relevant, the distinct market for testing and certification.

6.3 Assessment under Article 81(1)

162. Agreements to set standards may be either concluded between private undertakings or set under the aegis of public bodies or bodies entrusted with the operation of services of general economic interest, such as the standards bodies recognised under Directive 98/34/EC. The involvement of such bodies is subject to the obligations of Member States regarding the preservation of non-distorted competition in the Community.

6.3.1. *Nature of the agreement*

6.3.1.1. *Agreements that do not fall under Article 81(1)*

163. Where participation in standard setting is unrestricted and transparent, standardisation agreements as defined above, which set no obligation to comply with the standard or which are parts of a wider agreement to ensure compatibility of products, do not restrict competition. This normally applies to standards adopted by the recognised standards bodies which are based on non-discriminatory, open and transparent procedures.

164. No appreciable restriction exists for those standards that have a negligible coverage of the relevant market, as long as it remains so. No appreciable restriction is found either in agreements which pool together SMEs to standardise access forms or conditions to collective tenders or those that standardise aspects such as minor product characteristics, forms and reports, which have an insignificant effect on the main factors affecting competition in the relevant markets.

6.3.1.2. *Agreements that almost always fall under Article 81(1)*

165. Agreements that use a standard as a means amongst other parts of a broader restrictive agreement aimed at excluding actual or potential competitors will almost always be caught by Article 81(1). For instance, an agreement whereby a national association of manufacturers set a standard and put pressure on third parties not to market products that did not comply with the standard would be in this category.

6.3.1.3. *Agreements that may fall under Article 81(1)*

166. Standardisation agreements may be caught by Article 81(1) in so far as they grant the parties joint control over production and/or innovation, thereby restricting their ability to compete on product characteristics, while affecting third parties like suppliers or purchasers of the standardised products. The assessment of each agreement must take into account the nature of the standard and its likely effect on the markets concerned, on the one hand, and the scope of possible restrictions that go beyond the primary objective of standardisation, as defined above, on the other.

167. The existence of a restriction of competition in standardisation agreements depends upon the extent to which the parties remain free to develop alternative standards or products that do not comply with the agreed standard. Standardisation agreements may restrict competition where they prevent the parties from either developing alternative standards or commercialising products that do not comply with the standard. Agreements that entrust certain bodies with the exclusive right to test compliance with the standard go beyond the primary objective of defining the standard and may also restrict competition. Agreements that impose restrictions on marking of conformity with standards, unless imposed by regulatory provisions, may also restrict competition.

6.3.2. *Market power and market structures*

168. High market shares held by the parties in the market(s) affected will not necessarily be a concern for standardisation agreements. Their effectiveness is often proportional to the share of the industry involved in setting and/or applying the standard. On the other hand, standards that are not accessible to third parties may discriminate or foreclose third parties or segment markets according to their geographic scope of application. Thus, the assessment whether the agreement restricts competition will focus, necessarily on an individual basis, on the extent to which such barriers to entry are likely to be overcome.

6.4   Assessment under Article 81(3)

6.4.1. *Economic benefits*

169. The Commission generally takes a positive approach towards agreements that promote economic interpenetration in the common market or encourage the development of new markets and improved supply conditions. To materialise those economic benefits, the necessary information to apply the standard must be available to those wishing to enter the market and an appreciable proportion of the industry must be involved in the setting of the standard in a transparent manner. It will be for the parties to demonstrate that any restrictions on the setting, use or access to the standard provide economic benefits.

170. In order to reap technical or economic benefits, standards should not limit innovation. This will depend primarily on the lifetime of the associated products, in connection with the market development stage (fast growing, growing, stagnant …). The effects on innovation must be analysed on a case-by-case basis. The parties may also have to provide evidence that collective standardisation is efficiency-enhancing for the consumer when a new standard may trigger unduly rapid obsolescence of existing products, without objective additional benefits.

6.4.2. *Indispensability*

171. By their nature, standards will not include all possible specifications or technologies. In some cases, it would be necessary for the benefit of the consumers or the economy at large to have only one technological solution. However, this standard must be set on a non-discriminatory basis. Ideally, standards should be technology neutral. In any event, it must be justifiable why one standard is chosen over another.

172. All competitors in the market(s) affected by the standard should have the possibility of being involved in discussions. Therefore, participation in standard setting should be open to all, unless the parties demonstrate important inefficiencies in such participation or unless recognised procedures are foreseen for the collective representation of interests, as in formal standards bodies.

173. As a general rule there should be a clear distinction between the setting of a standard and, where necessary, the related R & D, and the commercial exploitation of that standard. Agreements on standards should cover no more than what is necessary to ensure their aims, whether this is technical compatibility or a certain level of quality. For instance, it should be very clearly demonstrated why it is indispensable to the emergence of the economic benefits that an agreement to disseminate a standard in an industry where only one competitor offers an alternative should oblige the parties to the agreement to boycott the alternative.

6.4.3. *No elimination of competition*

174. There will clearly be a point at which the specification of a private standard by a group of firms that are jointly dominant is likely to lead to the creation of a de facto industry standard. The main concern will then be to ensure that these standards are as open as possible and applied in a clear non-discriminatory manner. To avoid elimination of competition in the relevant market(s), access to the standard must be possible for third parties on fair, reasonable and non-discriminatory terms.

175. To the extent that private organisations or groups of companies set a standard or their proprietary technology becomes a de facto standard, then competition will be eliminated if third parties are foreclosed from access to this standard.

6.5   Examples

176. Example 1

Situation: EN 60603-7:1993 defines the requirements to connect television receivers to video-generating accessories such as video recorders and video games. Although the standard is not legally binding, in practice manufacturers both of television receivers and of video games use the standard, as the market requires so.

Analysis: Article 81(1) is not infringed. The standard has been adopted by recognised standards bodies, at national, European and international level, through open and transparent procedures, and is based on national consensus reflecting the position of manufacturers and consumers. All manufacturers are allowed to use the standard.

177. Example 2

Situation: A number of video cassette manufacturers agree to develop a quality mark or standard to denote the fact that the videocassette meets certain minimum technical specifications. The manufacturers are free to produce videocassettes which do not conform to the standard and the standard is freely available to other developers.

Analysis: Provided that the agreement does not otherwise restrict competition, Article 81 (1) is not infringed, as participation in standard setting is unrestricted and transparent, and the standardisation agreement does not set an obligation to comply with the standard. If the parties agreed only to produce videocassettes which conform to the new standard, the agreement would limit technical development and prevent the parties from selling different products, which would infringe Article 81(1).

178. Example 3

Situation: A group of competitors active in various markets which are interdependent with products that must be compatible, and with over 80% of the relevant markets, agree to jointly develop a new standard that will be introduced in competition with other standards already present in the market, widely applied by their competitors. The various products complying with the new standard will not be compatible with existing standards. Because of the significant investment needed to shift and to maintain production under the new standard, the parties agree to commit a certain volume of sales to products complying with the new standard so as to create a 'critical mass' in the market. They also agree to limit their individual production volume of products not complying with the standard to the level attained last year.

Analysis: This agreement, owing to the parties' market power and the restrictions on production, falls under Article 81(1) while not being likely to fulfil the conditions of paragraph 3, unless access to technical information were provided on a non-discriminatory basis and reasonable terms to other suppliers wishing to compete.

7. ENVIRONMENTAL AGREEMENTS

7.1 Definition

179. Environmental agreements are those by which the parties undertake to achieve pollution abatement, as defined in environmental law, or environmental objectives, in particular, those set out in Article 174 of the Treaty. Therefore, the target or the measures agreed need to be directly linked to the reduction of a pollutant or a type of waste identified as such in relevant regulations. This excludes agreements that trigger pollution abatement as a by-product of other measures.

180. Environmental agreements may set out standards on the environmental performance of products (inputs or outputs) or production processes. Other possible categories may include agreements at the same level of trade, whereby the parties provide for the common attainment of an environmental target such as recycling of certain materials, emission reductions, or the improvement of energy-efficiency.

181. Comprehensive, industry-wide schemes are set up in many Member States for complying with environmental obligations on take-back or recycling. Such schemes usually comprise a complex set of arrangements, some of which are horizontal, while others are vertical in character. To the extent that these arrangements contain vertical restraints they are not subject to these guidelines.

7.2 Relevant markets

182. The effects are to be assessed on the markets to which the agreement relates, which will be defined according to the Notice on the definition of the relevant market for the purposes of Community competition law. When the pollutant is not itself a product, the relevant market encompasses that of the product into which the pollutant is incorporated. As for collection/recycling agreements, in addition to their effects on the market(s) on which the parties are active as producers or

distributors, the effects on the market of collection services potentially covering the good in question must be assessed as well.

7.3   Assessment under Article 81(1)

183.   Some environmental agreements may be encouraged or made necessary by State authorities in the exercise of their public prerogatives. The present guidelines do not deal with the question of whether such State intervention is in conformity with the Member State's obligations under the Treaty. They only address the assessment that must be made as to the compatibility of the agreement with Article 81.

7.3.1. *Nature of the agreement*

7.3.1.1. *Agreements that do not fall under Article 81(1)*

184.   Some environmental agreements are not likely to fall within the scope of the prohibition of Article 81(1), irrespective of the aggregated market share of the parties.

185.   This may arise if no precise individual obligation is placed upon the parties or if they are loosely committed to contributing to the attainment of a sector-wide environmental target. In this latter case, the assessment will focus on the discretion left to the parties as to the means that are technically and economically available in order to attain the environmental objective agreed upon. The more varied such means, the less appreciable the potential restrictive effects.

186.   Similarly, agreements setting the environmental performance of products or processes that do not appreciably affect product and production diversity in the relevant market or whose importance is marginal for influencing purchase decisions do not fall under Article 81(1). Where some categories of a product are banned or phased out from the market, restrictions cannot be deemed appreciable in so far as their share is minor in the relevant geographic market or, in the case of Community-wide markets, in all Member States.

187.   Finally, agreements which give rise to genuine market creation, for instance recycling agreements, will not generally restrict competition, provided that and for as long as, the parties would not be capable of conducting the activities in isolation, whilst other alternatives and/or competitors do not exist.

7.3.1.2. *Agreements that almost always come under Article 81(1)*

188.   Environmental agreements come under Article 81(1) by their nature if the cooperation does not truly concern environmental objectives, but serves as a tool to engage in a disguised cartel, i.e. otherwise prohibited price fixing, output limitation or market allocation, or if the cooperation is used as a means amongst other parts of a broader restrictive agreement which aims at excluding actual or potential competitors.

7.3.1.3. *Agreements that may fall under Article 81(1)*

189.   Environmental agreements covering a major share of an industry at national or EC level are likely to be caught by Article 81(1) where they appreciably restrict the parties' ability to devise the characteristics of their products or the way in which they produce them, thereby granting them influence over each other's production or sales. In addition to restrictions between the parties, an environmental agreement may also reduce or substantially affect the output of third parties, either as suppliers or as purchasers.

190.   For instance, environmental agreements, which may phase out or significantly affect an important proportion of the parties' sales as regards their products or production processes, may fall under Article 81(1) when the parties hold a significant proportion of the market. The same applies to agreements whereby the parties allocate individual pollution quotas.

191.   Similarly, agreements whereby parties holding significant market shares in a substantial part of the common market appoint an undertaking as exclusive provider of collection and/or recycling services for their products, may also appreciably restrict competition, provided other actual or realistic potential providers exist.

7.4   Assessment under Article 81(3)

7.4.1. *Economic benefits*

192.   The Commission takes a positive stance on the use of environmental agreements as a policy instrument to achieve the goals enshrined in Article 2 and Article 174 of the Treaty as well as in Community environmental action plans, provided such agreements are compatible with competition rules.

193.   Environmental agreements caught by Article 81(1) may attain economic benefits which, either at individual or aggregate consumer level, outweigh their negative effects on competition. To fulfil this condition, there must be net benefits in terms of reduced environmental pressure resulting from the agreement, as compared to a baseline where no action is taken. In other words, the expected economic benefits must outweigh the costs.

194.   Such costs include the effects of lessened competition along with compliance costs for economic operators and/or effects on third parties. The benefits might be assessed in two stages. Where consumers individually have a positive rate of return from the agreement under reasonable payback periods, there is no need for the aggregate environmental benefits to be objectively established. Otherwise, a cost-benefit analysis may be necessary to assess whether net benefits for consumers in general are likely under reasonable assumptions.

7.4.2. *Indispensability*

195.   The more objectively the economic efficiency of an environmental agreement is demonstrated, the more clearly each provision might be deemed indispensable to the attainment of the environmental goal within its economic context.

196.   An objective evaluation of provisions which might 'prima facie' be deemed not to be indispensable must be supported with a cost-effectiveness analysis showing that alternative means of attaining the expected environmental benefits, would be more economically or financially costly, under reasonable assumptions. For instance, it should be very clearly demonstrated that a uniform fee, charged irrespective of individual costs for waste collection, is indispensable for the functioning of an industry-wide collection system.

7.4.3. *No elimination of competition*

197.   Whatever the environmental and economic gains and the necessity of the intended provisions, the agreement must not eliminate competition in terms of product or process differentiation, technological innovation or market entry in the short or, where relevant, medium run. For instance, in the case of exclusive collection rights granted to a collection/recycling operator who has potential competitors, the duration of such rights should take into account the possible emergence of an alternative to the operator.

7.5   Examples

198.   Example

Situation: Almost all Community producers and importers of a given domestic appliance (e.g. washing machines) agree, with the encouragement of a public body, to no longer manufacture and import into the Community products which do not comply with certain environmental criteria (e.g. energy efficiency). Together, the parties hold 90% of the Community market. The products which will be thus phased out of the market account for a significant proportion of total sales. They will be replaced with more environmentally friendly, but also more expensive products. Furthermore, the agreement indirectly reduces the output of third parties (e.g. electric utilities, suppliers of components incorporated in the products phased out).

Analysis: The agreement grants the parties control of individual production and imports and concerns an appreciable proportion of their sales and total output, whilst also reducing third parties' output. Consumer choice, which is partly focused on the environmental characteristics of the product, is reduced and prices will probably rise. Therefore, the agreement is caught by Article 81(1). The involvement of the public authority is irrelevant for this assessment.

However, newer products are more technically advanced and by reducing the environmental problem indirectly aimed at (emissions from electricity generation), they will not inevitably create or increase another environmental problem (e.g. water consumption, detergent use). The net contribution to the improvement of the environmental situation overall outweighs increased costs. Furthermore, individual purchasers of more expensive products will also rapidly recoup the cost increase as the more environmentally friendly products have lower running costs. Other alternatives to the agreement are shown to be less certain and less cost-effective in delivering the same net benefits. Varied technical means are economically available to the parties in order to manufacture products which do comply with the environmental characteristics agreed upon and competition will still take place for other product characteristics. Therefore, the conditions for an exemption under Article 81 (3) are fulfilled.

Commission Notice on agreements of minor importance which do not appreciably restrict competition under Article 81(1) of the Treaty establishing the European Community (de minimis)

(OJ 2001, No. C368/13)

(Text with EEA relevance)

I

1. Article 81(1) prohibits agreements between undertakings which may affect trade between Member States and which have as their object or effect the prevention, restriction or distortion of competition within the common market. The Court of Justice of the European Communities has clarified that this provision is not applicable where the impact of the agreement on intra-Community trade or on competition is not appreciable.

2. In this notice the Commission quantifies, with the help of market share thresholds, what is not an appreciable restriction of competition under Article 81 of the EC Treaty. This negative definition of appreciability does not imply that agreements between undertakings which exceed the thresholds set out in this notice appreciably restrict competition. Such agreements may still have only a negligible effect on competition and may therefore not be prohibited by Article 81(1).

3. Agreements may in addition not fall under Article 81(1) because they are not capable of appreciably affecting trade between Member States. This notice does not deal with this issue. It does not quantify what does not constitute an appreciable effect on trade. It is however acknowledged that agreements between small and medium-sized undertakings, as defined in the Annex to Commission Recommendation 96/280/EC, are rarely capable of appreciably affecting trade between Member States. Small and medium-sized undertakings are currently defined in that recommendation as undertakings which have fewer than 250 employees and have either an annual turnover not exceeding EUR 40 million or an annual balance-sheet total not exceeding EUR 27 million.

4. In cases covered by this notice the Commission will not institute proceedings either upon application or on its own initiative. Where undertakings assume in good faith that an agreement is covered by this notice, the Commission will not impose fines. Although not binding on them, this notice also intends to give guidance to the courts and authorities of the Member States in their application of Article 81.

5. This notice also applies to decisions by associations of undertakings and to concerted practices.

6. This notice is without prejudice to any interpretation of Article 81 which may be given by the Court of Justice or the Court of First Instance of the European Communities.

II

7. The Commission holds the view that agreements between undertakings which affect trade between Member States do not appreciably restrict competition within the meaning of Article 81(1):

    (a) if the aggregate market share held by the parties to the agreement does not exceed 10% on any of the relevant markets affected by the agreement, where the agreement is made between undertakings which are actual or potential competitors on any of these markets (agreements between competitors); or

    (b) if the market share held by each of the parties to the agreement does not exceed 15% on any of the relevant markets affected by the agreement, where the agreement is made between undertakings which are not actual or potential competitors on any of these markets (agreements between non-competitors).

In cases where it is difficult to classify the agreement as either an agreement between competitors or an agreement between non-competitors the 10% threshold is applicable.

8. Where in a relevant market competition is restricted by the cumulative effect of agreements for the sale of goods or services entered into by different suppliers or distributors (cumulative foreclosure effect of parallel networks of agreements having similar effects on the market), the market share thresholds under point 7 are reduced to 5%, both for agreements between competitors and for agreements between non-competitors. Individual suppliers or distributors with a market share not exceeding 5% are in general not considered to contribute significantly to a cumulative foreclosure effect. A cumulative foreclosure effect is unlikely to exist if less than 30% of the relevant market is covered by parallel (networks of) agreements having similar effects.

9. The Commission also holds the view that agreements are not restrictive of competition if the market shares do not exceed the thresholds of respectively 10%, 15% and 5% set out in point 7 and 8 during two successive calendar years by more than 2 percentage points.

10. In order to calculate the market share, it is necessary to determine the relevant market. This consists of the relevant product market and the relevant geographic market. When defining the relevant market, reference should be had to the notice on the definition of the relevant market for the purposes of Community competition law. The market shares are to be calculated on the basis of sales value data or, where appropriate, purchase value data. If value data are not available, estimates based on other reliable market information, including volume data, may be used.

11. Points 7, 8 and 9 do not apply to agreements containing any of the following hardcore restrictions:

    (1) as regards agreements between competitors as defined in point 7, restrictions which, directly or indirectly, in isolation or in combination with other factors under the control of the parties, have as their object:

        (a) the fixing of prices when selling the products to third parties;

        (b) the limitation of output or sales;

        (c) the allocation of markets or customers;

    (2) as regards agreements between non-competitors as defined in point 7, restrictions which, directly or indirectly, in isolation or in combination with other factors under the control of the parties, have as their object:

        (a) the restriction of the buyer's ability to determine its sale price, without prejudice to the possibility of the supplier imposing a maximum sale price or recommending a sale price, provided that they do not amount to a fixed or minimum sale price as a result of pressure from, or incentives offered by, any of the parties;

        (b) the restriction of the territory into which, or of the customers to whom, the buyer may sell the contract goods or services, except the following restrictions which are not hardcore:

    – the restriction of active sales into the exclusive territory or to an exclusive customer group reserved to the supplier or allocated by the supplier to another buyer, where such a restriction does not limit sales by the customers of the buyer,

    – the restriction of sales to end users by a buyer operating at the wholesale level of trade,

    – the restriction of sales to unauthorised distributors by the members of a selective distribution system, and

    – the restriction of the buyer's ability to sell components, supplied for the purposes of incorporation, to customers who would use them to manufacture the same type of goods as those produced by the supplier;

(c) the restriction of active or passive sales to end users by members of a selective distribution system operating at the retail level of trade, without prejudice to the possibility of prohibiting a member of the system from operating out of an unauthorised place of establishment;

(d) the restriction of cross-suppliers between distributors within a selective distribution system, including between distributors operating at different levels of trade;

(e) the restriction agreed between a supplier of components and a buyer who incorporates those components, which limits the supplier's ability to sell the components as spare parts to end users or to repairers or other service providers not entrusted by the buyer with the repair or servicing of its goods;

    (3) as regards agreements between competitors as defined in point 7, where the competitors operate, for the purposes of the agreement, at a different level of the production or distribution chain, any of the hardcore restrictions listed in paragraph (1) and (2) above.

    12. (1) For the purposes of this notice, the terms 'undertaking', 'party to the agreement', 'distributor', 'supplier' and 'buyer' shall include their respective connected undertakings.

    (2) 'Connected undertakings' are:

(a) undertakings in which a party to the agreement, directly or indirectly:

    – has the power to exercise more than half the voting rights, or

    – has the power to appoint more than half the members of the supervisory board, board of management or bodies legally representing the undertaking, or

    – has the right to manage the undertaking's affairs;

(b) undertakings which directly or indirectly have, over a party to the agreement, the rights or powers listed in (a);

(c) undertakings in which an undertaking referred to in (b) has, directly or indirectly, the rights or powers listed in (a);

(d) undertakings in which a party to the agreement together with one or more of the undertakings referred to in (a), (b) or (c), or in which two or more of the latter undertakings, jointly have the rights or powers listed in (a);

(e) undertakings in which the rights or the powers listed in (a) are jointly held by:

    – parties to the agreement or their respective connected undertakings referred to in (a) to (d), or

    – one or more of the parties to the agreement or one or more of their connected undertakings referred to in (a) to (d) and one or more third parties.

    (3) For the purposes of paragraph 2(e), the market share held by these jointly held undertakings shall be apportioned equally to each undertaking having the rights or the powers listed in paragraph 2(a).

Guidelines on the assessment of horizontal mergers under the Council Regulation on the control of concentrations between undertakings

(OJ 2004, No. C31/03)

I. INTRODUCTION

1. Article 2 of Council Regulation (EC) No 139/2004 of 20 January 2004 on the control of concentrations between undertakings (hereinafter: the 'Merger Regulation') provides that the Commission has to appraise concentrations within the scope of the Merger Regulation with a view to establishing whether or not they are compatible with the common market. For that purpose, the Commission must assess, pursuant to Article 2(2) and (3), whether or not a concentration would significantly impede effective competition, in particular as a result of the creation or strengthening

2. Accordingly, the Commission must take into account any significant impediment to effective competition likely to be caused by a concentration. The creation or the strengthening of a dominant position is a primary form of such competitive harm. The concept of dominance was defined in the context of Council Regulation (EEC) No 4064/89 of 21 December 1989 on the control of concentrations between undertakings (hereinafter 'Regulation No 4064/89') as:

"a situation where one or more undertakings wield economic power which would enable them to prevent effective competition from being maintained in the relevant market by giving them the opportunity to act to a considerable extent independently of their competitors, their customers and, ultimately, of consumers".

3. For the purpose of interpreting the concept of dominance in the context of Regulation No 4064/89, the Court of Justice referred to the fact that it 'is intended to apply to all concentrations with a Community dimension insofar as they are likely, because of their effect on the structure of competition within the Community, to prove incompatible with the system of undistorted competition envisaged by the Treaty'.

4. The creation or strengthening of a dominant position held by a single firm as a result of a merger has been the most common basis for finding that a concentration would result in a significant impediment to effective competition. Furthermore, the concept of dominance has also been applied in an oligopolistic setting to cases of collective dominance. As a consequence, it is expected that most cases of incompatibility of a concentration with the common market will continue to be based upon a finding of dominance. That concept therefore provides an important indication as to the standard of competitive harm that is applicable when determining whether a concentration is likely to impede effective competition to a significant degree, and hence, as to the likelihood of intervention. To that effect, the present notice is intended to preserve the guidance that can be drawn from past decisional practice and to take full account of past case-law of the Community Courts.

5. The purpose of this notice is to provide guidance as to how the Commission assesses concentrations when the undertakings concerned are actual or potential competitors on the same relevant market. In this notice such mergers will be denoted 'horizontal mergers'. While the notice presents the analytical approach used by the Commission in its appraisal of horizontal mergers it cannot provide details of all possible applications of this approach. The Commission applies the approach described in the notice to the particular facts and circumstances of each case.

6. The guidance set out in this notice draws and elaborates on the Commission's evolving experience with the appraisal of horizontal mergers under Regulation No 4064/89 since its entry into force on 21 September 1990 as well as on the case-law of the Court of Justice and the Court of First Instance of the European Communities. The principles contained here will be applied and further developed and refined by the Commission in individual cases. The Commission may revise this notice from time to time in the light of future developments.

7. The Commission's interpretation of the Merger Regulation as regards the appraisal of horizontal mergers is without prejudice to the interpretation which may be given by the Court of Justice or the Court of First Instance of the European Communities.

II. OVERVIEW

8. Effective competition brings benefits to consumers, such as low prices, high quality products, a wide selection of goods and services, and innovation. Through its control of mergers, the Commission prevents mergers that would be likely to deprive customers of these benefits by significantly increasing the market power of firms. By 'increased market power' is meant the ability of one or more firms to profitably increase prices, reduce output, choice or quality of goods and services, diminish innovation, or otherwise influence parameters of competition. In this notice, the expression 'increased prices' is often used as shorthand for these various ways in which a merger may result in competitive harm. Both suppliers and buyers can have market power. However, for clarity, market power will usually refer here to a supplier's market power. Where a buyer's market power is the issue, the term 'buyer power' is employed.

9. In assessing the competitive effects of a merger, the Commission compares the competitive conditions that would result from the notified merger with the conditions that would have prevailed without the merger. In most cases the competitive conditions existing at the time of the merger constitute the relevant comparison for evaluating the effects of a merger. However, in some circumstances, the Commission may take into account future changes to the market that can reasonably be predicted. It may, in particular, take account of the likely entry or exit of firms if the merger did not take place when considering what constitutes the relevant comparison.

10. The Commission's assessment of mergers normally entails:
   (a) definition of the relevant product and geographic markets;
   (b) competitive assessment of the merger.

The main purpose of market definition is to identify in a systematic way the immediate competitive constraints facing the merged entity. Guidance on this issue can be found in the Commission's Notice on the definition of the relevant market for the purposes of Community competition law. Various considerations leading to the delineation of the relevant markets may also be of importance for the competitive assessment of the merger.

11. This notice is structured around the following elements:
   (a) The approach of the Commission to market shares and concentration thresholds (Section III).
   (b) The likelihood that a merger would have anticompetitive effects in the relevant markets, in the absence of countervailing factors (Section IV).
   (c) The likelihood that buyer power would act as a countervailing factor to an increase in market power resulting from the merger (Section V).
   (d) The likelihood that entry would maintain effective competition in the relevant markets (Section VI).
   (e) The likelihood that efficiencies would act as a factor counteracting the harmful effects on competition which might otherwise result from the merger (Section VII).
   (f) The conditions for a failing firm defence (Section VIII).

12. In order to assess the foreseeable impact of a merger on the relevant markets, the Commission analyses its possible anti-competitive effects and the relevant countervailing factors such as buyer power, the extent of entry barriers and possible efficiencies put forward by the parties. In exceptional circumstances, the Commission considers whether the conditions for a failing firm defence are met.

13. In the light of these elements, the Commission determines, pursuant to Article 2 of the Merger Regulation, whether the merger would significantly impede effective competition, in particular through the creation or the strengthening of a dominant position, and should therefore be declared incompatible with the common market. It should be stressed that these factors are not a 'checklist' to

be mechanically applied in each and every case. Rather, the competitive analysis in a particular case will be based on an overall assessment of the foreseeable impact of the merger in the light of the relevant factors and conditions. Not all the elements will always be relevant to each and every horizontal merger, and it may not be necessary to analyse all the elements of a case in the same detail.

III. MARKET SHARE AND CONCENTRATION LEVELS

14. Market shares and concentration levels provide useful first indications of the market structure and of the competitive importance of both the merging parties and their competitors.

15. Normally, the Commission uses current market shares in its competitive analysis. However, current market shares may be adjusted to reflect reasonably certain future changes, for instance in the light of exit, entry or expansion. Post-merger market shares are calculated on the assumption that the post-merger combined market share of the merging parties is the sum of their pre-merger market shares. Historic data may be used if market shares have been volatile, for instance when the market is characterised by large, lumpy orders. Changes in historic market shares may provide useful information about the competitive process and the likely future importance of the various competitors, for instance, by indicating whether firms have been gaining or losing market shares. In any event, the Commission interprets market shares in the light of likely market conditions, for instance, if the market is highly dynamic in character and if the market structure is unstable due to innovation or growth.

16. The overall concentration level in a market may also provide useful information about the competitive situation. In order to measure concentration levels, the Commission often applies the Herfindahl-Hirschman Index (HHI). The HHI is calculated by summing the squares of the individual market shares of all the firms in the market. The HHI gives proportionately greater weight to the market shares of the larger firms. Although it is best to include all firms in the calculation, lack of information about very small firms may not be important because such firms do not affect the HHI significantly. While the absolute level of the HHI can give an initial indication of the competitive pressure in the market post-merger, the change in the HHI (known as the 'delta') is a useful proxy for the change in concentration directly brought about by the merger.

Market share levels

17. According to well-established case law, very large market shares—50% or more—may in themselves be evidence of the existence of a dominant market position. However, smaller competitors may act as a sufficient constraining influence if, for example, they have the ability and incentive to increase their supplies. A merger involving a firm whose market share will remain below 50% after the merger may also raise competition concerns in view of other factors such as the strength and number of competitors, the presence of capacity constraints or the extent to which the products of the merging parties are close substitutes. The Commission has thus in several cases considered mergers resulting in firms holding market shares between 40% and 50% and in some cases below 40% to lead to the creation or the strengthening of a dominant position.

18. Concentrations which, by reason of the limited market share of the undertakings concerned, are not liable to impede effective competition may be presumed to be compatible with the common market. Without prejudice to Articles 81 and 82 of the Treaty, an indication to this effect exists, in particular, where the market share of the undertakings concerned does not exceed 25% either in the common market or in a substantial part of it.

HHI levels

19. The Commission is unlikely to identify horizontal competition concerns in a market with a post-merger HHI below 1 000. Such markets normally do not require extensive analysis.

20. The Commission is also unlikely to identify horizontal competition concerns in a merger with a post-merger HHI between 1 000 and 2 000 and a delta below 250, or a merger with a post-

merger HHI above 2 000 and a delta below 150, except where special circumstances such as, for instance, one or more of the following factors are present:

(a) a merger involves a potential entrant or a recent entrant with a small market share;

(b) one or more merging parties are important innovators in ways not reflected in market shares;

(c) there are significant cross-shareholdings among the market participants;

(d) one of the merging firms is a maverick firm with a high likelihood of disrupting coordinated conduct;

(e) indications of past or ongoing coordination, or facilitating practices, are present;

(f) one of the merging parties has a pre-merger market share of 50 % of more.

21. Each of these HHI levels, in combination with the relevant deltas, may be used as an initial indicator of the absence of competition concerns. However, they do not give rise to a presumption of either the existence or the absence of such concerns.

IV. POSSIBLE ANTI-COMPETITIVE EFFECTS OF HORIZONTAL MERGERS

22. There are two main ways in which horizontal mergers may significantly impede effective competition, in particular by creating or strengthening a dominant position:

(a) by eliminating important competitive constraints on one or more firms, which consequently would have increased market power, without resorting to coordinated behaviour (non-coordinated effects);

(b) by changing the nature of competition in such a way that firms that previously were not coordinating their behaviour, are now significantly more likely to coordinate and raise prices or otherwise harm effective competition. A merger may also make coordination easier, more stable or more effective for firms which were coordinating prior to the merger (coordinated effects).

23. The Commission assesses whether the changes brought about by the merger would result in any of these effects. Both instances mentioned above may be relevant when assessing a particular transaction.

Non-coordinated effects

24. A merger may significantly impede effective competition in a market by removing important competitive constraints on one or more sellers, who consequently have increased market power. The most direct effect of the merger will be the loss of competition between the merging firms. For example, if prior to the merger one of the merging firms had raised its price, it would have lost some sales to the other merging firm. The merger removes this particular constraint. Non-merging firms in the same market can also benefit from the reduction of competitive pressure that results from the merger, since the merging firms' price increase may switch some demand to the rival firms, which, in turn, may find it profitable to increase their prices. The reduction in these competitive constraints could lead to significant price increases in the relevant market.

25. Generally, a merger giving rise to such non-coordinated effects would significantly impede effective competition by creating or strengthening the dominant position of a single firm, one which, typically, would have an appreciably larger market share than the next competitor post-merger. Furthermore, mergers in oligopolistic markets involving the elimination of important competitive constraints that the merging parties previously exerted upon each other together with a reduction of competitive pressure on the remaining competitors may, even where there is little likelihood of coordination between the members of the oligopoly, also result in a significant impediment to competition. The Merger Regulation clarifies that all mergers giving rise to such non-coordinated effects shall also be declared incompatible with the common market.

26. A number of factors, which taken separately are not necessarily decisive, may influence whether significant non-coordinated effects are likely to result from a merger. Not all of these factors need to be present for such effects to be likely. Nor should this be considered an exhaustive list.

Merging firms have large market shares

27. The larger the market share, the more likely a firm is to possess market power. And the larger the addition of market share, the more likely it is that a merger will lead to a significant increase in market power. The larger the increase in the sales base on which to enjoy higher margins after a price increase, the more likely it is that the merging firms will find such a price increase profitable despite the accompanying reduction in output. Although market shares and additions of market shares only provide first indications of market power and increases in market power, they are normally important factors in the assessment.

Merging firms are close competitors

28. Products may be differentiated within a relevant market such that some products are closer substitutes than others. The higher the degree of substitutability between the merging firms' products, the more likely it is that the merging firms will raise prices significantly. For example, a merger between two producers offering products which a substantial number of customers regard as their first and second choices could generate a significant price increase. Thus, the fact that rivalry between the parties has been an important source of competition on the market may be a central factor in the analysis. High pre-merger margins may also make significant price increases more likely. The merging firms' incentive to raise prices is more likely to be constrained when rival firms produce close substitutes to the products of the merging firms than when they offer less close substitutes. It is therefore less likely that a merger will significantly impede effective competition, in particular through the creation or strengthening of a dominant position, when there is a high degree of substitutability between the products of the merging firms and those supplied by rival producers.

29. When data are available, the degree of substitutability may be evaluated through customer preference surveys, analysis of purchasing patterns, estimation of the cross-price elasticities of the products involved, or diversion ratios. In bidding markets it may be possible to measure whether historically the submitted bids by one of the merging parties have been constrained by the presence of the other merging party.

30. In some markets it may be relatively easy and not too costly for the active firms to reposition their products or extend their product portfolio. In particular, the Commission examines whether the possibility of repositioning or product line extension by competitors or the merging parties may influence the incentive of the merged entity to raise prices. However, product repositioning or product line extension often entails risks and large sunk costs and may be less profitable than the current line.

Customers have limited possibilities of switching supplier

31. Customers of the merging parties may have difficulties switching to other suppliers because there are few alternative suppliers or because they face substantial switching costs. Such customers are particularly vulnerable to price increases. The merger may affect these customers' ability to protect themselves against price increases. In particular, this may be the case for customers that have used dual sourcing from the two merging firms as a means of obtaining competitive prices. Evidence of past customer switching patterns and reactions to price changes may provide important information in this respect.

Competitors are unlikely to increase supply if prices increase

32. When market conditions are such that the competitors of the merging parties are unlikely to increase their supply substantially if prices increase, the merging firms may have an incentive to reduce output below the combined pre-merger levels, thereby raising market prices. The merger increases the incentive to reduce output by giving the merged firm a larger base of sales on

which to enjoy the higher margins resulting from an increase in prices induced by the output reduction.

33. Conversely, when market conditions are such that rival firms have enough capacity and find it profitable to expand output sufficiently, the Commission is unlikely to find that the merger will create or strengthen a dominant position or otherwise significantly impede effective competition.

34. Such output expansion is, in particular, unlikely when competitors face binding capacity constraints and the expansion of capacity is costly or if existing excess capacity is significantly more costly to operate than capacity currently in use.

35. Although capacity constraints are more likely to be important when goods are relatively homogeneous, they may also be important where firms offer differentiated products.

Merged entity able to hinder expansion by competitors

36. Some proposed mergers would, if allowed to proceed, significantly impede effective competition by leaving the merged firm in a position where it would have the ability and incentive to make the expansion of smaller firms and potential competitors more difficult or otherwise restrict the ability of rival firms to compete. In such a case, competitors may not, either individually or in the aggregate, be in a position to constrain the merged entity to such a degree that it would not increase prices or take other actions detrimental to competition. For instance, the merged entity may have such a degree of control, or influence over, the supply of inputs or distribution possibilities that expansion or entry by rival firms may be more costly. Similarly, the merged entity's control over patents or other types of intellectual property (e.g. brands) may make expansion or entry by rivals more difficult. In markets where interoperability between different infrastructures or platforms is important, a merger may give the merged entity the ability and incentive to raise the costs or decrease the quality of service of its rivals. In making this assessment the Commission may take into account, *inter alia,* the financial strength of the merged entity relative to its rivals.

Merger eliminates an important competitive force

37. Some firms have more of an influence on the competitive process than their market shares or similar measures would suggest. A merger involving such a firm may change the competitive dynamics in a significant, anticompetitive way, in particular when the market is already concentrated. For instance, a firm may be a recent entrant that is expected to exert significant competitive pressure in the future on the other firms in the market.

38. In markets where innovation is an important competitive force, a merger may increase the firms' ability and incentive to bring new innovations to the market and, thereby, the competitive pressure on rivals to innovate in that market. Alternatively, effective competition may be significantly impeded by a merger between two important innovators, for instance between two companies with 'pipeline' products related to a specific product market. Similarly, a firm with a relatively small market share may nevertheless be an important competitive force if it has promising pipeline products.

Coordinated effects

39. In some markets the structure may be such that firms would consider it possible, economically rational, and hence preferable, to adopt on a sustainable basis a course of action on the market aimed at selling at increased prices. A merger in a concentrated market may significantly impede effective competition, through the creation or the strengthening of a collective dominant position, because it increases the likelihood that firms are able to coordinate their behaviour in this way and raise prices, even without entering into an agreement or resorting to a concerted practice within the meaning of Article 81 of the Treaty. A merger may also make coordination easier, more stable or more effective for firms, that were already coordinating before the merger, either by making the coordination more robust or by permitting firms to coordinate on even higher prices.

40. Coordination may take various forms. In some markets, the most likely coordination may involve keeping prices above the competitive level. In other markets, coordination may aim at limiting production or the amount of new capacity brought to the market. Firms may also coordinate by dividing the market, for instance by geographic area or other customer characteristics, or by allocating contracts in bidding markets.

41. Coordination is more likely to emerge in markets where it is relatively simple to reach a common understanding on the terms of coordination. In addition, three conditions are necessary for coordination to be sustainable. First, the coordinating firms must be able to monitor to a sufficient degree whether the terms of coordination are being adhered to. Second, discipline requires that there is some form of credible deterrent mechanism that can be activated if deviation is detected. Third, the reactions of outsiders, such as current and future competitors not participating in the coordination, as well as customers, should not be able to jeopardise the results expected from the coordination.

42. The Commission examines whether it would be possible to reach terms of coordination and whether the coordination is likely to be sustainable. In this respect, the Commission considers the changes that the merger brings about. The reduction in the number of firms in a market may, in itself, be a factor that facilitates coordination. However, a merger may also increase the likelihood or significance of coordinated effects in other ways. For instance, a merger may involve a 'maverick' firm that has a history of preventing or disrupting coordination, for example by failing to follow price increases by its competitors, or has characteristics that gives it an incentive to favour different strategic choices than its coordinating competitors would prefer. If the merged firm were to adopt strategies similar to those of other competitors, the remaining firms would find it easier to coordinate, and the merger would increase the likelihood, stability or effectiveness of coordination.

43. In assessing the likelihood of coordinated effects, the Commission takes into account all available relevant information on the characteristics of the markets concerned, including both structural features and the past behaviour of firms. Evidence of past coordination is important if the relevant market characteristics have not changed appreciably or are not likely to do so in the near future. Likewise, evidence of coordination in similar markets may be useful information.

Reaching terms of coordination

44. Coordination is more likely to emerge if competitors can easily arrive at a common perception as to how the coordination should work. Coordinating firms should have similar views regarding which actions would be considered to be in accordance with the aligned behaviour and which actions would not.

45. Generally, the less complex and the more stable the economic environment, the easier it is for the firms to reach a common understanding on the terms of coordination. For instance, it is easier to coordinate among a few players than among many. It is also easier to coordinate on a price for a single, homogeneous product, than on hundreds of prices in a market with many differentiated products. Similarly, it is easier to coordinate on a price when demand and supply conditions are relatively stable than when they are continuously changing. In this context volatile demand, substantial internal growth by some firms in the market or frequent entry by new firms may indicate that the current situation is not sufficiently stable to make coordination likely. In markets where innovation is important, coordination may be more difficult since innovations, particularly significant ones, may allow one firm to gain a major advantage over its rivals.

46. Coordination by way of market division will be easier if customers have simple characteristics that allow the coordinating firms to readily allocate them. Such characteristics may be based on geography; on customer type or simply on the existence of customers who typically buy from one specific firm. Coordination by way of market division may be relatively straightforward if it is easy to identify each customer's supplier and the coordination device is the allocation of existing customers to their incumbent supplier.

47. Coordinating firms may, however, find other ways to overcome problems stemming from complex economic environments short of market division. They may, for instance, establish simple pricing rules that reduce the complexity of coordinating on a large number of prices. One example of such a rule is establishing a small number of pricing points, thus reducing the coordination problem. Another example is having a fixed relationship between certain base prices and a number of other prices, such that prices basically move in parallel. Publicly available key information, exchange of information through trade associations, or information received through cross-shareholdings or participation in joint ventures may also help firms reach terms of coordination. The more complex the market situation is, the more transparency or communication is likely to be needed to reach a common understanding on the terms of coordination.

48. Firms may find it easier to reach a common understanding on the terms of coordination if they are relatively symmetric, especially in terms of cost structures, market shares, capacity levels and levels of vertical integration. Structural links such as cross-shareholding or participation in joint ventures may also help in aligning incentives among the coordinating firms.

Monitoring deviations

49. Coordinating firms are often tempted to increase their share of the market by deviating from the terms of coordination, for instance by lowering prices, offering secret discounts, increasing product quality or capacity or trying to win new customers. Only the credible threat of timely and sufficient retaliation keeps firms from deviating. Markets therefore need to be sufficiently transparent to allow the coordinating firms to monitor to a sufficient degree whether other firms are deviating, and thus know when to retaliate.

50. Transparency in the market is often higher, the lower the number of active participants in the market. Further, the degree of transparency often depends on how market transactions take place in a particular market. For example, transparency is likely to be high in a market where transactions take place on a public exchange or in an open outcry auction. Conversely, transparency may be low in a market where transactions are confidentially negotiated between buyers and sellers on a bilateral basis. When evaluating the level of transparency in the market, the key element is to identify what firms can infer about the actions of other firms from the available information. Coordinating firms should be able to interpret with some certainty whether unexpected behaviour is the result of deviation from the terms of coordination. For instance, in unstable environments it may be difficult for a firm to know whether its lost sales are due to an overall low level of demand or due to a competitor offering particularly low prices. Similarly, when overall demand or cost conditions fluctuate, it may be difficult to interpret whether a competitor is lowering its price because it expects the coordinated prices to fall or because it is deviating.

51. In some markets where the general conditions may seem to make monitoring of deviations difficult, firms may nevertheless engage in practices which have the effect of easing the monitoring task, even when these practices are not necessarily entered into for such purposes. These practices, such as meeting-competition or most-favoured customer clauses, voluntary publication of information, announcements, or exchange of information through trade associations, may increase transparency or help competitors interpret the choices made. Cross-directorships, participation in joint ventures and similar arrangements may also make monitoring easier.

Deterrent mechanisms

52. Coordination is not sustainable unless the consequences of deviation are sufficiently severe to convince coordinating firms that it is in their best interest to adhere to the terms of coordination. It is thus the threat of future retaliation that keeps the coordination sustainable. However the threat is only credible if, where deviation by one of the firms is detected, there is sufficient certainty that some deterrent mechanism will be activated.

53. Retaliation that manifests itself after some significant time lag, or is not certain to be activated, is less likely to be sufficient to offset the benefits from deviating. For example, if a market is

characterised by infrequent, large volume orders, it may be difficult to establish a sufficiently severe deterrent mechanism, since the gain from deviating at the right time may be large, certain and immediate, whereas the losses from being punished may be small and uncertain and only materialise after some time. The speed with which deterrent mechanisms can be implemented is related to the issue of transparency. If firms are only able to observe their competitors' actions after a substantial delay, then retaliation will be similarly delayed and this may influence whether it is sufficient to deter deviation.

54. The credibility of the deterrence mechanism depends on whether the other coordinating firms have an incentive to retaliate. Some deterrent mechanisms, such as punishing the deviator by temporarily engaging in a price war or increasing output significantly, may entail a short-term economic loss for the firms carrying out the retaliation. This does not necessarily remove the incentive to retaliate since the short-term loss may be smaller than the long-term benefit of retaliating resulting from the return to the regime of coordination.

55. Retaliation need not necessarily take place in the same market as the deviation. If the coordinating firms have commercial interaction in other markets, these may offer various methods of retaliation. The retaliation could take many forms, including cancellation of joint ventures or other forms of cooperation or selling of shares in jointly owned companies.

Reactions of outsiders

56. For coordination to be successful, the actions of non-coordinating firms and potential competitors, as well as customers, should not be able to jeopardise the outcome expected from coordination. For example, if coordination aims at reducing overall capacity in the market, this will only hurt consumers if non-coordinating firms are unable or have no incentive to respond to this decrease by increasing their own capacity sufficiently to prevent a net decrease in capacity, or at least to render the coordinated capacity decrease unprofitable.

57. The effects of entry and countervailing buyer power of customers are analysed in later sections. However, special consideration is given to the possible impact of these elements on the stability of coordination. For instance, by concentrating a large amount of its requirements with one supplier or by offering long-term contracts, a large buyer may make coordination unstable by successfully tempting one of the coordinating firms to deviate in order to gain substantial new business.

Merger with a potential competitor

58. Concentrations where an undertaking already active on a relevant market merges with a potential competitor in this market can have similar anti-competitive effects to mergers between two undertakings already active on the same relevant market and, thus, significantly impede effective competition, in particular through the creation or the strengthening of a dominant position.

59. A merger with a potential competitor can generate horizontal anti-competitive effects, whether coordinated or non-coordinated, if the potential competitor significantly constrains the behaviour of the firms active in the market. This is the case if the potential competitor possesses assets that could easily be used to enter the market without incurring significant sunk costs. Anticompetitive effects may also occur where the merging partner is very likely to incur the necessary sunk costs to enter the market in a relatively short period of time after which this company would constrain the behaviour of the firms currently active in the market.

60. For a merger with a potential competitor to have significant anti-competitive effects, two basic conditions must be fulfilled. First, the potential competitor must already exert a significant constraining influence or there must be a significant likelihood that it would grow into an effective competitive force. Evidence that a potential competitor has plans to enter a market in a significant way could help the Commission to reach such a conclusion. Second, there must not be a sufficient number of other potential competitors, which could maintain sufficient competitive pressure after the merger.

Mergers creating or strengthening buyer power in upstream markets

61. The Commission may also analyse to what extent a merged entity will increase its buyer power in upstream markets. On the one hand, a merger that creates or strengthens the market power of a buyer may significantly impede effective competition, in particular by creating or strengthening a dominant position. The merged firm may be in a position to obtain lower prices by reducing its purchase of inputs. This may, in turn, lead it also to lower its level of output in the final product market, and thus harm consumer welfare. Such effects may in particular arise when upstream sellers are relatively fragmented. Competition in the downstream markets could also be adversely affected if, in particular, the merged entity were likely to use its buyer power vis-a-vis its suppliers to foreclose its rivals.

62. On the other hand, increased buyer power may be beneficial for competition. If increased buyer power lowers input costs without restricting downstream competition or total output, then a proportion of these cost reductions are likely to be passed onto consumers in the form of lower prices.

63. In order to assess whether a merger would significantly impede effective competition by creating or strengthening buyer power, an analysis of the competitive conditions in upstream markets and an evaluation of the possible positive and negative effects described above are therefore required.

V. COUNTERVAILING BUYER POWER

64. The competitive pressure on a supplier is not only exercised by competitors but can also come from its customers. Even firms with very high market shares may not be in a position, post-merger, to significantly impede effective competition, in particular by acting to an appreciable extent independently of their customers, if the latter possess countervailing buyer power. Countervailing buyer power in this context should be understood as the bargaining strength that the buyer has vis-à-vis the seller in commercial negotiations due to its size, its commercial significance to the seller and its ability to switch to alternative suppliers.

65. The Commission considers, when relevant, to what extent customers will be in a position to counter the increase in market power that a merger would otherwise be likely to create. One source of countervailing buyer power would be if a customer could credibly threaten to resort, within a reasonable timeframe, to alternative sources of supply should the supplier decide to increase prices or to otherwise deteriorate quality or the conditions of delivery. This would be the case if the buyer could immediately switch to other suppliers, credibly threaten to vertically integrate into the upstream market or to sponsor upstream expansion or entry for instance by persuading a potential entrant to enter by committing to placing large orders with this company. It is more likely that large and sophisticated customers will possess this kind of countervailing buyer power than smaller firms in a fragmented industry. A buyer may also exercise countervailing buying power by refusing to buy other products produced by the supplier or, particularly in the case of durable goods, delaying purchases.

66. In some cases, it may be important to pay particular attention to the incentives of buyers to utilise their buyer power. For example, a downstream firm may not wish to make an investment in sponsoring new entry if the benefits of such entry in terms of lower input costs could also be reaped by its competitors.

67. Countervailing buyer power cannot be found to sufficiently off-set potential adverse effects of a merger if it only ensures that a particular segment of customers, with particular bargaining strength, is shielded from significantly higher prices or deteriorated conditions after the merger. Furthermore, it is not sufficient that buyer power exists prior to the merger, it must also exist and remain effective following the merger. This is because a merger of two suppliers may reduce buyer power if it thereby removes a credible alternative.

VI. ENTRY

68. When entering a market is sufficiently easy, a merger is unlikely to pose any significant anti-competitive risk. Therefore, entry analysis constitutes an important element of the overall competitive assessment. For entry to be considered a sufficient competitive constraint on the merging parties, it must be shown to be likely, timely and sufficient to deter or defeat any potential anti-competitive effects of the merger.

Likelihood of entry

69. The Commission examines whether entry is likely or whether potential entry is likely to constrain the behaviour of incumbents post-merger. For entry to be likely, it must be sufficiently profitable taking into account the price effects of injecting additional output into the market and the potential responses of the incumbents. Entry is thus less likely if it would only be economically viable on a large scale, thereby resulting in significantly depressed price levels. And entry is likely to be more difficult if the incumbents are able to protect their market shares by offering long-term contracts or giving targeted pre-emptive price reductions to those customers that the entrant is trying to acquire. Furthermore, high risk and costs of failed entry may make entry less likely. The costs of failed entry will be higher, the higher is the level of sunk cost associated with entry.

70. Potential entrants may encounter barriers to entry which determine entry risks and costs and thus have an impact on the profitability of entry. Barriers to entry are specific features of the market, which give incumbent firms advantages over potential competitors. When entry barriers are low, the merging parties are more likely to be constrained by entry. Conversely, when entry barriers are high, price increases by the merging firms would not be significantly constrained by entry. Historical examples of entry and exit in the industry may provide useful information about the size of entry barriers.

71. Barriers to entry can take various forms:
   (a) Legal advantages encompass situations where regulatory barriers limit the number of market participants by, for example, restricting the number of licences. They also cover tariff and non-tariff trade barriers.
   (b) The incumbents may also enjoy technical advantages, such as preferential access to essential facilities, natural resources, innovation and R & D, or intellectual property rights, which make it difficult for any firm to compete successfully. For instance, in certain industries, it might be difficult to obtain essential input materials, or patents might protect products or processes. Other factors such as economies of scale and scope, distribution and sales networks, access to important technologies, may also constitute barriers to entry.
   (c) Furthermore, barriers to entry may also exist because of the established position of the incumbent firms on the market. In particular, it may be difficult to enter a particular industry because experience or reputation is necessary to compete effectively, both of which may be difficult to obtain as an entrant. Factors such as consumer loyalty to a particular brand, the closeness of relationships between suppliers and customers, the importance of promotion or advertising, or other advantages relating to reputation will be taken into account in this context. Barriers to entry also encompass situations where the incumbents have already committed to building large excess capacity, or where the costs faced by customers in switching to a new supplier may inhibit entry.

72. The expected evolution of the market should be taken into account when assessing whether or not entry would be profitable. Entry is more likely to be profitable in a market that is expected to experience high growth in the future than in a market that is mature or expected to decline. Scale economies or network effects may make entry unprofitable unless the entrant can obtain a sufficiently large market share.

73. Entry is particularly likely if suppliers in other markets already possess production facilities that could be used to enter the market in question, thus reducing the sunk costs of entry. The smaller the difference in profitability between entry and non-entry prior to the merger, the more likely such a reallocation of production facilities.

Timeliness

74. The Commission examines whether entry would be sufficiently swift and sustained to deter or defeat the exercise of market power. What constitutes an appropriate time period depends on the characteristics and dynamics of the market, as well as on the specific capabilities of potential entrants. However, entry is normally only considered timely if it occurs within two years.

Sufficiency

75. Entry must be of sufficient scope and magnitude to deter or defeat the anti-competitive effects of the merger. Small-scale entry, for instance into some market 'niche', may not be considered sufficient.

VII. EFFICIENCIES

76. Corporate reorganisations in the form of mergers may be in line with the requirements of dynamic competition and are capable of increasing the competitiveness of industry, thereby improving the conditions of growth and raising the standard of living in the Community. It is possible that efficiencies brought about by a merger counteract the effects on competition and in particular the potential harm to consumers that it might otherwise have. In order to assess whether a merger would significantly impede effective competition, in particular through the creation or the strengthening of a dominant position, within the meaning of Article 2(2) and (3) of the Merger Regulation, the Commission performs an overall competitive appraisal of the merger. In making this appraisal, the Commission takes into account the factors mentioned in Article 2(1), including the development of technical and economic progress provided that it is to the consumers' advantage and does not form an obstacle to competition.

77. The Commission considers any substantiated efficiency claim in the overall assessment of the merger. It may decide that, as a consequence of the efficiencies that the merger brings about, there are no grounds for declaring the merger incompatible with the common market pursuant to Article 2(3) of the Merger Regulation. This will be the case when the Commission is in a position to conclude on the basis of sufficient evidence that the efficiencies generated by the merger are likely to enhance the ability and incentive of the merged entity to act pro-competitively for the benefit of consumers, thereby counteracting the adverse effects on competition which the merger might otherwise have.

78. For the Commission to take account of efficiency claims in its assessment of the merger and be in a position to reach the conclusion that as a consequence of efficiencies, there are no grounds for declaring the merger to be incompatible with the common market, the efficiencies have to benefit consumers, be merger-specific and be verifiable. These conditions are cumulative.

Benefit to consumers

79. The relevant benchmark in assessing efficiency claims is that consumers will not be worse off as a result of the merger. For that purpose, efficiencies should be substantial and timely, and should, in principle, benefit consumers in those relevant markets where it is otherwise likely that competition concerns would occur.

80. Mergers may bring about various types of efficiency gains that can lead to lower prices or other benefits to consumers. For example, cost savings in production or distribution may give the merged entity the ability and incentive to charge lower prices following the merger. In line with the need to ascertain whether efficiencies will lead to a net benefit to consumers, cost efficiencies that lead to reductions in variable or marginal costs are more likely to be relevant to the assessment of efficiencies than reductions in fixed costs; the former are, in principle, more likely to result in lower prices for consumers. Cost reductions, which merely result from anti-competitive reductions in output, cannot be considered as efficiencies benefiting consumers.

81. Consumers may also benefit from new or improved products or services, for instance resulting from efficiency gains in the sphere of R & D and innovation. A joint venture company set up in order to develop a new product may bring about the type of efficiencies that the Commission can take into account.

82. In the context of coordinated effects, efficiencies may increase the merged entity's incentive to increase production and reduce prices, and thereby reduce its incentive to coordinate its market behaviour with other firms in the market. Efficiencies may therefore lead to a lower risk of coordinated effects in the relevant market.

83. In general, the later the efficiencies are expected to materialise in the future, the less weight the Commission can assign to them. This implies that, in order to be considered as a counteracting factor, the efficiencies must be timely.

84. The incentive on the part of the merged entity to pass efficiency gains on to consumers is often related to the existence of competitive pressure from the remaining firms in the market and from potential entry. The greater the possible negative effects on competition, the more the Commission has to be sure that the claimed efficiencies are substantial, likely to be realised, and to be passed on, to a sufficient degree, to the consumer. It is highly unlikely that a merger leading to a market position approaching that of a monopoly, or leading to a similar level of market power, can be declared compatible with the common market on the ground that efficiency gains would be sufficient to counteract its potential anti-competitive effects.

Merger specificity

85. Efficiencies are relevant to the competitive assessment when they are a direct consequence of the notified merger and cannot be achieved to a similar extent by less anticompetitive alternatives. In these circumstances, the efficiencies are deemed to be caused by the merger and thus, merger-specific. It is for the merging parties to provide in due time all the relevant information necessary to demonstrate that there are no less anticompetitive, realistic and attainable alternatives of a non-concentrative nature (e.g. a licensing agreement, or a cooperative joint venture) or of a concentrative nature (e.g. a concentrative joint venture, or a differently structured merger) than the notified merger which preserve the claimed efficiencies. The Commission only considers alternatives that are reasonably practical in the business situation faced by the merging parties having regard to established business practices in the industry concerned.

Verifiability

86. Efficiencies have to be verifiable such that the Commission can be reasonably certain that the efficiencies are likely to materialise, and be substantial enough to counteract a merger's potential harm to consumers. The more precise and convincing the efficiency claims are, the better the Commission can evaluate the claims. Where reasonably possible, efficiencies and the resulting benefit to consumers should therefore be quantified. When the necessary data are not available to allow for a precise quantitative analysis, it must be possible to foresee a clearly identifiable positive impact on consumers, not a marginal one. In general, the longer the start of the efficiencies is projected into the future, the less probability the Commission may be able to assign to the efficiencies actually being brought about.

87. Most of the information, allowing the Commission to assess whether the merger will bring about the sort of efficiencies that would enable it to clear a merger, is solely in the possession of the merging parties. It is, therefore, incumbent upon the notifying parties to provide in due time all the relevant information necessary to demonstrate that the claimed efficiencies are merger-specific and likely to be realised. Similarly, it is for the notifying parties to show to what extent the efficiencies are likely to counteract any adverse effects on competition that might otherwise result from the merger, and therefore benefit consumers.

88. Evidence relevant to the assessment of efficiency claims includes, in particular, internal documents that were used by the management to decide on the merger, statements from the management to the owners and financial markets about the expected efficiencies, historical examples of efficiencies and consumer benefit, and pre-merger external experts' studies on the type and size of efficiency gains, and on the extent to which consumers are likely to benefit.

VIII. FAILING FIRM

89. The Commission may decide that an otherwise problematic merger is nevertheless compatible with the common market if one of the merging parties is a failing firm. The basic requirement is that the deterioration of the competitive structure that follows the merger cannot be said to be caused by the merger. This will arise where the competitive structure of the market would deteriorate to at least the same extent in the absence of the merger.

90. The Commission considers the following three criteria to be especially relevant for the application of a 'failing firm defence'. First, the allegedly failing firm would in the near future be forced out of the market because of financial difficulties if not taken over by another undertaking. Second, there is no less anti-competitive alternative purchase than the notified merger. Third, in the absence of a merger, the assets of the failing firm would inevitably exit the market ([111]).

91. It is for the notifying parties to provide in due time all the relevant information necessary to demonstrate that the deterioration of the competitive structure that follows the merger is not caused by the merger.

Commission Notice on cooperation within the Network of Competition Authorities

(OJ 2004, No. C 101/03)

(Text with EEA relevance)

1. INTRODUCTION

1. Council Regulation (EC) No 1/2003 of 16 December 2002 on the implementation of the rules on competition laid down in Articles 81 and 82 of the Treaty (hereafter the 'Council Regulation') creates a system of parallel competences in which the Commission and the Member States' competition authorities (hereafter the 'NCAs') can apply Article 81 and Article 82 of the EC Treaty (hereafter the 'Treaty'). Together the NCAs and the Commission form a network of public authorities: they act in the public interest and cooperate closely in order to protect competition. The network is a forum for discussion and cooperation in the application and enforcement of EC competition policy. It provides a framework for the cooperation of European competition authorities in cases where Articles 81 and 82 of the Treaty are applied and is the basis for the creation and maintenance of a common competition culture in Europe. The network is called 'European Competition Network' (ECN).

2. The structure of the NCAs varies between Member States. In some Member States, one body investigates cases and takes all types of decisions. In other Member States, the functions are divided between two bodies, one which is in charge of the investigation of the case and another, often a college, which is responsible for deciding the case. Finally, in certain Member States, prohibition decisions and/or decisions imposing a fine can only be taken by a court: another competition authority acts as a prosecutor bringing the case before that court. Subject to the general principle of effectiveness, Article 35 of the Council Regulation allows Member States to choose the body or bodies which will be designated as national competition authorities and to allocate functions between them. Under general principles of Community law, Member States are under an obligation to set up a sanctioning system providing for sanctions which are effective, proportionate and dissuasive for infringements of EC law. The enforcement systems of the Member States differ but they have recognised the standards of each other's systems as a basis for cooperation.

3. The network formed by the competition authorities should ensure both an efficient division of work and an effective and consistent application of EC competition rules. The Council Regulation together with the joint statement of the Council and the Commission on the functioning of the European Competition Network sets out the main principles of the functioning of the network. This notice presents the details of the system.

4. Consultations and exchanges within the network are matters between public enforcers and do not alter any rights or obligations arising from Community or national law for companies. Each competition authority remains fully responsible for ensuring due process in the cases it deals with.

2 DIVISION OF WORK

2.1 Principles of allocation

5. The Council Regulation is based on a system of parallel competences in which all competition authorities have the power to apply Articles 81 or 82 of the Treaty and are responsible for an efficient division of work with respect to those cases where an investigation is deemed to be necessary. At the same time each network member retains full discretion in deciding whether or not to investigate a case. Under this system of parallel competences, cases will be dealt with by:

- a single NCA, possibly with the assistance of NCAs of other Member States; or
- several NCAs acting in parallel; or
- the Commission.

6. In most instances the authority that receives a complaint or starts an ex-officio procedure will remain in charge of the case. Re-allocation of a case would only be envisaged at the outset of a procedure (see paragraph 18 below) where either that authority considered that it was not well placed to act or where other authorities also considered themselves well placed to act (see paragraphs 8 to 15 below).

7. Where re-allocation is found to be necessary for an effective protection of competition and of the Community interest, network members will endeavour to re-allocate cases to a single well placed competition authority as often as possible. In any event, re-allocation should be a quick and efficient process and not hold up ongoing investigations.

8. An authority can be considered to be well placed to deal with a case if the following three cumulative conditions are met:

1. the agreement or practice has substantial direct actual or foreseeable effects on competition within its territory, is implemented within or originates from its territory;
2. the authority is able to effectively bring to an end the entire infringement, i.e. it can adopt a cease-and-desist order the effect of which will be sufficient to bring an end to the infringement and it can, where appropriate, sanction the infringement adequately;
3. it can gather, possibly with the assistance of other authorities, the evidence required to prove the infringement.

9. The above criteria indicate that a material link between the infringement and the territory of a Member State must exist in order for that Member State's competition authority to be considered well placed. It can be expected that in most cases the authorities of those Member States where

competition is substantially affected by an infringement will be well placed provided they are capable of effectively bringing the infringement to an end through either single or parallel action unless the Commission is better placed to act (see below paragraphs 14 and 15).

10. It follows that a single NCA is usually well placed to deal with agreements or practices that substantially affect competition mainly within its territory.

> Example 1: *Undertakings situated in Member State A are involved in a price fixing cartel on products that are mainly sold in Member State A.*
> *The NCA in A is well placed to deal with the case.*

11. Furthermore single action of an NCA might also be appropriate where, although more than one NCA can be regarded as well placed, the action of a single NCA is sufficient to bring the entire infringement to an end.

> Example 2: *Two undertakings have set up a joint venture in Member State A. The joint venture provides services in Member States A and B and gives rise to a competition problem. A cease-and-desist order is considered to be sufficient to deal with the case effectively because it can bring an end to the entire infringement. Evidence is located mainly at the offices of the joint venture in Member State A.*
> *The NCAs in A and B are both well placed to deal with the case but single action by the NCA in A would be sufficient and more efficient than single action by NCA in B or parallel action by both NCAs.*

12. Parallel action by two or three NCAs may be appropriate where an agreement or practice has substantial effects on competition mainly in their respective territories and the action of only one NCA would not be sufficient to bring the entire infringement to an end and/or to sanction it adequately.

> Example 3: *Two undertakings agree on a market sharing agreement, restricting the activity of the company located in Member State A to Member State A and the activity of the company located in Member State B to Member State B.*
> *The NCAs in A and B are well placed to deal with the case in parallel, each one for its respective territory.*

13. The authorities dealing with a case in parallel action will endeavour to coordinate their action to the extent possible. To that effect, they may find it useful to designate one of them as a lead authority and to delegate tasks to the lead authority such as for example the coordination of investigative measures, while each authority remains responsible for conducting its own proceedings.

14. The Commission is particularly well placed if one or several agreement(s) or practice(s), including networks of similar agreements or practices, have effects on competition in more than three Member States (crossborder markets covering more than three Member States or several national markets).

> Example 4: *Two undertakings agree to share markets or fix prices for the whole territory of the Community. The Commission is well placed to deal with the case.*
> Example 5: *An undertaking, dominant in four different national markets, abuses its position by imposing fidelity rebates on its distributors in all these markets. The Commission is well placed to deal with the case. It could also deal with one national market so as to create a 'leading' case and other national markets could be dealt with by NCAs, particularly if each national market requires a separate assessment.*

15. Moreover, the Commission is particularly well placed to deal with a case if it is closely linked to other Community provisions which may be exclusively or more effectively applied by the Commission, if the Community interest requires the adoption of a Commission decision to develop Community competition policy when a new competition issue arises or to ensure effective enforcement.

2.2   Mechanisms of cooperation for the purpose of case allocation and assistance

2.2.1. *Information at the beginning of the procedure (Article 11 of the Council Regulation)*
16. In order to detect multiple procedures and to ensure that cases are dealt with by a well placed competition authority, the members of the network have to be informed at an early stage of the cases pending before the various competition authorities. If a case is to be re-allocated, it is indeed in the best interest both of the network and of the undertakings concerned that the re-allocation takes place quickly.

17. The Council Regulation creates a mechanism for the competition authorities to inform each other in order to ensure an efficient and quick re-allocation of cases. Article 11(3) of the Council Regulation lays down an obligation for NCAs to inform the Commission when acting under Article 81 or 82 of the Treaty before or without delay after commencing the first formal investigative measure. It also states that the information may be made available to other NCAs. The rationale of Article 11(3) of the Council Regulation is to allow the network to detect multiple procedures and address possible case re-allocation issues as soon as an authority starts investigating a case. Information should therefore be provided to NCAs and the Commission before or just after any step similar to the measures of investigation that can be undertaken by the Commission under Articles 18 to 21 of the Council Regulation. The Commission has accepted an equivalent obligation to inform NCAs under Article 11(2) of the Council Regulation. Network members will inform each other of pending cases by means of a standard form containing limited details of the case, such as the authority dealing with the case, the product, territories and parties concerned, the alleged infringement, the suspected duration of the infringement and the origin of the case. They will also provide each other with updates when a relevant change occurs.

18. Where case re-allocation issues arise, they should be resolved swiftly, normally within a period of two months, starting from the date of the first information sent to the network pursuant to Article 11 of the Council Regulation. During this period, competition authorities will endeavour to reach an agreement on a possible re-allocation and, where relevant, on the modalities for parallel action.

19. In general, the competition authority or authorities that is/are dealing with a case at the end of the re-allocation period should continue to deal with the case until the completion of the proceedings. Re-allocation of a case after the initial allocation period of two months should only occur where the facts known about the case change materially during the course of the proceedings.

2.2.2. *Suspension or termination of proceedings (Article 13 of the Council Regulation)*
20. If the same agreement or practice is brought before several competition authorities, be it because they have received a complaint or have opened a procedure on their own initiative, Article 13 of the Council Regulation provides a legal basis for suspending proceedings or rejecting a complaint on the grounds that another authority is dealing with the case or has dealt with the case. In Article 13 of the Council Regulation, 'dealing with the case' does not merely mean that a complaint has been lodged with another authority. It means that the other authority is investigating or has investigated the case on its own behalf.

21. Article 13 of the Council Regulation applies when another authority has dealt or is dealing with the competition issue raised by the complainant, even if the authority in question has acted or acts on the basis of a complaint lodged by a different complainant or as a result of an *ex-officio* procedure. This implies that Article 13 of the Council Regulation can be invoked when

the agreement or practice involves the same infringement (s) on the same relevant geographic and product markets.

22. An NCA may suspend or close its proceedings but it has no obligation to do so. Article 13 of the Council Regulation leaves scope for appreciation of the peculiarities of each individual case. This flexibility is important: if a complaint was rejected by an authority following an investigation of the substance of the case, another authority may not want to re-examine the case. On the other hand, if a complaint was rejected for other reasons (e.g. the authority was unable to collect the evidence necessary to prove the infringement), another authority may wish to carry out its own investigation and deal with the case. This flexibility is also reflected, for pending cases, in the choice open to each NCA as to whether it closes or suspends its proceedings. An authority may be unwilling to close a case before the outcome of another authority's proceedings is clear. The ability to suspend its proceedings allows the authority to retain its ability to decide at a later point whether or not to terminate its proceedings. Such flexibility also facilitates consistent application of the rules.

23. Where an authority closes or suspends proceedings because another authority is dealing with the case, it may transfer—in accordance with Article 12 of the Council Regulation—the information provided by the complainant to the authority which is to deal with the case.

24. Article 13 of the Council Regulation can also be applied to part of a complaint or to part of the proceedings in a case. It may be that only part of a complaint or of an ex-officio procedure overlaps with a case already dealt or being dealt with by another competition authority. In that case, the competition authority to which the complaint is brought is entitled to reject part of the complaint on the basis of Article 13 of the Council Regulation and to deal with the rest of the complaint in an appropriate manner. The same principle applies to the termination of proceedings.

25. Article 13 of the Council Regulation is not the only legal basis for suspending or closing ex-officio proceedings or rejecting complaints. NCAs may also be able to do so according to their national procedural law. The Commission may also reject a complaint for lack of Community interest or other reasons pertaining to the nature of the complaint.

2.2.3. *Exchange and use of confidential information (Article 12 of the Council Regulation)*

26. A key element of the functioning of the network is the power of all the competition authorities to exchange and use information (including documents, statements and digital information) which has been collected by them for the purpose of applying Article 81 or Article 82 of the Treaty. This power is a precondition for efficient and effective allocation and handling of cases.

27. Article 12 of the Council Regulation states that for the purpose of applying Articles 81 and 82 of the Treaty, the Commission and the competition authorities of the Member States shall have the power to provide one another with and use in evidence any matter of fact or of law, including confidential information. This means that exchanges of information may not only take place between an NCA and the Commission but also between and amongst NCAs. Article 12 of the Council Regulation takes precedence over any contrary law of a Member State. The question whether information was gathered in a legal manner by the transmitting authority is governed on the basis of the law applicable to this authority. When transmitting information the transmitting authority may inform the receiving authority whether the gathering of the information was contested or could still be contested.

28. The exchange and use of information contains in particular the following safeguards for undertakings and individuals.

    (a) First, Article 28 of the Council Regulation states that 'the Commission and the competition authorities of the Member States, their officials, servants and other persons working under the supervision of these authorities (...) shall not disclose information acquired or exchanged by them pursuant to the' Council Regulation which is 'of the kind covered by the obligation of professional secrecy'. However, the legitimate interest of undertakings in the protection of their business secrets may not prejudice the disclosure of information necessary to prove an infringement of Articles 81 and 82 of the Treaty. The term 'professional secrecy' used in Article 28 of the Council Regulation is a Community law concept and includes in particular business secrets and other confidential information. This will create a common minimum level of protection throughout the Community.

(b) The second safeguard given to undertakings relates to the use of information which has been exchanged within the network. Under Article 12(2) of the Council Regulation, information so exchanged can only be used in evidence for the application of Articles 81 and 82 of the Treaty and for the subject matter for which it was collected. According to Article 12(2) of the Council Regulation, the information exchanged may also be used for the purpose of applying national competition law in parallel in the same case. This is, however, only possible if the application of national law does not lead to an outcome as regards the finding of an infringement different from that under Articles 81 and 82 of the Treaty.

(c) The third safeguard given by the Council Regulation relates to sanctions on individuals on the basis of information exchanged pursuant to Article 12(1). The Council Regulation only provides for sanctions on undertakings for violations of Articles 81 and 82 of the Treaty. Some national laws also provide for sanctions on individuals in connection with violations of Articles 81 and 82 of the Treaty. Individuals normally enjoy more extensive rights of defence (e.g. a right to remain silent compared to undertakings which may only refuse to answer questions which would lead them to admit that they have committed an infringement). Article 12(3) of the Council Regulation ensures that information collected from undertakings cannot be used in a way which would circumvent the higher protection of individuals. This provision precludes sanctions being imposed on individuals on the basis of information exchanged pursuant to the Council Regulation if the laws of the transmitting and the receiving authorities do not provide for sanctions of a similar kind in respect of individuals, unless the rights of the individual concerned as regards the collection of evidence have been respected by the transmitting authority to the same standard as they are guaranteed by the receiving authority. The qualification of the sanctions by national law ('administrative' or 'criminal') is not relevant for the purpose of applying Article 12(3) of the Council Regulation. The Council Regulation intends to create a distinction between sanctions which result in custody and other types of sanctions such as fines on individuals and other personal sanctions. If both the legal system of the transmitting and that of the receiving authority provide for sanctions of a similar kind (e.g. in both Member States, fines can be imposed on a member of the staff of an undertaking who has been involved in the violation of Article 81 or 82 of the Treaty), information exchanged pursuant to Article 12 of the Council Regulation can be used by the receiving authority. In that case, procedural safeguards in both systems are considered to be equivalent. If on the other hand, both legal systems do not provide for sanctions of a similar kind, the information can only be used if the same level of protection of the rights of the individual has been respected in the case at hand (see Article 12(3) of the Council Regulation). In that latter case however, custodial sanctions can only be imposed where both the transmitting and the receiving authority have the power to impose such a sanction.

2.2.4. *Investigations (Article 22 of the Council Regulation)*

29. The Council Regulation provides that an NCA may ask another NCA for assistance in order to collect information on its behalf. An NCA can ask another NCA to carry out fact-finding measures on its behalf. Article 12 of the Council Regulation empowers the assisting NCA to transmit the information it has collected to the requesting NCA. Any exchange between or amongst NCAs and use in evidence by the requesting NCA of such information shall be carried out in accordance with Article 12 of the Council Regulation. Where an NCA acts on behalf of another NCA, it acts pursuant to its own rules of procedure, and under its own powers of investigation.

30. Under Article 22(2) of the Council Regulation, the Commission can ask an NCA to carry out an inspection on its behalf. The Commission can either adopt a decision pursuant to Article 20 (4) of

the Council Regulation or simply issue a request to the NCA. The NCA officials will exercise their powers in accordance with their national law. The agents of the Commission may assist the NCA during the inspection.

2.3   Position of undertakings

2.3.1. *General*

31. All network members will endeavour to make the allocation of cases a quick and efficient process. Given the fact that the Council Regulation has created a system of parallel competences, the allocation of cases between members of the network constitutes a mere division of labour where some authorities abstain from acting. The allocation of cases therefore does not create individual rights for the companies involved in or affected by an infringement to have the case dealt with by a particular authority.

32. If a case is re-allocated to a given competition authority, it is because the application of the allocation criteria set out above led to the conclusion that this authority is well placed to deal with the case by single or parallel action. The competition authority to which the case is re-allocated would have been in a position, in any event, to commence an *ex-officio* procedure against the infringement.

33. Furthermore, all competition authorities apply Community competition law and the Council Regulation sets out mechanisms to ensure that the rules are applied in a consistent way.

34. If a case is re-allocated within the network, the undertakings concerned and the complainant(s) are informed as soon as possible by the competition authorities involved.

2.3.2. *Position of complainants*

35. If a complaint is lodged with the Commission pursuant to Article 7 of the Council Regulation and if the Commission does not investigate the complaint or prohibit the agreement or practice complained of, the complainant has a right to obtain a decision rejecting his complaint. This is without prejudice to Article 7(3) of the Commission implementing regulation. The rights of complainants who lodge a complaint with an NCA are governed by the applicable national law.

36. In addition, Article 13 of the Council Regulation gives all NCAs the possibility of suspending or rejecting a complaint on the ground that another competition authority is dealing or has dealt with the same case. That provision also allows the Commission to reject a complaint on the ground that a competition authority of a Member State is dealing or has dealt with the case. Article 12 of the Council Regulation allows the transfer of information between competition authorities within the network subject to the safeguards provided in that Article (see paragraph 28 above).

2.3.3. *Position of applicants claiming the benefit of a leniency programme*

37. The Commission considers that it is in the Community interest to grant favourable treatment to undertakings which co-operate with it in the investigation of cartel infringements. A number of Member States have also adopted leniency programmes relating to cartel investigations. The aim of these leniency programmes is to facilitate the detection by competition authorities of cartel activity and also thereby to act as a deterrent to participation in unlawful cartels.

38. In the absence of a European Union-wide system of fully harmonised leniency programmes, an application for leniency to a given authority is not to be considered as an application for leniency to any other authority. It is therefore in the interest of the applicant to apply for leniency to all competition authorities which have competence to apply Article 81 of the Treaty in the territory which is affected by the infringement and which may be considered well placed to act against the infringement in question. In view of the importance of timing in most existing leniency programmes, applicants will also need to consider whether it would be appropriate to file leniency applications with the relevant authorities simultaneously. It is for the applicant to take the steps which it considers appropriate to protect its position with respect to possible proceedings by these authorities.

39. As for all cases where Articles 81 and 82 of the Treaty are applied, where an NCA deals with a case which has been initiated as a result of a leniency application, it must inform the Commission

and may make the information available to other members of the network pursuant to Article 11(3) of the Council Regulation (cf. paragraphs 16 *et subseq.*). The Commission has accepted an equivalent obligation to inform NCAs under Article 11(2) of the Council Regulation. In such cases, however, information submitted to the network pursuant to Article 11 will not be used by other members of the network as the basis for starting an investigation on their own behalf whether under the competition rules of the Treaty or, in the case of NCAs, under their national competition law or other laws. This is without prejudice to any power of the authority to open an investigation on the basis of information received from other sources or, subject to paragraphs 40 and 41 below, to request, be provided with and use information pursuant to Article 12 from any member of the network, including the network member to whom the leniency application was submitted.

40. Save as provided under paragraph 41, information voluntarily submitted by a leniency applicant will only be transmitted to another member of the network pursuant to Article 12 of the Council Regulation with the consent of the applicant. Similarly other information that has been obtained during or following an inspection or by means of or following any other fact-finding measures which, in each case, could not have been carried out except as a result of the leniency application will only be transmitted to another authority pursuant to Article 12 of the Council Regulation if the applicant has consented to the transmission to that authority of information it has voluntarily submitted in its application for leniency. The network members will encourage leniency applicants to give such consent, in particular as regards disclosure to authorities in respect of which it would be open to the applicant to obtain lenient treatment. Once the leniency applicant has given consent to the transmission of information to another authority, that consent may not be withdrawn. This paragraph is without prejudice, however, to the responsibility of each applicant to file leniency applications to whichever authorities it may consider appropriate.

41. Notwithstanding the above, the consent of the applicant for the transmission of information to another authority pursuant to Article 12 of the Council Regulation is not required in any of the following circumstances:

1. No consent is required where the receiving authority has also received a leniency application relating to the same infringement from the same applicant as the transmitting authority, provided that at the time the information is transmitted it is not open to the applicant to withdraw the information which it has submitted to that receiving authority.

2. No consent is required where the receiving authority has provided a written commitment that neither the information transmitted to it nor any other information it may obtain following the date and time of transmission as noted by the transmitting authority, will be used by it or by any other authority to which the information is subsequently transmitted to impose sanctions:

    (a) on the leniency applicant;

    (b) on any other legal or natural person covered by the favourable treatment offered by the transmitting authority as a result of the application made by the applicant under its leniency programme;

    (c) on any employee or former employee of any of the persons covered by (a) or (b).

    A copy of the receiving authority's written commitment will be provided to the applicant.

3. In the case of information collected by a network member under Article 22(1) of the Council Regulation on behalf of and for the account of the network member to whom the leniency application was made, no consent is required for the transmission of such information to, and its use by, the network member to whom the application was made.

42. Information relating to cases initiated as a result of a leniency application and which has been submitted to the Commission under Article 11(3) of the Council Regulation will only be made available to those NCAs that have committed themselves to respecting the principles set out above (see paragraph 72). The same principle applies where a case has been initiated by the Commission as a result of a leniency application made to the Commission. This does not affect the power of any authority to be provided with information under Article 12 of the Council Regulation, provided however that the provisions of paragraphs 40 and 41 are respected.

3 CONSISTENT APPLICATION OF EC COMPETITION RULES

3.1 Mechanism of cooperation (Article 11(4) and 11(5) of the Council Regulation)

43. The Council Regulation pursues the objective that Articles 81 and 82 of the Treaty are applied in a consistent manner throughout the Community. In this respect NCAs will respect the convergence rule contained in Article 3(2) of the Council Regulation. In line with Article 16(2) they cannot—when ruling on agreements, decisions and practices under Article 81 or Article 82 of the Treaty which are already the subject of a Commission decision—take decisions, which would run counter to the decisions adopted by the Commission. Within the network of competition authorities the Commission, as the guardian of the Treaty, has the ultimate but not the sole responsibility for developing policy and safeguarding consistency when it comes to the application of EC competition law.

44. According to Article 11(4) of the Council Regulation, no later than 30 days before the adoption of a decision applying Articles 81 or 82 of the Treaty and requiring that an infringement be brought to an end, accepting commitments or withdrawing the benefit of a blockexemption regulation, NCAs shall inform the Commission. They have to send to the Commission, at the latest 30 days before the adoption of the decision, a summary of the case, the envisaged decision or, in the absence thereof, any other document indicating the proposed course of action.

45. As under Article 11(3) of the Council Regulation, the obligation is to inform the Commission, but the information may be shared by the NCA informing the Commission with the other members of the network.

46. Where an NCA has informed the Commission pursuant to Article 11(4) of the Council Regulation and the 30 days deadline has expired, the decision can be adopted as long as the Commission has not initiated proceedings. The Commission may make written observations on the case before the adoption of the decision by the NCA. The NCA and the Commission will make the appropriate efforts to ensure the consistent application of Community law (cf. paragraph 3 above).

47. If special circumstances require that a national decision is taken in less than 30 days following the transmission of information pursuant to Article 11(4) of the Council Regulation, the NCA concerned may ask the Commission for a swifter reaction. The Commission will endeavour to react as quickly as possible.

48. Other types of decisions, i.e. decisions rejecting complaints, decisions closing an *ex-officio* procedure or decisions ordering interim measures, can also be important from a competition policy point of view, and the network members may have an interest in informing each other about them and possibly discussing them. NCAs can therefore on the basis of Article 11(5) of the Council Regulation inform the Commission and thereby inform the network of any other case in which EC competition law is applied.

49. All members of the network should inform each other about the closure of their procedures which have been notified to the network pursuant to Article 11(2) and (3) of the Council Regulation.

3.2 The initiation of proceedings by the Commission under Article 11(6) of the Council Regulation

50. According to the case law of the Court of Justice, the Commission, entrusted by Article 85 (1) of the Treaty with the task of ensuring the application of the principles laid down in Articles 81 and 82 of the Treaty, is responsible for defining and implementing the orientation of Community competition policy. It can adopt individual decisions under Articles 81 and 82 of the Treaty at any time.

51. Article 11(6) of the Council Regulation states that the initiation by the Commission of proceedings for the adoption of a decision under the Council Regulation shall relieve all NCAs of their competence to apply Articles 81 and 82 of the Treaty. This means that once the Commission has

opened proceedings, NCAs cannot act under the same legal basis against the same agreement (s) or practice (s) by the same undertaking(s) on the same relevant geographic and product market.

52. The initiation of proceedings by the Commission is a formal act by which the Commission indicates its intention to adopt a decision under Chapter III of the Council Regulation. It can occur at any stage of the investigation of the case by the Commission. The mere fact that the Commission has received a complaint is not in itself sufficient to relieve NCAs of their competence.

53. Two situations can arise. First, where the Commission is the first competition authority to initiate proceedings in a case for the adoption of a decision under the Council Regulation, national competition authorities may no longer deal with the case. Article 11(6) of the Council Regulation provides that once the Commission has initiated proceedings, the NCAs can no longer start their own procedure with a view to applying Articles 81 and 82 of the Treaty to the same agreement (s) or practice(s) by the same undertaking(s) on the same relevant geographic and product market.

54. The second situation is where one or more NCAs have informed the network pursuant to Article 11(3) of the Council Regulation that they are acting on a given case. During the initial allocation period (indicative time period of two months, see paragraph 18 above), the Commission can initiate proceedings with the effects of Article 11(6) of the Council Regulation after having consulted the authorities concerned. After the allocation phase, the Commission will in principle only apply Article 11(6) of the Council Regulation if one of the following situations arises:

  (a) Network members envisage conflicting decisions in the same case;
  (b) Network members envisage a decision which is obviously in conflict with consolidated case law; the standards defined in the judgements of the Community courts and in previous decisions and regulations of the Commission should serve as a yardstick; concerning the assessment of the facts (e.g. market definition), only a significant divergence will trigger an intervention of the Commission;
  (c) Network member (s) is (are) unduly drawing out proceedings in the case;
  (d) There is a need to adopt a Commission decision to develop Community competition policy in particular when a similar competition issue arises in several Member States or to ensure effective enforcement;
  (e) The NCA(s) concerned do not object.

55. If an NCA is already acting on a case, the Commission will explain the reasons for the application of Article 11(6) of the Council Regulation in writing to the NCA concerned and to the other members of the Network.

56. The Commission will announce to the network its intention of applying Article 11(6) of the Council Regulation in due time, so that Network members will have the possibility of asking for a meeting of the Advisory Committee on the matter before the Commission initiates proceedings.

57. The Commission will normally not—and to the extent that Community interest is not at stake—adopt a decision which is in conflict with a decision of an NCA after proper information pursuant to both Article 11(3) and (4) of the Council Regulation has taken place and the Commission has not made use of Article 11 (6) of the Council Regulation.

4 THE ROLE AND THE FUNCTIONING OF THE ADVISORY COMMITTEE IN THE NEW SYSTEM

58. The Advisory Committee is the forum where experts from the various competition authorities discuss individual cases and general issues of Community competition law.

4.1 Scope of the consultation

4.1.1. *Decisions of the Commission*

59. The Advisory Committee is consulted prior to the Commission taking any decision pursuant to Articles 7, 8, 9, 10, 23, 24(2) or 29(1) of the Council Regulation. The Commission must take the utmost account of the opinion of the Advisory Committee and inform the Committee of the manner in which its opinion has been taken into account.

60. For decisions adopting interim measures, the Advisory Committee is consulted following a swifter and lighter procedure, on the basis of a short explanatory note and the operative part of the decision.

4.1.2. *Decisions of NCAs*

61. It is in the interest of the network that important cases dealt with by NCAs under Articles 81 and 82 of the Treaty can be discussed in the Advisory Committee. The Council Regulation enables the Commission to put a given case being dealt with by an NCA on the agenda of the Advisory Committee. Discussion can be requested by the Commission or by any Member State. In either case, the Commission will put the case on the agenda after having informed the NCA(s) concerned. This discussion in the Advisory Committee will not lead to a formal opinion.

62. In important cases, the Advisory Committee could also serve as a forum for the discussion of case allocation. In particular, where the Commission intends to apply Article 11(6) of the Council Regulation after the initial allocation period, the case can be discussed in the Advisory Committee before the Commission initiates proceedings. The Advisory Committee may issue an informal statement on the matter.

4.1.3. *Implementing measures, block-exemption regulations, guidelines and other notices (Article 33 of the Council Regulation)*

63. The Advisory Committee will be consulted on draft Commission regulations as provided for in the relevant Council Regulations.

64. Beside regulations, the Commission may also adopt notices and guidelines. These more flexible tools are very useful for explaining and announcing the Commission's policy, and for explaining its interpretation of the competition rules. The Advisory Committee will also be consulted on these notices and guidelines.

4.2 Procedure

4.2.1. *Normal procedure*

65. For consultation on Commission draft decisions, the meeting of the Advisory Committee takes place at the earliest 14 days after the invitation to the meeting is sent by the Commission. The Commission attaches to the invitation a summary of the case, a list of the most important documents, i.e. the documents needed to assess the case, and a draft decision. The Advisory Committee gives an opinion on the Commission draft decision. At the request of one or several members, the opinion shall be reasoned.

66. The Council Regulation allows for the possibility of the Member States agreeing upon a shorter period of time between the sending of the invitation and the meeting.

4.2.2. *Written procedure*

67. The Council Regulation provides for the possibility of a written consultation procedure. If no Member State objects, the Commission can consult the Member States by sending the documents to them and setting a deadline within which they can comment on the draft. This deadline would not normally be shorter than 14 days, except for decisions on interim measures pursuant to Article 8 of the Council Regulation. Where a Member State requests that a meeting takes place, the Commission will arrange for such a meeting.

4.3 Publication of the opinion of the Advisory Committee

68. The Advisory Committee can recommend the publication of its opinion. In that event, the Commission will carry out such publication simultaneously with the decision, taking into account the legitimate interest of undertakings in the protection of their business secrets.

5 FINAL REMARKS

69. This Notice is without prejudice to any interpretation of the applicable Treaty and regulatory provisions by the Court of First Instance and the Court of Justice.

70. This Notice will be the subject of periodic review carried out jointly by the NCAs and the Commission. On the basis of the experience acquired, it will be reviewed no later than at the end of the third year after its adoption.

71. This notice replaces the Commission notice on cooperation between national competition authorities and the Commission in handling cases falling within the scope of Articles 81 and 82 of the Treaty published in 1997.

6 STATEMENT BY OTHER NETWORK MEMBERS

72. The principles set out in this notice will also be abided by those Member States' competition authorities which have signed a statement in the form of the Annex to this Notice. In this statement they acknowledge the principles of this notice, including the principles relating to the protection of applicants claiming the benefit of a leniency programme and declare that they will abide by them. A list of these authorities is published on the website of the European Commission. It will be updated if appropriate.

Annex
Statement regarding the Commission Notice on cooperation within the Network of Competition Authorities

In order to cooperate closely with a view to protecting competition within the European Union in the interest of consumers, the undersigned competition authority:

1. Acknowledges the principles set out in the Commission Notice on Cooperation within the Network of Competition Authorities; and

2. Declares that it will abide by those principles, which include principles relating to the protection of applicants claiming the benefit of a leniency programme, in any case in which it is acting or may act and to which those principles apply.

....
(place)   (date)

Commission Notice on the co-operation between the Commission and the courts of the EU Member States in the application of Articles 81 and 82 EC

(OJ 2004, No. C 101/4)

(Text with EEA relevance)

I THE SCOPE OF THE NOTICE

1. The present notice addresses the co-operation between the Commission and the courts of the EU Member States, when the latter apply Articles 81 and 82 EC. For the purpose of this notice, the 'courts of the EU Member States' (hereinafter 'national courts') are those courts and tribunals within an EU Member State that can apply Articles 81 and 82 EC and that are authorised to ask a preliminary question to the Court of Justice of the European Communities pursuant to Article 234 EC.

2. The national courts may be called upon to apply Articles 81 or 82 EC in lawsuits between private parties, such as actions relating to contracts or actions for damages. They may also act as public enforcer or as review court. A national court may indeed be designated as a competition authority of a Member State (hereinafter 'the national competition authority') pursuant to Article 35(1) of

Regulation (EC) No 1/2003 (hereinafter 'the regulation'). In that case, the co-operation between the national courts and the Commission is not only covered by the present notice, but also by the notice on the co-operation within the network of competition authorities.

II THE APPLICATION OF EC COMPETITION RULES BY NATIONAL COURTS

A   The competence of national courts to apply EC competition rules

3. To the extent that national courts have jurisdiction to deal with a case, they have the power to apply Articles 81 and 82 EC. Moreover, it should be remembered that Articles 81 and 82 EC are a matter of public policy and are essential to the accomplishment of the tasks entrusted to the Community, and, in particular, for the functioning of the internal market. According to the Court of Justice, where, by virtue of domestic law, national courts must raise of their own motion points of law based on binding domestic rules which have not been raised by the parties, such an obligation also exists where binding Community rules, such as the EC competition rules, are concerned. The position is the same if domestic law confers on national courts a discretion to apply of their own motion binding rules of law: national courts must apply the EC competition rules, even when the party with an interest in application of those provisions has not relied on them, where domestic law allows such application by the national court. However, Community law does not require national courts to raise of their own motion an issue concerning the breach of provisions of Community law where examination of that issue would oblige them to abandon the passive role assigned to them by going beyond the ambit of the dispute defined by the parties themselves and relying on facts and circumstances other than those on which the party with an interest in application of those provisions bases his claim.

4. Depending on the functions attributed to them under national law, national courts may be called upon to apply Articles 81 and 82 EC in administrative, civil or criminal proceedings. In particular, where a natural or legal person asks the national court to safeguard his individual rights, national courts play a specific role in the enforcement of Articles 81 and 82 EC, which is different from the enforcement in the public interest by the Commission or by national competition authorities. Indeed, national courts can give effect to Articles 81 and 82 EC by finding contracts to be void or by awards of damages.

5. National courts can apply Articles 81 and 82 EC, without it being necessary to apply national competition law in parallel. However, where a national court applies national competition law to agreements, decisions by associations of undertakings or concerted practices which may affect trade between Member States within the meaning of Article 81(1) EC or to any abuse prohibited by Article 82 EC, they also have to apply EC competition rules to those agreements, decisions or practices.

6. The regulation does not only empower the national courts to apply EC competition law. The parallel application of national competition law to agreements, decisions of associations of undertakings and concerted practices which affect trade between Member States may not lead to a different outcome from that of EC competition law. Article 3(2) of the regulation provides that agreements, decisions or concerted practices which do not infringe Article 81 (1) EC or which fulfil the conditions of Article 81(3) EC cannot be prohibited either under national competition law. On the other hand, the Court of Justice has ruled that agreements, decisions or concerted practices that violate Article 81(1) and do not fulfil the conditions of Article 81(3) EC cannot be upheld under national law. As to the parallel application of national competition law and Article 82 EC in the case of unilateral conduct, Article 3 of the regulation does not provide for a similar convergence obligation. However, in case of conflicting provisions, the general principle of primacy of Community law requires national courts to disapply any provision of national law which contravenes a Community rule, regardless of whether that national law provision was adopted before or after the Community rule.

7. Apart from the application of Articles 81 and 82 EC, national courts are also competent to apply acts adopted by EU institutions in accordance with the EC Treaty or in accordance with the measures adopted to give the Treaty effect, to the extent that these acts have direct effect. National courts may thus have to enforce Commission decisions or regulations applying Article 81(3) EC to certain categories of agreements, decisions or concerted practices. When applying these EC competition rules, national courts act within the framework of Community law and are consequently bound to observe the general principles of Community law.

8. The application of Articles 81 and 82 EC by national courts often depends on complex economic and legal assessments. When applying EC competition rules, national courts are bound by the case law of the Community courts as well as by Commission regulations applying Article 81(3) EC to certain categories of agreements, decisions or concerted practices. Furthermore, the application of Articles 81 and 82 EC by the Commission in a specific case binds the national courts when they apply EC competition rules in the same case in parallel with or subsequent to the Commission. Finally, and without prejudice to the ultimate interpretation of the EC Treaty by the Court of Justice, national courts may find guidance in Commission regulations and decisions which present elements of analogy with the case they are dealing with, as well as in Commission notices and guidelines relating to the application of Articles 81 and 82 EC and in the annual report on competition policy.

B Procedural aspects of the application of EC competition rules by national courts

9. The procedural conditions for the enforcement of EC competition rules by national courts and the sanctions they can impose in case of an infringement of those rules, are largely covered by national law. However, to some extent, Community law also determines the conditions in which EC competition rules are enforced. Those Community law provisions may provide for the faculty of national courts to avail themselves of certain instruments, e.g. to ask for the Commission's opinion on questions concerning the application of EC competition rules or they may create rules that have an obligatory impact on proceedings before them, e.g. allowing the Commission and national competition authorities to submit written observations. These Community law provisions prevail over national rules. Therefore, national courts have to set aside national rules which, if applied, would conflict with these Community law provisions. Where such Community law provisions are directly applicable, they are a direct source of rights and duties for all those affected, and must be fully and uniformly applied in all the Member States from the date of their entry into force.

10. In the absence of Community law provisions on procedures and sanctions related to the enforcement of EC competition rules by national courts, the latter apply national procedural law and—to the extent that they are competent to do so—impose sanctions provided for under national law. However, the application of these national provisions must be compatible with the general principles of Community law. In this regard, it is useful to recall the case law of the Court of Justice, according to which:

(a) where there is an infringement of Community law, national law must provide for sanctions which are effective, proportionate and dissuasive;

(b) where the infringement of Community law causes harm to an individual, the latter should under certain conditions be able to ask the national court for damages;

(c) the rules on procedures and sanctions which national courts apply to enforce Community law

  – must not make such enforcement excessively difficult or practically impossible (the principle of effectiveness) and they

  – must not be less favourable than the rules applicable to the enforcement of equivalent national law (the principle of equivalence).

On the basis of the principle of primacy of Community law, a national court may not apply national rules that are incompatible with these principles.

C   Parallel or consecutive application of EC competition rules by the Commission and by national courts

11. A national court may be applying EC competition law to an agreement, decision, concerted practice or unilateral behaviour affecting trade between Member States at the same time as the Commission or subsequent to the Commission. The following points outline some of the obligations national courts have to respect in those circumstances.

12. Where a national court comes to a decision before the Commission does, it must avoid adopting a decision that would conflict with a decision contemplated by the Commission. To that effect, the national court may ask the Commission whether it has initiated proceedings regarding the same agreements, decisions or practices and if so, about the progress of proceedings and the likelihood of a decision in that case. The national court may, for reasons of legal certainty, also consider staying its proceedings until the Commission has reached a decision. The Commission, for its part, will endeavour to give priority to cases for which it has decided to initiate proceedings within the meaning of Article 2(1) of Commission Regulation (EC) No 773/ 2004 and that are the subject of national proceedings stayed in this way, in particular when the outcome of a civil dispute depends on them. However, where the national court cannot reasonably doubt the Commission's contemplated decision or where the Commission has already decided on a similar case, the national court may decide on the case pending before it in accordance with that contemplated or earlier decision without it being necessary to ask the Commission for the information mentioned above or to await the Commission's decision.

13. Where the Commission reaches a decision in a particular case before the national court, the latter cannot take a decision running counter to that of the Commission. The binding effect of the Commission's decision is of course without prejudice to the interpretation of Community law by the Court of Justice. Therefore, if the national court doubts the legality of the Commission's decision, it cannot avoid the binding effects of that decision without a ruling to the contrary by the Court of Justice. Consequently, if a national court intends to take a decision that runs counter to that of the Commission, it must refer a question to the Court of Justice for a preliminary ruling (Article 234 EC). The latter will then decide on the compatibility of the Commission's decision with Community law. However, if the Commission's decision is challenged before the Community courts pursuant to Article 230 EC and the outcome of the dispute before the national court depends on the validity of the Commission's decision, the national court should stay its proceedings pending final judgment in the action for annulment by the Community courts unless it considers that, in the circumstances of the case, a reference to the Court of Justice for a preliminary ruling on the validity of the Commission decision is warranted.

14. When a national court stays proceedings, e.g. awaiting the Commission's decision (situation described in point 12 of this notice) or pending final judgement by the Community courts in an action for annulment or in a preliminary ruling procedure (situation described in point 13), it is incumbent on it to examine whether it is necessary to order interim measures in order to safeguard the interests of the parties.

III   THE CO-OPERATION BETWEEN THE COMMISSION AND NATIONAL COURTS

15. Other than the co-operation mechanism between the national courts and the Court of Justice under Article 234 EC, the EC Treaty does not explicitly provide for co-operation between the national courts and the Commission. However, in its interpretation of Article 10 EC, which obliges the Member States to facilitate the achievement of the Community's tasks, the Community courts found that this Treaty provision imposes on the European institutions and the Member States mutual duties of loyal co-operation with a view to attaining the objectives of the EC Treaty. Article 10 EC thus implies that the Commission must assist national courts when they apply Community law. Equally, national courts may be obliged to assist the Commission in the fulfilment of its tasks.

16. It is also appropriate to recall the co-operation between national courts and national authorities, in particular national competition authorities, for the application of Articles 81 and 82 EC. While the co-operation between these national authorities is primarily governed by national rules, Article 15(3) of the regulation provides for the possibility for national competition authorities to submit observations before the national courts of their Member State. Points 31 and 33 to 35 of this notice are *mutatis mutandis* applicable to those submissions.

A The Commission as amicus curiae

17. In order to assist national courts in the application of EC competition rules, the Commission is committed to help national courts where the latter find such help necessary to be able to decide on a case. Article 15 of the regulation refers to the most frequent types of such assistance: the transmission of information (points 21 to 26) and the Commission's opinions (points 27 to 30), both at the request of a national court and the possibility for the Commission to submit observations (points 31 to 35). Since the regulation provides for these types of assistance, it cannot be limited by any Member States' rule. However, in the absence of Community procedural rules to this effect and to the extent that they are necessary to facilitate these forms of assistance, Member States must adopt the appropriate procedural rules to allow both the national courts and the Commission to make full use of the possibilities the regulation offers.

18. The national court may send its request for assistance in writing to
European Commission
Directorate General for Competition
B-1049 Brussels
Belgium
or send it electronically to comp-amicus@cec.eu.int

19. It should be recalled that whatever form the co-operation with national courts takes, the Commission will respect the independence of national courts. As a consequence, the assistance offered by the Commission does not bind the national court. The Commission has also to make sure that it respects its duty of professional secrecy and that it safeguards its own functioning and independence. In fulfilling its duty under Article 10 EC, of assisting national courts in the application of EC competition rules, the Commission is committed to remaining neutral and objective in its assistance. Indeed, the Commission's assistance to national courts is part of its duty to defend the public interest. It has therefore no intention to serve the private interests of the parties involved in the case pending before the national court. As a consequence, the Commission will not hear any of the parties about its assistance to the national court. In case the Commission has been contacted by any of the parties in the case pending before the court on issues which are raised before the national court, it will inform the national court thereof, independent of whether these contacts took place before or after the national court's request for co-operation.

20. The Commission will publish a summary concerning its co-operation with national courts pursuant to this notice in its annual Report on Competition Policy. It may also make its opinions and observations available on its website.

1. *The Commission's duty to transmit information to national courts*

21. The duty for the Commission to assist national courts in the application of EC competition law is mainly reflected in the obligation for the Commission to transmit information it holds to national courts. A national court may, e.g., ask the Commission for documents in its possession or for information of a procedural nature to enable it to discover whether a certain case is pending before the Commission, whether the Commission has initiated a procedure or whether it has already taken a position. A national court may also ask the Commission when a decision is likely to be taken, so as to be able to determine the conditions for any decision to stay proceedings or whether interim measures need to be adopted.

22. In order to ensure the efficiency of the co-operation with national courts, the Commission will endeavour to provide the national court with the requested information within one month from

the date it receives the request. Where the Commission has to ask the national court for further clarification of its request or where the Commission has to consult those who are directly affected by the transmission of the information, that period starts to run from the moment that it receives the required information.

23. In transmitting information to national courts, the Commission has to uphold the guarantees given to natural and legal persons by Article 287 EC. Article 287 EC prevents members, officials and other servants of the Commission from disclosing information covered by the obligation of professional secrecy. The information covered by professional secrecy may be both confidential information and business secrets. Business secrets are information of which not only disclosure to the public but also mere transmission to a person other than the one that provided the information might seriously harm the latter's interests.

24. The combined reading of Articles 10 and 287 EC does not lead to an absolute prohibition for the Commission to transmit information which is covered by the obligation of professional secrecy to national courts. The case law of the Community courts confirms that the duty of loyal co-operation requires the Commission to provide the national court with whatever information the latter asks for, even information covered by professional secrecy. However, in offering its co-operation to the national courts, the Commission may not in any circumstances undermine the guarantees laid down in Article 287 EC.

25. Consequently, before transmitting information covered by professional secrecy to a national court, the Commission will remind the court of its obligation under Community law to uphold the rights which Article 287 EC confers on natural and legal persons and it will ask the court whether it can and will guarantee protection of confidential information and business secrets. If the national court cannot offer such guarantee, the Commission shall not transmit the information covered by professional secrecy to the national court. Only when the national court has offered a guarantee that it will protect the confidential information and business secrets, will the Commission transmit the information requested, indicating those parts which are covered by professional secrecy and which parts are not and can therefore be disclosed.

26. There are further exceptions to the disclosure of information by the Commission to national courts. Particularly, the Commission may refuse to transmit information to national courts for overriding reasons relating to the need to safeguard the interests of the Community or to avoid any interference with its functioning and independence, in particular by jeopardising the accomplishment of the tasks entrusted to it. Therefore, the Commission will not transmit to national courts information voluntarily submitted by a leniency applicant without the consent of that applicant.

2. Request for an opinion on questions concerning the application of EC competition rules

27. When called upon to apply EC competition rules to a case pending before it, a national court may first seek guidance in the case law of the Community courts or in Commission regulations, decisions, notices and guidelines applying Articles 81 and 82 EC. Where these tools do not offer sufficient guidance, the national court may ask the Commission for its opinion on questions concerning the application of EC competition rules. The national court may ask the Commission for its opinion on economic, factual and legal matters. The latter is of course without prejudice to the possibility or the obligation for the national court to ask the Court of Justice for a preliminary ruling regarding the interpretation or the validity of Community law in accordance with Article 234 EC.

28. In order to enable the Commission to provide the national court with a useful opinion, it may request the national court for further information. In order to ensure the efficiency of the co-operation with national courts, the Commission will endeavour to provide the national court with the requested opinion within four months from the date it receives the request. Where the Commission has requested the national court for further information in order to enable it to formulate its opinion, that period starts to run from the moment that it receives the additional information.

29. When giving its opinion, the Commission will limit itself to providing the national court with the factual information or the economic or legal clarification asked for, without considering the merits of the case pending before the national court. Moreover, unlike the authoritative interpretation of Community law by the Community courts, the opinion of the Commission does not legally bind the national court.

30. In line with what has been said in point 19 of this notice, the Commission will not hear the parties before formulating its opinion to the national court. The latter will have to deal with the Commission's opinion in accordance with the relevant national procedural rules, which have to respect the general principles of Community law.

3. The Commission's submission of observations to the national court

31. According to Article 15(3) of the regulation, the national competition authorities and the Commission may submit observations on issues relating to the application of Articles 81 or 82 EC to a national court which is called upon to apply those provisions. The regulation distinguishes between written observations, which the national competition authorities and the Commission may submit on their own initiative, and oral observations, which can only be submitted with the permission of the national court.

32. The regulation specifies that the Commission will only submit observations when the coherent application of Articles 81 or 82 EC so requires. That being the objective of its submission, the Commission will limit its observations to an economic and legal analysis of the facts underlying the case pending before the national court.

33. In order to enable the Commission to submit useful observations, national courts maybe asked to transmit or ensure the transmission to the Commission of a copy of all documents that are necessary for the assessment of the case. In line with Article 15(3), second subparagraph, of the regulation, the Commission will only use those documents for the preparation of its observations.

34. Since the regulation does not provide for a procedural framework within which the observations are to be submitted, Member States' procedural rules and practices determine the relevant procedural framework. Where a Member State has not yet established the relevant procedural framework, the national court has to determine which procedural rules are appropriate for the submission of observations in the case pending before it.

35. The procedural framework should respect the principles set out in point 10 of this notice. That implies amongst others that the procedural framework for the submission of observations on issues relating to the application of Articles 81 or 82 EC

(a) has to be compatible with the general principles of Community law, in particular the fundamental rights of the parties involved in the case;

(b) cannot make the submission of such observations excessively difficult or practically impossible (the principle of effectiveness); and

(c) cannot make the submission of such observations more difficult than the submission of observations in court proceedings where equivalent national law is applied (the principle of equivalence).

B   The national courts facilitating the role of the Commission in the enforcement of EC competition rules

36. Since the duty of loyal co-operation also implies that Member States' authorities assist the European institutions with a view to attaining the objectives of the EC Treaty, the regulation provides for three examples of such assistance: (1) the transmission of documents necessary for the assessment of a case in which the Commission would like to submit observations (see point 33), (2) the transmission of judgements applying Articles 81 or 82 EC; and (3) the role of national courts in the context of a Commission inspection.

1. *The transmission of judgements of national courts applying Articles 81 or 82 EC*

37. According to Article 15(2) of the regulation, Member States shall send to the Commission a copy of any written judgement of national courts applying Articles 81 or 82 EC without delay after the full written judgement is notified to the parties. The transmission of national judgements on the application of Articles 81 or 82 EC and the resulting information on proceedings before national courts primarily enable the Commission to become aware in a timely fashion of cases for which it might be appropriate to submit observations where one of the parties lodges an appeal against the judgement.

2. *The role of national courts in the context of a Commission inspection*

38. Finally, national courts may play a role in the context of a Commission inspection of undertakings and associations of undertakings. The role of the national courts depends on whether the inspections are conducted in business premises or in non-business premises.

39. With regard to the inspection of business premises, national legislation may require authorisation from a national court to allow a national enforcement authority to assist the Commission in case of opposition of the undertaking concerned. Such authorisation may also be sought as a precautionary measure. When dealing with the request, the national court has the power to control that the Commission's inspection decision is authentic and that the coercive measures envisaged are neither arbitrary nor excessive having regard to the subject matter of the inspection. In its control of the proportionality of the coercive measures, the national court may ask the Commission, directly or through the national competition authority, for detailed explanations in particular on the grounds the Commission has for suspecting infringement of Articles 81 and 82 EC, as well as on the seriousness of the suspected infringement and on the nature of the involvement of the undertaking concerned.

40. With regard to the inspection of non-business premises, the regulation requires the authorisation from a national court before a Commission decision ordering such an inspection can be executed. In that case, the national court may control that the Commission's inspection decision is authentic and that the coercive measures envisaged are neither arbitrary nor excessive having regard in particular to the seriousness of the suspected infringement, to the importance of the evidence sought, to the involvement of the undertaking concerned and to the reasonable likelihood that business books and records relating to the subject matter of the inspection are kept in the premises for which the authorisation is requested. The national court may ask the Commission, directly or through the national competition authority, for detailed explanations on those elements that are necessary to allow its control of the proportionality of the coercive measures envisaged.

41. In both cases referred to in points 39 and 40, the national court may not call into question the lawfulness of the Commission's decision or the necessity for the inspection nor can it demand that it be provided with information in the Commission's file. Furthermore, the duty of loyal co-operation requires the national court to take its decision within an appropriate timeframe that allows the Commission to effectively conduct its inspection.

IV FINAL PROVISIONS

42. This notice is issued in order to assist national courts in the application of Articles 81 and 82 EC. It does not bind the national courts, nor does it affect the rights and obligations of the EU Member States and natural or legal persons under Community law.

43. This notice replaces the 1993 notice on co-operation between national courts and the Commission in applying Articles 85 and 86 of the EEC Treaty.

Commission Notice: Guidelines on the effect on trade concept contained in Articles 81 and 82 of the Treaty

(OJ 2004, No. C 101/07)

(Text with EEA relevance)

1 INTRODUCTION

1. Articles 81 and 82 of the Treaty are applicable to horizontal and vertical agreements and practices on the part of undertakings which 'may affect trade between Member States'.

2. In their interpretation of Articles 81 and 82, the Community Courts have already substantially clarified the content and scope of the concept of effect on trade between Member States.

3. The present guidelines set out the principles developed by the Community Courts in relation to the interpretation of the effect on trade concept of Articles 81 and 82. They further spell out a rule indicating when agreements are in general unlikely to be capable of appreciably affecting trade between Member States (the non-appreciable affectation of trade rule or NAAT-rule). The guidelines are not intended to be exhaustive. The aim is to set out the methodology for the application of the effect on trade concept and to provide guidance on its application in frequently occurring situations. Although not binding on them, these guidelines also intend to give guidance to the courts and authorities of the Member States in their application of the effect on trade concept contained in Articles 81 and 82.

4. The present guidelines do not address the issue of what constitutes an appreciable restriction of competition under Article 81(1). This issue, which is distinct from the ability of agreements to appreciably affect trade between Member States, is dealt with in the Commission Notice on agreements of minor importance which do not appreciably restrict competition under Article 81(1) of the Treaty (the *de minimis* rule). The guidelines are also not intended to provide guidance on the effect on trade concept contained in Article 87(1) of the Treaty on State aid.

5. These guidelines, including the NAAT-rule, are without prejudice to the interpretation of Articles 81 and 82 which may be given by the Court of Justice and the Court of First Instance.

2 THE EFFECT ON TRADE CRITERION

2.1 General principles

6. Article 81(1) provides that 'the following shall be prohibited as incompatible with the common market: all agreements between undertakings, decisions of associations of undertakings and concerted practices which may affect trade between Member States and which have as their object or effect the prevention, restriction or distortion of competition within the common market'. For the sake of simplicity the terms 'agreements, decisions of associations of undertakings and concerted practices' are collectively referred to as 'agreements'.

7. Article 82 on its part stipulates that 'any abuse by one or more undertakings of a dominant position within the common market or in a substantial part thereof shall be prohibited as incompatible with the common market insofar as it may affect trade between Member States.' In what follows the term 'practices' refers to the conduct of dominant undertakings.

8. The effect on trade criterion also determines the scope of application of Article 3 of Regulation 1/2003 on the implementation of the rules on competition laid down in Articles 81 and 82 of the Treaty.

9. According to Article 3(1) of that Regulation the competition authorities and courts of the Member States must apply Article 81 to agreements, decisions by associations of undertakings or concerted practices within the meaning of Article 81(1) of the Treaty which may affect trade between Member States within the meaning of that provision, when they apply national competition law to such agreements, decisions or concerted practices. Similarly, when the competition

authorities and courts of the Member States apply national competition law to any abuse prohibited by Article 82 of the Treaty, they must also apply Article 82 of the Treaty. Article 3(1) thus obliges the competition authorities and courts of the Member States to also apply Articles 81 and 82 when they apply national competition law to agreements and abusive practices which may affect trade between Member States. On the other hand, Article 3(1) does not oblige national competition authorities and courts to apply national competition law when they apply Articles 81 and 82 to agreements, decisions and concerted practices and to abuses which may affect trade between Member States. They may in such cases apply the Community competition rules on a stand alone basis.

10. It follows from Article 3(2) that the application of national competition law may not lead to the prohibition of agreements, decisions by associations of undertakings or concerted practices which may affect trade between Member States but which do not restrict competition within the meaning of Article 81 (1) of the Treaty, or which fulfil the conditions of Article 81 (3) of the Treaty or which are covered by a Regulation for the application of Article 81(3) of the Treaty. Member States, however, are not under Regulation 1/2003 precluded from adopting and applying on their territory stricter national laws which prohibit or sanction unilateral conduct engaged in by undertakings.

11. Finally it should be mentioned that Article 3(3) stipulates that without prejudice to general principles and other provisions of Community law, Article 3(1) and (2) do not apply when the competition authorities and the courts of the Member States apply national merger control laws, nor do they preclude the application of provisions of national law that predominantly pursue an objective different from that pursued by Articles 81 and 82 of the Treaty.

12. The effect on trade criterion is an autonomous Community law criterion, which must be assessed separately in each case. It is a jurisdictional criterion, which defines the scope of application of Community competition law. Community competition law is not applicable to agreements and practices that are not capable of appreciably affecting trade between Member States.

13. The effect on trade criterion confines the scope of application of Articles 81 and 82 to agreements and practices that are capable of having a minimum level of cross-border effects within the Community. In the words of the Court of Justice, the ability of the agreement or practice to affect trade between Member States must be 'appreciable'.

14. In the case of Article 81 of the Treaty, it is the agreement that must be capable of affecting trade between Member States. It is not required that each individual part of the agreement, including any restriction of competition which may flow from the agreement, is capable of doing so. If the agreement as a whole is capable of affecting trade between Member States, there is Community law jurisdiction in respect of the entire agreement, including any parts of the agreement that individually do not affect trade between Member States. In cases where the contractual relations between the same parties cover several activities, these activities must, in order to form part of the same agreement, be directly linked and form an integral part of the same overall business arrangement. If not, each activity constitutes a separate agreement.

15. It is also immaterial whether or not the participation of a particular undertaking in the agreement has an appreciable effect on trade between Member States. An undertaking cannot escape Community law jurisdiction merely because of the fact that its own contribution to an agreement, which itself is capable of affecting trade between Member States, is insignificant.

16. It is not necessary, for the purposes of establishing Community law jurisdiction, to establish a link between the alleged restriction of competition and the capacity of the agreement to affect trade between Member States. Non-restrictive agreements may also affect trade between Member States. For example, selective distribution agreements based on purely qualitative selection criteria justified by the nature of the products, which are not restrictive of competition within the meaning of Article 81(1), may nevertheless affect trade between Member States. However, the alleged restrictions arising from an agreement may provide a clear indication as to the capacity of the agreement to affect trade between Member States. For instance, a distribution agreement prohibiting exports is by its very nature capable of affecting trade between Member States, although not necessarily to an appreciable extent.

17. In the case of Article 82 it is the abuse that must affect trade between Member States. This does not imply, however, that each element of the behaviour must be assessed in isolation. Conduct that forms part of an overall strategy pursued by the dominant undertaking must be assessed in terms of its overall impact. Where a dominant undertaking adopts various practices in pursuit of the same aim, for instance practices that aim at eliminating or foreclosing competitors, in order for Article 82 to be applicable to all the practices forming part of this overall strategy, it is sufficient that at least one of these practices is capable of affecting trade between Member States.

18. It follows from the wording of Articles 81 and 82 and the case law of the Community Courts that in the application of the effect on trade criterion three elements in particular must be addressed:

    (a) The concept of 'trade between Member States',

    (b) The notion of 'may affect', and

    (c) The concept of 'appreciability'.

2.2 The concept of 'trade between Member States'

19. The concept of 'trade' is not limited to traditional exchanges of goods and services across borders. It is a wider concept, covering all cross-border economic activity including establishment. This interpretation is consistent with the fundamental objective of the Treaty to promote free movement of goods, services, persons and capital.

20. According to settled case law the concept of 'trade' also encompasses cases where agreements or practices affect the competitive structure of the market. Agreements and practices that affect the competitive structure inside the Community by eliminating or threatening to eliminate a competitor operating within the Community may be subject to the Community competition rules. When an undertaking is or risks being eliminated the competitive structure within the Community is affected and so are the economic activities in which the undertaking is engaged.

21. The requirement that there must be an effect on trade 'between Member States' implies that there must be an impact on cross-border economic activity involving at least two Member States. It is not required that the agreement or practice affect trade between the whole of one Member State and the whole of another Member State. Articles 81 and 82 may be applicable also in cases involving part of a Member State, provided that the effect on trade is appreciable.

22. The application of the effect on trade criterion is independent of the definition of relevant geographic markets. Trade between Member States may be affected also in cases where the relevant market is national or sub-national.

2.3 The notion 'may affect'

23. The function of the notion 'may affect' is to define the nature of the required impact on trade between Member States. According to the standard test developed by the Court of Justice, the notion 'may affect' implies that it must be possible to foresee with a sufficient degree of probability on the basis of a set of objective factors of law or fact that the agreement or practice may have an influence, direct or indirect, actual or potential, on the pattern of trade between Member States. As mentioned in paragraph 20 above the Court of Justice has in addition developed a test based on whether or not the agreement or practice affects the competitive structure. In cases where the agreement or practice is liable to affect the competitive structure inside the Community, Community law jurisdiction is established.

24. The 'pattern of trade'-test developed by the Court of Justice contains the following main elements, which are dealt with in the following sections:

    (a) 'A sufficient degree of probability on the basis of a set of objective factors of law or fact',

    (b) An influence on the 'pattern of trade between Member States',

    (c) 'A direct or indirect, actual or potential influence' on the pattern of trade.

2.3.1. *A sufficient degree of probability on the basis of a set of objective factors of law or fact*

25. The assessment of effect on trade is based on objective factors. Subjective intent on the part of the undertakings concerned is not required. If, however, there is evidence that undertakings

have intended to affect trade between Member States, for example because they have sought to hinder exports to or imports from other Member States, this is a relevant factor to be taken into account.

26. The words 'may affect' and the reference by the Court of Justice to 'a sufficient degree of probability' imply that, in order for Community law jurisdiction to be established, it is not required that the agreement or practice will actually have or has had an effect on trade between Member States. It is sufficient that the agreement or practice is 'capable' of having such an effect.

27. There is no obligation or need to calculate the actual volume of trade between Member States affected by the agreement or practice. For example, in the case of agreements prohibiting exports to other Member States there is no need to estimate what would have been the level of parallel trade between the Member States concerned, in the absence of the agreement. This interpretation is consistent with the jurisdictional nature of the effect on trade criterion. Community law jurisdiction extends to categories of agreements and practices that are capable of having cross-border effects, irrespective of whether a particular agreement or practice actually has such effects.

28. The assessment under the effect on trade criterion depends on a number of factors that individually may not be decisive. The relevant factors include the nature of the agreement and practice, the nature of the products covered by the agreement or practice and the position and importance of the undertakings concerned.

29. The nature of the agreement and practice provides an indication from a qualitative point of view of the ability of the agreement or practice to affect trade between Member States. Some agreements and practices are by their very nature capable of affecting trade between Member States, whereas others require more detailed analysis in this respect. Cross-border cartels are an example of the former, whereas joint ventures confined to the territory of a single Member State are an example of the latter. This aspect is further examined in section 3 below, which deals with various categories of agreements and practices.

30. The nature of the products covered by the agreements or practices also provides an indication of whether trade between Member States is capable of being affected. When by their nature products are easily traded across borders or are important for undertakings that want to enter or expand their activities in other Member States, Community jurisdiction is more readily established than in cases where due to their nature there is limited demand for products offered by suppliers from other Member States or where the products are of limited interest from the point of view of cross-border establishment or the expansion of the economic activity carried out from such place of establishment. Establishment includes the setting-up by undertakings in one Member State of agencies, branches or subsidiaries in another Member State.

31. The market position of the undertakings concerned and their sales volumes are indicative from a quantitative point of view of the ability of the agreement or practice concerned to affect trade between Member States. This aspect, which forms an integral part of the assessment of appreciability, is addressed in section 2.4 below.

32. In addition to the factors already mentioned, it is necessary to take account of the legal and factual environment in which the agreement or practice operates. The relevant economic and legal context provides insight into the potential for an effect on trade between Member States. If there are absolute barriers to cross-border trade between Member States, which are external to the agreement or practice, trade is only capable of being affected if those barriers are likely to disappear in the foreseeable future. In cases where the barriers are not absolute but merely render cross-border activities more difficult, it is of the utmost importance to ensure that agreements and practices do not further hinder such activities. Agreements and practices that do so are capable of affecting trade between Member States.

2.3.2. *An influence on the 'pattern of trade between Member States'*

33. For Articles 81 and 82 to be applicable there must be an influence on the 'pattern of trade between Member States'.

34. The term 'pattern of trade' is neutral. It is not a condition that trade be restricted or reduced. Patterns of trade can also be affected when an agreement or practice causes an increase in trade. Indeed, Community law jurisdiction is established if trade between Member States is likely to develop differently with the agreement or practice compared to the way in which it would probably have developed in the absence of the agreement or practice.

35. This interpretation reflects the fact that the effect on trade criterion is a jurisdictional one, which serves to distinguish those agreements and practices which are capable of having cross-border effects, so as to warrant an examination under the Community competition rules, from those agreements and practices which do not.

2.3.3. A 'direct or indirect, actual or potential influence' on the pattern of trade

36. The influence of agreements and practices on patterns of trade between Member States can be 'direct or indirect, actual or potential'.

37. Direct effects on trade between Member States normally occur in relation to the products covered by an agreement or practice. When, for example, producers of a particular product in different Member States agree to share markets, direct effects are produced on trade between Member States on the market for the products in question. Another example of direct effects being produced is when a supplier limits distributor rebates to products sold within the Member State in which the distributors are established. Such practices increase the relative price of products destined for exports, rendering export sales less attractive and less competitive.

38. Indirect effects often occur in relation to products that are related to those covered by an agreement or practice. Indirect effects may, for example, occur where an agreement or practice has an impact on cross-border economic activities of undertakings that use or otherwise rely on the products covered by the agreement or practice. Such effects can, for instance, arise where the agreement or practice relates to an intermediate product, which is not traded, but which is used in the supply of a final product, which is traded. The Court of Justice has held that trade between Member States was capable of being affected in the case of an agreement involving the fixing of prices of spirits used in the production of cognac. Whereas the raw material was not exported, the final product—cognac—was exported. In such cases Community competition law is thus applicable, if trade in the final product is capable of being appreciably affected.

39. Indirect effects on trade between Member States may also occur in relation to the products covered by the agreement or practice. For instance, agreements whereby a manufacturer limits warranties to products sold by distributors within their Member State of establishment create disincentives for consumers from other Member States to buy the products because they would not be able to invoke the warranty. Export by official distributors and parallel traders is made more difficult because in the eyes of consumers the products are less attractive without the manufacturer's warranty.

40. Actual effects on trade between Member States are those that are produced by the agreement or practice once it is implemented. An agreement between a supplier and a distributor within the same Member State, for instance one that prohibits exports to other Member States, is likely to produce actual effects on trade between Member States. Without the agreement the distributor would have been free to engage in export sales. It should be recalled, however, that it is not required that actual effects are demonstrated. It is sufficient that the agreement or practice be capable of having such effects.

41. Potential effects are those that may occur in the future with a sufficient degree of probability. In other words, foreseeable market developments must be taken into account. Even if trade is not capable of being affected at the time the agreement is concluded or the practice is implemented, Articles 81 and 82 remain applicable if the factors which led to that conclusion are likely to change in the foreseeable future. In this respect it is relevant to consider the impact of liberalisation measures adopted by the Community or by the Member State in question and other foreseeable measures aiming at eliminating legal barriers to trade.

42. Moreover, even if at a given point in time market conditions are unfavourable to cross-border trade, for example because prices are similar in the Member States in question, trade may still be capable of being affected if the situation may change as a result of changing market conditions. What matters is the ability of the agreement or practice to affect trade between Member States and not whether at any given point in time it actually does so.

43. The inclusion of indirect or potential effects in the analysis of effects on trade between Member States does not mean that the analysis can be based on remote or hypothetical effects. The likelihood of a particular agreement to produce indirect or potential effects must be explained by the authority or party claiming that trade between Member States is capable of being appreciably affected. Hypothetical or speculative effects are not sufficient for establishing Community law jurisdiction. For instance, an agreement that raises the price of a product which is not tradable reduces the disposable income of consumers. As consumers have less money to spend they may purchase fewer products imported from other Member States. However, the link between such income effects and trade between Member States is generally in itself too remote to establish Community law jurisdiction.

2.4   The concept of appreciability

2.4.1. *General principle*

44. The effect on trade criterion incorporates a quantitative element, limiting Community law jurisdiction to agreements and practices that are capable of having effects of a certain magnitude. Agreements and practices fall outside the scope of application of Articles 81 and 82 when they affect the market only insignificantly having regard to the weak position of the undertakings concerned on the market for the products in question. Appreciability can be appraised in particular by reference to the position and the importance of the relevant undertakings on the market for the products concerned.

45. The assessment of appreciability depends on the circumstances of each individual case, in particular the nature of the agreement and practice, the nature of the products covered and the market position of the undertakings concerned. When by its very nature the agreement or practice is capable of affecting trade between Member States, the appreciability threshold is lower than in the case of agreements and practices that are not by their very nature capable of affecting trade between Member States. The stronger the market position of the undertakings concerned, the more likely it is that an agreement or practice capable of affecting trade between Member States can be held to do so appreciably.

46. In a number of cases concerning imports and exports the Court of Justice has considered that the appreciability requirement was fulfilled when the sales of the undertakings concerned accounted for about 5% of the market. Market share alone, however, has not always been considered the decisive factor. In particular, it is necessary also to take account of the turnover of the undertakings in the products concerned.

47. Appreciability can thus be measured both in absolute terms (turnover) and in relative terms, comparing the position of the undertaking(s) concerned to that of other players on the market (market share). This focus on the position and importance of the undertakings concerned is consistent with the concept 'may affect', which implies that the assessment is based on the ability of the agreement or practice to affect trade between Member States rather than on the impact on actual flows of goods and services across borders. The market position of the undertakings concerned and their turnover in the products concerned are indicative of the ability of an agreement or practice to affect trade between Member States. These two elements are reflected in the presumptions set out in paragraphs and 53 below.

48. The application of the appreciability test does not necessarily require that relevant markets be defined and market shares calculated. The sales of an undertaking in absolute terms may be sufficient to support a finding that the impact on trade is appreciable. This is particularly so in the case of agreements and practices that by their very nature are liable to affect trade between Member States, for example because they concern imports or exports or because they cover several Member States. The fact that in such circumstances turnover in the products covered by the agreement may

be sufficient for a finding of an appreciable effect on trade between Member States is reflected in the positive presumption set out in paragraph below.

49. Agreements and practices must always be considered in the economic and legal context in which they occur. In the case of vertical agreements it may be necessary to have regard to any cumulative effects of parallel networks of similar agreements. Even if a single agreement or network of agreements is not capable of appreciably affecting trade between Member States, the effect of parallel networks of agreements, taken as a whole, may be capable of doing so. For that to be the case, however, it is necessary that the individual agreement or network of agreements makes a significant contribution to the overall effect on trade.

2.4.2. *Quantification of appreciability*

50. It is not possible to establish general quantitative rules covering all categories of agreements indicating when trade between Member States is capable of being appreciably affected. It is possible, however, to indicate when trade is normally not capable of being appreciably affected. Firstly, in its notice on agreements of minor importance which do not appreciably restrict competition in the meaning of Article 81(1) of the Treaty (the *de minimis* rule) the Commission has stated that agreements between small and medium-sized undertakings (SMEs) as defined in the Annex to Commission Recommendation 96/280/EC are normally not capable of affecting trade between Member States. The reason for this presumption is the fact that the activities of SMEs are normally local or at most regional in nature. However, SMEs may be subject to Community law jurisdiction in particular where they engage in cross-border economic activity. Secondly, the Commission considers it appropriate to set out general principles indicating when trade is normally not capable of being appreciably affected, i.e. a standard defining the absence of an appreciable effect on trade between Member States (the NAAT-rule). When applying Article 81, the Commission will consider this standard as a negative rebuttable presumption applying to all agreements within the meaning of Article 81(1) irrespective of the nature of the restrictions contained in the agreement, including restrictions that have been identified as hardcore restrictions in Commission block exemption regulations and guidelines. In cases where this presumption applies the Commission will normally not institute proceedings either upon application or on its own initiative. Where the undertakings assume in good faith that an agreement is covered by this negative presumption, the Commission will not impose fines.

51. Without prejudice to paragraph below, this negative definition of appreciability does not imply that agreements, which do not fall within the criteria set out below, are automatically capable of appreciably affecting trade between Member States. A case by case analysis is necessary.

52. The Commission holds the view that in principle agreements are not capable of appreciably affecting trade between Member States when the following cumulative conditions are met:

(a) The aggregate market share of the parties on any relevant market within the Community affected by the agreement does not exceed 5 %, and

(b) In the case of horizontal agreements, the aggregate annual Community turnover of the undertakings concerned in the products covered by the agreement does not exceed 40 million euro. In the case of agreements concerning the joint buying of products the relevant turnover shall be the parties' combined purchases of the products covered by the agreement.In the case of vertical agreements, the aggregate annual Community turnover of the supplier in the products covered by the agreement does not exceed 40 million euro. In the case of licence agreements the relevant turnover shall be the aggregate turnover of the licensees in the products incorporating the licensed technology and the licensor's own turnover in such products. In cases involving agreements concluded between a buyer and several suppliers the relevant turnover shall be the buyer's combined purchases of the products covered by the agreements.

The Commission will apply the same presumption where during two successive calendar years the above turnover threshold is not exceeded by more than 10 % and the above market threshold is not exceeded by more than 2 percentage points. In cases where the agreement concerns an emerging not yet existing market and where as a consequence the parties neither generate relevant turnover nor accumulate any relevant market share, the Commission will not apply this presumption. In such cases appreciability may have to be assessed on the basis of the position of the parties on related product markets or their strength in technologies relating to the agreement.

53.   The Commission will also hold the view that where an agreement by its very nature is capable of affecting trade between Member States, for example, because it concerns imports and exports or covers several Member States, there is a rebuttable positive presumption that such effects on trade are appreciable when the turnover of the parties in the products covered by the agreement calculated as indicated in paragraphs 52 and 54 exceeds 40 million euro. In the case of agreements that by their very nature are capable of affecting trade between Member States it can also often be presumed that such effects are appreciable when the market share of the parties exceeds the 5% threshold set out in the previous paragraph. However, this presumption does not apply where the agreement covers only part of a Member State (see paragraph 90 below).

54.   With regard to the threshold of 40 million euro (cf. paragraph 52 above), the turnover is calculated on the basis of total Community sales excluding tax during the previous financial year by the undertakings concerned, of the products covered by the agreement (the contract products). Sales between entities that form part of the same undertaking are excluded.

55.   In order to apply the market share threshold, it is necessary to determine the relevant market. This consists of the relevant product market and the relevant geographic market. The market shares are to be calculated on the basis of sales value data or, where appropriate, purchase value data. If value data are not available, estimates based on other reliable market information, including volume data, may be used.

56.   In the case of networks of agreements entered into by the same supplier with different distributors, sales made through the entire network are taken into account.

57.   Contracts that form part of the same overall business arrangement constitute a single agreement for the purposes of the NAAT-rule. Undertakings cannot bring themselves inside these thresholds by dividing up an agreement that forms a whole from an economic perspective.

3   THE APPLICATION OF THE ABOVE PRINCIPLES TO COMMON TYPES OF AGREEMENTS AND ABUSES

58.   The Commission will apply the negative presumption set out in the preceding section to all agreements, including agreements that by their very nature are capable of affecting trade between Member States as well as agreements that involve trade with undertakings located in third countries (cf. section 3.3 below).

59.   Outside the scope of negative presumption, the Commission will take account of qualitative elements relating to the nature of the agreement or practice and the nature of the products that they concern (see paragraphs and above). The relevance of the nature of the agreement is also reflected in the positive presumption set out in paragraph 53 above relating to appreciability in the case of agreements that by their very nature are capable of affecting trade between Member States. With a view to providing additional guidance on the application of the effect on trade concept it is therefore useful to consider various common types of agreements and practices.

60.   In the following sections a primary distinction is drawn between agreements and practices that cover several Member States and agreements and practices that are confined to a single Member State or to part of a single Member State. These two main categories are broken down into further subcategories based on the nature of the agreement or practice involved. Agreements and practices involving third countries are also dealt with.

3.1   Agreements and abuse covering or implemented in several Member States

61.   Agreements and practices covering or implemented in several Member States are in almost all cases by their very nature capable of affecting trade between Member States. When the relevant turnover exceeds the threshold set out in paragraph above it will therefore in most cases not be necessary

to conduct a detailed analysis of whether trade between Member States is capable of being affected. However, in order to provide guidance also in these cases and to illustrate the principles developed in section 2 above, it is useful to explain what are the factors that are normally used to support a finding of Community law jurisdiction.

3.1.1. *Agreements concerning imports and exports*

62. Agreements between undertakings in two or more Member States that concern imports and exports are by their very nature capable of affecting trade between Member States. Such agreements, irrespective of whether they are restrictive of competition or not, have a direct impact on patterns of trade between Member States. In Kerpen & Kerpen, for example, which concerned an agreement between a French producer and a German distributor covering more than 10% of exports of cement from France to Germany, amounting in total to 350 000 tonnes per year, the Court of Justice held that it was impossible to take the view that such an agreement was not capable of (appreciably) affecting trade between Member States.

63. This category includes agreements that impose restrictions on imports and exports, including restrictions on active and passive sales and resale by buyers to customers in other Member States. In these cases there is an inherent link between the alleged restriction of competition and the effect on trade, since the very purpose of the restriction is to prevent flows of goods and services between Member States, which would otherwise be possible. It is immaterial whether the parties to the agreement are located in the same Member State or in different Member States.

3.1.2. *Cartels covering several Member States*

64. Cartel agreements such as those involving price fixing and market sharing covering several Member States are by their very nature capable of affecting trade between Member States. Cross-border cartels harmonise the conditions of competition and affect the interpenetration of trade by cementing traditional patterns of trade. When undertakings agree to allocate geographic territories, sales from other areas into the allocated territories are capable of being eliminated or reduced. When undertakings agree to fix prices, they eliminate competition and any resulting price differentials that would entice both competitors and customers to engage in cross-border trade. When undertakings agree on sales quotas traditional patterns of trade are preserved. The undertakings concerned abstain from expanding output and thereby from serving potential customers in other Member States.

65. The effect on trade produced by cross-border cartels is generally also by its very nature appreciable due to the market position of the parties to the cartel. Cartels are normally only formed when the participating undertakings together hold a large share of the market, as this allows them to raise price or reduce output.

3.1.3. *Horizontal cooperation agreements covering several Member States*

66. This section covers various types of horizontal cooperation agreements. Horizontal cooperation agreements may for instance take the form of agreements whereby two or more undertakings cooperate in the performance of a particular economic activity such as production and distribution. Often such agreements are referred to as joint ventures. However, joint ventures that perform on a lasting basis all the functions of an autonomous economic entity are covered by the Merger Regulation. At the level of the Community such full function joint ventures are not dealt with under Articles 81 and 82 except in cases where Article 2(4) of the Merger Regulation is applicable. This section therefore does not deal with full-function joint ventures. In the case of non-full function joint ventures the joint entity does not operate as an autonomous supplier (or buyer) on any market. It merely serves the parents, who themselves operate on the market.

67. Joint ventures which engage in activities in two or more Member States or which produce an output that is sold by the parents in two or more Member States affect the commercial activities of the parties in those areas of the Community. Such agreements are therefore normally by their very nature capable of affecting trade between Member States compared to the situation without the agreement. Patterns of trade are affected when undertakings switch their activities to the joint venture or use it for the purpose of establishing a new source of supply in the Community.

68. Trade may also be capable of being affected where a joint venture produces an input for the parent companies, which is subsequently further processed or incorporated into a product by the parent undertakings. This is likely to be the case where the input in question was previously sourced from suppliers in other Member States, where the parents previously produced the input in other Member States or where the final product is traded in more than one Member State.

69. In the assessment of appreciability it is important to take account of the parents' sales of products related to the agreement and not only those of the joint entity created by the agreement, given that the joint venture does not operate as an autonomous entity on any market.

3.1.4. *Vertical agreements implemented in several Member States*

70. Vertical agreements and networks of similar vertical agreements implemented in several Member States are normally capable of affecting trade between Member States if they cause trade to be channelled in a particular way. Networks of selective distribution agreements implemented in two or more Member States for example, channel trade in a particular way because they limit trade to members of the network, thereby affecting patterns of trade compared to the situation without the agreement.

71. Trade between Member States is also capable of being affected by vertical agreements that have foreclosure effects. This may for instance be the case of agreements whereby distributors in several Member States agree to buy only from a particular supplier or to sell only its products. Such agreements may limit trade between the Member States in which the agreements are implemented, or trade from Member States not covered by the agreements. Foreclosure may result from individual agreements or from networks of agreements. When an agreement or networks of agreements that cover several Member States have foreclosure effects, the ability of the agreement or agreements to affect trade between Member States is normally by its very nature appreciable.

72. Agreements between suppliers and distributors which provide for resale price maintenance (RPM) and which cover two or more Member States are normally also by their very nature capable of affecting trade between Member States. Such agreements alter the price levels that would have been likely to exist in the absence of the agreements and thereby affect patterns of trade.

3.1.5. *Abuses of dominant positions covering several Member States*

73. In the case of abuse of a dominant position it is useful to distinguish between abuses that raise barriers to entry or eliminate competitors (exclusionary abuses) and abuses whereby the dominant undertaking exploits its economic power for instance by charging excessive or discriminatory prices (exploitative abuses). Both kinds of abuse may be carried out either through agreements, which are equally subject to Article 81(1), or through unilateral conduct, which as far as Community competition law is concerned is subject only to Article 82.

74. In the case of exploitative abuses such as discriminatory rebates, the impact is on downstream trading partners, which either benefit or suffer, altering their competitive position and affecting patterns of trade between Member States.

75. When a dominant undertaking engages in exclusionary conduct in more than one Member State, such abuse is normally by its very nature capable of affecting trade between Member States. Such conduct has a negative impact on competition in an area extending beyond a single Member State, being likely to divert trade from the course it would have followed in the absence of the abuse. For example, patterns of trade are capable of being affected where the dominant undertaking grants loyalty rebates. Customers covered by the exclusionary rebate system are likely to purchase less from competitors of the dominant firm than they would otherwise have done. Exclusionary conduct that aims directly at eliminating a competitor such as predatory pricing is also capable of affecting trade between Member States because of its impact on the competitive market structure inside the Community. When a dominant firm engages in behaviour with a view to eliminating a competitor operating in more than one Member State, trade is capable of being

affected in several ways. First, there is a risk that the affected competitor will cease to be a source of supply inside the Community. Even if the targeted undertaking is not eliminated, its future competitive conduct is likely to be affected, which may also have an impact on trade between Member States. Secondly, the abuse may have an impact on other competitors. Through its abusive behaviour the dominant undertaking can signal to its competitors that it will discipline attempts to engage in real competition. Thirdly, the very fact of eliminating a competitor may be sufficient for trade between Member States to be capable of being affected. This may be the case even where the undertaking that risks being eliminated mainly engages in exports to third countries. Once the effective competitive market structure inside the Community risks being further impaired, there is Community law jurisdiction.

76. Where a dominant undertaking engages in exploitative or exclusionary abuse in more than one Member State, the capacity of the abuse to affect trade between Member States will normally also by its very nature be appreciable. Given the market position of the dominant undertaking concerned, and the fact that the abuse is implemented in several Member States, the scale of the abuse and its likely impact on patterns of trade is normally such that trade between Member States is capable of being appreciably affected. In the case of an exploitative abuse such as price discrimination, the abuse alters the competitive position of trading partners in several Member States. In the case of exclusionary abuses, including abuses that aim at eliminating a competitor, the economic activity engaged in by competitors in several Member States is affected. The very existence of a dominant position in several Member States implies that competition in a substantial part of the common market is already weakened. When a dominant undertaking further weakens competition through recourse to abusive conduct, for example by eliminating a competitor, the ability of the abuse to affect trade between Member States is normally appreciable.

3.2 Agreements and abuses covering a single, or only part of a, Member State

77. When agreements or abusive practices cover the territory of a single Member State, it may be necessary to proceed with a more detailed inquiry into the ability of the agreements or abusive practices to affect trade between Member States. It should be recalled that for there to be an effect on trade between Member States it is not required that trade is reduced. It is sufficient that an appreciable change is capable of being caused in the pattern of trade between Member States. Nevertheless, in many cases involving a single Member State the nature of the alleged infringement, and in particular, its propensity to foreclose the national market, provides a good indication of the capacity of the agreement or practice to affect trade between Member States. The examples mentioned hereafter are not exhaustive. They merely provide examples of cases where agreements confined to the territory of a single Member State can be considered capable of affecting trade between Member States.

3.2.1. *Cartels covering a single Member State*

78. Horizontal cartels covering the whole of a Member State are normally capable of affecting trade between Member States. The Community Courts have held in a number of cases that agreements extending over the whole territory of a Member State by their very nature have the effect of reinforcing the partitioning of markets on a national basis by hindering the economic penetration which the Treaty is designed to bring about.

79. The capacity of such agreements to partition the internal market follows from the fact that undertakings participating in cartels in only one Member State, normally need to take action to exclude competitors from other Member States. If they do not, and the product covered by the agreement is tradable, the cartel risks being undermined by competition from undertakings from other Member States. Such agreements are normally also by their very nature capable of having an appreciable effect on trade between Member States, given the market coverage required for such cartels to be effective.

80. Given the fact that the effect on trade concept encompasses potential effects, it is not decisive whether such action against competitors from other Member States is in fact adopted at any

given point in time. If the cartel price is similar to the price prevailing in other Member States, there may be no immediate need for the members of the cartel to take action against competitors from other Member States. What matters is whether or not they are likely to do so, if market conditions change. The likelihood of that depends on the existence or otherwise of natural barriers to trade in the market, including in particular whether or not the product in question is tradable. In a case involving certain retail banking services the Court of Justice has, for example, held that trade was not capable of being appreciably affected because the potential for trade in the specific products concerned was very limited and because they were not an important factor in the choice made by undertakings from other Member States regarding whether or not to establish themselves in the Member State in question.

81. The extent to which the members of a cartel monitor prices and competitors from other Member States can provide an indication of the extent to which the products covered by the cartel are tradable. Monitoring suggests that competition and competitors from other Member States are perceived as a potential threat to the cartel. Moreover, if there is evidence that the members of the cartel have deliberately fixed the price level in the light of the price level prevailing in other Member States (limit pricing), it is an indication that the products in question are tradable and that trade between Member States is capable of being affected.

82. Trade is normally also capable of being affected when the members of a national cartel temper the competitive constraint imposed by competitors from other Member States by inducing them to join the restrictive agreement, or if their exclusion from the agreement places the competitors at a competitive disadvantage. In such cases the agreement either prevents these competitors from exploiting any competitive advantage that they have, or raises their costs, thereby having a negative impact on their competitiveness and their sales. In both cases the agreement hampers the operations of competitors from other Member States on the national market in question. The same is true when a cartel agreement confined to a single Member State is concluded between undertakings that resell products imported from other Member States.

3.2.2. *Horizontal cooperation agreements covering a single Member State*

83. Horizontal cooperation agreements and in particular non-full function joint ventures (cf. paragraph 66 above), which are confined to a single Member State and which do not directly relate to imports and exports, do not belong to the category of agreements that by their very nature are capable of affecting trade between Member States. A careful examination of the capacity of the individual agreement to affect trade between Member States may therefore be required.

84. Horizontal cooperation agreements may, in particular, be capable of affecting trade between Member States where they have foreclosure effects. This may be the case with agreements that establish sector-wide standardisation and certification regimes, which either exclude undertakings from other Member States or which are more easily fulfilled by undertakings from the Member State in question due to the fact that they are based on national rules and traditions. In such circumstances the agreements make it more difficult for undertakings from other Member States to penetrate the national market.

85. Trade may also be affected where a joint venture results in undertakings from other Member States being cut off from an important channel of distribution or source of demand. If, for example, two or more distributors established within the same Member State, and which account for a substantial share of imports of the products in question, establish a purchasing joint venture combining their purchases of that product, the resulting reduction in the number of distribution channels limits the possibility for suppliers from other Member States of gaining access to the national market in question. Trade is therefore capable of being affected. Trade may also be affected where undertakings which previously imported a particular product form a joint venture which is entrusted with the production of that same product. In this case the agreement causes a change in the patterns of trade between Member States compared to the situation before the agreement.

3.2.3. *Vertical agreements covering a single Member State*

86. Vertical agreements covering the whole of a Member State may, in particular, be capable of affecting patterns of trade between Member States when they make it more difficult for undertakings from other Member States to penetrate the national market in question, either by means of exports or by means of establishment (foreclosure effect). When vertical agreements give rise to such foreclosure effects, they contribute to the partitioning of markets on a national basis, thereby hindering the economic interpenetration which the Treaty is designed to bring about.

87. Foreclosure may, for example, occur when suppliers impose exclusive purchasing obligations on buyers. In Delimitis, which concerned agreements between a brewer and owners of premises where beer was consumed whereby the latter undertook to buy beer exclusively from the brewer, the Court of Justice defined foreclosure as the absence, due to the agreements, of real and concrete possibilities of gaining access to the market. Agreements normally only create significant barriers to entry when they cover a significant proportion of the market. Market share and market coverage can be used as an indicator in this respect. In making the assessment account must be taken not only of the particular agreement or network of agreements in question, but also of other parallel networks of agreements having similar effects.

88. Vertical agreements which cover the whole of a Member State and which relate to tradable products may also be capable of affecting trade between Member States, even if they do not create direct obstacles to trade. Agreements whereby undertakings engage in resale price maintenance (RPM) may have direct effects on trade between Member States by increasing imports from other Member States and by decreasing exports from the Member State in question. Agreements involving RPM may also affect patterns of trade in much the same way as horizontal cartels. To the extent that the price resulting from RPM is higher than that prevailing in other Member States this price level is only sustainable if imports from other Member States can be controlled.

3.2.4. *Agreements covering only part of a Member State*

89. In qualitative terms the assessment of agreements covering only part of a Member State is approached in the same way as in the case of agreements covering the whole of a Member State. This means that the analysis in section 2 applies. In the assessment of appreciability, however, the two categories must be distinguished, as it must be taken into account that only part of a Member State is covered by the agreement. It must also be taken into account what proportion of the national territory is susceptible to trade. If, for example, transport costs or the operating radius of equipment render it economically unviable for undertakings from other Member States to serve the entire territory of another Member State, trade is capable of being affected if the agreement forecloses access to the part of the territory of a Member State that is susceptible to trade, provided that this part is not insignificant.

90. Where an agreement forecloses access to a regional market, then for trade to be appreciably affected, the volume of sales affected must be significant in proportion to the overall volume of sales of the products concerned inside the Member State in question. This assessment cannot be based merely on geographic coverage. The market share of the parties to the agreement must also be given fairly limited weight. Even if the parties have a high market share in a properly defined regional market, the size of that market in terms of volume may still be insignificant when compared to total sales of the products concerned within the Member State in question. In general, the best indicator of the capacity of the agreement to (appreciably) affect trade between Member States is therefore considered to be the share of the national market in terms of volume that is being foreclosed. Agreements covering areas with a high concentration of demand will thus weigh more heavily than those covering areas where demand is less concentrated. For Community jurisdiction to be established the share of the national market that is being foreclosed must be significant.

91. Agreements that are local in nature are in themselves not capable of appreciably affecting trade between Member States. This is the case even if the local market is located in a border region. Conversely, if the foreclosed share of the national market is significant, trade is capable of being affected even where the market in question is not located in a border region.

92. In cases in this category some guidance may be derived from the case law concerning the concept in Article 82 of a substantial part of the common market. Agreements that, for example, have the effect of hindering competitors from other Member States from gaining access to part of a Member State, which constitutes a substantial part of the common market, should be considered to have an appreciable effect on trade between Member States.

3.2.5. *Abuses of dominant positions covering a single Member State*

93. Where an undertaking, which holds a dominant position covering the whole of a Member State, engages in exclusionary abuses, trade between Member States is normally capable of being affected. Such abusive conduct will generally make it more difficult for competitors from other Member States to penetrate the market, in which case patterns of trade are capable of being affected. In Michelin, for example, the Court of Justice held that a system of loyalty rebates foreclosed competitors from other Member States and therefore affected trade within the meaning of Article 82. In Rennet the Court similarly held that an abuse in the form of an exclusive purchasing obligation on customers foreclosed products from other Member States.

94. Exclusionary abuses that affect the competitive market structure inside a Member State, for instance by eliminating or threatening to eliminate a competitor, may also be capable of affecting trade between Member States. Where the undertaking that risks being eliminated only operates in a single Member State, the abuse will normally not affect trade between Member States. However, trade between Member States is capable of being affected where the targeted undertaking exports to or imports from other Member States and where it also operates in other Member States. An effect on trade may arise from the dissuasive impact of the abuse on other competitors. If through repeated conduct the dominant undertaking has acquired a reputation for adopting exclusionary practices towards competitors that attempt to engage in direct competition, competitors from other Member States are likely to compete less aggressively, in which case trade may be affected, even if the victim in the case at hand is not from another Member State.

95. In the case of exploitative abuses such as price discrimination and excessive pricing, the situation may be more complex. Price discrimination between domestic customers will normally not affect trade between Member States. However, it may do so if the buyers are engaged in export activities and are disadvantaged by the discriminatory pricing or if this practice is used to prevent imports. Practices consisting of offering lower prices to customers that are the most likely to import products from other Member States may make it more difficult for competitors from other Member States to enter the market. In such cases trade between Member States is capable of being affected.

96. As long as an undertaking has a dominant position which covers the whole of a Member State it is normally immaterial whether the specific abuse engaged in by the dominant undertaking only covers part of its territory or affects certain buyers within the national territory. A dominant firm can significantly impede trade by engaging in abusive conduct in the areas or vis-à-vis the customers that are the most likely to be targeted by competitors from other Member States. For example, it may be the case that a particular channel of distribution constitutes a particularly important means of gaining access to broad categories of consumers. Hindering access to such channels can have a substantial impact on trade between Member States. In the assessment of appreciability it must also be taken into account that the very presence of the dominant undertaking covering the whole of a Member State is likely to make market penetration more difficult. Any abuse which makes it more difficult to enter the national market should therefore be considered to appreciably affect trade. The combination of the market position of the dominant undertaking and the anti-competitive nature of its conduct implies that such abuses have normally by their very nature an appreciable effect on trade. However, if the abuse is purely local in nature or involves only an insignificant share of the sales of the dominant undertaking within the Member State in question, trade may not be capable of being appreciably affected.

3.2.6. *Abuse of a dominant position covering only part of a Member State*

97. Where a dominant position covers only part of a Member State some guidance may, as in the case of agreements, be derived from the condition in Article 82 that the dominant position must cover a substantial part of the common market. If the dominant position covers part of a Member State that constitutes a substantial part of the common market and the abuse makes it more difficult for competitors from other Member States to gain access to the market where the undertaking is dominant, trade between Member States must normally be considered capable of being appreciably affected.

98. In the application of this criterion regard must be had in particular to the size of the market in question in terms of volume. Regions and even a port or an airport situated in a Member State may, depending on their importance, constitute a substantial part of the common market. In the latter cases it must be taken into account whether the infrastructure in question is used to provide crossborder services and, if so, to what extent. When infrastructures such as airports and ports are important in providing cross-border services, trade between Member States is capable of being affected.

99. As in the case of dominant positions covering the whole of a Member State (cf. paragraph 95 above), trade may not be capable of being appreciably affected if the abuse is purely local in nature or involves only an insignificant share of the sales of the dominant undertaking.

3.3 Agreements and abuses involving imports and exports with undertakings located in third countries, and agreements and practices involving undertakings located in third countries

3.3.1. *General remarks*

100. Articles 81 and 82 apply to agreements and practices that are capable of affecting trade between Member States even if one or more of the parties are located outside the Community. Articles 81 and 82 apply irrespective of where the undertakings are located or where the agreement has been concluded, provided that the agreement or practice is either implemented inside the Community, or produce effects inside the Community. Articles 81 and 82 may also apply to agreements and practices that cover third countries, provided that they are capable of affecting trade between Member States. The general principle set out in section 2 above according to which the agreement or practice must be capable of having an appreciable influence, direct or indirect, actual or potential, on the pattern of trade between Member States, also applies in the case of agreements and abuses which involve undertakings located in third countries or which relate to imports or exports with third countries.

101. For the purposes of establishing Community law jurisdiction it is sufficient that an agreement or practice involving third countries or undertakings located in third countries is capable of affecting cross-border economic activity inside the Community. Import into one Member State may be sufficient to trigger effects of this nature. Imports can affect the conditions of competition in the importing Member State, which in turn can have an impact on exports and imports of competing products to and from other Member States. In other words, imports from third countries resulting from the agreement or practice may cause a diversion of trade between Member States, thus affecting patterns of trade.

102. In the application of the effect on trade criterion to the above mentioned agreements and practices it is relevant to examine, inter alia, what is the object of the agreement or practice as indicated by its content or the underlying intent of the undertakings involved.

103. Where the object of the agreement is to restrict competition inside the Community the requisite effect on trade between Member States is more readily established than where the object is predominantly to regulate competition outside the Community. Indeed in the former case the agreement or practice has a direct impact on competition inside the Community and trade between Member States. Such agreements and practices, which may concern both imports and exports, are normally by their very nature capable of affecting trade between Member States.

3.3.2. *Arrangements that have as their object the restriction of competition inside the Community*

104. In the case of imports, this category includes agreements that bring about an isolation of the internal market. This is, for instance, the case of agreements whereby competitors in the Community and in third countries share markets, e.g. by agreeing not to sell in each other's home markets or by concluding reciprocal (exclusive) distribution agreements.

105. In the case of exports, this category includes cases where undertakings that compete in two or more Member States agree to export certain (surplus) quantities to third countries with a view to co-ordinating their market conduct inside the Community. Such export agreements serve to reduce price competition by limiting output inside the Community, thereby affecting trade between Member States. Without the export agreement these quantities might have been sold inside the Community.

3.3.3. *Other arrangements*

106. In the case of agreements and practices whose object is not to restrict competition inside the Community, it is normally necessary to proceed with a more detailed analysis of whether or not cross-border economic activity inside the Community, and thus patterns of trade between Member States, are capable of being affected.

107. In this regard it is relevant to examine the effects of the agreement or practice on customers and other operators inside the Community that rely on the products of the undertakings that are parties to the agreement or practice. In Compagnie maritime belge, which concerned agreements between shipping companies operating between Community ports and West African ports, the agreements were held to be capable of indirectly affecting trade between Member States because they altered the catchment areas of the Community ports covered by the agreements and because they affected the activities of other undertakings inside those areas. More specifically, the agreements affected the activities of undertakings that relied on the parties for transportation services, either as a means of transporting goods purchased in third countries or sold there, or as an important input into the services that the ports themselves offered.

108. Trade may also be capable of being affected when the agreement prevents re-imports into the Community. This may, for example, be the case with vertical agreements between Community suppliers and third country distributors, imposing restrictions on resale outside an allocated territory, including the Community. If in the absence of the agreement resale to the Community would be possible and likely, such imports may be capable of affecting patterns of trade inside the Community.

109. However, for such effects to be likely, there must be an appreciable difference between the prices of the products charged in the Community and those charged outside the Community, and this price difference must not be eroded by customs duties and transport costs. In addition, the product volumes exported compared to the total market for those products in the territory of the common market must not be insignificant. If these product volumes are insignificant compared to those sold inside the Community, the impact of any re-importation on trade between Member States is considered not to be appreciable. In making this assessment, regard must be had not only to the individual agreement concluded between the parties, but also to any cumulative effect of similar agreements concluded by the same and competing suppliers. It may be, for example, that the product volumes covered by a single agreement are quite small, but that the product volumes covered by several such agreements are significant. In that case the agreements taken as a whole may be capable of appreciably affecting trade between Member States. It should be recalled, however (cf. paragraph 49 above), that the individual agreement or network of agreements must make a significant contribution to the overall effect on trade.

Communication from the Commission Notice
Guidelines on the application of Article 81(3) of the Treaty

(OJ 2004, No. C 101/08)

(Text with EEA relevance)

1 INTRODUCTION

1. Article 81(3) of the Treaty sets out an exception rule, which provides a defence to undertakings against a finding of an infringement of Article 81(1) of the Treaty. Agreements, decisions of associations of undertakings and concerted practices caught by Article 81(1) which satisfy the conditions of Article 81(3) are valid and enforceable, no prior decision to that effect being required.

2. Article 81(3) can be applied in individual cases or to categories of agreements and concerted practices by way of block exemption regulation. Regulation 1/2003 on the implementation of the competition rules laid down in Articles 81 and 82 does not affect the validity and legal nature of block exemption regulations. All existing block exemption regulations remain in force and agreements covered by block exemption regulations are legally valid and enforceable even if they are restrictive of competition within the meaning of Article 81(1). Such agreements can only be prohibited for the future and only upon formal withdrawal of the block exemption by the Commission or a national competition authority. Block exempted agreements cannot be held invalid by national courts in the context of private litigation.

3. The existing guidelines on vertical restraints, horizontal cooperation agreements and technology transfer agreements deal with the application of Article 81 to various types of agreements and concerted practices. The purpose of those guidelines is to set out the Commission's view of the substantive assessment criteria applied to the various types of agreements and practices.

4. The present guidelines set out the Commission's interpretation of the conditions for exception contained in Article 81(3). It thereby provides guidance on how it will apply Article 81 in individual cases. Although not binding on them, these guidelines also intend to give guidance to the courts and authorities of the Member States in their application of Article 81(1) and (3) of the Treaty.

5. The guidelines establish an analytical framework for the application of Article 81(3). The purpose is to develop a methodology for the application of this Treaty provision. This methodology is based on the economic approach already introduced and developed in the guidelines on vertical restraints, horizontal co-operation agreements and technology transfer agreements. The Commission will follow the present guidelines, which provide more detailed guidance on the application of the four conditions of Article 81(3) than the guidelines on vertical restraints, horizontal cooperation agreements and technology transfer agreements, also with regard to agreements covered by those guidelines.

6. The standards set forth in the present guidelines must be applied in light of the circumstances specific to each case. This excludes a mechanical application. Each case must be assessed on its own facts and the guidelines must be applied reasonably and flexibly.

7. With regard to a number of issues, the present guidelines outline the current state of the case law of the Court of Justice. However, the Commission also intends to explain its policy with regard to issues that have not been dealt with in the case law, or that are subject to interpretation. The Commission's position, however, is without prejudice to the case law of the Court of Justice and the Court of First Instance concerning the interpretation of Article 81(1) and (3), and to the interpretation that the Community Courts may give to those provisions in the future.

2 THE GENERAL FRAMEWORK OF ARTICLE 81 EC

2.1 The Treaty provisions

8. Article 81(1) prohibits all agreements between undertakings, decisions by associations of undertakings and concerted practices which may affect trade between Member States and which have as their object or effect the prevention, restriction or distortion of competition.

9. As an exception to this rule Article 81(3) provides that the prohibition contained in Article 81(1) may be declared inapplicable in case of agreements which contribute to improving the production or distribution of goods or to promoting technical or economic progress, while allowing consumers a fair share of the resulting benefits, and which do not impose restrictions which are not indispensable to the attainment of these objectives, and do not afford such undertakings the possibility of eliminating competition in respect of a substantial part of the products concerned.

10. According to Article 1(1) of Regulation 1/2003 agreements which are caught by Article 81(1) and which do not satisfy the conditions of Article 81(3) are prohibited, no prior decision to that effect being required. According to Article 1(2) of the same Regulation agreements which are caught by Article 81(1) but which satisfy the conditions of Article 81(3) are not prohibited, no prior decision to that effect being required. Such agreements are valid and enforceable from the moment that the conditions of Article 81(3) are satisfied and for as long as that remains the case.

11. The assessment under Article 81 thus consists of two parts. The first step is to assess whether an agreement between undertakings, which is capable of affecting trade between Member States, has an anti-competitive object or actual or potential anti-competitive effects. The second step, which only becomes relevant when an agreement is found to be restrictive of competition, is to determine the pro-competitive benefits produced by that agreement and to assess whether these pro-competitive effects outweigh the anti-competitive effects. The balancing of anticompetitive and pro-competitive effects is conducted exclusively within the framework laid down by Article 81(3).

12. The assessment of any countervailing benefits under Article 81(3) necessarily requires prior determination of the restrictive nature and impact of the agreement. To place Article 81(3) in its proper context it is appropriate to briefly outline the objective and principal content of the prohibition rule of Article 81(1). The Commission guidelines on vertical restraints, horizontal co-operation agreements and technology transfer agreements contain substantial guidance on the application of Article 81(1) to various types of agreements. The present guidelines are therefore limited to recalling the basic analytical framework for applying Article 81(1).

2.2 The prohibition rule of Article 81(1)

2.2.1. *General remarks*

13. The objective of Article 81 is to protect competition on the market as a means of enhancing consumer welfare and of ensuring an efficient allocation of resources. Competition and market integration serve these ends since the creation and preservation of an open single market promotes an efficient allocation of resources throughout the Community for the benefit of consumers.

14. The prohibition rule of Article 81(1) applies to restrictive agreements and concerted practices between undertakings and decisions by associations of undertakings in so far as they are capable of affecting trade between Member States. A general principle underlying Article 81(1) which is expressed in the case law of the Community Courts is that each economic operator must determine independently the policy, which he intends to adopt on the market. In view of this the Community Courts have defined 'agreements', 'decisions' and 'concerted practices' as Community law concepts which allow a distinction to be made between the unilateral conduct of an undertaking and co-ordination of behaviour or collusion between undertakings. Unilateral conduct is subject only to Article 82 of the Treaty as far as Community competition law is concerned. Moreover, the convergence rule set out in Article 3(2) of Regulation 1/2003 does not apply to unilateral conduct. This provision applies only to agreements, decisions and concerted practices, which are capable of affecting trade between Member States. Article 3(2) provides that when such agreements, decisions and concerted practices are not prohibited by Article 81, they cannot be prohibited by national

competition law. Article 3 is without prejudice to the fundamental principle of primacy of Community law, which entails in particular that agreements and abusive practices that are prohibited by Articles 81 and 82 cannot be upheld by national law.

15. The type of co-ordination of behaviour or collusion between undertakings falling within the scope of Article 81(1) is that where at least one undertaking vis-à-vis another undertaking undertakes to adopt a certain conduct on the market or that as a result of contacts between them uncertainty as to their conduct on the market is eliminated or at least substantially reduced. It follows that co-ordination can take the form of obligations that regulate the market conduct of at least one of the parties as well as of arrangements that influence the market conduct of at least one of the parties by causing a change in its incentives. It is not required that co-ordination is in the interest of all the undertakings concerned. Co-ordination must also not necessarily be express. It can also be tacit. For an agreement to be capable of being regarded as having been concluded by tacit acceptance there must be an invitation from an undertaking to another undertaking, whether express or implied, to fulfil a goal jointly. In certain circumstances an agreement may be inferred from and imputed to an ongoing commercial relationship between the parties. However, the mere fact that a measure adopted by an undertaking falls within the context of on-going business relations is not sufficient.

16. Agreements between undertakings are caught by the prohibition rule of Article 81(1) when they are likely to have an appreciable adverse impact on the parameters of competition on the market, such as price, output, product quality, product variety and innovation. Agreements can have this effect by appreciably reducing rivalry between the parties to the agreement or between them and third parties.

2.2.2. *The basic principles for assessing agreements under Article 81(1)*

17. The assessment of whether an agreement is restrictive of competition must be made within the actual context in which competition would occur in the absence of the agreement with its alleged restrictions. In making this assessment it is necessary to take account of the likely impact of the agreement on inter-brand competition (i.e. competition between suppliers of competing brands) and on intra-brand competition (i.e. competition between distributors of the same brand). Article 81(1) prohibits restrictions of both inter-brand competition and intra-brand competition.

18. For the purpose of assessing whether an agreement or its individual parts may restrict inter-brand competition and/or intra-brand competition it needs to be considered how and to what extent the agreement affects or is likely to affect competition on the market. The following two questions provide a useful framework for making this assessment. The first question relates to the impact of the agreement on inter-brand competition while the second question relates to the impact of the agreement on intra-brand competition. As restraints may be capable of affecting both inter-brand competition and intra-brand competition at the same time, it may be necessary to analyse a restraint in light of both questions before it can be concluded whether or not competition is restricted within the meaning of Article 81(1):

(1) Does the agreement restrict actual or potential competition that would have existed without the agreement? If so, the agreement may be caught by Article 81(1). In making this assessment it is necessary to take into account competition between the parties and competition from third parties. For instance, where two undertakings established in different Member States undertake not to sell products in each other's home markets, (potential) competition that existed prior to the agreement is restricted. Similarly, where a supplier imposes obligations on his distributors not to sell competing products and these obligations foreclose third party access to the market, actual or potential competition that would have existed in the absence of the agreement is restricted. In assessing whether the parties to an agreement are actual or potential competitors the economic and legal context must be taken into account. For instance, if due to the financial risks involved and the technical capabilities of the parties it is unlikely on the basis of objective factors that each party would be able to carry out on its own the activities covered by the agreement the parties are deemed to be non-competitors in respect of that activity. It is for the parties to bring forward evidence to that effect.

(2) Does the agreement restrict actual or potential competition that would have existed in the absence of the contractual restraint (s)? If so, the agreement may be caught by Article 81(1). For instance, where a supplier restricts its distributors from competing with each other, (potential) competition that could have existed between the distributors absent the restraints is restricted. Such restrictions include resale price maintenance and territorial or customer sales restrictions between distributors. However, certain restraints may in certain cases not be caught by Article 81(1) when the restraint is objectively necessary for the existence of an agreement of that type or that nature. Such exclusion of the application of Article 81(1) can only be made on the basis of objective factors external to the parties themselves and not the subjective views and characteristics of the parties. The question is not whether the parties in their particular situation would not have accepted to conclude a less restrictive agreement, but whether given the nature of the agreement and the characteristics of the market a less restrictive agreement would not have been concluded by undertakings in a similar setting. For instance, territorial restraints in an agreement between a supplier and a distributor may for a certain period of time fall outside Article 81(1), if the restraints are objectively necessary in order for the distributor to penetrate a new market. Similarly, a prohibition imposed on all distributors not to sell to certain categories of end users may not be restrictive of competition if such restraint is objectively necessary for reasons of safety or health related to the dangerous nature of the product in question. Claims that in the absence of a restraint the supplier would have resorted to vertical integration are not sufficient. Decisions on whether or not to vertically integrate depend on a broad range of complex economic factors, a number of which are internal to the undertaking concerned.

19. In the application of the analytical framework set out in the previous paragraph it must be taken into account that Article 81(1) distinguishes between those agreements that have a restriction of competition as their object and those agreements that have a restriction of competition as their effect. An agreement or contractual restraint is only prohibited by Article 81(1) if its object or effect is to restrict inter-brand competition and/or intra-brand competition.

20. The distinction between restrictions by object and restrictions by effect is important. Once it has been established that an agreement has as its object the restriction of competition, there is no need to take account of its concrete effects. In other words, for the purpose of applying Article 81(1) no actual anti-competitive effects need to be demonstrated where the agreement has a restriction of competition as its object. Article 81(3), on the other hand, does not distinguish between agreements that restrict competition by object and agreements that restrict competition by effect. Article 81(3) applies to all agreements that fulfil the four conditions contained therein.

21. Restrictions of competition *by object* are those that by their very nature have the potential of restricting competition. These are restrictions which in light of the objectives pursued by the Community competition rules have such a high potential of negative effects on competition that it is unnecessary for the purposes of applying Article 81(1) to demonstrate any actual effects on the market. This presumption is based on the serious nature of the restriction and on experience showing that restrictions of competition by object are likely to produce negative effects on the market and to jeopardise the objectives pursued by the Community competition rules. Restrictions by object such as price fixing and market sharing reduce output and raise prices, leading to a misallocation of resources, because goods and services demanded by customers are not produced. They also lead to a reduction in consumer welfare, because consumers have to pay higher prices for the goods and services in question.

22. The assessment of whether or not an agreement has as its object the restriction of competition is based on a number of factors. These factors include, in particular, the content of the agreement and the objective aims pursued by it. It may also be necessary to consider the context in which it is (to be) applied and the actual conduct and behaviour of the parties on the market. In other words, an examination of the facts underlying the agreement and the specific circumstances in which it operates may be required before it can be concluded whether a particular restriction constitutes a restriction of

competition by object. The way in which an agreement is actually implemented may reveal a restriction by object even where the formal agreement does not contain an express provision to that effect. Evidence of subjective intent on the part of the parties to restrict competition is a relevant factor but not a necessary condition.

23. Non-exhaustive guidance on what constitutes restrictions by object can be found in Commission block exemption regulations, guidelines and notices. Restrictions that are black-listed in block exemptions or identified as hardcore restrictions in guidelines and notices are generally considered by the Commission to constitute restrictions by object. In the case of horizontal agreements restrictions of competition by object include price fixing, output limitation and sharing of markets and customers. As regards vertical agreements the category of restrictions by object includes, in particular, fixed and minimum resale price maintenance and restrictions providing absolute territorial protection, including restrictions on passive sales.

24. If an agreement is not restrictive of competition by object it must be examined whether it has restrictive effects on competition. Account must be taken of both actual and potential effects. In other words the agreement must have likely anti-competitive effects. In the case of restrictions of competition by effect there is no presumption of anti-competitive effects. For an agreement to be restrictive by effect it must affect actual or potential competition to such an extent that on the relevant market negative effects on prices, output, innovation or the variety or quality of goods and services can be expected with a reasonable degree of probability. Such negative effects must be appreciable. The prohibition rule of Article 81(1) does not apply when the identified anti-competitive effects are insignificant. This test reflects the economic approach which the Commission is applying. The prohibition of Article 81(1) only applies where on the basis of proper market analysis it can be concluded that the agreement has likely anti-competitive effects on the market. It is insufficient for such a finding that the market shares of the parties exceed the thresholds set out in the Commission's *de minimis* notice. Agreements falling within safe harbours of block exemption regulations may be caught by Article 81(1) but this is not necessarily so. Moreover, the fact that due to the market shares of the parties, an agreement falls outside the safe harbour of a block exemption is in itself an insufficient basis for finding that the agreement is caught by Article 81 (1) or that it does not fulfil the conditions of Article 81 (3). Individual assessment of the likely effects produced by the agreement is required.

25. Negative effects on competition within the relevant market are likely to occur when the parties individually or jointly have or obtain some degree of market power and the agreement contributes to the creation, maintenance or strengthening of that market power or allows the parties to exploit such market power. Market power is the ability to maintain prices above competitive levels for a significant period of time or to maintain output in terms of product quantities, product quality and variety or innovation below competitive levels for a significant period of time. In markets with high fixed costs undertakings must price significantly above their marginal costs of production in order to ensure a competitive return on their investment. The fact that undertakings price above their marginal costs is therefore not in itself a sign that competition in the market is not functioning well and that undertakings have market power that allows them to price above the competitive level. It is when competitive constraints are insufficient to maintain prices and output at competitive levels that undertakings have market power within the meaning of Article 81(1).

26. The creation, maintenance or strengthening of market power can result from a restriction of competition between the parties to the agreement. It can also result from a restriction of competition between any one of the parties and third parties, e.g. because the agreement leads to foreclosure of competitors or because it raises competitors' costs, limiting their capacity to compete effectively with the contracting parties. Market power is a question of degree. The degree of market power normally required for the finding of an infringement under Article 81(1) in the case of agreements that are restrictive of competition by effect is less than the degree of market power required for a finding of dominance under Article 82.

27. For the purposes of analysing the restrictive effects of an agreement it is normally necessary to define the relevant market. It is normally also necessary to examine and assess, *inter alia,* the nature

of the products, the market position of the parties, the market position of competitors, the market position of buyers, the existence of potential competitors and the level of entry barriers. In some cases, however, it may be possible to show anti-competitive effects directly by analysing the conduct of the parties to the agreement on the market. It may for example be possible to ascertain that an agreement has led to price increases. The guidelines on horizontal cooperation agreements and on vertical restraints set out a detailed framework for analysing the competitive impact of various types of horizontal and vertical agreements under Article 81(1).

2.2.3. *Ancillary restraints*

28. Paragraph 18 above sets out a framework for analysing the impact of an agreement and its individual restrictions on inter-brand competition and intra-brand competition. If on the basis of those principles it is concluded that the main transaction covered by the agreement is not restrictive of competition, it becomes relevant to examine whether individual restraints contained in the agreement are also compatible with Article 81(1) because they are ancillary to the main non-restrictive transaction.

29. In Community competition law the concept of ancillary restraints covers any alleged restriction of competition which is directly related and necessary to the implementation of a main non-restrictive transaction and proportionate to it. If an agreement in its main parts, for instance a distribution agreement or a joint venture, does not have as its object or effect the restriction of competition, then restrictions, which are directly related to and necessary for the implementation of that transaction, also fall outside Article 81(1). These related restrictions are called ancillary restraints. A restriction is directly related to the main transaction if it is subordinate to the implementation of that transaction and is inseparably linked to it. The test of necessity implies that the restriction must be objectively necessary for the implementation of the main transaction and be proportionate to it. It follows that the ancillary restraints test is similar to the test set out in paragraph 18(2) above. However, the ancillary restraints test applies in all cases where the main transaction is not restrictive of competition. It is not limited to determining the impact of the agreement on intra-brand competition.

30. The application of the ancillary restraint concept must be distinguished from the application of the defence under Article 81(3) which relates to certain economic benefits produced by restrictive agreements and which are balanced against the restrictive effects of the agreements. The application of the ancillary restraint concept does not involve any weighing of pro-competitive and anticompetitive effects. Such balancing is reserved for Article 81(3).

31. The assessment of ancillary restraints is limited to determining whether, in the specific context of the main non-restrictive transaction or activity, a particular restriction is necessary for the implementation of that transaction or activity and proportionate to it. If on the basis of objective factors it can be concluded that without the restriction the main non-restrictive transaction would be difficult or impossible to implement, the restriction may be regarded as objectively necessary for its implementation and proportionate to it. If, for example, the main object of a franchise agreement does not restrict competition, then restrictions, which are necessary for the proper functioning of the agreement, such as obligations aimed at protecting the uniformity and reputation of the franchise system, also fall outside Article 81(1). Similarly, if a joint venture is not in itself restrictive of competition, then restrictions that are necessary for the functioning of the agreement are deemed to be ancillary to the main transaction and are therefore not caught by Article 81(1). For instance in *TPS* the Commission concluded that an obligation on the parties not to be involved in companies engaged in distribution and marketing of television programmes by satellite was ancillary to the creation of the joint venture during the initial phase. The restriction was therefore deemed to fall outside Article 81(1) for a period of three years. In arriving at this conclusion the Commission took account of the heavy investments and commercial risks involved in entering the market for pay-television.

2.3 The exception rule of Article 81(3)

32. The assessment of restrictions by object and effect under Article 81(1) is only one side of the analysis. The other side, which is reflected in Article 81(3), is the assessment of the positive economic effects of restrictive agreements.

33. The aim of the Community competition rules is to protect competition on the market as a means of enhancing consumer welfare and of ensuring an efficient allocation of resources. Agreements that restrict competition may at the same time have pro-competitive effects by way of efficiency gains. Efficiencies may create additional value by lowering the cost of producing an output, improving the quality of the product or creating a new product. When the pro-competitive effects of an agreement outweigh its anti-competitive effects the agreement is on balance pro-competitive and compatible with the objectives of the Community competition rules. The net effect of such agreements is to promote the very essence of the competitive process, namely to win customers by offering better products or better prices than those offered by rivals. This analytical framework is reflected in Article 81(1) and Article 81(3). The latter provision expressly acknowledges that restrictive agreements may generate objective economic benefits so as to outweigh the negative effects of the restriction of competition.

34. The application of the exception rule of Article 81(3) is subject to four cumulative conditions, two positive and two negative:

   (a) The agreement must contribute to improving the production or distribution of goods or contribute to promoting technical or economic progress,
   (b) Consumers must receive a fair share of the resulting benefits,
   (c) The restrictions must be indispensable to the attainment of these objectives, and finally
   (d) The agreement must not afford the parties the possibility of eliminating competition in respect of a substantial part of the products in question.

When these four conditions are fulfilled the agreement enhances competition within the relevant market, because it leads the undertakings concerned to offer cheaper or better products to consumers, compensating the latter for the adverse effects of the restrictions of competition.

35. Article 81(3) can be applied either to individual agreements or to categories of agreements by way of a block exemption regulation. When an agreement is covered by a block exemption the parties to the restrictive agreement are relieved of their burden under Article 2 of Regulation 1/ 2003 of showing that their individual agreement satisfies each of the conditions of Article 81(3). They only have to prove that the restrictive agreement benefits from a block exemption. The application of Article 81(3) to categories of agreements by way of block exemption regulation is based on the presumption that restrictive agreements that fall within their scope fulfil each of the four conditions laid down in Article 81(3).

36. If in an individual case the agreement is caught by Article 81(1) and the conditions of Article 81(3) are not fulfilled the block exemption may be withdrawn. According to Article 29(1) of Regulation 1/2003 the Commission is empowered to withdraw the benefit of a block exemption when it finds that in a particular case an agreement covered by a block exemption regulation has certain effects which are incompatible with Article 81(3) of the Treaty. Pursuant to Article 29(2) of Regulation 1/2003 a competition authority of a Member State may also withdraw the benefit of a Commission block exemption regulation in respect of its territory (or part of its territory), if this territory has all the characteristics of a distinct geographic market. In the case of withdrawal it is for the competition authorities concerned to demonstrate that the agreement infringes Article 81(1) and that it does not fulfil the conditions of Article 81(3).

37. The courts of the Member States have no power to withdraw the benefit of block exemption regulations. Moreover, in their application of block exemption regulations Member State courts may not modify their scope by extending their sphere of application to agreements not covered by the block exemption regulation in question. Outside the scope of block exemption regulations Member State courts have the power to apply Article 81 in full (cf. Article 6 of Regulation 1/2003).

3 THE APPLICATION OF THE FOUR CONDITIONS OF ARTICLE 81(3)

38. The remainder of these guidelines will consider each of the four conditions of Article 81(3). Given that these four conditions are cumulative it is unnecessary to examine any remaining conditions

once it is found that one of the conditions of Article 81(3) is not fulfilled. In individual cases it may therefore be appropriate to consider the four conditions in a different order.

39. For the purposes of these guidelines it is considered appropriate to invert the order of the second and the third condition and thus deal with the issue of indispensability before the issue of pass-on to consumers. The analysis of pass-on requires a balancing of the negative and positive effects of an agreement on consumers. This analysis should not include the effects of any restrictions, which already fail the indispensability test and which for that reason are prohibited by Article 81.

3.1   General principles

40. Article 81(3) of the Treaty only becomes relevant when an agreement between undertakings restricts competition within the meaning of Article 81(1). In the case of non-restrictive agreements there is no need to examine any benefits generated by the agreement.

41. Where in an individual case a restriction of competition within the meaning of Article 81(1) has been proven, Article 81(3) can be invoked as a defence. According to Article 2 of Regulation 1/2003 the burden of proof under Article 81(3) rests on the undertaking(s) invoking the benefit of the exception rule. Where the conditions of Article 81(3) are not satisfied the agreement is null and void, cf. Article 81 (2). However, such automatic nullity only applies to those parts of the agreement that are incompatible with Article 81, provided that such parts are severable from the agreement as a whole. If only part of the agreement is null and void, it is for the applicable national law to determine the consequences thereof for the remaining part of the agreement.

42. According to settled case law the four conditions of Article 81(3) are cumulative, i.e. they must all be fulfilled for the exception rule to be applicable. If they are not, the application of the exception rule of Article 81(3) must be refused. The four conditions of Article 81(3) are also exhaustive. When they are met the exception is applicable and may not be made dependant on any other condition. Goals pursued by other Treaty provisions can be taken into account to the extent that they can be subsumed under the four conditions of Article 81(3).

43. The assessment under Article 81(3) of benefits flowing from restrictive agreements is in principle made within the confines of each relevant market to which the agreement relates. The Community competition rules have as their objective the protection of competition on the market and cannot be detached from this objective. Moreover, the condition that consumers must receive a fair share of the benefits implies in general that efficiencies generated by the restrictive agreement within a relevant market must be sufficient to outweigh the anti-competitive effects produced by the agreement within that same relevant market. Negative effects on consumers in one geographic market or product market cannot normally be balanced against and compensated by positive effects for consumers in another unrelated geographic market or product market. However, where two markets are related, efficiencies achieved on separate markets can be taken into account provided that the group of consumers affected by the restriction and benefiting from the efficiency gains are substantially the same. Indeed, in some cases only consumers in a downstream market are affected by the agreement in which case the impact of the agreement on such consumers must be assessed. This is for instance so in the case of purchasing agreements.

44. The assessment of restrictive agreements under Article 81(3) is made within the actual context in which they occur and on the basis of the facts existing at any given point in time. The assessment is sensitive to material changes in the facts. The exception rule of Article 81(3) applies as long as the four conditions are fulfilled and ceases to apply when that is no longer the case. When applying Article 81(3) in accordance with these principles it is necessary to take into account the initial sunk investments made by any of the parties and the time needed and the restraints required to commit and recoup an efficiency enhancing investment. Article 81 cannot be applied without taking due account of such *ex ante* investment. The risk facing the parties and the sunk investment that must be committed to implement the agreement can thus lead to the agreement falling outside Article 81(1) or fulfilling the conditions of Article 81(3), as the case may be, for the period of time required to recoup the investment.

45. In some cases the restrictive agreement is an irreversible event. Once the restrictive agreement has been implemented the *ex ante* situation cannot be re-established. In such cases the assessment must be made exclusively on the basis of the facts pertaining at the time of implementation. For instance, in the case of a research and development agreement whereby each party agrees to abandon its respective research project and pool its capabilities with those of another party, it may from an objective point of view be technically and economically impossible to revive a project once it has been abandoned. The assessment of the anti-competitive and pro-competitive effects of the agreement to abandon the individual research projects must therefore be made as of the time of the completion of its implementation. If at that point in time the agreement is compatible with Article 81, for instance because a sufficient number of third parties have competing research and development projects, the parties' agreement to abandon their individual projects remains compatible with Article 81, even if at a later point in time the third party projects fail. However, the prohibition of Article 81 may apply to other parts of the agreement in respect of which the issue of irreversibility does not arise. If for example in addition to joint research and development, the agreement provides for joint exploitation, Article 81 may apply to this part of the agreement if due to subsequent market developments the agreement becomes restrictive of competition and does not (any longer) satisfy the conditions of Article 81(3) taking due account of *ex ante* sunk investments, cf. the previous paragraph.

46. Article 81(3) does not exclude a *priori* certain types of agreements from its scope. As a matter of principle all restrictive agreements that fulfil the four conditions of Article 81(3) are covered by the exception rule. However, severe restrictions of competition are unlikely to fulfil the conditions of Article 81(3). Such restrictions are usually black-listed in block exemption regulations or identified as hardcore restrictions in Commission guidelines and notices. Agreements of this nature generally fail (at least) the two first conditions of Article 81(3). They neither create objective economic benefits nor do they benefit consumers. For example, a horizontal agreement to fix prices limits output leading to misallocation of resources. It also transfers value from consumers to producers, since it leads to higher prices without producing any countervailing value to consumers within the relevant market. Moreover, these types of agreements generally also fail the indispensability test under the third condition.

47. Any claim that restrictive agreements are justified because they aim at ensuring fair conditions of competition on the market is by nature unfounded and must be discarded. The purpose of Article 81 is to protect effective competition by ensuring that markets remain open and competitive. The protection of fair conditions of competition is a task for the legislator in compliance with Community law obligations and not for undertakings to regulate themselves.

3.2 First condition of Article 81(3): efficiency gains

3.2.1. *General remarks*

48. According to the first condition of Article 81(3) the restrictive agreement must contribute to improving the production or distribution of goods or to promoting technical or economic progress. The provision refers expressly only to goods, but applies by analogy to services.

49. It follows from the case law of the Court of Justice that only objective benefits can be taken into account. This means that efficiencies are not assessed from the subjective point of view of the parties. Cost savings that arise from the mere exercise of market power by the parties cannot be taken into account. For instance, when companies agree to fix prices or share markets they reduce output and thereby production costs. Reduced competition may also lead to lower sales and marketing expenditures. Such cost reductions are a direct consequence of a reduction in output and value. The cost reductions in question do not produce any pro-competitive effects on the market. In particular, they do not lead to the creation of value through an integration of assets and activities. They merely allow the undertakings concerned to increase their profits and are therefore irrelevant from the point of view of Article 81(3).

50. The purpose of the first condition of Article 81(3) is to define the types of efficiency gains that can be taken into account and be subject to the further tests of the second and third conditions of Article 81(3). The aim of the analysis is to ascertain what are the objective benefits created by the

agreement and what is the economic importance of such efficiencies. Given that for Article 81(3) to apply the pro-competitive effects flowing from the agreement must outweigh its anti-competitive effects, it is necessary to verify what is the link between the agreement and the claimed efficiencies and what is the value of these efficiencies.

51. All efficiency claims must therefore be substantiated so that the following can be verified:
   (a) The *nature* of the claimed efficiencies;
   (b) The *link* between the agreement and the efficiencies;
   (c) The *likelihood* and *magnitude* of each claimed efficiency; and
   (d) *How* and *when* each claimed efficiency would be achieved.

52. Letter (a) allows the decision-maker to verify whether the claimed efficiencies are objective in nature, cf. paragraph 49 above.

53. Letter (b) allows the decision-maker to verify whether there is a sufficient causal link between the restrictive agreement and the claimed efficiencies. This condition normally requires that the efficiencies result from the economic activity that forms the object of the agreement. Such activities may, for example, take the form of distribution, licensing of technology, joint production or joint research and development. To the extent, however, that an agreement has wider efficiency enhancing effects within the relevant market, for example because it leads to a reduction in industry wide costs, these additional benefits are also taken into account.

54. The causal link between the agreement and the claimed efficiencies must normally also be direct. Claims based on indirect effects are as a general rule too uncertain and too remote to be taken into account. A direct causal link exists for instance where a technology transfer agreement allows the licensees to produce new or improved products or a distribution agreement allows products to be distributed at lower cost or valuable services to be produced. An example of indirect effect would be a case where it is claimed that a restrictive agreement allows the undertakings concerned to increase their profits, enabling them to invest more in research and development to the ultimate benefit of consumers. While there maybe a link between profitability and research and development, this link is generally not sufficiently direct to be taken into account in the context of Article 81(3).

55. Letters (c) and (d) allow the decision-maker to verify the value of the claimed efficiencies, which in the context of the third condition of Article 81(3) must be balanced against the anti-competitive effects of the agreement, see paragraph 101 below. Given that Article 81(1) only applies in cases where the agreement has likely negative effects on competition and consumers (in the case of hardcore restrictions such effects are presumed) efficiency claims must be substantiated so that they can be verified. Unsubstantiated claims are rejected.

56. In the case of claimed cost efficiencies the undertakings invoking the benefit of Article 81(3) must as accurately as reasonably possible calculate or estimate the value of the efficiencies and describe in detail how the amount has been computed. They must also describe the method(s) by which the efficiencies have been or will be achieved. The data submitted must be verifiable so that there can be a sufficient degree of certainty that the efficiencies have materialised or are likely to materialise.

57. In the case of claimed efficiencies in the form of new or improved products and other non-cost based efficiencies, the undertakings claiming the benefit of Article 81(3) must describe and explain in detail what is the nature of the efficiencies and how and why they constitute an objective economic benefit.

58. In cases where the agreement has yet to be fully implemented the parties must substantiate any projections as to the date from which the efficiencies will become operational so as to have a significant positive impact in the market.

3.2.2. *The different categories of efficiencies*

59. The types of efficiencies listed in Article 81 (3) are broad categories which are intended to cover all objective economic efficiencies. There is considerable overlap between the various categories mentioned in Article 81(3) and the same agreement may give rise to several kinds of efficiencies. It is therefore not appropriate to draw clear and firm distinctions between the various categories. For

the purpose of these guidelines, a distinction is made between cost efficiencies and efficiencies of a qualitative nature whereby value is created in the form of new or improved products, greater product variety etc.

60. In general, efficiencies stem from an integration of economic activities whereby undertakings combine their assets to achieve what they could not achieve as efficiently on their own or whereby they entrust another undertaking with tasks that can be performed more efficiently by that other undertaking.

61. The research and development, production and distribution process may be viewed as a value chain that can be divided into a number of stages. At each stage of this chain an undertaking must make a choice between performing the activity itself, performing it together with (an)other undertaking(s) or outsourcing the activity entirely to (an)other undertaking(s).

62. In each case where the choice made involves cooperation on the market with another undertaking, an agreement within the meaning of Article 81(1) normally needs to be concluded. These agreements can be vertical, as is the case where the parties operate at different levels of the value chain or horizontal, as is the case where the firms operate at the same level of the value chain. Both categories of agreements may create efficiencies by allowing the undertakings in question to perform a particular task at lower cost or with higher added value for consumers. Such agreements may also contain or lead to restrictions of competition in which case the prohibition rule of Article 81(1) and the exception rule of Article 81(3) may become relevant.

63. The types of efficiencies mentioned in the following are only examples and are not intended to be exhaustive.

3.2.2.1. *Cost efficiencies*

64. Cost efficiencies flowing from agreements between undertakings can originate from a number of different sources. One very important source of cost savings is the development of new production technologies and methods. In general, it is when technological leaps are made that the greatest potential for cost savings is achieved. For instance, the introduction of the assembly line led to a very substantial reduction in the cost of producing motor vehicles.

65. Another very important source of efficiency is synergies resulting from an integration of existing assets. When the parties to an agreement combine their respective assets they may be able to attain a cost/output configuration that would not otherwise be possible. The combination of two existing technologies that have complementary strengths may reduce production costs or lead to the production of a higher quality product. For instance, it may be that the production assets of firm A generate a high output per hour but require a relatively high input of raw materials per unit of output, whereas the production assets of firm B generate lower output per hour but require a relatively lower input of raw materials per unit of output. Synergies are created if by establishing a production joint venture combining the production assets of A and B the parties can attain a high(er) level of output per hour with a low(er) input of raw materials per unit of output. Similarly, if one undertaking has optimised one part of the value chain and another undertaking has optimised another part of the value chain, the combination of their operations may lead to lower costs. Firm A may for instance have a highly automated production facility resulting in low production costs per unit whereas B has developed an efficient order processing system. The system allows production to be tailored to customer demand, ensuring timely delivery and reducing warehousing and obsolescence costs. By combining their assets A and B may be able to obtain cost reductions.

66. Cost efficiencies may also result from economies of scale, i.e. declining cost per unit of output as output increases. To give an example: investment in equipment and other assets often has to be made in indivisible blocks. If an undertaking cannot fully utilise a block, its average costs will be higher than if it could do so. For instance, the cost of operating a truck is virtually the same regardless of whether it is almost empty, half-full or full. Agreements whereby undertakings combine their logistics operations may allow them to increase the load factors and reduce the number of vehicles employed. Larger scale may also allow for better division of labour leading to lower unit costs. Firms may achieve economies of scale in respect of all parts of the value chain, including research and

development, production, distribution and marketing. Learning economies constitute a related type of efficiency. As experience is gained in using a particular production process or in performing particular tasks, productivity may increase because the process is made to run more efficiently or because the task is performed more quickly.

67. Economies of scope are another source of cost efficiency, which occur when firms achieve cost savings by producing different products on the basis of the same input. Such efficiencies may arise from the fact that it is possible to use the same components and the same facilities and personnel to produce a variety of products. Similarly, economies of scope may arise in distribution when several types of goods are distributed in the same vehicles. For instance, a producer of frozen pizzas and a producer of frozen vegetables may obtain economies of scope by jointly distributing their products. Both groups of products must be distributed in refrigerated vehicles and it is likely that there are significant overlaps in terms of customers. By combining their operations the two producers may obtain lower distribution costs per distributed unit.

68. Efficiencies in the form of cost reductions can also follow from agreements that allow for better planning of production, reducing the need to hold expensive inventory and allowing for better capacity utilisation. Efficiencies of this nature may for example stem from the use of 'just in time' purchasing, i.e. an obligation on a supplier of components to continuously supply the buyer according to its needs thereby avoiding the need for the buyer to maintain a significant stock of components which risks becoming obsolete. Cost savings may also result from agreements that allow the parties to rationalise production across their facilities.

3.2.2.2 *Qualitative efficiencies*

69. Agreements between undertakings may generate various efficiencies of a qualitative nature which are relevant to the application of Article 81(3). In a number of cases the main efficiency enhancing potential of the agreement is not cost reduction; it is quality improvements and other efficiencies of a qualitative nature. Depending on the individual case such efficiencies may therefore be of equal or greater importance than cost efficiencies.

70. Technical and technological advances form an essential and dynamic part of the economy, generating significant benefits in the form of new or improved goods and services. By cooperating undertakings may be able to create efficiencies that would not have been possible without the restrictive agreement or would have been possible only with substantial delay or at higher cost. Such efficiencies constitute an important source of economic benefits covered by the first condition of Article 81(3). Agreements capable of producing efficiencies of this nature include, in particular, research and development agreements. An example would be A and B creating a joint venture for the development and, if successful, joint production of a cell-based tyre. The puncture of one cell does not affect other cells, which means that there is no risk of collapse of the tyre in the event of a puncture. The tyre is thus safer than traditional tyres. It also means that there is no immediate need to change the tyre and thus to carry a spare. Both types of efficiencies constitute objective benefits within the meaning of the first condition of Article 81(3).

71. In the same way that the combination of complementary assets can give rise to cost savings, combinations of assets may also create synergies that create efficiencies of a qualitative nature. The combination of production assets may for instance lead to the production of higher quality products or products with novel features. This may for instance be the case for licence agreements, and agreements providing for joint production of new or improved goods or services. Licence agreements may, in particular, ensure more rapid dissemination of new technology in the Community and enable the licensee (s) to make available new products or to employ new production techniques that lead to quality improvements. Joint production agreements may, in particular, allow new or improved products or services to be introduced on the market more quickly or at lower cost. In the telecommunications sector, for example, cooperation agreements have been held to create efficiencies by making available more quickly new global services. In the banking sector cooperation agreements that made available improved facilities for making cross-border payments have also been held to create efficiencies falling within the scope of the first condition of Article 81(3).

72. Distribution agreements may also give rise to qualitative efficiencies. Specialised distributors, for example, may be able to provide services that are better tailored to customer needs or to provide quicker delivery or better quality assurance throughout the distribution chain.

3.3   Third condition of Article 81(3): indispensability of the restrictions

73. According to the third condition of Article 81(3) the restrictive agreement must not impose restrictions, which are not indispensable to the attainment of the efficiencies created by the agreement in question. This condition implies a two-fold test. First, the restrictive agreement as such must be reasonably necessary in order to achieve the efficiencies. Secondly, the individual restrictions of competition that flow from the agreement must also be reasonably necessary for the attainment of the efficiencies.

74. In the context of the third condition of Article 81(3) the decisive factor is whether or not the restrictive agreement and individual restrictions make it possible to perform the activity in question more efficiently than would likely have been the case in the absence of the agreement or the restriction concerned. The question is not whether in the absence of the restriction the agreement would not have been concluded, but whether more efficiencies are produced with the agreement or restriction than in the absence of the agreement or restriction.

75. The first test contained in the third condition of Article 81(3) requires that the efficiencies be specific to the agreement in question in the sense that there are no other economically practicable and less restrictive means of achieving the efficiencies. In making this latter assessment the market conditions and business realities facing the parties to the agreement must be taken into account. Undertakings invoking the benefit of Article 81(3) are not required to consider hypothetical or theoretical alternatives. The Commission will not second guess the business judgment of the parties. It will only intervene where it is reasonably clear that there are realistic and attainable alternatives. The parties must only explain and demonstrate why such seemingly realistic and significantly less restrictive alternatives to the agreement would be significantly less efficient.

76. It is particularly relevant to examine whether, having due regard to the circumstances of the individual case, the parties could have achieved the efficiencies by means of another less restrictive type of agreement and, if so, when they would likely be able to obtain the efficiencies. It may also be necessary to examine whether the parties could have achieved the efficiencies on their own. For instance, where the claimed efficiencies take the form of cost reductions resulting from economies of scale or scope the undertakings concerned must explain and substantiate why the same efficiencies would not be likely to be attained through internal growth and price competition. In making this assessment it is relevant to consider, *inter alia,* what is the minimum efficient scale on the market concerned. The minimum efficient scale is the level of output required to minimise average cost and exhaust economies of scale. The larger the minimum efficient scale compared to the current size of either of the parties to the agreement, the more likely it is that the efficiencies will be deemed to be specific to the agreement. In the case of agreements that produce substantial synergies through the combination of complementary assets and capabilities the very nature of the efficiencies give rise to a presumption that the agreement is necessary to attain them.

77. These principles can be illustrated by the following hypothetical example: A and B combine within a joint venture their respective production technologies to achieve higher output and lower raw material consumption. The joint venture is granted an exclusive licence to their respective production technologies. The parties transfer their existing production facilities to the joint venture. They also transfer key staff in order to ensure that existing learning economies can be exploited and further developed. It is estimated that these economies will reduce production costs by a further 5%. The output of the joint venture is sold independently by A and B. In this case the indispensability condition necessitates an assessment of whether or not the benefits could be substantially achieved by means of a licence agreement, which would be likely to be less restrictive because A and B would continue to produce independently. In the circumstances described this is unlikely to be the case since under a licence agreement the parties would not be able to benefit

in the same seamless and continued way from their respective experience in operating the two technologies, resulting in significant learning economies.

78. Once it is found that the agreement in question is necessary in order to produce the efficiencies, the indispensability of each restriction of competition flowing from the agreement must be assessed. In this context it must be assessed whether individual restrictions are reasonably necessary in order to produce the efficiencies. The parties to the agreement must substantiate their claim with regard to both the nature of the restriction and its intensity.

79. A restriction is indispensable if its absence would eliminate or significantly reduce the efficiencies that follow from the agreement or make it significantly less likely that they will materialise. The assessment of alternative solutions must take into account the actual and potential improvement in the field of competition by the elimination of a particular restriction or the application of a less restrictive alternative. The more restrictive the restraint the stricter the test under the third condition. Restrictions that are black listed in block exemption regulations or identified as hardcore restrictions in Commission guidelines and notices are unlikely to be considered indispensable.

80. The assessment of indispensability is made within the actual context in which the agreement operates and must in particular take account of the structure of the market, the economic risks related to the agreement, and the incentives facing the parties. The more uncertain the success of the product covered by the agreement, the more a restriction may be required to ensure that the efficiencies will materialise. Restrictions may also be indispensable in order to align the incentives of the parties and ensure that they concentrate their efforts on the implementation of the agreement. A restriction may for instance be necessary in order to avoid hold-up problems once a substantial sunk investment has been made by one of the parties. Once for instance a supplier has made a substantial relationship-specific investment with a view to supplying a customer with an input, the supplier is locked into the customer. In order to avoid that *ex post* the customer exploits this dependence to obtain more favourable terms, it may be necessary to impose an obligation not to purchase the component from third parties or to purchase minimum quantities of the component from the supplier.

81. In some cases a restriction may be indispensable only for a certain period of time, in which case the exception of Article 81 (3) only applies during that period. In making this assessment it is necessary to take due account of the period of time required for the parties to achieve the efficiencies justifying the application of the exception rule. In cases where the benefits cannot be achieved without considerable investment, account must, in particular, be taken of the period of time required to ensure an adequate return on such investment, see also paragraph 44 above.

82. These principles can be illustrated by the following hypothetical examples:

P produces and distributes frozen pizzas, holding 15% of the market in Member State X. Deliveries are made directly to retailers. Since most retailers have limited storage capacity, relatively frequent deliveries are required, leading to low capacity utilisation and use of relatively small vehicles. T is a wholesaler of frozen pizzas and other frozen products, delivering to most of the same customers as P. The pizza products distributed by T hold 30% of the market. T has a fleet of larger vehicles and has excess capacity. P concludes an exclusive distribution agreement with T for Member State X and undertakes to ensure that distributors in other Member States will not sell into T's territory either actively or passively. T undertakes to advertise the products, survey consumer tastes and satisfaction rates and ensure delivery to retailers of all products within 24 hours. The agreement leads to a reduction in total distribution costs of 30% as capacity is better utilised and duplication of routes is eliminated. The agreement also leads to the provision of additional services to consumers. Restrictions on passive sales are hardcore restrictions under the block exemption regulation on vertical restraints and can only be considered indispensable in exceptional circumstances. The established market position of T and the nature of the obligations imposed on it indicate this is not an exceptional case. The ban on active selling, on the other hand, is likely to be indispensable. T is likely to have less incentive to sell and advertise the P brand, if distributors in other Member States could sell actively in Member State X and thus get a free ride on the efforts of T. This is particularly so, as T also distributes competing brands and thus has the possibility of pushing more of the brands that are the least exposed to free riding.

S is a producer of carbonated soft drinks, holding 40% of the market. The nearest competitor holds 20%. S concludes supply agreements with customers accounting for 25% of demand, whereby they undertake to purchase exclusively from S for 5 years. S concludes agreements with other customers accounting for 15% of demand whereby they are granted quarterly target rebates, if their purchases exceed certain individually fixed targets. S claims that the agreements allow it to predict demand more accurately and thus to better plan production, reducing raw material storage and warehousing costs and avoiding supply shortages. Given the market position of S and the combined coverage of the restrictions, the restrictions are very unlikely to be considered indispensable. The exclusive purchasing obligation exceeds what is required to plan production and the same is true of the target rebate scheme. Predictability of demand can be achieved by less restrictive means. S could, for example, provide incentives for customers to order large quantities at a time by offering quantity rebates or by offering a rebate to customers that place firm orders in advance for delivery on specified dates.

3.4   Second condition of Article 81(3): fair share for consumers

3.4.1. *General remarks*

83. According to the second condition of Article 81(3) consumers must receive a fair share of the efficiencies generated by the restrictive agreement.

84. The concept of *'consumers'* encompasses all direct or indirect users of the products covered by the agreement, including producers that use the products as an input, wholesalers, retailers and final consumers, i.e. natural persons who are acting for purposes which can be regarded as outside their trade or profession. In other words, consumers within the meaning of Article 81(3) are the customers of the parties to the agreement and subsequent purchasers. These customers can be undertakings as in the case of buyers of industrial machinery or an input for further processing or final consumers as for instance in the case of buyers of impulse ice-cream or bicycles.

85. The concept of *'fair share'* implies that the pass-on of benefits must at least compensate consumers for any actual or likely negative impact caused to them by the restriction of competition found under Article 81(1). In line with the overall objective of Article 81 to prevent anti-competitive agreements, the net effect of the agreement must at least be neutral from the point of view of those consumers directly or likely affected by the agreement. If such consumers are worse off following the agreement, the second condition of Article 81(3) is not fulfilled. The positive effects of an agreement must be balanced against and compensate for its negative effects on consumers. When that is the case consumers are not harmed by the agreement. Moreover, society as a whole benefits where the efficiencies lead either to fewer resources being used to produce the output consumed or to the production of more valuable products and thus to a more efficient allocation of resources.

86. It is not required that consumers receive a share of each and every efficiency gain identified under the first condition. It suffices that sufficient benefits are passed on to compensate for the negative effects of the restrictive agreement. In that case consumers obtain a fair share of the overall benefits. If a restrictive agreement is likely to lead to higher prices, consumers must be fully compensated through increased quality or other benefits. If not, the second condition of Article 81(3) is not fulfilled.

87. The decisive factor is the overall impact on consumers of the products within the relevant market and not the impact on individual members of this group of consumers. In some cases a certain period of time may be required before the efficiencies materialise. Until such time the agreement may have only negative effects. The fact that pass-on to the consumer occurs with a certain time lag does not in itself exclude the application of Article 81(3). However, the greater the time lag, the greater must be the efficiencies to compensate also for the loss to consumers during the period preceding the pass-on.

88. In making this assessment it must be taken into account that the value of a gain for consumers in the future is not the same as a present gain for consumers. The value of saving 100 euro today is greater than the value of saving the same amount a year later. A gain for consumers in the future therefore does not fully compensate for a present loss to consumers of equal nominal size. In order to allow for an appropriate comparison of a present loss to consumers with a future gain to con-

sumers, the value of future gains must be discounted. The discount rate applied must reflect the rate of inflation, if any, and lost interest as an indication of the lower value of future gains.

89. In other cases the agreement may enable the parties to obtain the efficiencies earlier than would otherwise be possible. In such circumstances it is necessary to take account of the likely negative impact on consumers within the relevant market once this lead-time has lapsed. If through the restrictive agreement the parties obtain a strong position on the market, they may be able to charge a significantly higher price than would otherwise have been the case. For the second condition of Article 81(3) to be satisfied the benefit to consumers of having earlier access to the products must be equally significant. This may for instance be the case where an agreement allows two tyre manufacturers to bring to market three years earlier a new substantially safer tyre but at the same time, by increasing their market power, allows them to raise prices by 5%. In such a case it is likely that having early access to a substantially improved product outweighs the price increase.

90. The second condition of Article 81(3) incorporates a sliding scale. The greater the restriction of competition found under Article 81(1) the greater must be the efficiencies and the pass-on to consumers. This sliding scale approach implies that if the restrictive effects of an agreement are relatively limited and the efficiencies are substantial it is likely that a fair share of the cost savings will be passed on to consumers. In such cases it is therefore normally not necessary to engage in a detailed analysis of the second condition of Article 81(3), provided that the three other conditions for the application of this provision are fulfilled.

91. If, on the other hand, the restrictive effects of the agreement are substantial and the cost savings are relatively insignificant, it is very unlikely that the second condition of Article 81 (3) will be fulfilled. The impact of the restriction of competition depends on the intensity of the restriction and the degree of competition that remains following the agreement.

92. If the agreement has both substantial anti-competitive effects and substantial pro-competitive effects a careful analysis is required. In the application of the balancing test in such cases it must be taken into account that competition is an important long-term driver of efficiency and innovation. Undertakings that are not subject to effective competitive constraints - such as for instance dominant firms - have less incentive to maintain or build on the efficiencies. The more substantial the impact of the agreement on competition, the more likely it is that consumers will suffer in the long run.

93. The following two sections describe in more detail the analytical framework for assessing consumer pass-on of efficiency gains. The first section deals with cost efficiencies, whereas the section that follows covers other types of efficiencies such as new or improved products (qualitative efficiencies). The framework, which is developed in these two sections, is particularly important in cases where it is not immediately obvious that the competitive harms exceed the benefits to consumers or vice versa.

94. In the application of the principles set out below the Commission will have regard to the fact that in many cases it is difficult to accurately calculate the consumer pass-on rate and other types of consumer pass-on. Undertakings are only required to substantiate their claims by providing estimates and other data to the extent reasonably possible, taking account of the circumstances of the individual case.

3.4.2. Pass-on and balancing of cost efficiencies

95. When markets, as is normally the case, are not perfectly competitive, undertakings are able to influence the market price to a greater or lesser extent by altering their output. They may also be able to price discriminate amongst customers.

96. Cost efficiencies may in some circumstances lead to increased output and lower prices for the affected consumers. If due to cost efficiencies the undertakings in question can increase profits by expanding output, consumer pass-on may occur. In assessing the extent to which cost efficiencies are likely to be passed on to consumers and the outcome of the balancing test contained in Article 81(3) the following factors are in particular taken into account:

    (a) The characteristics and structure of the market,

    (b) The nature and magnitude of the efficiency gains,

(c) The elasticity of demand, and

(d) The magnitude of the restriction of competition.

All factors must normally be considered. Since Article 81 (3) only applies in cases where competition on the market is being appreciably restricted, see paragraph 24 above, there can be no presumption that residual competition will ensure that consumers receive a fair share of the benefits. However, the degree of competition remaining on the market and the nature of this competition influences the likelihood of pass-on.

97. The greater the degree of residual competition the more likely it is that individual undertakings will try to increase their sales by passing on cost efficiencies. If undertakings compete mainly on price and are not subject to significant capacity constraints, pass-on may occur relatively quickly. If competition is mainly on capacity and capacity adaptations occur with a certain time lag, pass-on will be slower. Pass-on is also likely to be slower when the market structure is conducive to tacit collusion. If competitors are likely to retaliate against an increase in output by one or more parties to the agreement, the incentive to increase output may be tempered, unless the competitive advantage conferred by the efficiencies is such that the undertakings concerned have an incentive to break away from the common policy adopted on the market by the members of the oligopoly. In other words, the efficiencies generated by the agreement may turn the undertakings concerned into so-called 'mavericks'.

98. The nature of the efficiency gains also plays an important role. According to economic theory undertakings maximise their profits by selling units of output until marginal revenue equals marginal cost. Marginal revenue is the change in total revenue resulting from selling an additional unit of output and marginal cost is the change in total cost resulting from producing that additional unit of output. It follows from this principle that as a general rule output and pricing decisions of a profit maximising undertaking are not determined by its fixed costs (i.e. costs that do not vary with the rate of production) but by its variable costs (i.e. costs that vary with the rate of production). After fixed costs are incurred and capacity is set, pricing and output decisions are determined by variable cost and demand conditions. Take for instance a situation in which two companies each produce two products on two production lines operating only at half their capacities. A specialisation agreement may allow the two undertakings to specialise in producing one of the two products and scrap their second production line for the other product. At the same time the specialisation may allow the companies to reduce variable input and stocking costs. Only the latter savings will have a direct effect on the pricing and output decisions of the undertakings, as they will influence the marginal costs of production. The scrapping by each undertaking of one of their production lines will not reduce their variable costs and will not have an impact on their production costs. It follows that undertakings may have a direct incentive to pass on to consumers in the form of higher output and lower prices efficiencies that reduce marginal costs, whereas they have no such direct incentive with regard to efficiencies that reduce fixed costs. Consumers are therefore more likely to receive a fair share of the cost efficiencies in the case of reductions in variable costs than they are in the case of reductions in fixed costs.

99. The fact that undertakings may have an incentive to pass on certain types of cost efficiencies does not imply that the pass-on rate will necessarily be 100%. The actual pass-on rate depends on the extent to which consumers respond to changes in price, i.e. the elasticity of demand. The greater the increase in demand caused by a decrease in price, the greater the pass-on rate. This follows from the fact that the greater the additional sales caused by a price reduction due to an increase in output the more likely it is that these sales will offset the loss of revenue caused by the lower price resulting from the increase in output. In the absence of price discrimination the lowering of prices affects all units sold by the undertaking, in which case marginal revenue is less than the price obtained for the marginal product. If the undertakings concerned are able to charge different prices to different customers, i.e. price discriminate, pass-on will normally only benefit price-sensitive consumers.

100. It must also be taken into account that efficiency gains often do not affect the whole cost structure of the undertakings concerned. In such event the impact on the price to consumers is reduced. If for example an agreement allows the parties to reduce production costs by 6%, but

production costs only make up one third of the costs on the basis of which prices are determined, the impact on the product price is 2%, assuming that the full amount is passed-on.

101. Finally, and very importantly, it is necessary to balance the two opposing forces resulting from the restriction of competition and the cost efficiencies. On the one hand, any increase in market power caused by the restrictive agreement gives the undertakings concerned the ability and incentive to raise price. On the other hand, the types of cost efficiencies that are taken into account may give the undertakings concerned an incentive to reduce price, see paragraph 98 above. The effects of these two opposing forces must be balanced against each other. It is recalled in this regard that the consumer pass-on condition incorporates a sliding scale. When the agreement causes a substantial reduction in the competitive constraint facing the parties, extraordinarily large cost efficiencies are normally required for sufficient pass-on to occur.

3.4.3 *Pass-on and balancing of other types of efficiencies*

102. Consumer pass-on can also take the form of qualitative efficiencies such as new and improved products, creating sufficient value for consumers to compensate for the anticompetitive effects of the agreement, including a price increase.

103. Any such assessment necessarily requires value judgment. It is difficult to assign precise values to dynamic efficiencies of this nature. However, the fundamental objective of the assessment remains the same, namely to ascertain the overall impact of the agreement on the consumers within the relevant market. Undertakings claiming the benefit of Article 81(3) must substantiate that consumers obtain countervailing benefits (see in this respect paragraphs 57 and 86 above).

104. The availability of new and improved products constitutes an important source of consumer welfare. As long as the increase in value stemming from such improvements exceeds any harm from a maintenance or an increase in price caused by the restrictive agreement, consumers are better off than without the agreement and the consumer pass-on requirement of Article 81 (3) is normally fulfilled. In cases where the likely effect of the agreement is to increase prices for consumers within the relevant market it must be carefully assessed whether the claimed efficiencies create real value for consumers in that market so as to compensate for the adverse effects of the restriction of competition.

3.5 Fourth condition of Article 81(3): no elimination of competition

105. According to the fourth condition of Article 81(3) the agreement must not afford the undertakings concerned the possibility of eliminating competition in respect of a substantial part of the products concerned. Ultimately the protection of rivalry and the competitive process is given priority over potentially pro-competitive efficiency gains which could result from restrictive agreements. The last condition of Article 81(3) recognises the fact that rivalry between undertakings is an essential driver of economic efficiency, including dynamic efficiencies in the shape of innovation. In other words, the ultimate aim of Article 81 is to protect the competitive process. When competition is eliminated the competitive process is brought to an end and short-term efficiency gains are outweighed by longer-term losses stemming *inter alia* from expenditures incurred by the incumbent to maintain its position (rent seeking), misallocation of resources, reduced innovation and higher prices.

106. The concept in Article 81(3) of elimination of competition in respect of a substantial part of the products concerned is an autonomous Community law concept specific to Article 81(3). However, in the application of this concept it is necessary to take account of the relationship between Article 81 and Article 82. According to settled case law the application of Article 81(3) cannot prevent the application of Article 82 of the Treaty. Moreover, since Articles 81 and 82 both pursue the aim of maintaining effective competition on the market, consistency requires that Article 81 (3) be interpreted as precluding any application of this provision to restrictive agreements that constitute an abuse of a dominant position. However, not all restrictive agreements concluded by a dominant undertaking constitute an abuse of a dominant position. This is for instance the case where a dominant undertaking is party to a non-full function joint venture, which is found to be restrictive of competition but at the same time involves a substantial integration of assets.

107. Whether competition is being eliminated within the meaning of the last condition of Article 81(3) depends on the degree of competition existing prior to the agreement and on the impact of the restrictive agreement on competition, i.e. the reduction in competition that the agreement brings about. The more competition is already weakened in the market concerned, the slighter the further reduction required for competition to be eliminated within the meaning of Article 81(3). Moreover, the greater the reduction of competition caused by the agreement, the greater the likelihood that competition in respect of a substantial part of the products concerned risks being eliminated.

108. The application of the last condition of Article 81(3) requires a realistic analysis of the various sources of competition in the market, the level of competitive constraint that they impose on the parties to the agreement and the impact of the agreement on this competitive constraint. Both actual and potential competition must be considered.

109. While market shares are relevant, the magnitude of remaining sources of actual competition cannot be assessed exclusively on the basis of market share. More extensive qualitative and quantitative analysis is normally called for. The capacity of actual competitors to compete and their incentive to do so must be examined. If, for example, competitors face capacity constraints or have relatively higher costs of production their competitive response will necessarily be limited.

110. In the assessment of the impact of the agreement on competition it is also relevant to examine its influence on the various parameters of competition. The last condition for exception under Article 81(3) is not fulfilled, if the agreement eliminates competition in one of its most important expressions. This is particularly the case when an agreement eliminates price competition or competition in respect of innovation and development of new products.

111. The actual market conduct of the parties can provide insight into the impact of the agreement. If following the conclusion of the agreement the parties have implemented and maintained substantial price increases or engaged in other conduct indicative of the existence of a considerable degree of market power, it is an indication that the parties are not subject to any real competitive pressure and that competition has been eliminated with regard to a substantial part of the products concerned.

112. Past competitive interaction may also provide an indication of the impact of the agreement on future competitive interaction. An undertaking may be able to eliminate competition within the meaning of Article 81(3) by concluding an agreement with a competitor that in the past has been a 'maverick'. Such an agreement may change the competitive incentives and capabilities of the competitor and thereby remove an important source of competition in the market.

113. In cases involving differentiated products, i.e. products that differ in the eyes of consumers, the impact of the agreement may depend on the competitive relationship between the products sold by the parties to the agreement. When undertakings offer differentiated products the competitive constraint that individual products impose on each other differs according to the degree of substitutability between them. It must therefore be considered what is the degree of substitutability between the products offered by the parties, i.e. what is the competitive constraint that they impose on each other. The more the products of the parties to the agreement are close substitutes the greater the likely restrictive effect of the agreement. In other words, the more substitutable the products the greater the likely change brought about by the agreement in terms of restriction of competition on the market and the more likely it is that competition in respect of a substantial part of the products concerned risks being eliminated.

114. While sources of actual competition are usually the most important, as they are most easily verified, sources of potential competition must also be taken into account. The assessment of potential competition requires an analysis of barriers to entry facing undertakings that are not already competing within the relevant market. Any assertions by the parties that there are low barriers to market entry must be supported by information identifying the sources of potential competition and the parties must also substantiate why these sources constitute a real competitive pressure on the parties.

115. In the assessment of entry barriers and the real possibility for new entry on a significant scale, it is relevant to examine, *inter alia,* the following:

    (i)   The regulatory framework with a view to determining its impact on new entry,

(ii)   The cost of entry including sunk costs. Sunk costs are those that cannot be recovered if the entrant subsequently exits the market. The higher the sunk costs the higher the commercial risk for potential entrants.

(iii)   The minimum efficient scale within the industry, i.e. the rate of output where average costs are minimised. If the minimum efficient scale is large compared to the size of the market, efficient entry is likely to be more costly and risky.

(iv)   The competitive strengths of potential entrants. Effective entry is particularly likely where potential entrants have access to at least as cost efficient technologies as the incumbents or other competitive advantages that allow them to compete effectively. When potential entrants are on the same or an inferior technological trajectory compared to the incumbents and possess no other significant competitive advantage entry is more risky and less effective.

(v)   The position of buyers and their ability to bring onto the market new sources of competition. It is irrelevant that certain strong buyers may be able to extract more favourable conditions from the parties to the agreement than their weaker competitors. The presence of strong buyers can only serve to counter a prima facie finding of elimination of competition if it is likely that the buyers in question will pave the way for effective new entry.

(vi)   The likely response of incumbents to attempted new entry. Incumbents may for example through past conduct have acquired a reputation of aggressive behaviour, having an impact on future entry.

(vii)   The economic outlook for the industry may be an indicator of its longer-term attractiveness. Industries that are stagnating or in decline are less attractive candidates for entry than industries characterised by growth.

(viii) Past entry on a significant scale or the absence thereof.

116. The above principles can be illustrated by the following hypothetical examples, which are not intended to establish thresholds:

Firm A is brewer, holding 70% of the relevant market, comprising the sale of beer through cafés and other on-trade premises. Over the past 5 years A has increased its market share from 60%. There are four other competitors in the market, B, C, D and E with market shares of 10%, 10%, 5% and 5%. No new entry has occurred in the recent past and price changes implemented by A have generally been followed by competitors. A concludes agreements with 20% of the on-trade premises representing 40% of sales volumes whereby the contracting parties undertake to purchase beer only from A for a period of 5 years. The agreements raise the costs and reduce the revenues of rivals, which are foreclosed from the most attractive outlets. Given the market position of A, which has been strengthened in recent years, the absence of new entry and the already weak position of competitors it is likely that competition in the market is eliminated within the meaning of Article 81(3).

Shipping firms A, B, C, and D, holding collectively more than 70% of the relevant market, conclude an agreement whereby they agree to coordinate their schedules and their tariffs. Following the implementation of the agreement prices rise between 30% and 100%. There are four other suppliers, the largest holding about 14% of the relevant market. There has been no new entry in recent years and the parties to the agreement did not lose significant market share following the price increases. The existing competitors brought no significant new capacity to the market and no new entry occurred. In light of the market position of the parties and the absence of competitive response to their joint conduct it can reasonably be concluded that the parties to the agreement are not subject to real competitive pressures and that the agreement affords them the possibility of eliminating competition within the meaning of Article 81(3).

A is a producer of electric appliances for professional users with a market share of 65% of a relevant national market. B is a competing manufacturer with 5% market share which has developed a new type of motor that is more powerful while consuming less electricity. A and B conclude an agreement whereby they establish a production joint venture for the production of the new motor. B undertakes to grant an exclusive licence to the joint venture. The joint venture combines the new technology of

B with the efficient manufacturing and quality control process of A. There is one other main competitor with 15% of the market. Another competitor with 5% market share has recently been acquired by C, a major international producer of competing electric appliances, which itself owns efficient technologies. C has thus far not been active on the market mainly due to the fact that local presence and servicing is desired by customers. Through the acquisition C gains access to the service organisation required to penetrate the market. The entry of C is likely to ensure that competition is not being eliminated.

Commission Notice on Case Referral in respect of concentrations

(OJ 2005, No. C 56/02)

(Text with EEA relevance)

1. The purpose of this Notice is to describe in a general way the rationale underlying the case referral system in Article 4(4) and (5), Article 9 and Article 22 of Council Regulation (EC) No 139/ 2004 of 20 January 2004 on the control of concentrations between undertakings (the EC Merger Regulation) (hereinafter 'the Merger Regulation'), including the recent changes made to the system, to catalogue the legal criteria that must be fulfilled in order for referrals to be possible, and to set out the factors which may be taken into consideration when referrals are decided upon. The Notice also provides practical guidance regarding the mechanics of the referral system, in particular regarding the pre-notification referral mechanism provided for in Article 4(4) and (5) of the Merger Regulation. The guidance provided in this notice applies, *mutatis mutandis,* to the referral rules contained in the EEA Agreement.

I INTRODUCTION

2. Community jurisdiction in the field of merger control is defined by the application of the turnoverrelated criteria contained in Articles 1(2) and 1(3) of the Merger Regulation. When dealing with concentrations, the Commission and Member States do not have concurrent jurisdiction. Rather, the Merger Regulation establishes a clear division of competence. Concentrations with a 'Community dimension', i.e. those above the turnover thresholds in Article 1 of the Merger Regulation, fall within the exclusive jurisdiction of the Commission; Member States are precluded from applying national competition law to such concentrations by virtue of Article 21 of the Merger Regulation. Concentrations falling below the thresholds remain within the competence of the Member States; the Commission has no jurisdiction to deal with them under the Merger Regulation.

3. Determining jurisdiction exclusively by reference to fixed turnover-related criteria provides legal certainty for merging companies. While the financial criteria generally serve as effective proxies for the category of transactions for which the Commission is the more appropriate authority, Regulation (EEC) No 4064/89 complemented this 'bright-line' jurisdictional scheme with a possibility for cases to be re-attributed by the Commission to Member States and vice versa, upon request and provided certain criteria were fulfilled.

4. When Regulation (EEC) No 4064/89 was first introduced, it was envisaged by the Council and Commission that case referrals would only be resorted to in 'exceptional circumstances' and where 'the interests in respect of competition of the Member State concerned could not be adequately protected in any other way'. There have, however, been a number of developments since the adoption of Regulation (EEC) No 4064/89. First, merger control laws have been introduced in almost all Member States. Second, the Commission has exercised its discretion to refer a number of cases to Member States pursuant to Article 9 in circumstances where it was felt that the Member State in question was in a better position to carry out the investigation than the Commission. Likewise, in a number of cases, several Member States decided to make a joint referral of a case pursuant to Article 22 in

circumstances where it was felt that the Commission was the authority in a better position to carry out the investigation. Third, there has been an increase in the number of transactions not meeting the thresholds in Article 1 of the Merger Regulation which must be filed in multiple Member State jurisdictions, a trend which is likely to continue in line with the Community's growing membership. Many of these transactions affect competition beyond the territories of individual Member States.

5. The revisions made to the referral system in the Merger Regulation are designed to facilitate the reattribution of cases between the Commission and Member States, consistent with the principle of subsidiarity, so that the more appropriate authority or authorities for carrying out a particular merger investigation should in principle deal with the case. At the same time, the revisions are intended to preserve the basic features of the Community merger control system introduced in 1989, in particular the provision of a 'one-stop-shop' for the competition scrutiny of mergers with a cross-border impact and an alternative to multiple merger control notifications within the Community. Such multiple filings often entail considerable cost for competition authorities and businesses alike.

6. The case re-attribution system now provides that a referral may also be triggered before a formal filing has been made in any Member State jurisdiction, thereby affording merging companies the possibility of ascertaining, at as early as possible a stage, where jurisdiction for scrutiny of their transaction will ultimately lie. Such pre-notification referrals have the advantage of alleviating the additional cost, notably in terms of time delay, associated with post-filing referral.

7. The revisions made to the referral system in Regulation (EC) No. 139/2004 were motivated by a desire that it should operate as a jurisdictional mechanism which is flexible but which at the same time ensures effective protection of competition and limits the scope for 'forum shopping' to the greatest extent possible. However, having regard in particular to the importance of legal certainty, it should be stressed that referrals remain a derogation from the general rules which determine jurisdiction based upon objectively determinable turnover thresholds. Moreover, the Commission and Member States retain a considerable margin of discretion in deciding whether to refer cases falling within their 'original jurisdiction', or whether to accept to deal with cases not falling within their 'original jurisdiction', pursuant to Article 4(4) and (5), Article 9(2)(a) and Article 22. To that extent, the current Notice is intended to provide no more than general guidance regarding the appropriateness of particular cases or categories of cases for referral.

II REFERRAL OF CASES

Guiding principles

8. The system of merger control established by the Merger Regulation, including the mechanism for reattributing cases between the Commission and Member States contained therein, is consistent with the principle of subsidiarity enshrined in the EC Treaty. Decisions taken with regard to the referral of cases should accordingly take due account of all aspects of the application of the principle of subsidiarity in this context, in particular which is the authority more appropriate for carrying out the investigation, the benefits inherent in a 'one-stop-shop' system, and the importance of legal certainty with regard to jurisdiction. These factors are inter-linked and the respective weight placed upon each of them will depend upon the specificities of a particular case. Above all, in considering whether or not to exercise their discretion to make or accede to a referral, the Commission and Member States should bear in mind the need to ensure effective protection of competition in all markets affected by the transaction.

More appropriate authority

9. In principle, jurisdiction should only be re-attributed to another competition authority in circumstances where the latter is the more appropriate for dealing with a merger, having regard to the specific characteristics of the case as well as the tools and expertise available to the authority. Particular regard should be had to the likely locus of any impact on competition resulting from the

merger. Regard may also be had to the implications, in terms of administrative effort, of any contemplated referral.

10. The case for re-attributing jurisdiction is likely to be more compelling where it appears that a particular transaction may have a significant impact on competition and thus may deserve careful scrutiny.

One-stop-shop

11. Decisions on the referral of cases should also have regard to the benefits inherent in a 'one-stop-shop', which is at the core of the Merger Regulation. The provision of a one-stop-shop is beneficial to competition authorities and businesses alike. The handling of a merger by a single competition authority normally increases administrative efficiency, avoiding duplication and fragmentation of enforcement effort as well as potentially incoherent treatment (regarding investigation, assessment and possible remedies) by multiple authorities. It normally also brings advantages to businesses, in particular to merging firms, by reducing the costs and burdens arising from multiple filing obligations and by eliminating the risk of conflicting decisions resulting from the concurrent assessment of the same transaction by a number of competition authorities under diverse legal regimes.

12. Fragmentation of cases through referral should therefore be avoided where possible, unless it appears that multiple authorities would be in a better position to ensure that competition in all markets affected by the transaction is effectively protected. Accordingly, while partial referrals are possible under Article 4(4) and Article 9, it would normally be appropriate for the whole of a case (or at least all connected parts thereof) to be dealt with by a single authority.

Legal certainty

13. Due account should also be taken of the importance of legal certainty regarding jurisdiction over a particular concentration, from the perspective of all concerned. Accordingly, referral should normally only be made when there is a compelling reason for departing from 'original jurisdiction' over the case in question, particularly at the post-notification stage. Similarly, if a referral has been made prior to notification, a post-notification referral in the same case should be avoided to the greatest extent possible.

14. The importance of legal certainty should also be borne in mind with regard to the legal criteria for referral, and particularly—given the tight deadlines—at the pre-notification stage. Accordingly, pre-filing referrals should in principle be confined to those cases where it is relatively straightforward to establish, from the outset, the scope of the geographic market and/or the existence of a possible competitive impact, so as to be able to promptly decide upon such requests

Case referrals: legal requirements and other factors to be considered

Pre-notification referrals

15. The system of pre-notification referrals is triggered by a reasoned submission lodged by the parties to the concentration. When contemplating such a request, the parties to the concentration are required, first, to verify whether the relevant legal requirements set out in the Merger Regulation are fulfilled, and second, whether a pre-notification referral would be consistent with the guiding principles outlined above.

Referral of cases by the Commission to Member States under Article 4(4)

Legal requirements

16. In order for a referral to be made by the Commission to one or more Member States pursuant to Articles 4(4), two legal requirements must be fulfilled
   (i)   there must be indications that the *concentration may significantly affect competition* in a market or markets;
   (ii) the market(s) in question must be within a Member State and *present all the characteristics of a distinct market.*

17. As regards the *first criterion,* the requesting parties are in essence required to demonstrate that the transaction is liable to have a potential impact on competition on a distinct market in a Member State, which may prove to be significant, thus deserving close scrutiny. Such indications may be no more than preliminary in nature, and would be without prejudice to the outcome of the investigation. While the parties are not required to demonstrate that the effect on competition is likely to be an adverse one, they should point to indicators which are generally suggestive of the existence of some competitive effects stemming from the transaction.

18. As regards the *second criterion,* the requesting parties are required to show that a geographic market in which competition is affected by the transaction in the manner just described (paragraph 17) is national, or narrower than national in scope.

Other factors to be considered

19. Other than verification of the legal requirements, in order to anticipate to the greatest extent possible the likely outcome of a referral request, merging parties contemplating a request should also consider whether referral of the case is likely to be considered appropriate. This will involve an examination of the application of the guiding principles referred to above (paragraphs 8 to 14), and in particular whether the competition authority or authorities to which they are contemplating requesting the referral of the case is the most appropriate authority for dealing with the case. To this end, consideration should be given in turn both to the likely locus of the competitive effects of the transaction and to how appropriate the national competition authority (NCA) would be for scrutinising the operation.

20. Concentrations with a Community dimension which are likely to affect competition in markets that have a national or narrower than national scope, and the effects of which are likely to be confined to, or have their main economic impact in, a single Member State, are the most appropriate candidate cases for referral to that Member State. This applies in particular to cases where the impact would occur on a distinct market which does not constitute a substantial part of the common market. To the extent that referral is made to one Member State only, the benefit of a 'one-stop-shop' is also preserved.

21. The extent to which a concentration with a Community dimension which, despite having a potentially significant impact on competition in a nation-wide market, nonetheless potentially engenders substantial cross-border effects (e.g. because the effects of the concentration in one geographic market may have significant repercussions in geographic markets in other Member States, or because it may involve potential foreclosure effects and consequent fragmentation of the common market), may be an appropriate candidate for referral will depend on the specific circumstances of the case. As both the Commission and Member States may be equally well equipped or be in an equally good position to deal with such cases, a considerable margin of discretion should be retained in deciding whether or not to refer such cases.

22. The extent to which concentrations with a Community dimension, and potentially affecting competition in a series of national or narrower than national markets in more than one Member State, may be appropriate candidates for referral to Member States will depend on factors specific to each individual case, such as the number of national markets likely to be significantly affected, the prospect of addressing any possible concerns by way of proportionate, non-conflicting remedies, and the investigative efforts that the case may require. To the extent that a case may engender competition concerns in a number of Member States, and require coordinated investigations and remedial action, this may militate in favour of the Commission retaining jurisdiction over the entirety of the case in question. On the other hand, to the extent that the case gives rise to competition concerns which, despite involving national markets in more than one Member State, do not appear to require coordinated investigation and/or remedial action, a referral may be appropriate. In a limited number of cases, the Commission has even found it appropriate to refer a concentration to more than one Member State, in view of the significant differences in competitive conditions that characterised the affected markets in the Member States concerned. While fragmentation of the treatment of a case deprives the merging parties of the benefit of a one-stop-

shop in such cases, this consideration is less pertinent at the pre-notification stage, given that the referral is triggered by a voluntary request from the merging parties.

23. Consideration should also, to the extent possible, be given to whether the NCA(s) to which referral of the case is contemplated may possess specific expertise concerning local markets, or be examining, or about to examine, another transaction in the sector concerned.

Referral of cases from Member States to the Commission under Article 4(5)
Legal requirements

24. Under Article 4(5), only two legal requirements must be met in order for the parties to the transaction to request the referral of the case to the Commission: the transaction must be a concentration within the meaning of Article 3 of the Merger Regulation, and the concentration must be *capable of being reviewed under the national competition laws for the control of mergers of at least three Member States* (see also paragraphs 65 et seq and 70 et seq).

Other factors to be considered

25. Other than verification of the legal requirements, in order to anticipate to the greatest extent possible the likely outcome of a referral request, merging parties contemplating a request should also consider whether referral of the case is likely to be considered appropriate. This will involve an examination of the application of the guiding principles referred to above, and in particular whether the Commission is the more appropriate authority for dealing with the case.

26. In this regard, Recital 16 to the Merger Regulation states that 'requests for pre-notification referrals to the Commission would be particularly pertinent in situations where the concentration would affect competition beyond the territory of one Member State.' Particular consideration should therefore be given to the likely locus of any competitive effects resulting from the transaction, and to how appropriate it would be for the Commission to scrutinise the operation.

27. It should in particular be assessed whether the case is genuinely cross-border in nature, having regard to elements such as its likely effects on competition and the investigative and enforcement powers likely to be required to address any such effects. In this regard, particular consideration should be given to whether the case is liable to have a potential impact on competition in one or more markets affected by the concentration. In any case, indications of possible competitive impact may be no more than preliminary in nature, and would be without prejudice to the outcome of the investigation. Nor would it be necessary for the parties to demonstrate that the effect on competition is likely to be an adverse one.

28. Cases where the market(s) in which there may be a potential impact on competition is/ are wider than national in geographic scope, or where some of the potentially affected markets are wider than national and the main economic impact of the concentration is connected to such markets, are the most appropriate candidate cases for referral to the Commission. In such cases, as the competitive dynamics extend over territories reaching beyond national boundaries, and may consequently require investigative efforts in several countries as well as appropriate enforcement powers, the Commission is likely to be in the best position to carry out the investigation.

29. The Commission may be more appropriately placed to treat cases (including investigation, assessment and possible remedial action) that give rise to potential competition concerns in a series of national or narrower than national markets located in a number of different Member States. The Commission is likely to be in the best position to carry out the investigation in such cases, given the desirability of ensuring consistent and efficient scrutiny across the different countries, of employing appropriate investigative powers, and of addressing any competition concerns by way of coherent remedies.

30. Similarly to what has been said above in relation to Article 4(4), the appropriateness of referring concentrations which, despite having a potentially significant impact on competition in a nationwide market, nonetheless potentially engender substantial cross-border effects, will depend on the specific circumstances of the case. As both the Commission and Member States may be in an equally good position to deal with such cases, a considerable margin of discretion should be retained in deciding whether or not to refer such cases.

31. Consideration should also, to the extent possible, be given to whether the Commission is particularly well equipped to properly scrutinise the case, in particular having regard to factors such

as specific expertise, or past experience in the sector concerned. The greater a merger's potential to affect competition beyond the territory of one Member State, the more likely it is that the Commission will be better equipped to conduct the investigation, particularly in terms of fact finding and enforcement powers.

32. Finally, the parties to the concentration might submit that, despite the apparent absence of an effect on competition, there is a compelling case for having the operation treated by the Commission, having regard in particular to factors such as the cost and time delay involved in submitting multiple Member State filings.

Post-notification referrals
Referrals from the Commission to Member States pursuant to Article 9

33. Under Article 9 there are two options for a Member State wishing to request referral of a case following its notification to the Commission: Articles 9(2) (a) and 9(2) (b) respectively.

Article 9(2)(a)
Legal requirements

34. In order for a referral to be made to a Member State or States pursuant to Article 9(2) (a), the following legal requirements must be fulfilled:
    (i)   the concentration must *threaten* to *affect significantly competition in a market;* and
    (ii) the market in question must be *within the requesting Member State, and present all the characteristics of a distinct market.*

35. As regards the *first criterion,* in essence a requesting Member State is required to demonstrate that, based on a preliminary analysis, there is a real risk that the transaction may have a significant adverse impact on competition, and thus that it deserves close scrutiny. Such preliminary indications may be in the nature of *prima facie* evidence of such a possible significant adverse impact, but would be without prejudice to the outcome of a full investigation.

36. As regards the *second criterion,* the Member State is required to show that a geographic market(s) in which competition is affected by the transaction in the manner just described (paragraph 35) is/are national, or narrower than national in scope.

Other factors to be considered

37. Other than verification of the legal requirements, other factors should also be considered in assessing whether referral of a case is likely to be considered appropriate. This will involve an examination of the application of the guiding principles referred to above, and in particular whether the competition authority or authorities requesting the referral of the case is/are in the best position to deal with the case. To this end, consideration should be given in turn both to the likely locus of the competitive effects of the transaction and to how well equipped the NCA would be to scrutinise the operation (see above at paragraphs 19–23).

Article 9(2)(b)
Legal requirements

38. In order for a referral to be made to a Member State or States pursuant to Article 9(2)(b), the following legal requirements must be fulfilled:
    (i)   the concentration must *affect competition in a market;* and
    (ii) the market in question must be *within the requesting Member State, present all the characteristics of a distinct market, and must not constitute a substantial part of the common market.*

39. As regards the *first criterion,* a requesting Member State is required to show, based on a preliminary analysis, that the concentration is liable to have an impact on competition in a market. Such preliminary indications may be in the nature of *prima facie* evidence of a possible adverse impact, but would be without prejudice to the outcome of a full investigation.

40. As to the *second criterion,* a requesting Member State is required to show not only that the market in which competition is affected by the operation in the manner just described (paragraph 38) constitutes a distinct market within a Member State, but also that the market in question does not constitute a substantial part of the common market. In this respect, based on the past practice and

caselaw, it appears that such situations are generally limited to markets with a narrow geographic scope, within a Member State.

41. If these conditions are met, the Commission has an obligation to refer the case.

Referrals from Member States to the Commission pursuant to Article 22

Legal requirement

42. In order for a referral to be made by one or more Member States to the Commission pursuant to Article 22, two legal requirements must be fulfilled:

    (i)   the concentration must *affect trade between Member States;* and

    (ii) it must *threaten to significantly affect competition within the territory of the Member State or States making the request.*

43. As to the *first criterion,* a concentration fulfils this requirement to the extent that it is liable to have some discernible influence on the pattern of trade between Member States.

44. As to the *second criterion,* as under Article 9(2)(a), a referring Member State or States is/are required in essence to demonstrate that, based on a preliminary analysis, there is a real risk that the transaction may have a significant adverse impact on competition, and thus that it deserves close scrutiny. Such preliminary indications may be in the nature of *prima facie* evidence of such a possible significant adverse impact, but would be without prejudice to the outcome of a full investigation.

Other factors to be considered

45. As post-notification referrals to the Commission may entail additional cost and time delay for the merging parties, they should normally be limited to those cases which appear to present a real risk of negative effects on competition and trade between Member States, and where it appears that these would be best addressed at the Community level. The categories of cases normally most appropriate for referral to the Commission pursuant to Article 22 are accordingly the following:

    – cases which give rise to serious competition concerns in one or more markets which are wider than national in geographic scope, or where some of the potentially affected markets are wider than national, and where the main economic impact of the concentration is connected to such markets,

    – cases which give rise to serious competition concerns in a series of national or narrower than national markets located in a number of Member States, in circumstances where coherent treatment of the case (regarding possible remedies, but also, in appropriate cases, the investigative efforts as such) is considered desirable, and where the main economic impact of the concentration is connected to such markets.

III MECHANICS OF THE REFERRAL SYSTEM

A Overview of the referral system

46. The Merger Regulation sets out the relevant legal rules for the functioning of the referral system. The rules contained in Article 4(4) and (5), Article 9 and Article 22 set out in detail the various steps required for a case to be referred from the Commission to Member States and vice versa.

47. Each of the four relevant referral provisions establishes a self-contained mechanism for the referral of a given category of concentration. The provisions can be categorised in the following way:

    (a) Pre-notification referrals:

        (i)   From the Commission to Member States (Article 4(4))

        (ii) From Member States to the Commission (Article 4(5))

    (b) Post-notification referrals:

        (i)   From the Commission to Member States (Article 9)

        (ii) From Member States to the Commission (Article 22).

48. The flowcharts in Annex I to this Notice describe in graphical form the various procedural steps to be followed in the referral mechanisms set out in Articles 4(4) and (5), Article 9 and Article 22.

Pre-notification referrals

49.   Pre-notification referrals can only be requested by the undertakings concerned. It is for the undertakings concerned to verify whether the concentration meets the criteria specified in Article 4(4) (that the concentration has a Community dimension but may significantly affect competition in a distinct market within a Member State) or Article 4(5) (that the concentration does not have a Community dimension but is capable of being reviewed under the national competition laws of at least three Member States). The undertakings concerned may then decide to request a referral to or from the Commission by submitting a reasoned request on Form RS. The request is transmitted without delay by the Commission to all Member States. The remainder of the process differs under Article 4(4) and Article 4(5).

- Under Article 4(4), the Member State or States concerned have 15 working days from the date they receive the submission to express agreement or disagreement with the request. Silence on the part of a Member State is deemed to constitute agreement. If the Member State or States concerned agree to the referral, the Commission has an additional period of approximately 10 working days (25 working days from the date the Commission received Form RS) in which it may decide to refer the case. Silence on the part of the Commission is deemed to constitute assent. If the Commission assents, the case (or one or more parts thereof) is referred to the Member States or States as requested by the undertakings concerned. If the referral is made, the Member State or States concerned apply their national law to the referred part of the case). Articles 9(6) to 9(9) apply.

- Under Article 4(5), the Member States concerned have 15 working days from the date they receive the submission to express agreement or disagreement with the request. At the end of that period, the Commission checks whether any Member State competent to examine the concentration under its national competition law has expressed disagreement. If there is no expression of disagreement by any such competent Member State, the case is deemed to acquire a Community dimension and is thus referred to the Commission which has exclusive jurisdiction over it. It is then for the parties to notify the case to the Commission, using Form CO. On the other hand, if one or more competent Member States have expressed their disagreement, the Commission informs all Member States and the undertakings concerned without delay of any such expression of disagreement and the referral process ends. It is then for the parties to comply with any applicable national notification rules.

Post-notification referrals

50.   Pursuant to Article 9(2) and Article 22(1), post-notification referrals are triggered by Member States either on their own initiative or following an invitation by the Commission pursuant to Article 9(2) and Article 22(5) respectively. The procedures differ according to whether the referral is from or to the Commission.

- Under Article 9, a Member State may request that the Commission refer to it a concentration with Community dimension, or a part thereof, which has been notified to the Commission and which threatens to significantly affect competition within a distinct market within that Member State (Article 9(2)(a)), or which affects such a distinct market not constituting a substantial part of the common market (Article 9(2)(b)). The request must be made within 15 working days from the date the Member State received a copy of Form CO. The Commission must first verify whether those legal criteria are met. It may then decide to refer the case, or a part thereof, exercising its administrative discretion. In the case of a referral request made pursuant to Article 9(2)(b), the Commission must (i.e. has no discretion) make the referral if the legal criteria are met. The decision must be taken within 35 working days from notification or, where the Commission has initiated proceedings, within 65 working days. If the referral is made, the Member State concerned applies its own national competition law, subject only to Article 9(6) and (8).

- Under Article 22, a Member State may request that the Commission examine a concentration which has no Community dimension but which affects trade between Member States and threatens to significantly affect competition within its territory. The request must be made within 15 working days from the date of national notification or, where no notification is required, the date when the concentration was 'made known' to the Member State concerned. The Commission transmits the request to all Member States. Any other Member States can decide to join the request within a period of 15 working days from the date they receive a copy of the initial request. All national time limits relating to the concentration are suspended a decision has been taken as to where it will be examined; a Member State can restart the national time limits before the expiry of the 15 working day period by informing the Commission and the merging parties that it does not wish to join the request. At the latest 10 working days following the expiry of the 15 working day period, the Commission must decide whether to accept the case from the requesting Member State (s). If the Commission accepts jurisdiction, national proceedings in the referring Member State (s) are terminated and the Commission examines the case pursuant to Article 22(4) of the Merger Regulation on behalf of the requesting State(s). Non-requesting States can continue to apply national law.

51. The following section of the Notice focuses on a number of detailed elements of the system with the aim in particular of providing further guidance to undertakings contemplating making requests at the pre-notification stage, or who may be party to transactions subject to the possibility of post-notification referral.

B Details of the referral mechanism

52. This section of this Notice provides guidance regarding certain aspects of the functioning of the referral system set out in Article 4(4) and (5), Article 9 and Article 22 of the Merger Regulation.

1. The network of competition authorities

53. Article 19(2) of the Merger Regulation provides that the Commission is to carry out the procedures set out in that Regulation in close and constant liaison with the competent authorities of the Member States (the NCAs). Cooperation and dialogue between the Commission and the NCAs, and between the NCAs themselves, is particularly important in the case of concentrations which are subject to the referral system set out in the Merger Regulation.

54. According to Recital 14 to the Merger Regulation, 'the Commission and the NCAs should form together a network of public authorities, applying their respective competences in close cooperation using efficient arrangements for information sharing and consultation with a view to ensuring that a case is dealt with by the most appropriate authority, in the light of the principle of subsidiarity, and with a view to ensuring that multiple notifications of a given concentration are avoided to the greatest extent possible'.

55. The network should ensure the efficient re-attribution of concentrations according to the principles described in section II above. This involves facilitating the smooth operation of the pre-notification referral mechanism, as well as providing, to the extent foreseeable, a system whereby potential postnotification referral requests are identified as soon as possible.

56. Pursuant to Article 4(4) and (5), the Commission must transmit reasoned requests made by the undertakings concerned 'without delay'. The Commission will endeavour to transmit such documents on the working day following that on which they are received or issued. Information within the network will be exchanged by various means, depending on the circumstances: e-mail, surface mail, courier, fax, telephone. It should be noted that for sensitive information or confidential information exchanges will be carried out by secure e-mail or by any other protected means of communication between these contact points.

57. All members of the network, including the Commission and all NCAs, their officials and other servants, and other persons working under the supervision of those authorities as well as officials and civil servants of other authorities of the Member States, will be bound by the professional secrecy obligations set out in Article 17 of the Merger Regulation. They must not disclose non-public information they have acquired through the application of the Merger Regulation, unless the natural or legal person who provided that information has consented to its disclosure.

58. Consultations and exchanges within the network is a matter between public enforcement agencies and do not alter any rights or obligations arising from Community or national law for companies. Each competition authority remains fully responsible for ensuring that due process is observed in the cases it deals with.

2. Triggering the pre-notification referral system; information to be provided by the requesting parties

59. For the referral system to work swiftly and smoothly, it is crucial that the requesting parties, provide complete and accurate information, whenever required, in a timely fashion and in the most efficient way possible. Legal requirements concerning the information to be provided and the consequences of providing incorrect, incomplete or misleading information are set out in the Merger Regulation, Regulation (EC) No 802/2004 (hereinafter 'the Merger Implementing Regulation') and Form RS.

60. Form RS states that all information submitted in a reasoned submission must be correct and complete. If parties submit incorrect or incomplete information, the Commission has the power to either adopt a decision pursuant to Article 6(1)(a) of the Merger Regulation (where failure to fulfil the conditions of Article 4(5) comes to its attention during the course of the investigation), or to revoke any decision it adopts pursuant to Article 6 or Article 8, following an Article 4(5) referral, pursuant to Article 6(3)(a) or 8(6)(a) of the Merger Regulation. Following the adoption of a decision pursuant to Article 6(1) (a) or following revocation, national competition laws would once again be applicable to the transaction. In the case of referrals under Article 4(4) made on the basis of incorrect or incomplete information, the Commission may require a notification pursuant to Article 4(1). In addition, the Commission has the power to impose fines under Article 14(1)(a) of the Merger Regulation. Finally, parties should also be aware that, if a referral is made on the basis of incorrect or incomplete information included in Form RS, the Commission and/or the Member States may consider making a post-notification referral reversing a pre-notification referral based on such incorrect or incomplete information.

61. When providing information on Form RS or generally in making a request for a pre-notification referral, it is not envisaged or necessary for the undertakings concerned to show that their concentration will lead to detrimental effects on competition. They should, however, provide as much information as possible showing clearly in what way the concentration meets the relevant legal criteria set out in Article 4(4) and (5) and why the concentration would be most appropriately dealt with by the competition authority or authorities specified in the request. The Merger Regulation does not require publication of the fact that a Form RS has been lodged, and it is not intended to do so. A non-public transaction can consequently be the subject of a pre-notification referral request.

62. Even though, according to the Merger Implementing Regulation, the Commission will accept Form RS in any official Community language, undertakings concerned providing information which is to be distributed to the network are strongly encouraged to use a language which will be understood by all addressees of the information. This will facilitate Member State treatment of such requests. Moreover, as regards requests for referral to a Member State or States, the requesting parties are strongly encouraged to include a copy of the request in the language (s) of the Member State (s) to which the referral is being requested.

63. Beyond the legal requirements specified in Form RS, the undertakings concerned should be prepared to provide additional information, if required, and to discuss the matter with the Commission and the NCAs in a frank and open manner in order to enable the Commission and the NCAs to assess whether the concentration in question should be the subject of referral.

64. Informal contacts between merging parties contemplating lodging a pre-filing referral request, on the one hand, and the Commission and/or Member State authorities, on the other, are actively encouraged, even following the submission of Form RS. The Commission is committed to providing informal, early guidance to firms wishing to use the pre-notification referrals system set out in Article 4(4) and (5) of the Merger Regulation.

3. Concentrations eligible for referral

65. Only concentrations within the meaning of Article 3 of the Merger Regulation are eligible for referral pursuant to Article 4(5) and Article 22. Only concentrations falling within the ambit of the relevant national competition laws for the control of mergers are eligible for referral pursuant to Article 4(4) and Article 9.

66. Pre-filing referral requests pursuant to Article 4(4) and (5) of the Merger Regulation must concern concentrations the plans for which are sufficiently concrete. In that regard, there must at least exist a good faith intention to merge on the part of the undertakings concerned, or, in the case of a public bid, at least a public announcement of an intention to make such a bid.

4. The concept of 'prior to notification' under Article 4(4) and (5)

67. Article 4(4) and (5) only apply at the pre-notification stage.

68. Article 4(4) specifies that the undertakings concerned may make a referral request by means of reasoned submission (Form RS), 'prior to the notification of a concentration within the meaning of paragraph 1'. This means that the request can only be made where no Form CO has been submitted pursuant to Article 4(1).

69. Likewise, Article 4(5) specifies that the request may be made 'before any notification to the competent [national] authorities'. This means that the concentration in question must not have been formally notified in any Member State jurisdiction for that provision to apply. Even one notification anywhere in the Community will preclude the undertakings concerned from triggering the mechanism of Article 4(5). In the Commission's view, no penalty should be imposed for non-notification of a transaction at the national level while a request pursuant to Article 4(5) is pending.

5. The concept of a 'concentration capable of being reviewed under national competition law' and the concept of 'competent Member State' in Article 4(5)

70. Article 4(5) enables the undertakings concerned to request a pre-notification referral of a concentration which does not have a Community dimension and which is 'capable of being reviewed under the national competition laws of at least three Member States'.

71. 'Capable of being reviewed' or reviewable should be interpreted as meaning a concentration which falls within the jurisdiction of a Member State under its national competition law for the control of mergers. There is no need for a mandatory notification requirement, i.e. it is not necessary for the concentration to be required to be notified under national law.

72. Pursuant to the third and fourth subparagraphs of Article 4(5), where at least one Member State 'competent to examine the concentration under its national competition law' has expressed its disagreement with the referral, the case must not be referred. A 'competent' Member State is one where the concentration is reviewable and which therefore has the power to examine the concentration under its national competition law.

73. All Member States, and not only those 'competent' to review the case, receive a copy of the Form RS. However, only Member States 'competent' to review the case are counted for the purposes of the third and fourth subparagraphs of Article 4(5). Pursuant to the third subparagraph of Article 4(5), 'competent' Member States have 15 working days from the date they receive the Form RS to express their agreement or disagreement with the referral. If they all agree, the case will be deemed to acquire a Community dimension pursuant to the fifth subparagraph of Article 4(5). According to the fourth subparagraph of Article 4(5), by contrast, if even only one 'competent' Member State disagrees, no referral will take place from any Member State.

74. Given the above mechanism, it is crucial to the smooth operation of Article 4(5) that *all* Member States where the case is reviewable under national competition law, and which are hence 'competent' to examine the case under national competition law, are identified correctly. Form RS therefore requires the undertakings concerned to provide sufficient information to enable each and every Member State to identify whether or not it is competent to review the concentration pursuant to its own national competition law.

75. In situations where Form RS has been filled in correctly, no complications should arise. The undertakings concerned will have identified correctly all Member States which are competent to

review the case. In situations, however, where the undertakings concerned have not filled in Form RS correctly, or where there is a genuine disagreement as to which Member States are 'competent' to review the case, complications may arise.

– Within the period of 15 working days provided for in the third subparagraph of Article 4(5), a Member State which is not identified in Form RS as being competent may inform the Commission that it is competent and may, like any other competent Member State, express its agreement or disagreement with the referral.

– Likewise, within the period of 15 working days provided for in the third subparagraph of Article 4(5), a Member State which has been identified as competent in Form RS may inform the Commission that it is not 'competent'. That Member State would then be disregarded for the purposes of Article 4(5).

76. Once the period of 15 working days has expired without any disagreement having been expressed, the referral, will be considered valid. This ensures the validity of Commission decisions taken under Articles 6 or 8 of the Merger Regulation following an Article 4(5) referral.

77. This is not to say, however, that undertakings concerned can abuse the system by negligently or intentionally providing incorrect information, including as regards the reviewability of the concentration in the Member States, on Form RS. As noted at paragraph 60 above, the Commission may take measures to rectify the situation and to deter such violations. The undertakings concerned should also be aware that, in such circumstances, where a referral has been made on the basis of incorrect or incomplete information, a Member State which believes it was competent to deal with the case but did not have the opportunity to veto the referral due to incorrect information being supplied, may request a post-notification referral.

6. Notification and publication of decisions

78. According to the fourth subparagraph of Article 4(4), the fourth subparagraph of Article 4(5), Article 9(1) and the second subparagraph of Article 22(3), the Commission is obliged to inform the undertakings or persons concerned and all Member States of any decision taken pursuant to those provisions as to the referral of a concentration.

79. The information will be provided by means of a letter addressed to the undertakings concerned (or for decisions adopted pursuant to Article 9(1) or Article 22(3), a letter addressed to the Member State concerned). All Member States will receive a copy thereof.

80. There is no requirement that such decisions be published in the *Official Journal of the European Union*. The Commission will, however, give adequate publicity to such decisions on DG Competition's website, subject to confidentiality requirements.

7. Article 9(6)

81. Article 9(6) provides that, when the Commission refers a notified concentration to a Member State in accordance with Article 4(4) or Article 9(3), the NCA concerned must deal with the case 'without undue delay'. Accordingly, the competent authority concerned should deal as expeditiously as possible with the case under national law.

82. In addition, Article 9(6) provides that the competent national authority must, within 45 working days after the Commission's referral or following receipt of a notification at the national level if requested inform the undertakings concerned of the result of the 'preliminary competition assessment' and what 'further action', if any, it proposes to take. Accordingly, within 45 working days after the referral or notification, as appropriate, the merging parties should be provided with sufficient information to enable them to understand the nature of any preliminary competition concerns the authority may have and be informed of the likely extent and duration of the investigation. The Member State concerned may only exceptionally suspend this time limit, where necessary information has not been provided to it by the undertakings concerned as required under its national competition law.

IV FINAL REMARKS

83. This Notice will be the subject of periodic review, in particular following any revision of the referral provisions in the Merger Regulation. In that regard, it should be noted that, according to Article 4(6) of the Merger Regulation, the Commission must report to the Council on the operation of the pre-notification referral provisions in Article 4(4) and (5), by 1 July 2009.

84. This Notice is without prejudice to any interpretation of the applicable Treaty and regulatory provisions by the Court of First Instance and the Court of Justice of the European Communities.

Annexes

Referral Charts

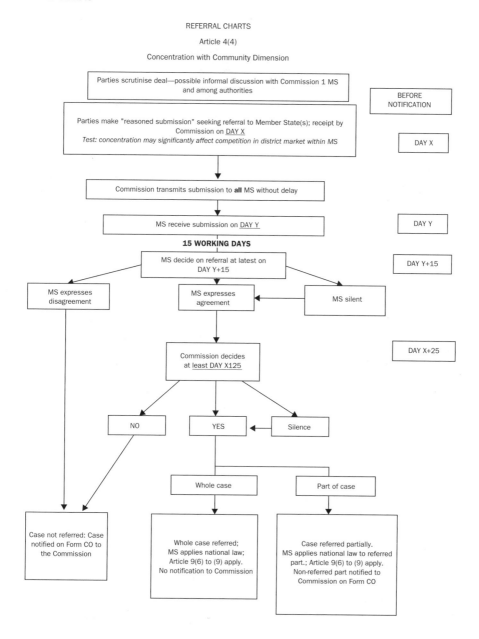

REFERRAL CHARTS

Article 4(4)

Concentration with Community Dimension

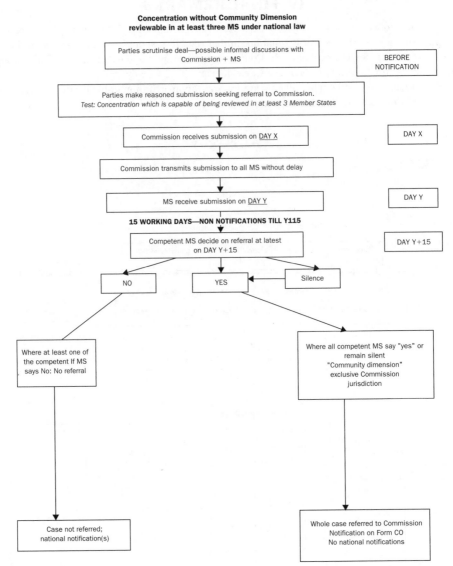

Article 4(5)

**Concentration without Community Dimension
reviewable in at least three MS under national law**

| Parties scrutinise deal—possible informal discussions with Commission + MS | BEFORE NOTIFICATION |

Parties make reasoned submission seeking referral to Commission.
Test: Concentration which is capable of being reviewed in at least 3 Member States

| Commission receives submission on <u>DAY X</u> | DAY X |

Commission transmits submission to all MS without delay

| MS receive submission on <u>DAY Y</u> | DAY Y |

15 WORKING DAYS—NON NOTIFICATIONS TILL Y115

| Competent MS decide on referral at latest on DAY Y+15 | DAY Y+15 |

NO   YES   Silence

Where at least one of the competent If MS says No: No referral

Where all competent MS say "yes" or remain silent
"Community dimension"
exclusive Commission jurisdiction

Case not referred;
national notification(s)

Whole case referred to Commission
Notification on Form CO
No national notifications

Article 9

Concentration with Community Dimension

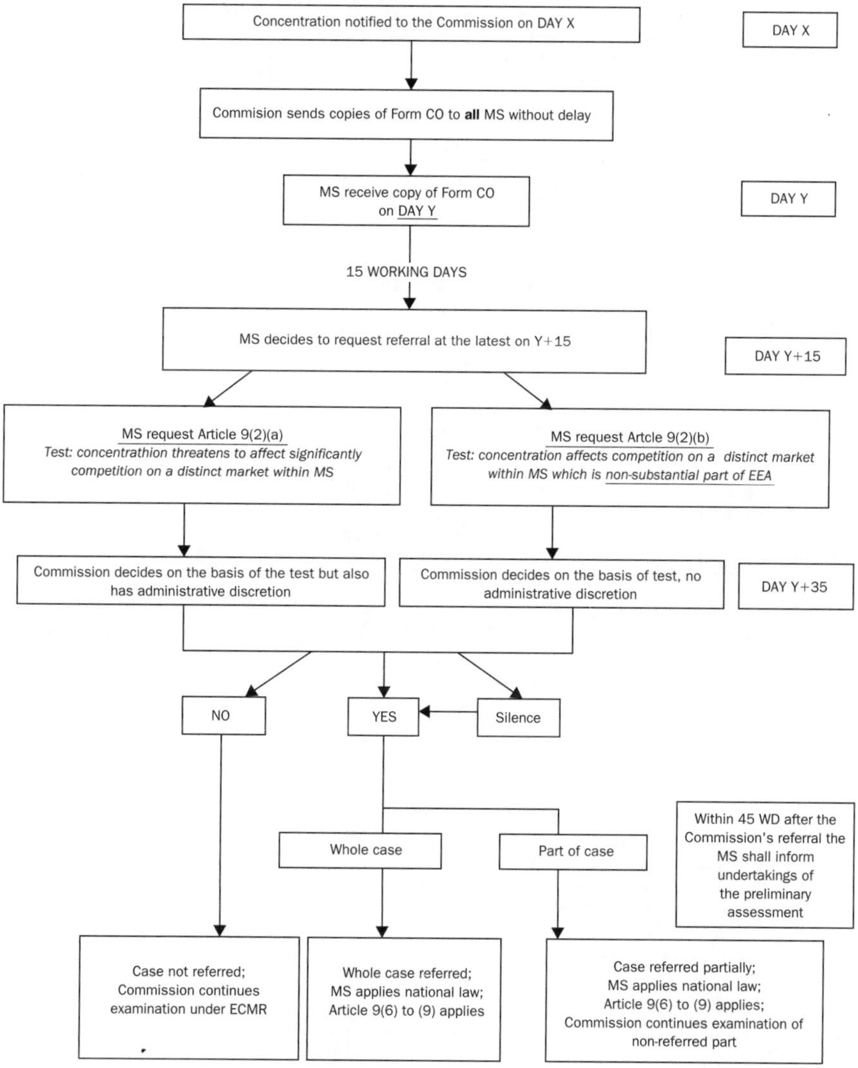

Article 22

Concentration without Community dimension

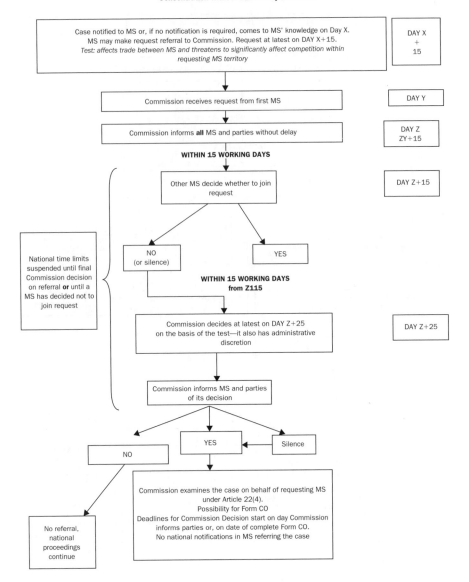

Commission Notice on restrictions directly related and necessary to concentrations

(OJ 2005, No. C 56/03)

(Text with EEA relevance)

I INTRODUCTION

1. Council Regulation (EC) No 139/2004 of 20 January 2004 on the control of concentrations between undertakings (the EC Merger Regulation) provides in Article 6(1) (b), second subparagraph, in Article 8(1), second subparagraph and in Article 8(2), third subparagraph that a decision declaring a concentration compatible with the common market *'shall be deemed* to *cover restrictions directly related and necessary to the implementation of the concentration'*.

2. The amendment of the rules governing the assessment of restrictions directly related and necessary to the implementation of the concentration (hereinafter also referred to as 'ancillary restraints') introduces a principle of self-assessment of such restrictions. This reflects the intention of the legislature not to oblige the Commission to assess and individually address ancillary restraints. The treatment of ancillary restraints under the EC Merger Regulation is further explained in recital 21 in the preamble to the EC Merger Regulation, which states that *'Commission decisions declaring concentrations compatible with the common market in application of this Regulation should automatically cover such restrictions, without the Commission having to assess such restrictions in individual cases'*. While the Recital envisages that the Commission will exercise a residual function with regard to specific novel or unresolved issues giving rise to genuine uncertainty, it is in all other scenarios the task of the undertakings concerned to assess for themselves whether and to what extent their agreements can be regarded as ancillary to a transaction. Disputes as to whether restrictions are directly related and necessary to the implementation of the concentration, and thus automatically covered by the Commission's clearance decision, may be resolved before national courts.

3. The Commission's residual function is addressed in recital 21 of the Merger Regulation, where it is stated that the Commission should, at the request of the undertakings concerned, expressly assess the ancillary character of restrictions if a case presents *'novel and unresolved questions giving rise to genuine uncertainty'*. The Recital subsequently defines a 'novel or unresolved question giving rise to genuine uncertainty' as a question that is 'not *covered by the relevant Commission notice in force or a published Commission decision.'*

4. In order to provide legal certainty to the undertakings concerned, this Notice provides guidance on the interpretation of the notion of ancillary restraints. The guidance given in the following sections reflects the essence of the Commission's practice, and sets out principles for assessing whether and to what extent the most common types of agreements are deemed to be ancillary restraints.

5. However, cases involving exceptional circumstances that are not covered by this Notice may justify departing from these principles. Parties may find further guidance in published Commission decisions as to whether their agreements can be regarded as ancillary restraints or not. To the extent that cases involving exceptional circumstances have been previously addressed by the Commission in its published decisions, they do not constitute 'novel or unresolved questions' within the meaning of recital 21) of the Merger Regulation.

6. Accordingly, a case presents a 'novel and unresolved question giving rise to genuine uncertainty' if those restrictions are not covered by this Notice and have not been previously addressed by the Commission in its published decisions. As envisaged in recital 21 of the Merger Regulation, the Commission will, at the request of the parties, expressly assess such restrictions in these cases. Subject to confidentiality requirements, the Commission will provide adequate publicity as regards such assessments that further develop the principles set out in this Notice.

7. To the extent that restrictions are directly related and necessary to the implementation of the concentration, Article 21(1) of the Merger Regulation provides that this Regulation alone applies, to the exclusion of Council Regulations (EC) No 1/2003, (EEC) No 1017/68 and (EEC) No 4056/86.

By contrast, for restrictions that cannot be regarded as directly related and necessary to the implementation of the concentration, Articles 81 and 82 of the EC Treaty remain potentially applicable. However, the mere fact that an agreement or arrangement is not deemed to be ancillary to a concentration is not, as such, prejudicial to the legal status thereof. Such agreements or arrangements are to be assessed in accordance with Article 81 and 82 of the EC Treaty and the related regulatory texts and notices. They may also be subject to any applicable national competition rules. Hence, agreements which contain a restriction on competition, but are not considered directly related and necessary to the implementation of the concentration pursuant to this notice, may nevertheless be covered by those provisions.

8. The Commission's interpretation of Article 6(1)(b), second subparagraph, and Article 8 (1), second subparagraph, and (2), third subparagraph, of the Merger Regulation is without prejudice to the interpretation which maybe given by the Court of Justice or the Court of First Instance of the European Communities.

9. This Notice replaces the Commission's previous Notice regarding restrictions directly related and necessary to concentrations.

II GENERAL PRINCIPLES

10. A concentration consists of contractual arrangements and agreements establishing control within the meaning of Article 3(2) of the Merger Regulation. All agreements which carry out the main object of the concentration, such as those relating to the sale of shares or assets of an undertaking, are integral parts of the concentration. In addition to these arrangements and agreements, the parties to the concentration may enter into other agreements which do not form an integral part of the concentration but can restrict the parties' freedom of action in the market. If such agreements contain ancillary restraints, these are automatically covered by the decision declaring the concentration compatible with the Common Market.

11. The criteria of direct relation and necessity are objective in nature. Restrictions are not directly related and necessary to the implementation of a concentration simply because the parties regard them as such.

12. For restrictions to be considered 'directly related to the implementation of the concentration', they must be closely linked to the concentration itself. It is not sufficient that an agreement has been entered into in the same context or at the same time as the concentration. Restrictions which are directly related to the concentration are economically related to the main transaction and intended to allow a smooth transition to the changed company structure after the concentration.

13. Agreements must be 'necessary to the implementation of the concentration', which means that, in the absence of those agreements, the concentration could not be implemented or could only be implemented under considerably more uncertain conditions, at substantially higher cost, over an appreciably longer period or with considerably greater difficulty. Agreements necessary to the implementation of a concentration are typically aimed at protecting the value transferred, maintaining the continuity of supply after the break-up of a former economic entity, or enabling the start-up of a new entity. In determining whether a restriction is necessary, it is appropriate not only to take account of its nature, but also to ensure that its duration, subject matter and geographical field of application does not exceed what the implementation of the concentration reasonably requires. If equally effective alternatives are available for attaining the legitimate aim pursued, the undertakings must choose the one which is objectively the least restrictive of competition.

14. For concentrations which are carried out in stages, the contractual arrangements relating to the stages before the establishment of control within the meaning of Article 3(1) and (2) of the Merger Regulation cannot normally be considered directly related and necessary to the implementation of the concentration. However, an agreement to abstain from material changes in the target's business until completion is considered directly related and necessary to the implementation of the joint bid. The same applies, in the context of a joint bid, to an agreement by the joint purchasers of an

undertaking to abstain from making separate competing offers for the same undertaking, or otherwise acquiring control.

15. Agreements which serve to facilitate the joint acquisition of control are to be considered directly related and necessary to the implementation of the concentration. This will apply to arrangements between the parties for the joint acquisition of control aimed at implementing the division of assets in order to divide the production facilities or distribution networks among themselves, together with the existing trademarks of the undertaking acquired jointly.

16. To the extent that such a division involves the break-up of a pre-existing economic entity, arrangements that make the break-up possible under reasonable conditions are to be considered directly related and necessary to the implementation of the concentration, under the principles set out below.

III PRINCIPLES APPLICABLE TO COMMONLY ENCOUNTERED RESTRICTIONS IN CASES OF ACQUISITION OF AN UNDERTAKING

17. Restrictions agreed between the parties in the context of a transfer of an undertaking may be to the benefit of the purchaser or of the vendor. In general terms, the need for the purchaser to benefit from certain protection is more compelling than the corresponding need for the vendor. It is the purchaser who needs to be assured that she/he will be able to acquire the full value of the acquired business. Thus, as a general rule, restrictions which benefit the vendor are either not directly related and necessary to the implementation of the concentration at all, or their scope and/or duration need to be more limited than that of clauses which benefit the purchaser.

A Non-competition clauses

18. Non-competition obligations which are imposed on the vendor in the context of the transfer of an undertaking or of part of it can be directly related and necessary to the implementation of the concentration. In order to obtain the full value of the assets transferred, the purchaser must be able to benefit from some protection against competition from the vendor in order to gain the loyalty of customers and to assimilate and exploit the know-how. Such non-competition clauses guarantee the transfer to the purchaser of the full value of the assets transferred, which in general include both physical assets and intangible assets, such as the goodwill accumulated or the know-how developed by the vendor. These are not only directly related to the concentration but are also necessary to its implementation because, without them, there would be reasonable grounds to expect that the sale of the undertaking or of part of it could not be accomplished.

19. However, such non-competition clauses are only justified by the legitimate objective of implementing the concentration when their duration, their geographical field of application, their subject matter and the persons subject to them do not exceed what is reasonably necessary to achieve that end.

20. Non-competition clauses are justified for periods of up to three years, when the transfer of the undertaking includes the transfer of customer loyalty in the form of both goodwill and know-how. When only goodwill is included, they are justified for periods of up to two years.

21. By contrast, non-competition clauses cannot be considered necessary when the transfer is in fact limited to physical assets (such as land, buildings or machinery) or to exclusive industrial and commercial property rights (the holders of which could immediately take action against infringements by the transferor of such rights).

22. The geographical scope of a non-competition clause must be limited to the area in which the vendor has offered the relevant products or services before the transfer, since the purchaser does not need to be protected against competition from the vendor in territories not previously penetrated by the vendor. That geographical scope can be extended to territories which the vendor was planning to enter at the time of the transaction, provided that he had already invested in preparing this move.

23. Similarly, non-competition clauses must remain limited to products (including improved versions or updates of products as well as successor models) and services forming the economic activity of the undertaking transferred. This can include products and services at an advanced stage of development at the time of the transaction, or products which are fully developed but not yet marketed. Protection against competition from the vendor in product or service markets in which the transferred undertaking was not active before the transfer is not considered necessary.

24. The vendor may bind herself/himself, her/his subsidiaries and commercial agents. However, an obligation to impose similar restrictions on others would not be regarded as directly related and necessary to the implementation of the concentration. This applies, in particular, to clauses which would restrict the freedom of resellers or users to import or export.

25. Clauses which limit the vendor's right to purchase or hold shares in a company competing with the business transferred shall be considered directly related and necessary to the implementation of the concentration under the same conditions as outlined above for non-competition clauses, unless they prevent the vendor from purchasing or holding shares purely for financial investment purposes, without granting him/her, directly or indirectly, management functions or any material influence in the competing company.

26. Non-solicitation and confidentiality clauses have a comparable effect and are therefore evaluated in a similar way to non-competition clauses.

B   Licence agreements

27. The transfer of an undertaking or of part of it can include the transfer to the purchaser, with a view to the full exploitation of the assets transferred, of intellectual property rights or know-how. However, the vendor may remain the owner of the rights in order to exploit them for activities other than those transferred. In these cases, the usual means for ensuring that the purchaser will have the full use of the assets transferred is to conclude licensing agreements in his/her favour. Likewise, where the vendor has transferred intellectual property rights with the business, she/he may still want to continue using some or all of these rights for activities other than those transferred; in such a case the purchaser will grant a licence to the vendor.

28. Licences of patents, of similar rights, or of know-how, can be considered necessary to the implementation of the concentration. They may equally be considered an integral part of the concentration and, in any event, need not be limited in time. These licences can be simple or exclusive and may be limited to certain fields of use, to the extent that they correspond to the activities of the undertaking transferred.

29. However, territorial limitations on manufacture reflecting the territory of the transferred activity are not necessary to the implementation of the operation. As regards licences granted by the seller of a business to the buyer, the seller can be made subject to territorial restrictions in the licence agreement under the same conditions as laid down for non-competition clauses in the context of the sale of a business.

30. Restrictions in licence agreements going beyond the above provisions, such as those which protect the licensor rather than the licensee, are not necessary to the implementation of the concentration.

31. Similarly, in the case of licences of trademarks, business names, design rights, copyrights or similar rights, there may be situations in which the vendor wishes to remain the owner of such rights in relation to activities retained, but the purchaser needs those rights in order to market the goods or services produced by the undertaking or part of the undertaking transferred. Here, the same considerations as above apply.

C   Purchase and supply obligations

32. In many cases, the transfer of an undertaking or of part of it can entail the disruption of traditional lines of purchase and supply which have existed as a result of the previous integration of activities within the economic unity of the vendor. In order to enable the break-up of the economic unity of the vendor and the partial transfer of the assets to the purchaser under reasonable conditions, it is often necessary to maintain, for a transitional period, the existing or similar links between the

vendor and the purchaser. This objective is normally attained by purchase and supply obligations for the vendor and/or the purchaser of the undertaking or of part of it. Taking into account the particular situation resulting from the break-up of the economic unity of the vendor, such obligations can be recognised as directly related and necessary to the implementation of the concentration. They may be in favour of the vendor as well as the purchaser, depending on the particular circumstances of the case.

33. The aim of such obligations may be to ensure the continuity of supply to either of the parties of products necessary for carrying out the activities retained by the vendor or taken over by the purchaser. However, the duration of purchase and supply obligations must be limited to a period necessary for the replacement of the relationship of dependency by autonomy in the market. Thus, purchase or supply obligations aimed at guaranteeing the quantities previously supplied can be justified for a transitional period of up to five years.

34. Both supply and purchase obligations providing for fixed quantities, possibly with a variation clause, are recognised as directly related and necessary to the implementation of the concentration. However, obligations providing for unlimited quantities, exclusivity or conferring preferred-supplier or preferred-purchaser status, are not necessary to the implementation of the concentration.

35. Service and distribution agreements are equivalent in their effect to supply arrangements; consequently the same considerations as above shall apply.

IV PRINCIPLES APPLICABLE TO COMMONLY ENCOUNTERED RESTRICTIONS IN CASES OF JOINT VENTURES WITHIN THE MEANING OF ARTICLE 3(4) OF THE MERGER REGULATION

A Non-competition obligations

36. A non-competition obligation between the parent undertakings and a joint venture may be considered directly related and necessary to the implementation of the concentration where such obligations correspond to the products, services and territories covered by the joint venture agreement or its bylaws. Such non-competition clauses reflect, *inter alia,* the need to ensure good faith during negotiations; they may also reflect the need to fully utilise the joint venture's assets or to enable the joint venture to assimilate know-how and goodwill provided by its parents; or the need to protect the parents' interests in the joint venture against competitive acts facilitated, *inter alia,* by the parents' privileged access to the know-how and goodwill transferred to or developed by the joint venture. Such non-competition obligations between the parent undertakings and a joint venture can be regarded as directly related and necessary to the implementation of the concentration for the lifetime of the joint venture.

37. The geographical scope of a non-competition clause must be limited to the area in which the parents offered the relevant products or services before establishing the joint venture. That geographical scope can be extended to territories which the parent companies were planning to enter at the time of the transaction, provided that they had already invested in preparing this move.

38. Similarly, non-competition clauses must be limited to products and services constituting the economic activity of the joint venture. This may include products and services at an advanced stage of development at the time of the transaction, as well as products and services which are fully developed but not yet marketed.

39. If the joint venture is set up to enter a new market, reference will be made to the products, services and territories in which it is to operate under the joint venture agreement or by-laws. However, the presumption is that one parent's interest in the joint venture does not need to be protected against competition from the other parent in markets other than those in which the joint venture will be active from the outset.

40. Additionally, non-competition obligations between non-controlling parents and a joint venture are not directly related and necessary to the implementation of the concentration.

41. The same principles as for non-competition clauses apply to non-solicitation and confidentiality clauses.

B Licence agreements

42. A licence granted by the parent undertakings to the joint venture may be considered directly related and necessary to the implementation of the concentration. This applies regardless of whether or not the licence is an exclusive one and whether or not it is limited in time. The licence may be restricted to a particular field of use which corresponds to the activities of the joint venture.

43. Licences granted by the joint venture to one of its parents, or cross-licence agreements, can be regarded as directly related and necessary to the implementation of the concentration under the same conditions as in the case of the acquisition of an undertaking. Licence agreements between the parents are not considered directly related and necessary to the implementation of a joint venture.

C Purchase and supply obligations

44. If the parent undertakings remain present in a market upstream or downstream of that of the joint venture, any purchase and supply agreements, including service and distribution agreements are subject to the principles applicable in the case of the transfer of an undertaking.

Commission Notice on a simplified procedure for treatment of certain concentrations under Council Regulation (EC) No 139/2004

(OJ 2005, No. C 56/04)

(Text with EEA relevance)

I INTRODUCTION

1. This Notice sets out a simplified procedure under which the Commission intends to treat certain concentrations pursuant to Council Regulation (EC) No 139/2004 of 20 January 2004, on the control of concentrations between undertakings (the EC Merger Regulation) on the basis that they do not raise competition concerns. This Notice replaces the Notice on a simplified procedure for treatment of certain concentrations under Council Regulation (EEC) No 4064/89. The Commission's experience gained in applying Council Regulation (EEC) No 4064/89 of 21 December 1989 on the control of concentrations between undertakings has shown that certain categories of notified concentrations are normally cleared without having raised any substantive doubts, provided that there were no special circumstances.

2. The purpose of this Notice is to set out the conditions under which the Commission usually adopts a short-form decision declaring a concentration compatible with the common market pursuant to the simplified procedure and to provide guidance in respect of the procedure itself. When all necessary conditions set forth at point 5 of this Notice are met and provided there are no special circumstances, the Commission adopts a short-form clearance decision within 25 working days from the date of notification, pursuant to Article 6(1) (b) of the EC Merger Regulation.

3. However, if the safeguards or exclusions set forth at points 6 to 11 of this Notice are applicable, the Commission may launch an investigation and/or adopt a full decision under the EC Merger Regulation.

4. By following the procedure outlined in the following sections, the Commission aims to make Community merger control more focused and effective.

II CATEGORIES OF CONCENTRATIONS SUITABLE FOR TREATMENT UNDER THE SIMPLIFIED PROCEDURE

Eligible concentrations

5. The Commission will apply the simplified procedure to the following categories of concentrations:

(a) two or more undertakings acquire joint control of a joint venture, provided that the joint venture has no, or negligible, actual or foreseen activities within the territory of the European Economic Area (EEA). Such cases occur where:

(i) the turnover of the joint venture and/or the turnover of the contributed activities is less than EUR 100 million in the EEA territory; and

(ii) the total value of assets transferred to the joint venture is less than EUR 100 million in the EEA territory;

(b) two or more undertakings merge, or one or more undertakings acquire sole or joint control of another undertaking, provided that none of the parties to the concentration are engaged in business activities in the same product and geographical market, or in a product market which is upstream or downstream of a product market in which any other party to the concentration is engaged;

(c) two or more undertakings merge, or one or more undertakings acquire sole or joint control of another undertaking and:

(i) two or more of the parties to the concentration are engaged in business activities in the same product and geographical market (horizontal relationships) provided that their combined market share is less than 15%; or

(ii) one or more of the parties to the concentration are engaged in business activities in a product market which is upstream or downstream of a product market in which any other party to the concentration is engaged (vertical relationships), provided that none of their individual or combined market shares is at either level 25% or more;

(d) a party is to acquire sole control of an undertaking over which it already has joint control.

Safeguards and exclusions

6. In assessing whether a concentration falls into one of the categories referred to in point 5, the Commission will ensure that all relevant circumstances are established with sufficient clarity. Given that market definitions are likely to be a key element in this assessment, the parties should provide information on all plausible alternative market definitions during the pre-notification phase (see point 15). Notifying parties are responsible for describing all alternative relevant product and geographic markets on which the notified concentration could have an impact and for providing data and information relating to the definition of such markets. The Commission retains the discretion to take the ultimate decision on market definition, basing its decision on an analysis of the facts of the case. Where it is difficult to define the relevant markets or to determine the parties' market shares, the Commission will not apply the simplified procedure. In addition, to the extent that concentrations involve novel legal issues of a general interest, the Commission would normally abstain from adopting short-form decisions, and would normally revert to a normal first phase merger procedure.

7. While it can normally be assumed that concentrations falling into the categories referred to in point 5 will not raise serious doubts as to their compatibility with the common market, there may nonetheless be certain situations, which exceptionally require a closer investigation and/or a full decision. In such cases, the Commission may revert to a normal first phase merger procedure.

8. The following are indicative examples of types of cases which may be excluded from the simplified procedure. Certain types of concentrations may increase the parties' market power, for instance by combining technological, financial or other resources, even if the parties to the concentration do not operate in the same market. Concentrations where at least two parties to the concentration are present in closely related neighbouring markets may also be unsuitable for the simplified

procedure, in particular, where one or more of the parties to the concentration holds individually a market share of 25% or more in any product market in which there is no horizontal or vertical relationship between the parties but which is a neighbouring market to a market where another party is active. In other cases, it may not be possible to determine the parties' precise market shares. This is often the case when the parties operate in new or little developed markets. Concentrations in markets with high entry barriers, with a high degree of concentration or other known competition problems may also be unsuitable.

9. The Commission's experience to date has shown that a change from joint to sole control may exceptionally require closer investigation and/or a full decision. A particular competition concern could arise in circumstances where the former joint venture is integrated into the group or network of its remaining single controlling shareholder, whereby the disciplining constraints exercised by the potentially diverging incentives of the different controlling shareholders are removed and its strategic market position could be strengthened. For example, in a scenario in which undertaking A and undertaking B jointly control a joint venture C, a concentration pursuant to which A acquires sole control of C may give rise to competition concerns in circumstances in which C is a direct competitor of A and where C and A will hold a substantial combined market position and where this removes a degree of independence previously held by C. In cases where such scenarios require a closer analysis, the Commission may revert to a normal first phase merger procedure.

10. The Commission may also revert to a normal first phase merger procedure where neither the Commission nor the competent authorities of Member States have reviewed the prior acquisition of joint control of the joint venture in question.

11. Furthermore, the Commission may revert to a normal first phase merger procedure where an issue of coordination as referred to in Article 2(4) of the EC Merger Regulation arises.

12. If a Member State expresses substantiated concerns about the notified concentration within 15 working days of receipt of the copy of the notification, or if a third party expresses substantiated concerns within the time-limit laid down for such comments, the Commission will adopt a full decision. The time-limits set out in Article 10(1) of the EC Merger Regulation apply.

Referral requests

13. The simplified procedure will not be applied if a Member State requests the referral of a notified concentration pursuant to Article 9 of the EC Merger Regulation or if the Commission accepts a request from one or more Member States for referral of a notified concentration pursuant to Article 22 of the EC Merger Regulation.

Pre-notification referrals at the request of the notifying parties

14. Subject to the safeguards and exclusions set out in this Notice, the Commission may apply the simplified procedure to concentrations where:

   (i)   following a reasoned submission pursuant to Article 4(4) of the EC Merger Regulation, the Commission decides not to refer the case to a Member State; or

   (ii) following a reasoned submission pursuant to Article 4(5) of the EC Merger Regulation the case is referred to the Commission.

III PROCEDURAL PROVISIONS

Pre-notification contacts

15. The Commission has found pre-notification contacts between notifying parties and the Commission beneficial even in seemingly unproblematic cases. The Commission's experience of the simplified procedure has shown that candidate cases for the simplified procedure may raise complex issues for instance, of market definition (see point 6) which should preferably be resolved prior to notification. Such contacts allow the Commission and the notifying parties to determine the precise amount of information to be provided in a notification. Pre-notification contacts should be initiated at least two weeks prior to the expected date of notification. Notifying parties are therefore advised to engage in pre-notification contacts, particularly where they request the Commission to waive full-form

notification in accordance with Article 3(1) of Commission Regulation (EC) No 802/2004 of 7 April 2004 implementing Council Regulation (EC) No 139/ 2004 on the control of concentrations between undertakings on the grounds that the operation to be notified will not raise competition concerns.

Publication of the fact of notification

16. The information to be published in the *Official Journal of the European Union* upon receipt of a notification will include the names of the parties to the concentration, their country of origin, the nature of the concentration and the economic sectors involved, as well as an indication that, on the basis of the information provided by the notifying party, the concentration may qualify for a simplified procedure. Interested parties will then have the opportunity to submit observations, in particular on circumstances which might require an investigation.

Short-form decision

17. If the Commission is satisfied that the concentration fulfils the criteria for the simplified procedure (see point 5), it will normally issue a short-form decision. This includes appropriate cases not giving rise to any competition concerns where it receives a full form notification. The concentration will thus be declared compatible with the common market, within 25 working days from the date of notification, pursuant to Article 10(1) and (6) of the EC Merger Regulation. The Commission will endeavour to issue a short-form decision as soon as practicable following expiry of the 15 working day period during which Member States may request referral of a notified concentration pursuant to Article 9 of the EC Merger Regulation. However, in the period leading up to the 25 working day deadline, the option of reverting to a normal first phase merger procedure and thus launching investigations and/or adopting a full decision remains open to the Commission, should it judge such action appropriate in the case in question.

Publication of the short-form decision

18. The Commission will publish a notice of the fact of the decision in the *Official Journal of the European Union* as it does for full clearance decisions. The public version of the decision will be made available on DG Competition's Internet website for a limited period. The short-form decision will contain the information about the notified concentration published in the Official Journal at the time of notification (names of the parties, their country of origin, nature of the concentration and economic sectors concerned) and a statement that the concentration is declared compatible with the common market because it falls within one or more of the categories described in this Notice, with the applicable category(ies) being explicitly identified.

IV ANCILLARY RESTRICTIONS

19. The simplified procedure is not suited to cases in which the undertakings concerned request an express assessment of restrictions which are directly related to, and necessary for, the implementation of the concentration.

Commission Notice on Immunity from fines and reduction of fines in cartel cases

(OJ 2006, No. C 298/11)

(Text with EEA relevance)

I INTRODUCTION

(1) This notice sets out the framework for rewarding cooperation in the Commission investigation by undertakings which are or have been party to secret cartels affecting the Community. Cartels are agreements and/or concerted practices between two or more competitors aimed at coordinating

their competitive behaviour on the market and/or influencing the relevant parameters of competition through practices such as the fixing of purchase or selling prices or other trading conditions, the allocation of production or sales quotas, the sharing of markets including bid-rigging, restrictions of imports or exports and/or anti-competitive actions against other competitors. Such practices are among the most serious violations of Article 81 EC.

(2) By artificially limiting the competition that would normally prevail between them, undertakings avoid exactly those pressures that lead them to innovate, both in terms of product development and the introduction of more efficient production methods. Such practices also lead to more expensive raw materials and components for the Community companies that purchase from such producers. They ultimately result in artificial prices and reduced choice for the consumer. In the long term, they lead to a loss of competitiveness and reduced employment opportunities.

(3) By their very nature, secret cartels are often difficult to detect and investigate without the cooperation of undertakings or individuals implicated in them. Therefore, the Commission considers that it is in the Community interest to reward undertakings involved in this type of illegal practices which are willing to put an end to their participation and co-operate in the Commission's investigation, independently of the rest of the undertakings involved in the cartel. The interests of consumers and citizens in ensuring that secret cartels are detected and punished outweigh the interest in fining those undertakings that enable the Commission to detect and prohibit such practices.

(4) The Commission considers that the collaboration of an undertaking in the detection of the existence of a cartel has an intrinsic value. A decisive contribution to the opening of an investigation or to the finding of an infringement may justify the granting of immunity from any fine to the undertaking in question, on condition that certain additional requirements are fulfilled.

(5) Moreover, co-operation by one or more undertakings may justify a reduction of a fine by the Commission. Any reduction of a fine must reflect an undertaking's actual contribution, in terms of quality and timing, to the Commission's establishment of the infringement. Reductions are to be limited to those undertakings that provide the Commission with evidence that adds significant value to that already in the Commission's possession.

(6) In addition to submitting pre-existing documents, undertakings may provide the Commission with voluntary presentations of their knowledge of a cartel and their role therein prepared specially to be submitted under this leniency programme. These initiatives have proved to be useful for the effective investigation and termination of cartel infringements and they should not be discouraged by discovery orders issued in civil litigation. Potential leniency applicants might be dissuaded from cooperating with the Commission under this Notice if this could impair their position in civil proceedings, as compared to companies who do not cooperate. Such undesirable effect would significantly harm the public interest in ensuring effective public enforcement of Article 81 EC in cartel cases and thus its subsequent or parallel effective private enforcement.

(7) The supervisory task conferred on the Commission by the Treaty in competition matters does not only include the duty to investigate and punish individual infringements, but also encompasses the duty to pursue a general policy. The protection of corporate statements in the public interest is not a bar to their disclosure to other addressees of the statement of objections in order to safeguard their rights of defence in the procedure before the Commission, to the extent that it is technically possible to combine both interests by rendering corporate statements accessible only at the Commission premises and normally on a single occasion following the formal notification of the objections. Moreover, the Commission will process personal data in the context of this notice in conformity with its obligations under Regulation (EC) No 45/2001.

II IMMUNITY FROM FINES

A. Requirements to qualify for immunity from fines

(8) The Commission will grant immunity from any fine which would otherwise have been imposed to an undertaking disclosing its participation in an alleged cartel affecting the Community if

that undertaking is the first to submit information and evidence which in the Commission's view will enable it to:

    (a) carry out a targeted inspection in connection with the alleged cartel; or

    (b) find an infringement of Article 81 EC in connection with the alleged cartel.

(9) For the Commission to be able to carry out a targeted inspection within the meaning of point (8)(a), the undertaking must provide the Commission with the information and evidence listed below, to the extent that this, in the Commission's view, would not jeopardize the inspections:

    (a) A corporate statement which includes, in so far as it is known to the applicant at the time of the submission:

        – A detailed description of the alleged cartel arrangement, including for instance its aims, activities and functioning; the product or service concerned, the geographic scope, the duration of and the estimated market volumes affected by the alleged cartel; the specific dates, locations, content of and participants in alleged cartel contacts, and all relevant explanations in connection with the pieces of evidence provided in support of the application;

        – The name and address of the legal entity submitting the immunity application as well as the names and addresses of all the other undertakings that participate (d) in the alleged cartel;

        – The names, positions, office locations and, where necessary, home addresses of all individuals who, to the applicant's knowledge, are or have been involved in the alleged cartel, including those individuals which have been involved on the applicant's behalf;

        – Information on which other competition authorities, inside or outside the EU, have been approached or are intended to be approached in relation to the alleged cartel; and

    (b) Other evidence relating to the alleged cartel in possession of the applicant or available to it at the time of the submission, including in particular any evidence contemporaneous to the infringement.

(10) Immunity pursuant to point (8) (a) will not be granted if, at the time of the submission, the Commission had already sufficient evidence to adopt a decision to carry out an inspection in connection with the alleged cartel or had already carried out such an inspection.

(11) Immunity pursuant to point (8)(b) will only be granted on the cumulative conditions that the Commission did not have, at the time of the submission, sufficient evidence to find an infringement of Article 81 EC in connection with the alleged cartel and that no undertaking had been granted conditional immunity from fines under point (8)(a) in connection with the alleged cartel. In order to qualify, an undertaking must be the first to provide contemporaneous, incriminating evidence of the alleged cartel as well as a corporate statement containing the kind of information specified in point (9)(a), which would enable the Commission to find an infringement of Article 81 EC.

(12) In addition to the conditions set out in points (8)(a), (9) and (10) or in points (8)(b) and 11, all the following conditions must be met in any case to qualify for any immunity from a fine:

    (a) The undertaking cooperates genuinely, fully, on a continuous basis and expeditiously from the time it submits its application throughout the Commission's administrative procedure. This includes:

        – providing the Commission promptly with all relevant information and evidence relating to the alleged cartel that comes into its possession or is available to it;

        – remaining at the Commission's disposal to answer promptly to any request that may contribute to the establishment of the facts;

        – making current (and, if possible, former) employees and directors available for interviews with the Commission;

        – not destroying, falsifying or concealing relevant information or evidence relating to the alleged cartel; and

        – not disclosing the fact or any of the content of its application before the Commission has issued a statement of objections in the case, unless otherwise agreed;

(b) The undertaking ended its involvement in the alleged cartel immediately following its application, except for what would, in the Commission's view, be reasonably necessary to preserve the integrity of the inspections;

(c) When contemplating making its application to the Commission, the undertaking must not have destroyed, falsified or concealed evidence of the alleged cartel nor disclosed the fact or any of the content of its contemplated application, except to other competition authorities.

(13) An undertaking which took steps to coerce other undertakings to join the cartel or to remain in it is not eligible for immunity from fines. It may still qualify for a reduction of fines if it fulfils the relevant requirements and meets all the conditions therefor.

B. Procedure

(14) An undertaking wishing to apply for immunity from fines should contact the Commission's Directorate General for Competition. The undertaking may either initially apply for a marker or immediately proceed to make a formal application to the Commission for immunity from fines in order to meet the conditions in points (8)(a) or (8)(b), as appropriate. The Commission may disregard any application for immunity from fines on the ground that it has been submitted after the statement of objections has been issued.

(15) The Commission services may grant a marker protecting an immunity applicant's place in the queue for a period to be specified on a case-by-case basis in order to allow for the gathering of the necessary information and evidence. To be eligible to secure a marker, the applicant must provide the Commission with information concerning its name and address, the parties to the alleged cartel, the affected product(s) and territory(-ies), the estimated duration of the alleged cartel and the nature of the alleged cartel conduct. The applicant should also inform the Commission on other past or possible future leniency applications to other authorities in relation to the alleged cartel and justify its request for a marker. Where a marker is granted, the Commission services determine the period within which the applicant has to perfect the marker by submitting the information and evidence required to meet the relevant threshold for immunity. Undertakings which have been granted a marker cannot perfect it by making a formal application in hypothetical terms. If the applicant perfects the marker within the period set by the Commission services, the information and evidence provided will be deemed to have been submitted on the date when the marker was granted.

(16) An undertaking making a formal immunity application to the Commission must:

(a) provide the Commission with all information and evidence relating to the alleged cartel available to it, as specified in points (8) and (9), including corporate statements; or

(b) initially present this information and evidence in hypothetical terms, in which case the undertaking must present a detailed descriptive list of the evidence it proposes to disclose at a later agreed date. This list should accurately reflect the nature and content of the evidence, whilst safeguarding the hypothetical nature of its disclosure. Copies of documents, from which sensitive parts have been removed, may be used to illustrate the nature and content of the evidence. The name of the applying undertaking and of other undertakings involved in the alleged cartel need not be disclosed until the evidence described in its application is submitted. However, the product or service concerned by the alleged cartel, the geographic scope of the alleged cartel and the estimated duration must be clearly identified.

(17) If requested, the Directorate General for Competition will provide an acknowledgement of receipt of the undertaking's application for immunity from fines, confirming the date and, where appropriate, time of the application.

(18) Once the Commission has received the information and evidence submitted by the undertaking under point (16)(a) and has verified that it meets the conditions set out in points (8)(a) or (8)(b), as appropriate, it will grant the undertaking conditional immunity from fines in writing.

(19) If the undertaking has presented information and evidence in hypothetical terms, the Commission will verify that the nature and content of the evidence described in the detailed list

referred to in point (16)(b) will meet the conditions set out in points (8)(a) or (8)(b), as appropriate, and inform the undertaking accordingly. Following the disclosure of the evidence no later than on the date agreed and having verified that it corresponds to the description made in the list, the Commission will grant the undertaking conditional immunity from fines in writing.

(20) If it becomes apparent that immunity is not available or that the undertaking failed to meet the conditions set out in points (8)(a) or (8)(b), as appropriate, the Commission will inform the undertaking in writing. In such case, the undertaking may withdraw the evidence disclosed for the purposes of its immunity application or request the Commission to consider it under section III of this notice. This does not prevent the Commission from using its normal powers of investigation in order to obtain the information.

(21) The Commission will not consider other applications for immunity from fines before it has taken a position on an existing application in relation to the same alleged infringement, irrespective of whether the immunity application is presented formally or by requesting a marker.

(22) If at the end of the administrative procedure, the undertaking has met the conditions set out in point (12), the Commission will grant it immunity from fines in the relevant decision. If at the end of the administrative procedure, the undertaking has not met the conditions set out in point (12), the undertaking will not benefit from any favorable treatment under this Notice. If the Commission, after having granted conditional immunity ultimately finds that the immunity applicant has acted as a coercer, it will withhold immunity.

III REDUCTION OF A FINE

A. Requirements to qualify for reduction of a fine

(23) Undertakings disclosing their participation in an alleged cartel affecting the Community that do not meet the conditions under section II above may be eligible to benefit from a reduction of any fine that would otherwise have been imposed.

(24) In order to qualify, an undertaking must provide the Commission with evidence of the alleged infringement which represents significant added value with respect to the evidence already in the Commission's possession and must meet the cumulative conditions set out in points (12)(a) to (12)(c) above.

(25) The concept of 'added value' refers to the extent to which the evidence provided strengthens, by its very nature and/or its level of detail, the Commission's ability to prove the alleged cartel. In this assessment, the Commission will generally consider written evidence originating from the period of time to which the facts pertain to have a greater value than evidence subsequently established. Incriminating evidence directly relevant to the facts in question will generally be considered to have a greater value than that with only indirect relevance. Similarly, the degree of corroboration from other sources required for the evidence submitted to be relied upon against other undertakings involved in the case will have an impact on the value of that evidence, so that compelling evidence will be attributed a greater value than evidence such as statements which require corroboration if contested.

(26) The Commission will determine in any final decision adopted at the end of the administrative procedure the level of reduction an undertaking will benefit from, relative to the fine which would otherwise be imposed. For the:

- first undertaking to provide significant added value: a reduction of 30–50 %,
- second undertaking to provide significant added value: a reduction of 20–30 %,
- subsequent undertakings that provide significant added value: a reduction of up to 20 %.

In order to determine the level of reduction within each of these bands, the Commission will take into account the time at which the evidence fulfilling the condition in point (24) was submitted and the extent to which it represents added value.

If the applicant for a reduction of a fine is the first to submit compelling evidence in the sense of point (25) which the Commission uses to establish additional facts increasing the gravity or the duration of the infringement, the Commission will not take such additional facts into account when setting any fine to be imposed on the undertaking which provided this evidence.

B. Procedure

(27) An undertaking wishing to benefit from a reduction of a fine must make a formal application to the Commission and it must present it with sufficient evidence of the alleged cartel to qualify for a reduction of a fine in accordance with point (24) of this Notice. Any voluntary submission of evidence to the Commission which the undertaking that submits it wishes to be considered for the beneficial treatment of section III of this Notice must be clearly identified at the time of its submission as being part of a formal application for a reduction of a fine.

(28) If requested, the Directorate General for Competition will provide an acknowledgement of receipt of the undertaking's application for a reduction of a fine and of any subsequent submissions of evidence, confirming the date and, where appropriate, time of each submission. The Commission will not take any position on an application for a reduction of a fine before it has taken a position on any existing applications for conditional immunity from fines in relation to the same alleged cartel.

(29) If the Commission comes to the preliminary conclusion that the evidence submitted by the undertaking constitutes significant added value within the meaning of points (24) and (25), and that the undertaking has met the conditions of points (12) and (27), it will inform the undertaking in writing, no later than the date on which a statement of objections is notified, of its intention to apply a reduction of a fine within a specified band as provided in point (26). The Commission will also, within the same time frame, inform the undertaking in writing if it comes to the preliminary conclusion that the undertaking does not qualify for a reduction of a fine. The Commission may disregard any application for a reduction of fines on the grounds that it has been submitted after the statement of objections has been issued.

(30) The Commission will evaluate the final position of each undertaking which filed an application for a reduction of a fine at the end of the administrative procedure in any decision adopted. The Commission will determine in any such final decision:

(a) whether the evidence provided by an undertaking represented significant added value with respect to the evidence in the Commission's possession at that same time;

(b) whether the conditions set out in points (12) (a) to (12) (c) above have been met;

(c) the exact level of reduction an undertaking will benefit from within the bands specified in point (26).

If the Commission finds that the undertaking has not met the conditions set out in point (12), the undertaking will not benefit from any favourable treatment under this Notice.

IV CORPORATE STATEMENTS MADE TO QUALIFY UNDER THIS NOTICE

(31) A corporate statement is a voluntary presentation by or on behalf of an undertaking to the Commission of the undertaking's knowledge of a cartel and its role therein prepared specially to be submitted under this Notice. Any statement made vis-à-vis the Commission in relation to this notice, forms part of the Commission's file and can thus be used in evidence.

(32) Upon the applicant's request, the Commission may accept that corporate statements be provided orally unless the applicant has already disclosed the content of the corporate statement to third parties. Oral corporate statements will be recorded and transcribed at the Commission's premises. In accordance with Article 19 of Council Regulation (EC) No 1/2003 and Articles 3 and 17 of Commission Regulation (EC) No 773/2004, undertakings making oral corporate statements will be granted the opportunity to check the technical accuracy of the recording, which will be available at the Commission's premises and to correct the substance of their oral statements within a given time limit. Undertakings may waive these rights within the said time-limit, in which case the recording will from that moment on be deemed to have been approved. Following the explicit or implicit approval of the oral statement or the submission of any corrections to it, the undertaking shall listen to the recordings at the Commission's premises and check the accuracy of the transcript within a given

time limit. Non-compliance with the last requirement may lead to the loss of any beneficial treatment under this Notice.

(33) Access to corporate statements is only granted to the addressees of a statement of objections, provided that they commit,—together with the legal counsels getting access on their behalf—, not to make any copy by mechanical or electronic means of any information in the corporate statement to which access is being granted and to ensure that the information to be obtained from the corporate statement will solely be used for the purposes mentioned below. Other parties such as complainants will not be granted access to corporate statements. The Commission considers that this specific protection of a corporate statement is not justified as from the moment when the applicant discloses to third parties the content thereof.

(34) In accordance with the Commission Notice on rules for access to the Commission file, access to the file is only granted to the addressees of a statement of objections on the condition that the information thereby obtained may only be used for the purposes of judicial or administrative proceedings for the application of the Community competition rules at issue in the related administrative proceedings. The use of such information for a different purpose during the proceeding may be regarded as lack of cooperation within the meaning of points (12) and (27) of this Notice. Moreover, if any such use is made after the Commission has already adopted a prohibition decision in the proceeding, the Commission may, in any legal proceedings before the Community Courts, ask the Court to increase the fine in respect of the responsible undertaking. Should the information be used for a different purpose, at any point in time, with the involvement of an outside counsel, the Commission may report the incident to the bar of that counsel, with a view to disciplinary action.

(35) Corporate statements made under the present Notice will only be transmitted to the competition authorities of the Member States pursuant to Article 12 of Regulation No 1/2003, provided that the conditions set out in the Network Notice are met and provided that the level of protection against disclosure awarded by the receiving competition authority is equivalent to the one conferred by the Commission.

V GENERAL CONSIDERATIONS

(36) The Commission will not take a position on whether or not to grant conditional immunity, or otherwise on whether or not to reward any application, if it becomes apparent that the application concerns infringements covered by the five years limitation period for the imposition of penalties stipulated in Article 25(1)(b) of Regulation 1/2003, as such applications would be devoid of purpose.

(37) From the date of its publication in the Official Journal, this notice replaces the 2002 Commission notice on immunity from fines and reduction of fines in cartel cases for all cases in which no undertaking has contacted the Commission in order to take advantage of the favourable treatment set out in that notice. However, points (31) to (35) of the current notice will be applied from the moment of its publication to all pending and new applications for immunity from fines or reduction of fines.

(38) The Commission is aware that this notice will create legitimate expectations on which undertakings may rely when disclosing the existence of a cartel to the Commission.

(39) In line with the Commission's practice, the fact that an undertaking cooperated with the Commission during its administrative procedure will be indicated in any decision, so as to explain the reason for the immunity or reduction of the fine. The fact that immunity or reduction in respect of fines is granted cannot protect an undertaking from the civil law consequences of its participation in an infringement of Article 81 EC.

(40) The Commission considers that normally public disclosure of documents and written or recorded statements received in the context of this notice would undermine certain public or private interests, for example the protection of the purpose of inspections and investigations, within the meaning of Article 4 of Regulation (EC) No 1049/2001 (1), even after the decision has been taken.

Guidelines on the method of setting fines imposed pursuant to Article 23(2)(a) of Regulation No 1/2003

(OJ 2006, No. C 210/02)

(Text with EEA relevance)

INTRODUCTION

1. Pursuant to Article 23(2)(a) of Regulation No 1/2003, the Commission may, by decision, impose fines on undertakings or associations of undertakings where, either intentionally or negligently, they infringe Article 81 or 82 of the Treaty.

2. In exercising its power to impose such fines, the Commission enjoys a wide margin of discretion within the limits set by Regulation No 1/2003. First, the Commission must have regard both to the gravity and to the duration of the infringement. Second, the fine imposed may not exceed the limits specified in Article 23(2), second and third subparagraphs, of Regulation No 1/2003.

3. In order to ensure the transparency and impartiality of its decisions, the Commission published on 14 January 1998 guidelines on the method of setting fines. After more than eight years of implementation, the Commission has acquired sufficient experience to develop further and refine its policy on fines.

4. The Commission's power to impose fines on undertakings or associations of undertakings which, intentionally or negligently, infringe Article 81 or 82 of the Treaty is one of the means conferred on it in order for it to carry out the task of supervision entrusted to it by the Treaty. That task not only includes the duty to investigate and sanction individual infringements, but it also encompasses the duty to pursue a general policy designed to apply, in competition matters, the principles laid down by the Treaty and to steer the conduct of undertakings in the light of those principles. For this purpose, the Commission must ensure that its action has the necessary deterrent effect. Accordingly, when the Commission discovers that Article 81 or 82 of the Treaty has been infringed, it may be necessary to impose a fine on those who have acted in breach of the law. Fines should have a sufficiently deterrent effect, not only in order to sanction the undertakings concerned (specific deterrence) but also in order to deter other undertakings from engaging in, or continuing, behaviour that is contrary to Articles 81 and 82 of the EC Treaty (general deterrence).

5. In order to achieve these objectives, it is appropriate for the Commission to refer to the value of the sales of goods or services to which the infringement relates as a basis for setting the fine. The duration of the infringement should also play a significant role in the setting of the appropriate amount of the fine. It necessarily has an impact on the potential consequences of the infringement on the market. It is therefore considered important that the fine should also reflect the number of years during which an undertaking participated in the infringement.

6. The combination of the value of sales to which the infringement relates and of the duration of the infringement is regarded as providing an appropriate proxy to reflect the economic importance of the infringement as well as the relative weight of each undertaking in the infringement. Reference to these factors provides a good indication of the order of magnitude of the fine and should not be regarded as the basis for an automatic and arithmetical calculation method.

7. It is also considered appropriate to include in the fine a specific amount irrespective of the duration of the infringement, in order to deter companies from even entering into illegal practices.

8. The sections below set out the principles which will guide the Commission when it sets fines imposed pursuant to Article 23 (2) (a) of Regulation No 1/2003.

METHOD FOR THE SETTING OF FINES

9. Without prejudice to point 37 below, the Commission will use the following two-step methodology when setting the fine to be imposed on undertakings or associations of undertakings.

10. First, the Commission will determine a basic amount for each undertaking or association of undertakings (see Section 1 below).

11. Second, it may adjust that basic amount upwards or downwards (see Section 2 below).

1.   Basic amount of the fine

12. The basic amount will be set by reference to the value of sales and applying the following methodology.

A. Calculation of the value of sales

13. In determining the basic amount of the fine to be imposed, the Commission will take the value of the undertaking's sales of goods or services to which the infringement directly or indirectly relates in the relevant geographic area within the EEA. It will normally take the sales made by the undertaking during the last full business year of its participation in the infringement (hereafter 'value of sales').

14. Where the infringement by an association of undertakings relates to the activities of its members, the value of sales will generally correspond to the sum of the value of sales by its members.

15. In determining the value of sales by an undertaking, the Commission will take that undertaking's best available figures.

16. Where the figures made available by an undertaking are incomplete or not reliable, the Commission may determine the value of its sales on the basis of the partial figures it has obtained and/or any other information which it regards as relevant and appropriate.

17. The value of sales will be determined before VAT and other taxes directly related to the sales.

18. Where the geographic scope of an infringement extends beyond the EEA (e.g. worldwide cartels), the relevant sales of the undertakings within the EEA may not properly reflect the weight of each undertaking in the infringement. This may be the case in particular with worldwide market-sharing arrangements.

In such circumstances, in order to reflect both the aggregate size of the relevant sales within the EEA and the relative weight of each undertaking in the infringement, the Commission may assess the total value of the sales of goods or services to which the infringement relates in the relevant geographic area (wider than the EEA), may determine the share of the sales of each undertaking party to the infringement on that market and may apply this share to the aggregate sales within the EEA of the undertakings concerned. The result will be taken as the value of sales for the purpose of setting the basic amount of the fine.

B. Determination of the basic amount of the fine

19. The basic amount of the fine will be related to a proportion of the value of sales, depending on the degree of gravity of the infringement, multiplied by the number of years of infringement.

20. The assessment of gravity will be made on a case-by-case basis for all types of infringement, taking account of all the relevant circumstances of the case.

21. As a general rule, the proportion of the value of sales taken into account will be set at a level of up to 30 % of the value of sales.

22. In order to decide whether the proportion of the value of sales to be considered in a given case should be at the lower end or at the higher end of that scale, the Commission will have regard to a number of factors, such as the nature of the infringement, the combined market share of all the undertakings concerned, the geographic scope of the infringement and whether or not the infringement has been implemented.

23. Horizontal price-fixing, market-sharing and output-limitation agreements, which are usually secret, are, by their very nature, among the most harmful restrictions of competition. As a matter of policy, they will be heavily fined. Therefore, the proportion of the value of sales taken into account for such infringements will generally be set at the higher end of the scale.

24. In order to take fully into account the duration of the participation of each undertaking in the infringement, the amount determined on the basis of the value of sales (see points 20 to 23 above) will be multiplied by the number of years of participation in the infringement. Periods of less

than six months will be counted as half a year; periods longer than six months but shorter than one year will be counted as a full year.

25. In addition, irrespective of the duration of the undertaking's participation in the infringement, the Commission will include in the basic amount a sum of between 15 % and 25 % of the value of sales as defined in Section A above in order to deter undertakings from even entering into horizontal price-fixing, market-sharing and output limitation agreements. The Commission may also apply such an additional amount in the case of other infringements. For the purpose of deciding the proportion of the value of sales to be considered in a given case, the Commission will have regard to a number of factors, in particular those referred in point 22.

26. Where the value of sales by undertakings participating in the infringement is similar but not identical, the Commission may set for each of them an identical basic amount. Moreover, in determining the basic amount of the fine, the Commission will use rounded figures.

2. Adjustments to the basic amount

27. In setting the fine, the Commission may take into account circumstances that result in an increase or decrease in the basic amount as determined in Section 1 above. It will do so on the basis of an overall assessment which takes account of all the relevant circumstances.

A. Aggravating circumstances

28. The basic amount may be increased where the Commission finds that there are aggravating circumstances, such as:
- where an undertaking continues or repeats the same or a similar infringement after the Commission or a national competition authority has made a finding that the undertaking infringed Article 81 or 82: the basic amount will be increased by up to 100 % for each such infringement established;
- refusal to cooperate with or obstruction of the Commission in carrying out its investigations;
- role of leader in, or instigator of, the infringement; the Commission will also pay particular attention to any steps taken to coerce other undertakings to participate in the infringement and/or any retaliatory measures taken against other undertakings with a view to enforcing the practices constituting the infringement.

B. Mitigating circumstances

29. The basic amount may be reduced where the Commission finds that mitigating circumstances exist, such as:
- where the undertaking concerned provides evidence that it terminated the infringement as soon as the Commission intervened: this will not apply to secret agreements or practices (in particular, cartels);
- where the undertaking provides evidence that the infringement has been committed as a result of negligence;
- where the undertaking provides evidence that its involvement in the infringement is substantially limited and thus demonstrates that, during the period in which it was party to the offending agreement, it actually avoided applying it by adopting competitive conduct in the market: the mere fact that an undertaking participated in an infringement for a shorter duration than others will not be regarded as a mitigating circumstance since this will already be reflected in the basic amount;
- where the undertaking concerned has effectively cooperated with the Commission outside the scope of the Leniency Notice and beyond its legal obligation to do so;
- where the anti-competitive conduct of the undertaking has been authorized or encouraged by public authorities or by legislation.

C. Specific increase for deterrence

30. The Commission will pay particular attention to the need to ensure that fines have a sufficiently deterrent effect; to that end, it may increase the fine to be imposed on undertakings which

have a particularly large turnover beyond the sales of goods or services to which the infringement relates.

31.   The Commission will also take into account the need to increase the fine in order to exceed the amount of gains improperly made as a result of the infringement where it is possible to estimate that amount.

D. Legal maximum

32.   The final amount of the fine shall not, in any event, exceed 10 % of the total turnover in the preceding business year of the undertaking or association of undertakings participating in the infringement, as laid down in Article 23(2) of Regulation No 1/2003.

33.   Where an infringement by an association of undertakings relates to the activities of its members, the fine shall not exceed 10 % of the sum of the total turnover of each member active on the market affected by that infringement.

E. Leniency notice

34.   The Commission will apply the leniency rules in line with the conditions set out in the applicable notice.

F. Ability to pay

35.   In exceptional cases, the Commission may, upon request, take account of the undertaking's inability to pay in a specific social and economic context. It will not base any reduction granted for this reason in the fine on the mere finding of an adverse or loss-making financial situation. A reduction could be granted solely on the basis of objective evidence that imposition of the fine as provided for in these Guidelines would irretrievably jeopardise the economic viability of the undertaking concerned and cause its assets to lose all their value.

FINAL CONSIDERATIONS

36.   The Commission may, in certain cases, impose a symbolic fine. The justification for imposing such a fine should be given in its decision.

37.   Although these Guidelines present the general methodology for the setting of fines, the particularities of a given case or the need to achieve deterrence in a particular case may justify departing from such methodology or from the limits specified in point 21.

38.   These Guidelines will be applied in all cases where a statement of objections is notified after their date of publication in the Official Journal, regardless of whether the fine is imposed pursuant to Article 23(2) of Regulation No 1/2003 or Article 15(2) of Regulation 17/62.

Commission Consolidated Jurisdictional Notice under Council Regulation (EC) No 139/2004 on the control of concentrations between undertakings

(OJ 2008, No. C 95/01)

A. INTRODUCTION

(1)   The purpose of this Notice is to provide guidance as to jurisdictional issues under Council Regulation (EC) No 139/2004, OJ L 24, 29.1.2003, page 1 (the Merger Regulation). This formal guidance should enable firms to establish more quickly, in advance of any contact with the Commission, whether and to what extent their operations may be covered by Community control of concentrations.

(2) This Notice replaces the Notice on the concept of concentration, the Notice on the concept of full function joint ventures, the Notice on the concept of undertakings concerned and the Notice on calculation of turnover.

(3) This Notice deals with the concepts of a concentration and of a full-function joint venture, undertakings concerned and the calculation of turnover as set out in Articles 1, 3 and 5 of the Merger Regulation. Issues concerning referrals are dealt with in the Notice on referrals. The Commission's interpretation of Articles 1, 3 and 5 in the present Notice is without prejudice to the interpretation which may be given by the Court of Justice or by the Court of First Instance of the European Communities.

(4) The guidance set out in this Notice reflects the Commission's experience in applying the recast Merger Regulation and the former Merger Regulation since the latter entered into force on 21 September 1990. The general principles governing the issues dealt with in this Notice have not been changed by the entry into force of Regulation (EC) No 139/2004, but where changes have occurred, the Notice deals with them explicitly. The principles contained in the Notice will be applied and further developed by the Commission in individual cases.

(5) According to Article 1, the Merger Regulation only applies to operations that satisfy two conditions. First, there must be a concentration of two or more undertakings within the meaning of Article 3 of the Merger Regulation. Secondly, the turnover of the undertakings concerned, calculated in accordance with Article 5, must satisfy the thresholds set out in Article 1 of the Regulation. The notion of a concentration (including the particular requirements for joint ventures), as the first condition, is dealt with under Part B; the identification of undertakings concerned and the calculation of their turnover as relevant for the second condition are dealt with under Part C.

(6) The Commission addresses the question of its jurisdiction over a concentration in decisions according to Article 6 of the Merger Regulation.

B. THE CONCEPT OF CONCENTRATION

(7) According to Article 3(1) of the Merger Regulation, a concentration only covers operations where a change of control in the undertakings concerned occurs on a lasting basis. Recital 20 in the preamble to the Merger Regulation further explains that the concept of concentration is intended to relate to operations which bring about a lasting change in the structure of the market. Because the test in Article 3 is centred on the concept of control, the existence of a concentration is to a great extent determined by qualitative rather than quantitative criteria.

(8) Article 3(1) of the Merger Regulation defines two categories of concentrations:
– those arising from a merger between previously independent undertakings (point (a));
– those arising from an acquisition of control (point (b)).
These are treated respectively in Sections I and II below.

I. MERGERS BETWEEN PREVIOUSLY INDEPENDENT UNDERTAKINGS

(9) A merger within the meaning of Article 3(1)(a) of the Merger Regulation occurs when two or more independent undertakings amalgamate into a new undertaking and cease to exist as separate legal entities. A merger may also occur when an undertaking is absorbed by another, the latter retaining its legal identity while the former ceases to exist as a legal entity.

(10) A merger within the meaning of Article 3(1)(a) may also occur where, in the absence of a legal merger, the combining of the activities of previously independent undertakings results in the creation of a single economic unit. This may arise in particular where two or more undertakings, while retaining their individual legal personalities, establish contractually a common economic management or the structure of a dual listed company. If this leads to a *de facto* amalgamation of the undertakings concerned into a single economic unit, the operation is considered to be a merger. A prerequisite for the determination of such a *de facto* merger is the existence of a permanent, single

economic management. Other relevant factors may include internal profit and loss compensation or a revenue distribution as between the various entities within the group, and their joint liability or external risk sharing. The *de facto* amalgamation may be solely based on contractual arrangements, but it can also be reinforced by cross-shareholdings between the undertakings forming the economic unit.

II. ACQUISITION OF CONTROL

1. CONCEPT OF CONTROL

1.1. Person or undertaking acquiring control

(11) Article 3 (1)(b) provides that a concentration occurs in the case of an acquisition of control. Such control may be acquired by one undertaking acting alone or by several undertakings acting jointly.

Person controlling another undertaking

(12) Control may also be acquired by a person in circumstances where that person already controls (whether solely or jointly) at least one other undertaking or, alternatively, by a combination of persons (which control another undertaking) and undertakings. The term 'person' in this context extends to public bodies and private entities, as well as natural persons. Acquisitions of control by natural persons are only considered to bring about a lasting change in the structure of the undertakings concerned if those natural persons carry out further economic activities on their own account or if they control at least one other undertaking.

Acquirer of control

(13) Control is normally acquired by persons or undertakings which are the holders of the rights or are entitled to rights conferring control under the contracts concerned (Article 3(3)(a)). However, there are also situations where the formal holder of a controlling interest differs from the person or undertaking having in fact the real power to exercise the rights resulting from this interest. This may be the case, for example, where an undertaking uses another person or undertaking for the acquisition of a controlling interest and has the power to exercise the rights conferring control through this person or undertaking, i.e. the latter is formally the holder of the rights, but acts only as a vehicle. In such a situation, control is acquired by the undertaking which in reality is behind the operation and in fact enjoys the power to control the target undertaking (Article 3(3)(b)). The Court of First Instance concluded from this provision that control held by commercial companies can be attributed to their exclusive shareholder, their majority shareholders or to those jointly controlling the companies since these companies comply in any event with the decisions of those shareholders. A controlling shareholding which is held by different entities in a group is normally attributed to the undertaking exercising control over the different formal holders of the rights. In other cases, the evidence needed to establish this type of indirect control may include, either separately or in combination and to be assessed on a case-by-case basis, factors such as shareholdings, contractual relations, source of financing or family links.

Acquisition of control by investment funds

(14) Specific issues may arise in the case of acquisitions of control by investment funds. The Commission will analyse structures involving investment funds on a case-by-case basis, but some general features of such structures can be set out on the basis of the Commission's past experience.

(15) Investment funds are often set up in the legal form of limited partnerships, in which the investors participate as limited partners and normally do not exercise control, either individually or collectively. The investment funds usually acquire the shares and voting rights which confer control over the portfolio companies. Depending on the circumstances, control is normally exercised by the investment company which has set up the fund as the fund itself is typically a mere investment vehicle;

in more exceptional circumstances, control may be exercised by the fund itself. The investment company usually exercises control by means of the organisational structure, *e.g.* by controlling the general partner of fund partnerships, or by contractual arrangements, such as advisory agreements, or by a combination of both. This may be the case even if the investment company itself does not own the company acting as a general partner, but their shares are held by natural persons (who may be linked to the investment company) or by a trust. Contractual arrangements with the investment company, in particular advisory agreements, will become even more important if the general partner does not have any own resources and personnel for the management of the portfolio companies, but only constitutes a company structure whose acts are performed by persons linked to the investment company. In these circumstances, the investment company normally acquires indirect control within the meaning of Article 3(1)(b) and 3(3)(b) of the Merger Regulation, and has the power to exercise the rights which are directly held by the investment fund.

1.2. Means of control

(16) Control is defined by Article 3(2) of the Merger Regulation as the possibility of exercising decisive influence on an undertaking. It is therefore not necessary to show that the decisive influence is or will be actually exercised. However, the possibility of exercising that influence must be effective. Article 3(2) further provides that the possibility of exercising decisive influence on an undertaking can exist on the basis of rights, contracts or any other means, either separately or in combination, and having regard to the considerations of fact and law involved. A concentration therefore may occur on a legal or a *de facto* basis, may take the form of sole or joint control, and extend to the whole or parts of one or more undertakings (cf. Article 3(1)(b)).

Control by the acquisition of shares or assets

(17) Whether an operation gives rise to an acquisition of control therefore depends on a number of legal and/or factual elements. The most common means for the acquisition of control is the acquisition of shares, possibly combined with a shareholders' agreement in cases of joint control, or the acquisition of assets.

Control on a contractual basis

(18) Control can also be acquired on a contractual basis. In order to confer control, the contract must lead to a similar control of the management and the resources of the other undertaking as in the case of acquisition of shares or assets. In addition to transferring control over the management and the resources, such contracts must be characterised by a very long duration (ordinarily without a possibility of early termination for the party granting the contractual rights). Only such contracts can result in a structural change in the market. Examples of such contracts are organisational contracts under national company law or other types of contracts, *e.g.* in the form of agreements for the lease of the business, giving the acquirer control over the management and the resources despite the fact that property rights or shares are not transferred. In this respect, Article 3(2)(a) specifies that control may also be constituted by a right to use the assets of an undertaking. Such contracts may also lead to a situation of joint control if both the owner of the assets as well as the undertaking controlling the management enjoy veto rights over strategic business decisions.

Control by other means

(19) In line with these considerations, franchising agreements as such do not normally confer control over the franchisee's business on the franchisor. The franchisee usually exploits the entrepreneurial resources on its own account even if essential parts of the assets may belong to the franchisor. Furthermore, purely financial agreements, such as sale-and-lease-back transactions with arrangements for a buyback of the assets at the end of the term, do not normally constitute a concentration as they do not change control over the management and the resources.

(20) Furthermore, control can also be established by any other means. Purely economic relationships may play a decisive role for the acquisition of control. In exceptional circumstances, a situation of economic dependence may lead to control on a *de facto* basis where, for example, very important long-term supply agreements or credits provided by suppliers or customers, coupled with structural

links, confer decisive influence. In such a situation, the Commission will carefully analyse whether such economic links, combined with other links, are sufficient to lead to a change of control on a lasting basis.

(21) There may be an acquisition of control even if it is not the declared intention of the parties or if the acquirer is only passive and the acquisition of control is triggered by action of third parties. Examples are situations where the change of control results from the inheritance of a shareholder or where the exit of a shareholder triggers a change of control, in particular a change from joint to sole control. Article 3(1)(b) covers such scenarios in specifying that control may also be acquired 'by any other means'.

Control and national company law

(22) National legislation within a Member State may provide specific rules on the structure of bodies representing the organization of decision-making within an undertaking. While such legislation may confer some power of control upon persons other than the shareholders, in particular on representatives of employees, the concept of control under the Merger Regulation is not related to such a means of influence as the Merger Regulation focuses on decisive influence enjoyed on the basis of rights, assets or contracts or equivalent *de facto* means. Restrictions in the articles of association or in general law concerning the persons eligible to sit on the board, such as a provisions requiring the appointment of independent members or excluding persons holding office or employment in the parent companies, do not exclude the existence of control as long as the shareholders decide the composition of the decision-making bodies (27). Similarly, despite provisions of national law foreseeing that decisions of a company must be taken by its company organs in its interests, those persons holding the voting rights have the power to adopt those decisions and therefore have the possibility to exercise decisive influence on the company.

Control in other areas of legislation

(23) The concept of control under the Merger Regulation may be different from that applied in specific areas of Community and national legislation concerning, for example, prudential rules, taxation, air transport or the media. The interpretation of 'control' in other areas is therefore not necessarily decisive for the concept of control under the Merger Regulation.

1.3. Object of control

(24) The Merger Regulation provides in Article 3(1)(b), (2) that the object of control can be one or more, or also parts of, undertakings which constitute legal entities, or the assets of such entities, or only some of these assets. The acquisition of control over assets can only be considered a concentration if those assets constitute the whole or a part of an undertaking, *i.e.* a business with a market presence, to which a market turnover can be clearly attributed. The transfer of the client base of a business can fulfil these criteria if this is sufficient to transfer a business with a market turnover. A transaction confined to intangible assets such as brands, patents or copyrights may also be considered to be a concentration if those assets constitute a business with a market turnover. In any case, the transfer of licences for brands, patents or copyrights, without additional assets, can only fulfil these criteria if the licences are exclusive at least in a certain territory and the transfer of such licences will transfer the turnover-generating activity. For non-exclusive licences it can be excluded that they may constitute on their own a business to which a market turnover is attached.

(25) Specific issues arise in cases where an undertaking outsources in-house activities, such as the provision of services or the manufacturing of products, to a service provider. Typical cases are the outsourcing of IT services to specialised IT companies. Outsourcing contracts can take several forms; their common characteristic is that the outsourcing service supplier shall provide those services to the customer which the latter has performed in-house before. Cases of simple outsourcing do not involve any transfer of assets or employees to the outsourcing service suppliers, but it is usually the case that any assets or employees are retained by the customer. Such an outsourcing contract is akin to a normal service contract and even if the outsourcing service supplier acquires a right to direct those

assets and employees of the customer, no concentration arises if the assets and employees will be used exclusively to service the customer.

(26) The situation may be different if the outsourcing service supplier, in addition to taking over a certain activity which was previously provided internally, is transferred the associated assets and/or personnel. A concentration only arises in these circumstances if the assets constitute the whole or part of an undertaking, i.e. a business with access to the market. This requires that the assets previously dedicated to in-house activities of the seller will enable the outsourcing service supplier to provide services not only to the outsourcing customer but also to third parties, either immediately or within a short period after the transfer. This will be the case if the transfer relates to an internal business unit or a subsidiary already engaged in the provision of services to third parties. If third parties are not yet supplied, the assets transferred in the case of manufacturing should contain production facilities, the product know-how (it is sufficient if the assets transferred allow the build-up of such capabilities in the near future) and, if there is no existing market access, the means for the purchaser to develop a market access within a short period of time (e.g. including existing contracts or brands). As regards the provision of services, the assets transferred should include the required know-how (e.g. the relevant personnel and intellectual property) and those facilities which allow market access (such as, e.g., marketing facilities). The assets transferred therefore have to include at least those core elements that would allow an acquirer to build up a market presence in a time-frame similar to the start-up period for joint ventures as set out below under paragraphs 97, 100. As in the case of joint ventures, the Commission will take account of substantiated business plans and general market features for assessing this.

(27) If the assets transferred do not allow the purchaser to at least develop a market presence, it is likely that they will be used only for providing services to the outsourcing customer. In such circumstances, the transaction will not result in a lasting change in the market structure and the outsourcing contract is again similar to a service contract. The transaction will not constitute a concentration. The specific requirements under which a joint venture for the provision of outsourcing services is qualified as a concentration are assessed in the present Notice in the section on full-function joint ventures.

1.4. Change of control on a lasting basis

(28) Article 3(1) of the Merger Regulation defines the concept of a concentration in such a manner as to cover operations only if they bring about a lasting change in the control of the undertakings concerned and, as recital 20 adds, in the structure of the market. The Merger Regulation therefore does not deal with transactions resulting only in a temporary change of control. However, a change of control on a lasting basis is not excluded by the fact that the underlying agreements are entered into for a definite period of time, provided those agreements are renewable. A concentration may arise even in cases in which agreements envisage a definite end-date, if the period envisaged is sufficiently long to lead to a lasting change in the control of the undertakings concerned.

(29) The question whether an operation results in a lasting change in the market structure is also relevant for the assessment of several operations occurring in succession, where the first transaction is only transitory in nature. Several scenarios can be distinguished in this respect.

(30) In one scenario, several undertakings come together solely for the purpose of acquiring another company on the basis of an agreement to divide up the acquired assets according to a pre-existing plan immediately upon completion of the transaction. In such circumstances, in a first step, the acquisition of the entire target company is carried out by one or several undertakings. In a second step, the acquired assets are divided among several undertakings. The question is then whether the first transaction is to be considered as a separate concentration, involving an acquisition of sole control (in the case of a single purchaser) or of joint control (in the case of a joint purchase) of the entire target undertaking, or whether only the acquisitions in the second step constitute concentrations, whereby each of the acquiring undertakings acquires its relevant part of the target undertaking.

(31) The Commission considers that the first transaction does not constitute a concentration, and examines the acquisitions of control by the ultimate acquirers, provided a number of conditions are met: First, the subsequent break-up must be agreed between the different purchasers in a legally binding way. Second, there must not be any uncertainty that the second step, the division of the acquired

assets, will take place within a short time period after the first acquisition. The Commission considers that normally the maximum time-frame for the division of the assets should be one year.

(32) If both conditions are met, the first acquisition does not result in a structural change on a lasting basis. There is no effective concentration of economic power between the acquirer(s) and the target company as a whole since the acquired assets are not held in an undivided way on a lasting basis, but only for the time necessary to carry out the immediate split-up of the acquired assets. In those circumstances, only the acquisitions of the different parts of the undertaking in the second step will constitute concentrations, whereby each of these acquisitions by different purchasers will constitute a separate concentration. This is irrespective of whether the first acquisition is carried out by only one undertaking or jointly by the undertakings which are also involved in the second step. In any case, it must be noted that the scope of a clearance decision will only allow for a takeover of the entire target if the break-up can proceed within a short time-frame afterwards and the different parts of the target undertaking are directly sold on to the respective ultimate buyer.

(33) However, if these conditions are not fulfilled, in particular if it is not certain that the second step will proceed within a short time-frame after the first acquisition, the Commission will consider the first transaction as a separate concentration, involving the entire target undertaking. This, e.g., is the case if the first transaction may also proceed independently of the second transaction or if a longer transitory period is needed to divide up the target undertaking.

(34) A second scenario is an operation leading to joint control for a starting-up period but, according to legally binding agreements, this joint control will be converted to sole control by one of the shareholders. As the joint control situation may not constitute a lasting change of control, the whole operation may be considered to be an acquisition of sole control. In the past, the Commission accepted that such a start-up period could last up to three years. Such a period seems to be too long to exclude that the joint control scenario has an impact on the structure of the market. The period therefore should, in general, not exceed one year and the joint control period should be only transitory in nature. Only such a relatively short period will make it unlikely that the joint control period will have a distinct impact on the market structure and can therefore be considered as not leading to a change in control on a lasting basis.

(35) In a third scenario, an undertaking is 'parked' with an interim buyer, often a bank, on the basis of an agreement on the future onward sale of the business to an ultimate acquirer. The interim buyer generally acquires shares 'on behalf' of the ultimate acquirer, which often bears the major part of the economic risks and may also be granted specific rights. In such circumstances, the first transaction is only undertaken to facilitate the second transaction and the first buyer is directly linked to the ultimate acquirer. Contrary to the situation described in the first scenario in paragraphs 30–33, no other ultimate acquirer is involved, the target business remains unchanged, and the sequence of transactions is initiated alone by the sole ultimate acquirer. From the date of the adoption of this Notice, the Commission will examine the acquisition of control by the ultimate acquirer, as provided for in the agreements entered into by the parties. The Commission will consider the transaction by which the interim buyer acquires control in such circumstances as the first step of a single concentration comprising the lasting acquisition of control by the ultimate buyer.

1.5. Interrelated transactions

1.5.1. Relation between Article 3 and Article 5(2) second subparagraph

(36) Several transactions can be treated as a single concentration under the Merger Regulation either according to the general rule of Article 3—as the transactions are interdependent—or according to the specific provision of Article 5(2) second subparagraph.

(37) Article 5(2) second subparagraph governs a different question from that referred to by Article 3 of the Merger Regulation. Article 3 defines the existence of a 'concentration' in general and material terms, but does not directly determine the question of the Commission's competence in respect of concentrations. Article 5 intends to specify the scope of the Merger Regulation, in particular by defining the turnover to be taken into account for the purpose of determining whether a concentration has Community dimension, and Article 5(2) second subparagraph allows the Commission in

this respect to consider two or more concentrative transactions to constitute a single concentration for the purposes of calculating the turnover of the undertakings concerned. The assessment whether, in application of Article 3, a number of transactions give rise to a single concentration or whether those transactions must be regarded as giving rise to a number of concentrations, is thereby logically precedent to the question addressed in Article 5(2) second subparagraph.

1.5.2. Interdependent transactions under Article 3

(38) The general and teleological definition of a concentration set out in Article 3(1)—the result being control of one or more undertakings—implies that it makes no difference whether control was acquired by one or several legal transactions, provided that the end result constitutes a single concentration. Two or more transactions constitute a single concentration for the purposes of Article 3 if they are unitary in nature. It should therefore be determined whether the result leads to conferring one or more undertakings direct or indirect economic control over the activities of one or more other undertakings. For the assessment, the economic reality underlying the transactions is to be identified and thus the economic aim pursued by the parties. In other words, in order to determine the unitary nature of the transactions in question, it is necessary, in each individual case, to ascertain whether those transactions are interdependent, in such a way that one transaction would not have been carried out without the other.

(39) Recital 20 to the Merger Regulation explains in this respect that it is appropriate to treat as a single concentration transactions that are closely connected in that they are linked by condition. The requirement that the transactions are interdependent as set out by the Court of First Instance in the *Cementbouw* judgment (44) thereby corresponds to the explanation set out in recital 20 that the transactions are linked by condition.

(40) This general approach reflects, on the one hand, that under the Merger Regulation transactions which stand or fall together according to the economic objectives pursued by the parties should also be analysed in one procedure. In these circumstances, the change of the market structure is brought about by these transactions together. On the other hand, if different transactions are not interdependent and if the parties would proceed with one of the transactions if the other ones would not succeed, it seems appropriate to assess these transactions individually under the Merger Regulation.

(41) However, several transactions, even if linked by condition upon each other, can only be treated as a single concentration, if control is acquired ultimately by the same undertaking(s). Only in these circumstances two or more transactions can be considered to be unitary in nature and therefore to constitute a single concentration for the purposes of Article 3. This excludes de-mergers of joint ventures by which different parts of an undertaking are split between its former parent companies. The Commission will consider those transactions as separate concentrations. The same applies to transactions where two (or more) companies exchange assets in transactions involving de-mergers of joint ventures or assets swaps. Although the parties will normally consider those transactions as interdependent, the purpose of the Merger Regulation requires a separate assessment of the results of each of the transactions: Several undertakings acquire control of different assets; a separate combination of resources takes place for each of the acquiring undertakings; and the impact on the market of each of those acquisitions of control needs to be analysed separately under the Merger Regulation.

(42) The acquisition of different degrees of control (for example joint control of one business and sole control of another business) raises specific questions. An operation involving the acquisition of joint control of one part of an undertaking and sole control of another part is in principle regarded as two separate concentrations under the Merger Regulation. Those transactions constitute only one concentration if they are interdependent and if the undertaking acquiring sole control is also acquiring joint control. In any case, such a scenario is considered to constitute one concentration where a corporate entity is acquired to which both the solely controlled and the jointly controlled undertaking belong. On the basis of the interpretation in recital 20, the situation where the same undertaking acquires sole and joint control of other undertakings based on interdependent agreements is

not to be treated differently. These transactions, if they are interdependent, therefore constitute a single concentration.

Requirement of conditionality of transactions

(43) The required conditionality implies that none of the transactions would take place without the others and they therefore constitute a single operation. Such conditionality is normally demonstrated if the transactions are linked *de jure*, i.e. the agreements themselves are linked by mutual conditionality. If *de facto* conditionality can be satisfactorily demonstrated, it may also suffice for treating the transactions as a single concentration. This requires an economic assessment of whether each of the transactions necessarily depends on the conclusion of the others. Further indications of the interdependence of several transactions may be the statements of the parties themselves or the simultaneous conclusion of the relevant agreements. A conclusion of *de facto* interconditionality of several transactions will be difficult to reach in the absence of their simultaneity. A pronounced lack of simultaneity of legally interconditional transactions may likewise put into doubt their true interdependence.

(44) The principle that several transactions can be treated as a single concentration under the mentioned conditions only applies if the result is that control of one or more undertakings is acquired by the same person(s) or undertaking(s). First, this may be the case if a single business or undertaking is acquired via several legal transactions. Second, also the acquisition of control of several undertakings—which could constitute concentrations in themselves—can be linked in such a way that it constitutes a single concentration. However, it is not possible under the Merger Regulation to link different legal transactions which only partly concern the acquisition of control of undertakings, but partly also the acquisition of other assets, such as non-controlling minority stakes in other companies. It would not be in line with the general framework and the purpose of the Merger Regulation if different transactions, linked by conditionality, were assessed as a whole under the Merger Regulations if only some of these transactions lead to a change in control of a given target.

Acquisition of a single business

(45) A single concentration may therefore exist if the same purchaser(s) acquire control of a single business, i.e. a single economic entity, via several legal transactions if those are inter-conditional. This is the case irrespective of whether the business is acquired in a corporate structure, consisting of one or several companies, or whether various assets are acquired which form a single business, i.e. a single economic entity managed for a common commercial purpose to which all the assets contribute. Such a business may comprise majority and minority stakes in companies as well as tangible and intangible assets. If several legal transactions which are interdependent are required to transfer such a business, these transactions constitute one concentration.

Parallel and serial acquisitions of control

(46) For the treatment of several acquisitions of control as a single concentration, several scenarios have arisen in the Commission's past decisional practice. One such scenario is a parallel acquisition of control, i.e. undertaking A acquires control of undertaking B and C in parallel from separate sellers on condition that A is not obliged to buy either and neither seller is obliged to sell, unless both transactions proceed. Another scenario is a serial acquisition of control, i.e. undertaking A acquires control of undertaking B conditional on B's prior or simultaneous acquisition of undertaking C, as illustrated by the Kingfisher case.

Serial acquisition of sole/joint control

(47) In the same way as the Kingfisher scenario, the Commission approaches cases where, in a serial transaction, an undertaking agrees to acquire first sole control of a target undertaking, with a view to directly selling on parts of the acquired stake in the target to another undertaking, finally resulting in joint control of both acquirers over the target company. If both acquisitions are inter-conditional, the two transactions constitute a single concentration and only the acquisition of joint control, as the final result of the transactions, will be considered by the Commission.

1.5.3. Series of transactions in securities

(48) Recital 20 of the Merger Regulation further explains that a single concentration will also arise in cases where control over one undertaking is acquired by a series of transactions in securities from one or several sellers taking place within a reasonably short period of time. The concentration in these scenarios is not limited to the acquisition of the 'one and decisive' share, but will cover all the acquisitions of securities which take place in the reasonably short period of time.

1.5.4. Article 5(2) subparagraph 2

(49) Article 5(2) subparagraph 2 provides a specific rule which allows the Commission to consider successive transactions occurring in a fixed period of time a single concentration for the purposes of calculating the turnover of the undertakings concerned. The purpose of this provision is to ensure that the same persons do not break a transaction down into series of sales of assets over a period of time, with the aim of avoiding the competence conferred on the Commission by the Merger Regulation.

(50) If two or more transactions (each of them bringing about an acquisition of control) take place within a two-year period between the same persons or undertakings, they shall be qualified as a single concentration, irrespective of whether or not those transactions relate to parts of the same business or concern the same sector. This does not apply where the same persons or undertakings are joined by other persons or undertakings for only some of the transactions involved. It is sufficient if the transactions, although not carried out between the same companies, are carried out between companies belonging to the same respective groups. The provision also applies to two or more transactions between the same persons or undertakings if they are carried out simultaneously. Whenever they lead to acquisitions of control by the same undertaking, such simultaneous transactions between the same parties form a single concentration even if they are not conditional upon each other. However, Article 5(2) subparagraph 2 would not appear to apply to different transactions at least one of which involves an undertaking concerned which is distinct from the common seller(s) and buyer(s). In situations involving two transactions where one transaction results in sole control and the other in joint control, Article 5(2) subparagraph 2 therefore does not apply unless the other jointly controlling parent(s) in the latter transaction are the seller(s) of the solely controlling stake in the former transaction.

1.6. Internal restructuring

(51) A concentration within the meaning of the Merger Regulation is limited to changes in control. An internal restructuring within a group of companies does not constitute a concentration. This applies, e.g., to increases in shareholdings not accompanied by changes of control or to restructuring operations such as a merger of a dual listed company into a single legal entity or a merger of subsidiaries. A concentration could only arise if the operation leads to a change in the quality of control of one undertaking and therefore is no longer purely internal.

1.7. Concentrations involving State-owned undertakings

(52) An exceptional situation exists where both the acquiring and acquired undertakings are companies owned by the same State (or by the same public body or municipality). In this case, whether the operation is to be regarded as an internal restructuring depends in turn on the question whether both undertakings were formerly part of the same economic unit. Where the undertakings were formerly part of different economic units having an independent power of decision, the operation will be deemed to constitute a concentration and not an internal restructuring. However, where the different economic units will continue to have an independent power of decision also after the operation, the operation is only to be regarded as an internal restructuring, even if the shares of the undertakings, constituting different economic units, should be held by a single entity, such as a pure holding company.

(53) However, the prerogatives exercised by a State acting as a public authority rather than as a shareholder, in so far as they are limited to the protection of the public interest, do not constitute control within the meaning of the Merger Regulation to the extent that they have neither the aim nor the effect of enabling the State to exercise a decisive influence over the activity of the undertaking.

2. SOLE CONTROL

(54) Sole control is acquired if one undertaking alone can exercise decisive influence on an undertaking. Two general situations in which an undertaking has sole control can be distinguished. First, the solely controlling undertaking enjoys the power to determine the strategic commercial decisions of the other undertaking. This power is typically achieved by the acquisition of a majority of voting rights in a company. Second, a situation also conferring sole control exists where only one shareholder is able to veto strategic decisions in an undertaking, but this shareholder does not have the power, on his own, to impose such decisions (the so-called negative sole control). In these circumstances, a single shareholder possesses the same level of influence as that usually enjoyed by an individual shareholder which jointly controls a company, i.e. the power to block the adoption of strategic decisions. In contrast to the situation in a jointly controlled company, there are no other shareholders enjoying the same level of influence and the shareholder enjoying negative sole control does not necessarily have to cooperate with specific other shareholders in determining the strategic behaviour of the controlled undertaking. Since this shareholder can produce a deadlock situation, the shareholder acquires decisive influence within the meaning of Article 3(2) and therefore control within the meaning of the Merger Regulation.

(55) Sole control can be acquired on a *de jure* and/or *de facto* basis.

De jure sole control

(56) Sole control is normally acquired on a legal basis where an undertaking acquires a majority of the voting rights of a company. In the absence of other elements, an acquisition which does not include a majority of the voting rights does not normally confer control even if it involves the acquisition of a majority of the share capital. Where the company statutes require a supermajority for strategic decisions, the acquisition of a simple majority of the voting rights may not confer the power to determine strategic decisions, but may be sufficient to confer a blocking right on the acquirer and therefore negative control.

(57) Even in the case of a minority shareholding, sole control may occur on a legal basis in situations where specific rights are attached to this shareholding. These may be preferential shares to which special rights are attached enabling the minority shareholder to determine the strategic commercial behaviour of the target company, such as the power to appoint more than half of the members of the supervisory board or the administrative board. Sole control can also be exercised by a minority shareholder who has the right to manage the activities of the company and to determine its business policy on the basis of the organisational structure (e.g. as a general partner in a limited partnership which often does not even have a shareholding).

(58) A typical situation of negative sole control occurs where one shareholder holds 50 % in an undertaking whilst the remaining 50 % is held by several other shareholders (assuming this does not lead to positive sole control on a *de facto* basis), or where there is a supermajority required for strategic decisions which in fact confers a veto right upon only one shareholder, irrespective of whether it is a majority or a minority shareholder.

De facto sole control

(59) A minority shareholder may also be deemed to have sole control on a *de facto* basis. This is in particular the case where the shareholder is highly likely to achieve a majority at the shareholders' meetings, given the level of its shareholding and the evidence resulting from the presence of shareholders in the shareholders' meetings in previous years. Based on the past voting pattern, the Commission will carry out a prospective analysis and take into account foreseeable changes of the shareholders' presence which might arise in future following the operation. The Commission will further analyse the position of other shareholders and assess their role. Criteria for such an assessment are in particular whether the remaining shares are widely dispersed, whether other important shareholders have structural, economic or family links with the large minority shareholder or whether other shareholders have a strategic or a purely financial interest in the target company; these criteria will be assessed on a case-by-case basis. Where, on the basis of its shareholding, the historic voting pattern at the shareholders' meeting and the position of other shareholders, a minority shareholder

is likely to have a stable majority of the votes at the shareholders' meeting, then that large minority shareholder is taken to have sole control.

(60) An option to purchase or convert shares cannot in itself confer sole control unless the option will be exercised in the near future according to legally binding agreements. However, in exceptional circumstances an option, together with other elements, may lead to the conclusion that there is *de facto* sole control.

Sole control acquired by other means than voting rights

(61) Apart from the acquisition of sole control on the basis of voting rights, the considerations outlined in section 1.2 concerning the acquisition of sole control by purchase of assets, by contract, or by any other means also apply.

3. JOINT CONTROL

(62) Joint control exists where two or more undertakings or persons have the possibility of exercising decisive influence over another undertaking. Decisive influence in this sense normally means the power to block actions which determine the strategic commercial behaviour of an undertaking. Unlike sole control, which confers upon a specific shareholder the power to determine the strategic decisions in an undertaking, joint control is characterized by the possibility of a deadlock situation resulting from the power of two or more parent companies to reject proposed strategic decisions. It follows, therefore, that these shareholders must reach a common understanding in determining the commercial policy of the joint venture and that they are required to cooperate.

(63) As in the case of sole control, the acquisition of joint control can also be established on a *de jure* or *de facto* basis. There is joint control if the shareholders (the parent companies) must reach agreement on major decisions concerning the controlled undertaking (the joint venture).

3.1. Equality in voting rights or appointment to decision-making bodies

(64) The clearest form of joint control exists where there are only two parent companies which share equally the voting rights in the joint venture. In this case, it is not necessary for a formal agreement to exist between them. However, where there is a formal agreement, it must be consistent with the principle of equality between the parent companies, by laying down, for example, that each is entitled to the same number of representatives in the management bodies and that none of the members has a casting vote. Equality may also be achieved where both parent companies have the right to appoint an equal number of members to the decision-making bodies of the joint venture.

3.2. Veto rights

(65) Joint control may exist even where there is no equality between the two parent companies in votes or in representation in decision-making bodies or where there are more than two parent companies. This is the case where minority shareholders have additional rights which allow them to veto decisions which are essential for the strategic commercial behaviour of the joint venture. These veto rights may be set out in the statute of the joint venture or conferred by agreement between its parent companies. The veto rights themselves may operate by means of a specific quorum required for decisions taken at the shareholders' meeting or by the board of directors to the extent that the parent companies are represented on this board. It is also possible that strategic decisions are subject to approval by a body, e.g. supervisory board, where the minority shareholders are represented and form part of the quorum needed for such decisions.

(66) These veto rights must be related to strategic decisions on the business policy of the joint venture. They must go beyond the veto rights normally accorded to minority shareholders in order to protect their financial interests as investors in the joint venture. This normal protection of the rights of minority shareholders is related to decisions on the essence of the joint venture, such as changes in the statute, an increase or decrease in the capital or liquidation. A veto right, for example, which prevents the sale or winding-up of the joint venture does not confer joint control on the minority shareholder concerned.

(67) In contrast, veto rights which confer joint control typically include decisions on issues such as the budget, the business plan, major investments or the appointment of senior management. The acquisition of joint control, however, does not require that the acquirer has the power to exercise decisive influence on the day-to-day running of an undertaking. The crucial element is that the veto rights are sufficient to enable the parent companies to exercise such influence in relation to the strategic business behaviour of the joint venture. Moreover, it is not necessary to establish that an acquirer of joint control of the joint venture will actually make use of its decisive influence. The possibility of exercising such influence and, hence, the mere existence of the veto rights, is sufficient.

(68) In order to acquire joint control, it is not necessary for a minority shareholder to have all the veto rights mentioned above. It may be sufficient that only some, or even one such right, exists. Whether or not this is the case depends upon the precise content of the veto right itself and also the importance of this right in the context of the specific business of the joint venture.

Appointment of senior management and determination of budget

(69) Very important are the veto rights concerning decisions on the appointment and dismissal of the senior management and the approval of the budget. The power to co-determine the structure of the senior management, such as the members of the board, usually confers upon the holder the power to exercise decisive influence on the commercial policy of an undertaking. The same is true with respect to decisions on the budget since the budget determines the precise framework of the activities of the joint venture and, in particular, the investments it may make.

Business plan

(70) The business plan normally provides details of the aims of a company together with the measures to be taken in order to achieve those aims. A veto right over this type of business plan may be sufficient to confer joint control even in the absence of any other veto right. In contrast, where the business plan contains merely general declarations concerning the business aims of the joint venture, the existence of a veto right will be only one element in the general assessment of joint control but will not, on its own, be sufficient to confer joint control.

Investments

(71) In the case of a veto right on investments, the importance of this right depends, first, on the level of investments which are subject to the approval of the parent companies and, secondly, on the extent to which investments constitute an essential feature of the market in which the joint venture is active. In relation to the first criterion, where the level of investments necessitating approval of the parent companies is extremely high, this veto right may be closer to the normal protection of the interests of a minority shareholder than to a right conferring a power of co-determination over the commercial policy of the joint venture. With regard to the second, the investment policy of an undertaking is normally an important element in assessing whether or not there is joint control. However, there may be some markets where investment does not play a significant role in the market behaviour of an undertaking.

Market-specific rights

(72) Apart from the typical veto rights mentioned above, there exist a number of other possible veto rights related to specific decisions which are important in the context of the particular market of the joint venture. One example is the decision on the technology to be used by the joint venture where technology is a key feature of the joint venture's activities. Another example relates to markets characterized by product differentiation and a significant degree of innovation. In such markets, a veto right over decisions relating to new product lines to be developed by the joint venture may also be an important element in establishing the existence of joint control.

Overall context

(73) In assessing the relative importance of veto rights, where there are a number of them, these rights should not be evaluated in isolation. On the contrary, the determination of whether or not joint control exists is based upon an assessment of these rights as a whole. However, a veto right which does

not relate either to strategic commercial policy, to the appointment of senior management or to the budget or business plan cannot be regarded as giving joint control to its owner.

3.3.   Joint exercise of voting rights

(74) Even in the absence of specific veto rights, two or more undertakings acquiring minority shareholdings in another undertaking may obtain joint control. This may be the case where the minority shareholdings together provide the means for controlling the target undertaking. This means that the minority shareholders, together, will have a majority of the voting rights; and they will act together in exercising these voting rights. This can result from a legally binding agreement to this effect, or it may be established on a *de facto* basis.

(75) The legal means to ensure the joint exercise of voting rights can be in the form of a (jointly controlled) holding company to which the minority shareholders transfer their rights, or an agreement by which they undertake to act in the same way (pooling agreement).

(76) Very exceptionally, collective action can occur on a *de facto* basis where strong common interests exist between the minority shareholders to the effect that they would not act against each other in exercising their rights in relation to the joint venture. The greater the number of parent companies involved in such a joint venture, however, the more remote is the likelihood of this situation occurring.

(77) Indicative for such a commonality of interests is a high degree of mutual dependency as between the parent companies to reach the strategic objectives of the joint venture. This is in particular the case when each parent company provides a contribution to the joint venture which is vital for its operation (e.g. specific technologies, local know-how or supply agreements). In these circumstances, the parent companies may be able to block the strategic decisions of the joint venture and, thus, they can operate the joint venture successfully only with each other's agreement on the strategic decisions even if there is no express provision for any veto rights. The parent companies will therefore be required to cooperate. Further factors are decision making procedures which are tailored in such a way as to allow the parent companies to exercise joint control even in the absence of explicit agreements granting veto rights or other links between the minority shareholders related to the joint venture.

(78) Such a scenario may not only occur in a situation where two or more minority shareholders jointly control an undertaking on a de facto basis, but also where there is high degree of dependency of a majority shareholder on a minority shareholder. This may be the case where the joint venture economically and financially depends on the minority shareholder or where only the minority shareholder has the required know-how for, and will play a major role in, the operation of the joint undertaking whereas the majority shareholder is a mere financial investor. In such circumstances, the majority shareholder will not be able to enforce its position, but the joint venture partner may be able to block strategic decisions so that both parent undertakings will be required to cooperate permanently. This leads to a situation of *de facto* joint control which prevails over a pure *de jure* assessment according to which the majority shareholder could have been considered to have sole control.

(79) These criteria apply to the formation of a new joint venture as well as to acquisitions of minority shareholdings, together conferring joint control. In case of acquisitions of shareholdings, there is a higher probability of a commonality of interests if the shareholdings are acquired by means of concerted action. However, an acquisition by way of a concerted action is not alone sufficient for the purposes of establishing *de facto* joint control. In general, a common interest as financial investors (or creditors) of a company in a return on investment does not constitute a commonality of interests leading to the exercise of *de facto* joint control.

(80) In the absence of strong common interests such as those outlined above, the possibility of changing coalitions between minority shareholders will normally exclude the assumption of joint control. Where there is no stable majority in the decision-making procedure and the majority can on each occasion be any of the various combinations possible amongst the minority shareholders, it cannot be assumed that the minority shareholders (or a certain group thereof) will jointly control the undertaking. In this context, it is not sufficient that there are agreements between two or more parties having an equal shareholding in the capital of an undertaking which establish identical rights and

powers between the parties, where these fall short of strategic veto rights. For example, in the case of an undertaking where three shareholders each own one-third of the share capital and each elect one-third of the members of the Board of Directors, the shareholders do not have joint control since decisions are required to be taken on the basis of a simple majority.

3.4. Other considerations related to joint control

Unequal role of the parent companies

(81) Joint control is not incompatible with the fact that one of the parent companies enjoys specific knowledge of and experience in the business of the joint venture. In such a case, the other parent company can play a modest or even non-existent role in the daily management of the joint venture where its presence is motivated by considerations of a financial, long-term-strategy, brand image or general policy nature. Nevertheless, it must always retain the real possibility of contesting the decisions taken by the other parent company on the basis of equality in voting rights or rights of appointment to decision making bodies or of veto rights related to strategic issues. Without this, there would be sole control.

Casting vote

(82) For joint control to exist, there should not be a casting vote for one parent company only as this would lead to sole control of the company enjoying the casting vote. However, there can be joint control when this casting vote is in practice of limited relevance and effectiveness. This may be the case when the casting vote can be exercised only after a series of stages of arbitration and attempts at reconciliation or in a very limited field or if the exercise of the casting vote triggers a put option implying a serious financial burden or if the mutual interdependence of the parent companies would make the exercise of the casting vote unlikely.

III. CHANGES IN THE QUALITY OF CONTROL

(83) The Merger Regulation covers operations resulting in the acquisition of sole or joint control, including operations leading to changes in the quality of control. First, such a change in the quality of control, resulting in a concentration, occurs if there is a change between sole and joint control. Second, a change in the quality of control occurs between joint control scenarios before and after the transaction if there is an increase in the number or a change in the identity of controlling shareholders. However, there is no change in the quality of control if a change from negative to positive sole control occurs. Such a change affects neither the incentives of the negatively controlling shareholder nor the nature of the control structure, as the controlling shareholder did not necessarily have to cooperate with specific shareholders at the time when it enjoyed negative control. In any case, mere changes in the level of shareholdings of the same controlling shareholders, without changes of the powers they hold in a company and of the composition of the control structure of the company, do not constitute a change in the quality of control and therefore are not a notifiable concentration.

(84) These changes in the quality of control will be discussed in two categories: first, an entrance of one or more new controlling shareholders irrespective of whether or not they replace existing controlling shareholders and, second, a reduction of the number of controlling shareholders.

1. ENTRY OF CONTROLLING SHAREHOLDERS

(85) An entry of new controlling shareholders leading to a joint control scenario can either result from a change from sole to joint control, or from the entry of an additional shareholder or a replacement of an existing shareholder in an already jointly controlled undertaking.

(86) A move from sole control to joint control is considered a notifiable operation as this changes the quality of control of the joint venture. First, there is a new acquisition of control for the shareholder entering the controlled undertaking. Second, only the new acquisition of control makes the controlled undertaking to a joint venture which changes decisively also the situation for the remaining controlling undertaking under the Merger Regulation: In the future, it has to take into account the interests

of one or more other controlling shareholder(s) and it is required to cooperate permanently with the new shareholder(s). Before, it could either determine the strategic behaviour of the controlled undertaking alone (in the case of sole control) or was not forced to take into account the interests of specific other shareholders and was not forced to cooperate with those shareholders permanently.

(87) The entry of a new shareholder in a jointly controlled undertaking—either in addition to the already controlling shareholders or in replacement of one of them—also constitutes a notifiable concentration, although the undertaking is jointly controlled before and after the operation. First, also in this scenario there is a shareholder newly acquiring control of the joint venture. Second, the quality of control of the joint venture is determined by the identity of all controlling shareholders. It lies in the nature of joint control that, since each shareholder alone has a blocking right concerning strategic decisions, the jointly controlling shareholders have to take into account each others interests and are required to cooperate for the determination of the strategic behaviour of the joint venture. The nature of joint control therefore does not exhaust itself in a pure mathematical addition of the blocking rights exercised by several shareholders, but is determined by the composition of the jointly controlling shareholders. One of the most obvious scenarios leading to a decisive change in the nature of the control structure of a jointly controlled undertaking is a situation where in a joint venture, jointly controlled by a competitor of the joint venture and a financial investor, the financial investor is replaced by another competitor. In these circumstances, the control structure and the incentives of the joint venture may entirely change, not only because of the entry of the new controlling shareholder, but also due to the change in the behaviour of the remaining shareholder. The replacement of a controlling shareholder or the entry of a new shareholder in a jointly controlled undertaking therefore constitutes a change in the quality of control.

(88) However, the entry of new shareholders only results in a notifiable concentration if one or several shareholders acquire sole or joint control by virtue of the operation. The entry of new shareholders may lead to a situation where joint control can neither be established on a *de jure* basis nor on a *de facto* basis as the entry of the new shareholder leads to the consequence that changing coalitions between minority shareholders are possible.

2. REDUCTION IN THE NUMBER OF SHAREHOLDERS

(89) A reduction in the number of controlling shareholders constitutes a change in the quality of control and is thus to be considered as a concentration if the exit of one or more controlling shareholders results in a change from joint to sole control. Decisive influence exercised alone is substantially different from decisive influence exercised jointly, since in the latter case the jointly controlling shareholders have to take into account the potentially different interests of the other party or parties involved.

(90) Where the operation involves a reduction in the number of jointly controlling shareholders, without leading to a change from joint to sole control, the transaction will normally not lead to a notifiable concentration.

IV. JOINT VENTURES—THE CONCEPT OF FULL-FUNCTIONALITY

(91) Article 3(1)(b) provides that a concentration shall be deemed to arise where control is acquired by *one or more* undertakings of the whole or parts of another undertaking. The new acquisition of another undertaking by several jointly controlling undertakings therefore constitutes a concentration under the Merger Regulation. As in the case of the acquisition of sole control of an undertaking, such an acquisition of joint control will lead to a structural change in the market even if, according to the plans of the acquiring undertakings, the acquired undertaking would no longer be considered full-function after the transaction (e.g. because it will sell exclusively to the parent undertakings in future). Thus, a transaction involving several undertakings acquiring joint control of

another undertaking or parts of another undertaking, fulfilling the criteria set out in paragraph 24, from third parties will constitute a concentration according to Article 3(1) without it being necessary to consider the full-functionality criterion.

(92) Article 3(4) provides in addition that the creation of a joint venture performing on a lasting basis all the functions of an autonomous economic entity (so called full-function joint ventures) shall constitute a concentration within the meaning of the Merger Regulation. The full-functionality criterion therefore delineates the application of the Merger Regulation for the creation of joint ventures by the parties, irrespective of whether such a joint venture is created as a 'greenfield operation' or whether the parties contribute assets to the joint venture which they previously owned individually. In these circumstances, the joint venture must fulfil the full-functionality criterion in order to constitute a concentration.

(93) The fact that a joint venture may be a full-function undertaking and therefore economically autonomous from an operational viewpoint does not mean that it enjoys autonomy as regards the adoption of its strategic decisions. Otherwise, a jointly controlled undertaking could never be considered a full-function joint venture and therefore the condition laid down in Article 3(4) would never be complied with. It is therefore sufficient for the criterion of full-functionality if the joint venture is autonomous in operational respect.

1. SUFFICIENT RESOURCES TO OPERATE INDEPENDENTLY ON A MARKET

(94) Full function character essentially means that a joint venture must operate on a market, performing the functions normally carried out by undertakings operating on the same market. In order to do so the joint venture must have a management dedicated to its day-to-day operations and access to sufficient resources including finance, staff, and assets (tangible and intangible) in order to conduct on a lasting basis its business activities within the area provided for in the joint-venture agreement. The personnel do not necessarily need to be employed by the joint venture itself. If it is standard practice in the industry where the joint venture is operating, it may be sufficient if third parties envisage the staffing under an operational agreement or if staff is assigned by an interim employment agency. The secondment of personnel by the parent companies may also be sufficient if this is done either only for a start-up period or if the joint venture deals with the parent companies in the same way as with third parties. The latter case requires that the joint venture deals with the parents at arm's length on the basis of normal commercial conditions and that the joint venture is also free to recruit its own employees or to obtain staff via third parties.

2. ACTIVITIES BEYOND ONE SPECIFIC FUNCTION FOR THE PARENTS

(95) A joint venture is not full-function if it only takes over one specific function within the parent companies' business activities without its own access to or presence on the market. This is the case, for example, for joint ventures limited to R&D or production. Such joint ventures are auxiliary to their parent companies' business activities. This is also the case where a joint venture is essentially limited to the distribution or sales of its parent companies' products and, therefore, acts principally as a sales agency. However, the fact that a joint venture makes use of the distribution network or outlet of one or more of its parent companies normally will not disqualify it as 'full-function' as long as the parent companies are acting only as agents of the joint venture.

(96) A frequent example where this question arises are joint ventures involved in the holding of real estate property, which are typically set up for tax and other financial reasons. As long as the purpose of the joint venture is limited to the acquisition and/or holding of certain real estate for the parents and based on financial resources provided by the parents, it will not usually be considered to be full-function, as it lacks an autonomous, long term business activity on the market and will typically

also lack the necessary resources to operate independently. This has to be distinguished from joint ventures that are actively managing a real estate portfolio and who act on their own behalf on the market, which typically indicates full-functionality.

3. SALE/PURCHASE RELATIONS WITH THE PARENTS

(97) The strong presence of the parent companies in upstream or downstream markets is a factor to be taken into consideration in assessing the full-function character of a joint venture where this presence results in substantial sales or purchases between the parent companies and the joint venture. The fact that, for an initial start-up period only, the joint venture relies almost entirely on sales to or purchases from its parent companies does not normally affect its full-function character. Such a start-up period may be necessary in order to establish the joint venture on a market. But the period will normally not exceed a period of three years, depending on the specific conditions of the market in question.

Sales to the parents

(98) Where sales from the joint venture to the parent companies are intended to be made on a lasting basis, the essential question is whether, regardless of these sales, the joint venture is geared to play an active role on the market and can be considered economically autonomous from an operational viewpoint. In this respect the relative proportion of sales made to its parents compared with the total production of the joint venture is an important factor. Due to the particularities of each individual case, it is impossible to define a specific turnover ratio which distinguishes full-function from other joint ventures. If the joint venture achieves more than 50 % of its turnover with third parties, this will typically be an indication of full-functionality. Below this indicative threshold, a case-by-case analysis is required, whereby, for the finding of operational autonomy, the relationship between the joint venture and its parents must be truly commercial in character. For this purpose, it is to be demonstrated that the joint venture will supply its goods or services to the purchaser who values them most and will pay most and that the joint venture will also deal with its parents' companies at arm's length on the basis of normal commercial conditions. Under these circumstances, i.e. if the joint venture will treat its parent companies in the same commercial way as third parties, it may be sufficient that at least 20 % of the joint venture's predicted sales will go to third parties. However, the greater the proportion of sales likely to be made to the parents, the greater will be the need for clear evidence of the commercial character of the relationship.

(99) For the determination of the proportion between sales to the parents and to third parties, the Commission will take past accounts and substantiated business plans into account. However, especially where substantial third-party sales cannot be readily foreseen, the Commission will base its finding also on the general market structure. This may be a relevant factor as well for the assessment whether the joint venture will deal with its parents on an arm's length basis.

(100) These issues frequently arise with regard to outsourcing agreements, where an undertaking creates a joint venture with a service provider (91) which will carry out functions that were previously dealt with by the undertaking in-house. The JV typically cannot be considered to be full-function in these scenarios: it provides its services exclusively to the client undertaking, and it is dependent for its services on input from the service provider. The fact that the joint venture's business plan often at least does not exclude that the joint venture can provide its services to third parties does not alter this assessment, as in the typical outsourcing setup any third party revenues are likely to remain ancillary to the joint venture's main activities for the client undertaking. However, this general rule does not exclude that there are outsourcing situations where the joint venture partners, for example for reasons of economies of scale, set up a joint venture with the perspective of significant market access. This could qualify the joint venture as full function if significant third-party sales are foreseen and if the relationship between the joint venture and its parent will be truly commercial in character and if the joint venture deals with its parents on the basis of normal commercial conditions.

Purchases from the parents

(101) In relation to purchases made by the joint venture from its parent companies, the full-function character of the joint venture is questionable in particular where little value is added to the products or services concerned at the level of the joint venture itself. In such a situation, the joint venture may be closer to a joint sales agency.

Trade markets

(102) However, in contrast to this situation where a joint venture is active in a trade market and performs the normal functions of a trading company in such a market, it normally will not be an auxiliary sales agency but a full-function joint venture. A trade market is characterised by the existence of companies which specialise in the selling and distribution of products without being vertically integrated in addition to those which are integrated, and where different sources of supply are available for the products in question. In addition, many trade markets may require operators to invest in specific facilities such as outlets, stockholding, warehouses, depots, transport fleets and sales and service personnel. In order to constitute a full-function joint venture in a trade market, an undertaking must have the necessary facilities and be likely to obtain a substantial proportion of its supplies not only from its parent companies but also from other competing sources.

4. OPERATION ON A LASTING BASIS

(103) Furthermore, the joint venture must be intended to operate on a lasting basis. The fact that the parent companies commit to the joint venture the resources described above normally demonstrates that this is the case. In addition, agreements setting up a joint venture often provide for certain contingencies, for example, the failure of the joint venture or fundamental disagreement as between the parent companies. This may be achieved by the incorporation of provisions for the eventual dissolution of the joint venture itself or the possibility for one or more parent companies to withdraw from the joint venture. This kind of provision does not prevent the joint venture from being considered as operating on a lasting basis. The same is normally true where the agreement specifies a period for the duration of the joint venture where this period is sufficiently long in order to bring about a lasting change in the structure of the undertakings concerned, or where the agreement provides for the possible continuation of the joint venture beyond this period.

(104) By contrast, the joint venture will not be considered to operate on a lasting basis where it is established for a short finite duration. This would be the case, for example, where a joint venture is established in order to construct a specific project such as a power plant, but it will not be involved in the operation of the plant once its construction has been completed.

(105) A joint venture also lacks the sufficient operations on a lasting basis at a stage where there are decisions of third parties outstanding that are of an essential core importance for starting the joint venture's business activity. Only decisions that go beyond mere formalities and the award of which is typically uncertain qualify for these scenarios. Examples are the award of a contract (e.g., in public tenders), licences (e.g., in the telecoms sector) or access rights to property (e.g., exploration rights for oil and gas). Pending the decision on such factors, it is unclear whether the joint venture will become operational at all. Thus, at that stage the joint venture cannot be considered to perform economic functions on a lasting basis and consequently does not qualify as full function. However, once a decision has been taken in favour of the joint venture in question, this criterion is fulfilled and a concentration arises.

5. CHANGES IN THE ACTIVITIES OF
THE JOINT VENTURE

(106) The parents may decide to enlarge the scope of the activities of the joint venture in the course of its lifetime. This will be considered as a new concentration that may trigger a notification requirement if this enlargement entails the acquisition of the whole or part of another undertaking

from the parents that would, considered in isolation, qualify as a concentration as explained in paragraph 24 of this Notice.

(107) A concentration may also arise if the parent companies transfer significant additional assets, contracts, know-how or other rights to the joint venture and these assets and rights constitute the basis or nucleus of an extension of the activities of the joint venture into other product or geographic markets which were not the object of the original joint venture, and if the joint venture performs such activities on a full-function basis. As the transfer of the assets or rights shows that the parents are the real players behind the extension of the joint venture's scope, the enlargement of the activities of the joint venture can be considered in the same way as the creation of a new joint venture within the meaning of Article 3(4).

(108) If the scope of a joint venture is enlarged without additional assets, contracts, know-how or rights being transferred, no concentration will be deemed to arise.

(109) A concentration arises if a change in the activity of an existing non-full-function joint venture occurs so that a full-function joint venture within the meaning of Article 3(4) is created. The following examples may be given: a change of the organisational structure of a joint venture so that it fulfils the full functionality criterion; a joint venture that used to supply only the parent companies, which subsequently starts a significant activity on the market; or scenarios, as described in paragraph 105 above, where a joint venture can only start its activity on the market once it has essential input (such as a licence for a joint venture in the telecoms sector). Such a change in the activity of the joint venture will frequently require a decision by its shareholders or its management. Once the decision is taken that leads to the joint venture meeting the full functionality criterion, a concentration arises.

V. EXCEPTIONS

(110) Article 3(5) sets out three exceptional situations where the acquisition of a controlling interest does not constitute a concentration under the Merger Regulation.

(111) First, the acquisition of securities by companies whose normal activities include transactions and dealing in securities for their own account or for the account of others is not deemed to constitute a concentration if such an acquisition is made in the framework of these businesses and if the securities are held on only a temporary basis (Article 3(5)(a)). In order to fall within this exception, the following requirements must be fulfilled:—the acquiring undertaking must be a credit or other financial institution or insurance company the normal activities of which are described above;

- the securities must be acquired with a view to their resale;
- the acquiring undertaking must not exercise the voting rights with a view to determining the strategic commercial behaviour of the target company or must exercise these rights only with a view to preparing the total or partial disposal of the undertaking, its assets or the securities;
- the acquiring undertaking must dispose of its controlling interest within one year of the date of the acquisition, that is, it must reduce its shareholding within this one-year period at least to a level which no longer confers control. This period, however, may be extended by the Commission where the acquiring undertaking can show that the disposal was not reasonably possible within the one year period.

(112) Second, there is no change of control, and hence no concentration within the meaning of the Merger Regulation, where control is acquired by an office-holder according to the law of a Member State relating to liquidation, winding-up, insolvency, cessation of payments, compositions or analogous proceedings (Article 3(5)(b));

(113) Third, a concentration does not arise where a financial holding company within the meaning of Article 5(3) of the Council Directive 78/660/EEC acquires control. The notion of 'financial holding company' is thus limited to companies whose sole purpose it is to acquire holdings in other undertakings without involving themselves directly or indirectly in the management of those undertakings, the foregoing without prejudice to their rights as shareholders. Such investment companies

must be further structured in a way that compliance with these limitations can be supervised by an administrative or judicial authority. The Merger Regulation provides for an additional condition for this exception to apply: such companies may exercise the voting rights in the other undertakings only to maintain the full value of those investments and not to determine directly or indirectly the strategic commercial conduct of the controlled undertaking.

(114) The exceptions under Article 3(5) of the Merger Regulation only apply to a very limited field. First, these exceptions only apply if the operation would otherwise be a concentration in its own right, but not if the transaction is part of a broader, single concentration, in circumstances in which the ultimate acquirer of control would not fall within the terms of Article 3(5) (see e.g. paragraph 35 above). Second, the exceptions under Article 3(5)(a) and (c) only apply to acquisitions of control by way of purchase of securities, not to acquisitions of assets.

(115) The exceptions do not apply to typical investment fund structures. According to their objectives, these funds usually do not limit themselves in the exercise of the voting rights, but adopt decisions to appoint the members of the management and the supervisory bodies of the undertakings or to even restructure those undertakings. This would not be compatible with the requirement under both Article 3(5)(a) and (c) that the acquiring companies do not exercise the voting rights with a view to determine the competitive conduct of the other undertaking.

(116) The question may arise whether an operation to rescue an undertaking before or from insolvency proceedings constitutes a concentration under the Merger Regulation. Such a rescue operation typically involves the conversion of existing debt into a new company, through which a syndicate of banks may acquire joint control of the company concerned. Where such an operation meets the criteria for joint control, as outlined above, it will normally be considered to be a concentration. Although the primary intention of the banks is to restructure the financing of the undertaking concerned for its subsequent resale, the exception set out in Article 3(5)(a) is normally not applicable to such an operation. In a similar way as set out for investment funds, the restructuring programme normally requires the controlling banks to determine the strategic commercial behaviour of the rescued undertaking. Furthermore, it is not normally a realistic proposition to transform a rescued company into a commercially viable entity and to resell it within the permitted one-year period. Moreover, the length of time needed to achieve this aim may be so uncertain that it would be difficult to grant an extension of the disposal period.

VI. ABANDONMENT OF CONCENTRATIONS

(117) A concentration ceases to exist and the Merger Regulation ceases to be applicable if the undertakings concerned abandon the concentration.

(118) In this respect, the revised Merger Regulation 139/2004 introduced a new provision related to the closure of procedures concerning the control of concentrations without a final decision after the Commission has initiated proceedings under Article 6(1)(c), first sentence. That sentence reads as follows: 'Without prejudice to Article 9, such proceedings shall be closed by means of a decision as provided for in Article 8(1) to (4), unless the undertakings concerned have demonstrated to the satisfaction of the Commission that they have abandoned the concentration'. Prior to the initiation of proceedings, such requirements do not apply.

(119) As a general principle, the requirements for the proof of the abandonment must correspond in terms of legal form, intensity etc. to the initial act that was considered sufficient to make the concentration notifiable. In case the parties proceed from that initial act to a strengthening of their contractual links during the procedure, for example by concluding a binding agreement after the transaction was notified on the basis of a good faith intention, the requirements for the proof of the abandonment must correspond also to the nature of the latest act.

(120) In line with this principle, in case of implementation of the concentration prior to a Commission decision, the re-establishment of the *status quo ante* has to be shown. The mere withdrawal of the notification is not considered as sufficient proof that the concentration has been

abandoned in the sense of Article 6(1)(c). Likewise, minor modifications of a concentration which do not affect the change in control or the quality of that change, cannot be considered as an abandonment of the original concentration.

— Binding agreement: proof of the legally binding cancellation of the agreement in the form envisaged by the initial agreement (i.e. usually a document signed by all the parties) will be required. Expressions of intention to cancel the agreement or not to implement the notified concentration, as well as unilateral declarations by (one of) the parties will not be considered sufficient.

— Good faith intention to conclude an agreement: In case of a letter of intent or memorandum of understanding reflecting such good faith intention, documents proving that this basis for the good faith intention has been cancelled will be required. As for possible other forms that indicated the good faith intention, the abandonment must reverse this good faith intention and correspond in terms of form and intensity to the initial expression of intent.

— Public announcement of a public bid or of the intention to make a public bid: a public announcement terminating the bidding procedure or renouncing to the intention to make a public bid will be required. The format and public reach of this announcement must be comparable to the initial announcement.

— Implemented concentrations: In case the concentration has been implemented prior to a Commission decision, the parties will be required to show that the situation prevailing before the implementation of the concentration has been re-established.

(121) It is for the parties to submit the necessary documentation to meet these requirements in due time.

VII. CHANGES OF TRANSACTIONS AFTER A COMMISSION AUTHORISATION DECISION

(122) In some cases, parties may wish not to implement the concentration in the form foreseen after authorisation of the concentration by the Commission. The question arises whether the Commission's authorisation decision still covers the changed structure of the transaction.

(123) Broadly speaking, if, before implementation of the authorised concentration, the transactional structure is changed from an acquisition of control, falling under Article 3(1)(b), to a merger according to Article 3(1)(a), or *vice versa*, then the change in the transactional structure is considered a different concentration under the Merger Regulation and a new notification is required. However, less significant modifications of the transaction, for example minor changes in the shareholding percentages which do not affect the change in control or the quality of that change, changes in the offer price in the case of public bids or changes in the corporate structure by which the transaction is implemented without effects on the relevant control situation under the Merger Regulation, are considered as being covered by the Commission's authorisation decision.

C. COMMUNITY DIMENSION

I. THRESHOLDS

(124) A two fold test defines the operations to which the Merger Regulation applies. The first test is that the operation must be a concentration within the meaning of Article 3. The second comprises the turnover thresholds contained in Article 1, designed to identify those operations which have an impact upon the Community and can be deemed to be of 'Community dimension'. Turnover is used as a proxy for the economic resources being combined in a concentration, and is allocated geographically in order to reflect the geographic distribution of those resources.

(125) Two sets of thresholds are set out in Article 1 to establish whether the operation has a Community dimension. Article 1(2) establishes three different criteria: The worldwide turnover threshold is intended to measure the overall dimension of the undertakings concerned; the Community turnover threshold seek to determine whether the concentration involves a minimum level of activities in the Community; and the two-thirds rule aims to exclude purely domestic transactions from Community jurisdiction.

(126) This second set of thresholds, contained in Article 1(3), is designed to tackle those concentrations which fall short of achieving Community dimension under Article 1(2), but would have a substantial impact in at least three Member States leading to multiple notifications under national competition rules of those Member States. For this purpose, Article 1(3) provides for lower turnover thresholds, both worldwide and Community-wide, and for a minimum level of activities of the undertakings concerned, jointly and individually, in at least three Member States. Similarly to Article 1(2), Article 1(3) also contains a two thirds rule excluding predominantly domestic concentrations.

(127) The thresholds as such are designed to govern jurisdiction and not to assess the market position of the parties to the concentration nor the impact of the operation. In so doing they include turnover derived from, and thus the resources devoted to, all areas of activity of the parties, and not just those directly involved in the concentration. The thresholds are purely quantitative, since they are only based on turnover calculation instead of market share or other criteria. They pursue the objective to provide a simple and objective mechanism that can be easily handled by the companies involved in a merger in order to determine if their transaction has a Community dimension and is therefore notifiable.

(128) Whereas Article 1 sets out the numerical thresholds to establish jurisdiction, the purpose of Article 5 is to explain how turnover should be calculated to ensure that the resulting figures are a true representation of economic reality.

II. NOTION OF UNDERTAKING CONCERNED

1. GENERAL

(129) From the point of view of determining jurisdiction, the undertakings concerned are those participating in a concentration, i.e. a merger or an acquisition of control as foreseen in Article 3(1). The individual and aggregate turnover of those undertakings will be decisive in determining whether the thresholds are met.

(130) Once the undertakings concerned have been identified in a given transaction, their turnover for the purposes of determining jurisdiction is to be calculated according to the rules set out in Article 5. Article 5(4) sets out detailed criteria to identify undertakings whose turnover may be attributed to the undertaking concerned because of certain direct or indirect links with the latter. The legislator's intention was to lay down concrete rules which, seen together, can be taken to establish the notion of a 'group' for the purposes of the turnover thresholds in the Merger Regulation. The term 'group' will be used in the following sections exclusively to refer to the collection of undertakings whose relations with an undertaking concerned come within the terms of one or more of the subparagraphs of Article 5(4) of the Merger Regulation.

(131) It is important, when referring to the various undertakings which may be involved in a procedure, not to confuse the concept of 'undertakings concerned' under Articles 1 and 5 with the terminology used elsewhere in the Merger Regulation and in Commission Regulation (EC) No 802/2004 of 7 April 2004 implementing Council Regulation (EC) No 139/2004 on the control of concentrations between undertakings (hereinafter referred to as the 'Implementing Regulation') (106) referring to the various undertakings which may be involved in a procedure. This terminology refers to the notifying parties, other involved parties, third parties and parties who may be subject to fines or periodic penalty payments, and they are defined in Chapter IV of the Implementing Regulation, along with their respective rights and duties.

2. MERGERS

(132) In a merger the undertakings concerned are each of the merging entities.

3. ACQUISITION OF CONTROL

(133) In the remaining cases, it is the concept of 'acquiring control' that will determine which are the undertakings concerned. On the acquiring side, there can be one or more undertakings acquiring sole or joint control. On the acquired side, there can be one or more undertakings as a whole or parts thereof. As a general rule, each of these undertakings will be an undertaking concerned within the meaning of the Merger Regulation.

Acquisition of sole control

(134) Acquisition of sole control of the whole undertaking is the most straightforward case of acquisition of control. The undertakings concerned will be the acquiring undertaking and the target undertaking.

(135) Where the target undertaking is acquired by a group through one of its subsidiaries, the undertakings concerned are the target undertaking and the acquiring subsidiary if this is not a mere acquisition vehicle. However, even though the subsidiary is normally the undertaking concerned for the purpose of calculating turnover, the turnover of all undertakings with which the undertaking concerned has the links as specified in Article 5(4) shall be included in the threshold calculations. In this respect, the group is considered to be a single economic unit and the different companies belonging to the same group cannot be considered as different undertakings concerned for jurisdictional purposes under the Merger Regulation. The actual notification can be made by the subsidiary concerned or by its parent company.

Acquisition of parts of an undertaking and staggered operations—Article 5(2)

(136) The first subparagraph of Article 5(2) of the Merger Regulation provides that when the operation concerns the acquisition of parts of one or more undertakings, only those parts which are the subject of the transaction shall be taken into account with regard to the seller. The possible impact of the transaction on the market will depend only on the combination of the economic and financial resources that are the subject of the transaction with those of the acquirer and not on the remaining business of the seller. In this case, the undertakings concerned will be the acquirer(s) and the acquired part(s) of the target undertaking, but the remaining businesses of the seller will be ignored.

(137) The second subparagraph of Article 5(2) includes a special provision on staggered operations or follow up deals. The previous concentrations (within two years) involving the same parties become (re)notifiable with the most recent transaction, provided this constitutes a concentration, if the thresholds are met whether for one or more of the transactions taken in isolation or cumulatively. In this case, the undertakings concerned are the acquirer(s) and the different acquired part(s) of the target company taken as a whole.

Change from joint to sole control

(138) If the acquisition of control occurs by way of a change from joint control to sole control, one shareholder normally acquires the stake previously held by the other shareholder(s). In this situation, the undertakings concerned are the acquiring shareholder and the joint venture. As is the case for any other seller, the 'exiting' shareholder is not an undertaking concerned.

Acquisition of joint control

(139) In the case of acquisition of joint control of a newly-created undertaking, the undertakings concerned are each of the companies acquiring control of the newly set-up joint venture (which, as it does not yet exist, cannot be considered to be an undertaking concerned and moreover, as yet, has no turnover of its own). The same rule applies where one undertaking contributes a pre-existing subsidiary or a business (over which it previously exercised sole control) to a newly created joint venture. In these circumstances, each of the jointly-controlling undertakings is considered an undertaking

concerned whereas any company or business contributed to the joint venture is not an undertaking concerned, and its turnover is part of the turnover of the initial parent company.

(140) The situation is different if undertakings newly acquire joint control of a pre-existing undertaking or business. The undertakings concerned are each of the undertakings acquiring joint control on the one hand, and the pre-existing acquired undertaking or business on the other.

(141) The acquisition of a company with a view to immediately split up the assets is, as explained above in paragraph 32, mostly not considered as an acquisition of joint control of the entire target company, but as the acquisition of sole control by each of the ultimate acquirers of the respective parts of the target company. In line with the considerations for the acquisition of sole control, undertakings concerned are the acquiring undertakings and the acquired parts in each of the transactions.

Changes of controlling shareholders in cases of joint control of an existing joint venture

(142) A notifiable concentration may arise, as explained above, where a change in the quality of control occurs in a joint control structure due to the entrance of new controlling shareholders, irrespective of whether or not they replace existing controlling shareholders.

(143) In the case where one or more shareholders acquire control, either by entry or by substitution of one or more shareholders, in a situation of joint control both before and after the operation, the undertakings concerned are the shareholders (both existing and new) who exercise joint control and the joint venture itself. On the one hand, similar to the acquisition of joint control of an existing company, the joint venture itself can be considered as an undertaking concerned as it is an already pre-existing undertaking. On the other hand, as set out above, the entry of a new shareholder is not only in itself a new acquisition of control, but also leads to a change in the quality of control for the remaining controlling shareholders as the quality of control of the joint venture is determined by the identity and composition of the controlling shareholders and therefore also by the relationship between them. Furthermore, the Merger Regulation considers a joint venture as a combination of the economic resources of the parent companies, together with the joint venture if it already generates turnover on the market. For these reasons, the newly entering controlling shareholders are undertakings concerned alongside with the remaining controlling shareholders. Due to the change of the quality in control, all of them are considered to undertake an acquisition of control.

(144) As Article 4(2) first sentence of the Merger Regulation foresees that all acquisitions of joint control shall be notified jointly by the undertakings acquiring joint control, existing and new shareholders in principle have to notify concentrations arising from such changes in joint control scenarios jointly.

Acquisition of control by a joint venture

(145) In transactions where a joint venture acquires control of another company, the question arises whether or not the joint venture should be regarded as the undertaking concerned (the turnover of which would include the turnover of its parent companies), or whether each of its parent companies should individually be regarded as undertakings concerned. This question may be decisive for jurisdictional purposes. Whereas, in principle, the undertaking concerned is the joint venture as the direct participant in the acquisition of control, there may be circumstances where companies set up 'shell' companies and the parent companies will individually be considered as undertakings concerned. In this type of situation, the Commission will look at the economic reality of the operation to determine which are the undertakings concerned.

(146) Where the acquisition is carried out by a full-function joint venture, with the features set out above, and already operates on the same market, the Commission will normally consider the joint venture itself and the target undertaking to be the undertakings concerned (and not the joint venture's parent companies).

(147) Conversely, where the joint venture can be regarded as a mere vehicle for an acquisition by the parent companies, the Commission will consider each of the parent companies themselves to be the undertakings concerned, rather than the joint venture, together with the target company. This is the case in particular where the joint venture is set up especially for the purpose of acquiring the target company or has not yet started to operate, where an existing joint venture has no full-function

character as referred to above or where the joint venture is an association of undertakings. The same applies where there are elements which demonstrate that the parent companies are in fact the real players behind the operation. These elements may include a significant involvement by the parent companies themselves in the initiation, organisation and financing of the operation. In those cases, the parent companies are regarded as undertakings concerned.

Break-up of joint ventures and exchange of assets

(148) When two (or more) undertakings break up a joint venture and split the assets (constituting businesses) between them, this will normally be considered as more than one acquisition of control, as explained above in paragraph 41. For example, undertakings A and B form a joint venture and subsequently split it up, in particular with a new asset configuration. The break-up of the joint venture involves a change from joint control over the joint venture's entire assets to sole control over the divided assets by each of the acquiring undertakings.

(149) For each break-up operation, and in line with the consideration to the acquisition of sole control, the undertakings concerned will be, on the one hand, the acquiring party and, on the other, the assets that this undertaking will acquire.

(150) Similar to the break-up scenario is the situation where two (or more) companies exchange assets constituting a business on each side. In this case, each acquisition of control is considered an independent acquisition of sole control. The undertakings concerned will be, for each transaction, the acquiring companies and the acquired undertaking or assets.

Acquisitions of control by natural persons

(151) Control may also be acquired by natural persons, within the meaning of Article 3 of the Merger Regulation, if those persons themselves carry out further economic activities (and are therefore classified as economic undertakings in their own right) or if they control one or more other economic undertakings. In such a situation, the undertakings concerned are the target undertaking and the individual acquirer (with the turnover of the undertaking(s) controlled by that natural person being included in the calculation of the natural person's turnover to the extent that the terms of Article 5(4) are satisfied).

(152) An acquisition of control of an undertaking by its managers is also an acquisition by natural persons, and paragraph 151 above is also relevant. However, the managers may pool their interests through a 'vehicle company', so that it acts with a single voice and also to facilitate decision-making. Such a vehicle company may be, but is not necessarily, an undertaking concerned. The general guidance given above in paragraphs 145–147 on acquisitions of control by a joint venture also applies here.

Acquisition of control by a State-owned undertaking

(153) As described above, a merger or an acquisition of control arising between two undertakings owned by the same State (or the same public body) may constitute a concentration if the undertakings were formerly part of different economic units having an independent power of decision. If this is the case, both of them will qualify as undertakings concerned although both are owned by the same State.

III. RELEVANT DATE FOR ESTABLISHING JURISDICTION

(154) The legal situation for establishing the Commission's jurisdiction has been changed under the recast Merger Regulation. Under the former Merger Regulation, the relevant date was the triggering event for a notification according to Article 4(1) of this Regulation—the conclusion of a final agreement or the announcement of a public bid or the acquisition of a controlling interest—or, at the latest, the time when the parties were obliged to notify (i.e. one week after a triggering event for a notification).

(155) Under the recast Merger Regulation, there is no longer an obligation for the parties to notify within a certain time-frame (provided the parties do not implement the planned concentration before notification). Moreover, according to Article 4(1) second subparagraph, the undertakings concerned can already notify the transaction on the basis of a good faith intention to conclude an agreement or, in the case of a public bid, where they have publicly announced an intention to make such a bid. At the time of the notification at the latest, the Commission—as well as national competition authorities—must be able to determine their jurisdiction. Article 4(1) subparagraph 1 of the Merger Regulation provides, generally, that concentrations shall be notified following the conclusion of the agreement, the announcement of the public bid, or the acquisition of a controlling interest. The dates of these events are therefore still decisive under the recast Merger Regulation in order to determine the relevant date for establishing jurisdiction, if a notification does not occur before such events on the basis of a good faith intention or an announced intention.

(156) The relevant date for establishing Community jurisdiction over a concentration is therefore the date of the conclusion of the binding legal agreement, the announcement of a public bid or the acquisition of a controlling interest or the date of the first notification, whichever date is earlier. Regarding the date of notification, a notification to either the Commission or to a Member State authority is relevant. The relevant date needs in particular to be considered for the question whether acquisitions or divestitures which occur after the period covered by the relevant account, but before the relevant date, require adaptations to those accounts according to the principles set out in paragraphs 172 and 173.

IV. TURNOVER

1. THE CONCEPT OF TURNOVER

(157) The concept of turnover as used in Article 5 of the Merger Regulation comprises 'the amounts derived [...] from the sale of products and the provision of services'. Those amounts generally appear in company accounts under the heading 'sales'. In the case of products, turnover can be determined without difficulty, namely by identifying each commercial act involving a transfer of ownership.

(158) In the case of services, the method of calculating turnover in general does not differ from that used in the case of products: the Commission takes into consideration the total amount of sales. However, the calculation of the amounts derived from the provision of services may be more complex as this depends on the exact service provided and the underlying legal and economic arrangements in the sector in question. Where one undertaking provides the entire service directly to the customer, the turnover of the undertaking concerned consists of the total amount of sales for the provision of services in the last financial year.

(159) In other areas, this general principle may have to be adapted to the specific conditions of the service provided. In certain sectors of activity (such as package holidays and advertising), the service may be sold through intermediaries. Even if the intermediary invoices the entire amount to the final customer, the turnover of the undertaking acting as an intermediary consists solely of the amount of its commission. For package holidays, the entire amount paid by the final customer is then allocated to the tour operator which uses the travel agency as distribution network. In the case of advertising, only the amounts received (without the commission) are considered to constitute the turnover of the TV channel or the magazine since media agencies, as intermediaries, do not constitute the distribution channel for the sellers of advertising space, but are chosen by the customers, i.e. those undertakings wishing to place advertising.

(160) The examples mentioned show that, due to the diversity of services, many different situations may arise and the underlying legal and economic relations have to be carefully analysed. Similarly, specific situations for the calculation of turnover may arise in the areas of credit, financial services and insurance. These issues will be dealt with in Section VI.

2. ORDINARY ACTIVITIES

(161) Article 5(1) provides that the amounts to be included in the calculation of turnover should correspond to the 'ordinary activities' of the undertakings concerned. This is the turnover achieved from the sale of products or the provision of services in the normal course of its business. It generally excludes those items which are listed under the headers 'financial income' or 'extraordinary income' in the company's accounts. Such extraordinary income may be derived from the sale of businesses or of fixed assets. However, company accounts do not necessarily delineate the revenues derived from ordinary activities in the way required for the purposes of turnover calculation under the Merger Regulation. In some cases, the qualification of the items in the accounts may have to be adapted to the requirements of the Merger Regulation.

(162) The revenues do not necessarily have to be derived from the customer of the products or services. With regard to aid granted to undertakings by public bodies, any aid has to be included in the calculation of turnover if the undertaking is itself the recipient of the aid and if the aid is directly linked to the sale of products and the provision of services by the undertaking. The aid is therefore an income of the undertaking from the sale of products or provision of services in addition to the price paid by the consumer.

(163) Specific issues have arisen for the calculation of turnover of a business unit which only had internal revenues in the past. This may in particular apply for transactions involving the outsourcing of services by transfer of a business unit. If such a transaction constitutes a concentration on the basis of the considerations outlined in paragraphs 25 ff. of this Notice, the Commission's practice is that the turnover should normally be calculated on the basis of the previously internal turnover or of publicly quoted prices where such prices exist (e.g. in the oil industry). Where the previously internal turnover does not appear to correspond to a market valuation of the activities in question (and, thus, to the expected future turnover on the market), the forecast revenues to be received on the basis of an agreement with the former parent may be a suitable proxy.

3. 'NET' TURNOVER

(164) The turnover to be taken into account is 'net' turnover, after deduction of a number of components specified in the Regulation. The aim is to adjust turnover in such a way as to enable it to reflect the real economic strength of the undertaking.

3.1. Deduction of rebates and taxes

(165) Article 5(1) provides for the 'deduction of sales rebates and of value added tax and other taxes directly related to turnover'. 'Sales rebates' mean all rebates or discounts which are granted by the undertakings to their customers and which have a direct influence on the amounts of sales.

(166) As regards the deduction of taxes, the Merger Regulation refers to VAT and 'other taxes directly related to turnover'. The concept of 'taxes directly related to turnover' refers to indirect taxation linked to turnover, such as, for example, taxes on alcoholic beverages or cigarettes.

3.2. The treatment of 'internal' turnover

(167) The first subparagraph of Article 5(1) states that 'the aggregate turnover of an undertaking concerned shall not include the sale of products or the provision of services between any of the undertakings referred to in paragraph 4', i.e. the group to which the undertaking concerned belongs. The aim is to exclude the proceeds of business dealings within a group so as to take account of the real economic weight of each entity in the form of market turnover. Thus, the 'amounts' taken into account by the Merger Regulation reflect only the transactions which take place between the group of undertakings on the one hand and third parties on the other.

(168) Article 5(5)(a) of the Merger Regulation applies the principle that double counting is to be avoided specifically to the situation where two or more undertakings concerned in a concentration jointly have the rights or powers listed in Article 5(4)(b) in another company. According to this provision, the turnover resulting from the sale of products or the provision of services between the joint

venture and each of the undertakings concerned (or any other undertaking connected with any one of them in the sense of Article 5(4)) should be excluded. As regards joint ventures between undertakings concerned and third parties, insofar as their turnover is taken into account according to Article 5(4)(b) as set out in paragraph 181 below, the turnover generated by sales between the joint venture and the undertaking concerned (as well as undertakings linked to the undertaking concerned in accordance with the criteria set out in Article 5(4)) is not taken into account according to Article 5(1).

4. TURNOVER CALCULATION AND FINANCIAL ACCOUNTS

4.1. The general rule

(169) The Commission seeks to base itself upon the most accurate and reliable figures available. Generally, the Commission will refer to accounts which relate to the closest financial year to the date of the transaction and which are audited under the standard applicable to the undertaking in question and compulsory for the relevant financial year. An adjustment of the audited figures should only take place if this is required by the provisions of the Merger Regulation, including the cases explained in more detail in paragraph 172.

(170) The Commission is reluctant to rely on management or any other form of provisional accounts in any but exceptional circumstances. Where a concentration takes place within the first months of the year and audited accounts are not yet available for the most recent financial year, the figures to be taken into account are those relating to the previous year. Where there is a major divergence between the two sets of accounts, due to significant and permanent changes in the undertaking concerned, and, in particular, when the final draft figures for the most recent year have been approved by the board of management, the Commission may decide to take those figures into account.

(171) Despite the general rule, in cases where major differences between the Community's accounting standards and those of a non-member country are observed, the Commission may consider it necessary to restate these accounts in accordance with Community standards in respect of turnover.

4.2. Adjustments after the date of the last audited accounts

(172) Notwithstanding the foregoing paragraphs, an adjustment must always be made to account for permanent changes in the economic reality of the undertakings concerned, such as acquisitions or divestments which are not or not fully reflected in the audited accounts. Such changes have to be taken into account in order to identify the true resources being concentrated and to better reflect the economic situation of the undertakings concerned. Those adjustments are only selective in nature and do not endanger the principle that there should be a simple and objective mechanism to determine the Commission's jurisdiction as they do not require a complete revision of the audited accounts. First, this applies to acquisitions, divestments or closure of part of its business subsequent to the date of the audited accounts. This is relevant if a company closes a transaction concerning the divestment and closure of part of its business at any time before the relevant date for establishing jurisdiction (see paragraph 154) or where such a divestment or closure of a business is a pre-condition for the operation. In this case, the turnover to be attributed to that part of the business must be subtracted from the turnover of the notifying party as shown in its last audited accounts. If an agreement for the sale of part of its business is signed, but the closing of the sale (in other words, its legal implementation and the transfer of the legal title to the shares or assets acquired) has not yet occurred, such a change is not taken into account, unless the sale is a pre-condition for the notified operation. Conversely, the turnover of those businesses whose acquisition has been closed subsequent to the preparation of the most recent audited accounts, but before the relevant date for establishing jurisdiction, must be added to a company's turnover for notification purposes.

(173) Second, an adjustment may also be necessary for acquisitions, divestments or closure of part of the business which have taken place during the financial year for which the audited accounts are drawn up. If acquisitions, divestments or closure of part of the business within this period are made, the changes in the economic resources may only partly be reflected in the audited accounts of

the undertaking concerned. As the turnover of the businesses acquired may be included in the accounts only from the time of their acquisition, this may not reflect the full annual turnover of the acquired business. Conversely, the turnover of the businesses divested or closed may still be included in the audited accounts up to the point in time of their actual divestment or closure. In these cases, adjustments have to be made to remove the turnover generated by the divested or closed businesses from the audited accounts until the time of de-consolidation and to add the turnover which the acquired businesses have generated in the year until the time they have been consolidated in the accounts. As a result, the turnover of the businesses divested or closed must be excluded in full and the full annual turnover of the businesses acquired must be included.

(174) Other factors that may affect turnover on a temporary basis such as a decrease in orders for the product or a slow-down in the production process within the period prior to the transaction will be ignored for the purposes of calculating turnover. No adjustment to the definitive accounts will be made to incorporate them.

5.   ATTRIBUTION OF TURNOVER UNDER ARTICLE 5(4)

5.1. Identification of undertakings whose turnover is taken into account

(175) When an undertaking concerned by a concentration belongs to a group, not only the turnover of the undertaking concerned is considered, but the Merger Regulation requires to also take into account the turnover of those undertakings with which the undertaking concerned has links consisting in the rights or powers listed in Article 5(4) in order to determine whether the thresholds contained in Article 1 of the Merger Regulation are met. The aim is again to capture the total volume of the economic resources that are being combined through the operation irrespective of whether the economic activities are carried out directly by the undertaking concerned or whether they are undertaken indirectly via undertakings with which the undertaking concerned possesses the links described in Article 5(4).

(176) The Merger Regulation does not delineate the concept of a group in a single abstract definition, but sets out in Article 5(4)(b) certain rights or powers. If an undertaking concerned directly or indirectly has such links with other companies, those are to be regarded as part of its group for purposes of turnover calculation under the Merger Regulation.

(177) Article 5(4) of the Merger Regulation provides the following:

'Without prejudice to paragraph 2 [acquisitions of parts], the aggregate turnover of an undertaking concerned within the meaning of Article 1(2) and (3) shall be calculated by adding together the respective turnovers of the following:

    (a) the undertaking concerned;

    (b) those undertakings in which the undertaking concerned directly or indirectly:

        (i)   owns more than half the capital or business assets, or

        (ii)   has the power to exercise more than half the voting rights, or

        (iii) has the power to appoint more than half the members of the supervisory board, the administrative board or bodies legally representing the undertakings, or

        (iv) has the right to manage the undertaking's affairs;

    (c) those undertakings which have in an undertaking concerned the rights or powers listed in (b);

    (d) those undertakings in which an undertaking as referred to in (c) has the rights or powers listed in (b);

    (e) those undertakings in which two or more undertakings as referred to in (a) to (d) jointly have the rights or powers listed in (b).'

An undertaking which has in another undertaking the rights and powers mentioned in Article 5(4)(b) will be referred to as the 'parent' of the latter in the present section of this Notice dealing with the calculation of turnover, whereas the latter is referred to as 'subsidiary' of the former. In short, Article 5(4) therefore provides that the turnover of the undertaking concerned by the concentration (point (a)) should include its subsidiaries (point (b)), its parent companies (point (c)), the other subsidiaries of its parent undertakings (point (d)) and any other subsidiary jointly held by two or more of the undertakings identified under (a)–(d) (point (e)).

(178) A graphic example is as follows:

The undertaking concerned and its group:

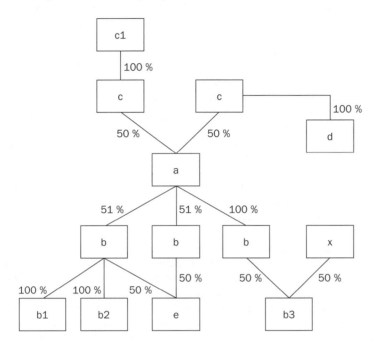

a: The undertaking concerned

b: Its subsidiaries, jointly held companies together with third parties (b3) and their own subsidiaries (b1 and b2)

c: Its parent companies and their own parent companies (c1)

d: Other subsidiaries of the parent companies of the undertaking concerned

e: Companies jointly held by two (or more) companies of the group

x: Third party

Note: the letters a—e correspond to the relevant points of Article 5(4). Percentages set out in the graph relate to the percentage of voting rights held by the respective parent company.

(179) The rights or powers listed in Article 5(4)(b)(i)–(iii) can be identified in a rather straightforward way as they refer to quantitative thresholds. These thresholds are fulfilled if the undertaking concerned owns more than half of the capital or business assets of other undertakings, has more than half of the voting rights or has legally the power to appoint more than half of the board members in other undertakings. However, the thresholds are also met if the undertaking concerned *de facto* has the power to exercise more than half of the voting rights in the shareholders' assembly or the power to appoint more than half of the board members in other undertakings.

(180) The provision contained in Article 5(4)(b)(iv) refers to the right to manage the undertaking's affairs. Such a right to manage exists under company law in particular on the basis of organisational contracts such as a *'Beherrschungsvertrag'* under German law, on the basis of business lease agreements or on the basis of the organisation structure for the general partner in a limited partnership. However, the 'right to manage' may also result from the holding of voting rights (alone or in combination with contractual arrangements, such as a shareholders' agreement) which enable, on a stable, *de jure* basis, to determine the strategic behaviour of an undertaking.

(181) The right to manage also covers situations in which the undertaking concerned jointly has the right to manage an undertaking's affairs together with third parties. The underlying consideration is that the undertakings exercising joint control have jointly the right to manage the controlled undertakings' affairs even if each of them individually may have those rights only in a negative sense, *i.e.* in the form of veto rights. In the example, the undertaking (b3) which is jointly controlled by the undertaking concerned (a) and a third party (x) is taken into account as both (a) and (x) have veto rights in (b3) on the basis of their equal shareholding in (b3). Under Article 5(4)(b)(iv) the Commission only takes into account those joint ventures in which the undertaking concerned and third parties have *de jure* rights that give rise to a clear-cut right to manage. The inclusion of joint ventures is therefore limited to situations where the undertaking concerned and third parties have a joint *right* to manage on the basis of an agreement, *e.g.* a shareholders' agreement, or where the undertaking concerned and a third party have an equality of voting rights to the effect that they have the right to appoint an equal number of members to the decision-making bodies of the joint venture.

(182) In the same way, where two or more companies jointly control the undertaking concerned in the sense that the agreement of each and all of them is needed in order to manage the undertaking affairs, the turnover of all of them is included. In the example, the two parent companies (c) of the undertaking concerned (a) would be taken into account as well as their own parent companies (c1 in the example). This interpretation results from the referral from Article 5(4)(c), dealing with this case, to Article 5(4)(b), which is applicable to jointly controlled companies as set out in the preceding paragraph.

(183) When any of the companies identified on the basis of Article 5(4) also has links as defined in Article 5(4) with other undertakings, these should also be brought into the calculation. In the example, one of the subsidiaries of the undertaking concerned a (called b) has in turn its own subsidiaries b1 and b2 and one of the parent companies (called c) has its own subsidiary (d).

(184) Article 5(4) sets out specific criteria for identifying undertakings whose turnover can be attributed to the undertaking concerned. These criteria, including the 'right to manage the undertaking's affairs', are not coextensive with the notion of 'control' under Article 3(2). There are significant differences between Articles 3 and 5, as those provisions fulfil different roles. The differences are most apparent in the field of *de facto* control. Whereas under Article 3(2) even a situation of economic dependence may lead to control on a *de facto* basis (see in detail above), a solely controlled subsidiary is only taken into account on a *de facto* basis under Article 5(4)(b) if it is clearly demonstrated that the undertaking concerned has the power to exercise more than half of the voting rights or to appoint more than half of the board members. Concerning joint control scenarios, Article 5(4)(b)(iv) covers those scenarios where the controlling undertakings jointly have a right to manage on the basis of individual veto rights. However, Article 5(4) would not cover situations where joint control occurs on a *de facto* basis due to strong common interests between different minority shareholders of the joint venture company on the basis of shareholders' attendance. The difference is reflected in the fact that Article 5(4)(b)(iv) refers to the *right* to manage, and not a *power* (as in subparagraph (b)(ii) and (iii)) and is explained by the need for precision and certainty in the criteria used for calculating turnover so that jurisdiction can be readily verified.

Under Article 3(3), however, the question whether a concentration arises can be much more comprehensively investigated. In addition, situations of negative sole control are only exceptionally covered (if the conditions of Article 5(4)(b)(i)–(iii) are met in the specific case); the 'right to manage' under Article 5(4)(b)(iv) does not cover negative control scenarios. Finally, Article 5(4)(b)(i), for example, covers situations where 'control' under Article 3(2) may not exist.

5.2. Allocation of turnover of the undertakings identified

(185) In general, as long as the test under Article 5(4)(b) is fulfilled, the whole turnover of the subsidiary in question will be taken into account regardless of the actual shareholding which the undertaking concerned holds in the subsidiary. In the chart, the whole turnover of the subsidiaries called b of the undertaking concerned a will be taken into account.

(186) However, the Merger Regulation includes specific rules for joint ventures. Article 5(5)(b) provides that for joint ventures between two or more undertakings concerned, the turnover of the

joint venture (as far as the turnover is generated from activities with third parties as set out above in paragraph 168) should be apportioned equally amongst the undertakings concerned, irrespective of their share of the capital or the voting rights.

(187) The principle contained in Article 5(5)(b) is followed by analogy for the allocation of turnover for joint ventures between undertakings concerned and third parties if their turnover is taken into account according to Article 5(4)(b) as set out above in paragraph 181. The Commission's practice has been to allocate to the undertaking concerned the turnover of the joint venture on a per capita basis according to the number of undertakings exercising joint control. In the example, half of the turnover of b3 is taken into account.

(188) The rules of Article 5(4) also have to be adapted in situations involving a change from joint to sole control in order to avoid double counting of the turnover of the joint venture. Even if the acquiring undertaking has rights or powers in the joint venture which satisfy the requirements of Article 5(4), the turnover of the acquiring shareholder has to be calculated without the turnover of the joint venture, and the turnover of the joint venture has to be taken without the turnover of the acquiring shareholder.

5.3. Allocation of turnover in case of investment funds

(189) The investment company, as set out above in paragraph 15, normally acquires indirect control over portfolio companies held by an investment fund. In the same way, the investment company may be considered to indirectly have the powers and rights which are set out in Article 5(4)(b), in particular to indirectly have the power to exercise the voting rights held by the investment fund in the portfolio companies.

(190) The same considerations, as set out above in the framework of Article 3 (paragraph 15), may also apply if an investment company sets up several investment funds with possibly different investors. Typically, on the basis of the organisational structure, in particular links between the investment company and the general partner(s) of the different funds organised as limited partnerships, or contractual arrangements, especially advisory agreements between the general partner or the investment fund and the investment company, the investment company will indirectly have the power to exercise the voting rights held by the investment fund in the portfolio companies or indirectly have one of the other powers or rights set out in Article 5(4)(b). In these circumstances, the investment company may exercise a common control structure over the different funds which it has set up and the common operation of the different funds by the investment company is often indicated by a common brand for the funds.

(191) Consequently, such an organisation of the different funds by the investment company may lead to the result that the turnover of all portfolio companies held by different funds is taken into account for the purpose of assessing whether the turnover thresholds in Article 1 are met if the investment company acquires indirect control of a portfolio company via one of the funds.

5.4. Allocation of turnover for State-owned undertakings

(192) As regards the calculation of turnover of State-owned undertakings, Article 5(4) should be read in conjunction with recital 22 of the Merger Regulation. This recital declares that, in order to avoid discrimination between the public and private sectors, 'in the public sector, calculation of the turnover of an undertaking concerned in a concentration needs, therefore, to take account of undertakings making up an economic unit with an independent power of decision, irrespective of the way in which their capital is held or of the rules of administrative supervision applicable to them'.

(193) This recital clarifies that Member States (or other public bodies) are not considered as 'undertakings' under Article 5(4) simply because they have interests in other undertakings which satisfy the conditions of Article 5(4). Therefore, for the purposes of calculating turnover of State-owned undertakings, account is only taken of those undertakings which belong to the same economic unit, having the same independent power of decision.

(194) Thus, where a State-owned company is not subject to any coordination with other State-controlled holdings, it should be treated as independent for the purposes of Article 5, and the turnover of other companies owned by that State should not be taken into account. Where, however, several

State-owned companies are under the same independent centre of commercial decision-making, then the turnover of those businesses should be considered part of the group of the undertaking concerned for the purposes of Article 5.

V. GEOGRAPHIC ALLOCATION OF TURNOVER

(195) The thresholds concerning Community-wide and Member State turnover in Article 1(2) and (3) aim to identify cases which have sufficient turnover within the Community in order to be of Community interest and which are primarily cross-border in nature. They require turnover to be allocated geographically to the Community and to individual Member States. Since audited accounts often do not provide a geographical breakdown as required by the Merger Regulation, the Commission will rely on the best figures available provided by the undertakings. The second subparagraph of Article 5(1) provides that the location of turnover is determined by the location of the customer at the time of the transaction: 'Turnover, in the Community or in a Member State, shall comprise products sold and services provided to undertakings or consumers, in the Community or in that Member State as the case may be.'

General rule

(196) The Merger Regulation does not discriminate between 'products sold' and 'services provided' for the geographic allocation of turnover. In both cases, the general rule is that turnover should be attributed to the place where the customer is located. The underlying principle is that turnover should be allocated to the location where competition with alternative suppliers takes place. This location is normally also the place where the characteristic action under the contract in question is to be performed, *i.e.* where the service is actually provided and the product is actually delivered. In the case of Internet transactions, it may be difficult for the undertakings to determine the location of the customer at the time when the contract is concluded via the Internet. If the product or the service itself is not supplied via the Internet, focusing on the place where the characteristic action under the contract is performed may avoid those difficulties. In the following, the sale of goods and the provision of services are dealt with separately as they exhibit certain different features in terms of allocation of turnover.

Sale of goods

(197) For the sale of goods, particular situations may arise in situations in which the place where the customer was located at the time of concluding the purchase agreement is different from the billing address and/or the place of delivery. In these situations, the place where the purchase agreement was entered into and the place of delivery are more important than the billing address. As the delivery is in general the characteristic action for the sale of goods, the place of delivery may even be prevailing over the place where the customer was located at the time when the purchase agreement was concluded. This will depend on whether the place of delivery is to be considered the place where competition takes place for the sale of goods or whether competition rather takes place at the residence of the customer. In the case of a sale of mobile goods, such as a motor car, to a final consumer, the place where the car is delivered to the customer is decisive even if the agreement was concluded via the phone or the Internet before.

(198) A specific situation arises in cases where a multinational corporation has a Community buying strategy and sources all its requirements for a good from one location. As a central purchasing organisation can take different forms, it is necessary to consider its concrete form since this may determine how to allocate the turnover. Where goods are purchased by and delivered to the central purchasing organisation and are subsequently re-distributed internally to different plants in a variety of Member States, turnover is allocated only to the Member State where the central purchasing organisation is located. In this case, competition takes place at the location of the central purchasing organisation and this is also the place where the characteristic action under the sales contract is performed. The situation is different in case of direct links between the seller and the different subsidiaries. This

comprises the case where the central purchasing organisation concludes a mere framework agreement, but the individual orders are placed by and the products are directly delivered to the subsidiaries in different Member States as well as the case where the individual orders are placed via the central purchasing organisation, but the products are directly delivered to the subsidiaries. In both cases, turnover is to be allocated to the different Member States in which the subsidiaries are located, irrespective of whether the central purchasing organisation or the subsidiaries receive the bills and effect the payment. The reason is that in both cases competition with alternative suppliers takes place for the delivery of products to the different subsidiaries even though the contract is concluded centrally. In the first case, in addition, the subsidiaries actually decide upon the quantities to be delivered and on an element essential for competition on their own.

Provision of services

(199) For services, the Merger Regulation foresees that the place of their provision to the customer is relevant. Services containing cross-border elements can be considered to fall into three general categories. The first category comprises cases where the service provider travels, the second category cases where the customer travels. The third category comprises those cases where a service is provided without either the service provider or the customer having to travel. In the first two categories, the turnover generated is to be allocated to the place of destination of the traveller, *i.e.* the place where the service is actually provided to the customer. In the third category, the turnover is generally to be allocated to the location of the customer. For the central sourcing of services the above outlined principles for the central purchasing of goods apply in an analogous way.

(200) An example of the first category would be a situation where a non-European company provides special airplane maintenance services to a carrier in a Member State. In this case, the service provider travels to the Community where the service is actually provided and where also competition for this service takes place. If a European tourist hires a car or books a hotel directly in the United States, this falls into the second category as the service is provided outside the Community and also competition takes place between hotels and rental car companies at the location chosen. However, the case is different for package holidays. For this kind of holiday, the service starts with the sale of the package through a travel agent at the customer's location and competition for the sale of holidays through travel agents takes place locally, as with retail shopping, even though parts of the service may be provided in a number of distant locations. The case therefore falls into the third category and the turnover generated is to be allocated to the customer's location. The third category also comprises cases like the supply of software or the distribution of films which are made outside the Community, but are supplied to a customer in a Member State so that the service is actually provided to the customer within the Community.

(201) Cases concerning the transport of goods are different as the customer, to whom those services are provided, does not travel, but the transport service is provided to the customer at its location. Those cases fall into the third category and the location of the customer is the relevant criterion for the allocation of the turnover.

(202) In telecom cases, the qualification of call termination services may raise problems. Although call termination would appear to fall into the third category, there are reasons to treat it differently. Call termination services are provided, e.g., in situations where a call, originating from a European operator, is being terminated in the United States. Although neither the European nor the US operator travels, the signal travels and the service is provided by the US network to the European operator in the United States. This is also the place where competition takes place (if any). The turnover is therefore to be considered as non-Community turnover.

Specific sectors

(203) Certain sectors do, however, pose very particular problems with regard to the geographical allocation of turnover. These will be dealt with in Section VI below.

VI. CONVERSION OF TURNOVER INTO EURO

(204) When converting turnover figures into euro great care should be taken with the exchange rate used. The annual turnover of a company should be converted at the average rate for the twelve months concerned. This average can be obtained via DG Competition's website. The audited annual turnover figures should be converted as such and not be broken down into quarterly or monthly figures which would then be converted individually.

(205) When a company has sales in a range of currencies, the procedure is no different. The total turnover given in the consolidated audited accounts and in that company's reporting currency is converted into euros at the yearly average rate. Local currency sales should not be converted directly into euros since these figures are not from the consolidated audited accounts of the company.

VII. PROVISIONS FOR CREDIT AND OTHER FINANCIAL INSTITUTIONS AND INSURANCE UNDERTAKINGS

1. SCOPE OF APPLICATION

(206) Due to the specific nature of the sector, Article 5(3) contains specific rules for the calculation of turnover of credit and other financial institutions as well as insurance undertakings.

(207) In order to define the terms 'credit institutions and other financial institutions' under the Merger Regulation, the Commission in its practice has consistently adopted the definitions provided in the applicable European regulation in the banking sector. The Directive on the taking up and pursuit of the business of credit institutions foresees that:

- 'Credit institution shall mean an undertaking whose business is to receive deposits or other repayable funds from the public and to grant credits for its own account.'
- 'Financial institution shall mean an undertaking other than a credit institution, the principal activity of which is to acquire holdings or to carry on one or more of the activities listed in points 2 to 12 of Annex I.'

(208) Financial institutions within the meaning of Article 5(3) of the Merger Regulation are, accordingly, on the one hand holding companies and, on the other hand, undertakings which perform on a regular basis as a principal activity one or more activities expressly mentioned in points 2 to 12 of the Annex of the banking Directive. These activities include:—lending (comprising activities such as consumer credit, mortgage credit, factoring);

- financial leasing;
- money transmission services;
- issuing and administering means of payment (e.g. credit cards, travellers' cheques and bankers' drafts);
- guarantees and commitments;
- trading for own account or for account of customers in money market instruments, (cheques, bills, certificates of deposit, etc.), foreign exchange, financial futures and options, exchange and interestate instruments, transferable securities;
- participation in securities issues and the provision of services related to such issues;
- money broking;
- portfolio management and advice; and
- safekeeping and administration of securities.

2. CALCULATION OF TURNOVER

(209) Article 5(3) of the Merger Regulation sets out the methods of calculation of turnover for credit and other financial institutions and for insurance undertakings. In the following Section, some

supplementary questions related to turnover calculation for the abovementioned types of undertakings are addressed.

2.1. Calculation of turnover of credit and financial institutions (other than financial holding companies)

2.1.1. *General*

(210) There are normally no particular difficulties in applying the banking income criterion for the definition of the worldwide turnover to credit institutions and other kinds of financial institutions. For the geographic allocation of turnover to the Community and to individual Member States, the specific provision of Article 5 (3)(a) second subparagraph applies. It specifies that the turnover is to be allocated to the branch or division established in the Community or in the Member State which receives this income.

2.1.2. *Turnover of leasing companies*

(211) There is a fundamental distinction to be made between financial leases and operating leases. Basically, financial leases are made for longer periods than operating leases and ownership is generally transferred to the lessee at the end of the lease term by means of a purchase option included in the lease contract. Under an operating lease, on the contrary, ownership is not transferred to the lessee at the end of the lease term and the costs of maintenance, repair and insurance of the leased equipment are included in the lease payments. A financial lease therefore functions as a loan by the lessor to enable the lessee to purchase a given asset.

(212) As already mentioned above, a company performing as its principal activity financial leasing is a financial institution within the meaning of Article 5(3)(a) and its turnover is to be calculated according to the specific rules set out in this provision. All payments on financial leasing contracts, except for the redemption part, are to be taken into account; a sale of future leasing payments at the beginning of the contract for re-financing purposes is not relevant.

(213) Operational leasing activities are, however, not considered to be carried out by financial institutions, and therefore the general turnover calculation rules of Article 5(1) apply.

2.2. Insurance undertakings

(214) In order to measure the turnover of insurance undertakings, Article 5(3)(b) of the Merger Regulation provides that gross premiums written are taken into account. The gross premiums written are the sum of received premiums, including any received reinsurance premiums if the undertaking concerned has activities in the field of reinsurance. Outgoing or outward reinsurance premiums, i.e. all amounts paid and payable by the undertaking concerned to get reinsurance cover, are only costs related to the provision of insurance coverage and are not to be deducted from the gross premiums written.

(215) The premiums to be taken into account are not only related to new insurance contracts made during the accounting year being considered but also to all premiums related to contracts made in previous years which remain in force during the period taken into consideration.

(216) In order to constitute appropriate reserves allowing for the payment of claims, insurance undertakings, usually hold a portfolio of investments in shares, interest-bearing securities, land and property and other assets providing annual revenues. The annual revenues coming from those sources are not considered as turnover for insurance undertakings under Article 5(3)(b). However, a distinction has to be made between pure financial investments, which do not confer the rights and powers specified in Article 5(4) to the insurance undertaking in the undertakings in which the investment has been made, and those investments leading to the acquisition of an interest which meets the criteria specified in Article 5(4)(b). In the latter case, Article 5(4) of the Merger Regulation applies, and the turnover of this undertaking has to be added to the turnover of the insurance undertaking, as calculated according to Article 5(3)(b), for the determination of the thresholds laid down in the Merger Regulation.

2.3. Financial holding companies

(217) As an 'other financial institution' within the meaning of Article 5(3)(a) of the Merger Regulation, the turnover of a financial holding company has to be calculated according to the specific rules set out in this provision. However, in the same way as mentioned above for insurance undertakings, Article 5(4) applies to those participations which meet the criteria specified in Article 5(4)(b). Thus, the turnover of a financial holding is to be basically calculated according to Article 5(3), but it may be necessary to add turnover of undertakings falling within the categories set out in Article 5(4) ('Art. 5(4) companies').

(218) In practice, the turnover of the financial holding company (non-consolidated) must first be taken into account. Then the turnover of the Art. 5(4) companies must be added, whilst taking care to deduct dividends and other income distributed by those companies to the financial holdings. The following provides an example for this kind of calculation:

(*EUR million*)

1. Turnover related to financial activities (from non-consolidated P&L) 3 000
2. Turnover related to insurance Art. 5(4) companies (gross premiums written) 300
3. Turnover of industrial Article 5(4) companies 2 000
4. Deduct dividends and other income derived from Art. 5(4) companies 2 and 3

Total turnover financial holding and its group 5 100

(219) In such calculations different accounting rules may need to be taken into consideration. Whilst this consideration applies to any type of undertaking concerned by the Merger Regulation, it is particularly important in the case of financial holding companies where the number and the diversity of enterprises controlled and the degree of control the holding holds on its subsidiaries, affiliated companies and other companies in which it has shareholding requires careful examination.

(220) Turnover calculation for financial holding companies as described above may in practice prove onerous. Therefore a strict and detailed application of this method will be necessary only in cases where it seems that the turnover of a financial holding company is likely to be close to the Merger Regulation thresholds; in other cases it may well be obvious that the turnover is far from the thresholds of the Merger Regulation, and therefore the published accounts are adequate for the establishment of jurisdiction.

Commission Notice on the conduct of settlement procedures in view of the adoption of Decisions pursuant to Article 7 and Article 23 of Council Regulation (EC) No 1/2003 in cartel cases

(OJ 2008/No. C 167/01)

1. INTRODUCTION

1. This Notice sets out the framework for rewarding cooperation in the conduct of proceedings commenced in view of the application of Article 81 of the EC Treaty to cartel cases. The settlement procedure may allow the Commission to handle more cases with the same resources, thereby fostering the public interest in the Commission's delivery of effective and timely punishment, while increasing overall deterrence. The cooperation covered by this Notice is different from the voluntary production of evidence to trigger or advance the Commission's investigation, which is covered by the Commission Notice on Immunity from fines and reduction of fines in cartel cases (the Leniency Notice). Provided that the cooperation offered by an undertaking qualifies under both Commission Notices, it can be cumulatively rewarded accordingly.

2. When parties to the proceedings are prepared to acknowledge their participation in a cartel violating Article 81 of the Treaty and their liability therefore, they may also contribute to expediting

the proceedings leading to the adoption of the corresponding decision pursuant to Article 7 and Article 23 of Council Regulation (EC) No 1/2003 of 16 December 2002 on the implementation of the rules on competition laid down in Articles 81 and 82 of the Treaty in the way and with the safeguards specified in this Notice. Whilst the Commission, as the investigative authority and the guardian of the Treaty empowered to adopt enforcement decisions subject to judicial control by the Community Courts, does not negotiate the question of the existence of an infringement of Community law and the appropriate sanction, it can reward the cooperation described in this Notice.

3. Commission Regulation (EC) No 773/2004 of 7 April 2004 relating to the conduct of proceedings by the Commission pursuant to Articles 81 and 82 of the EC Treaty lays down the core practical rules concerning the conduct of proceedings in antitrust cases including those applicable in the variant for settlement. In this regard, Regulation (EC) No 773/2004 bestows on the Commission the discretion whether to explore the settlement procedure or not in cartel cases, while ensuring that the choice of the settlement procedure cannot be imposed on the parties.

4. Effective enforcement of Community competition law is compatible with full respect of the parties' rights of defence, which constitutes a fundamental principle of Community law to be respected in all circumstances, and in particular in antitrust procedures which may give rise to penalties. It follows that the rules established to conduct the Commission proceedings to enforce Article 81 of the Treaty should ensure that the undertakings and associations of undertakings concerned are afforded the opportunity effectively to make known their views on the truth and relevance of the facts, objections and circumstances put forward by the Commission, throughout the administrative procedure.

2. PROCEDURE

5. The Commission retains a broad margin of discretion to determine which cases may be suitable to explore the parties' interest to engage in settlement discussions, as well as to decide to engage in them or discontinue them or to definitely settle. In this regard, account may be taken of the probability of reaching a common understanding regarding the scope of the potential objections with the parties involved within a reasonable timeframe, in view of factors such as number of parties involved, foreseeable conflicting positions on the attribution of liability, extent of contestation of the facts. The prospect of achieving procedural efficiencies in view of the progress made overall in the settlement procedure, including the scale of burden involved in providing access to non-confidential versions of documents from the file, will be considered. Other concerns such as the possibility of setting a precedent might apply. The Commission may also decide to discontinue settlement discussions if the parties to the proceedings coordinate to distort or destroy any evidence relevant to the establishment of the infringement or any part thereof or to the calculation of the applicable fine. Distortion or destruction of evidence relevant to the establishment of the infringement or any part thereof may also constitute an aggravating circumstance within the meaning of point 28 of the Commission Guidelines on the method of setting fines imposed pursuant to Article 23(2)(a) of Regulation (EC) No 1/2003 (the Guidelines on fines), and may be regarded as lack of cooperation within the meaning of points 12 and 27 of the Leniency Notice. The Commission may only engage in settlement discussions upon the written request of the parties concerned.

6. While parties to the proceedings do not have a right to settle, should the Commission consider that a case may, in principle, be suitable for settlement, it will explore the interest in settlement of all parties to the same proceedings.

7. The parties to the proceedings may not disclose to any third party in any jurisdiction the contents of the discussions or of the documents which they have had access to in view of settlement, unless they have a prior explicit authorization by the Commission. Any breach in this regard may lead the Commission to disregard the undertaking's request to follow the settlement procedure. Such disclosure may also constitute an aggravating circumstance, within the meaning of point 28 of the Guidelines on fines and may be regarded as lack of cooperation within the meaning of points 12 and 27 of the Leniency Notice.

2.1. Initiation of proceedings and exploratory steps regarding settlement

8. Where the Commission contemplates the adoption of a decision pursuant to Article 7 and/or Article 23 of Regulation (EC) No 1/2003, it is required in advance to identify and recognize as parties to the proceedings the legal persons on whom a penalty may be imposed for an infringement of Article 81 of the Treaty.

9. To this end, the initiation of proceedings pursuant to Article 11(6) of Regulation (EC) No 1/2003 in view of adopting such a decision can take place at any point in time, but no later than the date on which the Commission issues a statement of objections against the parties concerned. Article 2(1) of Regulation (EC) No 773/2004 further specifies that, should the Commission consider it suitable to explore the parties' interest in engaging in settlement discussions, it will initiate proceedings no later than the date on which it either issues a statement of objections or requests the parties to express in writing their interest to engage in settlement discussions, whichever is the earlier.

10. After the initiation of proceedings pursuant to Article 11(6) of Regulation (EC) No 1/2003, the Commission becomes the only competition authority competent to apply Article 81 of the Treaty to the case in point.

11. Should the Commission consider it suitable to explore the parties' interest to engage in settlement discussions, it will set a time-limit of no less than two weeks pursuant to Articles 10a(1) and 17(3) of Regulation (EC) No 773/2004 within which parties to the same proceedings should declare in writing whether they envisage engaging in settlement discussions in view of possibly introducing settlement submissions at a later stage. This written declaration does not imply an admission by the parties of having participated in an infringement or of being liable for it.

12. Whenever the Commission initiates proceedings against two or more parties within the same undertaking, the Commission will inform each of them of the other legal entities which it identifies within the same undertaking and which are also concerned by the proceedings. In such a case, should the concerned parties wish to engage in settlement discussions, they must appoint joint representatives duly empowered to act on their behalf by the end of the time-limit referred to in point 11. The appointment of joint representatives aims solely to facilitate the settlement discussions and it does not prejudge in any way the attribution of liability for the infringement amongst the different parties.

13. The Commission may disregard any application for immunity from fines or reduction of fines on the ground that it has been submitted after the expiry of the time-limit referred to in point 11.

2.2. Commencing the settlement procedure: settlement discussions

14. Should some of the parties to the proceedings request settlement discussions and comply with the requirements referred to in points 11 and 12, the Commission may decide to pursue the settlement procedure by means of bilateral contacts between the Commission Directorate-General for Competition and the settlement candidates.

15. The Commission retains discretion to determine the appropriateness and the pace of the bilateral settlement discussions with each undertaking. In line with Article 10a(2) of Regulation (EC) No 773/2004, this includes determining, in view of the progress made overall in the settlement procedure, the order and sequence of the bilateral settlement discussions as well as the timing of the disclosure of information, including the evidence in the Commission file used to establish the envisaged objections and the potential fine. Information will be disclosed in a timely manner as settlement discussions progress.

16. Such an early disclosure in the context of settlement discussions pursuant to Article 10a(2) and Article 15(1a) of Regulation (EC) No 773/2004 will allow the parties to be informed of the essential elements taken into consideration so far, such as the facts alleged, the classification of those facts, the gravity and duration of the alleged cartel, the attribution of liability, an estimation of the range of likely fines, as well as the evidence used to establish the potential objections. This will enable the parties effectively to assert their views on the potential objections against them and will allow them to make an informed decision on whether or not to settle. Upon request by a party, the Commission services will also grant it access to non-confidential versions of any specified accessible document listed in the case file at that point in time, in so far as this is justified for the purpose of enabling the party to ascertain its position regarding a time period or any other aspect of the cartel.

17. When the progress made during the settlement discussions leads to a common understanding regarding the scope of the potential objections and the estimation of the range of likely fines to be imposed by the Commission, and the Commission takes the preliminary view that procedural efficiencies are likely to be achieved in view of the progress made overall, the Commission may grant a final time-limit of at least 15 working days for an undertaking to introduce a final settlement submission pursuant to Articles 10a(2) and 17(3) of Regulation (EC) No 773/2004. The time-limit can be extended following a reasoned request. Before granting such time-limit, the parties will be entitled to have the information specified in point 16 disclosed to them upon request.

18. The parties may call upon the Hearing Officer at any time during the settlement procedure in relation to issues that might arise relating to due process. The Hearing Officer's duty is to ensure that the effective exercise of the rights of defence is respected.

19. Should the parties concerned fail to introduce a settlement submission, the procedure leading to the final decision in their regard will follow the general provisions, in particular Articles 10(2), 12(1) and 15(1) of Regulation (EC) No 773/2004, instead of those regulating the settlement procedure.

2.3. Settlement submissions

20. Parties opting for a settlement procedure must introduce a formal request to settle in the form of a settlement submission. The settlement submission provided for in Article 10a(2) of Regulation (EC) No 773/2004 should contain:

(a) an acknowledgement in clear and unequivocal terms of the parties' liability for the infringement summarily described as regards its object, its possible implementation, the main facts, their legal qualification, including the party's role and the duration of their participation in the infringement in accordance with the results of the settlement discussions;

(b) an indication of the maximum amount of the fine the parties foresee to be imposed by the Commission and which the parties would accept in the framework of a settlement procedure;

(c) the parties' confirmation that, they have been sufficiently informed of the objections the Commission envisages raising against them and that they have been given sufficient opportunity to make their views known to the Commission;

(d) the parties' confirmation that, in view of the above, they do not envisage requesting access to the file or requesting to be heard again in an oral hearing, unless the Commission does not reflect their settlement submissions in the statement of objections and the decision;

(e) the parties' agreement to receive the statement of objections and the final decision pursuant to Articles 7 and 23 of Regulation (EC) No 1/2003 in an agreed official language of the European Community.

21. The acknowledgments and confirmations provided by the parties in view of settlement constitute the expression of their commitment to cooperate in the expeditious handling of the case following the settlement procedure. However, those acknowledgments and confirmations are conditional upon the Commission meeting their settlement request, including the anticipated maximum amount of the fine.

22. Settlement requests cannot be revoked unilaterally by the parties which have provided them unless the Commission does not meet the settlement requests by reflecting the settlement submissions first in a statement of objections and ultimately, in a final decision (see in this regard points 27 and 29). The statement of objections would be deemed to have endorsed the settlement submissions if it reflects their contents on the issues mentioned in point 20(a). Additionally, for a final decision to be deemed to have reflected the settlement submissions, it should also impose a fine which does not exceed the maximum amount indicated therein.

2.4. Statement of objections and reply

23. Pursuant to Article 10(1) of Regulation (EC) No 773/2004, the notification of a written statement of objections to each of the parties against whom objections are raised is a mandatory preparatory step before adopting any final decision. Therefore, the Commission will issue a statement of objections also in a settlement procedure.

24. For the parties' rights of defence to be exercised effectively, the Commission should hear their views on the objections against them and supporting evidence before adopting a final decision and take them into account by amending its preliminary analysis, where appropriate. The Commission must be able not only to accept or reject the parties' relevant arguments expressed during the administrative procedure, but also to make its own analysis of the matters put forward by them in order to either abandon such objections because they have been shown to be unfounded or to supplement and reassess its arguments both in fact and in law, in support of the objections which it maintains.

25. By introducing a formal settlement request in the form of a settlement submission prior to the notification of the statement of objections, the parties concerned enable the Commission to effectively take their views into account already when drafting the statement of objections, rather than only before the consultation of the Advisory Committee on Restrictive Practices and Dominant Positions (hereinafter the "Advisory Committee") or before the adoption of the final decision.

26. Should the statement of objections reflect the parties' settlement submissions, the parties concerned should within a time-limit of at least two weeks set by the Commission in accordance with Articles 10a(3) and 17(3) of Regulation (EC) No 773/2004, reply to it by simply confirming (in unequivocal terms) that the statement of objections corresponds to the contents of their settlement submissions and that they therefore remain committed to follow the settlement procedure. In the absence of such a reply, the Commission will take note of the party's breach of its commitment and may also disregard the party's request to follow the settlement procedure.

27. The Commission retains the right to adopt a statement of objections which does not reflect the parties' settlement submission. If so, the general provisions in Articles 10(2), 12(1) and 15(1) of Regulation (EC) No 773/2004 will apply. The acknowledgements provided by the parties in the settlement submission would be deemed to be withdrawn and could not be used in evidence against any of the parties to the proceedings. Hence, the parties concerned would no longer be bound by their settlement submissions and would be granted a time-limit allowing them, upon request, to present their defence anew, including the possibility to access the file and to request an oral hearing.

2.5. Commission decision and settlement reward

28. Upon the parties' replies to the statement of objections confirming their commitment to settle, Regulation (EC) No 773/2004 allows the Commission to proceed, without any other procedural step, to the adoption of the subsequent final decision pursuant to Articles 7 and/or 23 of Regulation (EC) No 1/2003, after consultation of the Advisory Committee pursuant to Article 14 of Regulation (EC) No 1/2003. In particular, this implies that no oral hearing or access to the file may be requested by those parties once their settlement submissions have been reflected by the statement of objections, in line with Articles 12(2) and 15(1a) of Regulation (EC) No 773/2004.

29. The Commission retains the right to adopt a final position which departs from its preliminary position expressed in a statement of objections endorsing the parties' settlement submissions, either in view of the opinion provided by the Advisory Committee or for other appropriate considerations in view of the ultimate decisional autonomy of the Commission to this effect. However, should the Commission opt to follow that course, it will inform the parties and notify to them a new statement of objections in order to allow for the exercise of their rights of defence in accordance with the applicable general rules of procedure. It follows that the parties would then be entitled to have access to the file, to request an oral hearing and to reply to the statement of objections. The acknowledgments provided by the parties in the settlement submissions would be deemed to have been withdrawn and could not be used in evidence against any of the parties to the proceedings.

30. The final amount of the fine in a particular case is determined in the decision finding an infringement pursuant to Article 7 and imposing a fine pursuant to Article 23 of Regulation (EC) No 1/2003.

31. In line with the Commission's practice, the fact that an undertaking cooperated with the Commission under this Notice during the administrative procedure will be indicated in the final decision, so as to explain the reason for the level of the fine.

32. Should the Commission decide to reward a party for settlement in the framework of this Notice, it will reduce by 10 % the amount of the fine to be imposed after the 10 % cap has been applied

having regard to the Guidelines on the method of setting fines imposed pursuant to Article 23(2)(a) of Regulation (EC) No 1/2003 [8]. Any specific increase for deterrence used in their regard will not exceed a multiplication by two.

33. When settled cases involve also leniency applicants, the reduction of the fine granted to them for settlement will be added to their leniency reward.

3. GENERAL CONSIDERATIONS

34. This Notice applies to any case pending before the Commission at the time of or after its publication in the Official Journal of the European Union.

35. Access to settlement submissions is only granted to those addressees of a statement of objections who have not requested settlement, provided that they commit—together with the legal counsels getting access on their behalf—not to make any copy by mechanical or electronic means of any information in the settlement submissions to which access is being granted and to ensure that the information to be obtained from the settlement submission will solely be used for the purposes of judicial or administrative proceedings for the application of the Community competition rules at issue in the related proceedings. Other parties such as complainants will not be granted access to settlement submissions.

36. The use of such information for a different purpose during the proceeding may be regarded as lack of cooperation within the meaning of points 12 and 27 of the Leniency Notice. Moreover, if any such use is made after the Commission has already adopted a prohibition decision in the proceedings, the Commission may, in any legal proceedings before the Community Courts, ask the Court to increase the fine in respect of the responsible undertaking. Should the information be used for a different purpose, at any point in time, with the involvement of an outside counsel, the Commission may report the incident to the bar of that counsel, with a view to disciplinary action.

37. Settlement submissions made under this Notice will only be transmitted to the competition authorities of the Member States pursuant to Article 12 of Regulation (EC) No 1/2003, provided that the conditions set out in the Network Notice are met and provided that the level of protection against disclosure awarded by the receiving competition authority is equivalent to the one conferred by the Commission.

38. Upon the applicant's request, the Commission may accept that settlement submissions be provided orally. Oral settlement submissions will be recorded and transcribed at the Commission's premises. In accordance with Article 19 of Regulation (EC) No 1/2003 and Articles 3(3) and 17(3) of Regulation (EC) No 773/2004 undertakings making oral settlement submissions will be granted the opportunity to check the technical accuracy of the recording, which will be available at the Commission's premises and to correct the substance of their oral settlement submissions and the accuracy of the transcript without delay.

39. The Commission will not transmit settlement submissions to national courts without the consent of the relevant applicants, in line with the provisions in the Commission Notice on the cooperation between the Commission and the courts of the EU Member States in the application of Articles 81 and 82 EC.

40. The Commission considers that normally public disclosure of documents and written or recorded statements (including settlement submissions) received in the context of this Notice would undermine certain public or private interests, for example the protection of the purpose of inspections and investigations, within the meaning of Article 4 of Regulation (EC) No 1049/2001 of the European Parliament and of the Council of 30 May 2001 regarding public access to European Parliament, Council and Commission documents [19], even after the decision has been taken.

41. Final decisions taken by the Commission under Regulation (EC) No 1/2003 are subject to judicial review in accordance with Article 230 of the Treaty. Moreover, as provided in Article 229 of the Treaty and Article 31 of Regulation (EC) No 1/2003, the Court of Justice has unlimited jurisdiction to review decisions on fines adopted pursuant to Article 23 of Regulation (EC) No 1/2003.

Guidelines on the assessment of non-horizontal mergers under the Council Regulation on the control of concentrations between undertakings

(2008/C 265/07)

I. INTRODUCTION

1. Article 2 of Council Regulation (EC) No 139/2004 of 20 January 2004 on the control of concentrations between undertakings (hereinafter: the 'Merger Regulation') provides that the Commission has to appraise concentrations within the scope of the Merger Regulation with a view to establishing whether or not they are compatible with the common market. For that purpose, the Commission must assess, pursuant to Article 2(2) and (3), whether or not a concentration would significantly impede effective competition, in particular as a result of the creation or strengthening of a dominant position in the common market or a substantial part of it.

2. This document develops guidance as to how the Commission assesses concentrations where the undertakings concerned are active on different relevant markets. In this document, these concentrations will be called 'non-horizontal mergers'.

3. Two broad types of non-horizontal mergers can be distinguished: vertical mergers and conglomerate mergers.

4. Vertical mergers involve companies operating at different levels of the supply chain. For example, when a manufacturer of a certain product (the 'upstream firm') merges with one of its distributors (the 'downstream firm'), this is called a vertical merger.

5. Conglomerate mergers are mergers between firms that are in a relationship which is neither horizontal (as competitors in the same relevant market) nor vertical (as suppliers or customers). In practice, the focus of the present guidelines is on mergers between companies that are active in closely related markets (e.g. mergers involving suppliers of complementary products or products that belong to the same product range).

6. The general guidance already given in the Notice on horizontal mergers is also relevant in the context of non-horizontal mergers. The purpose of the present document is to concentrate on the competition aspects that are relevant to the specific context of non-horizontal mergers. In addition, it will set out the Commission's approach to market shares and concentration thresholds in this context.

7. In practice, mergers may entail both horizontal and non-horizontal effects. This may for instance be the case where the merging firms are not only in a vertical or conglomerate relationship, but are also actual or potential competitors of each other in one or more of the relevant markets concerned. In such a case, the Commission will appraise horizontal, vertical and/or conglomerate effects in accordance with the guidance set out in the relevant notices.

8. The guidance set out in this document draws and elaborates on the Commission's evolving experience with the appraisal of non-horizontal mergers under Regulation (EEC) No 4064/89 since its entry into force on 21 September 1990, the Merger Regulation presently in force as well as on the case-law of the Court of Justice and the Court of First Instance of the European Communities. The principles contained here will be applied and further developed and refined by the Commission in individual cases. The Commission may revise the notice on non-horizontal mergers from time to time in the light of future developments and of evolving insight.

9. The Commission's interpretation of the Merger Regulation as regards the appraisal of non-horizontal mergers is without prejudice to the interpretation which may be given by the Court of Justice or the Court of First Instance of the European Communities.

II. OVERVIEW

10. Effective competition brings benefits to consumers, such as low prices, high quality products, a wide selection of goods and services, and innovation. Through its control of mergers, the Commission prevents mergers that would be likely to deprive customers of these benefits by significantly increasing the market power of firms. An 'increase in market power' in this context refers to the ability of one or more firms to profitably increase prices, reduce output, choice or quality of goods and services, diminish innovation, or otherwise negatively influence parameters of competition.

11. Non-horizontal mergers are generally less likely to significantly impede effective competition than horizontal mergers.

12. First, unlike horizontal mergers, vertical or conglomerate mergers do not entail the loss of direct competition between the merging firms in the same relevant market. As a result, the main source of anti-competitive effect in horizontal mergers is absent from vertical and conglomerate mergers.

13. Second, vertical and conglomerate mergers provide substantial scope for efficiencies. A characteristic of vertical mergers and certain conglomerate mergers is that the activities and/or the products of the companies involved are complementary to each other. The integration of complementary activities or products within a single firm may produce significant efficiencies and be pro-competitive. In vertical relationships for instance, as a result of the complementarity, a decrease in mark-ups down-stream will lead to higher demand also upstream. A part of the benefit of this increase in demand will accrue to the upstream suppliers. An integrated firm will take this benefit into account. Vertical integration may thus provide an increased incentive to seek to decrease prices and increase output because the integrated firm can capture a larger fraction of the benefits. This is often referred to as the 'internalisation of double mark-ups'. Similarly, other efforts to increase sales at one level (e.g. improve service or stepping up innovation) may provide a greater reward for an integrated firm that will take into account the benefits accruing at other levels.

14. Integration may also decrease transaction costs and allow for a better co-ordination in terms of product design, the organisation of the production process, and the way in which the products are sold. Similarly, mergers which involve products belonging to a range or portfolio of products that are generally sold to the same set of customers (be they complementary products or not) may give rise to customer benefits such as one-stop-shopping.

15. However, there are circumstances in which non-horizontal mergers may significantly impede effective competition, in particular as a result of the creation or strengthening of a dominant position. This is essentially because a non-horizontal merger may change the ability and incentive to compete on the part of the merging companies and their competitors in ways that cause harm to consumers.

16. In the context of competition law, the concept of 'consumers' encompasses intermediate and ultimate consumers. When intermediate customers are actual or potential competitors of the parties to the merger, the Commission focuses on the effects of the merger on the customers to which the merged entity and those competitors are selling. Consequently, the fact that a merger affects competitors is not in itself a problem. It is the impact on effective competition that matters, not the mere impact on competitors at some level of the supply chain. In particular, the fact that rivals may be harmed because a merger creates efficiencies cannot in itself give rise to competition concerns.

17. There are two main ways in which non-horizontal mergers may significantly impede effective competition: non-coordinated effects and coordinated effects.

18. Non-coordinated effects may principally arise when non-horizontal mergers give rise to *foreclosure*. In this document, the term 'foreclosure' will be used to describe any instance where actual or potential rivals' access to supplies or markets is hampered or eliminated as a result of the merger, thereby reducing these companies' ability and/or incentive to compete. As a result of such foreclosure, the merging companies—and, possibly, some of its competitors as well—may be able to profitably increase the price charged to consumers. These instances give rise to a significant impediment to effective competition and are therefore referred to hereafter as 'anticompetitive foreclosure'.

19. Coordinated effects arise where the merger changes the nature of competition in such a way that firms that previously were not coordinating their behaviour, are now significantly more likely to

coordinate to raise prices or otherwise harm effective competition. A merger may also make coordination easier, more stable or more effective for firms which were coordinating prior to the merger.

20. In assessing the competitive effects of a merger, the Commission compares the competitive conditions that would result from the notified merger with the conditions that would have prevailed without the merger (5). In most cases the competitive conditions existing at the time of the merger constitute the relevant comparison for evaluating the effects of a merger. However, in some circumstances, the Commission will take into account future changes to the market that can reasonably be predicted. It may, in particular, take account of the likely entry or exit of firms if the merger did not take place when considering what constitutes the relevant comparison. The Commission may take into account future market developments that result from impending regulatory changes.

21. In its assessment, the Commission will consider both the possible anti-competitive effects arising from the merger and the possible pro-competitive effects stemming from substantiated efficiencies benefiting consumers. The Commission examines the various chains of cause and effect with a view to ascertaining which of them is the most likely. The more immediate and direct the perceived anti-competitive effects of a merger, the more likely the Commission is to raise competition concerns. Likewise, the more immediate and direct the pro-competitive effects of a merger, the more likely the Commission is to find that they counteract any anti-competitive effects.

22. This document describes the main scenarios of competitive harm and sources of efficiencies in the context of vertical mergers and, subsequently, in the context of conglomerate mergers.

III. MARKET SHARE AND CONCENTRATION LEVELS

23. Non-horizontal mergers pose no threat to effective competition unless the merged entity has a significant degree of market power (which does not necessarily amount to dominance) in at least one of the markets concerned. The Commission will examine this issue before proceeding to assess the impact of the merger on competition.

24. Market shares and concentration levels provide useful first indications of the market power and the competitive importance of both the merging parties and their competitors.

25. The Commission is unlikely to find concern in non-horizontal mergers, be it of a coordinated or of a non-coordinated nature, where the market share post-merger of the new entity in each of the markets concerned is below 30 % and the post-merger HHI is below 2 000.

26. In practice, the Commission will not extensively investigate such mergers, except where special circumstances such as, for instance, one or more of the following factors are present:

   (a) a merger involves a company that is likely to expand significantly in the near future, e.g. because of a recent innovation;
   (b) there are significant cross-shareholdings or cross-directorships among the market participants;
   (c) one of the merging firms is a firm with a high likelihood of disrupting coordinated conduct;
   (d) indications of past or ongoing coordination, or facilitating practices, are present.

27. The Commission will use the above market share and HHI thresholds as an initial indicator of the absence of competition concerns. However, these thresholds do not give rise to a legal presumption. The Commission is of the opinion that it is less appropriate in this context to present market share and concentration levels above which competition concerns would be deemed to be likely, as the existence of a significant degree of market power in at least one of the markets concerned is a necessary condition for competitive harm, but is not a sufficient condition.

IV. VERTICAL MERGERS

28. This Section sets out the Commission's framework of analysis in the context of vertical mergers. In its assessment, the Commission will consider both the possible anti-competitive effects arising from vertical mergers and the possible pro-competitive effects stemming from efficiencies substantiated by the parties.

A. NON-COORDINATED EFFECTS: FORECLOSURE

29. A merger is said to result in foreclosure where actual or potential rivals' access to supplies or markets is hampered or eliminated as a result of the merger, thereby reducing these companies' ability and/or incentive to compete. Such foreclosure may discourage entry or expansion of rivals or encourage their exit. Foreclosure thus can be found even if the foreclosed rivals are not forced to exit the market: It is sufficient that the rivals are disadvantaged and consequently led to compete less effectively. Such foreclosure is regarded as anti-competitive where the merging companies—and, possibly, some of its competitors as well—are as a result able to profitably increase the price charged to consumers.

30. Two forms of foreclosure can be distinguished. The first is where the merger is likely to raise the costs of downstream rivals by restricting their access to an important input (input foreclosure). The second is where the merger is likely to foreclose upstream rivals by restricting their access to a sufficient customer base (customer foreclosure).

1. Input foreclosure

31. Input foreclosure arises where, post-merger, the new entity would be likely to restrict access to the products or services that it would have otherwise supplied absent the merger, thereby raising its downstream rivals' costs by making it harder for them to obtain supplies of the input under similar prices and conditions as absent the merger. This may lead the merged entity to profitably increase the price charged to consumers, resulting in a significant impediment to effective competition. As indicated above, for input foreclosure to lead to consumer harm, it is not necessary that the merged firm's rivals are forced to exit the market. The relevant benchmark is whether the increased input costs would lead to higher prices for consumers. Any efficiencies resulting from the merger may, however, lead the merged entity to reduce price, so that the overall likely impact on consumers is neutral or positive. A graphical presentation of this mechanism is provided in Figure 1.

Input foreclosure

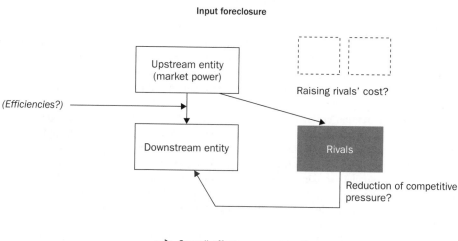

32. In assessing the likelihood of an anticompetitive input foreclosure scenario, the Commission examines, first, whether the merged entity would have, post-merger, the ability to substantially foreclose access to inputs, second, whether it would have the incentive to do so, and third, whether a foreclosure strategy would have a significant detrimental effect on competition downstream. In practice, these factors are often examined together since they are closely intertwined.

A. Ability to foreclose access to inputs

33. Input foreclosure may occur in various forms. The merged entity may decide not to deal with its actual or potential competitors in the vertically related market. Alternatively, the merged firm may decide to restrict supplies and/or to raise the price it charges when supplying competitors and/or to otherwise make the conditions of supply less favourable than they would have been absent the merger. Further, the merged entity may opt for a specific choice of technology within the new firm which is not compatible with the technologies chosen by rival firms. Foreclosure may also take more subtle forms, such as the degradation of the quality of input supplied. In its assessment, the Commission may consider a series of alternative or complementary possible strategies.

34. Input foreclosure may raise competition problems only if it concerns an important input for the downstream product. This is the case, for example, when the input concerned represents a significant cost factor relative to the price of the downstream product. Irrespective of its cost, an input may also be sufficiently important for other reasons. For instance, the input may be a critical component without which the downstream product could not be manufactured or effectively sold on the market, or it may represent a significant source of product differentiation for the downstream product. It may also be that the cost of switching to alternative inputs is relatively high.

35. For input foreclosure to be a concern, the vertically integrated firm resulting from the merger must have a significant degree of market power in the upstream market. It is only in these circumstances that the merged firm can be expected to have a significant influence on the conditions of competition in the upstream market and thus, possibly, on prices and supply conditions in the downstream market.

36. The merged entity would only have the ability to foreclose downstream competitors if, by reducing access to its own upstream products or services, it could negatively affect the overall availability of inputs for the downstream market in terms of price or quality. This may be the case where the remaining upstream suppliers are less efficient, offer less preferred alternatives, or lack the ability to expand output in response to the supply restriction, for example because they face capacity constraints or, more generally, face decreasing returns to scale. Also, the presence of exclusive contracts between the merged entity and independent input providers may limit the ability of downstream rivals to have adequate access to inputs.

37. When determining the extent to which input foreclosure may occur, it must be taken into account that the decision of the merged entity to rely on its upstream division's supply of inputs may also free up capacity on the part of the remaining input suppliers from which the downstream division used to purchase before. In fact, the merger may merely realign purchase patterns among competing firms.

38. When competition in the input market is oligopolistic, a decision of the merged entity to restrict access to its inputs reduces the competitive pressure exercised on remaining input suppliers, which may allow them to raise the input price they charge to non-integrated downstream competitors. In essence, input foreclosure by the merged entity may expose its downstream rivals to non-vertically integrated suppliers with increased market power. This increase in third-party market power will be greater the lower the degree of product differentiation between the merged entity and other upstream suppliers and the higher the degree of upstream concentration. However, the attempt to raise the input price may fail when independent input suppliers, faced with a reduction in the demand for their products (from the downstream division of the merged entity or from independent downstream firms), respond by pricing more aggressively.

39. In its assessment, the Commission will consider, on the basis of the information available, whether there are effective and timely counter-strategies that the rival firms would be likely to deploy. Such counterstrategies include the possibility of changing their production process so as to be less reliant on the input concerned or sponsoring the entry of new suppliers upstream.

B.   Incentive to foreclose access to inputs

40.   The incentive to foreclose depends on the degree to which foreclosure would be profitable. The vertically integrated firm will take into account how its supplies of inputs to competitors downstream will affect not only the profits of its upstream division, but also of its downstream division. Essentially, the merged entity faces a trade-off between the profit lost in the upstream market due to a reduction of input sales to (actual or potential) rivals and the profit gain, in the short or longer term, from expanding sales downstream or, as the case may be, being able to raise prices to consumers.

41.   The trade-off is likely to depend on the level of profits the merged entity obtains upstream and downstream. Other things constant, the lower the margins upstream, the lower the loss from restricting input sales. Similarly, the higher the downstream margins, the higher the profit gain from increasing market share downstream at the expense of foreclosed rivals.

42.   The incentive for the integrated firm to raise rivals' costs further depends on the extent to which downstream demand is likely to be diverted away from foreclosed rivals and the share of that diverted demand that the downstream division of the integrated firm can capture. This share will normally be higher the less capacity constrained the merged entity will be relative to non-foreclosed downstream rivals and the more the products of the merged entity and foreclosed competitors are close substitutes. The effect on downstream demand will also be higher if the affected input represents a significant proportion of downstream rivals' costs or if the affected input represents a critical component of the downstream product.

43.   The incentive to foreclose actual or potential rivals may also depend on the extent to which the downstream division of the integrated firm can be expected to benefit from higher price levels downstream as a result of a strategy to raise rivals' costs. The greater the market shares of the merged entity downstream, the greater the base of sales on which to enjoy increased margins.

44.   An upstream monopolist that is already able to fully extract all available profits in vertically related markets may not have any incentive to foreclose rivals following a vertical merger. The ability to extract available profits from the consumers does not follow immediately from a very high market share. Such a finding would require a more thorough analysis of the actual and future constraints under which the monopolist operates. When all available profits cannot be extracted, a vertical merger—even if it involves an upstream monopolist—may give the merged entity the incentive to raise the costs of downstream rivals, thereby reducing the competitive constraint they exert on the merged entity in the downstream market.

45.   In its assessment of the likely incentives of the merged firm, the Commission may take into account various considerations such as the ownership structure of the merged entity, the type of strategies adopted on the market in the past or the content of internal strategic documents such as business plans.

46.   In addition, when the adoption of a specific course of conduct by the merged entity is an essential step in foreclosure, the Commission examines both the incentives to adopt such conduct and the factors liable to reduce, or even eliminate, those incentives, including the possibility that the conduct is unlawful. Conduct may be unlawful *inter alia* because of competition rules or sector-specific rules at the EU or national levels. This appraisal, however, does not require an exhaustive and detailed examination of the rules of the various legal orders which might be applicable and of the enforcement policy practised within them. Moreover, the illegality of a conduct may be likely to provide significant disincentives for the merged entity to engage in such conduct only in certain circumstances. In particular, the Commission will consider, on the basis of a summary analysis: (i) the likelihood that this conduct would be clearly, or highly probably, unlawful under Community law, (ii) the likelihood that this illegal conduct could be detected, and (iii) the penalties which could be imposed.

C.   Overall likely impact on effective competition

47.   In general, a merger will raise competition concerns because of input foreclosure when it would lead to increased prices in the downstream market thereby significantly impeding effective competition.

48. First, anticompetitive foreclosure may occur when a vertical merger allows the merging parties to increase the costs of downstream rivals in the market thereby leading to an upward pressure on their sales prices. Significant harm to effective competition normally requires that the foreclosed firms play a sufficiently important role in the competitive process on the downstream market. The higher the proportion of rivals which would be foreclosed on the downstream market, the more likely the merger can be expected to result in a significant price increase in the downstream market and, therefore, to significantly impede effective competition therein. Despite a relatively small market share compared to other players, a specific firm may play a significant competitive role compared to other players, for instance because it is a close competitor of the vertically integrated firm or because it is a particularly aggressive competitor.

49. Second, effective competition may be significantly impeded by raising barriers to entry to potential competitors. A vertical merger may foreclose potential competition on the downstream market when the merged entity would be likely not to supply potential downstream entrants, or only on less favourable terms than absent the merger. The mere likelihood that the merged entity would carry out a foreclosure strategy post-merger may already create a strong deterrent effect on potential entrants. Effective competition on the downstream market may be significantly impeded by raising barriers to entry, in particular if input foreclosure would entail for such potential competitors the need to enter at both the downstream and the upstream level in order to compete effectively on either market. The concern of raising entry barriers is particularly relevant in those industries that are opening up to competition or are expected to do so in the foreseeable future.

50. If there remain sufficient credible downstream competitors whose costs are not likely to be raised, for example because they are themselves vertically integrated or they are capable of switching to adequate alternative inputs, competition from those firms may constitute a sufficient constraint on the merged entity and therefore prevent output prices from rising above pre-merger levels.

51. The effect on competition on the downstream market must also be assessed in light of countervailing factors such as the presence of buyer power or the likelihood that entry upstream would maintain effective competition.

52. Further, the effect on competition needs to be assessed in light of efficiencies substantiated by the merging parties. The Commission may decide that, as a consequence of the efficiencies that the merger brings about, there are no grounds for declaring the merger incompatible with the common market pursuant to Article 2(3) of the Merger Regulation. This will be the case when the Commission is in a position to conclude on the basis of sufficient evidence that the efficiencies generated by the merger are likely to enhance the ability and incentive of the merged entity to act pro-competitively for the benefit of consumers, thereby counteracting the adverse effects on competition which the merger might otherwise have.

53. When assessing efficiencies in the context of non-horizontal mergers, the Commission applies the principles already set out in Section VII of the Notice on Horizontal Mergers In particular, for the Commission to take account of efficiency claims in its assessment of the merger, the efficiencies have to benefit consumers, be merger-specific and be verifiable. These conditions are cumulative.

54. Vertical mergers may entail some specific sources of efficiencies, the list of which is not exhaustive.

55. In particular, a vertical merger allows the merged entity to internalise any pre-existing double mark-ups resulting from both parties setting their prices independently pre-merger. Depending on the market conditions, reducing the combined mark-up (relative to a situation where pricing decisions at both levels are not aligned) may allow the vertically integrated firm to profitably expand output on the downstream market.

56. A vertical merger may further allow the parties to better coordinate the production and distribution process, and therefore to save on inventories costs.

57. More generally, a vertical merger may align the incentives of the parties with regard to investments in new products, new production processes and in the marketing of products. For instance, whereas before the merger, a downstream distributor entity might have been reluctant to invest in advertising and informing customers about the qualities of products of the upstream entity when such

investment would also have benefited the sale of other downstream firms, the merged entity may reduce such incentive problems.

2. Customer foreclosure

58. Customer foreclosure may occur when a supplier integrates with an important customer in the downstream market. Because of this downstream presence, the merged entity may foreclose access to a sufficient customer base to its actual or potential rivals in the upstream market (the input market) and reduce their ability or incentive to compete. In turn, this may raise downstream rivals' costs by making it harder for them to obtain supplies of the input under similar prices and conditions as absent the merger. This may allow the merged entity profitably to establish higher prices on the downstream market. Any efficiencies resulting from the merger, however, may lead the merged entity to reduce price, so that there is overall not a negative impact on consumers. For customer foreclosure to lead to consumer harm, it is thus not necessary that the merged firm's rivals are forced to exit the market. The relevant benchmark is whether the increased input costs would lead to higher prices for consumers. A graphical presentation of this mechanism is provided in Figure 2.

Customer foreclosure

59. In assessing the likelihood of an anticompetitive customer foreclosure scenario, the Commission examines, first, whether the merged entity would have the ability to foreclose access to downstream markets by reducing its purchases from its upstream rivals, second, whether it would have the incentive to reduce its purchases upstream, and third, whether a foreclosure strategy would have a significant detrimental effect on consumers in the downstream market.

A. Ability to foreclose access to downstream markets

60. A vertical merger may affect upstream competitors by increasing their cost to access downstream customers or by restricting access to a significant customer base. Customer foreclosure may take various forms. For instance, the merged entity may decide to source all of its required goods or services from its upstream division and, as a result, may stop purchasing from its upstream competitors. It may also reduce its purchases from upstream rivals, or purchase from those rivals on less favourable terms than it would have done absent the merger.

61. When considering whether the merged entity would have the ability to foreclose access to downstream markets, the Commission examines whether there are sufficient economic alternatives in the downstream market for the upstream rivals (actual or potential) to sell their output. For customer foreclosure to be a concern, it must be the case that the vertical merger involves a company which is an important customer with a significant degree of market power in the downstream market. If, on the contrary, there is a sufficiently large customer base, at present or in the future, that is likely

to turn to independent suppliers, the Commission is unlikely to raise competition concerns on that ground.

62. Customer foreclosure can lead to higher input prices in particular if there are significant economies of scale or scope in the input market or when demand is characterised by network effects. It is mainly in such circumstances that the ability to compete of upstream rivals, be they actual or potential, can be impaired.

63. For instance, customer foreclosure can lead to higher input prices when existing upstream rivals operate at or close to their minimum efficient scale. To the extent that customer foreclosure and the corresponding loss of output for the upstream rivals increases their variable costs of production, this may result in an upward pressure on the prices they charge to their customers operating in the downstream market.

64. In the presence of economies of scale or scope, customer foreclosure may also render entry upstream by potential entrants unattractive by significantly reducing the revenue prospects of potential entrants. When customer foreclosure effectively results in entry deterrence, input prices may remain at a higher level than otherwise would have been the case, thereby raising the cost of input supply to downstream competitors of the merged firm.

65. Further, when customer foreclosure primarily impacts upon the revenue streams of upstream rivals, it may significantly reduce their ability and incentive to invest in cost reduction, R & D and product quality. This may reduce their ability to compete in the long run and possibly even cause their exit from the market.

66. In its assessment, the Commission may take into account the existence of different markets corresponding to different uses for the input. If a substantial part of the downstream market is foreclosed, an upstream supplier may fail to reach efficient scale and may also operate at higher costs in the other market(s). Conversely, an upstream supplier may continue to operate efficiently if it finds other uses or secondary markets for its input without incurring significantly higher costs.

67. In its assessment, the Commission will consider, on the basis of the information available, whether there are effective and timely counter-strategies, sustainable over time, that the rival firms would be likely to deploy. Such counterstrategies include the possibility that upstream rivals decide to price more aggressively to maintain sales levels in the downstream market, so as to mitigate the effect of foreclosure.

B.   Incentive to foreclose access to downstream markets

68. The incentive to foreclose depends on the degree to which it is profitable. The merged entity faces a trade-off between the possible costs associated with not procuring products from upstream rivals and the possible gains from doing so, for instance, because it allows the merged entity to raise price in the upstream or downstream markets.

69. The costs associated with reducing purchases from rival upstream suppliers are higher, when the upstream division of the integrated firm is less efficient than the foreclosed suppliers. Such costs are also higher if the upstream division of the merged firm is capacity constrained or rivals' products are more attractive due to product differentiation.

70. The incentive to engage in customer foreclosure further depends on the extent to which the upstream division of the merged entity can benefit from possibly higher price levels in the upstream market arising as a result of upstream rivals being foreclosed. The incentive to engage in customer foreclosure also becomes higher, the more the downstream division of the integrated firm can be expected to enjoy the benefits of higher price levels downstream resulting from the foreclosure strategy. In this context, the greater the market shares of the merged entity's downstream operations, the greater the base of sales on which to enjoy increased margins.

71. When the adoption of a specific conduct by the merged entity is an essential step in foreclosure, the Commission examines both the incentives to adopt such conduct and the factors liable to reduce, or even eliminate, those incentives, including the possibility that the conduct is unlawful.

C. Overall likely impact on effective competition

72. Foreclosing rivals in the upstream market may have an adverse impact in the downstream market and harm consumers. By denying competitive access to a significant customer base for the foreclosed rivals' (upstream) products, the merger may reduce their ability to compete in the foreseeable future. As a result, rivals downstream are likely to be put at a competitive disadvantage, for example in the form of raised input costs. In turn, this may allow the merged entity to profitably raise prices or reduce the overall output on the downstream market.

73. The negative impact on consumers may take some time to materialise when the primary impact of customer foreclosure is on the revenue streams of upstream rivals, reducing their incentives to make investments in cost reduction, product quality or in other competitive dimensions so as to remain competitive.

74. It is only when a sufficiently large fraction of upstream output is affected by the revenue decreases resulting from the vertical merger that the merger may significantly impede effective competition on the upstream market. If there remain a number of upstream competitors that are not affected, competition from those firms may be sufficient to prevent prices from rising in the upstream market and, consequently, in the downstream market. Sufficient competition from these non-foreclosed upstream firms requires that they do not face barriers to expansion e.g. through capacity constraints or product differentiation. When the reduction of competition upstream affects a significant fraction of output downstream, the merger is likely, as with input foreclosure, to result in a significant increase of the price level in the downstream market and, therefore, to significantly impede effective competition.

75. Effective competition on the upstream market may also be significantly impeded by raising barriers to entry to potential competitors. This may be so in particular if customer foreclosure would entail for such potential competitors the need to enter at both the downstream and the upstream level in order to compete effectively on either market. In such a context, customer foreclosure and input foreclosure may thus be part of the same strategy. The concern of raising entry barriers is particularly relevant in those industries that are opening up to competition or are expected to do so in the foreseeable future.

76. The effect on competition must be assessed in light of countervailing factors such as the presence of countervailing buyer power or the likelihood that entry would maintain effective competition in the upstream or downstream market.

77. Further, the effect on competition needs to be assessed in light of efficiencies substantiated by the merging parties.

B. OTHER NON-COORDINATED EFFECTS

78. The merged entity may, by vertically integrating, gain access to commercially sensitive information regarding the upstream or downstream activities of rivals (7). For instance, by becoming the supplier of a downstream competitor, a company may obtain critical information, which allows it to price less aggressively in the downstream market to the detriment of consumers (8). It may also put competitors at a competitive disadvantage, thereby dissuading them to enter or expand in the market.

C. COORDINATED EFFECTS

79. As set out in Section IV of the Notice on Horizontal Mergers, a merger may change the nature of competition in such a way that firms that previously were not coordinating their behaviour, are now significantly more likely to coordinate and raise prices or otherwise harm effective competition. A merger may also make coordination easier, more stable or more effective for firms which were co-ordinating prior to the merger.

80. Market coordination may arise where competitors are able, without entering into an agreement or resorting to a concerted practice within the meaning of Article 81 of the Treaty, to identify

and pursue common objectives, avoiding the normal mutual competitive pressure by a coherent system of implicit threats. In a normal competitive setting, each firm constantly has an incentive to compete. This incentive is ultimately what keeps prices low, and what prevents firms from jointly maximising their profits. Coordination involves a departure from normal competitive conditions in that firms are able to sustain prices in excess of what independent short term profit maximisation would yield. Firms will refrain from undercutting the high prices charged by their competitors in a coordinated way because they anticipate that such behaviour would jeopardise coordination in the future. For coordinated effects to arise, the profit that firms could make by competing aggressively in the short term ('deviating') has to be less than the expected reduction in revenues that this behaviour would entail in the longer term, as it would be expected to trigger an aggressive response by competitors ('a punishment').

81. Coordination is more likely to emerge in markets where it is relatively simple to reach a common understanding on the terms of coordination. In addition, three conditions are necessary for coordination to be sustainable. First, the coordinating firms must be able to monitor to a sufficient degree whether the terms of coordination are being adhered to. Second, discipline requires that there is some form of deterrent mechanism that can be activated if deviation is detected. Third, the reactions of outsiders, such as current and future competitors not participating in the coordination, as well as customers, should not be able to jeopardise the results expected from the coordination.

Reaching terms of coordination

82. A vertical merger may make it easier for the firms in the upstream or downstream market to reach a common understanding on the terms of coordination.

83. For instance, when a vertical merger leads to foreclosure, it results in a reduction in the number of effective competitors in the market. Generally speaking, a reduction in the number of players makes it easier to coordinate among the remaining market players.

84. Vertical mergers may also increase the degree of symmetry between firms active in the market. This may increase the likelihood of coordination by making it easier to reach a common understanding on the terms of coordination. Likewise, vertical integration may increase the level of market transparency, making it easier to coordinate among the remaining market players.

85. Further, a merger may involve the elimination of a maverick in a market. A maverick is a supplier that for its own reasons is unwilling to accept the co-ordinated outcome and thus maintains aggressive competition. The vertical integration of the maverick may alter its incentives to such an extent that co-ordination will no longer be prevented.

Monitoring deviations

86. Vertical integration may facilitate coordination by increasing the level of market transparency between firms through access to sensitive information on rivals or by making it easier to monitor pricing. Such concerns may arise, for example, if the level of price transparency is higher downstream than upstream. This could be the case when prices to final consumers are public, while transactions at the intermediate market are confidential. Vertical integration may give upstream producers control over final prices and thus monitor deviations more effectively.

87. When it leads to foreclosure, a vertical merger may also induce a reduction in the number of effective competitors in a market. A reduction in the number of players may make it easier to monitor each other's actions in the market.

Deterrent mechanisms

88. Vertical mergers may affect coordinating firms' incentives to adhere to the terms of coordination. For instance, a vertically integrated company may be in a position to more effectively punish rival companies when they choose to deviate from the terms of coordination, because it is either a crucial customer or supplier to them.

Reactions of outsiders

89. Vertical mergers may reduce the scope for outsiders to destabilise the coordination by increasing barriers to enter the market or otherwise limiting the ability to compete on the part of outsiders to the coordination.

90. A vertical merger may also involve the elimination of a disruptive buyer in a market. If upstream firms view sales to a particular buyer as sufficiently important, they may be tempted to deviate from the terms of co-ordination in an effort to secure their business. Similarly, a large buyer may be able to tempt the co-ordinating firms to deviate from these terms by concentrating a large amount of its requirements on one supplier or by offering long term contracts. The acquisition of such a buyer may increase the risk of co-ordination in a market.

V. CONGLOMERATE MERGERS

91. Conglomerate mergers are mergers between firms that are in a relationship which is neither purely horizontal (as competitors in the same relevant market) nor vertical (as supplier and customer). In practice, the focus is on mergers between companies that are active in closely related markets (e.g. mergers involving suppliers of complementary products or of products which belong to a range of products that is generally purchased by the same set of customers for the same end use).

92. Whereas it is acknowledged that conglomerate mergers in the majority of circumstances will not lead to any competition problems, in certain specific cases there may be harm to competition. In its assessment, the Commission will consider both the possible anti-competitive effects arising from conglomerate mergers and the possible pro-competitive effects stemming from efficiencies substantiated by the parties.

A. NON-COORDINATED EFFECTS: FORECLOSURE

93. The main concern in the context of conglomerate mergers is that of foreclosure. The combination of products in related markets may confer on the merged entity the ability and incentive to leverage a strong market position from one market to another by means of tying or bundling or other exclusionary practices. Tying and bundling as such are common practices that often have no anticompetitive consequences. Companies engage in tying and bundling in order to provide their customers with better products or offerings in cost-effective ways. Nevertheless, in certain circumstances, these practices may lead to a reduction in actual or potential rivals' ability or incentive to compete. This may reduce the competitive pressure on the merged entity allowing it to increase prices.

94. In assessing the likelihood of such a scenario, the Commission examines, first, whether the merged firm would have the ability to foreclose its rivals, second, whether it would have the economic incentive to do so and, third, whether a foreclosure strategy would have a significant detrimental effect on competition, thus causing harm to consumers. In practice, these factors are often examined together as they are closely intertwined.

A. Ability to foreclose

95. The most immediate way in which the merged entity may be able to use its market power in one market to foreclose competitors in another is by conditioning sales in a way that links the products in the separate markets together. This is done most directly either by tying or bundling.

96. 'Bundling' usually refers to the way products are offered and priced by the merged entity. One can distinguish in this respect between pure bundling and mixed bundling. In the case of pure bundling the products are only sold jointly in fixed proportions. With mixed bundling the products are also available separately, but the sum of the stand-alone prices is higher than the bundled price. Rebates, when made dependent on the purchase of other goods, may be considered a form of mixed bundling.

97. 'Tying' usually refers to situations where customers that purchase one good (the tying good) are required to also purchase another good from the producer (the tied good). Tying can take place on a technical or contractual basis. For instance, technical tying occurs when the tying product is designed in such a way that it only works with the tied product (and not with the alternatives offered by competitors). Contractual tying entails that the customer when purchasing the tying good undertakes only to purchase the tied product (and not the alternatives offered by competitors).

98. The specific characteristics of the products may be relevant for determining whether any of these means of linking sales between separate markets are available to the merged entity. For instance, pure bundling is very unlikely to be possible if products are not bought simultaneously or by the same customers. Similarly, technical tying is only an option in certain industries.

99. In order to be able to foreclose competitors, the new entity must have a significant degree of market power, which does not necessarily amount to dominance, in one of the markets concerned. The effects of bundling or tying can only be expected to be substantial when at least one of the merging parties' products is viewed by many customers as particularly important and there are few relevant alternatives for that product, e.g. because of product differentiation or capacity constraints on the part of rivals.

100. Further, for foreclosure to be a potential concern it must be the case that there is a large common pool of customers for the individual products concerned. The more customers tend to buy both products (instead of only one of the products), the more demand for the individual products may be affected through bundling or tying. Such a correspondence in purchasing behaviour is more likely to be significant when the products in question are complementary.

101. Generally speaking, the foreclosure effects of bundling and tying are likely to be more pronounced in industries where there are economies of scale and the demand pattern at any given point in time has dynamic implications for the conditions of supply in the market in the future. Notably, where a supplier of complementary goods has market power in one of the products (product A), the decision to bundle or tie may result in reduced sales by the non-integrated suppliers of the complementary good (product B). If further there are network externalities at play this will significantly reduce these rivals' scope for expanding sales of product B in the future. Alternatively, where entry into the market for the complementary product is contemplated by potential entrants, the decision to bundle by the merged entity may have the effect of deterring such entry. The limited availability of complementary products with which to combine may, in turn, discourage potential entrants to enter market A.

102. It can also be noted that the scope for foreclosure tends to be smaller where the merging parties cannot commit to making their tying or bundling strategy a lasting one, for example through technical tying or bundling which is costly to reverse.

103. In its assessment, the Commission considers, on the basis of the information available, whether there are effective and timely counter-strategies that the rival firms may deploy. One such example is when a strategy of bundling would be defeated by single-product companies combining their offers so as to make them more attractive to customers. Bundling is further less likely to lead to foreclosure if a company in the market would purchase the bundled products and profitably resell them unbundled. In addition, rivals may decide to price more aggressively to maintain market share, mitigating the effect of foreclosure.

104. Customers may have a strong incentive to buy the range of products concerned from a single source (one-stop-shopping) rather than from many suppliers, e.g. because it saves on transaction costs. The fact that the merged entity will have a broad range or portfolio of products does not, as such, raise competition concerns.

B. Incentive to foreclose

105. The incentive to foreclose rivals through bundling or tying depends on the degree to which this strategy is profitable. The merged entity faces a trade-off between the possible costs associated with bundling or tying its products and the possible gains from expanding market shares in the

market(s) concerned or, as the case may be, being able to raise price in those market(s) due to its market power.

106. Pure bundling and tying may entail losses for the merged company itself. For instance, if a significant number of customers are not interested in buying the bundle, but instead prefers to buy only one product (e.g. the product used to leverage), sales of that product (as contained in the bundle) may significantly fall. Furthermore, losses on the leveraging product may arise where customers who, before the merger, used to 'mix and match' the leveraging product of a merging party with the product of another company, decide to purchase the bundle offered by rivals or no longer to purchase at all.

107. In this context it may thus be relevant to assess the relative value of the different products. By way of example, it is unlikely that the merged entity would be willing to forego sales on one highly profitable market in order to gain market shares on another market where turnover is relatively small and profits are modest.

108. However, the decision to bundle and tie may also increase profits by gaining market power in the tied goods market, protecting market power in the tying goods market, or a combination of the two (see Section C below).

109. In its assessment of the likely incentives of the merged firm, the Commission may take into account other factors such as the ownership structure of the merged entity, the type of strategies adopted on the market in the past or the content of internal strategic documents such as business plans.

110. When the adoption of a specific conduct by the merged entity is an essential step in foreclosure, the Commission examines both the incentives to adopt such conduct and the factors liable to reduce, or even eliminate, those incentives, including the possibility that the conduct is unlawful.

C. Overall likely impact on prices and choice

111. Bundling or tying may result in a significant reduction of sales prospects faced by single-component rivals in the market. The reduction in sales by competitors is not in and of itself a problem. Yet, in particular industries, if this reduction is significant enough, it may lead to a reduction in rivals' ability or incentive to compete. This may allow the merged entity to subsequently acquire market power (in the market for the tied or bundled good) and/or to maintain market power (in the market for the tying or leveraging good).

112. In particular, foreclosure practices may deter entry by potential competitors. They may do so for a specific market by reducing sales prospects for potential rivals in that market to a level below minimum viable scale. In the case of complementary products, deterring entry in one market through bundling or tying may also allow the merged entity to deter entry in another market if the bundling or tying forces potential competitors to enter both product markets at the same time rather than entering only one of them or entering them sequentially. The latter may have a significant impact in particular in those industries where the demand pattern at any given point in time has dynamic implications for the conditions of supply in the market in the future.

113. It is only when a sufficiently large fraction of market output is affected by foreclosure resulting from the merger that the merger may significantly impede effective competition. If there remain effective single-product players in either market, competition is unlikely to deteriorate following a conglomerate merger. The same holds when few single-product rivals remain, but these have the ability and incentive to expand output.

114. The effect on competition needs to be assessed in light of countervailing factors such as the presence of countervailing buyer power or the likelihood that entry would maintain effective competition in the upstream or downstream markets.

115. Further, the effect on competition needs to be assessed in light of the efficiencies substantiated by the merging parties.

116. Many of the efficiencies identified in the context of vertical mergers may, mutatis mutandis, also apply to conglomerate mergers involving complementary products.

117. Notably, when producers of complementary goods are pricing independently, they will not take into account the positive effect of a drop in the price of their product on the sales of the other product. Depending on the market conditions, a merged firm may internalise this effect and may have a certain incentive to lower margins if this leads to higher overall profits (this incentive is often referred to as the 'Cournot effect'). In most cases, the merged firm will make the most out of this effect by means of mixed bundling, i.e. by making the price drop conditional upon whether or not the customer buys both products from the merged entity.

118. Specific to conglomerate mergers is that they may produce cost savings in the form of economies of scope (either on the production or the consumption side), yielding an inherent advantage to supplying the goods together rather than apart. For instance, it may be more efficient that certain components are marketed together as a bundle rather than separately. Value enhancements for the customer can result from better compatibility and quality assurance of complementary components. Such economies of scope however are necessary but not sufficient to provide an efficiency justification for bundling or tying. Indeed, benefits from economies of scope frequently can be realised without any need for technical or contractual bundling.

B.   CO-ORDINATED EFFECTS

119. Conglomerate mergers may in certain circumstances facilitate anticompetitive co-ordination in markets, even in the absence of an agreement or a concerted practice within the meaning of Article 81 of the Treaty. The framework set out in Section IV of the Notice on Horizontal Mergers also applies in this context. In particular, co-ordination is more likely to emerge in markets where it is fairly easy to identify the terms of co-ordination and where such co-ordination is sustainable.

120. One way in which a conglomerate merger may influence the likelihood of a coordinated outcome in a given market is by reducing the number of effective competitors to such an extent that tacit coordination becomes a real possibility. Also when rivals are not excluded from the market, they may find themselves in a more vulnerable situation. As a result, foreclosed rivals may choose not to contest the situation of co-ordination, but may prefer instead to live under the shelter of the increased price level.

121. Further, a conglomerate merger may increase the extent and importance of multi-market competition. Competitive interaction on several markets may increase the scope and effectiveness of disciplining mechanisms in ensuring that the terms of co-ordination are being adhered to.

Commission notice on remedies acceptable under Council Regulation (EC) No 139/2004 and under Commission Regulation (EC) No 802/2004

(2008/C 267/01)

I.   INTRODUCTION

1. Council Regulation (EC) No 139/2004 of 20 January 2004 on the control of concentrations between undertakings (hereinafter referred to as 'the Merger Regulation') in Articles 6(2) and 8(2) expressly provides that the Commission may decide to declare a concentration compatible with the common market following modification by the parties, both before and after the initiation of proceedings. To that end, the Commission may attach to its decision conditions and obligations intended to ensure that the undertakings concerned comply with the commitments they have entered into *vis-à-vis* the Commission with a view to rendering the concentration compatible with the common market.

2. The purpose of this Notice is to provide guidance on modifications to concentrations, in particular commitments by the undertakings concerned to modify a concentration. Such modifications

are more commonly described as 'remedies' since their object is to eliminate the competition concerns identified by the Commission. The guidance set out in this Notice reflects the Commission's evolving experience with the assessment, acceptance and implementation of remedies under the Merger Regulation since its entry into force on 21 September 1990. The revision of the Commission's 2001 Notice on remedies is entailed by the entry into force of the recast Merger Regulation (EC) No 139/2004 and of Commission Regulation (EC) No 802/2004 (the 'Implementing Regulation') on 1 May 2004, case-law of the Court of Justice and the Court of First Instance, the conclusions drawn from the systematic *ex post* review of the Commission of past remedies case, and decisional practice of the Commission in cases involving remedies in recent years. The principles contained herein will be applied and further developed and refined by the Commission in individual cases. The guidance provided in this Notice is without prejudice to the interpretation which may be given by the Court of Justice or by the Court of First Instance of the European Communities.

3. This Notice sets out the general principles applicable to remedies acceptable to the Commission, the main types of commitments that may be accepted by the Commission in cases under the Merger Regulation, the specific requirements which proposals of commitments need to fulfil in both phases of the procedure, and the main requirements for the implementation of commitments. In any case, the Commission will take due account of the particular circumstances of the individual case.

II.   GENERAL PRINCIPLES

4. Under the Merger Regulation, the Commission assesses the compatibility of a notified concentration with the common market on the basis of its effect on the structure of competition in the Community. The test for compatibility under Article 2(2) and (3) of the Merger Regulation is whether or not a concentration would significantly impede effective competition in the common market or a substantial part of it, in particular as a result of the creation or strengthening of a dominant position. A concentration that significantly impedes effective competition as described above is incompatible with the common market and the Commission is required to prohibit it. For the creation of a joint venture, the Commission will also examine the concentration under Article 2(4) of the Merger Regulation. The principles set out in this Notice will generally also apply to remedies submitted to eliminate competition concerns identified under Article 2(4).

5. Where a concentration raises competition concerns in that it could significantly impede effective competition, in particular as a result of the creation or strengthening of a dominant position, the parties may seek to modify the concentration in order to resolve the competition concerns and thereby gain clearance of their merger. Such modifications may be fully implemented in advance of a clearance decision. However, it is more common that the parties submit commitments with a view to rendering the concentration compatible with the common market and that those commitments are implemented following clearance.

6. Under the structure of the Merger Regulation, it is the responsibility of the Commission to show that a concentration would significantly impede competition. The Commission communicates its competition concerns to the parties to allow them to formulate appropriate and corresponding remedies proposals. It is then for the parties to the concentration to put forward commitments; the Commission is not in a position to impose unilaterally any conditions to an authorisation decision, but only on the basis of the parties' commitments. The Commission will inform the parties about its preliminary assessment of remedies proposals. If, however, the parties do not validly propose remedies adequate to eliminate the competition concerns, the only option for the Commission will be to adopt a prohibition decision.

7. The Commission has to assess whether the proposed remedies, once implemented, would eliminate the competition concerns identified. Only the parties have all the relevant information necessary for such an assessment, in particular as to the feasibility of the commitments proposed and the viability and competitiveness of the assets proposed for divestiture. It is therefore the responsibility of the parties to provide all such information available that is necessary for the Commission's assessment of the remedies proposal. To this end, the Implementing Regulation obliges the notifying

parties to provide, with the commitments, detailed information on the content of the commitments offered, the conditions for their implementation and showing their suitability to remove any significant impediment of effective competition, as set out in the annex to the Implementing Regulation ('Form RM'). For commitments consisting in the divestiture of a business, parties have to describe in detail in particular how the business to be divested is currently operated. This information will enable the Commission to assess the viability, competitiveness and marketability of the business by comparing its current operation to its proposed scope under the commitments. The Commission can adapt the precise requirements to the information necessary in the individual case at hand and will be available to discuss the scope of the information required with the parties in advance of submission of Form RM.

8. Whereas the parties have to propose commitments sufficient to remove the competition concerns and submit the necessary information to assess them, it is for the Commission to establish whether or not a concentration, as modified by commitments validly submitted, must be declared incompatible with the common market because it leads, despite the commitments, to a significant impediment of effective competition. The burden of proof for a prohibition or authorisation of a concentration modified by commitments is therefore subject to the same criteria as an unmodified concentration.

Basic conditions for acceptable commitments

9. Under the Merger Regulation, the Commission only has power to accept commitments that are deemed capable of rendering the concentration compatible with the common market so that they will prevent a significant impediment of effective competition. The commitments have to eliminate the competition concerns entirely and have to be comprehensive and effective from all points of view. Furthermore, commitments must be capable of being implemented effectively within a short period of time as the conditions of competition on the market will not be maintained until the commitments have been fulfilled.

10. Structural commitments, in particular divestitures, proposed by the parties will meet these conditions only in so far as the Commission is able to conclude with the requisite degree of certainty that it will be possible to implement them and that it will be likely that the new commercial structures resulting from them will be sufficiently workable and lasting to ensure that the significant impediment to effective competition will not materialise.

11. The requisite degree of certainty concerning the implementation of the proposed commitments may in particular be affected by risks in relation to the transfer of a business to be divested, such as conditions attached by the parties to the divestiture, third party rights in relation to the business or the risks of finding a suitable purchaser, as well as risks in relation to the degradation of the assets until the divestiture has taken place. It is incumbent on the parties to remove such uncertainties as to the implementation of the remedy when submitting it to the Commission.

12. In assessing the second condition, whether the proposed commitment will likely eliminate the competition concerns identified, the Commission will consider all relevant factors relating to the proposed remedy itself, including, *inter alia*, the type, scale and scope of the remedy proposed, judged by reference to the structure and particular characteristics of the market in which the competition concerns arise, including the position of the parties and other players on the market.

13. In order for the commitments to comply with these principles, there has to be an effective implementation and ability to monitor the commitments. Whereas divestitures, once implemented, do not require any further monitoring measures, other types of commitments require effective monitoring mechanisms in order to ensure that their effect is not reduced or even eliminated by the parties. Otherwise, such commitments would have to be considered as mere declarations of intention by the parties and would not amount to binding obligations, as, due to the lack of effective monitoring mechanisms, any breach of them could not result in the revocation of the decision according to the provisions of the Merger Regulation.

14. Where, however, the parties submit remedies proposals that are so extensive and complex that it is not possible for the Commission to determine with the requisite degree of certainty, at the

time of its decision, that they will be fully implemented and that they are likely to maintain effective competition in the market, an authorisation decision cannot be granted. The Commission may reject such remedies in particular on the grounds that the implementation of the remedies cannot be effectively monitored and that the lack of effective monitoring diminishes, or even eliminates, the effect of the commitments proposed.

Appropriateness of different types of remedies

15. According to the case law of the Court, the basic aim of commitments is to ensure competitive market structures. Accordingly, commitments which are structural in nature, such as the commitment to sell a business unit, are, as a rule, preferable from the point of view of the Merger Regulation's objective, inasmuch as such commitments prevent, durably, the competition concerns which would be raised by the merger as notified, and do not, moreover, require medium or long-term monitoring measures. Nevertheless, the possibility cannot automatically be ruled out that other types of commitments may also be capable of preventing the significant impediment of effective competition.

16. The Commission stresses that the question of whether a remedy and, more specifically, which type of remedy is suitable to eliminate the competition concerns identified, has to be examined on a case-by-case basis.

17. Nevertheless, a general distinction can be made between divestitures, other structural remedies, such as granting access to key infrastructure or inputs on non-discriminatory terms, and commitments relating to the future behaviour of the merged entity. Divestiture commitments are the best way to eliminate competition concerns resulting from horizontal overlaps, and may also be the best means of resolving problems resulting from vertical or conglomerate concerns. Other structural commitments may be suitable to resolve all types of concerns if those remedies are equivalent to divestitures in their effects, as explained in more detail below in paragraphs 61 *et seq.* Commitments relating to the future behaviour of the merged entity may be acceptable only exceptionally in very specific circumstances. In particular, commitments in the form of undertakings not to raise prices, to reduce product ranges o to remove brands, etc., will generally not eliminate competition concerns resulting from horizontal overlaps. In any case, those types of remedies can only exceptionally be accepted if their workability is fully ensured by effective implementation and monitoring in line with the considerations set out in paragraphs 13–14, 66, 69, and if they do not risk leading to distorting effects on competition.

Procedure

18. The Commission may accept commitments in either phase of the procedure. However, given the fact that an in-depth market investigation is only carried out in phase II, commitments submitted to the Commission in phase I must be sufficient to clearly rule out 'serious doubts' within the meaning of Article 6(1)(c) of the Merger Regulation. Pursuant to Article 10(2) of the Merger Regulation, the Commission has to take a clearance decision as soon as the serious doubts referred to in Article 6(1)(c) of the Merger Regulation are removed as a result of commitments submitted by the parties. This rule applies to commitments proposed in phase II-proceedings before the Commission issues a Statement of Objections. If the Commission reaches the preliminary view that the merger leads to a significant impediment to effective competition and issues a Statement of Objections, the commitments must be sufficient to eliminate such a significant impediment to effective competition.

19. Whilst commitments have to be offered by the parties, the Commission will ensure the enforceability of commitments by making the authorisation of the merger subject to compliance with the commitments. A distinction must be made between conditions and obligations. The requirement for achievement of the structural change of the market is a condition—for example, that a business is to be divested. The implementing steps which are necessary to achieve this result are generally obligations on the parties, e.g. such as the appointment of a trustee with an irrevocable mandate to sell the business.

20. Where the undertakings concerned commit a breach of an obligation, the Commission may revoke clearance decisions issued either under Article 6(2) or Article 8(2) of the Merger Regulation,

acting pursuant to Article 6(3) or Article 8(6), respectively. In case of a breach of an obligation, the parties may also be subject to fines and periodic penalty payments as provided in Article 14(2)(d) and 15(1)(c) respectively of the Merger Regulation. Where, however, a condition is breached, e.g. a business is not divested in the time-frame foreseen in the commitments or afterwards re-acquired, the compatibility decision is no longer applicable. In such circumstances, the Commission may, first, take interim measures appropriate to maintain conditions of effective competition pursuant to Article 8(5)(b) of the Merger Regulation. Second, it may, if the conditions of Article 8(4)(b) are met, order any appropriate measure to ensure that the undertakings concerned dissolve the concentration or take other restorative measures or, according to Article 8(7), take a decision pursuant to Article 8(1)–(3). In addition, the parties may also be subject to fines as provided in Article 14(2)(d).

Model Texts for divestiture commitments

21. The Commission services have issued Best Practice Guidelines for divestiture commitments, consisting of a Model Text for Divestiture Commitments and a Model Text for Trustee Mandates. These model texts are neither intended to provide an exhaustive coverage of all issues that may become relevant in all cases, nor are they legally binding upon parties in a merger procedure. They complement the present Notice as they outline the typical arrangements for divestiture commitments in a format which can be used by the parties. At the same time, the model texts leave the flexibility to adapt them to the requirements of the specific case.

III. DIFFERENT TYPES OF REMEDIES

1. DIVESTITURE OF A BUSINESS TO A SUITABLE PURCHASER

22. Where a proposed concentration threatens to significantly impede effective competition the most effective way to maintain effective competition, apart from prohibition, is to create the conditions for the emergence of a new competitive entity or for the strengthening of existing competitors via divestiture by the merging parties.

1.1. Divestiture of a viable and competitive business

23. The divested activities must consist of a viable business that, if operated by a suitable purchaser, can compete effectively with the merged entity on a lasting basis and that is divested as a going concern. For the business to be viable, it may also be necessary to include activities which are related to markets where the Commission did not identify competition concerns if this is required to create an effective competitor in the affected markets.

24. In proposing a viable business for divestiture, it is necessary to take into account the uncertainties and risks related to the transfer of a business to a new owner. These risks may limit the competitive impact of the divested business, and, therefore, may lead to a market situation where the competition concerns at stake will not necessarily be eliminated.

Scope of the business to be divested

25. The business has to include all the assets which contribute to its current operation or which are necessary to ensure its viability and competitiveness and all personnel which is currently employed or which is necessary to ensure the business' viability and competitiveness.

26. Personnel and assets which are currently shared between the business to be divested and other businesses of the parties, but which contribute to the operation of the business or which are necessary to ensure its viability and competitiveness, also have to be included. Otherwise, the viability and competitiveness of the business to be divested would be endangered. Therefore, the divested business as to contain the personnel providing essential functions for the business such as, for instance, group R & D and information technology staff even where such personnel is currently employed by another business unit of the parties—at least in a sufficient proportion to meet the on-going needs

of the divested business. In the same way shared assets have to be included even if those assets are owned by or allocated to another business unit.

27. In order for the Commission to be able to identify the scope of the business to be divested, the parties have to include a precise definition of the scope of the divested business in the commitments (the 'description of the business'). The description of the business has to be adapted to the individual case at hand and should contain all the elements that are part of the business to be divested: tangible (e.g. R & D, production, distribution, sales and marketing activities) and intangible assets (such as intellectual property rights, know-how and goodwill); licences, permits and authorisations by governmental organisations granted to the business; contracts, leases and commitments (e.g. arrangements with suppliers and customers) for the benefit of the business to be divested; and customer, credit and other records. In the description of the business, the parties have to include the personnel to be transferred in general terms, including staff seconded and temporary employees, and to insert a list of the key personnel, i.e. the personnel essential for the viability and competitiveness of the business. The transfer of those employees is without prejudice to the application of the Council Directives on collective redundancies; on safeguarding employees' rights in the event of transfers of undertakings; and on informing and consulting employees as well as national provisions implementing those Directives and other national laws. The remedy has to include a non-solicitation commitment by the parties with regard to the key personnel.

28. In the description of the business, the parties also have to set out the arrangements for the supply of products and services by them to the divested business or by the divested business to them. Such on-going relationships of the divested business may be necessary to maintain the full economic viability and competitiveness of the divested business for a transitional basis. The Commission will only accept such arrangements if they do not affect the independence of the divested business from the parties.

29. In order to avoid any misunderstanding about the business to be divested, assets or personnel that are used within or employed by the business but that should not, according to the parties, be transferred with the divestiture, have to be expressly excluded by the parties in the commitments text. The Commission will only be able to accept such exclusion of assets or personnel if the parties can clearly show that this does not affect the viability and competitiveness of the business.

30. The business to be divested has to be viable as such. Therefore, the resources of a possible or even presumed future purchaser are not taken into account by the Commission at the stage of assessing the remedy. The situation is different if already during the procedure a sale and purchase agreement with a specific purchaser is concluded whose resources can be taken into account at the time of the assessment of the commitment. This situation will be dealt with in more detail below in paragraphs 56 ff.

31. Once a purchaser is identified after adoption of an authorisation decision, some of the assets or personnel included in the divested business may not be needed by the proposed purchaser. In the purchaser approval process, the Commission may, upon request by the parties, approve the divestiture of the business to the proposed purchaser without one or more assets or parts of the personnel if this does not affect the viability and competitiveness of the business to be divested after the sale, taking account of the resources of the proposed purchaser.

1.2. Stand-alone business and conditions for acceptability of alternatives

32. Normally, a viable business is a business that can operate on a stand-alone-basis, which means independently of the merging parties as regards the supply of input materials or other forms of cooperation other than during a transitory period.

33. The Commission has a clear preference for an existing stand-alone business. This may take the form of a pre-existing company or group of companies, or of a business division which was not previously legally incorporated as such.

34. Where the competition concern results from a horizontal overlap, the parties may be able to choose between two businesses. In cases involving a hostile bid, a commitment to divest activities of the target company may, in such circumstances of limited information available to the notifying

parties about the business to be divested, increase the risk that this business might not, after a divestiture, result in a viable competitor which could effectively compete in the market on a lasting basis. It may therefore be more appropriate for the parties to propose to divest activities of the acquiring company in such scenarios.

Carve-outs

35. Even though normally the divestiture of an existing viable stand-alone business is required, the Commission, taking into account the principle of proportionality, may also consider the divestiture of businesses which have existing strong links or are partially integrated with businesses retained by the parties and therefore need to be 'carved out' in those respects. In order to reduce the risks for the viability and competitiveness to a minimum in such circumstances, an option for the parties is to submit commitments proposing to carve out those parts of an existing business which do not necessarily have to be divested. In effect, an existing, stand-alone business is being divested in those circumstances although, by way of a 'reverse carve-out', the parties may carve-out the limited parts which they may keep.

36. In any case, the Commission will only be able to accept commitments which require the carve-out of a business if it can be certain that, at least at the time when the business is transferred to the purchaser, a viable business on a stand-alone basis will be divested and the risks for the viability and competitiveness caused by the carve-out will thereby be reduced to a minimum. The parties therefore have to ensure, as set out in detail below in paragraph 113, that the carve-out is started in the interim period, i.e. the period between the adoption of the Commission decision up to the completion of the divestiture (meaning the legal and factual transfer of the business to the purchaser). Consequently, at the end of this period, a viable business on a stand-alone basis will be divested. If this should not be possible or if the carve-out should be particularly difficult, parties may provide the requisite degree of certainty for the Commission by proposing an up-front buyer solution, as further detailed below in paragraph 55.

Divestiture of assets, in particular of brands and licences

37. A divestiture consisting of a combination of certain assets which did not form a uniform and viable business in the past creates risks as to the viability and competitiveness of the resulting business. This is in particular the case if assets from more than one party are involved. Such an approach may be accepted by the Commission only if the viability of the business is ensured notwithstanding the fact that the assets did not form a uniform business in the past. This may be the case if the individual assets can already be considered a viable and competitive business. Similarly, only in exceptional cases a divestiture package including only brands and supporting production and/or distribution assets may be sufficient to create the conditions for effective competition. In such circumstances, the package consisting of brands and assets must be sufficient to allow the Commission to conclude that the resulting business will be immediately viable in the hands of a suitable purchaser.

38. Divestitures of a business generally appear preferable to the granting of licenses to IP rights, as the granting of a license involve more uncertainties, will not enable the licensee to compete immediately in the market, requires an on-going relationship with the parties which may allow the licensor to influence the licensee in its competitive behaviour and may give rise to disputes between the licensor and the licensee over the scope and the terms and conditions of the license. The granting of a license will therefore generally not be considered appropriate where a divestiture of a business seems feasible. Where the competition concerns arise from the market position held for such a technology or such IP rights, a divestiture of the technology or the IP rights is the preferable remedy as it eliminates a lasting relationship between the merged entity and its competitors. However, the Commission may accept licensing arrangements as an alternative to divestiture where, for instance, a divestiture would impede efficient, on-going research or where a divestiture would be impossible due to the nature of the business. Such licences will have to enable the licensee to compete effectively with the parties in a similar way as if a divestiture had taken place. They will normally be exclusive licences and have to be without any field-of-use and any geographical restrictions on the licensee. Where there might be

any uncertainty as regards the scope of the licence or its terms and conditions, the parties will have to divest the underlying IP right, but may obtain a licence back. If there is uncertainty that the license will actually be granted to a suitable licensee, the parties may consider to propose an up-front licensee or a fix-it-first solution according to the considerations set out below in paragraphs 56, in order to enable the Commission to conclude with the requisite degree of certainty that the remedy will be implemented.

Re-branding

39. In exceptional cases, the Commission has accepted commitments to grant an exclusive, time-limited licence for a brand with the purpose of allowing the licensee to re-brand the product in the period foreseen. After the first licence phase of these so-called re-branding commitments, the parties commit in a second phase to abstain from any use of the brand (blackout phase). The goal of such commitments is to allow the licensee to transfer the customers from the licensed brand to its own brand in order to create a viable competitor, without the licensed brand being permanently divested.

40. A re-branding remedy carries substantially higher risks for restoring effective competition than a divestiture, including the divestiture of a brand as there is considerable uncertainty whether the licensee will succeed in establishing itself as an active competitor in the market on the basis of the re-branded product. A re-branding remedy may be acceptable in circumstances where the brand at stake is widely used and a high proportion of its turnover is generated in markets outside those in which competition concerns have been identified. In those circumstances, a re-branding remedy has to be defined in such a way as to ensure that the granting of the licence will effectively maintain competition in the market on a lasting basis and that the licensee will be an effective competitor after re-branding the products.

41. As the success of re-branding commitments is substantially linked to the viability of the licensed brand a number of preconditions have to be met for the design of such commitments. Firstly, the brand to be transferred must be well-known and one of considerable strength to guarantee both immediate viability of the licensed brand and its economic survival in the re-branding period. Secondly, part of the assets related to the production or the distribution of the products marketed under the licensed brand or the transfer of know-how may be necessary to ensure the viability of the remedy. Thirdly, the licence has to be exclusive and normally comprehensive, i.e. not limited to a certain range of products within a specific market, and has to include the intellectual property rights to ensure that customers will acknowledge the familiarity of the re-branded product. The parties will not be allowed to use similar words or signs as this could undermine the effect of the re-branding exercise. Fourthly, both the licence and the black-out period have to be sufficiently long, account being taken of the particularities of the case, so that the re-branding remedy is in its effects similar to a divestiture.

42. The identity of the potential licensee will be a key factor for the success of the commitment. If there is uncertainty that a number of suitable licensees are available, being able and having strong incentives to carry out the re-branding exercise, the parties may consider proposing an up-front or fix-it-first solution, in line with the considerations set out in paragraph 53 below.

1.3. Non-reacquisition clause

43. In order to maintain the structural effect of a remedy, the commitments have to foresee that the merged entity cannot subsequently acquire influence over the whole or parts of the divested business. The commitments will normally have to foresee that no re-acquisition of material influence is possible for a significant period, generally of 10 years. However, the commitments can also provide for a waiver allowing the Commission to relieve the parties from this obligation if it subsequently finds that the structure of the market has changed to such an extent that the absence of influence over the divested business is no longer necessary to render the concentration compatible with the common market. Even in the absence of an explicit clause, a re-acquisition of the business would violate an implicit obligation on the parties under the commitments as this would affect the effectiveness of the remedies.

1.4. Alternative divestiture commitments: Crown Jewels

44. In certain cases, the implementation of the parties' preferred divestiture option (of a viable business solving the competition concerns) might be uncertain in view, for example, of third parties' pre-emption rights or uncertainty as to the transferability of key contracts, intellectual property rights, or the uncertainty of finding a suitable purchaser. Nevertheless, the parties may consider that they would be able to divest this business to a suitable purchaser within a very short time period.

45. In such circumstances, the Commission cannot take the risk that, in the end, effective competition will not be maintained. Accordingly, the Commission will only accept such divestiture commitments under the following conditions: (a) absent the uncertainty, the first divestiture proposed in the commitments would consist of a viable business, and (b) the parties will have to propose a second alternative divestiture which the parties will be obliged to implement if they are not able to implement the first commitment within the given time frame for the first divestiture. Such an alternative commitment normally has to be a 'crown jewel', i.e. it should be as least as good as the first proposed divestiture in terms of creating a viable competitor once implemented, it should not involve any uncertainties as to its implementation and it should be capable of being implemented quickly in order to avoid that the overall implementation period exceeds what would normally be regarded as acceptable in the conditions of the market in question. In order to limit the risks in the interim period, it is indispensable that interim preservation and holding separate measures apply to all assets included in both divestiture alternatives. Furthermore, the commitment has to establish clear criteria and a strict timetable as to how and when the alternative divestiture obligation will become effective and the Commission will require shorter periods for its implementation.

46. If there is uncertainty as to the implementation of the divestiture due to third party rights or as to finding a suitable purchaser crown jewel commitments and up-front buyers as discussed below in paragraphs 54 address the same concerns, and the parties may therefore choose between both structures.

1.5. Transfer to a suitable purchaser

47. The intended effect of the divestiture will only be achieved if and once the business is transferred to a suitable purchaser in whose hands it will become an active competitive force in the market. The potential of a business to attract a suitable purchaser is an important element already of the Commission's assessment of the appropriateness of the proposed commitment. In order to ensure that the business is divested to a suitable purchaser, the commitments have to include criteria to define its suitability which will allow the Commission to conclude that the divestiture of the business to such a purchaser will likely remove the competition concerns identified.

(a) Suitability of a purchaser

48. The standard purchaser requirements are the following:

— the purchaser is required to be independent of and unconnected to the parties,

— the purchaser must possess the financial resources, proven relevant expertise and have the incentive and ability to maintain and develop the divested business as a viable and active competitive force in competition with the parties and other competitors, and

— the acquisition of the business by a proposed purchaser must neither be likely to create new competition problems nor give rise to a risk that the implementation of the commitments will be delayed. Therefore, the proposed purchaser must reasonably be expected to obtain all necessary approvals from the relevant regulatory authorities for the acquisition of the business to be divested.

49. The standard purchaser requirements may have to be supplemented on a case-by-case basis. An example is the requirement, where appropriate, that the purchaser should be an industrial, rather than a financial purchaser. The commitments will normally contain such a clause where, due to the specific circumstances of the case, a financial buyer might not be able or might not have the incentives to develop the business as a viable and competitive force in the market even considering that it could

obtain the necessary management expertise (e.g. by recruiting managers experienced in the sector at stake) and therefore the acquisition by a financial buyer would not remove the competition concerns with sufficient certainty.

(b) Identification of a suitable purchaser

50. In general, there are three ways to ensure that the business is transferred to a suitable purchaser. First, the business is transferred within a fixed time-limit after adoption of the decision to a purchaser which is approved by the Commission on the basis of the purchaser requirements. Second, in addition to the conditions set out for the first category, the commitments foresee that the parties may not complete the notified operation before having entered into a binding agreement with a purchaser for the business, approved by the Commission (so-called 'up-front-buyer'). Third, the parties identify a purchaser for the business and enter into a binding agreement already during the Commission's procedure (so-called 'fix-it-first' remedy). The main difference between the two latter options is that in the case of an up-front buyer, the identity of the purchaser is not known to the Commission prior to the authorisation decision.

51. The choice of the category depends on the risks involved in the case and therefore on the measures which enable the Commission to conclude with the requisite degree of certainty that the commitment will be implemented. This will depend on the nature and the scope of the business to be divested, the risks of degradation of the business in the interim period up to divestiture and any uncertainties inherent in the transfer and implementation, in particular the risks of finding a suitable purchaser.

1. Sale of the divested business within a fixed time-limit after the decision

52. In the first category, the parties may proceed with the sale of the divested business on the basis of the purchaser requirements within a fixed time-limit after the adoption of the decision. This procedure is likely to be appropriate in the majority of cases, provided that a number of purchasers can be envisaged for a viable business and that no specific issues complicate or stand in the way of the divestiture. Where the purchaser needs to have special qualifications, this procedure may be appropriate if there are sufficient interested potential purchasers available which fulfil the specific purchaser requirements to be included in the commitments in such cases. In these circumstances the Commission may be able to conclude that the divestiture will be implemented and that there are no reasons for the implementation of the notified concentration to be suspended after the Commission decision.

2. Up-front buyer

53. There are cases where only the proposal of an up-front buyer will allow the Commission to conclude with the requisite degree of certainty that the business will be effectively divested to a suitable purchaser. The parties therefore have to undertake in the commitments that they are not going to complete the notified operation before having entered into a binding agreement with a purchaser for the divested business, approved by the Commission.

54. First, this concerns cases where there are considerable obstacles for a divestiture, such as third party rights, or uncertainties as to finding a suitable purchaser. In such cases, an up-front buyer will allow the Commission to conclude with the requisite degree of certainty that the commitments will be implemented, as such a commitment creates greater incentives for the parties to close the divestiture in order to be able to complete their own concentration. In these circumstances, parties may choose between proposing an up-front buyer and an alternative divestiture commitment, as set out above in paragraph 46.

55. Second, an up-front buyer may be necessary in cases which cause considerable risks of preserving the competitiveness and saleability of the divestment business in the interim period until divestiture. This category comprises cases where the risks of a degradation of the divestment business appear to be high, in particular due to a risk of losing employees being key for the business, or where the interim risks are increased as the parties are not able to undertake the carve-out process in the interim period, but the carve-out process can only take place once a sales and purchase agreement with a purchaser is entered into. The up-front buyer provision may accelerate the transfer of the business

to be divested—given the increased incentives for the parties to close the divestiture in order to be able to complete their own concentration—to such an extent that the commitments may allow the Commission to conclude with the requisite degree of certainty that those risks are limited and the divestiture will be effectively implemented.

3.   Fix-it-first remedies

56.   The third category involves cases where the parties identify and enter into a legally binding agreement with a buyer outlining the essentials of the purchase during the Commission procedure. The Commission will be able to decide in the final decision whether the transfer of the divested business to the identified purchaser will remove the competition concerns. If the Commission authorises the notified concentration, no additional Commission decision for the purchaser approval will be needed and the closing of the sale of the divested business may take place shortly afterwards.

57.   The Commission welcomes fix-it-first remedies in particular in cases where the identity of the purchaser is crucial for the effectiveness of the proposed remedy. This concerns cases where, given the circumstances, only very few potential purchasers can be considered suitable, in particular as the divested business is not a viable business in itself, but its viability will only be ensured by specific assets of the purchaser, or where the purchaser needs to have specific characteristics in order for the remedy to solve the competition concerns. If the parties choose to enter into a binding agreement with a suitable purchaser during the procedure by way of a fix-it-first solution, the Commission can in those circumstances conclude with the requisite degree of certainty that the commitments will be implemented with a sale to a suitable purchaser. In these situations, an 'upfront buyer' solution containing specific requirements as to the suitability of a buyer will generally be considered equivalent and acceptable.

2.   REMOVAL OF LINKS WITH COMPETITORS

58.   Divestiture commitments may also be used for removing links between the parties and competitors in cases where these links contribute to the competition concerns raised by the merger. The divestiture of a minority shareholding in a joint venture may be necessary in order to sever a structural link with a major competitor, or, similarly, the divestiture of a minority shareholding in a competitor.

59.   Although the divestiture of such stakes is the preferable solution, the Commission may exceptionally accept the waiving of rights linked to minority stakes in a competitor where it can be excluded, given the specific circumstances of the case, that the financial gains derived from a minority shareholding in a competitor would in themselves raise competition concerns. In such circumstances, the parties have to waive all the rights linked to such a shareholding which were relevant for behaviour in terms of competition, such as representations on the board, veto rights and also information rights. The Commission may only be able to accept such a severing of the link with a competitor if those rights are waived comprehensively and in a permanent way.

60.   Where competition concerns result from agreements with companies supplying the same products or providing the same services, a suitable remedy may be the termination of the respective agreement, such as distribution agreements with competitors or agreements resulting in the coordination of certain commercial behaviour. However, the termination of a distribution agreement alone will only remove the competition concerns if it is ensured that the product of a competitor will also be distributed in the future and exercise effective competitive pressure on the parties.

3.   OTHER REMEDIES

61.   Whilst being the preferred remedy, divestitures or the removal of links with competitors are not the only remedy possible to eliminate certain competition concerns. However, divestitures are the benchmark for other remedies in terms of effectiveness and efficiency. The Commission therefore may accept other types of commitments, but only in circumstances where the other remedy proposed is at least equivalent in its effects to a divestiture.

Access remedies

62. In a number of cases, the Commission has accepted remedies foreseeing the granting of access to key infrastructure, networks, key technology, including patents, know-how or other intellectual property rights, and essential inputs. Normally, the parties grant such access to third parties on a non-discriminatory and transparent basis.

63. Commitments granting access to infrastructure and networks may be submitted in order to facilitate market entry by competitors. They may be acceptable to the Commission in circumstances where it is sufficiently clear that there will be actual entry of new competitors that would eliminate any significant impediment to effective competition. Other examples of access commitments are commitments granting access to pay-TV platforms and to energy via gas release programs. Often, a sufficient reduction of entry barriers is not achieved by individual measures, but by a package comprising a combination of divestiture remedies and access commitments or a commitments package aimed at overall facilitating entry of competitors by a whole range of different measures. If those commitments actually make the entry of sufficient new competitors timely and likely, they can be considered to have a similar effect on competition in the market as a divestiture. If it cannot be concluded that the lowering of the entry barriers by the proposed commitments will likely lead to the entry of new competitors in the market, the Commission will reject such a remedies package.

64. Commitments granting non-discriminatory access to infrastructure or networks of the merging parties may also be submitted in order to ensure that competition is not significantly impeded as a result of foreclosure. In past Commission decisions, commitments have foreseen the granting of access to pipelines and to telecom or similar networks. The Commission will only accept such commitments if it can be concluded that these commitments will be effective and competitors will likely use them so that foreclosure concerns will be eliminated. In specific cases, it may be appropriate to link such a commitment with an up-front or fix-it-first provision in order to allow the Commission to conclude with the requisite degree of certainty that the commitment will be implemented.

65. Similarly, the control of key technology or IP rights may lead to concerns of foreclosure of competitors which depend on the technology or IP rights as essential input for the activities in a downstream market. This, for example, concerns cases where competition problems arise as the parties may withhold information necessary for the interoperability of different equipment. In such circumstances, commitments to grant competitors access to the necessary information may eliminate the competition concerns. Similarly, in sectors where players commonly have to cooperate by licensing patents to each other, concerns that the merged entity would no longer have the incentive to provide licences to the same extent and under the same conditions as before may be eliminated by commitments to grant licenses on the same basis also in the future. In those cases, commitments should foresee nonexclusive licences or the disclosure of information on a non-exclusive basis to all third parties which depend on the IP rights or information for their activities. It has to be further ensured that the terms and conditions under which the licenses are granted do not impede the effective implementation of such a license remedy. If no clearly determined terms and conditions for the granting of licenses exist in the market at stake, the terms and conditions, including the pricing, should be clearly apparent from the commitments (e.g. by way of pricing formulas). An alternative solution may be to rely on royalty-free licences. Furthermore, depending on the case, the granting of licenses may also transmit sensitive information to the licensor on the competitive behaviour of the licensees which are active as competitors in the downstream market, e.g. by transmitting the number of licenses used in the downstream market. In such cases, in order for the remedy to be suitable, the commitments will have to exclude such confidentiality problems. Generally, as set out in the preceding paragraph, the Commission will only accept such commitments if it can be concluded that they will be effective and competitors will likely use them.

66. Access commitments are often complex in nature and necessarily include general terms for determining the terms and conditions under which access is granted. In order to render them effective, those commitments have to contain the procedural requirements necessary for monitoring them, such as the requirement of separate accounts for the infrastructure in order to allow a review of the costs involved, and suitable monitoring devices. Normally, such monitoring has to be done by the

market participants themselves, e.g. by those undertakings wishing to benefit from the commitments. Measures allowing third parties themselves to enforce the commitments are in particular access to a fast dispute resolution mechanism via arbitration proceedings (together with trustees) or via arbitration proceedings involving national regulatory authorities if existing for the markets concerned. If the Commission can conclude that the mechanisms foreseen in the commitments will allow the market participants themselves to effectively enforce them in a timely manner, no permanent monitoring of the commitments by the Commission is required. In those cases, an intervention by the Commission would only be necessary in cases where the parties do not comply with the solutions found by those dispute resolution mechanisms. However, the Commission will only be able to accept such commitments where the complexity does not lead to a risk of their effectiveness from the outset and where the monitoring devices proposed ensure that those commitments will be effectively implemented and the enforcement mechanism will lead to timely results.

Change of long-term exclusive contracts

67. The change in the market structure resulting from a proposed concentration can cause existing contractual arrangements to be inimical to effective competition. This is in particular true for exclusive long-term supply agreements if such agreements foreclose either, up-stream, the input for competitors or, down-stream, their access to customers. Where the merged entity will have the ability and the incentives to foreclose competitors in this way, the foreclosure effects resulting from existing exclusive agreements may contribute to significantly impeding effective competition.

68. In such circumstances, the termination or change of existing exclusive agreements may be considered appropriate to eliminate the competition concerns. However, the available evidence must allow the Commission to clearly determine that no *de facto* exclusivity will be maintained. Furthermore, such change of long-term agreements will normally only be sufficient as part of a remedies package to remove the competition concerns identified.

Other non-divestiture remedies

69. As indicated above in paragraph 17, non-structural types of remedies, such as promises by the parties to abstain from certain commercial behaviour (e.g. bundling products), will generally not eliminate the competition concerns resulting from horizontal overlaps. In any case, it may be difficult to achieve the required degree of effectiveness of such a remedy due to the absence of effective monitoring of its implementation, as already set out above in paragraph 13(f). Indeed, it may be impossible for the Commission to verify whether or not the commitment is complied with and even other market participants, such as competitors, may not be able to establish at all or with the requisite degree of certainty whether the parties meet the conditions of the commitment in practice. In addition, competitors may also not have an incentive to alert the Commission as they do not directly benefit from the commitments. Therefore, the Commission may examine other types of non-divestiture remedies, such as behavioural promises, only exceptionally in specific circumstances, such as in respect of competition concerns arising in conglomerate structures.

Time limit for non-divestiture remedies

70. The Commission may accept that non-divestiture remedies are limited in their duration. The acceptability of a time limit and the duration will depend on the individual circumstances of the case and cannot be pre-defined in a general manner in the present Notice.

4. REVIEW CLAUSE

71. Irrespective of the type of remedy, commitments will usually include a review clause. This may allow the Commission, upon request by the parties showing good cause, to grant an extension of deadlines or, in exceptional circumstances, to waive, modify or substitute the commitments.

72. Modifying commitments by extending the deadlines is in particular relevant for divestiture commitments. Parties have to submit a request for an extension within the deadline. Where parties apply for an extension for the first divestiture period, the Commission will only accept that they have shown good cause if the parties were not able to meet the deadline for reasons outside their

responsibility and if it can be expected that the parties subsequently will succeed in divesting the business within a short time-frame. Otherwise, the divestiture trustee may be better placed to undertake the divestiture and to fulfil the commitments for the parties.

73. The Commission may grant waivers or accept modifications or substitutions of the commitments only in exceptional circumstances. This will very rarely be relevant for divestiture commitments. As divestiture commitments have to be implemented within a short time-frame after the decision, it is very unlikely that changes of market circumstances will have occurred in such a short time-frame and the Commission will normally not accept any modifications under the general review clause. For specific situations the commitments normally foresee more targeted review clauses.

74. A waiver, modification or substitution of commitments may be more relevant for non-divestiture commitments, such as access commitments, which may be on-going for a number of years and for which not all contingencies can be predicted at the time of the adoption of the Commission decision. Exceptional circumstances justifying a waiver, modification or substitution may, first, be accepted for such commitments if parties show that market circumstances have changed significantly and on a permanent basis. For showing this, a sufficient long time-span, normally at least several years, between the Commission decision and a request by the parties is required. Second, exceptional circumstances may also be present if the parties can show that the experience gained in the application of the remedy demonstrates that the objective pursued with the remedy will be better achieved if modalities of the commitment are changed. For any waiver, modification or substitution of commitments, the Commission will also take into account the view of third parties and the impact a modification may have on the position of third parties and thereby on the overall effectiveness of the remedy. In this regard, the Commission will also consider whether modifications affect the right already acquired by third parties after implementation of the remedy.

75. If at the time of the adoption of the decision the Commission for particular reasons cannot anticipate all contingencies in relation to the implementation of such commitments, it may also be appropriate for the parties to include a clause in the commitments, allowing the Commission to trigger a limited modification to the commitments. Such modifications may be necessary if the original commitments do not achieve the envisaged results set out in those commitments, and therefore do not effectively remove the competition concerns. Procedurally, the parties may be obliged in such cases to propose a change to the commitments in order to achieve the result defined in those commitments, or the Commission may itself, after hearing the parties, modify the conditions and obligations to this end. This type of clause will typically be limited to cases where specific modalities risk to jeopardise effective implementation of the commitments. Such clauses have been used, for example, in relation to the modalities of gas release programs.

76. The Commission may, upon request, adopt a formal decision for any waiver, modification or substitution of commitments or simply take note of satisfactory amendments of the remedy by the parties, where such amendments improve the effectiveness of the remedy and result in legally binding obligations of the parties, e.g. by contractual arrangements. A change of the commitments will normally only be effective *ex nunc*. Consequently, a modification of the commitments will not heal retroactively any breach of the commitments which has been committed before the time of the modification. The Commission may therefore, where appropriate, further pursue a breach under Articles 14, 15 of the Merger Regulation.

IV. ASPECTS OF PROCEDURE FOR SUBMISSION OF COMMITMENTS

1. PHASE I

77. Pursuant to Article 6(2) of the Merger Regulation the Commission may declare a concentration compatible with the common market also before the initiation of proceedings, where it is

confident that following modification a notified concentration no longer raises serious doubts within the meaning of paragraph 1(c).

78. Parties can submit proposals for commitments to the Commission on an informal basis, even before notification. Parties have to submit commitments within not more than 20 working days from the date of the receipt of the notification. The Commission informs the parties about its serious doubts in due time before that deadline. Where the parties submit commitments, the deadline for the Commission's decision pursuant to Article 6(1) of the Merger Regulation is extended from 25 to 35 working days.

79. In order to form the basis of a decision pursuant to Article 6(2), proposals for commitments must meet the following requirements:
   (a) they shall fully specify the substantive and implementing commitments entered into by the parties;
   (b) they shall be signed by a person duly authorised to do so;
   (c) they shall be accompanied by the information on the commitments offered as provided for in the Implementing Regulation (as explained above in paragraph 7); and
   (d) they shall be accompanied by a non-confidential version of the commitments for the purposes of market testing them with third parties. The non-confidential version of the commitments must allow third parties to fully assess the workability and the effectiveness of the proposed remedies to remove the competition concerns.

80. Proposals submitted by the parties in accordance with these requirements will be assessed by the Commission. The Commission will consult the authorities of the Member States on the proposed commitments and, when considered appropriate, also third parties in the form of a market test, including in particular those third parties and the recognised representatives of those employees whose positions are directly affected by the proposed remedies. In markets with national regulatory authorities the Commission may also, if appropriate, consult the competent national regulatory authorities. In addition, in cases involving a geographic market that is wider than the European Economic Area ('EEA') or where, for reasons related to the viability of the business, the scope of the business to be divested is wider than the EEA territory, the non-confidential version of the proposed remedies may also be discussed with non-EEA competition authorities in the framework of the Community's bilateral cooperation agreements with these countries.

81. Commitments in phase I can only be accepted where the competition problem is readily identifiable and can easily be remedied (4). The competition problem therefore needs to be so straightforward and the remedies so clear-cut that it is not necessary to enter into an in-depth investigation and that the commitments are sufficient to clearly rule out 'serious doubts' within the meaning of Article 6(1)(c) of the Merger Regulation. Where the assessment confirms that the proposed commitments remove the grounds for serious doubts on this basis, the Commission clears the merger in phase I.

82. Due to the time-constraints in phase I, it is particularly important for the parties to submit in a timely manner to the Commission the information required in the Implementing Regulation to properly assess the content and workability of the commitments and their suitability to maintain conditions of effective competition in the common market on a permanent basis. If the parties do not comply with the obligation in the Implementing Regulation, the Commission may not be able to conclude that the proposed commitments will remove the grounds for serious doubts.

83. Where the assessment shows that the commitments offered are not sufficient to remove the competition concerns raised by the concentration, the parties will be informed accordingly. Given that phase I remedies are designed to provide a clear-cut answer to a readily identifiable competition concern, only limited modifications can be accepted to the proposed commitments. Such modifications, presented as an immediate response to the result of the consultations, may include clarifications, refinements and/or other improvements designed to ensure that the commitments are workable and effective. However, such modifications may only be accepted in circumstances where it is ensured that the Commission can carry out a proper assessment of those commitments.

84. If the Commission's final assessment of a case shows that there are no competition concerns in one or more markets, the parties will be informed accordingly and may withdraw the unnecessary commitments for such markets. If the parties do not withdraw them, the Commission will normally

ignore them in the decision. In any event, such commitment proposals do not constitute a condition for clearance.

85. Where the parties are informed that the Commission intends to maintain in its final decision that the transaction raises competition concerns for a specific market, it is for the parties to propose commitments. The Commission is not in a position to impose unilaterally any conditions to an authorisation decision, but only on the basis of the parties' commitments. However, the Commission will review whether the commitments submitted by the parties are proportionate to the competition problem when assessing whether to attach them as conditions or obligations to its final decision. Nevertheless, it has to be stressed that, in a commitments proposal, all those elements which are required to fulfil the basic conditions for acceptable commitments as set out above in paragraphs 9 *et seq.* will be considered necessary. This paragraph as well as the previous one also applies to commitments in phase II.

86. If the Commission concludes that the commitments offered by the parties do not remove the serious doubts, it will issue an Article 6(1)(c) decision and open proceedings.

2. PHASE II

87. Pursuant to Article 8(2) of the Merger Regulation, the Commission must declare a concentration compatible with the common market, where following modification a notified concentration does no longer significantly impede effective competition within the meaning of Article 2(3) of the Merger Regulation.

88. Commitments proposed to the Commission pursuant to Article 8(2) must be submitted to the Commission within not more than 65 working days from the day on which proceedings were initiated. Where the deadlines for the final decision have been extended according to Article 10(3) of the Merger Regulation, also the deadline for remedies is automatically extended by the same number of days. Only in exceptional circumstances, the Commission may accept that commitments are submitted for the first time after the expiry of this period. The request by the parties for an extension of the deadline must be received within the period and has to set forth the exceptional circumstances which, according to the parties, justify it. In addition to the existence of exceptional circumstances, an extension is only possible where there is sufficient time to make a proper assessment of the proposal by the Commission and to allow adequate consultation with Member States and third parties.

89. The question whether or not submitting remedies will extend the deadline for the Commission to take a final decision depends on the time in the procedure when the commitments are submitted. Where the parties submit commitments within less than 55 working days after the initiation of proceedings, the Commission has to take a final decision within not more than 90 working days of the date of initiation of proceedings. Where the parties submit commitments on working day 55 or afterwards (even after working day 65, if those commitments should be acceptable due to exceptional circumstances as described above in paragraph 88), the period for the Commission to take a final decision is increased to 105 working days according to Article 10(3), subparagraph 2. Where the parties submit commitments within less than 55 working days, but submit a modified version on day 55 or thereafter, the period to take a final decision will also be extended to 105 working days.

90. The Commission is available to discuss suitable commitments well in advance of the end of the 65 working day period. The parties are encouraged to submit draft proposals dealing with both substantive and implementation aspects which are necessary to ensure that the commitments are fully workable. If the parties are of the opinion that more time is needed for the investigation of the competition concerns and for the corresponding design of appropriate commitments, they may also suggest to the Commission to extend the final deadline under Article 10(3), subparagraph 1. Such a request will have to be made before the end of the 65 working day period. Indeed, the Commission will normally not extend the period for adopting a final decision according to Article 10(3), subparagraph 1 where the request for extension is presented after the deadline for submitting remedies foreseen in the Implementing Regulation, i.e. after working day 65.

91. In order to meet the requirements for a decision pursuant to Article 8(2), commitments must meet the following requirements:

(a) they shall address all competition concerns raised by the concentration and shall fully specify the substantive and implementing commitments entered into by the parties;

(b) they shall be signed by a person duly authorised to do so;

(c) they shall by accompanied by the information on the commitments offered as provided for in the Implementing Regulation (as explained above in paragraph 7); and

(d) they shall be accompanied by a non-confidential version of the commitments for the purposes of market testing them with third parties, fulfilling the requirements set out above in paragraph 79.

92. Proposals submitted by the parties in accordance with these requirements will be assessed by the Commission. If the assessment confirms that the proposed commitments remove the serious doubts (if no Statement of Objection has been issued yet by the Commission) or the competition concerns raised in the Statement of Objections, following the consultations as set out in paragraph 80 above, the Commission will adopt a conditional clearance decision.

93. Conversely, where the assessment leads to the conclusion that the proposed commitments appear not to be sufficient to resolve the competition concerns raised by the concentration, the parties will be informed accordingly.

94. The Merger Regulation does not impose any obligation on the Commission to accept commitments after the legal deadline for remedies, unless the Commission voluntarily undertakes to assess commitments in specific circumstances. In view of this, where parties subsequently modify the proposed commitments after the deadline of 65 working days, the Commission will only accept these modified commitments where it can clearly determine—on the basis of its assessment of information already received in the course of the investigation, including the results of prior market testing, and without the need for any other market test—that such commitments, once implemented, fully and unambiguously resolve the competition concerns identified and where there is sufficient time to allow for an adequate assessment by the Commission and for proper consultation with Member States. The Commission will normally reject modified commitments which do not fulfil those conditions.

V. REQUIREMENTS FOR IMPLEMENTATION OF COMMITMENTS

95. Commitments are offered as a means of securing a clearance, with the implementation normally taking place after the decision. Commitments therefore require safeguards to ensure their effective and timely implementation. These implementing provisions will normally form part of the commitments entered into by the parties *vis-à-vis* the Commission.

96. In the following, detailed guidance is given on the implementation of divestiture commitments, as the most typical commitment. Afterwards, some aspects of the implementation of other types of commitments are discussed.

1. DIVESTITURE PROCESS

97. The divestiture has to be completed within a fixed time period agreed between the parties and the Commission. In the Commission's practice, the total time period is divided into a period for entering into a final agreement and a further period for the closing, the transfer of legal title, of the transaction. The period for entering into a binding agreement is further normally divided into a first period in which the parties can look for a suitable purchaser (the 'first divestiture period') and, if the parties do not succeed to divest the business, a second period in which a divestiture trustee obtains the mandate to divest the business at no minimum price (the 'trustee divestiture period').

98. The Commission's experience has shown that short divestiture periods contribute largely to the success of the divestiture as, otherwise, the business to be divested will be exposed to an extended period of uncertainty. The time periods should therefore be as short as feasible. The Commission will normally consider a period of around six months for the first divestiture period and an additional

period of three months for the trustee divestiture period as appropriate. A period of further three months is normally foreseen for closing the transaction. These periods may be modified on a case-by-case basis. In particular, they may have to be shortened if there is a high risk of degradation of the business' viability in the interim period.

99. The deadline for the divestiture shall normally start on the day of the adoption of the Commission decision. An exception might be justified for a transaction via public bid where the parties commit to divest a business belonging to the target. Where in such circumstances the parties cannot prepare for the divestiture of the target's business before closing of the notified concentration, the Commission might accept that the periods for such a divestiture only start with the date of closing the notified transaction. Similarly, such a solution may be considered if the date of closing of the concentration is not under the control of the parties as it, e.g. requires state approval. In return, it may be appropriate to shorten the deadlines in order to reduce the time of uncertainty for the business to be divested.

100. Whereas for up-front buyer solutions the above-described procedure applies, the procedure will be different for fix-it-first solutions. In general, a binding agreement with a purchaser will already be entered into during the procedure so that after the decision only a further period for the closing of the transaction has to be foreseen. If before the decision only a framework agreement has been concluded with the purchaser, the periods to be foreseen for entering into a full agreement and the closing afterwards will have to be decided on a case-by-case basis.

2. APPROVAL OF THE PURCHASER AND OF THE SALE AND PURCHASE AGREEMENT

101. In order to ensure the effectiveness of the commitment, the sale to a proposed purchaser is subject to prior approval by the Commission. When the parties (or the divestiture trustee) have reached a final agreement with a purchaser, they have to submit a reasoned and documented proposal to the Commission. The parties or the divestiture trustee, as the case may be, will be required to demonstrate to the satisfaction of the Commission that the proposed purchaser meets the purchaser requirements, and that the business is divested in a manner consistent with the Commission's decision and the commitments. Where the commitments allow that different purchasers are being proposed for different parts of the package, the Commission will assess whether each individual proposed purchaser is acceptable and that the total package solves the competition concern.

102. In assessing any proposed purchaser, the Commission will interpret the purchaser requirements in the light of the purpose of the commitments, to immediately maintain effective competition in the market where competition concerns had been found, and of the market circumstances as set out in the decision. Generally, the basis for the Commission's assessment of the purchaser requirements will be the submission of the parties, the assessment of the monitoring trustee and, in particular, discussions with the proposed purchaser and its business plan. The Commission will further analyse whether the underlying assumptions of the purchaser appear plausible according to the market circumstances.

103. The requirement that the purchaser has to have the necessary financial resources extends in particular to the way the acquisition is financed by the proposed purchaser. The Commission will normally not accept any financing of the divestiture by the seller, and, in particular, any seller financing if this were to give the seller a share in the profits of the divested business in the future.

104. In assessing whether the proposed purchaser threatens to create competition problems, the Commission will undertake a prima facie assessment in the light of the information available to the Commission in the purchaser approval process. Where the purchase results in a concentration that has a Community dimension, this new operation will have to be notified under the Merger Regulation and cleared under normal procedures. Where this is not the case, the Commission's approval of a proposed purchaser is without prejudice to the merger control jurisdiction of national authorities. In addition, the proposed purchaser must be expected to obtain all other necessary approvals from the relevant regulatory authorities. Where it can be foreseen, in the light of the information available to the Commission, that difficulties in obtaining merger control clearance or other approvals may

unduly delay the timely implementation of the commitment, it will be considered that the proposed purchaser does not meet the purchaser requirements. Otherwise, the competition concerns identified by the Commission would not be removed in the appropriate time-frame.

105. The requirement for an approval by the Commission does usually not only extend to the identity of the purchaser, but also to the sale and purchase agreement and any other agreement entered into between the parties and the proposed purchaser, including transitory agreements. The Commission will verify whether the divestiture according to the agreements is in line with the commitments.

106. The Commission will communicate its view as to the suitability of the proposed purchaser to the parties. If the Commission concludes that the proposed purchaser does not meet the purchaser requirements, it will adopt a decision that the proposed purchaser is not a purchaser under the commitments. If the Commission concludes that the sale and purchase agreement (or any ancillary agreements) does not foresee a divestiture in line with the commitments, the Commission will communicate this to the parties without necessarily rejecting the purchaser as such. If the Commission concludes that the purchaser is suitable under the commitments and that the contracts agree a divestiture in line with the commitments, the Commission will approve the divestiture to the proposed purchaser. The Commission will issue the necessary approvals as expeditiously as possible.

3. OBLIGATIONS OF THE PARTIES IN THE INTERIM PERIOD

107. Parties have to fulfil certain obligations in the interim period (as defined above in paragraph 36). The following should normally be included in the commitments in this respect: (i) safeguards for the interim preservation of the viability to the business; (ii) the necessary steps for a carve-out process, if relevant; and (iii) the necessary steps to prepare the divestiture of the business.

Interim preservation of the divested business

108. It is the parties' responsibility to reduce to the minimum any possible risk of loss of competitive potential of the business to be divested resulting from the uncertainties inherent in the transfer of a business. Up to the transfer of the business to the purchaser, the Commission will require the parties to offer commitments to maintain the independence, economic viability, marketability and competitiveness of the business. Only such commitments will allow the Commission to conclude with the requisite degree of certainty that the divestiture of the business will be implemented in the way as proposed by the parties in the commitments.

109. Generally, these commitments should be designed to keep the business separate from the business retained by the parties, and to ensure that it is managed as a distinct and saleable business in its best interest, with a view to ensuring its continued economic viability, marketability and competitiveness and its independence from the businesses retained by the parties.

110. The parties will be required to ensure that all assets of the business are maintained, pursuant to good business practice and in the ordinary course of business, and that no acts which might have a significant adverse impact on the business are carried out. This relates in particular to the maintenance of fixed assets, know-how or commercial information of a confidential or proprietary nature, the customer base and the technical and commercial competence of the employees. Furthermore, the parties must maintain the business in the same conditions as before the concentration, in particular provide sufficient resources, such as capital or a line of credit, on the basis and continuation of existing business plans, the same administrative and management functions, or other factors relevant for maintaining competition in the specific sector. The commitments also have to foresee that the parties should take all reasonable steps, including appropriate incentive schemes, to encourage all key personnel to remain with the business, and that the parties may not solicit or move any personnel to their remaining businesses.

111. The parties should further hold the business separate from its retained business and ensure that the key personnel of the business to be divested do not have any involvement into the retained

businesses and *vice versa*. If the business to be divested is in corporate form and a strict separation of the corporate structure appears necessary, the parties' rights as shareholders, in particular the voting rights, should be exercised by the monitoring trustee which should also have the power to replace the board members appointed on behalf of the parties. In relation to information, the parties must ring-fence the business to be divested and take all necessary measures to ensure that the parties do not obtain any business secrets or other confidential information. Any documents or information confidential to the business obtained by the parties before adoption of the decision have to be returned to the business or destroyed.

112. The parties are further generally required to appoint a hold-separate manager with the necessary expertise, who will be responsible for the management of the business and the implementation of the hold-separate and ring-fencing obligations. The hold-separate manager should act under the supervision of the monitoring trustee who may issue instructions to the hold-separate manager. The commitments have to provide that the appointment should take place immediately after the adoption of the decision and even before the parties may close the notified concentration. Whereas the parties can appoint the hold-separate manager on their own, the commitments have to foresee that the monitoring trustee is able to remove the hold-separate manager if s/he does not act in line with the commitments or endangers their timely and proper implementation. A new appointment of a hold separate manager afterwards will be subject to the approval of the monitoring trustee.

Steps for a carve-out

113. As outlined above in paragraph 35, the Commission may accept in appropriate circumstances that the divestiture of a business which needs to be carved out from the remaining businesses of the parties can be considered a suitable remedy. Nevertheless, also in such circumstances only the transfer of a viable business to a purchaser which can maintain and develop this business as an active competitive force in the market will remove the Commission's competition concerns. Therefore, the parties have to commit to a result-oriented obligation to carry out, in the interim period, a carve-out of the assets that contribute to the divested business. The result has to be that a viable and competitive business, which is stand-alone and separate from the other businesses of the parties, can be transferred to a suitable purchaser at the end of the interim period. The parties will have to bear the costs and risks of such a carve-out in the interim period.

114. The carve-out will need to be carried out by the parties under the supervision of the trustee and in cooperation with the hold-separate manager. First, those assets and parts of the personnel which are shared between the business to be divested and remaining businesses of the parties have to be allocated to the business to the extent that this is not excluded in the commitments. The allocation of the assets and the personnel will be monitored and has to be approved by the monitoring trustee. Second, the carve-out process may also require a replication for the business of assets held or functions performed by other parts of the parties' businesses if this is necessary to ensure the viability and competitiveness of the business to be divested. An example is the termination of the business' participation in a central information technology network and an installation of a separate IT system for the business. In general, the major steps of such a carve-out process and the functions to be replicated should be decided on a case-by-case basis and described in the commitments.

115. At the same time, it has to be ensured that the viability of the business to be divested is not affected by such measures. In the interim period, the parties therefore have to maintain the use of shared assets by and to continue to provide services to the business to the same extent as in the past as long as the business is not yet viable on a stand-alone basis.

Specific obligations of the parties concerning the divestiture process

116. For the divestiture process, the commitments should foresee that potential purchasers can carry out a due diligence exercise and obtain, dependent on the stage of the procedure, sufficient information concerning the divested business to allow the purchaser to fully assess the value, scope and commercial potential of the business, and have direct access to its personnel. The parties further have to submit periodic reports on potential purchasers and developments in the negotiations. The divestiture will only be implemented once the transaction is closed, that is the legal title has passed to

the approved purchaser, and the assets have been actually transferred. At the end of the process, the parties will have to send a final report, confirming the closing and the transfer of the assets.

4. THE MONITORING AND THE DIVESTITURE TRUSTEE

Role of the monitoring trustee

117. As the Commission cannot, on a daily basis, be directly involved in overseeing the implementation of the commitments, the parties have to propose the appointment of a trustee to oversee the parties' compliance with the commitments, in particular with their obligations in the interim period and the divestiture process (the so-called 'monitoring trustee'). Thereby, the parties guarantee the effectiveness of the commitments submitted by them and allow the Commission to ensure that the modification of the notified concentration, as proposed by the parties, will be carried out with the requisite degree of certainty.

118. The monitoring trustee will carry out its tasks under the supervision of the Commission and is to be considered the Commission's 'eyes and ears'. It shall be the guardian that the business is managed and kept properly on a stand-alone basis in the interim period. The Commission may therefore give any orders and instructions to the monitoring trustee in order to ensure compliance with the commitments, and the trustee may propose to the parties any measures it considers necessary for carrying out its tasks. The parties, however, may not issue any instructions to the trustee without approval by the Commission.

119. The Commitments will generally set out the tasks of the monitoring trustee. Its duties and obligations will be specified in detail in the trustee mandate, to be concluded between the parties and the trustee, and its tasks shall be further detailed in a work-plan. The tasks of the monitoring trustee will normally start immediately after the adoption of the Commission decision and last until the legal and actual transfer of the business to the approved purchaser. Five main, non-exhaustive tasks can be distinguished which the monitoring trustee should carry out under the supervision of the Commission:

— first, the monitoring trustee will be called upon to oversee the safeguards for the business to be divested in the interim period,

— second, in carve-out cases, the monitoring trustee has to monitor the splitting of assets and the allocation of the personnel between the divested business and retained businesses by the parties as well as the replication of assets and functions in the business previously provided by the parties,

— third, the monitoring trustee shall be responsible for overseeing the parties' efforts to find a potential purchaser and to transfer the business. In general, it shall review the progress of the divestiture process and the potential purchasers included in the process. It shall verify that potential purchasers receive sufficient information relating to the business—in particular by reviewing the information memorandum (if available), the data room or the due diligence process. Once a purchaser is proposed, the monitoring trustee shall submit to the Commission a reasoned opinion as to whether the proposed purchaser fulfils the purchaser requirements in the commitments and whether the business is sold in a manner consistent with the commitments. At the end of the process, the monitoring trustee has to oversee the legal and actual transfer of the business to the purchaser and make a final report, confirming the transfer,

— fourth, the monitoring trustee shall act as a contact point for any requests by third parties, in particular potential purchasers, in relation to the commitments. The parties shall inform interested third parties of the identity and the tasks of the monitoring trustee, including any potential purchasers. In case of disagreement between the parties and third parties in relation to matters dealt with by the commitments, the monitoring trustee shall discuss those matters with both sides and report to the Commission. In order to be able to carry out its role, the monitoring trustee will keep confidential any business secrets of the parties and third parties,

— fifth, the monitoring trustee shall report on these issues to the Commission in periodic compliance reports and shall also submit additional reports upon request by the Commission.

120. The commitments will also comprehensively set out the monitoring trustee's needs for support by and cooperation with the parties; the Commission will supervise the relationship between the parties and the trustee also in this respect. In order to fulfil its tasks, the trustee shall have access to books and records of the parties and of the divested business, insofar and as long as this is relevant for the implementation of the commitments, may ask for managerial and administrative support by the parties, shall be informed of potential purchasers and all developments in the divestiture process, and shall be provided with the information submitted to potential purchasers. In addition, the parties shall indemnify the trustee and allow the trustee to appoint advisors, if appropriate for the fulfilment of its tasks under the commitments. The commitments will also enable the Commission to share the parties' information with the monitoring trustee in order to allow the monitoring trustee to fulfil its tasks. The monitoring trustee will be bound to keep this information confidential.

Role of the divestiture trustee

121. As for the monitoring trustee, the parties have to propose to appoint a divestiture trustee in order to make the commitments submitted by them effective and allow the Commission to ensure that the modification of the notified concentration, as proposed by them, will be carried out. If the parties do not succeed in finding a suitable purchaser within the first divestiture period, then in the trustee divestiture period, the divestiture trustee will be given an irrevocable and exclusive mandate to dispose of the business, under the supervision of the Commission, within a specific deadline at no minimum price to a suitable purchaser. The commitments shall allow the divestiture trustee to include in the sale and purchase agreement such terms and conditions as it considers appropriate for an expedient sale, in particular customary representations, warranties and indemnities. The sale of the business by the divestiture trustee is in the same way subject to the prior approval of the Commission as the sale by the parties.

122. The commitments will set out that the parties shall support and inform the divestiture trustee and cooperate with the trustee in the same way as this is foreseen for the monitoring trustee. For the divestiture, the parties have to grant to the divestiture trustee comprehensive powers of attorney, covering all stages of the divestiture.

Approval of the trustee and the trustee mandate

123. Depending on the commitment, the monitoring trustee may or may not be the same person or institution as the divestiture trustee. The parties shall propose one or several potential trustees to the Commission, including the full terms of the mandate and an outline of a work-plan. It is of the essence that the monitoring trustee is in place immediately after the Commission decision. Therefore, the parties should propose a suitable trustee immediately after the Commission decision and the commitments normally have to foresee that the notified concentration can only be implemented once the monitoring trustee is appointed, after being approved by the Commission. The situation is different for the divestiture trustee who should be appointed well ahead of the end of the first divestiture period so that its mandate can take effect with the beginning of the trustee divestiture period.

124. Both types of trustees will be appointed by the parties on the basis of a trustee mandate, entered into by the parties and the trustee. The appointment and the mandate will be subject to the approval by the Commission which will have discretion in the selection of the trustee and will assess whether the proposed candidate is suitable for the tasks in the specific case. The trustee shall be independent of the parties, possess the necessary qualifications to carry out its mandate and shall not be, or become, exposed to a conflict of interests.

125. The Commission will assess the necessary qualifications in the light of the requirements of the specific case, including the geographic area and the sector concerned. According to the Commission's experience, auditing firms and other consulting firms may be particularly well placed to fulfil the tasks of a monitoring trustee. Individuals who have worked in the specific industry may also be suitable candidates for performing such a role if they have the necessary resources available to

deal with the tasks at stake. Investment banks seem to be particularly suitable for the role of a divestiture trustee. The independence of the trustee is crucial in order to enable the trustee to properly fulfil its role of monitoring the parties' compliance for the Commission and to ensure its credibility *vis-à-vis* third parties. In particular, the Commission will not accept persons or institutions as trustees which are at the same time the parties' auditors or their investment advisors in the divestiture. However, no conflicts of interests will arise by relations of the trustee with the parties if those relations will not impair the Trustee's objectivity and independence in discharging its tasks. It is the parties' responsibility to supply the Commission with adequate information for it to verify that the trustee fulfils the requirements. The appointment of the trustee after approval by the parties is irrevocable unless the trustee is replaced with the approval of or upon request by the Commission.

126. The trustee mandate shall define the tasks as specified in the commitments further and shall include all provisions necessary to enable the trustee to fulfil its tasks under the commitments accepted by the Commission. The parties are responsible for remuneration of the trustee under the mandate, and the remuneration structure must be such as to not impede the trustee's independence and effectiveness in fulfilling the mandate. The Commission will approve a trustee only together with a suitable mandate. In appropriate cases, it may publish the identity of the trustee and a summary of its tasks.

127. When the specific commitments with which the trustee has been entrusted have been implemented—that is to say, when legal title for the business to be divested has passed, the assets have been actually transferred to the purchaser and specific arrangements which may continue postdivestiture have been fulfilled—the mandate will provide for the trustee to request the Commission for a discharge from further responsibilities. Even after the discharge has been given, it may be necessary for the Commission to require the reappointment of the trustee on the basis of the commitments, if it appears subsequently to the Commission that the relevant commitments might not have been fully and properly implemented.

5. OBLIGATIONS OF THE PARTIES FOLLOWING IMPLEMENTATION OF THE DIVESTITURE

128. The Commitments also have to foresee that for a period of 10 years after the adoption of the decision accepting the commitments the Commission may request information from the parties. This will allow the Commission to monitor the effective implementation of the remedy.

6. IMPLEMENTATION OF OTHER COMMITMENTS

129. Many of the principles discussed above for the implementation of divestiture commitments can equally be applied to other types of commitments if those commitments need to be implemented subsequent to the Commission decision. For example, if it is foreseen that the beneficiary of a licence needs to be approved by the Commission, the considerations regarding the purchaser approval can be applied. Given the wide range of non-divestiture commitments, no general and comprehensive requirements for the implementation of non-divestiture commitments can be set out.

130. However, given the long duration of non-divestiture commitments and their frequent complexity, they often require a very high monitoring effort and specific monitoring tools in order to allow the Commission to conclude that they will effectively be implemented. Therefore, the Commission will often require the involvement of a trustee to oversee the implementation of such commitments and the establishment of a fast-track arbitration procedure in order to provide for a dispute resolution mechanism and to render the commitments enforceable by the market participants themselves. In past cases, the Commission has often required both the appointment of a trustee and an arbitration clause. In those circumstances, the trustee will oversee the implementation of the commitments, but will also be able to assist in arbitral proceedings to the effect that they may be finalised in a short period of time.

Index